PRAYERS THROUGH THE PANDEMIC
YEAR ONE

Joe Vitale Jr

VARI LOUD MUSIK™

This book is dedicated to my Lord & Savior Jesus Christ, my wonderful, beautiful & supportive wife Kathryn, my mother and father, my mother and father in law & all of our wonderful friends & family. Thank you all for always encouraging & believing in me.

©Copyright 2020 & 2021 Joe Vitale Jr
All Rights Reserved

No part of this book may be reproduced, or stored in a retrieval system, or transmitted in any form or by any means, electronic, mechanical, photocopying, recording, or otherwise, without express written permission of the publisher. IVXX

Cover design by: Joe Vitale Jr

Printed in the United States of America

TABLE OF CONTENTS
FOREWARD BY SUSIE VITALE

MARCH 2020	1
APRIL 2020	17
MAY 2020	45
JUNE 2020	83
JULY 2020	123
AUGUST 2020	163
SEPTEMBER 2020	203
OCTOBER 2020	241
NOVEMBER 2020	279
DECEMBER 2020	327
JANUARY 2021	373
FEBRUARY 2021	419
MARCH 2021	457
BIBLE VERSES FROM YEAR ONE	481
THE SINNER'S PRAYER	493
ABOUT THE AUTHOR	495
JOE VITALE JR'S TESTIMONY	497

"Lord of Lords" Photography by Joe Vitale Jr

At sunset on September 7th, 2015 I was driving home and this appeared in the sky above North East Ohio. I immediately saw Christ, Archangels & on the right side the hand of God. This image doesn't do justice to how amazing this truly was.

ABOUT THIS BOOK

In mid winter of 2020, the Covid-19 Pandemic hit the world & changed everyone's life in an incredibly short amount of time. There were lockdowns, masks & fear throughout the planet. My name is Joe Vitale Jr, my whole life I've been a Christian and I knew God would take care of us through this uncertain time. In March of 2020, when our state went into lockdown, I felt directed by God to start a nightly prayer through the length of the pandemic. I wanted to help others by spreading God's Word, sharing the Gospel of Jesus Christ & hopefully, through the name & power of Jesus, alleviate some anxieties many were feeling. At the time of the writing of this book, we are still in the pandemic & approaching the completion of year two. Soon after the publication of this book, I will be releasing "Prayers Through the Pandemic : Year Two."

This book contains every prayer from March 17th, 2020 through March 16th, 2021, all 365 days. The chapters are laid out in months & each day is numbered and dated. Every Bible verse mentioned in this book throughout the year is listed in the back. For those of you seeking God & wanting to have a relationship with Him, I have included the sinner's prayer throughout the book.

I had received many requests to release a book like this & once again, I felt directed by God to do this. This book is not only a day by day account of the prayers said, but it gives you a look into what we faced during that uncertain time. I hope that these prayers give you hope through the power of Jesus Christ. If you are reading this section, know that Jesus Christ loves you more than you could ever possibly know & has a personal destiny for you & for you alone. May God keep, protect you in the years to come & may God bless you in all ways.

ISAIAH 54:17

No weapon that is formed against you shall prosper.

FOREWARD
By Susie Vitale

Joe Vitale Jr. has been a remarkable person from the time he was born. He rarely slept, was fascinated with everything around him and barely ever stopped moving. He has a tremendous sense of humor, unlimited curiosity and kindness, and the intelligence to research, comprehend and to teach himself whatever he needs to know to accomplish his various dreams, which he follows with unbelievable tenacity. His creativity and talents are boundless.

He has had to deal with a tremendous amount of adversity with his health, which God has used to draw Joe near to Himself. He has always had a close relationship with Jesus Christ to the point that we used to joke that he had God on "speed dial." I've had the great honor of being his Mother, and his Father and I thank God every day for the quality of person he is. We will always love, respect and believe in Joe. Family, friends and even acquaintances often comment to us on the amazing, yet kind person he is.

His video career began with documentaries he made in Florida, starting with what was in his grandparents' refrigerator. During his many illnesses, he grew to love Star Trek, with Captain Kirk as a role model for him. He recreated Star Trek films, recruiting his friends, filming, directing and acting scene by scene and thereby learning cinematography.

Influenced by his father Joe Vitale's musical career, Joe Vitale Jr. learned to play drums, guitar, keyboards, sing and how to record, produce, mix and master his music. He married his incredibly beautiful, talented, creative and understanding wife, Kathryn Vitale, also a Christian, who is supportive of and sometimes inspires his projects.

Joe has always openly briefly shared his faith as a Christian toward the end of each show with his band "Joe Vitale Jr." and "Ravenwood."

At the beginning of the Covid-19 pandemic, Joe wanted to give people hope and wrote, recorded and produced the song, "We're All In This Together," which was posted with his accompanying video. His music themes have always been something he relates to...overcoming adversity with & through faith in The Lord. No one knew where the pandemic road would lead, and as family, friends and the world began experiencing Covid-19, Joe began posting a nightly prayer for anyone who would read, pray and receive it...a prayer of overcoming through faith in God, and His love, protection, encouragement, blessing and strength while we all look up waiting for His return. Hold on, He's coming.

This is Book One, the first year of Joe's nightly posted prayers during the pandemic.

DAY 1
March 17th, 2020

I just want to say hello to everyone tonight and I hope you are all safe and healthy. We are banding together and I'm seeing kindness towards people like I haven't seen in a very long time. And as I promised, every night I'm claiming Psalm 91 over all of you in Jesus name. This is a battle, it's pure war, and we are the warriors that will prevail. We have to stay together, stay united, not panic and when this viral foe is defeated and eradicated we will celebrate like never before!! I have faith in all of us. We CAN do this!! God bless and protect all of you in the name of Jesus I command victory for each and every one of you. BE HEALTHY! BE SAFE!!

DAY 2
March 18th, 2020

Hey everyone! I released this song, "Fight It Or Self Destruct", back in 2008. In these uncertain times, I hope this gives you some strength! We are going to get through this time, we're gonna beat this thing, we're going to prevail! God will see us through this and as I vowed I'm claiming Psalm 91 over all of you every night until this passes! God bless you all. Be healthy, be safe!!

DAY 3
March 19th, 2020

Hey everyone! I hope everyone is healthy and feeling good. As promised, I'm claiming Psalm 91 over all of you tonight. May this virus end in the name of Jesus! May a hedge of protection surround each and every one of you. Hold on everyone, we are going to get through this. God bless you all!

DAY 4
March 20th, 2020

Hey everyone, as we close out the week, I hope everyone is safe and healthy. We are entering day 4 and as promised, I am here to claim Psalm 91 over all of you tonight. I pray that this horrible virus doesn't come near you or your families. I pray and I know that this virus will end soon. We are truly living through a historic moment as each day passes. And when this is over by the grace of God we can shout we made it through this! As uncertain these times appear, I am seeing so much kindness and charity from not only the citizens but countless businesses that are retooling factories to make new respirators, medical equipment, hiring thousands of delivery personal, grocers working non stop to keep everything stocked. It's amazing to watch. And we will get through this difficult time. God bless you all this weekend. Be healthy, be safe, be vigilant and stay strong! We're all in this TOGETHER!!

DAY 5
March 21st, 2020

Hey everyone! We are ending day 5 and I hope you are having a great weekend. I hope you are all well and healthy. As promised, I will continue to do this every night of this virus.

I claim Psalm 91 over all of you, your friends and your families. In the name of Jesus I claim protection over you and that this horrible virus will end! We're gonna get through this everyone! I believe in the power of prayer so I'm asking everyone to please pray for everyone you know and even don't know. For those of you who know me, my over all message of my music is triumph over adversity, and adversity is what we are facing each and every single day. But I swear to you, through Christ we will triumph over this. Tonight I'm gonna share my debut music video "Never Look Back", This song is based on Psalm 23. I hope this song gives you some strength, hope and peace. God bless all of you my friends and family. We're gonna make it through this. Just keep holding on! Be Healthy Be Safe!

DAY 6
March 22nd, 2020

Hey everyone, It's now coming to the end of Day 6. I hope all of you are okay and healthy.

Tonight I am claiming two Psalms over everyone. I claim Psalm 91 and Psalm 23 over all of you, your friends and families. These are unprecedented times we are in, but we will persevere through this valley we are all walking through. I know this has been tough, I know everyone is scared but we will make it through this, we will beat this virus, life will return to normal, and there will be another tomorrow. We are ALL united in the destruction of this unseen enemy, and we will triumph! Be healthy, be safe! We are all in this TOGETHER! May God bless all of you!

DAY 7
March 23rd, 2020

Hello everyone, I hope all of you are having a good start to your week and for my fellow Ohioians, and at the end of day 7 of our initial lock down and the eve of our new lock down of day 1. I hope all of you are well, healthy and safe.

I'm here once again to claim Psalm 91 and 23 over all of you, your families and your friends. As we continue to pass through this dark valley I want each of you to realize one very important thing. For each step of this journey we are on, we are that much closer to victory. Tomorrow we will even be closer. This time of uncertainty will end, this virus will be eradicated and life will return to normal. We must stay strong, stay vigilant, and not allow fear of the unknown to infiltrate our minds. I want to share another passage that has been resonating in my mind the past few days. Isaiah 46:10 "Be still and know that I am God". We will make it through this everyone! We're all in this TOGETHER! Be Healthy, Be safe! God bless you all.

DAY 8
March 24th, 2020

Hey everyone, I hope everyone is well, healthy and safe tonight. I apologize that I am a little late in sending this message out but I have been battling a migraine all day. But that won't deter my promise to pray for all of you and your families tonight.

In the name of Jesus, I claim Psalm 91 and 23 over all of you, your families, your friends and neighbors. I pray this virus doesn't come near you and that a hedge of protection is around each of you.

Today we are one step closer to getting rid of this virus and stomping it out. I know we are going to be victorious & we will stop this pestilence. I hope these messages lift your spirits during these dark times but just know that there is an end to this valley and we will be triumphant on the mountain! God bless all of you! Be Healthy be safe!

DAY 9
March 25th, 2020

Hey everyone! Another day has passed and I hope you are all safe, healthy and it's that time again for prayer.

I claim Psalm 91 and 23 over all of you, your families, friends, and everyone that you know. I pray for the health and safety of the countless workers in the medical field tirelessly taking care of everyone who is ill. I pray that this horrible pandemic will cease around the globe and that we find a vaccine faster than we thought possible so no one ever has to suffer from this horrible illness. I claim this in the name of Jesus Christ!

We are another day closer to victory everyone! Just hang on! We're gonna get through this. I know it is tough but we will make it through! I walked outside today to get the mail and just the warm sun hitting my face felt like heaven. We are going to come out of this stronger as a people! In my lifetime I have never seen so many people and businesses all giving and donating to help others and eradicate this horrible virus. I'm working on something for all of you and I'm planning to share it on Friday morning if all goes well. That's all I'm going to say for now. But it's a surprise that I hope lifts your spirits. Everyone, we are all in this together and we will triumph! Be healthy! Be Safe! God bless all of you ☺

DAY 10
March 26th, 2020

Hey everyone! Good evening, I hope everyone is well, safe and healthy. I hope this nightly message helps lift your spirits and give you hope through these uncertain times. I really appreciate all the wonderful messages everyone has been sending me. Thank you. And it's that time again.

Dear Heavenly Father, I come to you in the name of Jesus, I claim Psalm 91 and 23 over everyone, all these families, friends, their friends & to the very ends of the earth that you protect them and put a hedge of protection around each and everyone of them from this horrible virus. We pray that this virus is eradicated and never can hurt anyone ever again. In Your precious name I pray Amen!

We're gonna get through this everyone! We're all in this together. I want to mention that tomorrow morning 3.27.20 at 7AM, I am releasing a surprise that I have been working on while in Isolation. It will be on the Ravenwood page. I will also post about it tomorrow as well. It's something that I truly hope lifts your spirits and gives you hope through these days. Stay strong everyone! Be healthy! Be Safe! May God bless all of you!

DAY 11
March 27th, 2020

Good evening everyone! My internet was out but we are back up and running! I hope you had a great week and that all of you're healthy & safe.

Dear Heavenly Father, I come to you with Heavenly praise. I claim Psalm 91 and Psalm 23 over all of you. I pray for protection for all of you, your families, and friends. I pray that this pestilence doesn't come near you and that each of you are surrounded by a hedge of protection. In Christ's name I pray! Amen!

If you didn't see my post earlier, I promised a surprise for all of you. This past week while in lock down I went to work on a new song for my band Ravenwood called "We're All in This Together". I wrote this to give all of you strength, peace and hope through these uncertain times. This is the official video. This is a tribute to all the amazing hard working men and women combating this terrible virus and to all those who this virus has affected. The past two weeks I kept hearing the same phrase "We're All in This Together" and I knew what I needed to do. The official release date is not until May 5th, but I wanted to surprise everyone with something that I hope gives you strength! We're gonna get through this everyone! This virus will be stopped and life will return to normal. Each of you is a soldier in this battle and with God we're already victorious over this invisible enemy we face! Be healthy! Be safe! God bless all of you!

DAY 12
March 28th, 2020

Good evening everyone, as we close another day I wanted to pray for all of you once again as promised.

Dear Heavenly Father, I come to you with Heavenly praise. I claim Psalm 91 and 23 over all of you, your families and friends tonight, tomorrow night and the next night. I pray for health, protection and safety for all of you. I pray that this virus is eradicated, and never causes harm to anyone again. I pray for safety and protection for all the brave men and women in the medical fields. I thank you that this too shall pass and that all will return to normal again. I pray for the workers, the families, everyone that you will have hope, peace and strength to preserver through this dark time. And I thank you Jesus for victory! In Christ's name I pray, amen!

I hope all of you are healthy, safe and well. I know I say this every night, and I don't want it to become old, but we are going to make through this everyone. We've never faced anything like this before in our lifetimes, but we will see victory over this. We will see the end of this virus! We will see all return to normal! We will be stronger as a people, as a nation and as a world. I mentioned this the other night but a passage I keep hearing in my head through these scary times is Psalm 46:10 "Be Still, and know that I am God". God is in control and He is with us each step of this journey. With the close of another day we are one step closer to winning this! We're gonna get through this! We're all in this together! Be healthy! Be Safe! May God bless all of you.

DAY 13
March 29th, 2020

Good evening everyone! As we close out another day of 2020, I hope that this message finds you healthy, well and safe.

Dear Heavenly Father, I come to you with Heavenly praise. Thank you that you each and every day You are leading us to the end of this horrible virus that is ravaging the planet. I claim Psalm 91 and 23 for all of you, your families and friends. I claim protection for all the essential workers in all fields. I pray for security and hope for all the small and large business owners. I pray for all the citizens. Thank you Lord that you are surrounding all of these people with your protective embrace and please bring this horrifying virus to an end. In Christ's name I pray! Amen!

Everyone, I know the future is unknown and very uncertain these days. But I also know that with God we'll push through this and defeat this invisible enemy that is plaguing the planet. We are living in historic and unprecedented times. I swear to you, we will make it through this. History books will be written about this time and you'll be shout I lived through this and made it! As a community, as a city, as a state, as a country, as a continent and as a world we are all fighting the same enemy and have been indelibly united together. WE'RE ALL IN THIS TOGETHER! Everyday we are one step closer, every step is one forward, every advance is a breakthrough and every moment is a possible end to this virus. By the grace of God and Christ this time and season will end. It hasn't been easy, it won't be easy, but we will persevere to victory. Be healthy! Be safe! May God bless you all!

DAY 14
March 30th, 2020

Good evening everyone! As we begin another week, I hope and pray you are all healthy, safe and well. I want to begin tonight by saying we are another day closer to victory!

Dear Heavenly Father, I come to you Heavenly praise. I claim Psalm 91 and 23 over all of you, your families and your friends. I pray for a hedge of protection around all of you and that this virus is stopped and never causes anyone anymore harm ever again. I lift up all the medical workers, scientists and businesses contributing and fighting to stop this terrible virus. Please give them strength and wisdom beyond themselves. I thank You Lord that You are in control and on the throne. Thank you that we will see victory because of You, In the name of Jesus I pray, Amen!

We're pushing through this everyone. We all need to hold on and keep moving forward. I know the isolation is difficult but by doing our part we will help to bring this to an end even faster. I know we can do this! We must do this. Failure must NEVER be in our vocabulary! I know times are uncertain but imagine how amazing the victory is going to feel when this pandemic ends. And through Jesus Christ I promise you it will end. We're gonna get through this! We're all in this TOGETHER! Be Healthy! Be Safe! God bless all of you!!

DAY 15
March 31st, 2020

Good evening everyone, as we close out this day on March 31st, 2020, I hope this message finds you healthy, safe and well. As promised I am here again to pray for all of you. And I just want to say

I really appreciate all the amazing messages I've received. I felt very compelled to do this by God and He deserves all the glory.

Dear Heavenly Father, I come to you with Heavenly praise and I claim Psalm 91 and 23 over you, your families, and friends and all their friends. Lord, we are entering a very difficult next few weeks of this virus in US and around the world, and I ask for a hedge of protection for all these people. I pray that this virus doesn't come across anyone's doorstep and causes no harm to anyone. Lord Jesus, I lift up the countless families impacted by this pestilence spreading across the world before You and that they are taken care of by Your hand. I thank you for their deliverance and health, in your Holy name I pray Lord Jesus, Amen!

The next 2 weeks are definitely going to be a fight against this virus. But we will prevail, we will get through this and through Christ we will be victorious and conquer this adversary. We must not lose heart, we must stay vigilant and have faith that we will get through this. We must stay positive every step of this journey. Please pray for the doctors, the scientists, medical workers, all of our leaders, grocers, pharmacies, businesses, and everyone involved. We must all stand strong and united against this invisible enemy. This difficult time will end and this virus will be eradicated. Life, as uncertain as it seems will return to normal again and we will be stronger! As of today, we another step closer to victory! Everyone, It's all going to be okay and we will get through this. We're all in this TOGETHER! Be healthy! Be Safe! Be Strong! May God bless all of you!

The Sinner's Prayer

      If you are not yet saved I want to personally invite you to read this prayer below. This could be the most profound decision of your entire life. This is a decision only you can make, as I am on a messenger. Please don't put off to tomorrow what can be done right now. Because tomorrow may never come.

If you would like to be saved, please read the prayer below out loud & believing in your heart.

"God, I'm a sinner. I'm sorry for my sins. I ask that You forgive me, and I believe that Jesus Christ is Your Son, and I want to invite Him to come into my heart and trust Him with my life. I'm willing to trust Him as my Savior and follow Him as my Lord forever, and I pray this in Jesus' Name.'"

DAY 16
April 1st, 2020

Good evening everyone, I hope tonight's post finds all of you healthy, safe and well. Let's begin.

Dear Heavenly Father, I come to you with Heavenly praise and claiming Psalm 91 and 23 over you, your family and friends. I pray for a hedge of protection, like an impenetrable force field around everyone that this virus cannot penetrate. I pray for complete healing and restoration for those who have contracted this horrible virus. I pray that this virus has no power against you or cause any harm. In the name of Jesus I command this virus be gone and eradicated from the entire planet. Essentially rendered extinct, inert, and never returns again. In Your Holy name I pray Lord Jesus, Amen.

If you have been watching the news lately, the numbers they have been giving us are very sobering. But we will prevail! I'm asking all of you to please pray along with me over the next few weeks for deliverance from this pestilence. As difficult as this has been for countless people, we will have victory over this. I will say it every night… Through Christ, this virus will end, we will see victory, we will prevail, we WILL eradicate it. We are in a war like none of us has ever seen but we will win. I know your scared and afraid, we all are. I know the future seems uncertain and the unknown can be the scariest realm. Our minds can imagine all the worst case scenarios, but I am telling you this... The passage in the Bible that continues to resonate in my mind is "Be still and know I am God". We are going to get this TOGETHER, we're all in this TOGETHER and through Christ we will be victorious TOGETHER. Be healthy! Be Safe! And may God bless and protect all of you!

DAY 17
April 2nd, 2020

Good evening everyone! I hope you had a wonderful Thursday and that this post again finds you Healthy, safe and well.

Dear Heavenly Father, I come to you again with Heavenly praise. I claim Psalm 91 and 23 over all of you, all of your friends and all of your family and coworkers. I pray that this virus never even touches the threshold of your homes and can't cause you or your loved ones harm. I lift up the families, small businesses and medical workers for peace, hope & prosperity through these uncertain times. And I pray for all of those who have contracted this illness that you have a full recovery and are fully restored to full health. I thank you Lord that this virus will be eradicated and eliminated. I ask for wisdom and strength for the doctors and all those working in the hospitals to keep going. And I pray that you have strength, peace and hope during these difficult uncertain days. In Your Holy name I pray Lord Jesus, Amen!

We are another day closer to victory everyone. It can't get here soon enough and one thing I hope that gives you peace is that every day we move forward, is one less day till we reach not only victory, the cure & new treatments but the elimination of this virus once & for all. I know this is tough & you are afraid but as it says in John 14:1 "Let not your hearts be troubled". I'm telling you, we are going to get through this. We face a great storm before us that seems to go to the edge of the horizon, but God is bigger than this & He will see us through this. We are closer to victory than ever before and tomorrow we will be even closer. We need to stay calm & actively not let our minds go to the worse case scenario. We can do this! Stay strong, vigilant, healthy & safe everyone! We're all in this together! We will all see victory together through Christ! Be Healthy! Be safe! God bless you all!

DAY 18
April 3rd, 2020

Good evening everyone, sorry for the lateness of this one but as promised I am here to pray for all of you again. I hope this post finds you healthy, well and safe.

Dear Heavenly Father, I come to you with Heavenly praise. In the name of Jesus, I claim Psalm 91 and 23 over all of you, your friends, family and coworkers. I pray for the protection of all of you and peace that surpasses all understanding to cover you and your families. I lift up all of you that are afraid and those who are on the front lines to battle this virus that you have strength, peace and hope through these difficult times we face. I pray for the safety of all the medical workers and all those at all levels in all lines of work fighting to keep us fed, safe, and taken care of while we have to stay home. I lift up those who are fighting for their very lives who have contracted this illness for complete restoration and healing. In Your holy name Lord Jesus I pray this, Amen.

Another day has gone by and we are another day closer to destroying this virus once and for all. Through the challenges we have faced and will face we will be stronger because of it. Victory is at hand, and we are closer today than we were yesterday and tomorrow even closer. All of us are afraid, all of us are in this fight together, but together we will win and together we will see this end. There will be a day not too far off when we can stand and shout we made it through this! Stay vigilant, stay healthy, stay safe! May God bless you all!

DAY 19
April 4th, 2020

Good evening everyone! My power was out for a few hours but we are back up and running. That is not stopping me from praying! I hope this post once again finds you healthy, well and safe!

Dear Heavenly Father, I come to you with Heavenly praise. I claim

Psalm 91 and 23 over all of you, your family, friends and coworkers. I pray that this virus is stopped in its tracks and can't even come close to you. I pray for a hedge of protection over all of you that this virus cannot penetrate. I pray for protection for all the health care workers at all levels are safe and given wisdom and strength to move forward through this and to keep going. I pray for the full recovery and restoration for all those who are sick And I pray for peace, safety, health and peace over all of you. In the name of Jesus I pray this, Amen!

As we finish out another day we are another day closer to victory everyone. It was a beautiful day outside today, and even though behind all of this we are in a constant battle, it was nice to see the sun, feel the warmth and know that we are now in spring. I will say going through this with all of you has made me extra appreciate everything even more so. And I swear to you life will return to normal again. We will see the end of this virus and we will see victory! Each step forward is our battle cry! Each discovery on the coming vaccines is a victory! Each advancement to combat this enemy is a victory! By the grace of the Lord almighty, we will prevail and win this war! It's tough, it's difficult, and I know all of you are afraid and the unknown is always scary. We can do this! Know that God is with us every step of this journey and we will win through Christ! Stay Healthy! Stay safe! And may God bless and protect all of you!

DAY 20
April 5th, 2020

Good evening everyone! I hope you are having a wonderful Palm Sunday and I hope that this post finds you healthy, safe and well. As promised I am praying over all of you every single night through this. I hope these messages & prayers give you peace, strength and hope.

Dear Heavenly Father I come to you with Heavenly praise. I claim Psalm 91 and 23 for you, your families, friends and coworkers. I pray that this virus is cast far from you and can never cause you harm. I pray that this virus is eradicated and the vaccine is developed faster then ever thought possible. I pray for the protection of all of you and that you are surrounded by an impenetrable hedge against this virus. I lift up all those who are sick and that they are fully restored and healed. I pray for our doctors, all medical workers, our leaders, our nation and all those affected by this pandemic that they will have strength, wisdom, peace and hope through the coming days. In your Holy name I pray this Lord Jesus, Amen!

It was another beautiful day out and reminded me again that we are in Spring. Spring is always a new beginning for everything. New leaves on the trees, new flowers, new grass, animals are waking up from their winter hibernation and warmth from the sun. And each new day is a day that we know we are one step closer to victory than we were the day before. I know all of you are tired, stressed, tired of sheltering at home and dying to go out, but this dark time will end. We are ever nearer to the cure and every day new treatments are coming together. We are going to beat this! We are going to win! We are going to see victory and we WILL prevail against this common invisible enemy. We're all in this together! Through Christ we will defeat this terrible virus and through Christ life will return to normal again. All of us have had to sacrifice for this but it will not be in vain. This too shall pass! Be healthy! Be Safe! May God bless all of you!

DAY 21
April 6th, 2020

Good evening everyone! As we close out another day on April 6th, 2020 I hope this post finds you safe, healthy and well. As promised, I am here to pray for you again. Let's begin tonight.

Dear Heavenly Father I come to you with Heavenly praise and thanksgiving. I claim Psalm 91 and 23 for you, your loved ones, family, friends and coworkers. I pray for a hedge of protection that cannot be breached by this virus. I pray for peace that surpasses all understanding for all of you. I lift up all those whom this virus has directly affected. I lift up our nation and all the nations affected by this virus to be saved. I pray for protection, wisdom and strength for all the medical workers, doctors, scientists, specialists, EMTs, small and large businesses, the workers, our leaders, and everyone. In Your name Lord Jesus I claim victory over this terrible virus. In Your Holy precious name I pray Lord Jesus, Amen!

We are moving forward everyone! Victory is coming! I know it's hard but we are doing it! We're gonna get through this! We're All in This together! It's tough, we've never had to face anything like this in our lifetime but we will prevail! We will persevere! We will have victory over this virus! I will shout this every night, through Christ we WILL WIN! We're yet another day closer to this being over. We have to stay strong and vigilant. Keep holding on everyone! Be healthy! Be safe! Be Well! God bless you all!

DAY 22
April 7th, 2020

Good evening everyone! I hope all of you had a great April 7th, 2020 and that this post finds you healthy, well and safe. It was a beautiful super moon tonight and a beautiful day here. Easter is upon us! And as promised I am here to pray for you all again tonight.

Dear Heavenly Father, I come to you tonight with Heavenly praise. I claim Psalm 91 and 23 over all of you, your friends, family and coworkers. I pray for a hedge of protection around you and all those you love that is impenetrable. I pray for the eradication of this virus and that it is rendered extinct. I pray for all those afflicted with coronavirus that they have a full recovery and completely restored to full health. I pray for all those working to fight against this virus for strength and wisdom. I pray for all the families that they have hope, peace and strength through this. I thank you Lord and praise Your name and I claim these things in the name of Jesus! Amen!

We're getting through this everyone! We're another day closer to victory! With each step, the journey to victory becomes shorter and it is at hand. As we've all been saying for the past month, We're all in this together, and we will prevail over this pestilence. Life will be restored to normal and we as a people will be stronger and better!

We are all united against a common invisible enemy and we are winning! We must continue to be strong and vigilant but we will see this dark time end. Through Christ we can do this! Be safe, Be Healthy! May God bless you all!

DAY 23
April 8th, 2020

Good evening everyone! It was beautiful out again today here in NE Ohio and we are again another day closer to the end of this virus! I hope this post finds you safe, healthy and well.

Dear Heavenly Father, I come to You with Heavenly praise. I claim Psalm 91 and 23 over all of you, your friends, family and coworkers. In the name of Jesus, I cast this virus from our land that it won't cause any more harm and not come near you. I pray for a hedge of protection around all of you and your loved ones. I thank you Lord that You are walking with us through this uncertain time and that you will deliver us from this terrible virus. I lift up all those afflicted and pray for their complete restoration and recovery. In Your holy name I pray Lord Jesus, Amen!

We are all pushing through this everyone! At this point the curves are looking better and we winning this battle. It's going to take all of us doing our part but we will prevail over this virus. We must stay vigilant, strong, and not let our guard down. I pray for all of you for peace and hope through this. I know a lot of you are still afraid but Let not your heart be troubled. Christ will see us through this! We are going to win! We are going to see victory! Be safe! Be healthy! May God bless you all!

DAY 24
April 9th, 2020

Good evening everyone! It is the end of the day on April 9th, 2020 and I hope you are well, safe and healthy! I'm here again to pray for you.

Dear Heavenly Father, I come to You with Heavenly praise. I claim Psalm 91 and 23 over all of you, your friends, family, coworkers and neighbors. I lift up all the health care workers at all levels that you give the wisdom and strength to continue fighting and taking care of the ill. I pray for complete restoration and recovery for all those who are sick with this terrible virus. I pray for protection for all of you that this virus won't even come near you and stays far away. I pray for all the businesses, workers and families that are afraid for the future, that they have peace and hope through this time. And I pray for the end of this virus that it is rendered extinct and never harms anyone ever again! I pray and claim these things in Your Holy name Lord Jesus! Amen!

Everyone, we are coming up on the weekend and we are another day closer to victory against this enemy! It's been a long journey and it isn't over yet but we will weather this storm and prevail. We are all warriors in a war that is encompassing the entire planet and in the end, we will win! Through Christ ALL things are possible and He is guiding us to victory! We are all in this together and through Christ, we WILL prevail! Stay strong, stay vigilant! Be Healthy! Be Safe! May God bless all of you!

DAY 25
April 10th, 2020

Good evening everyone! As we end April 10th, 2020 it is Good Friday! I hope that you are safe, well and healthy. As we enter Easter weekend I am here again to pray for all of you.

Dear Heavenly Father, on this Good Friday I come to You with Heavenly praise. I thank you Lord Jesus for your sacrifice on the cross over 2,000 years ago that we may be saved through You. I claim Psalm 91 and 23 over all of you, your friends, family, neighbors and coworkers. I pray for an impenetrable hedge of protection around you that this virus cannot penetrate. I pray for and lift up all the families, businesses, workers, medical personnel, our leaders, those who are sick, those who are healthy, our nation, and all the nations afflicted by this terrible virus that You will give them peace, hope, strength, wisdom, restoration and healing. I pray and claim all these things in Your name Lord Jesus and that Your will be done! Amen!

Some good news, things are starting to look up and we may be near the peak of this thing. But even after the peak we still need to be vigilant and strong. We aren't out of the woods yet but we are starting to see light at the edge! Victory is coming swiftly everyone! We are yet another day closer to victory and each day there are a ton of new advances that will help us through this time. Step by step, advance by advance we are nearing the end of this virus. We WILL prevail and through Christ we WILL win! It's a difficult journey and at war with an invisible enemy at the same time but this too shall pass! Let not your heart be troubled! Be safe! Be Healthy! May God bless all of you and Happy Good Friday!

DAY 26
April 11th, 2020

Good evening everyone! It is the night before Easter and I hope this post and message finds you healthy, safe and well. I'm back again to pray over all of you.

Dear Heavenly Father, I come to You with Heavenly praise. I claim Psalm 91 and 23 over all of you, your families, friends, and coworkers. I pray for protection against this virus and that this virus is eradicated and rendered extinct. I pray for wisdom and strength for all the medical workers at all levels to stay strong and healthy that take care of those who are sick. I lift up to You all those who are afflicted by this virus that they have a full recovery and health restored to their bodies. I pray for all of you that you have hope and peace that surpasses all understanding and I claim this in Your name Lord Jesus! Amen!

It is Saturday April 11th and we are closing out another day of this pandemic. We are getting closer to the end of this everyone. Each day that we go through is another day closer to the cure, treatments, a vaccine, victory and the end of this pandemic. We are adapting to the new norm but this will only be temporary. Life will return to normal and when it does we will be stronger and united like no other time in history! We are living through real history that will be taught to future generations and you will be able to tell others I lived through that! I made it! We made it! Through Christ all things are possible and I know He will guide us through this time. Let not your heart be troubled. Be Safe! Be Healthy! May God bless you all and Happy day before Easter everyone!

DAY 27
April 12th, 2020

Happy Easter everyone! I hope you had a wonderful day and that this message/post finds you healthy, well and safe.

Dear Heavenly Father, I come to you again tonight on this Easter Sunday April 12, 2020 with Heavenly praise! Thank You for Your sacrifice on the cross to save all of us who would believe in You. I claim Psalm 91 and 23 for all of you, your friends, family, and coworkers. I pray for an impenetrable hedge of protection around each of you against this virus. I pray for restoration, full recovery and pure health for all those afflicted by this deadly virus. I list up and pray for strength, wisdom, hope and peace for all the medical workers, families, small and large businesses, our leaders, our nation and all the nations affected by this terrible virus. I pray for the vaccine to come faster then ever thought possible and the eradication of this virus altogether. I cast this virus away from all of you in the Holy name of Jesus! And I claim all these things in Your name Lord Jesus Amen!

We are starting a new week and it's a new week of new possibilities to end this pandemic! Victory is coming! It's getting warmer out and we are starting to see the new beginnings of spring. Every step along this difficult journey will not be in vain. Each step is a victory unto itself. Each step is hope! Each step is peace! Each step is a battle won and a life saved. We are yet another day closer to victory and this all ending. We SHALL prevail over this time through Christ! All things are possible with God and He will guide us by His hand through these tumultuous waters we face. We can do this! We're ALL in this together! We WILL prevail in this together! Be strong, vigilant and safe! Be healthy! May God bless all of you!

DAY 28
April 13th, 2020

Hey everyone! It's April 13th, 2020 and it's a brand new day and a brand new week! I hope this message finds all of you well, safe and healthy. As promised I'm here again to pray for all of you.

Dear Heavenly Father, I come to You with Heavenly praise. I claim Psalm 91 and 23 over all of you, your friends, family, coworkers and neighbors. I lift all of you up before God that you are all surrounded by a hedge of protection that is impenetrable. I lift up all the nurses, doctors, scientists, EMTs, medical support workers, police, firemen and everyone else at all levels helping to fight this virus, that they are safe, healthy and have strength and wisdom to keep moving forward. I pray for complete healing and restoration for all the people who are afflicted by this terrible virus. I pray for all of you that you have hope, peace, faith and strength during these uncertain times in our lives. I lift up all the restaurants, small and large businesses and all the employees that are afraid for the future that they are all taken care of and financially sound. In the name of Jesus, I cast this virus AWAY from all of you and that it never crosses the threshold of your homes. I pray for and claim all these things in Your Holy name Lord Jesus, Amen!

I know how frustrating this time is for all of you, and we still have a ways to go on this journey but we are making progress every single day. Even as the numbers start to come down, we need to stay strong and vigilant. We can't let our guard down for even a moment. But we can do this! Failure is not an option and is not in our vocabulary. I swear to all of you that victory is coming soon! Through Christ we WILL prevail over this invisible enemy and we WILL be victorious. Yes life is somewhat different right now from our norm, and it will return to normal, but as in war, our sacrifices will not go in vain. WE WILL WIN! With each day, each step, each discovery, each breakthrough, we continue to move forward to victory. We are closer today then we were yesterday and tomorrow we'll even be closer! Say it with me… WE WILL PREVAIL!! Be strong! Be healthy! Be safe!! May God bless you all!

DAY 29
April 14th, 2020

Good evening everyone! It's April 14th, 2020 and I hope this message finds you healthy, safe and well. As we close another day in April, I'm here to pray for you all again.

Dear Heavenly Father, I come to You with Heavenly praise and thanksgiving. I claim Psalm 91 and 23 over all of you, your family, your friends, neighbors and coworkers tonight, tomorrow night and the night after that. I pray for safety, peace, hope, vigilance, perseverance, faith, health and protection over all of you. I pray for safety, strength and wisdom for all those fighting this terrible virus. I pray for all those who are sick with the virus that they are fully restored to complete health. In the name of Jesus, I cast this virus far from all of you that it cannot even come near you or your loved ones. I thank you Lord Jesus that You are leading us through this storm and that through You, victory is coming soon! I claim all these things in Your Holy name I pray Lord Jesus, Amen!

I want to personally thank all the medical workers at all levels on the front lines of this war. You are all TRUE heroes and all of us thank you! The numbers are continuing to drop and that is wonderful news. We have to continue to be vigilant and safe but things are definitely looking up! As I say every night… Through Christ WE WILL PREVAIL over this virus! Victory is coming with every day and every step! I know it's difficult right now, and I know how frustrated all of you are but keep holding on! We can do this! We will get through this! We're ALL in this together!! Say this with me! WE WILL PREVAIL!! Be Healthy! Be Safe! May God bless all of you!

DAY 30
April 15th, 2020

Greetings and hello everyone! I hope this message once again finds you healthy, safe and well. We are officially in the middle of the month and on this day April 15th, 2020 I am here to pray for you all once again.

Dear Heavenly Father I come before You once again with Heavenly praise and thanksgiving. Thank You Lord Jesus that You are with all of us through this terrible storm and pandemic. I claim Psalm 91 & 23 over all of you, your friends, family and coworkers that you may have a spiritual impenetrable hedge of protection surrounding all of you. In the name of Jesus I cast out the spirit of fear and uncertainty that follows so many people through this time far away from you. I lift up all the medical workers, scientists, businesses, citizens, leaders, everyone who is fighting this terrible virus and I pray for their protection, wisdom, strength and perseverance to keep going, keep fighting, and keep moving forward! I pray for all those who are afflicted around the world with this virus that they are restored to full health faster than thought possible and that this virus is eradicated from the very face of the planet! I claim all these things in Your Holy name Lord Jesus! Amen!

Everyone, we are still moving forward and the curve is not only flattening but seems to be on the downward turn which is great news. And as I say every night, we need to continue to be strong and vigilant to keep those numbers dropping. This time is very scary and uncertain but out of this apparent darkness we all will see light again soon! THIS TOO SHALL PASS! Victory is coming soon and through Christ WE SHALL PREVAIL! We are beating this virus, we are winning the battles and the war! Soon all of you will be able to shout WE HAVE WON! It will take a little more time but everything will return to normal again. As people, we are permanently united like no other time in our lifetime. Not just a city, a state, a country, a continent, a hemisphere but as the entire planet! We are going to get through this! We're ALL in this together! Be safe! Be Healthy! May God bless you all!

DAY 31
April 16th, 2020

Hey everyone! It is the end of the day on April 16th, 2020 and we are continuing to move forward! Before we start tonight I wanted to mention a passage that popped up on my screen today that I felt was very appropriate in our current circumstances. Psalm 56:3 "Whenever I am afraid, I will trust in You." God is in control! And as promised I am here again to pray for all of you.

Dear Heavenly Father, I come to You with Heavenly praise and thanksgiving. I claim Psalm 91, Psalm 23 and Psalm 56:3 over all of you, your friends, family, coworkers and neighbors. I pray for all of you that you are surrounded by a spiritual hedge of protection and that this virus has no power, no control, and cannot come near you or your loved ones. In the name of Jesus, I cast this virus far from your presence, and that it will be rendered extinct. I pray for all those afflicted by this virus that they are restored to full health. I pray that You, Lord Jesus, will provide for all the people who have been so greatly impacted by this virus. I pray for all of you that you have peace, hope, strength, and perseverance through this great storm we face. I thank you Lord for our coming victory!! I thank You Lord Jesus and claim all these things in Your name, AMEN!

It was chilly out today in Akron, Ohio but beautiful at the same time and a reminder that Spring is here and summer is around the corner. This journey continues that we are all on and we are continuing to press forward through this dark valley but light is ahead and we shall prevail! Please stay strong and vigilant through the coming weeks ahead. This time will come to a close and everything will return to normal but we can't become complacent. Failure is not an option and we will see victory! We ARE going to get through this! We ARE going to conquer and eradicate this virus! And through Christ, We ARE going to win! We are another day closer to victory! YELL it with me again! WE WILL PREVAIL!!! We're ALL in This Together!! Be healthy! Be Safe! May God bless you all!

DAY 32
April 17th, 2020

Good evening everyone! It's Friday, April 17th, 2020 and the end of another week. As always I hope this message finds you safe, well and healthy. I want to say this before I begin tonight, I believe very deeply in the power of prayer especially in this uncertain times and I truly believe it makes a huge difference.

Dear Heavenly Father, I come to You with Heavenly praise and thanksgiving. I claim Psalm 91 and 23 over all of you, your family, friends, coworkers and neighbors. I pray that you have health, peace, safety, healing, strength and wisdom through this storm. I lift up all the medical workers at all levels and everyone who is fighting this virus that they have strength and wisdom to combat this terrible illness. I lift up all the afflicted that they are healed and restored to full health. I pray that this terrible virus is eradicated and a vaccine is created in record time. I cast this virus far away from you and your homes in the name of Jesus. I claim all these things in Your Holy name Lord Jesus, Amen!

Tonight, I want to ask how all of you are doing? I know this is a difficult time for everyone but we are going to get through this! We're ALL in this Together and we ALL have each others backs. Sometime in the very near future this entire time will be a distant memory and you will have lived through true historic times. Books will be written about this time, lectures given in colleges and universities, and you are part of that history. You will be able to tell future generations that you lived through that time and made it. This journey is tough and each step sometimes seems more difficult than the last but we continue to press forward to victory. This season will end and through Christ we shall Prevail! Let not your heart be troubled as God is in control and is guiding us through this valley and storm. We must continue to be vigilant. But I truly tell you this, WE WILL WIN and VICTORY IS COMING!! Say this with me now… "VICTORY IS COMING" Be Safe! Be Healthy! May God bless all of you!

DAY 33
April 18th, 2020

Good evening everyone! It's the end of the day on April 18th, 2020 and I hope this message finds you once again healthy, safe and well.

Dear Heavenly Father I come to You with Heavenly praise and thanksgiving. Thank You Father for guiding us through another step forward in the battle against this terrible virus. I claim Psalm 91, Psalm 23 and Psalm 56:3 over all of you, your families, friends and coworkers. I pray for an impenetrable hedge of protection around each of you that this virus cannot and will not penetrate. As we near the reopening of the states and country I pray for Your protection even more so and that this virus is eradicated and rendered extinct. I pray for healing and full restoration for all those who are afflicted with this virus and those who are afraid. I cast the spirit of fear away from you. Greater is He who is in us then he who is in the world. I pray that all of you will receive peace that surpasses all understanding and know that God is in control and this time will end. I pray for wisdom and strength to all the people combating this virus at all levels around the planet. In the name of Jesus I command this pestilence to be removed and cast far from all of you and your loved ones. I claim all these things and thank you for the coming victory in the name of Jesus! Amen!

We are through another day and we are coming up on the reopening of the states and country. During this time we must not be complacent and must stay strong and vigilant. We are winning the battles and inevitably the war but we have to keep pressing forward without falter. As I imagine all of us combating this virus I visualize a Roman Phalanx, which is essentially a row of soldiers with shields linked together moving forward one step at a time pushing through the enemy without fear. We WILL prevail in this battle and we WILL see victory in the war! Victory is on our side and through Christ nothing is impossible. We're all in this together everyone! Shout this with me! FORWARD TO VICTORY! Be healthy! Be safe! May God bless you all!!

DAY 34
April 19th, 2020

Good evening everyone! It is the end of the day on April 19th, 2020 & I'm here once again to pray for all of you. I hope this message finds you healthy, safe & well. I also hope that these prayers give you peace, hope & strength through this difficult time we are all facing.

Dear Heavenly Father, I come to You once again with Heavenly praise & thanksgiving. I claim Psalm 91 & 23 over all of you, your friends, family & coworkers, tonight, tomorrow night & the next night. I thank you Lord Jesus, that with each passing day we are closer to the end of this uncertain time in all our lives. I pray for all the medical workers that they have health, strength, peace, wisdom & hope through each day & each difficult shift. I pray for all the afflicted that they are restored to full health. I lift up all the families & businesses around the country & world that you give them peace & hope through this dark time. In the name of Jesus, I cast this virus far from all of you & that it won't even come near the threshold of your house. I claim all these things in Your name & thank you Lord Jesus that victory is coming, Amen!

Everyone, we are about ready to start another week & that means another week of new possibilities for fighting this virus! Just think, at any one moment, there are millions upon millions of people fighting this virus all 24 hours of every day, seven days a week. So much can happen in just one 24 hour cycle. As of today, we are another step closer to victory! I can't stress this concept enough and I may say it every night but it is totally true. Through the power and guidance of Christ, WE SHALL PREVAIL! We have to keep moving forward but we shall prevail! We're going to win this thing! We're going to eradicate this virus! We're ALL in this together! Be Healthy! Be Safe! May God bless you all!

DAY 35
April 20th, 2020

Good evening everyone! As we end the day on April 20th, 2020, I hope you all are having a good start to your week and that this message once again finds you healthy, safe and well. Let's begin.

Dear Heavenly Father, I come to You with Heavenly praise and thanksgiving. I claim Psalm 91, Psalm 23 and 56:3 over all of you, your family, your friends, your neighbors and your coworkers. I pray that all of you have an impenetrable hedge of protection around each of you and in the name of Jesus I cast this virus far from you and your loved ones. I pray that each of you have peace, strength, and hope during this frustrating and difficult time. I thank You Lord Jesus that You are guiding us to victory with each day and walking this journey with us. I thank You and claim all these things in the name of Jesus, Amen!

This has been quite a journey we've all been on and we still have a ways to go before the end of this. But like so many difficult times in history, those dark days always end. Life always returns to normal, and we WILL defeat this invisible enemy. I know all of you are scared, frustrated and ready for all of this to be over with, and it will, but we all have to stay vigilant and strong until the end. We're another day closer to this pandemic ending and another day closer to the greatest victory this planet has ever seen! With Christ all things are possible and we WILL prevail! I will continue to pray this every night! We are going to beat this and victory is coming soon! Stay Strong! Stay Vigilant! Be Healthy! Be Safe! We are all in this together!! God bless you all!

DAY 36
April 21st, 2020

Good evening everyone! It's the end of the day on April 21st, 2020 and I hope you all had a great day and, as always, that this post finds you healthy, well and safe.

Dear Heavenly Father, I come to You with Heavenly praise and thanksgiving. I thank You Lord Jesus for continuing to guide and walk with us through this difficult journey and as You promised that You would never leave us or forsake us. I claim Psalm 91 and 23 over all of you, your friends, family, coworkers and neighbors. In the name of Jesus, I cast this virus away from you and all your loved ones. I call upon You Lord, the Great Physician, to heal and fully restore all those who are afflicted with this terrible virus and that You place a hedge of protection around all of you that nothing can penetrate. I lift up to You all the medical workers at all levels, businesses and everyone that has joined the fight that you give them protection, wisdom, peace, hope and strength to keep going & keep moving forward. I thank you Lord Jesus, that You are in control and that You will deliver us. I thank You Lord Jesus and claim all these things in Your Holy name, Amen!

Another day completed, another day forward and another day closer to victory! We're doing it everyone! We are pressing forward through the storm and this storm will end! Through Christ, we shall prevail! Let not your heart be troubled. We must continue to stay strong and vigilant over the coming weeks and months. And once again say it with me… "WE WILL SEE VICTORY!!" We're all in this together!! Be healthy! Be safe!! May God bless you all!

DAY 37
April 22nd, 2020

Good evening everyone! As we close out another day of lock down here in Ohio, it is April 22nd, 2020. I hope that this message once again finds you safe, healthy and well through this difficult time. As promised, I'm here again to pray for all of you.

Dear Heavenly Father, I come to You with Heavenly praise and thanksgiving. I claim Psalm 91, Psalm 23 and Psalm 56:3 over all of you, your family, friends, coworkers and neighbors. I pray for an impenetrable hedge of protection around each of you. I pray for all the health care workers that they are protected through their shifts and have more than enough supplies to do their jobs. I also pray for their safety, that they have wisdom and strength to get through every day. I lift up to You Lord Jesus all the sick and afflicted by this virus, that you restore them to full & complete health. I pray for peace, hope and strength for all the families who are afraid and have been affected by this virus. I also pray Lord Jesus for a blessing over all of the families, businesses (large and small) that through this time that all of you have more than enough to get through each and every day. I thank You Lord Jesus that You are in control and guiding us through this dark valley that all of us are walking through. In the name of Jesus, I cast this virus far from you and your loved ones. I claim all these things in Your Holy name Lord Jesus, Amen!

We are almost through another week everyone and we are coming up on the end of the lock down in Ohio. Through the coming weeks we need to continue to stay vigilant and safe. I know you're all tired, frustrated, and wanting everything to go back to normal again. And it will.. But we have to continue to keep moving forward and taking each step until we reach victory. Which we WILL see VICTORY! Through the power of Christ, we WILL PREVAIL! I truly believe that. With each step we take we are getting closer to this pandemic ending! It's coming! Let not your heart be troubled. We need to hold on and stay strong. We can do this. I have faith in all of you! We're gonna get through this! It's going to be okay! We're ALL in this together! Be healthy! Be safe! May God bless all of you!

DAY 38
April 23rd, 2020

Good evening everyone! It's April 23rd, 2020 & the end of another day of lock down & I'm back to pray for all of you again tonight. I hope you are all doing well, are safe, sound & healthy.

Dear Heavenly Father, I come to You with Heavenly praise & thanksgiving. I claim Psalm 91, Psalm 23 & 56:3 over all of you, your family, friends, coworkers, neighbors and all you love and hold dear. I pray for a protection for each of you that you are surrounded by a shield that the virus cannot penetrate. In the name of Jesus, I cast this virus far away from you & your loved ones & that it is completely eradicated & rendered extinct. I pray that all of you have hope, peace, strength, wisdom & an abundance through this difficult time. I lift up to You Lord Jesus all the afflicted and sick that You restore them to complete health. I pray for the Vaccine that it is created faster & more effective than ever thought possible. I lift up all the medical workers & pray for their safety, protection, wisdom & strength. I lift up our families, businesses, our leaders, our nation & all the nations affected by this virus that You will heal their lands & people. I claim all these things in Your Holy name Lord Jesus, Amen!

We are continuing to fight this virus & we are hitting it with everything in the arsenal. This is a true war & with each day and each saved life, we have a new victory. We ARE going to win this war! It continues to be a difficult journey & we still have many more days to go. But those days will not be in vain. I said this before but truly there are millions of people around the planet fighting this virus. Just imagine what 24 hours x millions fighting it can yield! Through Christ WE SHALL PREVAIL!! Coming soon will be a day when this virus is no more!! Coming soon there will NOT be a new case!! Coming soon this virus will be utterly destroyed! Say it with me!! COMING SOON IS VICTORY!! We're All in This Together! We're Gonna get through this! Be healthy! Be Safe & May God bless & protect all of you!!

DAY 39
April 24th, 2020

Good evening everyone! It is the end of the day on Friday April 24th, 2020 and it was another beautiful day out today. Once again I hope that this message finds all of you healthy, safe and well. As promised I am here once again to pray for all of you.

Dear Heavenly Father, I come to You with Heavenly praise and thanksgiving. I claim Psalm 91, Psalm 23 & Psalm 56:3 over all of you, your friends, your family, neighbors, coworkers & all whom you hold dear. I pray for an impenetrable hedge of protection around each of you. I lift up & pray for all those who are sick and afflicted with this terrible virus & that they are healed and fully restored by You Lord Jesus. I pray for all the medical workers, scientists, families, businesses, our leaders, our cities, states, nation & all who are affected by this virus that they have safety, protection, peace, hope, strength & an abundance to get through each and every single day of this pandemic. In the name of Jesus, I bind up and cast this virus and the spirit of fear to farthest ends of the earth away from you and your loved ones & that this virus is completed eradicated and rendered extinct I thank You Lord Jesus that you are guiding us through this difficult journey and that through You we shall prevail. I thank You & claim all these things in Your Holy name Lord Jesus, Amen!

Well everyone, we are through another day and another step of this journey is completed. We are now EVEN closer to victory then we were just yesterday. We are coming up on the beginning of reopening the cities and states and we need to continue to be strong and vigilant and continue to be safe. We are going to get through this and we are ALL in this together! It was beautiful out again today and once again reminded me that with the new beginnings of Spring, we are moving forward each new day. I know how difficult this has been for all of you including myself but this time will end and we will see victory in the end. Let not your heart be troubled! God is in control and through Christ we shall prevail! We can do this everyone! Let's take another great big step tomorrow and continue to press forward! LET'S DO IT!! Be healthy! Be safe! May God bless all of you!

DAY 40
April 25th, 2020

Good evening everyone! Apologies for this being a little later tonight but once again I'm here to pray for all of you. It is the end of another day of the pandemic, April 25th, 2020 and I hope that this message continues to find you safe, healthy and well. Let's begin.

Dear Heavenly Father, I come to You tonight with Heavenly praise & thanksgiving. Lord Jesus, I claim Psalm 91, Psalm 23 and Psalm 56:3 over all of you, your friends, your dear families, your coworkers and your neighbors. In the name of Jesus & through His name I command this virus and the spirit of fear to be gone and cast far from you and your loved ones, never to return. In Christ's name, It must go now! I lift up all those afflicted by this terrible pestilence that they are restored to full health. I pray for a hedge of protection around each of you and that nothing can penetrate and cause harm. I lift up everyone who has been affected by this pandemic that their lives will be restored to fullness & have abundance through this time. I pray for all the medical workers around the globe fighting this virus that they are protected and have strength and wisdom to treat their patients. If you are afraid tonight know this, Greater is He who is in you than He who is in the world & through Christ all things are possible. I claim all these things in Your Holy name Lord Jesus, Amen!

Here in NE Ohio, it was another beautiful day out & it was good to feel the sun on my face. We are ALL living through a difficult time but it is also good to take note of the beauty around us that we usually take for granted. I know all of you have been frustrated & ready for this pandemic to be over and it will soon. Like any war we face, when you are in the thick of it, you wonder if or when it will end. I'm telling all of you now that this war will end. We continue to win battle after battle & as I said in the prayer, through Christ WE SHALL PREVAIL! This dark valley will end! Each day we are one step CLOSER! We must stay strong, calm & vigilant! Each fight, each life saved, each medical breakthrough, each battle won, is another victory upon victory! We're all in this together!! Say this again with me. VICTORY IS COMING! Be healthy! Be safe! May God bless you all!!

DAY 41
April 26th, 2020

Good evening everyone, It is the ending of the day on April 26th, 2020 and we are getting ready to start a brand new week. As you read tonight's prayer, I hope that this message once again finds you healthy, safe and well. As promised I will pray over all of you every single night of this pandemic.

Dear Heavenly Father, I come to You with Heavenly praise and thanksgiving. In the name of Jesus I claim Psalm 91, Psalm 23 and Psalm 56:3 over all of you, your friends, family, coworkers and neighbors. I pray for an impenetrable hedge of protection around each of you and your loved ones that this virus cannot penetrate. In the name of Jesus, I command & cast this virus & the spirit of fear far from you and the very thresholds of your houses. I pray for everyone who has been affected by this virus that you will have more than enough to get through this uncertain time and that with each day, each of you has peace, wisdom, strength, and perseverance. I lift up all the afflicted of this virus, that You restore them to complete health and that they are made whole. I pray for the protection of all the medical workers that they are protected and given strength and wisdom to keep going through the most difficult shifts taking care of all their patients. I pray that a safe and powerful vaccine is developed faster than anyone thought possible. I thank You Lord Jesus that even in this dark valley we are walking through that You are right by our side and as You promised You would never leave us or forsake us. I claim all these things in Your Holy name Lord Jesus, Amen!

Everyone, I sincerely hope that all of you are safe and healthy. I know all of you can't wait for this time to be over & it will end one day soon. I hope that these messages and prayers I post every night help to give you strength and hope. Not from me, but from God. As scary as the numbers still are, they are dropping and we are pushing through this valley we are all in. We are winning these battles & soon, the war on this virus. It's been a difficult journey but we continue to weather the storm of uncertainty. We continue to wage war on the unknown as we proceed to glorious victory. Victory is coming &when the history books of time are written, you can say you survived this pandemic. Everyone who is alive this very moment is indelibly united together & through Christ WE SHALL PREVAIL!! We're All in this together!! Be Healthy! Be Safe! Be STRONG! May God bless all of you!

DAY 42
April 27th, 2020

Good evening everyone! It is the ending of the day on Monday April 27th, 2020 during this pandemic and I hope this message once again continues to find you healthy, safe and well. I said it back in March and I continue to say it today. We're gonna get through this everyone! We're ALL in this together! And as promised I am back to pray for all of you again.

Dear Heavenly Father, I come to You with Heavenly praise and thanksgiving. Thank You Lord Jesus, for guiding all of us through this uncertain time and walking with us step by step. I claim Psalm 91, Psalm 23, Psalm 56:3 and Isaiah 54:17 over all of you, your friends, family, coworkers, and neighbors. I lift up everyone who is afflicted by this terrible virus, and that all of them are restored to full health. I pray for all the families, businesses, and citizens that continue to be affected by this virus that you will have peace, hope, strength, and a blessing of abundance despite what is going on. In the name of Jesus, I cast this virus and the spirit of fear far from you, the threshold of your house and your loved ones and that this virus will be eradicated from the planet never to return. I lift up to You Father, all the hard working medical workers that they are given continued supernatural wisdom and strength to keep going. I thank You and claim all these things in Your Holy name Lord Jesus, Amen!

As we end another day, we are getting closer to things starting to open up around the country. We need to continue to stay strong and vigilant and not let our guard down. This dark valley we're all walking through will end. We are going to win! We're gonna make it! Through the power and guidance of Jesus Christ we shall PREVAIL! Keep strong everyone! Keep moving forward! Victory is coming! Be healthy! Be safe! Be strong! May God bless all of you!

DAY 43
April 28th, 2020

Good evening everyone! It's nearing the end of the day on April 28th, 2020 and I hope and pray that this message finds you healthy, safe and well once again. I am back to pray for all of you as promised.

Dear Heavenly Father, I come to You with Heavenly praise & thanksgiving. Thank You Lord Jesus for all that You have given us & that You are with us every step of this journey through this dark valley. I claim Psalm 91, Psalm 23, Psalm 56:3 & Isaiah 54:17 over all of you, your friends, family, coworkers & neighbors, tonight, tomorrow, and the day after that. I lift up all the afflicted that You restore all of them to complete health. I pray for the safety of all the medical workers at all levels that they are protected and given strength and wisdom to keep going. In the name of Jesus, I command and cast this virus, and the spirit of fear far from you and all your loved ones. I lift up and pray for all the families, businesses (large and small), our nation, our leaders, workers and people that You give them hope, peace, faith, strength, and an abundance through this difficult time. I claim all these things in Your Holy name Lord Jesus, Amen!

Everyone, I know that all of you are very frustrated, stressed and ready for this whole pandemic to be over with. Myself included. We're yet another day closer to victory. We all need to continue to stay strong, vigilant and not become complacent with the states getting ready to reopen. Even after the reopening begins, our journey continues and I will be here to pray for all of you each and every night. The message in my music has always been triumph over adversity and the only thing that has kept me going all these years is my faith in Jesus Christ. He has never failed me! He has given me strength when I've felt that I have none left, He has kept me fighting to victory when all has seemed lost and He will deliver all of us through this uncertain time. As I say every single night through Christ WE SHALL PREVAIL!!! VICTORY IS COMING! WE WILL WIN! Let not your heart be troubled! We're gonna get through this! We're all in this together! Be healthy! Be Safe! Be Strong! May God bless all of you!

DAY 44
April 29th, 2020

Good evening everyone! It's April 29th, 2020 and we are closing out another day of this pandemic. In these historic times we live in, I hope this message and all these messages find you healthy, well and safe. This is day 46 since I began these nightly prayers and as promised I am here once again to pray for all of you. Let's begin.

Dear Heavenly Father, I come to You with Heavenly praise and thanksgiving. Thank You Lord Jesus for all You have given to us and that You are walking with us every step of this journey. I claim Psalm 91, Psalm 23, Psalm 56:3 and Isaiah 54:17 over all of you, your families, your friends, your coworkers, and your neighbors. I pray for an impenetrable hedge of protection that surrounds you and completely protects you from this virus. In the name of Jesus I command and cast this virus and the spirit of fear away from all of you and that it will soon be eradicated and removed from this earth. I pray for full health and complete restoration for everyone who has been afflicted by this virus. I pray for all the medical workers, families, businesses, our leaders, our nation, and all the lives affected by this virus that they will have peace, hope, faith, strength, wisdom and abundance during these uncertain times. I lift up all the businesses and their employees that they will all be taken care of and able to reopen soon and safely. I pray and claim all these things in Your name Lord Jesus, Amen!

We are continuing to press forward through each day and we are continuing to win the war on this virus. I cannot wait for the day that we will celebrate the destruction of this virus with a unified shout of victory! Just think, every 24 hours, we're making leaps and bounds in combating this invisible enemy. We are going to be victorious! Through Christ, WE SHALL PREVAIL!! We have to hold on and stay strong. I know you're all frustrated, tired of this lock down and ready for all of this to be over. Please know this, with each day completed, VICTORY IS COMING!

Tonight I want to add something extra to this message. We are living in very uncertain times and if you're afraid for the future, for your family, your career, your business, your employees and you want to have peace in these uncertain times, I offer this... From what I have personally experienced throughout my life, everything leads back to one decision I made early on… That was accepting Jesus Christ as my Lord and Savior. I never force this on anyone, this is a decision you and only you can make. If this is something you would like to do, all you have to do is say this simple prayer.

"God, I'm a sinner. I'm sorry for my sins. I ask that You forgive me, and I believe that Jesus Christ is Your Son, and I want to invite Him to come into my heart and trust Him with my life. I'm willing to trust Him as my Savior and follow Him as my Lord forever, and I pray this in Jesus' Name. Amen'"

We're gonna get through this everyone! We're all in this together! Be healthy! Be safe! May God bless you all!

DAY 45
April 30th, 2020

Good evening everyone! We are closing out yet another day of this pandemic. It's April 30th, 2020 and I hope this message once again finds you healthy, well and safe. As promised I am here each and every night to pray for all of you.

Dear Heavenly Father, I come to You with Heavenly praise and thanksgiving. Thank You Father, for taking care of us, protecting us and walking with us each and every step of this very difficult journey. I claim Psalm 91, Psalm 23, Psalm 56:3 and Isaiah 54:17 over all of you, your friends, family, coworkers and neighbors tonight, tomorrow night and the night after that. I pray that each of you is completely protected by a spiritual hedge of protection that this virus cannot penetrate. I lift up all the afflicted from this virus that You please restore them to full and complete health. Please give strength, wisdom and protection to all the medical workers at all levels battling this virus. Father, please give all the people who are afraid for their future, frustrated and scared peace that surpasses all understanding that only You can provide. I pray that all of you have hope, strength, and wisdom during these uncertain times. In the name of Jesus I command and cast this virus and spirit of fear far from you, all your loved ones and the threshold of your homes. In the name of Jesus, Greater is He who lives in us than he who is in the world and if we resist the devil he must flee from us and by Your name the devil and all his agents of evil must go. I thank You, and claim all these things in Your Holy name Lord Jesus, Amen!

I know how frustrated all of you feel and that with each day all the negative news we hear can tend to pull down our spirits. But there is always good news to lift our spirits! That good news is that we are continuing to press forward every day, continually winning battles and inevitably the war on this virus. One day soon this will all behind us and we can look back with a united shout "I MADE IT THROUGH!" Through Christ we shall see victory and eradicate this virus! We're going to keep fighting! We're not going to stop and we're going to win! The history that is unfolding before us will shortly be only that… History! We're gonna make it through this everyone! We're all in this together. Let not your heart be troubled. Be healthy! Be safe! May God bless all of you!

DAY 46
May 1st, 2020

Good evening everyone! Well we are concluding another week of this pandemic and it is now May 1st, 2020 and as with every night I hope this message finds you healthy, well and safe wherever you are in the world. As we are starting a new month I am back as promised to pray for all of you again every night.

Dear Heavenly Father, I come to You with Heavenly praise and thanksgiving. I thank You for Your guidance and wisdom through this difficult journey. Please Lord Father Jesus, heal our lands. I claim Psalm 91, Psalm 23, Psalm 56:3 and Isaiah 54:17 over all of you, your loved ones, friends, family, neighbors and coworkers. In the name of Jesus I command and cast this virus away from you and that it is completely eradicated from this planet. I pray that through

Your wisdom our doctors and scientists continue to develop a safe vaccine faster than ever thought possible before in history. I pray for all the afflicted that they would be completely healed and full restored by Your hand. I pray for all the countless families, citizens, businesses, nations that they will be fully provided for and that they have abundance and more than enough to make it through this difficult dark time we all face. I lift up all the medical workers. They are exhausted and overworked, tirelessly taking care of all the sick that You would give them supernatural strength and wisdom to keep going. I claim all these things in Your Holy name Lord Jesus, Amen!

We are through another month as we begin the month of May and we are getting closer to the comforting warmth summer. We are now slowly starting to open up the country again and I know everyone is tired and ready for this all to be over with. We still need to keep pressing forward with wisdom and be strong and vigilant, but take a moment to appreciate the world around you outside. This time has made me appreciate the little things like looking at a freshly bloomed cherry tree against the sky in my backyard. The beauty that God has placed around us that we sometimes overlook is truly a miracle. I know how difficult this has been for all of you, myself included. But this too shall pass! Christ is leading us through this dark valley to victory and victory is coming soon. As I say each night, each day we are one day closer. I want you all to know that it's all going to be okay. Let not your hearts be troubled. We're gonna get through this. We are ALL in this together!! Shout it with me again! WE SHALL PREVAIL! Be healthy! Be safe! May God bless all of you!

DAY 47
May 2nd, 2020

Good evening everyone! We are coming to the end of the day on Saturday, May 2nd, 2020 and I hope all of you are safe, healthy and well. Tonight I am back to pray for all of you once again as I will be here every night of this pandemic. I truly believe in the power of prayer and that it is one of the MOST powerful weapons against the enemy. Let's begin.

Dear Heavenly Father, I come to You with Heavenly praise and thanksgiving. Thank You Lord Jesus for protecting us, walking with us and guiding us through this difficult journey. I thank You that You will lead us to victory over this virus and that You are in complete control. I claim Psalm 91, Psalm 23, Psalm 46:1, Psalm 56:3 and Isaiah 54:17 over all of you, your family, friends, neighbors, coworkers and all you hold dear. I pray for a spiritual hedge of protection to surround all of you that no evil can penetrate. In the name of Jesus, I command and cast this virus and spirit of fear away from you, your loved ones and that this pestilence never crosses the threshold of your homes. I lift up the sick and afflicted by this virus that are healed and restored to full health. I pray for miracle healing of those on the edge that they are brought back in complete health. I pray for all the medical workers that they have more than enough supplies, wisdom and strength to keep going. I pray for all the families, businesses, cities, counties, states, our nation, our leaders that they are given strength, wisdom, guidance, hope, peace, and abundance to make it through these difficult days. In the name of Jesus, I pray that this virus is eradicated from the planet and that You will please heal our lands. I thank You God that You are in control, on the Throne and that You will never leave us or forsake us. I claim all these things in Your Holy name Lord Jesus and thank You, we love You Father, In Jesus name I pray, Amen!

It's starting to warm up outside which means that spring is here and hopefully the heat will start to help destroy this virus. We are getting through this and we are going to be okay. Through Christ, ALL things are possible and someday soon this virus will be gone. One thing that I have appreciated more than anything through this time is how much I truly love my friends and family and how much I dearly miss all of them. Soon we will all be back together again and all of us as a people will bring forth a great shout of victory when this time ends. It's coming! Victory is coming! Through Christ WE SHALL PREVAIL! Keep moving forward!! We're ALL in this TOGETHER!! Let not your heart be troubled! Be healthy! Be safe! Be strong! May God bless all of you!

DAY 48
May 3rd, 2020

Good evening everyone! We are at the end of the day on May 3rd, 2020 and we're about to begin another week. If you haven't seen my prayers each night up to this point, I want to let you know that I will be praying over all of you each and every night of this pandemic. Thank you for the wonderful messages that I have received in regards to these prayers. I am just trying to do what I felt God was directing me to do. Let's begin.

Dear Heavenly Father, I come to You with Heavenly praise and thanksgiving. Thank You Lord Jesus for the blessings that You have given us, for Your guidance and wisdom and for walking with us and never leaving us through this difficult time. I claim Psalm 91, Psalm 23, Psalm 46:1, Psalm 56:3 and Isaiah 54:17 over all of you, your friends, family, coworkers, neighbors and all you hold dear. I pray for a continued spiritual hedge of protection around each of you that no evil can penetrate. I pray for all the families, all the businesses both large and small, the workers, our leaders, our nation and the world that through this time all of you will have peace, faith, wisdom, strength and abundance to make it through each day with more than enough. In the name of Jesus, I command, bind up and cast this virus and spirit of fear away from you as far as the east is from the west and that it never comes near you, your loved ones or even crosses the very threshold of your homes. I lift up all the afflicted that they are restored to full health. I pray for wisdom and strength for all the medical workers working tirelessly to fight this virus and help the sick. I claim all these things in Your name Lord Jesus and thank you for the coming victory. In Your Holy Precious name I pray, Amen!

Each day we wake up, be encouraged and know that we are another day closer to beating this pestilence. As a nation, we've always been innovative and when I look around, I see how all of us are adapting to these difficult times. We may get struck by something difficult, but we always adapt and keep fighting forward. We are going to beat this thing everyone! We are going to be okay! I'll say this every night because it is the truth. Through Christ WE SHALL PREVAIL!

We ARE going to see victory! Life WILL return to normal! WE WILL WIN! This very moment we are even closer than we were yesterday. It's coming! As it says in Isaiah 54:17 "No weapon formed against you shall prosper". This will take some time to traverse this dark valley but we are going to make it! Light is coming! We're ALL in this together! Let not your heart be troubled. God is in control!! Be healthy! Be safe! May God bless all of you!

DAY 49
May 4th, 2020

Good evening everyone! We are closing out another day of this pandemic. It is May 4th, 2020 and we are starting a brand new week. I hope all of you are healthy, safe, well and have peace.

Dear Heavenly Father, I come to You with Heavenly praise and thanksgiving. Thank You Lord Jesus for the blessings You have given us. Thank You that You are walking with us and guiding our path during this difficult journey. In the name of Jesus I claim Psalm 91, Psalm, 23, Psalm 46:1, Psalm 56:3 and Isaiah 54:17 over all of you, your friends, family, coworkers, neighbors and all you hold dear. I pray for an impenetrable hedge of protection around each of you. In the name of Jesus, I command, bind up and cast this virus and spirit of fear far from you, all those you love. It has to leave now! Greater is He who is in us, than he who is in the world. I lift up before You all that are afflicted with this terrible pestilence and that they are healed and restored to full health. I pray for all the families and businesses that have been affected by this pandemic that they have peace, hope, wisdom, strength and abundance to get through every day. I pray for all the medical workers at every level fighting this virus that they have protection, supplies, wisdom, strength and medical breakthroughs to keep going and fighting this virus. I claim all these things in Your Holy precious name Lord Jesus, Thank you Lord God, Amen!

I hope all of you are doing well. How are you doing through this pandemic? As we start to reopen the country, we need to continue to stay vigilant and strong. I swear to you, there is coming a day when all of this will be behind us. I've said this before but we are truly living in historic times and I believe that soon we will have victory over this virus. With Christ ALL things, not some things, but ALL things are possible. We could wake up tomorrow and the answer has been found. Each day, millions of people are working and fighting this virus and each day could be the day this all ends. This too shall pass! Let not your heart be troubled. God is in control and on the throne. He will lead us to victory and that day is coming soon! Say it with me again! WE SHALL PREVAIL! We're ALL in this together!! Be healthy! Be safe! Be strong! May God bless all of you!

DAY 50
May 5th, 2020

Good evening everyone! I hope you all had a great May 5th, 2020 and that this message finds you once again healthy, safe and well. As promised I am here once again to pray over all of you.

Dear Heavenly Father, I come to You with Heavenly praise and thanksgiving. Thank You Lord Jesus for blessing us, for protecting us and walking with us every step of this long journey. I claim Psalm 91, Psalm 23, Psalm 46:1, Psalm 56:3 and Isaiah 54:17 over all of you, your friends, family, neighbors, coworkers and all you hold dear. In the name of Jesus I command, bind up and cast this virus and spirit of fear to the farthest ends of the Earth away from you and your loved ones. I pray for all the medical workers that they have protection, more than enough supplies, wisdom and strength to keep fighting this virus. I lift up all the afflicted that they fully recover and are restored to full health. I pray for all the families, businesses, our states, our nation and all who have been affected by this virus that they are given strength, wisdom, abundance, hope, faith and especially peace that surpasses all understanding. I claim all these things in the name of Jesus! Thank You Lord Jesus, Amen!

This invisible enemy's days are numbered!! You all are going to witness its eradication and elimination from this planet once and for all. We are another day closer to victory and every single day there are more and more breakthroughs in combating this virus. This is a full on out war and we WILL WIN! God is on the Throne and in total control. He will lead us to victory and through Christ ALL things are possible. We're all tired and ready for all of this to be over with and it is coming! With a unified step forward, one by one, we will CRUSH this enemy into the dust and oblivion. Shout this with me! VICTORY IS COMING!! We're ALL in this together! Let not your heart be troubled! Be healthy! Be safe! Be strong! May God bless all of you!

DAY 51
May 6th, 2020

Good evening everyone! We are closing out May 6th, 2020 and another day of this pandemic is now completed. It was a beautiful day out today and I hope this message tonight once again finds you healthy, safe and well. For those of you who may not have seen these posts yet. Each and every night of this pandemic I am praying for protection over all of you. Let's begin.

Dear Heavenly Father, I come to You with Heavenly praise and thanksgiving. I thank You Lord Jesus for all Your blessings, Your wisdom, protection, guidance and walking with us each step of this journey through this long valley and that You will bring us to victory. I claim Psalm 91, Psalm 23, Psalm 46:1, Psalm 56:3 and Isaiah 54:17 over all of you, your friends, family, pets, neighbors, coworkers and all you hold dear. I pray for supernatural spiritual hedge of protection that surrounds you that is impenetrable. In the name of Jesus, I command, bind up and cast this virus far away from you and that it never even crosses the threshold of your homes. I pray for all the families, businesses and all who are affected by this virus that they are given peace, hope, faith, wisdom, strength and abundance to get through each and every day of this pandemic. Lord Jesus, please heal our lands and restore us. I pray for all the medical workers that they are protected, have far more than enough supplies, wisdom, peace and strength to keep fighting this virus. I lift up all the afflicted that they are healed and fully restored to health. I pray for our scientists and doctors that they are able to develop a safe and powerful vaccine against this virus faster than ever before in history. Thank You Lord Jesus that through You we will see victory over this virus. I claim all these things in the name of Jesus. Thank You Lord God, In Jesus name I pray, Amen!

Everyone, we are all warriors in this constant battle against this virus. Each and every one of us is at war with this virus but we are continuing to press forward to victory. It's been tough and we are all tired but we must remain strong and vigilant and we will win. It's another day completed, another day forward as we push back this invisible enemy. Through Christ ALL things are possible and we shall prevail! We shall see victory! We shall win this war! It is a mere matter of time before we hear the word that it's over and that it has been eradicated and decimated into the very dust it came from. We're going to get through this! We're ALL in this together! Be healthy! Be safe! Be strong! May God bless all of you!

DAY 52
May 7th, 2020

Good evening everyone! Well we are now closing out another day of this on going pandemic and it is May 7th, 2020. I hope all of you are healthy, safe and well.

Dear Heavenly Father, I come to You with Heavenly praise and thanksgiving. Thank You Lord Jesus for the blessings You have given us, for the wisdom You have given us, for protecting us and for guiding us through this difficult journey. I claim Psalm 91, Psalm 23, Psalm 46:1, Psalm 56:3 and Isaiah 54:17 over all of you, your friends, family, pets, neighbors and coworkers tonight, tomorrow night and the night after that. I pray for a spiritual hedge of protection around each of you that this virus cannot penetrate. In the name of Jesus, I command and bind up this pestilence and the spirit of fear and cast them to the very ends of the Earth far away from you and all you love and that this virus will not even pass over the very threshold of your home. I lift up all the afflicted that they may be healed and restored to full health. I pray for all those affected by this virus that they will be given, peace, hope, faith, wisdom, strength and abundance to get through each and every single day of this pandemic. I pray for all the hard working medical workers that they are given protection, more than enough supplies, strength and wisdom to keep fighting this virus. I also pray for all the people who work at restaurants, grocery stores and every single person in all the supply chains that are keeping us going that they are protected and given strength as well. I claim all these things in the name of Jesus, Thank You Lord Father! In Jesus name I pray! AMEN!

Well, another day has passed which means that we are another day and another step closer to victory. I cannot wait for the day that this pandemic is behind us. And that is coming soon! I know everyone is exhausted, frustrated, paranoid to go out, afraid, angry and unsure of what the future brings. This too shall pass! But we will make it through this difficult time. We are going to press forward! We ARE going to win this war. Through Christ ALL things are possible and He will lead us to victory. It's a mere matter of time before this is history and over! But take peace knowing that God is on the Throne, in control and that He will deliver us. Today is a national day of prayer and I'm asking everyone to pray to God that this time will soon end, that He will heal our lands, restore us and eradicate this virus. We're ALL in this together everyone! With each day we will crush this invisible enemy! WE SHALL PREVAIL! Be healthy! Be Safe! May God bless all of you!

DAY 53
May 8th, 2020

Good evening everyone! Well we are finishing out another week and today is May 8th, 2020. As you read this message tonight I hope that all of you are and continue to be healthy, safe and well.

Dear Heavenly Father, I come to You with Heavenly praise and thanksgiving. Thank You Lord Jesus for another day that we are waking up, thank You for Your blessings, for Your wisdom, guidance and walking with us through these uncertain times. I claim Psalm 91, Psalm 23, Psalm 46:1, Psalm 56:3 and Isaiah 54:17 over all of you, your family, pets, friends, neighbors and coworkers. Once again I pray for a spiritual hedge of protection that surrounds you with an impenetrable shield. I lift up and pray for all the afflicted that they are restored to full health. I pray for all the families, businesses and all who are affected by this terrible virus that you will have peace, health, wisdom, faith, hope, strength and abundance though each day of this pandemic. In the name of Jesus, I command, bind up and cast this virus and the spirit of fear away from you and your loved ones to the far corners of the Earth and that this pestilence never even crosses the thresholds of your homes. I thank You Lord Jesus that You are on the Throne and You are in complete control of the circumstances that are surrounding us. Please heal our lands father and restore our nation. I thank You and I claim all these things in Your Holy name Lord Jesus, Amen!

Well everyone, we are entering into another weekend and everything is continuing to open back up. As I have said before we still need to stay vigilant and strong but things are definitely moving forward. It's been a long journey from the start of this pandemic to where we are now but with each passing day we continue to win new battles on all fronts in the war on this virus. I keep hearing all the new medical breakthroughs and treatments that are currently being developed and this is a true global endeavor to end this virus once and for all. What we are living through right now is a true unifying time for everyone and we will come out of this stronger, better and victorious. Through Christ ALL things are possible and He is guiding us each step of the way. WE SHALL PREVAIL! I know things have been uncertain and the journey forward will continue to be difficult. But this too shall pass and we are going to come out of this time. We are seeing light at the end of the tunnel and that is where our victory lies. We're all in this together! Stay strong! Keep fighting FORWARD! Be healthy! Be safe! May God bless all of you!

DAY 54
May 9th, 2020

Good evening everyone! It is Saturday, May 9th, 2020 and we are once again closing out another day of this pandemic. We are having some strangely cold weather for May and I hope all of you are warm, healthy, safe and well. As promised, I am back to pray over all of you.

Dear Heavenly Father, I come to You with Heavenly praise and thanksgiving. Thank You Lord Jesus for the blessings You have given us, and for never leaving us or forsaking us. I claim Psalm 91, Psalm 23, Psalm 46:1, Psalm 56:3 and Isaiah 54:17 over all of you, your loved ones, family, friends, pets, neighbors and coworkers. In the name of Jesus, I command, bind up and cast this virus and spirit of fear away from all of you. I pray for a hedge of protection that surrounds all of you and all you hold dear. I pray for all the families and businesses that are still afraid for the future that they have peace, hope, wisdom, strength and abundance through this time. I lift up all the afflicted that they are restored to full and complete health. I pray for every single medical worker who is fighting this virus that they are protected, given wisdom, more than enough supplies, and strength to keep working through difficult and dangerous shifts. I pray for all the scientists and doctors working diligently to create a vaccine that they are given supernatural wisdom and that a safe vaccine is created faster than ever thought possible before in history. Thank You Father. I claim all these things in Your Holy name Lord Jesus, Amen!

We have never been through anything like what we've all experienced over the past few months but we are still here and everything is continuing to look up. Battle by battle, we continue to march forward and we are NOT slowing down. Through Christ this war will be won! I know all of you are still unsure about the future but know this, with Christ ALL things are possible and as this storm continues to rage around us, we need to keep our eyes on God and not the storm. He WILL deliver us through this difficult time. As it says in Psalm 91:5-7 "You will not fear the terror of night, nor the arrow that flies by day, nor the pestilence that stalks in the darkness, nor the plague that destroys at midday. A thousand may fall at your side, ten thousand at your right hand, but it will not come near you." Shout it with me again! WE SHALL PREVAIL! Be healthy! Be safe! Be strong! May God bless all of you!

DAY 55
May 10th, 2020

Good evening everyone! Today is a special day because it is Mother's Day, Sunday May 10th, 2020 and we are coming to the end of another day of quarantine of this pandemic. Along with celebrating Mother's Day, I hope that this message finds you healthy, safe and well.

Dear Heavenly Father, I come to You with Heavenly praise and thanksgiving on this Mother's Day 2020. I thank You for all the blessings You have given us, for giving us wisdom, guiding us and especially for our mother's. I claim Psalm 91, Psalm 23, Psalm 46:1, Psalm 56:3 and Isaiah 54:17 over all of you, your family, friends, pets, coworkers, neighbors, and all whom you hold dear. I claim and pray for an impenetrable, spiritual hedge of protection around each of you. In the name of Jesus, I command, bind up and cast away this terrible virus and the spirit of fear far away from all of you and that it cannot ever return or cross the very thresholds of your homes. I lift up all the sick and afflicted from this virus that they are miraculously and completely restored to full health with no trace of this pestilence. I pray for hope, peace, faith, wisdom, strength and abundance for all the families and businesses that have been affected by this virus. I pray for a safe vaccine that is created faster than anything like it in history and that there will be more than enough doses to protect everyone. I pray for the eradication of this virus, that it is not only de-clawed but also eliminated and rendered extinct. I pray for all the medical workers at every level working hard in the hospitals taking care of the sick that they will be provided for, have wisdom, more than enough supplies, and strength to keep fighting each day. I pray that, You Lord, will heal and restore our lands. Thank You Father! I claim all these things in Your Holy name Lord Jesus, Amen!

I know each night I claim these same Psalms over each of you and each night and I want to include some the passage too at the bottom of this message tonight. We are through another day and summer is right around the corner. Hopefully the summer heat will start to dissipate and help kill this virus as we move forward. We are going to throw everything we have at this virus till it's eliminated completely! One of the most powerful things we can do is to humble ourselves before God and pray each day for the end of this pandemic. We are all the warriors in the war on this virus and very soon we will shout a battle cry of victory when this virus is completely decimated. Christ will guide and deliver us to victory and in Him we can trust and we shall prevail against this invisible enemy. We're ALL in this together and we are going to win! Be healthy! Be safe! May God bless all of you!

DAY 56
May 11th, 2020

Good evening everyone! It is now approaching the middle of May and we are closing out another day of this pandemic. Today is Monday, May 11th, 2020 and if you are a first time reading this post, welcome. I want you to know that every day of this pandemic I am praying over all of you. Let's Begin.

Dear Heavenly Father, I come to You with Heavenly praise and thanksgiving. I thank You Lord Jesus for blessing us, guiding us, protecting us and walking with us every step of this difficult journey. I claim Psalm 91, Psalm 23, Psalm 46:1, Psalm 56:3 and Isaiah 54:17 over all of you, your family, friends, pets, neighbors, coworkers and all you hold dear. I pray for an impenetrable hedge of protection that this virus cannot penetrate. In the name of Jesus, I command, bind up and cast this horrible virus and the spirit of fear away from you to the furthest ends of the earth and that this virus will not and cannot cross the threshold of your homes. For all those afflicted by this pestilence, I lift you up before God that He restores you to full and complete health. For all those in the medical fields at every single level, I pray for full protection for you and your families and that all of you are given wisdom, more than enough supplies and strength to keep fighting every day to help those who are sick and to get through the dangerous shifts you heroically work. I pray for all the families and businesses that are afraid for the future, that they will be given a spirit of peace and hope. You are not given a spirit of fear and I pray that you will have peace that surpasses all understanding, faith, strength and abundance to get through this difficult journey with more than enough. In the name of Jesus, I pray that our lands will be healed and restored and that a safe and fully effective vaccine will be created faster than ever before. I claim all these things in Your Holy Name Lord Jesus! Amen!

Warriors! We continue to win these battles in this war. But we need to stay strong, vigilant and on the offensive! This invisible enemy WILL be destroyed, WILL be eradicated and through Christ, WE SHALL PREVAIL! Nothing is impossible for Christ and He will guide and deliver us to victory. And victory is coming very soon! I know all of you are tired and frustrated but know this, this too shall pass! This time will end and this deep, dark valley will soon explode into light and deliverance. It's been a difficult journey but we are strong and will persevere! We're All in this together!! Be healthy! Be safe! Be strong! Have hope! May God bless all of you!!

DAY 57
May 12th, 2020

Good evening everyone! I hope this message finds you once again healthy, safe and well. We are finishing up the day on Tuesday May 12th, 2020.

Dear Heavenly Father, I come to You once again with Heavenly praise and thanksgiving. Thank You Lord Jesus for the blessings You have given us, for giving us wisdom and leading us through this dark valley to victory. I claim Psalm 91, Psalm 23, Psalm 46:1, Psalm 56:3, Mark 5:36 and Isaiah 54:17. I pray for an impenetrable, spiritual hedge of protection that surrounds all of you that this virus can't penetrate. In the name of Jesus, I command, bind up and cast this virus and the spirit of fear far away from you and that it cannot come near you or anyone you love. I pray for all the medical workers at all levels, scientists, nurses, doctors, specialists, support staff that you have protection, more than enough supplies, wisdom and strength to fight this virus and keep going. I lift up all the families and businesses that are afraid, hurting and worried about the future that You will give all of them peace, hope, faith, wisdom, strength and abundance to get through this uncertain time. I pray for all the sick and all the afflicted that they are supernaturally healed and restored to complete health. I pray for our people, our leaders, cities, states, our country, and all the countries throughout the world that they are given wisdom, strength and restoration. I pray that this virus is eradicated and that a fully effective and safe vaccine is created faster that ever thought possible. Thank You Lord Father. I claim all these things in Your Holy precious name Lord Jesus, Amen!

Everyone, we are through another day, which means we are another day closer to victory and I will continue to keep praying protection over all of you every day. Through Christ, we are gonna get through this and we shall prevail! Though this has been a difficult journey and it will continue for a while, we are pressing forward and we are starting to see light at the end of the tunnel. We have to keep our minds off the storm and on God. Only He will get us through this valley. And we WILL get through it! Life WILL return to normal! We WILL end this virus! And We WILL be victorious! It's coming! We all have to be strong and hold on. Say this with me 3 times! Victory is coming! Victory is coming! VICTORY IS COMING! We're ALL in this together and we're all going to win this together! Be healthy! Be safe! Be strong! May God bless all of you!

DAY 58
May 13th, 2020

Good evening everyone! Today is Wednesday, May 13th, 2020 as we are closing out another day of this pandemic. I hope all of you are healthy, safe and well. It was a beautiful day out here in Ohio and things are looking up. As promised I am here to pray for all of you once again.

Dear Heavenly Father, I come to You with Heavenly praise and thanksgiving. Thank You Lord Jesus for helping us get through another day, for blessing us, for guiding us and walking with us every step of this journey. I claim Psalm 91, Psalm 23, Psalm 46:1, Psalm 56:3 and Isaiah 54:17 over all of you, your friends, family, pets, neighbors, coworkers and all you hold dear. I pray that all of you are protected by an impenetrable spiritual hedge of protection. I pray that through each day you are given peace that surpasses all understanding. In the name of Jesus I command, bind up and cast this virus and spirit of fear away from you and all you love. I pray that this virus is swiftly eradicated and eliminated from this planet. I lift up every medical worker at all levels across the planet that they are protected, given more than enough supplies, wisdom and strength to keep going through difficult and dangerous shifts. I lift up all the afflicted and sick from this virus that they are healed and fully restored to complete health. I pray that our doctors and scientists will make miraculous breakthroughs to create a safe and fully effective vaccine that is made faster than ever thought possible. I pray for all the families that are scared and afraid for the future that they are provided for, that they have peace, hope, wisdom, strength, and abundance to get through every day. Thank You Father for the victory that is coming through Your power, grace and majesty. I claim all these things in Your Holy name Lord Jesus, Amen!

This journey we have been on will be written in the books of history for all time and all of you are part of this historic unprecedented event. They will teach your kids, grand kids, great grand kids and beyond about this time. We are indelibly linked and united unlike anytime in our natural lives. I know this time has been difficult but through Christ and the grace of God almighty, WE SHALL PREVAIL! We are going to see victory soon. Though our foe is formidable, we are winning the battles and inevitably the war. This virus WILL be annihilated. We have to stay strong and vigilant and we will make it through all of this! We're all in this together! Be healthy! Be safe! Be strong! May God bless all of you!

DAY 59
May 14th, 2020

Good evening everyone! Today is May 14th, 2020 and I just looked at the cases in the USA and the case numbers seem to be trending downward which is great news. It's not over yet and we still need to be safe but things are starting to look up. I am back again to pray for protection over all of you.

Dear Heavenly Father, I come to You with Heavenly praise and thanksgiving. Thank You Lord Jesus for blessing us, guiding us, and walking with us each day and every step of this journey we are all on. I claim Psalm 91, Psalm 23, Psalm 46:1, Psalm 56:3 and Isaiah 53:5 and Isaiah 54:17 over all of you, your family, friends, pets, neighbors, and coworkers. I pray for a spiritual hedge of protection that is impenetrable. I lift up all those who are sick and afflicted by this virus all around the world that they are completely healed and restored to full health. I thank You Lord Jesus that the numbers are trending downwards and that each day of this journey we are one day closer to victory. In the name of Jesus I command, bind up and cast this virus away from you and that it is eradicated and rendered extinct. I pray for all the doctors and scientists that they are given supernatural wisdom to create a safe and fully effective vaccine. I pray for all the families and businesses that are hurting and are afraid for the future that they are given peace that surpasses all understanding, hope, faith, wisdom, strength and abundance to make through this difficult time. I pray for every single medical worker at every level that they are given peace, wisdom, protection, more than enough supplies and strength to keep fighting this virus. Thank You Father! I claim all these things in Your Holy name Lord Jesus! Amen!

This invisible enemy we face will be destroyed and completely eradicated. It's going to take some time but it will happen. Our victory is at hand and we are continuing to win battle after battle in this full on war. As I said earlier, the case numbers in the US are trending downwards and that is fantastic news! However, we can't become complacent. We need to stay strong and vigilant. We are all extremely frustrated from this virus but we WILL make it through this valley! We WILL see victory and through Christ WE SHALL PREVAIL! As I say every single night, We're ALL in this together! Say it with me again! VICTORY IS COMING! Be healthy! Be safe! Be strong! May God bless all of you!

DAY 60
May 15th, 2020

Good evening everyone! Well it is the end of the week and we are closing out another day of this pandemic. Today is Friday, May 15th, 2020 and I hope you are healthy, safe and well.

Dear Heavenly Father, I come to You with Heavenly praise and thanksgiving. Thank You Father for all the blessings You have given us, for wisdom, guidance and walking with us each step of this journey. I claim Psalm 91, Psalm 23, Psalm 46:1, Psalm 56:3, Isaiah 53:5 and Isaiah 54:17 over all of you, your entire family, your friends, pets, coworkers, and neighbors. In the name of Jesus, I command, bind up and cast this virus and spirit of fear to the furthest ends of the Earth away from you and all whom you love and care for. I thank You Lord Jesus that, through You, this virus will be eliminated, eradicated and a new vaccine will be created faster then ever before in history. I pray for all the families and businesses who are suffering or affected by this terrible virus that they are given, peace that surpasses all understanding, hope, faith, wisdom, strength and abundance to get through every day with more than enough. I lift up all the afflicted and ill that they are fully restored to complete and full health. I pray that our doctors and scientists will continue to find breakthrough treatments so that all have hope. I lift up before You Father all the medical workers that they are given peace, wisdom, rest, hope and strength to keep going and fighting this virus to help heal others. I pray for all those in the entertainment field that are unable to perform and are out of work that You will please provide for all of them through this difficult journey. I claim all these things in Your Holy precious name Lord Jesus, Thank You Father! Amen!

Well, we are in the middle of May and we are another day closer to victory and defeating this virus. We are going to do it everyone! Through Christ, He will deliver us and He has promised to never leave us or forsake us. If you are feeling anxious, know this, greater is He who lives in us than he who lives in this world. I know things are difficult and in some cases unbearable but please hold on. We are going to get through this. We are all in this together and we will see victory soon. The time to stand together is now. We all stand united against this invisible enemy and it will be vanquished and defeated! Period! We shall prevail and failure is not an option. We are truly living in unique times and you are seeing history being unveiled right before your eyes. Warriors! Shout with me! VICTORY IS COMING! Let not your heart be troubled. Be healthy! Be safe! Be strong! Have hope and faith! May God bless all of you!

DAY 61
May 16th, 2020

Good evening everyone! Ok, we are closing out Saturday May 16th, 2020 and I hope you all had a wonderful day and that you are all healthy, safe and well. Here in NE Ohio it was a truly beautiful day out and it felt good to be outside in the sun and fresh air. Let's begin tonight.

Dear Heavenly Father, I come to You with Heavenly praise and thanksgiving. Thank You Lord Jesus for this beautiful day, the blessings You have given us, guiding us and walking with us through each day of this pandemic. I claim Psalm 91, Psalm 23, Psalm 25:20-21, Psalm 46:1, Psalm 56:3, Isaiah 54:17 and Isaiah 53:5 over all of you, your family, pets, friends, neighbors and coworkers tonight, tomorrow night and the night after that. I pray that each of you are fully protected and surrounded by an impenetrable and indestructible spiritual hedge of protection. In the name of Jesus, I command, bind up and cast this virus and spirit of fear and anxiety away from you and your loved ones and command that it doesn't ever return. I pray for all the families and businesses that they are given continued hope, peace, faith, wisdom, strength and abundance to get through each and every day of this pandemic and that all the businesses that have had to shut down will be fully restored. I lift up all the afflicted and sick with the virus that they are supernaturally healed and restored to full health. I pray for all the medical workers at every level that they are given protection, more than enough supplies, wisdom and strength to care for their patients and keep fighting even when they are exhausted from long, dangerous shifts. I thank You Lord Jesus that a vaccine is in development and will be created faster than ever thought possible and that it will be safe and fully effective. I pray that more treatments to heal those with the virus are discovered so that everyone is able to be treated. Thank You Lord Jesus, I claim all these things in Your Holy precious name Lord Jesus, Amen!

I'm feeling very optimistic today. I know we are still in the valley and have a ways to go but I feel optimistic that we will soon see the end of this pandemic. I'll be honest I don't know when that will be yet, but we are all fighting this virus and we are all in this together. I feel such hope seeing everyone united against this common invisible enemy. The battles continue to rage on but I know we will win this war. It's inevitable and victory is truly coming. Christ continues to lead us every single day through this deep, dark valley but at the end of this valley is light and we will see it. And through Christ, WE SHALL PREVAIL and this time shall pass. Stay strong everyone! We aren't out of this yet but we are certainly on our way! Say it with me again! VICTORY IS COMING! Be healthy! Be safe! Be strong! May God bless all of you!

DAY 62
May 17th, 2020

Good evening everyone! We are finishing up the weekend and it is Sunday night May 17th, 2020. It is amazing how fast time flies and how much we have been though over the past few months, but we are still here standing strong! Once again, I hope this message finds you healthy, well and safe and as promised I am here to pray over all of you. Let's begin.

Dear Heavenly Father, I come to You with Heavenly praise and thanksgiving. I claim Psalm 91, Psalm 23, Psalm 25:20-21, Psalm 46:1, Psalm 56:3, Isaiah 54:17 and Isaiah 53:5 over you, your friends, family, pets, neighbors, coworkers and all who read this message. I pray that peace overtakes all of you and surpasses all understanding. I pray that you are surrounded and protected by a spiritual hedge of protection and in the name of Jesus, I command, bind up and cast this virus and spirit of fear & anxiety away from you and all you hold dear. I pray for all the afflicted that they are healed and supernaturally restored to full health. I pray for all the medical workers that they are given protection, more than enough supplies, wisdom and strength to keep going and keep fighting on the frontlines. I pray that our doctors and scientists are given supernatural wisdom to discover new miraculous medical breakthroughs, new treatments and a create a safe and fully effective vaccine in record time. I lift up and pray for every family and business that has suffered through this time and afraid for the future that they are given peace, hope, faith, wisdom, strength and abundance to make it through each day. I also pray that they have more than enough so that are able to be a blessing to others around them. Thank you Father! I claim all these things in Your Holy precious name Lord Jesus, Amen!

We are beginning a new week and with a new week come new beginnings and advances in combating this virus. Each day will have its difficulties but each day, each battle will be won through Christ. He is guiding us all to victory and through Him we shall prevail. I say it every night and I will continue to say it every night... VICTORY IS COMING! Each and every day brings us closer. Along this journey we are on, each day brings with it the combined work of millions of doctors and scientists on the planet and countless people praying to God for wisdom and answers to fight this virus. Can you imagine what we can accomplish in just 24 hours. We are going to win this war against this invisible enemy. We are ALL in this together! Stay healthy! Stay safe! Stay Strong! Stay hopeful! May God bless all of you!

DAY 63
May 18th, 2020

Good evening everyone! It is a brand new week & we are closing out the day on Monday May 18th, 2020. As promised, I'm here to pray protection over all of you each and every day of this pandemic. Let's begin.

Dear Heavenly Father, I come to You tonight with Heavenly praise & thanksgiving. Thank You Father for blessing us, for guiding us, giving us wisdom, strength & walking with us along this long journey.

I claim Psalm 91, Psalm 23, Psalm 25:20-21, Psalm 46:1, Psalm 56:3, 2 Chronicles 7:14, Isaiah 54:17 and Isaiah 53:5 over you, your family, friends, pets, neighbors, coworkers and all you love. In the name of Jesus, I command, bind up and cast this virus & the spirit of fear and anxiety away from you & all whom you love. I lift up all those who are afflicted with this virus that they are healed & fully restored. I pray for all the medical workers that they protected, given more than enough supplies, wisdom & strength to keep fighting this virus. I pray for all the families & businesses affected by this virus that they are given more than enough, abundance, blessings, faith, peace, wisdom, strength & hope to get through these difficult days. I pray for the doctors & scientists that they are able to develop the most effective safe treatments & vaccine in record time. Thank you Father! I claim these things in Your Holy & precious name Lord Jesus, Amen!

I was out today & I love seeing the ingenuity & creativeness of the American spirit to keep fighting. We will NOT go down without a fight & we are going to win this war! This virus WILL be eradicated & rendered extinct. Warriors, we need to stand firm & continue to push forward. Through Christ, we shall prevail, this time will pass & we'll be stronger at the end of this journey. With the start of today, we're that much closer. Soon, we're going to wake up one morning & we'll be welcomed by the phrase, "The Pandemic is OVER!" Victory is coming everyone! We need to stay strong, vigilant & keep fighting! We're all in this together! Let not your heart be troubled. Be healthy! Be safe! Be strong! Have faith! May God bless all of you!

DAY 64
May 19th, 2020

Good evening everyone! We are finishing out the day on Tuesday May, 19th, 2020 and I'm back as promised to pray protection over all of you.

Dear Heavenly Father, I come to You with Heavenly praise and thanksgiving. I thank You Lord Jesus for the blessings you have given us, Your peace, guidance, hope, strength and walking with us every step of this journey. Thank You Lord Jesus that as You promised us, that You would never leave us or forsake us. I claim Psalm 91, Psalm 23, Psalm 25:20-21, Psalm 46:1, Psalm 56:3, 2 Chronicles 7:14, 2 Timothy 1:7, Isaiah 54:17 and Isaiah 53:5 over all of you, your friends, family, pets, neighbors and coworkers tonight, tomorrow night and the night after that. In the name of Jesus, I command, bind up and cast this virus and the spirit of fear completely away from you and all you love. I pray that a supernatural spiritual hedge of protection surrounds you that is impenetrable. I lift up and pray for all those who are afflicted by this virus and that they are healed and completely restored to complete health. I pray for all the families and businesses that have suffered through this time that they are given peace, hope, faith, wisdom, strength and abundance to make it through this difficult time. I pray for all the medical workers that they are given protection, more than enough supplies, wisdom, peace and strength to keep fighting through difficult and dangerous shifts combating this virus. Thank You Father! I claim all these things in Your Holy, precious name Lord Jesus! Amen!

With the reopening of the country again, I know how frustrated many of you still are and I fully understand that. We have to hold on and be strong. Like you, I'm very ready for this pandemic to be over with, and soon, it will be. I'm truly telling you, this virus will be eradicated, we will have a safe and effective vaccine, life will return to normal and through Christ we shall prevail and see victory. It is coming. Even today we are 24 hours closer than we were yesterday at this same time. With each passing second, battles are being won, people are recovering, medical breakthroughs are being discovered and victory is at hand. It is a mere matter of time until this virus is eliminated. Do not be afraid. This too shall pass! Let not your hearts be troubled. VICTORY IS COMING AND WE SHALL PREVAIL! Be healthy! Be safe! Be strong! Have Hope! May God bless all of you!

DAY 65
May 20th, 2020

Good evening everyone! We are midway through the week, it's May 20th, 2020 and we are closing out another day of this pandemic. And as promised, I'm here every single night to pray over all of you & your loved ones.

Dear Heavenly Father, I come to You tonight with Heavenly praise & thanksgiving. Thank You Lord Jesus for the blessings You have given us, for guiding us, giving us protection, strength, wisdom & walking with us every step of this journey. I claim Psalm 91, Psalm 23, Psalm 25:20-21, Psalm 46:1, Psalm 56:3, 2 Chronicles 7:14, 2 Timothy 1:7, Isaiah 54:17 & Isaiah 53:5 over all of you, your friends, family, pets, neighbors, coworkers & all you hold dear. I pray that you are surrounded by Christ's love & a spiritual hedge of protection that this virus cannot penetrate. I pray for all the families, people, businesses, our leaders, our cities, states & nation and all who have been affected by this terrible virus that they are blessed, given health, hope, peace, faith, wisdom, strength & abundance to get through each day with more than enough so that they can be a blessing to others. I pray for all our medical workers that they are fully protected, given wisdom & strength to keep fighting this virus. I pray for our doctors and scientists that they have supernatural wisdom to develop a safe & fully effective vaccine. In the name of Jesus, I lift up the afflicted so that they are restored & fully healed. In the name of Jesus, I command, bind up & cast away this virus, spirit of fear and all agents of evil away from you, your families and all you love. Thank You Lord Jesus! I claim all these things in Your Holy precious name Lord Jesus, Amen!

Well it is the middle of the week & we are continuing to push back against this terrible virus. We are like a row of soldiers standing united against a common enemy & with each step forward this virus retreats. This war will continue to rage on through many more battles in the coming weeks & months, but in the end, we will inevitably win. Through Christ we shall prevail & as I say every night: VICTORY IS COMING! It is not a matter of if we will win, but rather when we will win. And that time is coming soon! We must stay united, vigilant and strong. We are going to make it through this. We're all in this together! Be healthy! Be strong! Have Hope! Stay safe! May God Bless you all!

DAY 66
May 21st, 2020

Good evening everyone! We are coming up on the weekend & we're closing out another day of this pandemic, Thursday May 21st, 2020. I hope that this message once again finds you healthy, safe and well.

Dear Heavenly Father, I come to You with Heavenly praise and thanksgiving. Thank You Lord Jesus for continuing to bless us, guide us, giving us strength, wisdom and never leaving our side through these difficult times. In the name of Jesus, I claim Psalm 91, Psalm 23, Psalm 25:20-21, Psalm 46:1, Psalm 56:3, 2 Chronicles 7:14, 2 Timothy 1:7, Isaiah 54:17 & Isaiah 53:5 over all of you, your friends, family, pets, neighbors, coworkers & all you hold dear tonight, tomorrow night and the night after that. I pray for a supernatural, impenetrable, spiritual hedge of complete protection around you, your loved ones and all you hold dear. In the name of Jesus, I command, bind up and through the power of Christ, cast this virus and the spirit of fear away from you and command it to never return. I thank You Lord Jesus that this virus will soon be eradicated from the planet where it can do no harm ever again. I lift up the countless families and businesses that have suffered and are afraid for their future, their children's future, their employees, their legacy, that they will be given peace that surpasses all understanding, hope, faith, guidance, wisdom, tenacity, and abundance to get through each and every day of this pandemic with more than enough so that their cup runneth over. I pray for all of our doctors & scientists that they are given wisdom beyond their years to develop a safe and fully effective vaccine. I lift up the afflicted and sick with this virus that they are healed and restored to complete and full health. Thank You Father! I claim all these things through the power and majesty of Your Holy precious name Lord Jesus. Amen!

We keep hearing in the news stories that break your hearts of people across our country and planet, but I am telling you this difficult time is going to end. This too shall pass! We didn't come this far, just be stopped by something one billionth our size. Through Christ this virus IS going to be eradicated and eliminated. Through Christ we WILL triumph! Through Christ WE SHALL PREVAIL! I know you are tired and over all of this. I am too, but we need to hold on, stay strong and fight this virus! We're going to get through this. We're all in this together and God is right by your side right now! God is on the throne! Say it with me! VICTORY IS COMING! Be healthy! Be safe! Be strong! Have Faith! Have hope! Have peace! May God bless all of you!

DAY 67
May 22nd, 2020

Good evening everyone! Well we are closing out another week of this pandemic & today is May 22nd, 2020. As always I hope that this message finds you healthy, safe & well. As promised I am here again to pray protection over all of you.

Dear Heavenly Father, I come to You with Heavenly praise & thanksgiving. Thank You Jesus for all the blessings You have given us, for never leaving us, for giving us wisdom, strength & courage. Thank You that You are walking with us each step of this difficult journey & that You will never forsake us ever. In the name of Jesus, I claim Psalm 91, Psalm 23, Psalm 25:20-21, Psalm 46:1, Psalm 56:3, Psalm 61:2, 2 Chronicles 7:14, 2 Timothy 1:7, Isaiah 54:17 & Isaiah 53:5 over all of you, your friends, family, pets, neighbors, coworkers & all you care for & love. I pray that as each of you go out each day that you are surrounded by a spiritual hedge of protection that no evil can penetrate. I lift up the afflicted that they are cared for & restored to full and complete health. I pray for all the families & businesses that have been afraid for the future of their lives that they are all given strength, peace that surpasses all understanding, abundance to get through each day, wisdom, faith, guidance & especially hope. In the name of Jesus I command, bind up and cast this virus, all agents of evil, and the spirit of fear away from you & that it never returns. Greater is He who is in us than he who is in the world. I pray for all the medical workers that they have protection, more than enough supplies, wisdom & strength to continue to keep fighting. I pray that a safe and fully effective vaccine is developed faster than ever thought possible. Thank You Lord Jesus for the deliverance that is coming only from You. I claim all these things in Your Holy & precious name Lord Jesus, Amen!

It is Memorial Day weekend & here in Ohio it is going to be in the upper 80s. Let's pray that this coming heat will help be the beginning of the end of this virus. Soon, there will be a time when this virus is only talked about in past tense & only included in the history books! Soon, there will no longer be social distancing! Soon, this virus will be eradicated from the face of this planet! And soon we will celebrate the victorious end of this pandemic! Through Christ all things are possible & I believe that victory is coming soon! We will prevail through this time! We need to stay strong & vigilant but this virus's days are numbered! We're gonna get through this! We're all in this together! Be healthy! Be safe! Be strong! Have hope! May God bless all of you!

DAY 68
May 23rd, 2020

Good evening everyone! Well it was a beautiful day outside here in NE Ohio on Saturday, May 23rd, 2020 & as always I hope that this message once again finds you healthy, safe and well. Things are opening up & it's great to see people outside again. As promised, I'm here each night of this pandemic to pray for all of you. Let's begin tonight.

Dear Heavenly Father, I come to You once again with Heavenly praise and thanksgiving. I thank you Jesus for blessing our lives, for health, wisdom, strength, peace, hope, faith & walking with us each step of this journey. In the name of Jesus, I claim Psalm 91, Psalm 23, Psalm 25:20-21, Psalm 46:1, Psalm 56:3, Psalm 61:2, 2 Chronicles 7:14, 2 Timothy 1:7, Isaiah 54:17 & Isaiah 53:5 over all of you, your friends, family, pets, neighbors, coworkers & all you love tonight, tomorrow and the next day. I pray for a supernatural hedge of protection that surrounds you & all your loved ones that is impenetrable by this virus. I pray for the afflicted that they are restored to complete & full health. I lift up all the medical workers still on the frontlines combating this virus and that they are given peace, more than enough supplies, wisdom & strength to fight this virus during long and dangerous shifts. In the name of Jesus, I command, bind up, and cast this virus and the spirit of fear far away from you & that it never crosses the very threshold of your homes. I pray for all the doctors and scientists that they can develop a safe & fully effective vaccine. I pray that this virus is eradicated from the very surface of the Earth & rendered harmless to anyone. I pray for all the families and business that have been affected by this virus that they are given blessings of hope, peace, strength, wisdom, faith, and abundance to take care of their families & be a blessing to others. Thank You Father! I claim all these things in Your Holy, majestic and precious name Lord Jesus, Amen!

Things are continuing to look up. The virus hasn't gone away yet but as we move forward, continue to be vigilant & strong it won't belong before it is eliminated. The most important thing to remember during this time is that God is on the throne, God is in control & through Christ we shall see victory. All wars come to an end & the end of this one is coming soon. Can you feel it? This time has been difficult for so many but we all have each others backs. Things are already starting to return to normal. The battles aren't over yet, but the conclusion to the war draws near. Say it with me again! WE SHALL PREVAIL! WE SHALL PREVAIL! WE SHALL PREVAIL! We're all in this together! Be Healthy! Be Safe! Be Strong Have hope! May God bless all of you!

DAY 69
May 24th, 2020

Good evening everyone! It is Sunday, May 24th, 2020 on Memorial Day weekend & we are closing out another day of this pandemic. I know this is a little later than normal but once again I am here to pray over all of you. Let's begin for tonight.

Dear Heavenly Father, I come to You with Heavenly praise, love & thanksgiving. Thank You Lord Jesus for the blessings You have given us, for giving us strength in our times of need, wisdom and guiding us along this difficult journey we are all on. In the name of Jesus, I claim Psalm 91, Psalm 23, Psalm 25:20-21, Psalm 46:1, Psalm 56:3, Psalm 61:2, 2 Chronicles 7:14, 2 Timothy 1:7, Isaiah 54:17 & Isaiah 53:5 over all of you, your friends, family, pets, neighbors, coworkers & all you love tonight, tomorrow night and the next night. I pray for an impenetrable spiritual hedge of protection to surround you and all you love. In the name of Jesus, I command, bind up and cast away this terrible virus and the spirit of fear from all of you to the very ends of the earth, commanding it to never return. I pray for all the families, businesses & people affected by this virus that they are given, peace, hope, wisdom, faith, strength & abundance to get through every day. I pray that the virus cases continue to drop and I pray to You Lord Jesus that You will restore our lands. I pray for the doctors, nurses, EMTs & all medical workers at all levels that they are given protection, more than enough supplies, wisdom & strength to keep fighting this virus. I lift up and pray for all the sick and afflicted that they are cured & supernaturally restored to complete and full health. Thank You Father! I claim all these things in Your Holy, majestic & precious name, Lord Jesus, Amen!

I am happy to say that things are continuing to look up. This virus is still here, but we are conquering it each and every day little by little. Jesus will deliver us from this terrible pestilence and through Christ all things are possible. This journey we are all on will continue for a time but the light at the end of the tunnel is getting brighter with each & every day. We will see victory! This virus will end! And soon, very soon, life will return to normal. We are going to beat this thing everyone! We shall prevail! Let not your hearts be troubled! Do not be afraid! Victory is at hand! We're All in this together! Be healthy! Be safe! Be strong! Have Hope! Have Joy! May God bless you all!

DAY 70
May 25th, 2020

Good evening everyone! Happy Memorial Day! I want to start tonight's prayer with a special thank you to all our brave men and women in the armed forces past, present and future for fighting for our liberty, way of life & freedom. We're now closing out Monday, May 25th, 2020. I hope all of you had a wonderful Memorial Day 2020 & I hope that this message once again finds you healthy, safe & well.

Dear Heavenly Father, I come to You with Heavenly praise & thanksgiving. Thank You Lord Jesus for another day on Earth, thank You for blessing our lives, for wisdom, hope, strength & always by our side through this difficult & long journey we have been on. In the name of Jesus, I claim Psalm 91, Psalm 23, Psalm 25:20-21, Psalm 46:1, Psalm 56:3, Psalm 61:2, 2 Chronicles 7:14, 2 Timothy 1:7, Isaiah 54:17 & Isaiah 53:5 over all of you, your friends, family, pets, neighbors, coworkers & all you love. I pray that each of you is surrounded by a spiritual hedge of protection that this virus & all evil cannot penetrate. In the name of Jesus, I command, bind up and cast this virus, all the agents of evil and spirit of fear away from you and all you hold dear. I pray for all the sick & afflicted that they are supernaturally healed by Your hand and restored to complete and full health. I lift up all those who have been affected by this pandemic & I pray that they are given hope, faith, peace, strength, wisdom, & abundance to get through each day and receive more than enough so they can be a blessing to others. I pray for all the hard working & brave medical workers fighting this virus that they are given full protection, wisdom & strength. I pray that our scientists and doctors are able to develop a fully effective & safe vaccine. I pray that this virus is completely eradicated & rendered extinct. I claim all these things in Your Holy, majestic & precious name Lord Jesus, Amen!
It's a brand new week and with that it's a brand new week of endless possibilities in combating this virus. Just think each day there are millions of medical professionals and scientists working on a vaccine and treatments to combat this virus. So much can happen in a 24 hour period. Tomorrow this could be all over! We just have to stay

strong and keep moving forward. Above all else when we are nervous about the future we need to do one main thing. That is, not to focus on the storm raging around us but to focus on God. Through Christ we shall prevail and He will guide us to the end of this pandemic. The journey is long & tough but we will see victory on the other side of this valley. Let not your heart be troubled and believe that victory is coming swiftly! We're all in this together! Be Healthy! Be safe! Be strong! Have Hope! Have faith! May God bless all of you!

DAY 71
May 26th, 2020

Good evening everyone! It was a beautiful day outside today in NE Ohio and we are closing out Tuesday May 26th, 2020. I hope this message continues to find you healthy, safe and well.

Dear Heavenly Father, I come to You with Heavenly praise, love & thanksgiving. Thank You Lord Jesus for giving us another day to wake up and praise You. Thank You for blessing us, giving us wisdom and guiding us through the storm of this virus to safety & ultimately victory. In the name of Jesus, I claim Psalm 91, Psalm 23, Psalm 25:20-21, Psalm 46:1, Psalm 56:3, Psalm 61:2, 2 Chronicles 7:14, 2 Timothy 1:7, Jeremiah 30:17, Isaiah 54:17 & Isaiah 53:5 over all of you, your friends, family, pets, neighbors, coworkers & all you love. I pray that wherever you go, that you are fully surrounded by a spiritual hedge of protection that nothing can penetrate. I pray that all those who have become infected by this virus will be supernaturally restored to complete health. In the name of Jesus the most High, I command, bind up and cast this horrible virus and the spirit of fear away from you and all your loved ones, never to return. I pray that as we are now reopening the country that all of you will see such abundance that you will be a blessing to many others. For the families and businesses still afraid for the future, I lift you up before almighty God the Father and pray that you are given hope, strength, faith, wisdom and to know deep down that it will all be alright. I pray that this virus will soon be eradicated with a powerful, safe and fully effective vaccine currently being developed. Thank You Jesus! I claim all these things in Your Holy, majestic, powerful and precious name I pray, Thank you Lord Jesus, Amen!!

Warriors! The time of our victory is at hand! Christ is leading us though this difficult journey and we shall not only prevail but as we move forward we are indelibly united unlike anytime in our lifetimes. We move as one force against this invisible enemy and we will not back down. Failure is not an option and all things are possible with Christ. Believe and know that Christ will deliver us! Believe and know that this time shall pass! Believe and know that we are going to come out stronger on the other side of this great storm! The battles will continue but believe and know that the war is already won by Christ! We're all in this together and we are going to win! Be healthy! Be safe! Have hope! Have joy! Have faith! May God bless all of you!

DAY 72
May 27th, 2020

Good evening everyone! We are closing out another day of this pandemic & it's Wednesday, May 27th, 2020. I hope on this warm summer evening that this message finds you healthy, safe & well.

Dear Heavenly Father, I come to You with Heavenly praise, love & thanksgiving. Thank You Jesus for the blessings you have given us, for strength in our times of weakness, for never leaving us & for walking with us each step of this long journey. In the name of Jesus, I claim Psalm 91, Psalm 23, Psalm 25:20-21, Psalm 46:1, Psalm 56:3, Psalm 61:2, 2 Chronicles 7:14, 2 Timothy 1:7, Jeremiah 30:17, Isaiah 54:17 & Isaiah 53:5 over all of you, your friends, family, pets, neighbors, coworkers & all you love this night, tomorrow & the day after that. I pray that each of you is surrounded by a supernatural & impenetrable hedge of protection that no evil can pass through. I pray for all the afflicted that they are healed & restored to full health. I pray for all the families & businesses that they are given hope for the future, faith, peace that surpasses all understanding, wisdom to move forward, strength to get through the coming days & abundance to be a blessing to many others around them. I pray for all the medical workers at every level that they are given protection, more than enough supplies, wisdom & strength to continue to fight this terrible virus. I pray that a safe & fully effective vaccine can be developed faster than ever thought possible. In the name of Jesus, I command, bind up & cast this virus, the spirit of fear & all agents of evil away from you to the farthest ends of existence. Thank You Father! In Your Holy, majestic & precious name I pray Lord Jesus, Amen!

As of today, we are another step closer to the end of this war. Battle after battle, fight after fight we continue to press forward to victory. It's a difficult & long journey but in the end we shall prevail over this virus! Christ is on the throne, in control & leading us to victory. I know all of you are tired & ready for this to be over, and it will soon. We need to hold on strong & keep fighting until its gone. But know this. Soon, very soon, this time will be a mere memory that we can draw strength from knowing that we stood together, we fought with everything we had, we had faith in the delivery of Christ & we prevailed and saw victory! We're all in this together everyone! Be healthy! Be safe! Be strong! Have hope! Have joy! May God bless all of you!

DAY 73
May 28th, 2020

Good evening everyone! We are approaching the weekend & we are closing out the day on Thursday May 28th, 2020. I hope that you have had a great week so far & that you are healthy, safe & well. If you haven't seen my posts up to this point, every night I am praying protection over all of you against the coronavirus.

Dear Heavenly Father, I come to you tonight with Heavenly praise, love & thanksgiving. Thank You Lord Jesus for blessing us, providing for us, giving us wisdom, strength during these stressful times, peace, hope & walking with us each step of this long journey. In the name of Jesus, I claim Psalm 91, Psalm 23, Psalm 25:20-21, Psalm 46:1, Psalm 56:3, Psalm 61:2, 2 Chronicles 7:14, 2 Timothy 1:7, Jeremiah 30:17, Isaiah 54:17 & Isaiah 53:5 over all of you, your friends, family, pets, neighbors, coworkers & all you love. I pray for a spiritual hedge of protection to surround you & all your loved ones that no evil can penetrate and shields you from all harm from this virus. In the name of Jesus, I command, bind up, and cast this virus, the spirit of fear & all forms of evil away from you and all you love. I pray that each of you is given peace that surpasses all understanding. I pray for all the families & businesses that they are blessed with hope, faith, wisdom, strength & abundance to be a blessing to many others. I pray for all the medical workers that they are protected, given more than enough supplies, wisdom, strength & peace during their difficult and dangerous shifts. I pray that this virus is eradicated and rendered extinct. I pray that a vaccine is developed swiftly that is fully effective and safe. Thank You Father! I claim all these things in Your Holy, majestic and precious name I pray Lord Jesus Amen!

The numbers are continuing to come down in the US. There's still a fluctuation up and down but it is definitely trending downward, which is wonderful news! We need to continue to be strong and vigilant but it's making a difference. Our continued journey through this valley is starting to see more light each and every day. Through Christ we will make it to the other side of all this. As I say each night and will continue to say each night, victory is coming soon! I can't phrase that any other way. Someday soon we are going to wake up & this pandemic will be over and you can rejoice with all of us that we made it through! Things are returning to normal, businesses are opening up again, summer is here & the cases are trending down. We can't let our guard down yet but with the end of today we are now another day closer to victory! We shall prevail and say it with me again. VICTORY IS COMING! VICTORY IS COMING! VICTORY IS COMING! We're all in this together! Be healthy! Be safe! Have hope! Have joy! Be strong! May God bless all of you!

DAY 74
May 29th, 2020

Good evening everyone! We are entering the weekend & we are closing out the day on Friday May 29th, 2020. On this summer evening I hope that this message once again finds you healthy, safe & well. There's a lot going all around us tonight & I am here to pray protection over all of you.

Dear Heavenly Father, I come to You tonight with Heavenly praise, love & thanksgiving. In the name of Jesus, I claim Psalm 91, Psalm 23, Psalm 25:20-21, Psalm 46:1, Psalm 56:3, Psalm 61:2, 2 Chronicles 7:14, 2 Timothy 1:7, Jeremiah 30:17, Isaiah 54:17 & Isaiah 53:5 over all of you, your friends, family, pets, neighbors, coworkers & all you love tonight, tomorrow and the next night. Dear Lord Jesus, tonight we need You. Please restore our lands & our nation. There are so many things going on beyond our control & we humble ourselves before You & ask for Your Holy intervention. For all of you reading tonight, I pray that you & your loved ones are surrounded by a hedge of protection that no evil can penetrate. I pray for all the families, businesses, our leaders and our nation that you are given hope, faith, peace, wisdom, strength, calmness and abundance to get through these trying days in our lives. I lift up all the afflicted before You Lord Jesus that they are restored to full health. In the name of Jesus, I command, bind up, rebuke and cast this virus, the spirit of fear, all agents of evil & the devil away from you & your loved ones. In the name of Jesus, this evil must go now. It has no option but to leave. Greater is He who is in us than he who is in the world & it is written if we resist the devil he has to leave. I pray for all the medical workers that they are given full protection, more than enough supplies, wisdom & strength to keep fighting. I pray for a vaccine to be developed swiftly. I pray for peace to fill this land. Thank You Father! I claim all these things in Your Holy, majestic & precious name I pray Lord Jesus, Amen!

Warriors! I know things seem out of control again tonight. But let not your hearts be troubled. Christ is on the Throne & totally in control. It's all going to be okay. We are facing more challenges than we've ever seen before, but this too shall pass. Have faith that we will be delivered from all of this. Through Christ we shall prevail. We will see victory over all of this. Focus on God & not the storm. We're gonna get through this. We're all in this together. Be healthy! Be safe! Have faith! Have hope! Have peace! Have Joy! May God bless all of you!

DAY 75
May 30th, 2020

Good evening everyone! We are closing out Saturday, May 30th, 2020 and let me start tonight's message with this... Wherever you are tonight across our nation, I pray that you and your family are safe & that peace fills your heart soul and mind. I pray that this message also finds you healthy & well.

Dear Heavenly Father, I come to you again tonight with Heavenly praise & thanksgiving. I thank You Lord Jesus for the blessings You have given us, wisdom, peace, protection through this new storm we are currently facing this evening, and for walking with us each step of this journey. I thank You that You are still in control and on the Throne. I plead with You Lord Jesus to please bring peace back to our nation and restore our lands. I plead to You that we as a nation are healed. I plead to You to help us get through this storm. In the name of Jesus, I claim Psalm 91, Psalm 23, Psalm 25:20-21, Psalm 46:1, Psalm 56:3, Psalm 61:2, 2 Chronicles 7:14, 2 Timothy 1:7, Jeremiah 30:17, Isaiah 54:17 and Isaiah 53:5 over all of you, your friends, family, pets, neighbors, coworkers & all you love tonight, tomorrow and the next night. I pray that you are all protected with a hedge of protection that this virus and all evil cannot penetrate and that it merely passes you by you. I pray for all the afflicted that they are restored to full health. In the Holy name of Jesus, I command, bind up, rebuke and cast this virus, the spirit of fear, this spirit of anger and hatred, all agents of evil and the devil away and that in the name of Christ that they never can return. I pray that peace covers this nation and our minds. I pray for all the medical workers fighting this virus that they are fully protected, have more than enough supplies, wisdom and strength to keep fighting. I pray for all the families and businesses affected by all that's going on around this country that you are given peace, protection, faith, a calm heart, wisdom, hope, strength and abundance. Dear Lord Jesus, I pray again, for peace to cover this nation tonight that surpasses all understanding. Thank You Father! In Your Holy, majestic and precious name I pray lord Jesus, Amen!

Warriors, with everything going on across our nation and the world, it is obviously difficult to be upbeat. But I swear to all of you this too shall pass. Christ is still in control no matter what we see going on around us. Through Christ we shall prevail. The thing we need to do right now is what Christ says, "Be still and know that I am God". We need to focus, not on the storm that is ravaging us, but to focus laser sharp on God. We need to stay united and we make it through. Like I say every night… We're all in this together! Be healthy! Be safe! Be strong! Be calm! Have peace! Have Strength! Have Joy! May God bless all of you!

DAY 76
May 31st, 2020

Good evening my friends! The end of the weekend is here & we are closing out May 31st, 2020. I'll start by saying this tonight. Needless to say, there's quite a lot going on all around us right now. But before I pray tonight & I said this last night, God is on the Throne and in control. This too shall pass. Let's begin.

Dear Heavenly Father, I come to You tonight with Heavenly praise, love & thanksgiving. Thank You Father that despite everything going on around us that is beyond our control and understanding that You are still in control. Thank You Father for the blessings You have given us, thank You that You went to the cross that we may have life through You & salvation. In the name of Jesus, I claim Psalm 91, Psalm 23, Psalm 25:20-21, Psalm 46:1, Psalm 56:3, Psalm 61:2, 2 Chronicles 7:14, 2 Timothy 1:7, Jeremiah 30:17, Philippians 4:7-9, Isaiah 54:17 & Isaiah 53:5 over all of you, your friends, family, pets, neighbors, coworkers & all you love. I pray that you, your families & all you hold dear are protected & shielded from the evil in this world by a hedge of protection that nothing can penetrate. I pray for the afflicted that they are healed & restored to full health. I pray for all the medical workers continually fighting this virus that they are protected, given more than enough supplies, wisdom & strength. I pray for the eradication of this virus & a powerful safe vaccine to be developed. I pray for all the families, people, businesses that have been affected by not only this virus, but the violence & destruction that has affected so many, that they are given peace that surpasses all understanding, hope, faith, restoration, healing, calmness, wisdom, more than enough strength & beyond abundance to be blessing to countless others. In the Holy name of Jesus, I command, bind up, rebuke & cast this virus, the spirit of fear, anger and hatred away, never to return. Father, I lift up our nation before You. Our cities are burning, lives have been lost, destroyed, and businesses & life savings have been lost. We humble ourselves before You & plead to You to restore our lands. We need a spiritual miracle to bring peace back to us. I pray that Your calming & restorative hands be placed on all the lives of everyone so we are united in You. Thank You Father! I claim all these things in Your Holy, majestic & precious name Lord Jesus, Amen!

Everyone, all of us are frustrated, angry & more than on edge. We've been in lock down for months, this virus is still present & now we are faced with a new storm before us, but I swear to all of you this too shall pass. I'm asking all of you tonight to pray for this country. We are all an army of warriors & our most powerful & effective weapon is prayer. We can do this. You have the power right now to make a difference wherever you are reading this. Take a moment, 5 minutes, even 10 seconds to say a prayer to restore us. Through Christ we shall prevail over this as well. We will not back down, we will only more forward! Failure is NOT an option! VICTORY IS COMING! We're all in this together! Be healthy! Be safe! Be strong! Have hope! Have peace! Have Joy! May God bless all of you!

DAY 77
June 1st, 2020

Good evening my friends! It is the end of the day on Monday June 1st, 2020 & I hope that tonight you, above all else, are safe, well & healthy. As promised I'm here to pray for all of you again tonight.

Dear Heavenly Father, I come to You with Heavenly praise, love & thanksgiving. Thank You Lord Jesus for the blessings that You have given us, thank You that through each & every storm You are by our side & will never leave us. Thank You that even when we don't understand, You are on the Throne & in total control. Father tonight we truly need You more than ever. Please Lord Jesus, restore our lands. We humble ourselves before You. Please help us. In the name of Jesus, I claim Psalm 91, Psalm 23, Psalm 25:20-21, Psalm 46:1, Psalm 56:3, Psalm 61:2, 2 Chronicles 7:14, 2 Timothy 1:7, Jeremiah 30:17, Philippians 4:7-9, Isaiah 54:17 & Isaiah 53:5 over all of you, your friends, family, pets, neighbors, coworkers, cities, our nation & all you love. Through this new storm we are facing along with the virus I pray for a hedge of protection to completely surround you that is impenetrable. I pray for all the families and business affected our current circumstances that You give them hope, peace, calmness, wisdom, strength, protection and abundance to be a blessing to many others. I pray that peace covers this nation tonight. I pray for the medical workers that they are protected, have more than enough supplies, wisdom and strength to keep fighting this virus. I pray that a safe and powerful vaccine is developed & that this virus is eradicated. In the name of Jesus, I command, bind up, rebuke and cast this terrible virus, the spirit of fear, anger and hatred away and command in the name of Jesus that it never returns. By His name IT MUST GO!!! This virus & violence MUST STOP! I lift up the afflicted that they are healed and restored to full health. Thank You Father for the coming miracle from You! I claim all these things in Your Holy, majestic, powerful and precious name I pray Lord Jesus, Amen!

Warriors, I'm asking all of you to once again to pray for our nation. We continue to face this new storm but through Christ we will be delivered. We shall prevail! I know all of you are angry, frustrated, scared and want all of this to stop. Please hold strong and have faith. Take a minute and pray before God for deliverance. Even if it is only 10 seconds, a minute, a day, whatever you can do. Through Christ and prayer we make our stand here and say NO MORE! Say it with me right now… WE SHALL PREVAIL!!! Let not your hearts be troubled. We're going to get through this as well. We're all in this together! Be healthy! Be safe! Be strong! Have hope! Have Joy! May God bless all of you!

DAY 78
June 2nd, 2020

Good evening friends! We are now closing out Tuesday June 2nd, 2020 & as always, I hope this message once again finds you safe, healthy & well.

Dear Heavenly Father I come to You with Heavenly praise, love & thanksgiving. Thank You Lord Jesus for all the blessings You have given us, for protecting us, giving us wisdom, guiding us & always walking with us & never ever leaving our side. Lord Father need You & we humble ourselves before You. Please restore our lands. In the name of Jesus, I claim Psalm 91, Psalm 23, Psalm 25:20-21, Psalm 46:1, Psalm 56:3, Psalm 61:2, 2 Chronicles 7:14, 2 Timothy 1:7, Jeremiah 30:17, Philippians 4:7-9, Isaiah 54:17 & Isaiah 53:5 over all of you, your friends, family, pets, neighbors, coworkers, cities, our nation & all you love. I pray that you are covered by the peace of Jesus Christ that surpasses all understanding. I pray that all of the families & businesses are given hope, protection, faith, guidance, wisdom & abundance to be a blessing to many others around you. I pray that a spiritual hedge of protection surrounds all of you that no evil can penetrate. I lift up all the afflicted that they would be supernaturally healed & restored to full health. I pray for all our medical workers that they are protected, given all the supplies they need, wisdom & strength. I pray for peace & calmness to cover all the citizens of the US tonight. I pray that a safe & effective vaccine is developed in record time. In the name of Jesus, I command, rebuke, bind up & cast this virus, the spirit of fear, anger & hatred away from you & your loved ones, never to return. I pray that we as Americans are reunited again. A house divided against it self cannot stand. Please Lord Jesus deliver all of us. Thank You Father! I claim all these things in Your Holy, majestic, powerful, glorified & precious name I pray Lord Jesus, Amen!

So far, 2020 has been a humbling year for all of us. It has been one storm after another for months & has pushed many of us to our limits. Everyone I know is frustrated, angry or afraid. The journey through this valley we're all in is dark, long & difficult. But despite ALL of this. DESPITE ALL OF THIS! God is on the throne & in control! We will get through this time! Peace & order will be restored! This virus will be destroyed & WE WILL WIN! Christ has a plan & through Him we shall Prevail! No matter what we see around us, victory is already ours! Let not your hearts be troubled. We need to get our eyes off the storm & on God. Only He can deliver us and He will. We're gonna get through this everyone! We're ALL in this together! We make our stand today and say NO MORE! Greater is He who is us than he who is in the world & in the name of Jesus I command this evil to LEAVE NOW! And by His name IT MUST GO!!! Be safe! Be healthy! Be strong! Have hope! Have Faith! Have strength! Have trust! May God bless all of you!

DAY 79
June 3rd, 2020

Good evening my friends! As we close out the middle of the week, Wednesday, June 3rd, 2020 once again I hope that this message finds all of you safe, healthy & well.

Dear Heavenly Father, I come to you tonight with Heavenly praise, love & thanksgiving. Thank You Father that You are on the Throne & in control, that You are leading us out of this valley. Thank You Lord Jesus for always supplying our needs & making ways when there were no ways. Thank You Father for blessing us & never leaving our sides. In the name of Jesus, I claim Psalm 91, Psalm 23, Psalm 25:20-21, Psalm 46:1, Psalm 56:3, Psalm 61:2, 2 Chronicles 7:14, 2 Timothy 1:7, Jeremiah 30:17, Philippians 4:7-9, Isaiah 54:17 & Isaiah 53:5 over all of you, your friends, family, pets, neighbors, coworkers,

cities, our nation & all you love. In the name of Jesus, as a child of God, covered in the blood of Christ, protected by Jesus & the Holy Spirit & saved by His grace, through You, with all Your power & majesty, I command, bind up, rebuke & cast out this virus, this spirit of fear, all the agents of evil, the spirit of anger, division, hatred, anxiety, worry & the devil away from all of you & by His name they cannot return. They must GO NOW! Greater is He that is in us than he who is in the world & it is written that if we, as children of God, resist the devil, he has to leave. I pray for protection for the countless families & businesses around the country & that they have peace, prosperity, hope, faith, wisdom, super natural strength, & abundance to bless countless others. In the name of Jesus, I pray that peace & order cover our nation & that this virus is completely eradicated. I pray that each & every person who is afflicted by this virus or violence be completely restored. I pray that all of you are shielded by an impenetrable hedge of protection. I lift up the medical workers, first responders, firefighters, police, EMTs, our leaders & all our citizens across our nation that they're all provided for & completely protected. I pray that we as a country are reunited as we humble ourselves before God & pray for the restoration of our lands. Thank You Lord Jesus that You are delivering us. Thank You Father & I claim all these things in Your Holy, majestic, powerful name Lord Jesus, Amen!
Warriors! Right here & now we make our stand! We stand united and through the power of Christ we shall not fall but we shall prevail! This year has been, for many of us, the most difficult time in our lives but we WILL NOT diminish! We WILL NOT falter! We WILL NOT FAIL! WE WILL SEE VICTORY! I know everything seems out of control with no end in sight & right as we get through one storm another rises but this too shall pass! Let not your hearts be troubled! Hold fast with a courageous unwavering heart & complete trust & faith that Christ will see us through this as well! And know this, through Christ, we are already victorious and have already won! We're all in this together! Be safe! Be healthy! Be strong! Be brave! Have hope! Have faith! May God bless all of you & protect you!

DAY 80
June 4th, 2020

Good evening my friends! We are approaching another weekend & we are closing out the day on Thursday, June 4th, 2020. If you haven't seen these messages before I'm praying protection over all of you each & every night. Thank you for all the wonderful messages I have received regarding these prayers each night. It means so much to me & I give all the Glory to God that these prayers are helping to give you peace. As always I hope this message finds you safe, healthy & well.

Dear Heavenly Father, I come to You tonight with a humble heart, Heavenly praise, love & thanksgiving. Thank You Father for all the blessings You have given us, for giving us strength, Your wisdom, for not leaving our sides & for walking with each of us each step of this journey. In the name of Jesus, I claim Psalm 91, Psalm 23, Psalm 25:20-21, Psalm 46:1, Psalm 56:3, Psalm 61:2, 2 Chronicles 7:14, 2 Timothy 1:7, Jeremiah 30:17, Philippians 4:7-9, Isaiah 54:17 & Isaiah 53:5 over all of you, your friends, family, pets, neighbors, coworkers, cities, our nation & all you love. Lord Jesus, we humble ourselves before You, turn from our sinful ways & pray that You restore our lands. In the name of Jesus, I command, bind up, rebuke & cast this virus, the spirit of fear, anger, hatred, violence, all agents of evil & the devil away from you to the very ends of the Earth. I pray for a powerful, spiritual & impenetrable hedge of protection to surround you & all you love. I pray for all the families & businesses that have been affected by this horrible virus & violence across our nation that they are given hope, peace, faith, strength, calmness & abundance to be a blessing to others. I pray for all the medical workers that they are protected, given more than enough supplies, wisdom & strength to keep combating this virus. Thank You Father for our coming victory through You. I claim all these things in Your Holy, powerful, majestic & precious name I pray Lord Jesus, Amen!

Warriors! I know that all of us are frustrated, angry, afraid, overwhelmed & that everything seems like it's completely out of control. But I swear to all of you Christ is in control & on the Throne! The storm that surrounds us is great but God is more powerful than anything thrown against us. Turn your eyes away from this storm and look away! JUST LOOK AWAY!! Turn your eyes to Christ and focus ONLY on Him! Lift your hand up & say this with me right now. "VICTORY IS COMING & WE SHALL PREVAIL!" We're ALL in this together! Be safe! Be healthy! Be strong! Have Hope! Have Faith! Have Joy! May God less you & protect you!

Normally I add one of the passages from above but tonight I am adding this. If you don't know Jesus & would like to, simply say this prayer below.

"God, I'm a sinner. I'm sorry for my sins. I believe Jesus Christ is your Son. And I want to invite Him to come into my heart, into my life. I'm willing to trust Him as my Savior and follow Him as my Lord. And I pray this in Jesus' name."

DAY 81
June 5th, 2020

Good evening my friends. We are closing out Friday June 5th, 2020 & on this warm summer night I hope this message finds all of you safe, healthy & well. Let's begin.

Dear Heavenly Father, I come to You tonight with Heavenly praise, trust, love & thanksgiving. Thank You Father for the blessings You've given us, for guiding us, walking with us & never forsaking us. In the name of Jesus, I claim Psalm 91, Psalm 23, Psalm 25:20-21, Psalm 46:1, Psalm 56:3, Psalm 61:2, 2 Chronicles 7:14, 2 Timothy 1:7, Jeremiah 30:17, Philippians 4:7-9, Isaiah 54:17 & Isaiah 53:5 over all of you, your friends, family, pets, neighbors, coworkers, cities, our nation & all you love. I claim & pray for a spiritual hedge of protection that surrounds you & all you hold dear. I pray for all the afflicted & sick that they are restored to full health & for a safe and fully effective vaccine. In the name of Jesus, I command, bind up, rebuke & cast this virus, the spirit of fear, anger, hatred, violence, all agents of evil & the devil away from you & all you love. I lift up all the families, businesses & countless people around the country that are afraid, frustrated, angry that all of you are blessed with peace, hope, faith, wisdom, strength & abundance. I pray, that we as a people, are reunited again & that peace & calmness covers this nation. I pray for all the medical workers, our leaders, firefighters, police, EMTs that all of you are given strength, wisdom & protection. I place all these situations we are facing in Your hands Lord Jesus. I Thank You Father for the coming deliverance & miracle that only You can deliver. Thank You Lord Jesus. I claim all these things in Your Holy, powerful, majestic & precious name Lord Jesus! Amen!

My friends, as we're walking along this difficult journey, have faith that even though everything seems uncertain & fearful that Christ has a plan & already has the solution & victory. We are going to make it through this! 2020 certainly has been one thing after another, but through Christ we SHALL PREVAIL! The history of the world has seen countless times when things seemed impossible, only to be miraculously turned around. I know it is difficult & painful but we are going to make it. Draw strength & find protection in Jesus. He WILL deliver us from this virus, violence & evil. Please take a moment again tonight & pray for our nation. We are an army of warriors & our commander has already signaled the victory. Say this with me now! BECAUSE OF CHRIST WE HAVE VICTORY! We're all in this together! Be safe! Be healthy! Be strong! Have wisdom! Have faith! Have hope! May God bless and protect all of you!

I want to add this at the end. Thank you for all your kind messages about these prayers I do every night. I'm glad that Christ's power is helping ease your fears & I pray that God blesses ALL of you this year.

DAY 82
June 6th, 2020

Good evening my friends! We're closing out Saturday, June 6th, 2020 & wherever you are reading this, I hope that this post finds you safe, healthy & well. Let's begin tonight.

Dear Heavenly Father, I come to You with Heavenly praise, love &

thanksgiving. Thank You for another day, thank You for the blessings that You've given us & for walking with us each step of this difficult journey. Jesus, I pray that everyone who's reading this prayer tonight would be truly abundantly blessed by You. Please supply all their needs & please give them peace that surpasses all understanding, hope, faith, wisdom & strength to face each day. In the name of Jesus, I claim Psalm 91, Psalm 23, Psalm 25:20-21, Psalm 46:1, Psalm 56:3, Psalm 61:2, 2 Chronicles 7:14, 2 Timothy 1:7, Jeremiah 30:17, Philippians 4:7-9, Isaiah 54:17 & Isaiah 53:5 over all of you, your friends, family, pets, neighbors, coworkers, cities & our nation. I pray for the sick to be healed & a powerful vaccine to be created swiftly. I pray for all the medical workers, EMTs firefighters, police, our leaders & our nation that peace would cover all of you & that all of you are protected & given strength. In the name of Jesus, I command, bind up & cast this virus, the spirit of fear, anger, hatred & violence away from you. I pray for peace in our nation tonight & calmness. I pray for a spiritual hedge of protection around all of you. I pray for our nation to be reunited through You Father. Thank You Lord Jesus, I claim all these things in Your Holy, majestic, powerful & precious name Lord Jesus, Amen!

Warriors, we're another day closer to victory & peace being restored to our nation. I know that everything seems out of control, but please know that God IS in control & on the Throne. None of this is a surprise to Him & He already has the perfect solution prepared. This violence IS going to end! This virus IS going to be eradicated! Peace WILL be restored! Life WILL return to normal again. Turn away from the storm! Focus ONLY on God. Through the protection of Christ you'll be observers of the storm, not destroyed by it. We need to hold on and not lose faith! We WILL be delivered through the power & majesty of Jesus Christ. Victory is coming! We're gonna get through this too! We're all in this together! Be safe! Be healthy! Be strong! Have faith! Have hope! Have Joy! May God bless & protect all of you!

DAY 83
June 7th, 2020

Good evening my friends! As we finish out the day on Sunday June 7th, 2020 & begin a brand new week, I hope that you're safe, healthy & well. In NE Ohio it was a beautiful weekend & despite all the challenges we're all facing, which have become highly accretive, it made me stop to reflect on the things we tend to take for granted. Even in the most aggressive storms of life, there's always beauty & magnificence to be found & observed. Let's begin.

Dear Heavenly Father, tonight, I come to You with a humble heart, Heavenly praise, love & thanksgiving. Thank You Jesus for another day, for Your infinite wisdom You freely give, for the strength we need to face each day and for never leaving our sides. In the name of Jesus, I claim Psalm 91, Psalm 23, Psalm 25:20-21, Psalm 46:1, Psalm 56:3, Psalm 61:2, 2 Chronicles 7:14, 2 Timothy 1:7, Jeremiah 30:17, Philippians 4:7-9, Isaiah 54:17 & Isaiah 53:5 over all of you, your friends, family, pets, neighbors, coworkers, cities and our nation. I pray for a powerful spiritual hedge of protection to surround you & your loved ones. I pray that the afflicted would be healed & restored. I pray that powerful treatments and vaccines be developed to combat this virus. I pray for all the families and businesses across this nation & world that you would be blessed with hope, peace, faith, wisdom, strength and abundance to bless others. I pray for peace, calmness & restoration to cover our nation and cities. I pray for our people to be reunited. I pray for protection of our medical workers, firefighters, EMTs, our leaders and our citizens. I pray Father, that You restore our lands. In the name of Jesus, I command, bind up, rebuke and cast this pestilence & the spirit of fear, anger, violence, hatred, animosity, anxiety, all the agents of evil & the devil away from you, your loved ones and all you hold dear. Greater is He who lives in us than he who lives in the world and by the Holy and majestic name of Jesus Christ, they have to LEAVE NOW! They have no other option but to go and never return. Thank You Father! I claim all these things in Your Holy, powerful, majestic and awesome name Lord Jesus, Amen!

Warriors, as we pray tonight, we have to pray as warriors on the offensive. We are under attack in the spiritual sense & we need to hold our ground, stand firm & say no more! We need to say to this evil be gone, leave & never return! I pray for all of your protection through this storm & I swear to you we will see victory because of what Christ has already done! With Christ, not some things, but ALL things are possible & we will not go quietly into the night but make our stand today. We are not weak but strong, not timid but bold, not afraid but brave! We draw the line in the sand this night & we are already victorious! Victory is coming soon my friends! And all of you are here to witness Christ's awesome power & might! Be safe! Be healthy! Be strong! Have faith! Have hope! Have joy! Have victory! May God keep, protect & bless all of you!

DAY 84
June 8th, 2020

Good evening my friends! As we close out the day on Monday, June 8th, 2020 I'm back to pray protection over you & wherever you are I hope that you're safe, healthy & well.

Dear Heavenly Father, I come to You with a humble heart, Heavenly praise, love & thanksgiving. Thank You Lord Jesus, that You're on the Throne & in control. Thank You Father for the blessings You've given us & never leaving our side. Father, please bless whoever is reading this tonight with peace, faith, hope, wisdom, strength & abundance to be a blessing to others. In the name of Jesus, I command, rebuke, bind up and cast away this virus, the spirit of fear, anger, violence, hatred, all agents of evil & the devil away from all of you & loved ones. Greater is He who is in us than he who is in the world & by the name of Jesus, it must go now! In the name of Jesus, I claim Psalm 91, Psalm 23, Psalm 25:20-21, Psalm 46:1, Psalm 56:3, Psalm 61:2, 2 Chronicles 7:14, 2 Timothy 1:7, Jeremiah 30:17, Philippians 4:7-9, Isaiah 54:17 & Isaiah 53:5 over all of you, your friends, family, pets, neighbors, coworkers, cities & our nation. I pray that you're protected by an impenetrable spiritual hedge of protection. I pray that the afflicted will be supernaturally restored to full health & that new treatments & a powerful vaccine are developed swiftly. In the name of Jesus, I pray for peace & calmness to cover this nation & reunite its people. Please Father restore our lands. I pray for protection over all the medical workers that they're have more than enough supplies, wisdom & strength. Thank You father. I claim all these things in Your Holy, powerful, majestic & precious name, Lord Jesus, Amen!

My friends, despite how everything looks right now! Despite how everything seems out of control! Despite all of the insanity we have seen over the past several months everywhere. God is IN control of everything. Do not fear what we cannot see, because God is working behind the scenes. We're living in a very uncertain & difficult time but WE ARE WARRIORS! Through Christ, we're going to make it through these storms. Today we are that much closer to victory. Don't worry about tomorrow as tomorrow has its own problems to deal with. Let not your heart be troubled. We're gonna break through this with the power of Christ! Stand firm! Stand tall! Stand ready warriors! Say it with me tonight! WE SHALL PREVAIL! Be safe! Be healthy! Be strong! Be blessed! Have wisdom! May God bless all of you!

DAY 85
June 9th, 2020

Good evening my friends! We're through another day & we're closing out Tuesday June 9th, 2020. As always, I hope this message finds you safe, healthy & well.

Dear Heavenly Father, I come to You tonight with Heavenly praise, a humble heart, love & thanksgiving. Thank You Lord Jesus, for all the blessings You have given us, that You are in control, on the Throne & that You'll never leave us. Jesus, I come to You tonight praying for our nation. I pray that Your peace & calmness will cover our country again. I pray that You'll deliver us out of the storms that have surrounded us. I pray that this virus is eradicated & that a powerful vaccine is developed swiftly. I pray for all the afflicted that they're restored to full & complete health. In the name of Jesus, I claim Psalm 91, Psalm 23, Psalm 25:20-21, Psalm 46:1, Psalm 56:3, Psalm 61:2, 2 Chronicles 7:14, 2 Timothy 1:7, Jeremiah 30:17,

Philippians 4:7-9, Isaiah 54:17 & Isaiah 53:5 over all of you, your friends, family, pets, neighbors, coworkers, cities & our nation. I pray that you're protected by an impenetrable spiritual hedge of protection. I pray that this violence & anger that has enveloped our nation is replaced with peace, calmness, love & hope. In the name of Jesus, I command, bind up, rebuke & cast this virus, the spirit of fear, anger, violence, hatred, all agents of evil & the devil away from you & your loved ones. By the name of Jesus Christ, it has to obey & leave now! It cannot stay & must go! I pray for all the families, businesses, our nation, our leaders & everyone affected by these storms that they'd be blessed with peace, hope, faith, wisdom, strength, perseverance & abundance. I pray that all the medical workers are given protection, supplies, wisdom & strength to keep fighting the virus. Thank You Father! I claim all these things in Your Holy, powerful, majestic & precious name I pray Lord Jesus, Amen!

Warriors! We're continuing to press forward & we're another day closer to victory! The path we've been on has been difficult but we'll not be deterred. Christ leads us to victory & only through Him, shall we prevail! These storms are no match for our God. I know you all are afraid, angry, frustrated but know this... We WILL WIN! We're going to stay strong! We're going to press forward! We're going to not back down! We're going to get through this! We're all in this together! Shout with me! VICTORY IS COMING! Be strong! Be safe! Be healthy! Have wisdom! Have hope! Have faith! May God bless & protect all of you!

DAY 86
June 10th, 2020

Good evening my friends! I apologize for this coming out a little late tonight but with the storms that came through NE, Ohio tonight I was offline for a little bit. As we close out this Wednesday June 10th, 2020 we're 1/3 of the way through June & I hope this message finds you healthy, safe & well. Let's begin tonight.

Dear Heavenly Father, I come to You with Heavenly praise, a humble heart, love & thanksgiving. Thank You Father for the blessings

You've given us, for walking with us through the challenges we face & for never leaving us. Father, I come to You & pray that peace completely covers this nation & this violence ceases. In the name of Jesus, I claim Psalm 91, Psalm 23, Psalm 25:20-21, Psalm 46:1, Psalm 56:3, Psalm 61:2, 2 Chronicles 7:14, 2 Timothy 1:7, Jeremiah 30:17, Philippians 4:7-9, Isaiah 43:2, Isaiah 54:17 & Isaiah 53:5 over all of you, your friends, family, pets, neighbors, coworkers, cities & our nation. I pray that you & all you love are completely surrounded by a spiritual impenetrable hedge of protection. I pray for all the afflicted by this terrible virus that they are restored to full health & that a powerful vaccine is developed swiftly. I lift up all our medical workers, first responders, police, firefighters, EMTs & our leaders that they would be given protection, more than enough supplies, wisdom & strength to keep going through long & dangerous shifts. I pray for all of you that you would be blessed & given peace, hope, faith, wisdom, strength & abundance through these difficult days. In the name of Jesus, as a child of the Living God, covered in Your blood & sealed with the Holy Spirit, I command, rebuke & cast this virus, the spirit of fear, anger, hatred, anxiety, violence, all agents of evil & the devil away from you & your loved ones. By the power of Christ IT MUST GO NOW! Thank You Father! I claim all these things in Your holy, powerful, majestic & precious name I pray Lord Jesus, Amen!

My fellow warriors, shout with me "FEAR NOT! THIS TOO SHALL PASS". We are about to see the amazing power of God as we continue to press forward through the storms we have been facing. Only through Christ will we be delivered & we must keep our focus on God & not the storm! I know you are tired, but know that victory is coming!. 2020 will go down in history as an immensely difficult time. But we faced adversity that kept coming & through Christ we saw victory. I know this journey is difficult, but we WILL come out of this time! This season will end & through the majestic power of Christ, we shall prevail! Stand firm! Stand Strong! Stand Ready! VICTORY IS COMING! We're all in this together! Be safe! Be healthy! Be strong! Have FAITH! Have hope! Have strength! Have peace! May God bless all of you !

DAY 87
June 11th, 2020

Good evening my friends! We're approaching the weekend & we're closing out Thursday, June 11th, 2020. As we end the week, I hope this message finds you safe, healthy & well.

Dear Heavenly Father, I come to You with a humble heart, Heavenly praise, love & thanksgiving. Thank You Father for the blessings You've given us, for guiding us along this journey & for never leaving our side. Lord Jesus, we humble ourselves before You, turn from our sins & pray that You please restore our lands. We pray Lord Jesus that You cover our nation with Your calming hands & please restore peace. In the name of Jesus, I claim Psalm 91, Psalm 23, Psalm 25:20-21, Psalm 46:1, Psalm 56:3, Psalm 61:2, 2 Chronicles 7:14, 2 Timothy 1:7, Jeremiah 30:17, Philippians 4:7-9, Isaiah 43:2, Isaiah 54:17 & Isaiah 53:5 over all of you, your friends, family, pets, neighbors, coworkers, cities & our nation. I pray that you & all you love are completely surrounded by a spiritual, powerful & impenetrable hedge of protection. I pray for all the afflicted that they're restored to full health & for a powerful vaccine to be swiftly developed. In the name of Jesus, I command, rebuke & cast this virus, the spirit of fear, anger, violence, hatred, all agents of evil & the devil away from you & all you love. I pray for all the families who have been affected by the virus & violence across this nation that they're blessed with peace, faith, hope, wisdom, strength & abundance to make it through this difficult journey. I lift up all the medical workers, our first responders & our leaders that they're protected & blessed with peace, wisdom, more than enough supplies & strength to keep going! Thank You Father for our coming victory! I claim all these things in Your Holy, powerful, majestic & precious name I pray Lord Jesus, Amen!

Warriors! We're continuing to push through these storms we face! These storms are great, but our God is GREATER! Christ is in control & on the Throne & only through Him will we prevail. I know this has been difficult for many of you & continues to be so, but this season will end! This too shall pass! Our victory is coming & we need to do our part & have faith & hold on. We must be strong in the face of adversity & stay united! Soon, ALL OF THIS, will be nothing more than a distant memory & life will return to normal. And know this, despite everything going on around us, through Christ we have ALREADY WON! We must keep our eyes only on Christ. Let not your heart be troubled! We're all in this together! VICTORY IS COMING! Be safe! Be healthy! Be strong! Have faith! Have hope! Have peace! Have Joy! May God bless all of you!

DAY 88
June 12th, 2020

Good evening my friends! It's the weekend & we're closing out Friday, June 12th, 2020. Tonight I want to start off by saying this. 2020 has been truly a difficult year but I believe in the restorative power of Christ & with that I pray that wherever you are reading this right now, this very moment that you're abundantly blessed & have joy knowing that despite everything going on around you, you're known & blessed by God almighty. I hope this message finds you safe, healthy & well.

Dear Heavenly Father, I come to You with Heavenly praise, love & thanksgiving. Thank You Father for the gift of salvation through Your son Jesus Christ. Truly, the most amazing blessing of all. In the name of Jesus, I claim Psalm 91, Psalm 23, Psalm 25:20-21, Psalm 46:1, Psalm 56:3, Psalm 61:2, 2 Chronicles 7:14, 2 Timothy 1:7, Jeremiah 30:17, Philippians 4:7-9, Isaiah 43:2, Isaiah 54:17 & Isaiah 53:5 over all of you & over everyone you love. I pray that you are supernaturally protected by a hedge of protection that this virus & all forms evil can't penetrate. I pray for the sick to be fully restored. I pray for a powerful vaccine to be developed. I pray that this violence, anger & hatred is replaced with peace, hope & faith. I pray Lord Jesus that You will restore our lands. For all of you that have been affected by the virus & the violence, I pray you're given supernatural peace, hope, faith, wisdom, guidance, calmness, love, wisdom, strength & abundance. I pray for all our medical workers, firefighters, first responders, police, leaders, EMTs that you're protected by the blood of Christ blessed with wisdom & strength. In the name of Jesus, as a child of the Living God, covered in Christ's blood & sealed with the

Holy Spirit, I command, rebuke & cast this virus, all forms of evil, the spirit of fear, anger, anxiety, violence, hatred & the devil from you & I command it by the name & power of Christ that it MUST GO NOW! Greater is He who is in us, than he who is in the world. Thank You Father for our coming victory! I claim all these things in Your Holy, majestic, powerful & precious name Lord Jesus, I Pray, Amen!

My fellow warriors! This battle field we live in called life will one day be replaced with 1,000 years of peace during the millennium rule of Christ Jesus. As we march forward each day, we continue to win battle after battle against the enemy. But know this, though our foe is formidable, God is more powerful & we have already won. We don't fight for victory, we fight from victory! I know life is uncertain but all things are certain with Christ & through Christ we SHALL PREVAIL! I pray for peace that surpasses all understanding to envelop & fill all of you. Let NOT your heart be troubled. We're going to get through this too! It's all going to be okay! Shout with me! OUR GOD IS GOD! Be safe! Be strong! Be healthy! Have faith! Have hope! Have wisdom! Have peace! Have joy! May God bless all of you!

DAY 89
June 13th, 2020

Good evening my friends! Tonight as we close out Saturday June 13th, 2020, I hope this message finds you safe, healthy & well. As promised I'm here to pray over all of you through these difficult times we face.

Dear Heavenly Father, I come to You with a humble heart, Heavenly praise, love & thanksgiving. Thank You Jesus for another day, for Your infinite wisdom, guidance & always staying by our sides. In the Holy name of Jesus, I claim Psalm 91, Psalm 23, Psalm 25:20-21, Psalm 46:1, Psalm 56:3, Psalm 61:2, 2 Chronicles 7:14, 2 Timothy 1:7, Jeremiah 30:17, Philippians 4:7-9, Isaiah 43:2, Isaiah 54:17 & Isaiah 53:5 over all of you & over everyone you love. I pray that you're supernaturally protected by a hedge of protection tonight, tomorrow night & the night after that. I pray for the sick to be fully restored to health & for a powerful vaccine to combat this virus. I pray for all our doctors, nurses & all medical workers that they be blessed with wisdom, peace, supplies & strength to keep going. I lift up & pray for everyone that has been affected by the virus & this violence that's spread across, not only our nation, but the world & that you would be blessed with hope, peace, faith, wisdom, strength & abundance to help bless others. In the name of Jesus, as a son of the Living God & covered in His blood, I command, rebuke & cast this virus, the spirit of fear, anger, anxiety, violence, hatred, all agents of evil & the devil away from you & all you love. In the name of Christ, IT MUST GO NOW & never return! Thank You Lord Jesus! I claim all these things in Your Holy, powerful, majestic & precious name I pray, Lord Jesus, Amen!

Warriors! Tonight we stand once again & must hold our ground against our enemy. This world we live in is fallen but we're protected & saved by Christ. One day, very soon, ALL of this will be made right. Until that day, we must continue to stay strong & press forward knowing that we're victorious in Christ Jesus. God is in control & on the Throne! None of what's going on is a surprise to Him & He already has a plan for deliverance. As it says in Isaiah, "no weapon formed against you shall prosper!" Through Christ we will triumph over the storms ravaging this world & through Christ we shall be victorious & prevail! Once again SHOUT WITH ME! WE SHALL PREVAIL!! We're all in this together! Be safe! Be healthy! Be strong! Have faith! Have hope! Have peace! Have joy! May God bless all of you!

DAY 90
June 14th, 2020

Good evening my friends! I hope all of you had a wonderful weekend as we close out Sunday June 14th, 2020. Let's begin tonight.

Dear Heavenly Father, I come to You with a humble heart, Heavenly praise, love & thanksgiving. Thank You Father for the blessings You've given us, for wisdom, guidance & never forsaking us ever. I thank You Father for our coming victory! In the name of Jesus, I claim Psalm 91, Psalm 23, Psalm 25:20-21, Psalm 46:1, Psalm 56:3, Psalm 61:2, 2 Chronicles 7:14, 2 Timothy 1:7, Jeremiah 30:17,

Philippians 4:7-9, Isaiah 43:2, Isaiah 54:17 & Isaiah 53:5 over all of you, everyone you love & hold dear. I pray that you're supernaturally protected by an impenetrable hedge of protection that, neither this virus nor any evil can penetrate. I pray for the afflicted that they're restored to complete health & that new treatments as well as a power vaccine is developed. I lift up all the families, businesses & everyone affected by the virus as well as the violence that has been spreading across the planet that you're blessed with peace that surpasses all understanding, hope for the future, wisdom, guidance, strength & abundance through these difficult storms. In the name of Jesus, as a son of the Living God & covered in His blood I command, rebuke & cast this virus, all agents of evil, the devil & the spirit of fear, hatred, violence & anxiety away from you & by His name it MUST GO NOW, never to return! I pray for all the medical workers continuing to fight this ongoing pandemic that they'd be blessed with protection, supplies, wisdom, & strength. I pray for Your infinite peace & calmness to cover this nation tonight. Thank You Father. I claim all these things in Your Holy, powerful, majestic & precious name I pray Lord Jesus, Amen!

Warriors, as we begin another week in 2020 we must continue to stay focused on God & not these compounding storms that seem to keep coming at us from all sides. No storm is too powerful for Christ & He'll lead us to victory & deliver us. When the voices of fear, anxiety & doubt come remember this passage from the Bible Psalm 46:10 He says, "Be still, and know that I am God". He fights our battles & has already won the war. Have faith & know that it's all going to be okay. Through Christ WE SHALL PREVAIL! Through Christ, WE WILL SEE VICTORY! Through Christ WE HAVE WON! Be safe! Be healthy! Be strong! Have faith! Have hope! Have joy! May God bless all of you!

DAY 91
June 15th, 2020

Good evening my friends. It's the beginning of a new week & we're closing out Monday, June 15th, 2020. I hope this message finds you safe, healthy & well. Dear Heavenly Father, I come to You tonight with a humble heart, Heavenly praise, love & thanksgiving.

Thank You Jesus for blessing us with guidance, wisdom, strength & never forsaking us. Father we need Your peace and calming hands to cover this nation tonight. Please restore our lands. In the name of Jesus, I claim Psalm 91, Psalm 23, Psalm 25:20-21, Psalm 46:1, Psalm 56:3, Psalm 61:2, 2 Chronicles 7:14, 2 Timothy 1:7, Jeremiah 30:17, Philippians 4:7-9, Isaiah 43:2, Isaiah 54:17 & Isaiah 53:5 over all of you, everyone you love. I pray, right now, that all of you are supernaturally protected by an impenetrable hedge of protection. I pray for the afflicted that they're miraculously restored to full health & for a powerful vaccine is developed swiftly. I pray for all the families, people, businesses that have been affected by the virus & all the violence spreading across this nation that you're blessed with protection, peace, hope, guidance, wisdom, strength & abundance to bless others. In the name of Jesus, as a son of the Living God, covered in His blood & sealed by the Holy Spirit, I come against & command through the authority of Christ that this virus, the spirit of fear, violence, hatred, animosity, all agents of evil & the devil are ALL CAST AWAY from you & your families. THEY MUST GO! Greater is He who is in us than he who is in the world & it is written that if we resist the devil he must flee from us. I pray for all the medical workers, police, firefighters, EMTs our leaders that you're blessed with wisdom & strength. I thank You Father for our coming victory! I claim all these things in Your Holy, powerful, majestic & precious name I pray Lord Jesus, Amen!

Warriors! I'll start with this tonight. Let not your heart's be troubled. As it's written "Be still & know that I am God". I know these storms continue but all storms end! This valley we're walking through is long & difficult but there's light coming! There's peace coming! There's victory coming! Through all of this, always know, God is in control & on the Throne! Stay strong & have faith! Only through Christ will we prevail! As I say each night, keep your eyes on God & away from the storm. We're gonna get through this! Shout with me! VICTORY IS COMING! Be safe! Be healthy! Be strong! Have faith! Have hope! Have Joy! May God bless all of you.

DAY 92
June 16th, 2020

Good evening my friends! As we close out the day on June 16th, 2020, I hope that you're safe, healthy & well. If you're new to my posts, every night I'm praying protection over all of you.

Dear Heavenly Father, I come to you with Heavenly praise & thanksgiving. Thank You Jesus for the blessings You've given us & for guiding us, giving us wisdom & never leaving us. In the name of Jesus, I claim Psalm 91, Psalm 23, Psalm 25:20-21, Psalm 46:1, Psalm 56:3, Psalm 61:2, 2 Chronicles 7:14, 2 Timothy 1:7, Jeremiah 30:17, Philippians 4:7-9, Isaiah 43:2, Isaiah 54:17 & Isaiah 53:5 over all of you, everyone you love. I pray for a supernatural & impenetrable hedge of protection. In the name of Jesus, as a son of the Living God, covered in Christ's blood & sealed by the Holy Spirit, I command, rebuke & cast the virus, all agents of evil, the spirit of fear & all forms of hatred & violence & the devil away from you & your loved ones. I pray for all the families & businesses affected by the pandemic & the violence spreading across the country & world that all of you, are blessed with peace, hope, faith, wisdom, guidance, tenacity, strength & abundance. I pray for all the afflicted that you're restored to full health & for the development of a powerfully effective vaccine. I pray for all the medical workers that you're protected & given peace, supplies, protection, wisdom & strength to keep going. I pray for peace to cover our nation once again & for restoration of our lands. Thank You Father. I claim all these things in Your Holy, powerful, majestic & precious name I pray Lord Jesus, Amen! Warriors! Notice around us how all the events & signs are escalating. Something very big is coming. And tonight, I am praying not only protection for you, but that all of you are truly blessed wherever you are in the world. We're here on this Earth but a mere blink of the eye in comparison to eternity. Throughout my life & all the challenges, trials & tribulations the one thing that's kept me going through all these years is my personal faith in Jesus Christ. Through Christ all things are possible & truly through him we WILL prevail through this uncertain time. Tonight, I'm asking everyone to once again pray for our nation & if we humble ourselves before God & turn from our wicked ways, I believe we'll be delivered through this storm & future storms. These storms that surround us are great & powerful, but they're NOT as powerful as Christ. God is in complete control & on the throne! Shout it with me again! VICTORY IS COMING! Be safe! Be healthy! Be strong! Have faith! Have hope! Have Joy! May God bless all of you!

DAY 93
June 17th, 2020

Good evening my friends! I hope this message finds you safe, healthy & well as we close out Wednesday, June 17th, 2020. Let's begin tonight.

Dear Heavenly Father, I come to You with a humble heart, praising Your name with love & thanksgiving. Thank You Father, for taking care of us & walking with us each step of this long, difficult journey. In the name of Jesus, I claim Psalm 91, Psalm 23, Psalm 25:20-21, Psalm 46:1, Psalm 56:3, Psalm 61:2, 2 Chronicles 7:14, 2 Timothy 1:7, Jeremiah 30:17, Philippians 4:7-9, Isaiah 43:2, Isaiah 54:17 & Isaiah 53:5 over all of you, everyone you love. I pray you & your loved ones are surrounded by an impenetrable hedge of protection each day & night. I pray that the afflicted are restored to full & complete health & for a powerful vaccine to combat the virus. I pray for all the families & businesses that have been affected by the virus & the violence spreading across our nation that you're blessed with peace, hope, faith, wisdom, strength & abundance to bless others. In the name of Jesus, as a child of God, covered in His blood & sealed by the Holy Spirit, I command, come against, rebuke & cast this virus, the spirit of fear, violence, hatred, all agents of evil & the devil away from you & your loved ones. Through the name and awesome power of Christ it MUST GO NOW! I lift up & pray for the medical workers fighting the virus that you're blessed with protection, peace, supplies, wisdom & strength. Lord Jesus, I pray that You cover this nation with Your calming hands & restore peace to our lands. Thank You Jesus for our coming deliverance. Thank You Jesus for our coming victory. Thank You Jesus for standing with us and sustaining us through these difficult days. I claim all these things in Your Holy, powerful, majestic & precious name I pray Lord Jesus, Thank You Father! Amen!

My fellow warriors! Stand with me now as we once again draw a line in the sand & say no more! We move as a united Phalanx standing our ground & pressing forward, all through the power of Christ Jesus. Let not your hearts be troubled as we move across this difficult terrain but know that Christ will deliver us to the other side of this valley. Storms may come against us but they will dwindle before the awesome power of God. We WILL make it through this valley! We WILL see victory! And through Christ we WILL PREVAIL! Hold fast & know that God is in complete control! Our victory is coming swiftly! Be safe! Be healthy! Be strong! Have faith! Have hope! Have joy! Have peace! May God bless all of you!

DAY 94
June 18th, 2020

Good evening my friends! We're coming up on the weekend as we close out Thursday June 18th, 2020. As with every night, I hope this message finds you safe, healthy & well wherever you are.

Dear Heavenly Father, I come to You with a humble heart, love & thanksgiving. Thank You Jesus for guiding us through another day & walking with us through this difficult journey. Father, I pray that You bless everyone who reads this prayer & that You give them abundant peace, hope, guidance, wisdom, strength & faith. In the Holy name of Jesus, I claim Psalm 91, Psalm 23, Psalm 25:20-21, Psalm 46:1, Psalm 56:3, Psalm 61:2, 2 Chronicles 7:14, 2 Timothy 1:7, Jeremiah 30:17, Philippians 4:7-9, Isaiah 43:2, Isaiah 54:17 & Isaiah 53:5 over all of you & everyone you love. I pray for an impenetrable hedge of protection to surround you & all you hold dear. I pray for protection, wisdom & strength for all the medical workers, firefighters, police, EMTs & our leaders. In the name of Jesus, as a child of the Living God, covered in His blood & sealed by the Holy Spirit I command, rebuke & cast this virus, the spirit of fear, violence, hatred, all agents of evil & the devil away from you through the awesome & amazing power of Jesus Christ. And through His name these evil forces must

GO NOW! Never to return! Greater is He who is in us than he who's in the world! And as it's written, if we resist the devil he must flee. I pray that a powerful vaccine is developed & that all the afflicted are restored to full health. Please Father, heal & cover our nation with Your calming hands & restore peace. Thank You Father! I claim all these things in Your Holy, powerful, majestic, awesome & precious name I pray Lord Jesus, Amen! Warriors! Let me hear you shout GOD IS IN CONTROL! Turn your eyes away from these great storms around us & focus on God as He's more powerful than any storm that comes against us. We stand with Christ through these battles & we shall prevail! I know you're all tired & frustrated but when the darkness falls around you, know that God is there to defend you & protect you. Let not your hearts be troubled! We're all in this together & we're going to get through this storm & soon come out of this valley in victory! Through Christ WE WILL WIN! Be safe! Be healthy! Be strong! Have faith! Have hope! Have Joy! May God bless all of you!

DAY 95
June 19th, 2020

Good evening my friends! It's finally the weekend & we're closing out Friday June 19th, 2020. As always, I hope this message finds you safe, healthy & well. Let's begin tonight.

Dear Heavenly Father I come to You with a humble heart, Heavenly praise, love & thanksgiving. Father, Thank You for blessing us this day, for Your guidance, infinite wisdom & love. We praise Your Holy name & say thank You Jesus. Father, we humble ourselves before You tonight praying for peace & restoration to our lands. I'm praying for protection for all that read this tonight. I'm praying that You restore the afflicted by this virus to complete & full health & for a vaccine that can eradicate this virus & help the countless people that are still afraid. I'm praying for Your calming hands to cover this nation with Your peace that surpasses all understanding. In the Holy name of Jesus, I claim Psalm 91, Psalm 23, Psalm 25:20-21, Psalm 46:1, Psalm 56:3, Psalm 61:2, 2 Chronicles 7:14, 2 Timothy 1:7, Jeremiah 30:17, Philippians 4:7-9, Isaiah 43:2, Isaiah 54:17 & Isaiah 53:5 over all of you & everyone you love. I pray for an impenetrable hedge of protection to surround you & all you love. Father, please abundantly bless all those affected by this terrible virus & violence that has plagued our nation & the world. In the Holy name of Jesus Christ, as a child of the Living God, covered in His blood, sealed by the Holy Spirit & through the power of Christ I command, rebuke & cast this virus, the spirits of fear, violence, hatred, all agents of evil & the devil away from you now. By the authority of Christ's name it has no hold or power over you or your loved ones and by His name it must go NOW! It has no right to you, it has no control over you. Greater is He who is in us than he who is in the world & as it's written, if we resist the devil he must flee from you now. Be gone & never return to cause anymore harm! I pray for the protection of all our medical workers as they continue to fight this virus daily. I pray for all of you reading this that you are given peace, hope, strength & wisdom to know that everything is going to be alright through the power & majesty of Christ Jesus. I thank You Father for our coming deliverance & victory! I claim all these things in Your Holy, powerful, majestic & precious name I pray Lord Jesus! Amen! Warriors! As we stand ready for battle against the enemy & storms against us, know that we don't fight for victory, we fight FROM victory! Through the power of Christ, we have already won. Storms may come & while it looks like evil is sometimes winning, know that God is totally in control, on the Throne & through His power WE ARE VICTORIOUS! This journey we're on leads only to victory, This journey we're on leads only to peace, this journey we're on leads only to salvation. Fear not the storm but know the awesome power of God! Shout with me! VICTORY THROUGH CHRIST! Be safe! Be healthy! Be strong! Have faith! Have hope! Have joy! May God bless all of you!

DAY 96
June 20th, 2020

Good evening my friends! It's the weekend & I hope all of you are healthy, safe & well as we close out Saturday, June 20th, 2020.

Dear Heavenly Father, I come to You tonight with a humble heart, Heavenly praise, love & thanksgiving. Thank You Jesus for the blessings You've given us, for wisdom You freely give & for salvation through You. I pray Lord Jesus for Your calming hands to cover this nation with peace that surpasses all understanding. I pray that everyone who's reading this message be blessed with protection, hope, peace, faith, wisdom, strength, guidance & abundance. In the Holy name of Jesus, I claim Psalm 91, Psalm 23, Psalm 25:20-21, Psalm 46:1, Psalm 56:3, Psalm 61:2, 2 Chronicles 7:14, 2 Timothy 1:7, Jeremiah 30:17, Philippians 4:7-9, Isaiah 43:2, Isaiah 54:17 & Isaiah 53:5 over all of you & everyone you love. In the name of Jesus, I lift up & pray for a spiritual & impenetrable hedge of protection to surround all of you & all you love tonight, tomorrow & the next day. I pray for the afflicted that they're restored to complete health & for a powerful vaccine to be developed. I pray for all the medical workers that they're given protection, wisdom & strength to keep fighting this virus. I pray for all the families & businesses, our leaders, firefighters, police, cities, states & nation affected by the virus & the violence that has spread across our nation that they are truly blessed abundantly. I pray that this virus is eradicated from the planet & rendered completely extinct. In the name of Jesus, as a child of God, covered in His blood, saved by His grace, protected by God almighty, sealed by the Holy Spirit & as a warrior of Christ, I command, rebuke & cast away this virus, the spirit of fear, violence, hatred, anxiety, all agents of evil & the devil completely away from you as the far as the east is from the west never to return or cause harm. Greater is He who is in us than he who is in the world & as it is written, if we resist the devil he must flee from us. By the power & authority in the name of Jesus Christ, IT MUST LEAVE NOW! BE GONE! Thank You Jesus! I claim all these things in Your Holy, majestic, powerful & precious name I pray Lord Jesus! Amen!

My fellow warriors, we are continuing to fight through these battles & storms that have encompassed us & through the awesome power of God, WE SHALL PREVAIL! I may say this every night, but it's important that we not ever lose heart or faith. Through Christ this spiritual war we fight both in the physical & spiritual realm has already been won. Do not fear the unknown but only trust that God will deliver us. Victory & peace are coming! Stand firm! Stand Tall stand ready! We're all in this together! Be safe! Be healthy! Be strong! Have faith! Have hope! Have joy! May God bless all of you!

DAY 97
June 21st, 2020

Good evening my friends! As we finish out the weekend on this Father's Day, Sunday, June 21st, 2020, I hope you're all healthy, safe & well.

Dear Heavenly Father, I come to You tonight with Heavenly praise, love & thanksgiving. Thank You Jesus for blessing us today. Thank you for providing for us, for instilling peace & never forsaking us. Father, we're all living through very troubling times & many of us are afraid for the future. That being said, we thank You that You have a plan for victory & prosperity even in this desert we cross. The storms of life may come against us but through You, we will persevere & see victory. In the Holy name of Jesus, I claim Psalm 91, Psalm 23, Psalm 25:20-21, Psalm 46:1, Psalm 56:3, Psalm 61:2, 2 Chronicles 7:14, 2 Timothy 1:7, Jeremiah 30:17, Philippians 4:7-9, Isaiah 43:2, Isaiah 54:17 & Isaiah 53:5 over all of you & everyone you love. I pray that each of you is surrounded by an invincible & spiritual hedge of protection that no evil can penetrate. In the name of Jesus, as a child of the Living God, protected by Christ, covered in His blood, sealed by the Holy Spirit & as a warrior of Christ I command, rebuke & cast this virus, the spirit of fear, anxiety, hatred, violence, all agents of evil & the devil away from you this very moment. By the name of Christ, it has to obey & leave now. It has no option but to GO & never return. I pray for all the afflicted that they're restored to full health & that our scientist's & doctors develop a powerful vaccine swiftly. I lift up & pray for all of you affected by this pandemic & violence spreading across the world that you're protected & blessed with peace, hope, faith, wisdom, strength & abundance to bless others. Jesus, I lift up our nation, we're so divided right now & I'm asking that you bring peace, order & restore our lands by Your hands. I pray for all the medical workers, firefighters, police, our leaders that you're all protected & blessed. I claim all these things in Your Holy, majestic, powerful & precious name I pray Lord Jesus, Amen!

Warriors, let not your hearts be troubled. Do not fear the unknown! As it says in Psalm 46:10 & Romans 8:31 "Be still and know that

I'm God" & "What, then, shall we say in response to these things? If God is for us, who can be against us?" We're going to pass through these storms. We're going to see victory soon! We're going to draw a spiritual line in the sand & say no more! Through Christ all things are possible & even though we don't understand the things that are happening around us, Christ will deliver us. We need not lean on our own understanding but trust in God. I know it is hard to let go of control. But that is what we need to do. Let go & let God. I pray that peace covers you all who read this tonight! I pray that anxiety flees from you! I pray that you are filled with comfort knowing that it's going to be okay. Shout it with me again! VICTORY IS COMING! Be healthy! Be safe! Be strong! Have faith! Have hope! Have calmness! Have joy! May God bless all of you!

DAY 98
June 22nd, 2020

Good evening my friends! It's the start of a brand new week & as we close out Monday, June 22nd, 2020 I hope this message finds you healthy, safe & well.

Dear Heavenly Father, I come to You with Heavenly praise, love & thanksgiving. Father, I thank You for protecting us, blessing us & guiding us each day. Jesus, we need You tonight. We humble ourselves before You, repent of our sins & pray that You'll restore our lands & return peace to our nation. I pray that You cover this nation with Your calming hands. In the Holy name of Jesus, I claim Psalm 91, Psalm 23, Psalm 25:20-21, Psalm 46:1, Psalm 56:3, Psalm 61:2, 2 Chronicles 7:14, 2 Timothy 1:7, Jeremiah 30:17, Philippians 4:7-9, Isaiah 43:2, Isaiah 54:17 & Isaiah 53:5 over all of you & everyone you love. I pray that you & your loved ones are surrounded by a hedge of protection. I pray for all the afflicted that they're supernaturally restored to health. I pray for our doctors & scientists to develop a safe & powerful vaccine to combat the virus & render it extinct. I pray for everyone who's been affected by the virus & this violence that's encompassed our nation that you're abundantly blessed with peace, hope, guidance, wisdom & strength. I pray for all our medical workers, that they're protected, given more than enough supplies, wisdom & strength. In the name of Jesus, as a child of the living God, protected by Christ, covered in His blood, sealed by the Holy Spirit & as a warrior of Christ, I command, rebuke & cast this virus, all agents of evil, the spirit of fear, anxiety, violence, hatred & the devil away from you now. In the name of Jesus Christ, it must go now! It has no other option but to leave you & your loved ones alone. As it is written, through the power of Christ, if we resist the devil, he must flee. Thank You Father. I claim all these things in Your Holy, powerful, majestic & precious name I pray Lord Jesus, Amen!

Warriors! As I have said before, each day we're one step closer to victory! These storms are great but our God is greater! As we move as a united army & through the power of Christ, we'll continue to win battle after battle until we see victory. Through Christ all things are possible & through Him we've already won the war! We stay vigilant, strong & as we draw a line in the sand we say with a collective voice. NO MORE! We WILL hold strong! We WILL press forward! We WILL see victory! Let not your heart be troubled! Have faith that through Christ we shall prevail! We're all in this together! Be safe! Be healthy! Be strong! Have faith! Have hope! Have joy! May God bless all of you!

DAY 99
June 23rd, 2020

Good evening my friends! It's Tuesday, June 23rd, 2020 & as we're closing out this day, I hope this message finds you healthy, safe & well.

Dear Heavenly Father, I come to You with Heavenly praise, love & thanksgiving. Thank You Jesus for blessing & protecting us. Thank You that despite everything going on around us, You are in total & complete control. Jesus, we come together to pray to You to please restore peace to this nation & that You place Your calming hands on every soul in this country. In the name of Jesus, I claim Psalm 91, Psalm 23, Psalm 25:20-21, Psalm 46:1, Psalm 56:3, Psalm 61:2, 2 Chronicles 7:14, 2 Timothy 1:7, Jeremiah 30:17, Philippians 4:7-9, Isaiah 43:2, Isaiah 54:17 & Isaiah 53:5 over all of you & everyone you love. I pray that you & everyone you love are protected by a spiritual & impenetrable hedge of protection that no evil can penetrate. In the name of Jesus, as a warrior of Christ, a child of the Living God, covered in Christ's blood & sealed by the Holy Spirit, I command, rebuke & cast this virus, the spirit of fear, hatred, anxiety, violence, all agents of evil & the devil away from you to the farthest corners of the Earth. Greater is He who dwells in us than he who is in the world & by the power & majesty of Christ Jesus this evil must leave now. It has no choice & must obey! BE GONE NOW! I pray for the sick & afflicted that they're miraculously restored to complete & full health. I pray for everyone that has been affected by the virus & violence spreading across this nation that you're abundantly & supernaturally blessed with peace, hope, wisdom, protection & strength. I pray for all our medical workers fighting the virus that they're protected, have an overflow of supplies, wisdom, peace & strength. I pray for a vaccine & that this virus is rendered extinct! Thank You Jesus, I claim all these things in Your Holy, majestic, powerful, awesome & precious name I pray Lord Jesus, Amen!

Warriors! If you've watched the news lately, I know it seems like evil is winning, but know this… All these things we're seeing now was prophesied nearly 2 millennia ago & despite the fear of the unknown, have peace because we've already won! There's no force in the known or unknown universe that's more powerful than God. Evil WILL NOT triumph! Evil WILL NOT over power us! Evil WILL NOT stop your destiny! EVIL WILL END! There's coming a day in the very near future when all of this is made right. We must not lose faith but remain strong in Christ & keep our focus on Him! I know these storms seem overwhelming, but this too shall pass! Victory is coming & through the power of Christ WE SHALL PREVAIL! Stand tall! Stand firm! Stand ready! Let your fear melt away & be filled with peace from Christ that surpasses all understanding! VICTORY IS COMING! Be safe! Be healthy! Be strong! Have faith! Have hope! Have peace! May God bless all of you!

DAY 100
June 24th, 2020

Good evening my friends! As we close out Wednesday, June 24th, 2020, I pray you're healthy, safe & well. I know things still seem completely out of control & I know many of you are wondering what the rest of this year holds for us. While the future is unknown, there is one thing that's certain… God is in control & on the Throne. There is a plan & there will be victory! Let's begin tonight.

Dear Heavenly Father, I come to You with Heavenly praise, love & thanksgiving. Thank You Jesus, that through the storms we're all facing that You're on the Throne and in control. Father, we need You more than ever! Jesus, we humble ourselves, repent of our sins & pray You restore our lands. Please return peace to this nation and its people. Jesus, please cover our nation with Your calming hands. In the name of Jesus, I claim Psalm 91, Psalm 23, Psalm 25:20-21, Psalm 46:1, Psalm 56:3, Psalm 61:2, 2 Chronicles 7:14, 2 Timothy 1:7, Jeremiah 30:17, Philippians 4:7-9, Isaiah 43:2, Isaiah 54:17 and Isaiah 53:5 over all of you & everyone you love. I pray that all of you are surrounded by a hedge of protection that no evil will even approach or penetrate. I pray that everyone who's been affected by this virus and violence spreading across our country that you'll be abundantly blessed with peace, hope, faith, wisdom, healing, strength and resources so you may be a blessing to many others. I pray for all the medical workers, police, firefighters and our leaders that they're blessed with protection, peace, guidance, wisdom & strength to keep going. In the name of Jesus, I stand here as a warrior of Christ, a son of the Living God, protected & covered in the blood of Christ & sealed by the Holy Spirit and through the name & awesome power of God I cast, rebuke and command that this virus, the spirits of fear, hatred, anxiety, violence, destruction, all agents of evil and the devil to be gone from your very presence. They have no option but to flee now. As it is written in the Bible, if we resist the devil, he must flee. Be GONE! It has no authority or power over you or your loved ones. I thank You Father for our coming victory! I thank You Father for our coming deliverance! I thank You Father for Your infinite power & love! I claim all these things in Your Holy, majestic, powerful, everlasting and precious name I pray Lord, Jesus!

Warriors! We press forward regardless of these storms! We press forward regardless of what we see because we walk by faith not by sight! Through the infinite power of Christ WE PRESS FORWARD & WE SHALL PREVAIL! I know you are tired, frustrated & angry. We all are, but this too shall pass! We must hold on & trust in God's timing because it's always perfect! Let not your hearts be troubled! We're going to get through this valley! We're gonna get through this storm! And we WILL get through any future storm that comes against us because OUR GOD IS GOD! Be safe! Be healthy! Be strong! Have faith! Have hope! Have wisdom! Have joy! May God bless all of you!

DAY 101
June 25th, 2020

Good evening my friends! We're closing out June 25th, 2020 & hope you're once again healthy, safe & well. As promised, I'm here every night of this pandemic & troubling times to pray for all of you as promised.

Dear Heavenly Father, I come to you with a humble heart, Heavenly praise, love & thanksgiving. Thank You Jesus for the blessings You've given us, protecting us, & guiding us. Jesus, we need You again tonight. Please restore peace to our nation & restore our lands. In the name of Jesus, I claim Psalm 91, Psalm 23, Psalm 25:20-21, Psalm 46:1, Psalm 56:3, Psalm 61:2, 2 Chronicles 7:14, 2 Timothy 1:7, Jeremiah 30:17, Philippians 4:7-9, Isaiah 43:2, Isaiah 54:17 & Isaiah 53:5 over all of you & everyone you love. I pray for a supernatural hedge of protection to surround you, your families & all you know & love. I pray for all the afflicted that they are restored to complete & full health. I pray for a powerful vaccine to eradicate this virus. I pray for peace from God's calming hands to cover this nation. I pray for everyone that's been affected by the virus & the violence that has been spreading across our nation, that you will be blessed with peace, hope, faith, protection, wisdom, strength & abundance to bless others. I pray for all our medical workers, scientists, firefighters, police & our leaders to give them powerful protection, peace, wisdom & strength to keep fighting the virus. In the name of Jesus, as a son of the living God, covered in His blood, protected by Christ, sealed by the Holy Spirit & as a warrior of Christ, I command, rebuke & cast this virus, all agents of evil, the devil & the spirit of fear, violence & hatred away from you, never to return! Greater is He who is in us than he who is in the world & by the name of Christ it MUST obey and leave now. Thank You Jesus, I claim all these things in Your Holy, majestic, powerful, everlasting & precious name I pray Lord Jesus, Amen!

Warriors! We're now more than half way through the year and each day we press forward we are that much closer to victory. We must stay vigilant against the virus but again this too shall pass. Through Christ, we're going to see victory soon. This journey has been a long, difficult & uncertain, but through these uncertain times, we cling to God & we must keep our focus on Him & look away from the storm! Let not your hearts be troubled as we move forward. Gain strength knowing that this season will end & through the awesome & amazing power of Christ WE SHALL PREVAIL! God is in total control! God is on the Throne! And God WILL deliver us to victory! SAY IT VICTORY IS COMING! Be safe! Be healthy! Be strong! Have faith! Have hope! Have peace! Have joy! Have trust! May God bless all of you!

DAY 102
June 26th, 2020

Good evening my friends. As we close out another week of 2020, it's Friday June 26th, 2020 & as with every night, I hope you & your loved ones are safe, healthy & well. Wherever you are in the world reading this tonight, I hope this message helps you gain strength, peace & hope as we continue to press forward through 2020. Let's begin

Dear Heavenly Father, I come to You tonight with Heavenly praise, a humble heart, love and thanksgiving. Thank You Jesus for being the light in the darkness, that You are on the Throne and in complete control of everything. Thank You Jesus, that our victory is coming soon through You. In the name of Jesus, I claim Psalm 91, Psalm 23,

Psalm 25:20-21, Psalm 46:1, Psalm 56:3, Psalm 61:2, 2 Chronicles 7:14, 2 Timothy 1:7, Jeremiah 30:17, Philippians 4:7-9, Isaiah 43:2, Isaiah 54:17 & Isaiah 53:5 over all of you and everyone you love. I pray Father that everyone reading this tonight is completely surrounded by a hedge of protection that no evil can penetrate or even approach. I pray that all the afflicted from the virus are swiftly restored to complete & full health. I pray for a powerful vaccine to be developed faster than ever thought possible. I pray that all of you are abundantly blessed with protection, hope, faith, peace, wisdom and strength through these uncertain times. I pray for all the medical workers, that through this surge, that you are double protected & doubled blessed with supplies, peace, wisdom and strength. I pray for all our firefighters, police, leaders, cities and nation that the violence that has surrounded you will return to peace & tranquility. Lord Jesus, please restore peace with Your calming hands. In the name of Jesus, as a son of the Living God, protected by Christ, covered in His blood, sealed by the Holy Spirit and as a warrior of Christ, I command, rebuke and cast this virus, the spirit of fear, hatred, violence, anxiety, animosity, all agents of evil and the devil away from you as far as the east is from the west and I command it to never return. It has no authority, power or claim to you and your loved ones and it must GO NOW. BE GONE! As it is written, greater is He who dwells in us than he who is in this world and if we resist the devil he has no other choice but to obey. Fear not because you are protected by Christ. Thank You Father! I claim all these things in Your Holy, majestic, powerful, everlasting and precious name I pray Lord Jesus, Amen!

Warriors! Another hour, day and week has been completed in 2020 and we continue to press forward to victory as we're another step closer. Can you all imagine what it'll be like when victory arrives? We will shout a collective shout of victory because we endured and prevailed through the storms of this year. I know everything seems uncertain right now but know that God is in control and through Christ all things are truly possible. We must not lean on our own understanding but keep our focus and trust in God almighty! Don't look at the storm! All of this will be history soon. We'll look back on this year and know beyond the shadow of a doubt that our victory came ONLY from Christ Jesus. We're gonna get through this!

VICTORY IS COMING! Be safe! Be healthy! Be strong! Have faith! Have wisdom! Have hope! Have peace! Have trust! May God bless all of you!

DAY 103
June 27th, 2020

Good evening my friends. I apologize for the lateness of this prayer. As we've just closed out Saturday, June 27, 2020, I hope this message once again finds you safe, healthy & well. As promised, I'm here every night to pray protection over you. Let's begin.

Dear Heavenly Father, I come to You with Heavenly praise, love & thanksgiving. Thank You Father for another day, thank You for blessing us & thank You for your guidance & wisdom that You freely give. In the name of Jesus, I claim Psalm 91, Psalm 23, Psalm 25:20-21, Psalm 46:1, Psalm 56:3, Psalm 61:2, 2 Chronicles 7:14, 2 Timothy 1:7, Jeremiah 30:17, Philippians 4:7-9, Isaiah 43:2, Isaiah 54:17 & Isaiah 53:5 over all of you & everyone you love. I pray for a spiritual & impenetrable hedge of protection that completely surrounds you & all you love every day & night. I pray for everyone who's been affected by this virus & violence that has been spreading across our nation that you're abundantly blessed with peace, hope, faith, joy, wisdom, guidance, protection & strength to get through each day of these uncertain times. I pray for & lift up all the afflicted by this virus that they're restored to full & complete health. I pray for all the medical workers that they're double protected, given peace, strength & wisdom to fight this virus. I pray that this horrible virus is finally eradicated from the face of the earth where it can no longer cause any harm. In the name of Jesus, as a warrior of Christ, a son of the Living God, protected by Christ, shielded in His armor & sealed by the Holy Spirit I command this virus, all agents of evil, the devil & the spirit of fear, violence, hatred & anxiety to be cast from your very presence never to return. Through the power of Christ I say to it BE GONE & it must obey. I pray for a powerful & safe vaccine to be developed swiftly. Thank You Lord Jesus for our coming deliverance! I claim all these things in Your Holy, powerful, majestic, everlasting & precious name I pray Lord Jesus, Amen!

Warriors! As we close out another day, remember that through each of these battles we face, each day we must remain vigilant & have faith. Through Christ we will prevail & see a victorious outcome. As that night on the Sea of Galilee, when the storms ravaged the boat & all were afraid, Christ was at peace & in total control of the situation & that is true today. Let not Your heart be troubled! We're going to get through this time. No matter what comes against us, Christ goes before us to clear the path for our deliverance. As I say each night. Keep your eyes on God & not the storm! WE WILL SEE VICTORY! Be safe! Be healthy! Be protected! Be strong! Have faith! Have peace! Have joy! May God bless all of you!

DAY 104
June 28th, 2020

Good evening my friends. We are now closing out Sunday June 28th, 2020 & about to start a brand new week & month. Let's begin tonight.

Dear Heavenly Father, I come to you once again tonight to pray for all the people who read these prayers each night. I come to You with Heavenly praise, love & thanksgiving. Father, please abundantly bless all who read this tonight with protection, peace, hope, faith, prosperity, happiness, wisdom & strength. I know that all things are possible through You Christ Jesus & I know you have a plan of deliverance for all those who have been suffering due to recent events that have been plaguing not only our nation, but countless people around the world. I lift up everyone who has been affected by this virus & violence & ask for your calming hands to give all healing, a miracle & peace that surpasses all understanding. In the name of Jesus, I claim Psalm 91, Psalm 23, Psalm 25:20-21, Psalm 46:1, Psalm 56:3, Psalm 61:2, 2 Chronicles 7:14, 2 Timothy 1:7, Jeremiah 30:17, Philippians 4:7-9, Isaiah 43:2, Isaiah 54:17 & Isaiah 53:5 over all of you, your family & everyone you love. I pray for a spiritual hedge of protection to surround all of you. I thank You Jesus that You are supplying the needs of all the medical workers fighting this virus. I thank You Jesus that You're restoring the afflicted to full health. I thank You Jesus that You're on the throne & in control of every second of our lives. In the name of Jesus, as a child of the Living true God, protected by Christ, covered in His blood, sealed by the Holy Spirit & as a warrior of Christ I command, rebuke & cast this virus & evil that's been plaguing us away to the farthest corners of the Earth. It has no authority, power or control over you & through the blood shed by Christ you are free of its influence & saved by Christ almighty. Through the name of Jesus Christ I command it to be gone! Leave now! I thank You Jesus for the vaccine that is being developed & that this virus will be eradicated & we shall be delivered. Thank You Father! I claim all these things in Your Holy, majestic, powerful & precious name I pray Lord Jesus! Amen!

Warriors! Put Your spiritual shields up & side by side as we once again press forward into another week of battle. We may not know what storms are coming, but we do know that no matter what comes against us, there is no power that can defeat Christ who goes before us to clear the path. The power of God is awesome & He has a plan for victory & deliverance. I know how difficult this time has been & I truly hope that these messages each week help to bring strength to your souls. Through Christ, we cannot fail & have already won the war! Know that these storms shall pass & peace shall return. Shout with me again! WE SHALL PREVAIL! VICTORY IS COMING! Be safe! Be healthy! Be strong! Have faith! Have joy! Have peace! Have hope! Have VICTORY! May God bless all of you!

DAY 105
June 29th, 2020

Good evening my friends! As we close out Monday, June 29th, 2020, I hope this message once again finds you healthy, safe & well. I'm here again to pray protection over all of you.

Dear Heavenly Father, I come to You tonight with Heavenly praise, love & thanksgiving. Thank You Jesus for all You have blessed us with today, for guidance in these uncertain times & for never leaving our sides. In the name of Jesus, I claim Psalm 91, Psalm 23, Psalm 25:20-21, Psalm 46:1, Psalm 56:3, Psalm 61:2, 2 Chronicles 7:14, 2 Timothy 1:7, Jeremiah 30:17, Philippians 4:7-9, Isaiah 43:2, Isaiah

54:17 & Isaiah 53:5 over all of you, your family & everyone you love. Wherever you are tonight in the world, I claim & pray for an impenetrable hedge of protection to completely surround & envelope you. I pray that the sick & afflicted will be supernaturally restored to full health with no sign of illness. I pray that a powerful & safe vaccine is developed faster than ever thought possible. I pray that all of you that are reading this tonight are abundantly blessed with complete protection, health, hope, peace, wisdom, guidance, prosperity & strength. I pray for all our medical workers, police, firefighters, our leaders, citizens, our nation that peace & protection will cover all of you. In the name of Jesus, as I stand here tonight as a child of the Living God, covered in His blood, protected by Jesus, sealed by the Holy Spirit & as a warrior of Christ I command, rebuke & cast this virus, the spirit of fear, violence, hatred, anxiety, all agents of evil & the devil away from you. By the name and power of Jesus Christ it MUST obey & leave NOW! It has no option & must GO NOW! Jesus I pray that You restore our lands & bring peace back to our nation. I thank You Father for our coming victory & deliverance. Thank You Father! I claim all these things in Your Holy, majestic, powerful, everlasting & precious name I pray Lord Jesus, Amen!

Warriors! We're continuing to press forward! This journey is long & difficult but we'll soon see our victory soon! Storms may come, battles, wars & other difficulties, but this too shall pass & through the awesome power of Christ we SHALL PREVAIL! Soon all this will be mere history! While this time has been truly difficult, I believe that God will bring miracles out of it everywhere. We're all unified like no other time in our lifetimes & indelibly linked. We'll tell our children & children's children about this time & how we survived it. Our victory & deliverance is coming swiftly. We must stay strong and vigilant and hold on, have faith and strength & know that we will be delivered by Christ Jesus. Be safe! Be healthy! Be strong! Have faith! Have hope! Have peace! Have joy! Have prosperity! May God bless all of you!

DAY 106
June 30th, 2020

Good evening my friends. As we close out Tuesday, June 30th, 2020, I hope this message finds you healthy, safe & well. Let's begin tonight..

Dear Heavenly Father, I come to You tonight with Heavenly praise, love & thanksgiving. Thank You Father for Your love, blessings, protection & guidance through each day we face. Jesus, we come before You tonight, humble ourselves, repent of our sins & pray that You will please restore our lands & bring peace back to our nation. In the name of Jesus, I claim Psalm 91, Psalm 23, Psalm 25:20-21, Psalm 46:1, Psalm 56:3, Psalm 61:2, 2 Chronicles 7:14, 2 Timothy 1:7, Jeremiah 30:17, Philippians 4:7-9, Isaiah 43:2, Isaiah 54:17 & Isaiah 53:5 over all of you, your family & everyone you love. I pray that you are surrounded by a hedge of protection that the virus & no evil can pass through. Father, please bless all those who are reading this prayer tonight with abundant peace, protection, wisdom, guidance, hope, faith, prosperity & strength. I pray that this virus is completely eradicated & that peace replaces the violence that has enveloped our country. I pray that all who are sick will be supernaturally restored back to complete and full health. I pray for our medical workers & scientists that they develop a safe vaccine & are protected, given supplies, peace, wisdom & strength to keep going through dangerous shifts. In the name of Jesus, as a warrior of Christ, a son of the Living God, protected by Jesus, clothed in spiritual armor, covered in Christ's blood & sealed by the Holy Spirit I command, rebuke & cast this virus, all agents of evil, the spirit of fear, hatred & the devil completely away from you. As it is written, greater is He who dwells in us than he who is in the world & if we resist the devil he MUST flee. Thank You Jesus for our coming deliverance & victory. I claim all these things in Your Holy, powerful, majestic & precious name I pray Lord Jesus, Amen!

Warriors! Today we're one day closer to victory! Every step, every battle, every breakthrough brings us closer to the end of this season & difficult journey. Whatever you're facing today, let it go & give it to

God. All things are possible with Christ. Because there's amazing & true power in prayer, take a moment tonight & pray for someone you know. They may not know you prayed for them but God will. Even though the future seems uncertain, through Christ we will prevail & see victory. It is coming on swift wings. Shout with me! VICTORY IS COMING! We must keep that thought laser focused in our thoughts. We're gonna get through this! We're all in this together! Be safe! Be healthy! Be well! Have faith! Have peace, Have strength! Have hope! Have joy! May God bless all of you!

The Sinner's Prayer

If you are not yet saved I want to personally invite you to read this prayer below. This could be the most profound decision of your entire life. This is a decision only you can make, as I am on a messenger. Please don't put off to tomorrow what can be done right now. Because tomorrow may never come.

If you would like to be saved, please read the prayer below out loud & believing in your heart.

"God, I'm a sinner. I'm sorry for my sins. I ask that You forgive me, and I believe that Jesus Christ is Your Son, and I want to invite Him to come into my heart and trust Him with my life. I'm willing to trust Him as my Savior and follow Him as my Lord forever, and I pray this in Jesus' Name.'"

DAY 107
July 1st, 2020

Good evening everyone! As we're starting a new month, we're closing out July 1st, 2020 & I'm here to pray over you again. Let's begin.

Dear Heavenly Father, I come to You again this summer night with Heavenly praise, love & thanksgiving. Thank You Jesus that You're always by our side as You've promised to never leave or forsake us ever. Thank You Jesus that Your calming hands will be returning peace to this nation. Thank You Jesus for You're death on the cross & for Your resurrection that we may have salvation through You in the belief that You are the son of God & that You died for our sins past present & future. In the name of Jesus, I claim Psalm 91, Psalm 23, Psalm 25:20-21, Psalm 46:1, Psalm 56:3, Psalm 61:2, 2 Chronicles 7:14, 2 Timothy 1:7, Jeremiah 30:17, Philippians 4:7-9, Isaiah 43:2, Isaiah 54:17 & Isaiah 53:5 over all of you, your family & everyone you love. I thank You Jesus that You're surrounding everyone reading this with a spiritual hedge of protection. I pray Father that everyone affected by the virus & this violence spreading across our nation that they're abundantly blessed with protection, peace, hope, faith, wisdom, prosperity & strength through these difficult days. I pray for all those afflicted that they're restored to full & complete health. I pray for all our medical workers, that they're blessed with protection, supplies, wisdom & strength to keep going & treating others. In the name of Jesus, as a child of the Living God, protected by Christ, covered in His blood, sealed by the Holy Spirit & as a warrior of Christ, I command, rebuke & cast this horrible virus, the spirit of fear, violence & hatred, all agents of evil & the devil away from you & through the name of Jesus Christ, it must leave now! BE GONE & never return! Thank You Father for our coming deliverance & for our coming victory. I claim all these things in Your Holy, majestic, everlasting & precious name I pray Lord Jesus, Amen!

Warriors! Tonight as we begin a new month, we draw another line in the sand & say NO MORE! This virus will be eradicated! This violence needs to & will stop! We all need to raise our hands to God

& pray for the restoration of our lands & for peace to fill the hearts of all of us. We're going to get through this deep, long & dark valley we are all walking through. Jesus will deliver us & through Christ all things are possible. Even when things seem at their darkest, Christ can bring about the brightest miracle. Let not your hearts be troubled as we WILL get through this time, we SHALL prevail & we WILL see victory! Stay strong, vigilant & hold on! God is in control & on the throne! Be safe! Be healthy! Be strong! Have faith! Have hope! Have peace! Have joy! May God bless all of you!

DAY 108
July 2nd, 2020

Good evening my friends. As we close out Thursday, July 2nd, 2020 I hope you & your family are safe, healthy & well. Let's begin tonight.

Dear Heavenly Father, I come to You on this warm summer evening with Heavenly praise, love & thanksgiving. Thank You Jesus for always guiding us along our daily path's, freely giving us wisdom when we ask & for always loving us unconditionally. In the name of Jesus, I claim Psalm 91, Psalm 23, Psalm 25:20-21, Psalm 46:1, Psalm 56:3, Psalm 61:2, 2 Chronicles 7:14, 2 Timothy 1:7, Jeremiah 30:17, Philippians 4:7-9, Isaiah 43:2, Isaiah 54:17 & Isaiah 53:5 over all of you, your family & everyone you love. I pray for all the afflicted that they're supernaturally restored to complete health. I pray for everyone affected by this virus & violence that's spread across our nation that you're abundantly blessed with protection, peace, hope, prosperity, forgiveness, faith, wisdom, guidance & strength. Lord Jesus, we pray that You please restore our lands & return peace to our nation. I pray for all the medical workers that they're blessed with everything mentioned above & double protection during their dangerous shifts. In the name of Jesus, as a child of the true Living God, protected by Christ, covered in His blood, sealed by the Holy Spirit & as a warrior of Christ I command that this virus, the spirit of fear, hatred & violence, all agents of evil & the devil are removed from your very presence & cast away never to return. By His name they MUST obey & be gone now! I pray that a powerful & safe vaccine is developed swiftly. I pray that all of you are surrounded by a hedge of protection that no evil can ever penetrate. Thank You Father for our coming deliverance & victory from this pestilence & violence. I claim all these things in Your Holy, everlasting, powerful & precious name I pray Lord Jesus, Amen!

Warriors! As we have now entered into a new month we're halfway through an already difficult year. But I believe that in an instant, everything can be turned around. As we move forward, we near the end of this valley with each & every step. Every day brings us closer. In fact, we are now closer today than we were yesterday & the day before. Though these times & tough, frustrating & uncertain, I believe that miracles & good will come out of this difficult time. We must stay strong, have faith & be vigilant & through the awesome power of Christ we SHALL be victorious! Hold strong! We're all in this together & we shall prevail! Be safe! Be healthy! Be strong! Have faith! Have Wisdom! Have joy! May God bless all of you!

DAY 109
July 3rd, 2020

Good evening my friends. As we close out Friday, July 3rd, 2020, this is a very important weekend for all of us in the USA. God bless all of you & God bless the USA. Let's begin tonight.

Dear Heavenly Father, I come to You tonight with Heavenly praise, love & thanksgiving on the eve of our Independence Day. Thank You Jesus for our nation. Thank You Father for guiding us & for our coming deliverance & victory. In the name of Jesus, I claim Psalm 91, Psalm 23, Psalm 25:20-21, Psalm 46:1, Psalm 56:3, Psalm 61:2, 2 Chronicles 7:14, 2 Timothy 1:7, Jeremiah 30:17, Philippians 4:7-9, John 14:27, Isaiah 43:2, Isaiah 54:17 & Isaiah 53:5 over all of you, your family & everyone you love. In the name of Jesus, I pray that all of you are continued to be surrounded by a hedge of protection. I thank You Jesus that You're in control & on the Throne. I pray for all those who have contracted this virus that they're fully restored to full health. I pray that all of you who've been affected by this terrible virus & violence are abundantly blessed with protection, peace, hope, faith, wisdom, prosperity & strength through these difficult times. I pray for all of our scientists, medical workers, police, firefighters, leaders, citizens & our nation that all of you will be blessed with protection, supplies, guidance, wisdom & strength. As it's written in the Bible, greater is He who dwells within us than he who is in the world & if we resist the devil, through the name of Christ, he must flee, obey and leave now. And in the name of Jesus Christ, as a child of the Living God, protected by Christ, covered in His blood, sealed by the Holy Spirit & as a warrior of Christ I command, rebuke & cast away this virus, the spirit of fear, hatred, violence, all agents of evil, & the devil from you this very moment. I pray that a vaccine is developed swiftly & I pray that our nation will be reunited again. Thank You Father! I claim all these things in Your Holy, majestic, powerful, everlasting & precious name I pray Lord Jesus, Amen!

Warriors! In these difficult times we face, it's always important to know what we've been truly blessed with. And I know how difficult the past few months have been for all of us, but I also know that because of this difficult time, we've been united as a people, like no other time in our lifetimes. These storms will pass, life will return to normal & we WILL get through this. No matter what storms we face, Christ is in complete control. While we may not understand why we go through times like this, God always works things out for our good. And as I stand here tonight I shout out that we will not lay down & go quietly into the night but through the power of Christ, WE SHALL PREVAIL! And though Christ, we've already won this war! THIS TOO SHALL PASS! Be safe! Be healthy! Be vigilant! Be strong! Have faith! Have hope! Have joy! May God bless all of you!

DAY 110
July 4th, 2020

Good evening my friends. I'm a little later than normal tonight but as promised I'm here to pray over all of you once again as we're closing out Saturday, July 4th, 2020. This day marks 244 years of the United States of America & truly a God blessed nation. We're all facing difficulties right now, but I believe that even in the uncertain times we find ourselves, God is still in control of everything.

Dear Heavenly Father, I come to You tonight on the birthday of our nation & I thank You that I was born in a country where I'm free to pray to You. Where Your Devine hand placed us in history, where even among our many differences, we're free to believe & speak about You Father. The road we've all been on has been difficult, long & trying but I know You have a plan for deliverance & victory even in the worst of storms. Tonight I pray over all of you protection as I claim Psalm 91, Psalm 23, Psalm 25:20-21, Psalm 46:1, Psalm 56:3, Psalm 61:2, 2 Chronicles 7:14, 2 Timothy 1:7, Jeremiah 30:17, Philippians 4:7-9, John 14:27, Isaiah 43:2, Isaiah 54:17 & Isaiah 53:5 over all of you, your family & everyone you love. I lift up all the families & businesses tonight that all of you will be blessed over the rest of this year & into the next year. I pray Father that Your loving hands will reach down & comfort all the lives affected by our recent events & that peace, tranquility, prosperity, forgiveness & love are restored to the people of this great nation. I pray that our lands, livelihoods, health, peace & kindness are restored. I pray that the sick are healed, the broken are given hope, the lost find the path that leads to You & our souls forgiven. In the name of Jesus, as a child of God & through the authority of Your name I command this evil spreading through our nation to end tonight! I pray for the complete eradication of this virus so no one will be harmed again & I pray for the healing of this great nation. Thank You Father! I claim all these things in Your Holy, majestic, everlasting, powerful & precious name I pray Lord Jesus, Amen!

Warriors! I can't say it enough times victory is coming & through Christ we shall prevail! This one unified thought needs to be laser focused in our minds & no matter what comes against us we need to know in our hearts that this difficult time WILL PASS! I know it is hard to see when everyone & everything is telling so many variations that you no longer no what to believe but believe this... OUR GOD IS GOD! AND NO POWER IN THE KNOWN OR UNKNOWN UNIVERSE IS MORE POWERFUL THAN HIM! We're in the middle of a spiritual battle but the war has already been won! Let not your heart be troubled! We're ALL in this together! Be safe! Be healthy! Be strong! Have faith! Have hope! Have prosperity! Have courage! Have wisdom, knowledge & guidance! May God bless all of you!

DAY 111
July 5th, 2020

Good evening my friends! As we close out the weekend it's Sunday night July 5th, 2020 & we just had the birthday of America at 244 years. I hope this message once again finds you safe, healthy & well.

Dear Heavenly Father, I come to You with a humble heart, Heavenly praise, love & thanksgiving. Thank You Jesus for the strength You give us when we need it, for wisdom that You freely give & for guiding us through the difficult & treacherous storms we face. Father, I'm praying for protection for everyone who's reading this message. I'm praying for surprise & abundant blessings for everyone who has been affected by the evil that has been spreading across our nation. In the name of Jesus, I claim Psalm 91, Psalm 23, Psalm 25:20-21, Psalm 46:1, Psalm 56:3, Psalm 61:2, 2 Chronicles 7:14, 2 Timothy 1:7, Jeremiah 30:17, Philippians 4:7-9, John 14:27, Isaiah 43:2, Isaiah 54:17 & Isaiah 53:5 over all of you, your family & everyone you love. I'm praying for a spiritual hedge of protection to encompass & surround you that cannot be penetrated. I'm praying for health for the afflicted, I'm praying for a safe & powerful vaccine. I'm praying for all our medical workers that they'll have protection, supplies & wisdom. I pray that this virus is eradicated from the very face of the Earth. I'm praying for Your loving, calming & hands of peace to cover this nation. In the name of Jesus, as a child of God, covered in Your blood, sealed by the Holy Spirit, protected by Jesus, & as a warrior of Christ I command this evil to be gone. Greater is He who is in us than he who is in this world & as it is written, if we resist the devil he must flee from us now. Be gone! Thank You Lord Jesus. I claim all these things in Your Holy, majestic, everlasting, precious name I pray Lord Jesus, Amen!

Warriors! We begin a new week, which will have its own challenges, so we need to continue to be vigilant & strong. When we look back at 2020, we'll never forget the difficulties, the fear, the anger, the uncertainness but through this time, take a moment to remember the victories, joy & answers to prayers, the "good stuff." It's always easy to remember the bad stuff, but sometimes we have to actively remember the good stuff especially while going through a difficult time. Through Christ, these difficulties will pass, through Christ, we WILL see victory & through Christ WE SHALL PREVAIL! Take a moment right now & thank God for something, it can be anything. Let not your hearts be troubled! Victory is coming! We're all in this together! Be safe! Be healthy! Be strong! Have hope! Have faith! Have wisdom! Have guidance! Have peace! Have joy! Have prosperity! May God bless all of you!

DAY 112
July 6th, 2020

Good evening my friends. It was another hot day of summer & we're closing out Monday, July 6th, 2020 & as with each night I hope this message once again finds you safe, healthy & well. Let's begin tonight.

Dear Heavenly Father, I come to You with Heavenly praise, love & thanksgiving. Thank you Jesus for giving us another day to praise You. Thank You for Your protection, guidance, wisdom & strength. In the Holy name of Jesus, I claim Psalm 91, Psalm 23, Psalm 25:20-21, Psalm 46:1, Psalm 56:3, Psalm 61:2, 2 Chronicles 7:14, 2 Timothy 1:7, Jeremiah 30:17, Philippians 4:7-9, John 14:27, Isaiah 43:2, Isaiah 54:17 & Isaiah 53:5 over all of you, your family & everyone you love. I pray for an impenetrable hedge of protection to surround you & protect you from all forms of evil & pestilence. I lift up the afflicted that they may be completely restored to full health. I'm praying that the cases of coronavirus start to radically drop back & that this virus is eradicated from the Earth. I pray for a powerful vaccine to be swiftly & safely created. I pray that everyone who reads this prayer tonight will be abundantly blessed with peace, hope, faith, wisdom, prosperity, protection & strength through these uncertain times. I pray for & lift up all our medical workers that they will be shielded from this virus & double protected working through long & dangerous shifts to heal others. I'm praying for peace to cover this nation & its cities. In the name of Jesus, as a warrior of Christ, a child of the Living God, covered in His blood, protected by Christ & sealed by the

Holy Spirit I command, rebuke & cast this virus, violence, all agents of evil, hatred & the devil to leave now. They have no power over you, no claim to you & no authority over you & by His name they MUST obey & be gone! Thank You Father! I claim all these things in Your holy, majestic, everlasting, power & precious name I pray Lord Jesus, Amen!

Warriors! It's a new week of opportunities! It's a new week to turn everything around! It's a new week of days leading to our coming victory! I know how unbelievably difficult 2020 has been for everyone, but this too shall pass. I know you're tired, frustrated, afraid & angry, but there's coming a day when all of this is replaced with peace, joy, hope & victory. Our journey continues forward & we won't be deterred. We stand tall, united & shout with a unified message of "THROUGH CHRIST ALL THINGS ARE POSSIBLE & WE SHALL PREVAIL! We ARE going to see victory! We're all in this together! Let not your hearts be troubled! Be safe! Be healthy! Be strong! Have peace! Have hope! Have faith! Have prosperity! Have wisdom! Have joy! May God bless all of you!

DAY 113
July 7th, 2020

Good evening my friends. It's Tuesday, July 7th, 2020 & we're closing out another day of this pandemic. As we approach the middle of the week, I hope this message finds you healthy, safe & well.

Dear Heavenly Father, I come to you tonight with a humble heart, love, Heavenly praise & thanksgiving. Thank You Jesus for being our Lord & savior, for loving us & accepting us even at our worst moments. In the Holy name of Jesus, I claim Psalm 91, Psalm 23, Psalm 25:20-21, Psalm 46:1, Psalm 56:3, Psalm 61:2, 2 Chronicles 7:14, 2 Timothy 1:7, Jeremiah 30:17, Philippians 4:7-9, John 14:27, Isaiah 43:2, Isaiah 54:17 & Isaiah 53:5 over all of you, your family & everyone you love. I pray that wherever you go that each of you is completely surrounded by a spiritual hedge of protection. Father, I pray that whoever reads this message tonight who's been affected by this terrible pandemic & violence that has spread across this nation, that You would abundantly bless them with protection, peace, hope, prosperity, wisdom, guidance & strength to get through these uncertain times. Thank You Father for our coming victory through You. I pray for protection for all our medical workers, EMTs, firefighters, police, our leaders, cities & nation. I pray for & lift up all the afflicted that they would be supernaturally healed & restored. In the name of Jesus, as a child of the Living God, covered in His blood, protected by Christ, sealed by the Holy Spirit & as a warrior of Christ, I command this virus, all agents of evil, the spirit of fear, anxiety, hatred & the devil to leave you now. Through the name & power of Christ, it must obey & leave. Thank you Father! I claim all these things in Your Holy, majestic, powerful, everlasting & precious name I pray Lord Jesus, Amen!

Warriors! Fear not! No matter what comes against you today, I want you to know that God is aware of you, your situation & whatever concerns you, concerns Him. One thing I have learned through my life is when we surrender & give complete control to God, it will always work out. Today we're that much closer to victory & leaving this valley. I'm telling you now, through Christ we WILL PREVAIL & see victory. It may take time, it may be difficult, but this too shall pass. One day soon, ALL OF THIS, will be mere history. Through this time we must continue to be strong & vigilant. We cannot afford to be complacent. Let not your heart be troubled! We're gonna get through this & we're all in this together. Be healthy! Be safe! Be strong! Be vigilant! Have faith! Have hope! Have peace! Have prosperity! Have joy! May God bless all of you!

Tonight, if you don't know Jesus, there's no better time than right now, I'm going to post a prayer below. All you have to do is simply pray this out loud, honestly & you will secure your eternity. Simply pray this: "God, I'm a sinner. I'm sorry for my sins. I ask that You forgive me, and I believe that Jesus Christ is Your Son, and I want to invite Him to come into my heart and trust Him with my life. I'm willing to trust Him as my Savior and follow Him as my Lord forever, and I pray this in Jesus' Name.'"

DAY 114
July 8th, 2020

Good evening my friends. As we close out Wednesday, July 8th, 2020 I hope this message finds you healthy, safe & well. If you're new to seeing my evening message, I'm praying protection over everyone.

Dear Heavenly Father, I come to You with Heavenly praise, love & thanksgiving. I thank You Father for protecting us, blessing us & guiding us each day. In the Holy name of Jesus, I claim Psalm 91, Psalm 23, Psalm 25:20-21, Psalm 46:1, Psalm 56:3, Psalm 61:2, 2 Chronicles 7:14, 2 Timothy 1:7, Jeremiah 30:17, Philippians 4:7-9, John 14:27, Isaiah 43:2, Isaiah 54:17 & Isaiah 53:5 over all of you, your family & everyone you love. Jesus I pray that everyone reading this is surrounded & protected by a hedge of protection. I lift up all the afflicted that they're restored to complete health. I pray that everyone who has been affected & suffered from this terrible virus & violence spreading across this nation, that all of you would be abundantly blessed with hope, peace, protection, prosperity, faith, wisdom, guidance & strength. I pray that this virus is eradicated & a safe & powerful vaccine developed. Father we pray that your calming hands will restore peace to our lands. I pray for all our medical workers to be protected through their difficult, long & dangerous shifts. In the name of Jesus, as a child of the living God, covered by Christ's blood, protected by Jesus, sealed by the Holy Spirit & as a warrior of Christ I command, rebuke & cast this evil away from you this very moment. By the name of Christ, it MUST leave now & not return! I thank You Father! I claim all these things in Your Holy, majestic, awesome, everlasting, powerful & precious name I pray Lord Jesus, Amen!

Warriors! Tonight as we close out another day, we stand firm & continue to press forward. Despite all these storms surrounding & ravaging us, they cannot stand up to Christ Jesus. They're no match to Him. God's more powerful than anything in the universe & He WILL deliver us to victory. We must do our part & have faith, stay strong & vigilant. Tonight, when you're done reading this message, please say a prayer. There is power in prayer! We are going to get through this difficult time & it's going to be glorious! There is coming a day when all of this is behind us & we can celebrate with a unified shout of victory! When fear comes in the night, remember that our God is God & through Christ all things are possible & command that fear away by His name! Let not your hearts be troubled! We're all in this together! Be safe! Be healthy! Be strong! Have faith! Have peace! Have hope! Have prosperity! Have joy! May God bless all of you!

DAY 115
July 9th, 2020

  Good evening my friends. We're closing out Thursday, July 9th, 2020 & as with each night I hope & pray that each of you are safe, healthy & well. Let's begin.

Dear Heavenly Father I come to You tonight with a humble heart, Heavenly praise, love & thanksgiving. Father thank You for giving us this day to praise You. Thank You for Your guidance, unconditional love, wisdom & strength. Father, there are many storms that we're facing & for many of us it's overwhelming. I thank You Father that You already have a plan for victory. I thank You that You are on the Throne & in control. In the name of Jesus, I claim Psalm 91, Psalm 23, Psalm 25:20-21, Psalm 46:1, Psalm 56:3, Psalm 61:2, 2 Chronicles 7:14, 2 Timothy 1:7, Jeremiah 30:17, Philippians 4:7-9, John 14:27, Isaiah 43:2, Isaiah 54:17 & Isaiah 53:5 over all of you, your family & everyone you love. Father, I'm praying that You will surround everyone reading this with a hedge of protection that no evil can penetrate. Jesus, we need Your calming hands to restore our lands & bring peace back to this nation & people. I'm praying that everyone affected by this virus & violence will be filled with Your peace, hope, guidance, prosperity, wisdom & strength. I pray for all the medical workers that they will be double protected as the numbers increase. I pray that the afflicted & fully restored. In the name of Jesus, as a child of the Living God, covered in His blood, protected by Jesus, sealed by the Holy Spirit & as a warrior of Christ I command, rebuke & cast this virus, the spirits of fear, violence, hatred, all agents of evil & the devil away from you to the furthest ends of the earth, as far as the east is from the west & through the power in His name they must obey, leave & never return. Greater is He who is in us than he who is in the world & it is written that if we resist the devil, he has no power or authority & must leave now. Thank You Jesus for our coming victory! I claim all these things in Your Holy, majestic, everlasting, powerful & precious name I pray Lord Jesus, Amen!

Warriors! I will start with this tonight! Let not your heart be troubled. Do NOT let the fears of the night fill your heart but have joy that He who saves us has already won the war. We must remember that as battles come & they will, we fight from victory not for victory! When everything seems like it's at its worst God brings miracles out of the darkest storms. He shows us His awesome power by turning situations around that were thought to be impossible. I know many of you are facing difficulties as we all are, but know that God knows what You are facing & already has a plan for deliverance. All we have to do is ask Him into our hearts. This dark time WILL pass! This long valley WILL end! These times of uncertainty WILL resolve! Take my hand & join me in unity as we say to this evil in our world NO MORE! Shout with me that OUR GOD IS GOD! And whatever comes against us know that through Christ, WE SHALL PREVAIL!! We're all in this together! Be safe! Be healthy! Be strong! Have hope! Have faith! Have prosperity! Have joy! May God bless all of you!

DAY 116
July 10th, 2020

Good evening my friends! Well it's Friday, July 10th, 2020 & we're closing out the week & bringing in the weekend. As always, I hope this message once again finds you safe, healthy & well.

Dear Heavenly Father, I come to You tonight with Heavenly praise, love & thanksgiving. Father, thank you for the continued blessings You give us each day, for guiding us, giving us wisdom & strength. Father, I pray tonight that You lay Your calming hands on this nation & all her people. We humble ourselves before You, turn from our wicked ways & pray that You will restore our lands & bring peace back into this nation. In the name of Jesus, I claim Psalm 91, Psalm 23,

Psalm 25:20-21, Psalm 46:1, Psalm 56:3, Psalm 61:2, 2 Chronicles 7:14, 2 Timothy 1:7, Jeremiah 30:17, Philippians 4:7-9, John 14:27, Isaiah 43:2, Isaiah 54:17 & Isaiah 53:5 over all of you, your family & everyone you love. I pray that You will bless everyone reading this message tonight with protection, peace, hope, faith, wisdom, prosperity & strength to get through each day. I pray that a spiritual hedge of protection completely encompasses you & all you love. I pray that all the afflicted with this virus will be fully restored to health. I pray for protection for all of our medical workers. In the Holy name of Jesus, as a child of the Living God, covered in His blood, protected by Jesus, sealed by the Holy Spirit & as a warrior of Christ, I command this virus, spirit of fear, all agents of evil, violence, hatred & the devil to leave now & be gone! Never to return! Thank You Father! I claim all these things in Your Holy, majestic, everlasting, powerful & precious name I pray Lord Jesus, Amen!

Warriors! It's the weekend & the end of another week, which means we're that much closer to victory! Day by day, step by step, inch by inch, we're walking through this valley guided by Christ. Along the way, we'll possibly see terrifying things, trials, face obstacles, storms, impossible moments, but through those moments we will see the awesome power of God. These trials in life build character & form you into who you are to become. We can either embrace the challenges or let them destroy us. We MUST face these trials with the knowledge that God is in control & when we let go of our control, surrender the situation & trust in Him we always come out victorious by His will not ours. Every storm we are facing today will end! Let not your hearts be troubled! Through Christ we shall prevail! We're all in this together! Be safe! Be healthy! Be strong! Have hope! Have faith! Have prosperity! Have joy! May God bless all of you!

DAY 117
July 11th, 2020

Good evening my friends. It's the middle of the weekend, we're closing out Saturday, July 11th, 2020 & as always, I hope this message finds you safe, healthy & well.

Dear Heavenly Father, I come to You tonight with love, Heavenly praise & thanksgiving. Thank You Father for our blessings, thank You for being our Lord & Savior & thank You for Your guiding wisdom and love. In the name of Jesus, I claim Psalm 91, Psalm 23, Psalm 25:20-21, Psalm 46:1, Psalm 56:3, Psalm 61:2, 2 Chronicles 7:14, 2 Timothy 1:7, Jeremiah 30:17, Philippians 4:7-9, John 14:27, Isaiah 43:2, Isaiah 54:17 & Isaiah 53:5 over all of you, your family & everyone you love. Wherever you are tonight reading this, I pray that you're surrounded by a spiritual hedge of protection. I pray for all the afflicted that their health is fully restored. I pray that this virus is eradicated & a safe & powerful vaccine is developed. I pray that Your calming hands cover this nation & its people & bring peace back to our lands. I pray Father that everyone reading this tonight would be abundantly blessed by Your loving hands. I pray for protection for all our medical workers working difficult & dangerous shifts. In the name of Jesus, I stand here tonight, as a child of the Living God, covered in His blood, protected by Jesus, sealed by the Holy Spirit & as a warrior of Christ, I command, rebuke, & cast this virus, violence & all forms of evil away from you & your loved ones this very moment & by His name & power it MUST obey & leave! Thank You Jesus! I claim all these things in Your Holy, majestic, everlasting, powerful & precious name I pray Lord Jesus, Amen!

Warriors! Tonight, we again stand on the front lines, ready for battle & at the ready. We draw a spiritual line in the sand & with a collective voice we shout! NO MORE! As we press forward, through Christ we'll win battle after battle having victory after victory. We will not go back or retreat but stand & fight! Right now, know deep in Your heart that no matter what you are facing today, God is still in control & has a plan. We must continue to be strong & vigilant! Let not your hearts be troubled & we must keep our eyes off the storm & on God. We're going to continue to get through this all the way to victory! We're going to get through this & we're all in this together! Be safe! Be healthy! Be strong! Have hope! Have faith! Have prosperity! Have joy! May God bless all of you!

DAY 118
July 12th, 2020

Good evening my friends! A new week is quickly coming upon us & we're closing out Sunday, July 12th, 2020. As with every night, wherever you are in the world reading this, I hope you are safe, healthy & well.

Dear Heavenly Father, I come to You tonight with a humble heart, Heavenly praise & thanksgiving. Thank You Father that no matter what storm we face that You're always in control & as You've promised You would never leave us nor forsake us. Jesus, tonight I'm coming to You praying for a Healing of this nation & protection for all those reading this message. There are so many people that need You're divine intervention in their lives for healing, protection & deliverance. Father thank You that even when we don't see the whole picture, that You do. Father I'm praying tonight for peace to return to this nation, for the health of this nation to be restored, for the eradication of this terrible virus, for You to please heal our lands. I pray that all who are reading this message tonight would be filled with the peace only You can supply & for light to fill their minds for their future knowing that in these uncertain times, that You will guide us to victory & restoration. I lift up the countless afflicted all across the world that they may be restored to complete health from this virus. I pray for the protection of all the medical workers at all levels working tirelessly to heal others. Father there are so many people afraid tonight that I pray that You please give them strength, hope, faith & courage. In the name of Jesus, I claim Psalm 91, Psalm 23, Psalm 25:20-21, Psalm 46:1, Psalm 56:3, Psalm 61:2, 2 Chronicles 7:14, 2 Timothy 1:7, Jeremiah 30:17, Philippians 4:7-9, John 14:27, Isaiah 43:2, Isaiah 54:17 & Isaiah 53:5 over all of you, your family & everyone you love. Jesus, as a warrior of Christ & in Your Holy name I command this virus & all forms of evil to depart & be gone & through Your name they must obey & leave now. Thank You Father! I claim all these things in Your Holy & precious name I pray Lord Jesus! Amen!

Warriors! Don't be dismayed at the growing number of virus cases or the continuing violence. This too shall pass. We may not understand what is going on or have the complete full & clear picture of what is happening right now but God does & He is in complete control. Like all of you I'm exhausted & frustrated but we all must hang on & be strong through this. Victory is coming. The last part of any difficult journey can be the hardest to endure but through Christ all things are possible & we will get through this storm as well. I'm not saying any of this is or will be easy for us as we press forward but know that no matter what we face we have already won. No weapon formed against you shall prosper & it is always darkest just before the dawn. And the dawn is upon us now. We're going to get through this! Be safe! Be healthy! Be strong! Have hope! Have faith! Have prosperity! Have joy! May God bless all of you!

DAY 119
July 13th, 2020

Good evening my friends. As we start a new week, I hope you're safe, healthy & well as we close out Monday, July 13th, 2020.

Dear Heavenly Father, I come to You with Heavenly praise & thanksgiving. Thank You Father for all the blessings You have given us & for Your unconditional love for us. Father, we're calling out to You tonight for the healing of our nation, protection, & peace. Father, I pray that everyone reading this will be abundantly blessed, surrounded by a spiritual hedge of protection & peace that surpasses all understanding. I pray that all the afflicted would be restored to full health & that a vaccine would be swiftly developed. I pray for protection for all our medical workers. In the name of Jesus, I claim Psalm 91, Psalm 23, Psalm 25:20-21, Psalm 46:1, Psalm 56:3, Psalm 61:2, 2 Chronicles 7:14, 2 Timothy 1:7, Jeremiah 30:17, Philippians 4:7-9, John 14:27, Isaiah 43:2, Isaiah 54:17 & Isaiah 53:5 over all of you, your family & everyone you love. Father I pray that You supernaturally restore our lands & peace with Your calming hands. In the name of Jesus, as a child of the Living God & covered in His blood, I command, rebuke & cast this terrible virus, violence, all agents of evil & the devil away from you to the furthest ends of the Earth. As it's written in the Bible, No weapon formed against you shall prosper & if we resist the devil he has to obey & leave now!

Greater is He who lives in us than he who is in the world. Thank You Father for our coming deliverance through You. I claim all these things in Your Holy & precious name I pray Lord Jesus, Amen!

Warriors! We may seem to be surrounded by storms on all sides, but God has the last word, is in complete control & will deliver us to victory. Storms may rage but we shall prevail through Christ! When we're wandering through the darkness it's hard to know which way to go, but Christ will always guide us in the way we should walk. I know many of you are afraid, frustrated & angry right now as we pass through uncertain waters, but know that this too shall pass. Everything can change in the twinkle of an eye. That twinkle is not a blink but the reflection of light moving at 186,000 miles per second or the speed of light. That's how fast all of this can change in an instant. Don't look at the storms, don't listen to the negativity, don't let the fears of the night envelop you but plant your feet, have faith & trust that God will deliver us to victory. We're going to get through this. Stay strong & hold fast! Be safe! Be healthy! Be strong! Have hope! Have faith! Have prosperity! Have joy! May God bless all of you!

DAY 120
July 14th, 2020

Good evening my friends. We're approaching the middle of the week & we're closing out Tuesday, July 14th, 2020. As with every night that I'm praying for all of you, I hope this message once again finds you healthy, safe & well.

Dear Heavenly Father, I come to You tonight with Heavenly praise & thanksgiving. Thank You Jesus for another day to praise You, thank You for Your wisdom, guidance & strength. In the name of Jesus, I claim Psalm 91, Psalm 23, Psalm 25:20-21, Psalm 46:1, Psalm 56:3, Psalm 61:2, 2 Chronicles 7:14, 2 Timothy 1:7, Jeremiah 30:17, Philippians 4:7-9, John 14:27, Isaiah 43:2, Isaiah 54:17 & Isaiah 53:5 over all of you, your family & everyone you love. Father, there is so much evil going on all around us & we turn to You for forgiveness of our sins, protection & healing. Jesus I pray that You'll bless everyone reading this with protection, prosperity, hope, faith, wisdom & strength. I pray that Your calming & healing hands will cover this nation with peace. I pray that all the sick with this virus will be restored to full health, a vaccine is swiftly developed & that this virus will be eradicated. I'm praying for & claiming a spiritual & impenetrable hedge of protection around each of you. I pray for protection for all our doctors, nurses & all medical workers. In the name of Jesus, as a child of God & covered in His blood I command, rebuke & cast this virus, violence, all agents of evil, fear & the devil away from all of you this moment & by His name it has to obey and be gone! Thank You Jesus for our coming deliverance & victory! I claim all these things in Your Holy, majestic, powerful, everlasting & precious name I pray Lord Jesus! Amen!

Warriors! Tonight I'm asking that each of you pray for someone you care about for their health & protection. As warriors, we're not only on the defensive but also on the offensive in each battle we face & all of us need to stand our ground. What we're facing is a spiritual war all around us but we need not be afraid we need only to be still & keep our eyes on God. This time will pass but we all need to stay vigilant & strong! There is true power in prayer & the enemy runs when we begin to pray. We're standing against a massive storm, but this too shall pass. Through Christ all things are possible & through Christ WE SHALL PREVAIL! Do NOT be afraid of the night! Do NOT be afraid for the future! Do NOT let the spirit of fear take hold of you but command it to leave by the name of Christ! We're not sheep led to the slaughter, but infinitely strong, powerful warriors in Christ & as I have said many times on here, we DO NOT fight for victory but FROM victory! We will NOT fall back! We will NOT run in retreat but to hold fast & say with a collective shout NO MORE! WE SHALL SEE VICTORY & WE SHALL PREVAIL! Be safe! Be healthy! Be strong! Have hope! Have faith! Have prosperity! Have joy! May God bless all of you!

DAY 121
July 15th, 2020

Good evening my friends. It's the middle of the week & we're closing out Wednesday, July 15th, 2020. As always, I hope this message finds you safe, healthy & well. Let's Begin tonight.

Dear Heavenly Father, I come to You with Heavenly praise & thanksgiving. Thank You Jesus that each & every day for the blessings You've given us, for Your unconditional love & Your infinite wisdom. Father, we're all facing massive storms around us & we're praying for Your Divine intervention to bring peace back to our nation & to please heal our lands. We thank You for our coming deliverance & victory through You. Thank You Father that You're healing the afflicted by this virus & giving wisdom to our scientists to develop a vaccine. In the name of Jesus, I claim Psalm 91, Psalm 23, Psalm 25:20-21, Psalm 46:1, Psalm 56:3, Psalm 61:2, 2 Chronicles 7:14, 2 Timothy 1:7, Jeremiah 30:17, Philippians 4:7-9, John 14:27, Isaiah 43:2, Isaiah 54:17 & Isaiah 53:5 over all of you, your family & everyone you love. I pray for protection for all of our doctors, nurses & all medical workers. I pray that all of you are continually protected by a hedge of protection. In the name of Jesus, as a child of the Living God, surrounded by Your protection, covered in Your blood, sealed by the Holy Spirit & as a warrior of Christ I come against, command, rebuke & cast this virus, this violence, all agents of evil, the spirit of fear & the devil away from you & in His name I command them to leave now. They must obey through the name of Christ. As it is written, if we resist the devil he must flee and greater is He who is in us than he who is in the world. By His name, we're saying to these storms, this virus, this violence NO MORE! They have no authority, no right, no claim, now power over us & must leave now! The Word of God is incorruptible, indestructible & true! Thank You Father! I claim all these things in Your Holy, powerful, everlasting & precious name I pray Lord Jesus! Amen!

Warriors! These storms around us are no match for the awesome & infinite power of God. His Word is all truth, no lies or errors & if He promises something You can count on Him always. Let not your hearts be troubled as these storms will pass & God's will, will prevail. Through Christ we're not weak but strong! Through the power of Christ, we're powerful! Through Christ we WILL see victory & we WILL be delivered! I know you're all tired, frustrated & fearful of the future but know that our victory is so close. So so close. We must be strong! We must be vigilant! We must stand firm & hold fast! We're moving forward & we're going to get through this valley! Be safe! Be healthy! Be strong! Have hope! Have faith! Have prosperity! Have joy! May God bless all of you!

DAY 122
July 16th, 2020

Good evening my friends. As we're approaching the weekend, we're closing out Thursday, July 16th, 2020. We're now in the middle of summer & I hope as you're reading this message tonight that you're healthy, safe & well.

Dear Heavenly Father, I come to You tonight with Heavenly praise & thanksgiving. Father thank You for Your grace, unconditional love, wisdom & guidance. Father, we come before You tonight, praying for our nation. Father, forgive us of our sins & please cover this country with Your calming hands of peace & restore our lands. I thank You Jesus that You're healing the afflicted with this virus & guiding the scientists & doctors to develop a vaccine. I pray that all of you are surrounded by an impenetrable hedge of protection. I pray that this virus is eradicated from the planet. Father, please abundantly bless all those reading this message tonight with peace, hope, faith, prosperity, wisdom, guidance & protection. I pray for protection for all our medical workers. In the name of Jesus, I claim Psalm 91, Psalm 23, Psalm 25:20-21, Psalm 46:1, Psalm 56:3, Psalm 61:2, 2 Chronicles 7:14, 2 Timothy 1:7, Jeremiah 30:17, Philippians 4:7-9, John 14:27, Isaiah 43:2, Isaiah 54:17 & Isaiah 53:5 over all of you, your family & everyone you love. Jesus, please calm the raging storms that surround us. In the name of Jesus, as a child of the true Living God, covered in His blood, protected by Jesus, sealed by the Holy Spirit & as a warrior of Christ, I command, rebuke & cast all this violence, the virus, the devil, the spirit of fear & all agents of evil away from you to the farthest corners of this earth never to return or cause harm. It has no authority over us & must leave now! By the name of Jesus Christ, it MUST obey! Thank you Father for our coming victory & deliverance. I claim all these things in Your Holy, majestic, everlasting & precious name I pray Lord Jesus, Amen!

Warriors! As we approach the weekend we're yet another second, another minute, another day, another week closer to victory! With every step we're making constant breakthroughs & through the awesome power of Christ, WE SHALL PREVAIL! We must not lose hope or faith. We must stay focused on Christ & turn away from the storms! We must simply be still & know that He is God. There's coming a day soon when all of this is over & we will be able to rejoice with a collective shout! It's been a continually tough journey & we've all traveled together through this difficult valley, but we'll see victory & the end of this difficult time. Through the coming weeks we must stay strong! We're going to get through this everyone! Be safe! Be healthy! Be strong! Have hope! Have faith! Have prosperity! Have joy! May God bless all of you!

DAY 123
July 17th, 2020

Good evening my friends. The weekend is here & we're closing out Friday, July 17th, 2020. As with every night, I hope this message finds you safe, healthy & well.

Dear Heavenly Father, I come to You tonight with Heavenly praise & thanksgiving. Thank You Father for Your continual presence & guidance through these difficult & uncertain times. In the name of Jesus, I claim Psalm 91, Psalm 23, Psalm 25:20-21, Psalm 46:1, Psalm 56:3, Psalm 61:2, 2 Chronicles 7:14, 2 Timothy 1:7, Jeremiah 30:17, Philippians 4:7-9, John 14:27, Isaiah 43:2, Isaiah 54:17 & Isaiah 53:5 over all of you, your family & everyone you love. I pray for a continual, spiritual & impenetrable hedge of protection around you & all you love. I pray for all the afflicted with this virus that they'd be miraculously restored to full health, for the development of a safe & powerful vaccine & that this terrible virus will be eradicated form the Earth. I pray for protection over all the medical workers working tirelessly to heal & help others. I pray that all of you reading this message tonight would be filled with God's peace, hope, faith & abundantly blessed. I pray for peace to be restored to our people & nation. In the name of Jesus, as a child of the Living God, covered in His blood, protected by Christ, sealed by the Holy Spirit & as a warrior of Christ I command, rebuke & cast this virus, violence, all agents of evil & the devil away from you this very moment & through His name they must obey and never return! I thank You Father for our coming victory through You. I claim all these things in Your Holy, majestic, powerful, everlasting & precious name I pray Lord Jesus, Amen!

Warriors! There's been a lot going on this week & this will continue but know that no matter what comes against us, Christ is in total control & on the Throne. He's never surprised by what happens down here & already has a plan in place, ready to deliver us to victory. Things are in a constant state of flux but God is constant throughout the ages. We can always count on Him & He's only working for our good. Tonight, we once again move forward & with another step forward, we move closer to victory. We WILL not be deterred! Through Christ WE SHALL PREVAIL! Be safe! Be healthy! Be strong! Have hope! Have faith! Have prosperity! Have joy! May God bless all of you!

DAY 124
July 18th, 2020

Good evening my friends. We're closing out Saturday, July 18th, 2020 & wherever you are in world reading this, I hope this message once again finds you healthy, safe & well.

Dear Heavenly Father, I come to You tonight with Heavenly praise & thanksgiving. Thank You Father for Your constant love, wisdom, guidance & salvation through You. Jesus, I'm praying for our nation tonight. Please cover every state, every city, neighborhood, street & corner with Your encompassing peace that surpasses all understanding. I thank You Jesus that this very moment the sick are being miraculously healed from this virus. I thank You that this very moment, scientists, guided by You, are developing a safe & powerful vaccine. I pray Jesus that You abundantly bless all those reading this with peace, hope, faith, protection, prosperity, wisdom & strength. I pray that each of you are surrounded by a spiritual hedge of protection. I claim Psalm 91, Psalm 23, Psalm 116:7, Psalm 62:5-8, Isaiah 26:3, Psalm 25:20-21, Psalm 46:1, Psalm 56:3, Psalm 61:2,

2 Chronicles 7:14, 2 Timothy 1:7, Jeremiah 30:17, Philippians 4:7-9, John 14:27, Isaiah 43:2, Isaiah 54:17 & Isaiah 53:5 over all of you, your family & everyone you love. I pray for the protection of all our medical workers. I lift up all the businesses that have suffered from this virus, pandemic, violence & uncertain times that You sustain & bless them. In the name of Jesus, as a child of the Living God, I command, rebuke & cast this virus, violence, all agents of evil, fear & the devil away from you that you may be in perfect peace through tonight & tomorrow night. I thank You Jesus that though we may not understand these difficult times, that You have a plan, deliverance & victory prepared. I claim all these things in Your Holy, majestic & precious name I pray Lord Jesus, Amen!

Warriors! As we're approaching another new week, we must continue to be strong & vigilant. These times may be uncertain & difficult, but don't allow that to steal your joy. That might seem counter-intuitive, but we all have each others backs through this, God has a plan for deliverance & victory & though this time we will see true miracles before our very eyes. No matter what storm or battles comes against us, know that we've already won. Fear not because our God is God! Let not your heart be troubled but be filled with peace knowing it's going to be okay. And keep saying this: Through Christ WE SHALL PREVAIL! Be safe! Be healthy! Be strong! Have hope! Have faith! Have prosperity! Have joy! May God bless all of you!

DAY 125
July 19th, 2020

Good evening my friends. We're finishing up the weekend & as we're closing out Sunday, July 19th, 2020, I hope all of you are healthy, safe & well.

Dear Heavenly Father, I come to You tonight with Heavenly praise & thanksgiving. Thank You Father for protecting us, blessing us & guiding us along this long & difficult journey. Jesus, I'm praying tonight, if it would be Your will, that peace will fill every corner of this nation from Your perfect calming hands. I claim Psalm 91, Psalm 23, Psalm 116:7, Psalm 62:5-8, Isaiah 26:3, Psalm 25:20-21, Psalm

46:1, Psalm 56:3, Psalm 61:2, 2 Chronicles 7:14, 2 Timothy 1:7, Jeremiah 30:17, Philippians 4:7-9, John 14:27, Isaiah 43:2, Isaiah 54:17 & Isaiah 53:5 over all of you, your family & everyone you love. I pray that you're continually & constantly surrounded buy a hedge of protection that no evil can penetrate. I pray for all the afflicted that they'd be completely restored to full health, for the development of a safe & powerful vaccine & that this terrible virus would be completely eradicated from the face of the earth. I pray that each of you would be abundantly & completely blessed by Christ in all areas of your lives. I pray for protection for all the medical workers. I pray that this violence would cease in this nation & peace return to the streets. In the name of Jesus, as a child of the Living God, covered in His blood, protected by Jesus, sealed by the Holy Spirit & as a warrior of Christ, I command this virus, this violence & destruction, the spirit of fear, all agents of evil & the devil to be cast away from your presence & away from all your loved ones. Greater is He who lives in you than he who lives in this world & by the name of Jesus it must obey & leave this very moment. I thank You Father for our coming victory & I claim all these things in Your Holy, powerful, everlasting, majestic & precious name I pray Lord Jesus, Amen!

Warriors! As we begin a brand new week, there will be new challenges we'll face, but don't be dismayed or afraid because Christ has gone before us to clear the path. The journey may be difficult & uncertain but know that all things are possible with Christ. We merely need to let go & let God. It took me a while to fully understand that statement but it's true. Let go of the fear in your heart, let go of the anger, let go of your own control & allow God to work through you. It's difficult & not easy sometimes, but when you do, you will see how everything works together for your good. Hold fast, stand firm & stand ready as we enter into battle this week. Let not your hearts be troubled because with every storm, every battle we face. We've already won! Through the very power of Jesus Christ, WE SHALL PREVAIL!! Be safe! Be healthy! Be strong! Have hope! Have faith! Have prosperity! Have joy! May God bless all of you!

DAY 126
July 20th, 2020

Good evening my friends. As we begin a new week we're closing out Monday, July 20th, 2020 & wherever you are reading this, I hope you are safe, healthy & well.

Dear Heavenly Father, I come to You tonight with Heavenly praise & thanksgiving. Thank You Father that through all these storms You are still in complete control & on the Throne. I claim Psalm 91, Psalm 23, Psalm 116:7, Psalm 62:5-8, Isaiah 26:3, Psalm 25:20-21, Psalm 46:10, Psalm 56:3, Psalm 61:2, 2 Chronicles 7:14, 2 Timothy 1:7, Jeremiah 30:17, Philippians 4:7-9, John 14:27, Isaiah 43:2, Isaiah 54:17 & Isaiah 53:5 over all of you, your family & everyone you love. I pray that you're surrounded by an impenetrable hedge of protection that no evil, violence or this virus can penetrate where you are a mere observer not touched by the storms around you. I pray for Your calming hands to cover every corner of this nation with complete peace that surpasses all understanding. I pray that this virus is eradicated, that the sick with this virus are restored to complete health & that a powerful & safe vaccine is developed swiftly. I pray for all the families & businesses affected by the virus & violence surrounding us that you will be abundantly blessed with protection, peace, hope, faith, prosperity, wisdom & strength. In the name of Jesus, as a child of the true Living God, covered in His blood, protected by Jesus, sealed by the Holy Spirit & as a warrior of Christ, I COMMAND, REBUKE & CAST this virus, violence, all agents of evil, these storms & the devil away from you now this very moment. It MUST leave now by the name of Christ. Greater is He who is in us than he who is in the world & as it is written, if we resist the devil he must flee. I thank You Father for our coming victory & deliverance. I claim all these things in Your Holy, majestic, everlasting & precious name I pray Lord Jesus, Amen & Amen!

Warriors! Once again tonight we draw another line in the sand as we press forward pushing through the storms. While we move forward, despite the difficulties we see before us, we must remember to keep our focus ONLY on God. While everything is seemingly out of control around us, there is a beacon of light of hope brighter & more powerful than anything in the known & unknown universe. Fear not! Let not your heart be troubled. Remember this Psalm, "Be still and know that I am God" (Psalm 46:10) We're going to get through this time & through Christ WE SHALL PREVAIL! Stay strong!! Be safe! Be healthy! Be strong! Have hope! Have faith! Have prosperity! Have joy! May God bless all of you!

DAY 127
July 21st, 2020

Good evening my friends. As we approach the middle of the week, we're closing out Tuesday, July 21st, 2020 & as with every night, I hope this message once again finds you safe, healthy & well. Let's begin tonight.

Dear Heavenly Father, I come to You tonight with Heavenly praise & thanksgiving. Thank You Jesus for always guiding us, protecting us, healing us & freely giving us Your wisdom when we ask. In the name of Jesus, I claim Psalm 91, Psalm 23, Psalm 116:7, Psalm 62:5-8, Isaiah 26:3, Psalm 25:20-21, Psalm 46:10, Psalm 56:3, Psalm 61:2, 2 Chronicles 7:14, 2 Timothy 1:7, Jeremiah 30:17, Philippians 4:7-9, John 14:27, Isaiah 43:2, Isaiah 54:17 & Isaiah 53:5 over all of you. Father I pray that You abundantly bless everyone reading this with protection, peace, prosperity, hope, faith, guidance, wisdom & strength. I pray for the protection of all our brave medical workers. I pray that Your calming hands cover this nation, as we pray Father that You please restore our lands. I pray that each of you is surrounded by an impenetrable hedge of protection. I pray that all the sick & afflicted are fully restored to complete health, that a safe & powerful vaccine is created & for the complete eradication of this terrible virus. In the name of Jesus, as a child of the Living God, covered in His blood, protected by Jesus & sealed by the Holy Spirit, I command, rebuke & cast this virus, violence, all agents of evil, fear & the devil completely away from you as far as the east is from the west. I thank You Father for our coming victory & deliverance through Your awesome power. I claim all these things in Your Holy, majestic, everlasting, precious name I pray Lord Jesus, Amen!

Warriors! As we move forward through this week, please take a moment to pray for the healing of, not only our people from this virus, but also the healing of this nation from the violence that has been also spreading. We're going to get through this too. Through the very power of Christ, we'll see victory, be delivered & prevail. Each day we take more steps forward. We will not retreat! We will not be deterred! We will not falter! Through Christ we move forward, only! Do not let the fear of the night take hold of your heart. The future may seem uncertain but God already has a plan of deliverance & victory. We must only be still and know that He is God. We're all in this together everyone! Hold fast! Be safe! Be healthy! Be strong! Have hope! Have faith! Have prosperity! Have joy! May God bless all of you!

DAY 128
July 22nd, 2020

Good evening my friends. Well it's the end of the day on Wednesday, July 22nd, 2020 & as with every single night I hope this message once again finds you safe, healthy & well.

Dear Heavenly Father, I come to You tonight with Heavenly Praise, love & thanksgiving. Thank You Jesus for all You've blessed us with & that You have a plan & a personal destiny for each & every one of us. Father, I'm praying tonight that You'll restore peace to our people & nation. Jesus, please restore our lands. I'm praying for all the families & businesses affected by this virus, violence & destruction that You will abundantly bless everyone reading this message with peace, protection, prosperity, hope, faith, wisdom, guidance & strength. I'm praying for all the afflicted that they will be restored to complete health, for a safe & powerful vaccine & that this virus is completely eradicated from the surface of the Earth. I'm praying for protection for all our brave medical workers working tirelessly every day during long & dangerous shifts to heal others. In the name of Jesus, I claim Psalm 91, Psalm 23, Psalm 116:7, Psalm 62:5-8, Isaiah 26:3, Psalm 25:20-21, Psalm 46:10, Psalm 56:3, Psalm 61:2, 2 Chronicles 7:14, 2 Timothy 1:7, Jeremiah 30:17, Philippians 4:7-9, John 14:27, Isaiah 43:2, Isaiah 54:17 & Isaiah 53:5 over all of you &

all you love. I'm praying that you all are continually surrounded by a hedge of protection. In the name of Jesus, as a child of the Living God, covered by His blood, protected by Christ, Sealed by the Holy Spirit & as a warrior of Christ, I command, rebuke & cast this virus, violence, destruction, all agents of evil & the devil away from you this very moment never to return. Greater is He who is in us than he who is in the world & by the name of Christ it must obey & must leave now. As it is written, if we resist the devil he MUST flee from us. He has no power, no authority or claim to you. I thank You Father! I claim all these things in Your Holy, majestic, powerful, everlasting & precious name I pray Lord Jesus, Amen!

Warriors! I know the events around the country have been difficult to hear as this virus & violence have permeated throughout. I know everything seems uncertain as we move forward. I know all of you are stressed, frustrated & angry. I know it seems like what more can happen today, this week or next? But know this… All of this is no surprise to God & He IS guiding us through this difficult & treacherous terrain. It's definitely not easy but there is victory on the other side of this deep chasm. Through Christ we WILL see victory over ALL of this. Through Christ we WILL be delivered! Through the awesome power of Christ WE SHALL PREVAIL! I know we all want everything to go back to the way it was before any of this started & it will, but as we push forward through this time & season know that there is victory coming! Let not your hearts be troubled! We're all in this together! Be safe! Be healthy! Be strong! Have hope! Have faith! Have prosperity! Have joy! May God bless all of you!

DAY 129
July 23rd, 2020

Good evening my friends. We're coming up on the weekend & we're closing out Thursday, July 23rd, 2020. As with every night of my prayers, I hope this message tonight finds you safe, healthy & well.

Dear Heavenly Father, I come to You tonight with Heavenly praise & thanksgiving. Thank You Jesus that You're leading us to victory.

Thank you Jesus that You're in control, have a plan for deliverance & on the Throne as we face these storms. I thank You Jesus that You have a plan for deliverance from the violence spreading across this nation. Thank You Father that You're healing the afflicted by this virus back to complete health. In the name of Jesus, I claim Psalm 91, Psalm 23, Psalm 116:7, Psalm 62:5-8, Isaiah 26:3, Psalm 25:20-21, Psalm 46:10, Psalm 56:3, Psalm 61:2, 2 Chronicles 7:14, 2 Timothy 1:7, Jeremiah 30:17, Philippians 4:7-9, John 14:27, Isaiah 43:2, Isaiah 54:17 & Isaiah 53:5 over all of you & all you love. I pray & thank You father for Your blessings & I pray that You abundantly bless everyone who is reading this tonight with protection, peace, hope, prosperity, wisdom & strength. I pray for the protection of all our medical workers, police, firefighters, our leaders & our nation. Father please cover this nation with Your calming hands & restore peace to every corner. In the name of Jesus, as a child of God & covered in His blood, protected by Jesus & sealed by the Holy Spirit, I command & cast this virus, this violence, all agents of evil, the spirit of fear & the devil away from you & all your loved ones. By His name it must LEAVE NOW! I pray for your continued protection with a hedge of protection that complete encompasses you & your loved ones. I thank You Father for our coming victory & deliverance! I claim all these things in Your Holy, powerful, everlasting & precious name I pray Lord Jesus, Amen!

Warriors! As we approach the weekend, we're another day closer to victory! Despite all the storms we face, despite the virus, despite the violence & uncertainty, we can rest in peace knowing that Christ is in complete control! As I have said many times, we must let go of our understanding, be still & know that He is God. Our God is God! We are not weak but strong! Through Christ all things are possible & through Christ WE SHALL PREVAIL! Let not your hearts be troubled. We're gonna get through this, we're all in this together! Be safe! Be healthy! Be strong! Have hope! Have faith! Have prosperity! Have joy! May God bless all of you!

DAY 130
July 24th, 2020

Good evening my friends. Well, the weekend is finally here, it's a beautiful night out here in NE Ohio & we're closing out Friday July 24th, 2020. As with every night I post these messages, I hope this message once again finds you safe, healthy & well.

Dear Heavenly Father, I come to You tonight with Heavenly praise & thanksgiving. Thank You Jesus that You unconditionally love us even at our worst moments & that You've promised to never leave nor forsake us. Father, there are a lot of people that are in need of You tonight, please fill their hearts with peace during these difficult times. I pray that You will protect & abundantly bless all those who have been affected by this terrible virus & violence. I pray that this virus will be eradicated at that all those afflicted will be fully restored to complete health. I pray for protection over all the medical workers working tirelessly to heal others. I don't know who needs this tonight but I'm praying for you that needed to hear this, It's all going to be okay & you'll be okay. In the name of Jesus, I claim Psalm 91, Psalm 23, Psalm 116:7, Psalm 62:5-8, Isaiah 26:3, Psalm 25:20-21, Psalm 46:10, Psalm 56:3, Psalm 61:2, 2 Chronicles 7:14, 2 Timothy 1:7, Jeremiah 30:17, Philippians 4:7-9, John 14:27, Isaiah 43:2, Isaiah 54:17 & Isaiah 53:5 over all of you & all you love. I'm praying for a hedge of protection to encompass you & all you love. In the name of Jesus, as a child of the Living & Most High God, Covered in His blood, I command & cast this virus, violence, all agents of evil & the devil away from you and by His name they must listen & obey. They have no other option but to leave now! I'm praying for all of you that are worried for the future of our nation, your loved ones, your careers, your lives that you all will be filled to the brim with God's peace that surpasses all understanding & blessings. I thank You Jesus that You are on the Throne & in complete control! I claim all these things in Your Holy, majestic, powerful, everlasting & precious name I pray Lord Jesus, Amen!

Warriors! We're another day forward & getting closer to our victory! I can't state this enough... No matter what storms we face, this season will end & this dark journey we've all been on will be over. It's been hard, it's been tough, it's not fun & it's not like anything we've ever faced, but there is a victory & deliverance coming swiftly. We must hold on strong. But do not worry because God is always on time! It won't be a second early or a second late but perfectly timed. So as we press forward & the lightning comes, know that this too shall pass! Through the power of Christ we shall prevail through this! Be safe! Be healthy! Be strong! Have hope! Have faith! Have prosperity! Have joy! May God bless all of you!

If you've never invited Jesus Christ into your heart, there's no better time to do it than right now & you can trust Him as your Savior. Just pray this prayer right now with me, just simply say, "God, I'm a sinner. I'm sorry for my sins. I ask that You forgive me & I believe that Jesus Christ is Your Son, and I want to invite Him to come into my heart and trust Him with my life. I'm willing to trust Him as my Savior and follow Him as my Lord forever, and I pray this in Jesus' Name.'"

DAY 131
July 25th, 2020

Good evening my friends. It's the weekend & we're closing out Saturday, July 25th, 2020. Wherever you are in the world reading this message, I hope you're healthy, safe & well.

Dear Heavenly Father, I come to You tonight with Heavenly praise & thanksgiving. Father, thank You that even in these uncertain times that You have a plan & are in complete & total control. In the name of Jesus, I claim Psalm 91, Psalm 23, Psalm 116:7, Psalm 62:5-8, Isaiah 26:3, Psalm 25:20-21, Psalm 46:10, Psalm 56:3, Psalm 61:2, 2 Chronicles 7:14, 2 Timothy 1:7, Jeremiah 30:17, Philippians 4:7-9, John 14:27, Isaiah 43:2, Isaiah 54:17 & Isaiah 53:5 over all of you & all you love. I pray for a spiritual hedge of protection to encompass & surround you, your family & loved ones. I pray that You will abundantly bless all those reading this prayer with protection, peace, prosperity, hope, faith, wisdom, guidance & strength. I lift up & pray for all the afflicted that they'll be supernaturally restored to full health, that this virus will be eradicated & for a powerful vaccine to be developed. I pray that all of our medical workers at all levels will be double protected from this virus. I pray for Your calming hands to restore peace to every corner of this nation. In the Holy name of Jesus, as a child of the Living God, covered in His blood & as a warrior of Christ I command, & cast this virus, violence, fear, all agents of evil & the devil away from you this very moment & by His name they MUST obey. Be gone now! I thank You Father for our coming victory & deliverance through You Lord Jesus. I claim all these things in Your Holy, majestic, everlasting & precious name I pray Lord Jesus, Amen!

Warriors! It's amazing how fast the past several months have gone by & we continue to hold strong through every battle & every storm. While this may be a year of uncertainty, we can be certain in God & His promises. We all want this time to end & it will. In the mean time, we must do our part & trust & have faith for our victory & deliverance. We're all indelibly linked, forever united by this time & we will never forget this season. But through even the worst storm there are always miracles & moments of Joy to remember as well. Through the very power of Christ, we shall see our victory & our deliverance will come to pass. We're going to get through this everyone! We're all in this together! Let not your hearts be troubled! Be safe! Be healthy! Be strong! Have hope! Have faith! Have prosperity! Have joy! May God bless all of you!

DAY 132
July 26th, 2020

Good evening my friends. I hope all of you had a wonderful weekend & as we're on the eve of a new week & closing out Sunday, July 26th, 2020, I hope this message once again finds you safe, healthy & well.

Dear Heavenly Father, I come to You with Heavenly praise & thanksgiving. Thank You Father for blessing us each day in ways we may never even know. Jesus, as we being a new week, I come before You praying for the restoration of our lands & people. Please cover this nation with Your perfect calming & restorative hands bringing health & peace to every corner. I claim a spiritual hedge of protection around each of you & please abundantly bless everyone reading this with protection, peace, prosperity, hope, faith, wisdom, guidance, health & strength. In the name of Jesus, I claim Psalm 91, Psalm 23, Psalm 116:7, Psalm 62:5-8, Isaiah 26:3, Psalm 25:20-21, Psalm 46:10, Psalm 56:3, Psalm 61:2, 2 Chronicles 7:14, 2 Timothy 1:7, Jeremiah 30:17, Philippians 4:7-9, John 14:27, Isaiah 43:2, Isaiah 54:17 & Isaiah 53:5 over all of you & all you love. I lift up & pray for all the afflicted they would be restored to complete & full health. I'm praying for all our brave medical workers that they'd be double protected & given supernatural strength to keep going. In the name of Jesus, as a child of the true Living God, covered in His blood, protected by Jesus, sealed by the Holy Spirit & as a warrior of Christ I command, rebuke & cast this virus, violence, fear, all agents of evil & the devil completely away from you, & by His name they MUST obey! As it is written, if we resist the devil he MUST flee from us. We need not fear because through the power of Christ we are strong. Thank You Father! I claim all these things in Your Holy, majestic, everlasting & precious name I pray Lord Jesus, Amen!

Warriors! As we begin a new week, please take a moment to pray for all those struggling right now through this difficult time. Through all the past months, as difficult as it's been, through the lock downs to the violence to the daily storms that have ravaged us, I still see amazing & wonderful acts of kindness towards others. Through this time, we must always remember while staying safe, we can always be a blessing to others. This difficult season will come to an end & when it does, we can rejoice that we are still here, stronger, better & more humble. Through the awesome power of Christ we will make it through this time & we will see our victory. Be safe! Be healthy! Be strong! Have hope! Have faith! Have prosperity! Have joy! May God bless all of you!

DAY 133
July 27th, 2020

Good evening my friends. We've begun a brand new week & we're now closing out Monday, July 27th, 2020. Where ever you are in the world reading this tonight, I hope you & all your loved ones are safe, healthy & well.

Dear Heavenly Father, I come to You tonight with Heavenly praise & thanksgiving. Thank You Jesus for Your death on the cross for our sins that we may have salvation & eternal life through You. Thank You Jesus for the victory that is coming swiftly. Jesus, I'm praying that You would abundantly bless all the families & businesses affected by this terrible pandemic & violence. I'm praying for a hedge of protection that encompasses & surrounds each of you where you're merely an observer & that no evil can touch you or your loved ones. I pray that all the afflicted would be supernaturally healed, that a safe vaccine will be developed & that this virus would be rendered extinct. I pray for all our medical workers that they all will be double protected. I pray for all our firefighters, police, EMTs, all our leaders & our nation that you would be protected, given wisdom & strength. I pray for the calming hands of Christ to be laid on the nation & people to bring peace that surpasses all understanding. In the name of Jesus, I claim Psalm 91, Psalm 23, Psalm 116:7, Psalm 62:5-8, Isaiah 26:3, Psalm 25:20-21, Psalm 46:10, Psalm 56:3, Psalm 61:2, 2 Chronicles 7:14, 2 Timothy 1:7, Jeremiah 30:17, Philippians 4:7-9, John 14:27, Isaiah 43:2, Isaiah 54:17 & Isaiah 53:5 over all of you & all you love. In the name of Jesus, as a child of the true Living God, covered in His blood, protected by Jesus & sealed by the Holy Spirit, I command this virus, evil, violence, all agents of evil & the devil to leave this very moment & by His name they MUST obey & LEAVE NOW! As it is written that greater is He who is in us than he who is in the world & if we resist the devil he must flee. BE GONE & LEAVE US ALONE! I thank You Father! I claim all these things in the Holy, majestic, everlasting, powerful & precious name, I pray Lord Jesus, Amen!

Warriors! It's already been an interesting start to the week but know that no matter what comes against you, it will inevitably fail because of the work on the Cross. Through the power of Jesus, we'll see victory, we'll see triumph & we shall prevail! This season will pass & we WILL continue to press forward. As I have said many times we will not be defeated, falter or be deterred! We MUST stay strong, have faith & we shall prevail! VICTORY IS COMING! Be safe! Be healthy! Be strong! Have hope! Have faith! Have prosperity! Have joy! May God bless all of you!

DAY 134
July 28th, 2020

Good evening my friends. We're approaching the middle of the week & we're closing out Tuesday, July 28th, 2020. As with each night, I hope this message finds you safe, healthy & well.

Dear Heavenly Father, I come to You with Heavenly praise & thanksgiving. Thank You Father that no matter what we face in this life, You're always by our side & as You've promised us You'll never leave us or forsake us. Jesus, I'm praying for the countless people across this nation who are afraid for the future of their lives, families, businesses, careers & all their loved ones that You would abundantly bless them with peace that surpasses all understanding, prosperity, protection, hope, faith, wisdom, guidance & strength. I pray that You will please restore peace to this nation & its people. I pray that this virus is swiftly eradicated & that all those who are sick with this virus be restored to full health. I pray for a hedge of protection to surround each of you that no evil can penetrate. I pray for protection for all medical workers across this planet. In the name of Jesus, I claim Psalm 91, Psalm 23, Psalm 116:7, Psalm 62:5-8, Isaiah 26:3, Psalm 25:20-21, Psalm 46:10, Psalm 56:3, Psalm 61:2, 2 Chronicles 7:14, 2 Timothy 1:7, Jeremiah 30:17, Philippians 4:7-9, John 14:27, Isaiah 43:2, Isaiah 54:17 & Isaiah 53:5 over all of you & all you love. In the Holy name of Jesus, as a child of the true Living God, covered in His blood, protected by Jesus, sealed by the Holy Spirit & as a warrior of Christ, I command, rebuke & cast this virus, all this violence, all agents of evil, the spirit of fear & the devil away from all of you & I command in His name that it MUST leave & be gone now. Greater is He who is in us than he who is in this world & as it is written, if we resist the devil he MUST flee. I thank You Father! I claim all these things in Your Holy, powerful, majestic, everlasting & precious name I pray Lord Jesus, Amen!

Warriors! Today we've taken another step forward & held our ground! Today, we've stood firm & said no more to the enemy! Today, we're 1 step closer to victory & deliverance. In a given 24 hour period there are millions of doctors, scientists, medical workers fighting this virus & each day we learn more & more how to beat it. It hasn't been easy & it's a slow journey but we WILL NOT fail because of the work on the Cross & the awesome power of Jesus Christ. I know you are all tired, overwhelmed, frustrated & angry but hold on strong with everything you've got & we will prevail! Through Christ all things are possible & He is in complete control & on the Throne. We're gonna get through this! Be safe! Be healthy! Be strong! Have hope! Have faith! Have prosperity! Have joy! May God bless all of you!

DAY 135
July 29th, 2020

Good evening my friends. As we close out Wednesday, July 29th, 2020, wherever you are, I hope this message finds you safe, healthy & well.

Dear Heavenly Father, I come to You tonight with Heavenly praise & thanksgiving. Thank You Jesus that through these ravaging storms surrounding us, that You go before us & clear the path. Only through You Lord, we will be victorious. In the name of Jesus, I claim Psalm 91, Psalm 23, Psalm 116:7, Psalm 62:5-8, Isaiah 26:3, Psalm 25:20-21, Psalm 46:10, Psalm 56:3, Psalm 61:2, 2 Chronicles 7:14, 2 Timothy 1:7, Jeremiah 30:17, Philippians 4:7-9, John 14:27, Isaiah 43:2, Isaiah 54:17 & Isaiah 53:5 over all of you & all you love. I pray that all of you & your loved ones are surrounded, encompassed & shielded by a powerful & impenetrable hedge of protection that no evil can ever pierce. Father, please cover this hurting nation with Your perfect calming hands & restore peace to every corner & please restore our lands. I pray that all the families, medical workers & businesses affected by this terrible virus & horrible violence spreading across our country that all of you will be abundantly blessed with protection, prosperity, peace, health, hope, faith, guidance, wisdom & strength through these trying times. In the Holy name of Jesus, as a child of the true Living God, covered in His blood, protected by

Jesus, sealed by the Holy Spirit & as a warrior of Christ, I command, rebuke, cast & come against this virus, violence, all agents of evil, the spirit of fear & the devil with all the power of Christ & command them to be gone & leave now. They have no power, authority, right or claim to you & by His name they MUST obey & leave this very moment! BE GONE & NEVER RETURN! As I will continue to say every night, greater is He who is in us than he who is in the world & if we resist the devil he MUST flee! I thank You Father that our coming deliverance & victory is coming swiftly & with intensity! I claim all these things in Your Holy, powerful, majestic, everlasting & precious name I pray Lord Jesus, Amen!

Warriors! Tonight, we stand firm & we draw another line in the sand. Through the very power of Christ we WILL prevail and these storms too shall pass. We must hold on & have faith through these difficult days. We MUST stay united! We MUST stay strong! We MUST stay vigilant! We MUST stay faithful! Like many of you, I'm frustrated & angry too but know this, we ARE going to make it through this time. This is not the time to back down or go quietly into the night but to stand tall, firm, confident & assured that we shall see victory through Christ. We ARE warriors that will NOT retreat, NOT falter & NOT be deterred! Above all else, we must take our eyes off the storm & keep them focused on Christ. Only through Jesus will we see victory! Let not your hearts be troubled! VICTORY IS COMING! Be safe! Be healthy! Be strong! Have hope! Have faith! Have prosperity! Have joy! May God bless all of you!

DAY 136
July 30th, 2020

Good evening my friends. As we approach the weekend we're closing out Thursday, July 30th, 2020 & wherever you are in the world reading this, I hope you once again, are healthy, safe & well.

Dear Heavenly Father, I come to You with Heavenly praise & thanksgiving. Thank You Jesus that though we may not understand what is happening all around us, that You are in complete control & aligning everything for our coming victory. Jesus, we bow before You tonight, asking forgiveness of our sins, repenting of our evil ways & praying that You will hear our prayers & please restore our lands & restore peace. Let Your will be done. Jesus, I pray tonight that You would please abundantly bless everyone reading this with protection, peace, hope, health, faith, prosperity, guidance, wisdom & strength. I pray that all of you are surrounded by a hedge of protection that completely encompasses you & all you love. I pray that all the afflicted are restored to complete health, for a safe vaccine to be developed, & that this virus will be eradicated for the Earth. I pray for all our medical workers to be extra protected from this virus. In the name of Jesus, I claim Psalm 91, Psalm 23, Psalm 116:7, Psalm 62:5-8, Isaiah 26:3, Psalm 25:20-21, Psalm 46:10, Psalm 56:3, Psalm 61:2, 2 Chronicles 7:14, 2 Timothy 1:7, Jeremiah 30:17, Philippians 4:7-9, John 14:27, Isaiah 43:2, Isaiah 54:17 & Isaiah 53:5 over all of you & all you love. In the name of Jesus, as a child of the Living God, covered in His blood, protected by Jesus, sealed by the Holy Spirit & as a warrior of Christ I command & cast this virus, violence, the spirit of fear, hatred, all agents of evil & the devil completely away from you, your family & all you love. I thank You Father for our coming victory & deliverance. I claim all these things in Your Holy, majestic, powerful, everlasting & precious name I pray Lord Jesus, Amen!

Warriors! As we approach the weekend, I pray for each of your protection from whatever storms may come tonight, tomorrow, & the next day. At any moment if you are feeling weak know that through Christ You are strong! If you are feeling lonely, Christ is always by your side! If you are afraid, trust that God will fight your battles & defend you & through the name & power of Christ you can tell the spirit of fear to be gone & it must obey. As warriors we are not only on the defensive but also on the offensive & there are times that we must command back the enemy through the name & awesome power of Christ. We're in the middle of an ongoing invisible war that surrounds us on all sides but we never need to be afraid. When you are saved you are surrounded & protected by Christ. Fear not! As it says in the Bible, "Be still & know that I am God" Psalm 46:10. Just know, that no matter what happens, OUR VICTORY IS COMING! Be safe! Be healthy! Be strong! Have hope! Have faith! Have prosperity! Have joy! May God bless all of you!

DAY 137
July 31st, 2020

     Good evening my friends. I hope you had a wonderful week & as we start a new weekend, we're closing out Friday, July 31st, 2020. I hope that wherever you are reading this, that each of you is safe, healthy & well.

Dear Heavenly Father, I come to You tonight with Heavenly praise & thanksgiving. Thank You Jesus for Your perfect wisdom, guidance & always staying by our sides no matter what we face. Father I pray that You cover this nation with Your perfect calming hands & restore peace to every corner. I pray for all the afflicted by this virus that they would be supernaturally healed. I pray for all the medical workers that they would be protected & that a safe & powerful vaccine will be developed. I pray for all those who have been affected by this virus & violence that You would abundantly bless them with protection, peace, hope, faith, health, guidance, wisdom & strength. I pray that each of you wherever you are, will be shielded from this virus & violence & that you're merely an observer, completely surrounded by a spiritual hedge of protection. In the name of Jesus, as a child of the Living God & covered in His blood & protected by Christ, I command, rebuke & cast away from you any & all evil, this virus, all this violence, the spirit of fear, all agents of evil & the devil away from you this very moment. By His name they have to obey & leave now! In the name of Jesus, I claim Psalm 91, Psalm 23, Psalm 116:7, Psalm 62:5-8, Isaiah 26:3, Psalm 25:20-21, Psalm 46:10, Psalm 56:3, Psalm 61:2, 2 Chronicles 7:14, 2 Timothy 1:7, Jeremiah 30:17, Philippians 4:7-9, John 14:27, Isaiah 43:2, Isaiah 54:17 & Isaiah 53:5 over all of you & all you love. I thank You Father for our coming deliverance & victory. I claim all these things in Your Holy, perfect, everlasting, powerful & precious name I pray Lord Jesus, Amen!

Warriors! It's the weekend & I hope that with each of these prayers I post each night that it's helping bring hope to you. I fully believe in the amazing power of prayer. When people pray, mountains are moved, so I'm asking that each of you please pray for someone tonight that needs it. We're living unprecedented & uncertain times but you can be certain of one thing. Our God is God! He is the only thing that stays consistent in an out of control world. There will be a day in the near future when all of this is over but for now, we must stay strong & hold on with everything we've got! Through the power of Christ we shall prevail! Don't give up, don't let go, don't give in. All of this is going to get better soon. Our victory & deliverance is coming. So as we once again move forward & draw another line in the sand, shout it with me... OUR GOD IS GOD! Be safe! Be healthy! Be strong! Have hope! Have faith! Have prosperity! Have joy! May God bless all of you!

DAY 138
August 1st, 2020

Good evening my friends. Well it's the middle of the weekend & we're closing out Saturday, August 1st, 2020 & I hope wherever you are, you're safe, healthy & well. Let's begin tonight.

Dear Heavenly Father, I come to You tonight with Heavenly praise & thanksgiving. Thank You Father for all You have blessed us with, for protecting us & for Your unconditional love for us. In the name of Jesus, I claim Psalm 91, Psalm 23, Psalm 116:7, Psalm 62:5-8, Isaiah 26:3, Psalm 25:20-21, Psalm 46:10, Psalm 56:3, Psalm 61:2, 2 Chronicles 7:14, 2 Timothy 1:7, Jeremiah 30:17, Philippians 4:7-9, Romans 12:18, John 14:27, Isaiah 43:2, Isaiah 54:17 & Isaiah 53:5 over all of you & all you love. I pray for a spiritual & impenetrable hedge of protection to surround you & all you love. I pray for all the afflicted with this virus that they'll be restored to complete health, for the development of a safe vaccine & for the protection of all our medical workers. I pray for Your calming hands to cover this nation with a blanket of peace. I pray that You will abundantly bless all those who have been affected by the virus & the violence. In the name of Jesus, as a child of the Living God, covered in His blood, protected by Jesus, sealed by the Holy Spirit & as a warrior of Christ I command & cast this virus, violence, all agents of evil, fear & the devil away from you as far as the east is from the west & by His name it MUST obey! I thank You father! I claim all these things in Your Holy, majestic, everlasting, powerful & precious name I pray Lord Jesus, Amen!

Warriors! As the lyrics go in my song "We're All in This Together" – "Stand Firm, Stand Tall Stand Ready", that is our stance tonight. As warriors we must always be alert & ready. Although the future is uncertain, do not worry because as it's in the Bible, we've already won. It's like reading the last page of a mystery novel in that you know the outcome, so no matter what comes our way or tries to stand against us, Christ has already defeated it & won the day. As I've said before, we do not fight for victory but from victory! We're gonna get through this everyone! Through the power of Christ we

WILL prevail! Shout this with me tonight! GOD IS GOOD ALL THE TIME! Be safe! Be healthy! Be strong! Have hope! Have faith! Have prosperity! Have joy! May God bless all of you!

DAY 139
August 2nd, 2020

Good evening my friends. I hope all of you had a wonderful weekend & as we approach the start of the new week, we're closing out Sunday, August 2nd, 2020. As with every night, I hope this message once again finds you safe, healthy & well.

Dear Heavenly Father, I come to You with Heavenly praise & thanksgiving. Jesus, thank You for Your death on the cross so that we may have eternal life through You. I pray for all those who have been affected by this virus & continuing violence spreading across our country & the world & I pray that You will abundantly bless them with protection, peace, prosperity, health, guidance, wisdom & strength. I pray for the afflicted with this virus that would be restore to full health & for protection for all the medical workers tirelessly working to help heal others. I pray for a spiritual hedge of protection to surround you & your loved ones. I pray for the development of a powerful, safe & effective vaccine against the virus. I pray that Your calming hands will restore peace to every corner of this country. In the name of Jesus, I claim Psalm 91, Psalm 23, Psalm 116:7, Psalm 62:5-8, Isaiah 26:3, Psalm 25:20-21, Psalm 46:10, Psalm 56:3, Psalm 61:2, 2 Chronicles 7:14, 2 Timothy 1:7, Jeremiah 30:17, Philippians 4:7-9, Romans 12:18, John 14:27, Isaiah 43:2, Isaiah 54:17 & Isaiah 53:5 over all of you & all you love. In the name of Jesus, as a child of God, covered in His blood, protected by Christ & sealed by the Holy Spirit, I command, rebuke & cast this terrible virus, the violence, the spirit of fear, all agents of evil & the devil away from you this very moment & command it through His name that it must go now! Greater is He who lives in us than he who is in the world & as it is written, if we resist the devil he must flee from us. I thank You Lord Jesus for our coming victory & deliverance. I claim all these things in Your Holy, majestic, everlasting, powerful & precious name I pray Lord Jesus, Amen!

Warriors! As we approach this coming week, be sure to put on the full armor of God wherever you go. 2020 has proven that literally anything can happen at any moment & we need to continue to be vigilant & strong. One day soon all of this will be done with & on that day we'll rejoice. I know this much, as of today, we are yet another day closer to victory. The storms may surround us, but the storms are no match for God. Through the very power of Christ we WILL prevail & we WILL make it through this. I know it's difficult & we're all frustrated by everything going on but there is an end to this rough season & it's going to get better. Let not your heart be troubled as we continue to move forward. We will not retreat but always press forward no matter what comes against us. Victory is coming! Be safe! Be healthy! Be strong! Have hope! Have faith! Have prosperity! Have joy! May God bless all of you!

DAY 140
August 3rd, 2020

Good evening my friends. Well we've started a new week & we're now closing out Monday, August 3rd, 2020 & I hope that wherever you are in the world reading this that you & your loved ones are safe, healthy & well. It's amazing how fast this year is going by already.

Dear Heavenly Father, I come to You with Heavenly praise & thanksgiving. Thank You Jesus for another day to praise You. Thank You, that even in our worst moments You still love us unconditionally. Father, I'm praying tonight for the healing & restoration of our lands & I'm praying that You'll cover every inch of this nation & please bring peace back to every corner. I pray for all the afflicted that they will be healed, that a powerful & safe vaccine will be developed & for protection of all our brave medical workers. For all those suffering due to the pandemic & violence, I pray that you are abundantly blessed with peace, protection, prosperity, hope, faith, guidance, wisdom & strength to get through these difficult times & to be a blessing to many others. I pray that all of you are surrounded by an impenetrable hedge of protection. In the name of Jesus, as a child of the Living God, covered in His blood, protected by Jesus, sealed by the Holy Spirit & as a warrior of Christ, I command, rebuke & cast this virus, violence, fear, all agents of evil & the devil away from you now. By His name it must GO. In the name of Jesus, I claim Psalm 91, Psalm 23, Psalm 116:7, Psalm 62:5-8, Isaiah 26:3, Psalm 25:20-21, Psalm 46:10, Psalm 56:3, Psalm 61:2, 2 Chronicles 7:14, 2 Timothy 1:7, Jeremiah 30:17, Philippians 4:7-9, Romans 12:18, John 14:27, Isaiah 43:2, Isaiah 54:17 & Isaiah 53:5 over all of you & all you love. I pray that Your will be done in each of our lives & I thank You Father for our coming victory! I claim all these things in Your Holy, majestic, power, everlasting & precious name I pray Lord Jesus, Amen!

Warriors! Though we may be in the middle of an ancient invisible war that is going on all around us at every moment, we need not be afraid. Through the power of Christ, not only will we get through this difficult time but we shall prevail & be victorious. I know how tough it is wondering when this pandemic will be over? When will the violence end? What does our future hold? But even in these uncertain times we must all be strong. Myself included. It's not easy, it's not fun & it's not what we're used to, but this season will end, these difficulties will be replaced with joy & life will return to normal. As of today we're 24 hours closer to victory than we were yesterday at this same time. It's like a saying a dear friend said to me once that has stayed with me through moments of overwhelming circumstances. "How do you eat an elephant? One bite at a time." So we WILL get through this together & with Christ leading us, we will only come out victorious! Be safe! Be healthy! Be strong! Have hope! Have faith! Have prosperity! Have joy! May God bless all of you!

DAY 141
August 4th, 2020

Good evening my friends. We're closing out Tuesday, August 4th, 2020 & I hope wherever you are in the world reading this that you & your loved ones are safe, healthy & well. Before I begin tonight, please say a prayer for the people of Lebanon in the aftermath of that deadly explosion in Beirut.

Dear Heavenly Father, I come to You tonight with Heavenly praise, love & thanksgiving. Thank You Father for being our Lord & Savior and that in these in uncertain times we can always be certain in You. I pray that You will cover our nation with your perfect calming hands and please restore peace. I pray that everyone affected by the virus and violence will be abundantly blessed so they can be a blessing to many others. I pray that peace returns to our nation & that this virus is completely eradicated. I pray for all those afflicted with the virus that they're restored to complete and full health. I pray for our brave medical workers that they would be protected from this virus & given strength during their difficult & dangerous shifts. I pray that a hedge of protection surrounds each of you where you are merely an observer & that no evil can come near you or your loved ones. In the name of Jesus, I claim Psalm 91, Psalm 23, Psalm 116:7, Psalm 62:5-8, Isaiah 26:3, Psalm 25:20-21, Psalm 46:10, Psalm 56:3, Psalm 61:2, 2 Chronicles 7:14, 2 Timothy 1:7, Jeremiah 30:17, Philippians 4:7-9, Romans 12:18, John 14:27, Isaiah 43:2, Isaiah 54:17 & Isaiah 53:5 over all of you and all you love. In the name of Jesus, as a child of the true Living God, covered in His blood, protected by Jesus, sealed by the Holy Spirit & as a warrior of Christ, I command. Rebuke & come against this virus, violence, fear, all agents of evil & the devil with the power of Jesus Christ & command it away from you. By His name & power it must GO NOW & leave you and your loved ones alone! I thank You Father! I claim all these things in Your Holy, majestic, everlasting, ever living, powerful & precious name I pray Lord Jesus, Amen!

Warriors! As we approach the middle of the week, I pray that you're blessed & protected. Each day it seems like more evil is occurring in the world because the devil knows he has very little time left, but we need not be afraid. Greater is He who lives in us than he who is in this world & the devil has no authority, no claim, no power over you. Through the name and power of Jesus it is written that if we resist the devil he must flee. We all take another step forward today & each day we are closer to victory. 1 day turns into 10 days which turns into 100 and so forth. We have come so far since March and we will continue to press forward through the storms. Through Christ we shall prevail & there is nothing in the known or unknown universe more powerful than God. He will deliver us. We must hold on and have faith in Him. Victory is coming!! Be safe! Be healthy! Be strong!

Have hope! Have faith! Have prosperity! Have joy! May God bless all of you!

DAY 142
August 5th, 2020

Good evening my friends. We're going over the middle of the week & closing out Wednesday, August 5th, 2020. As with every night, I hope wherever you & your loved ones are, you're all safe, healthy & well.

Dear Heavenly Father, I come to You tonight with Heavenly praise & thanksgiving. Thank You Jesus that You're leading us through this valley & that You'll deliver us to victory on the other side. In the name of Jesus, I claim Psalm 91, Psalm 23, Psalm 116:7, Psalm 62:5-8, Isaiah 26:3, Psalm 25:20-21, Psalm 46:10, Psalm 56:3, Psalm 61:2, 2 Chronicles 7:14, 2 Timothy 1:7, Jeremiah 30:17, Philippians 4:7-9, Romans 12:18, John 14:27, Isaiah 43:2, Isaiah 54:17 & Isaiah 53:5 over all of you & all you love. I pray that each of you is surrounded by a hedge of protection that no evil can penetrate. I pray for all the afflicted that they would be fully restored to complete health. I pray for the complete eradication of this virus & for the development of a powerful & safe vaccine. I pray that Your calming hands will cover & restore peace to this nation. I pray that this violence will stop. I pray that everyone who has been affected by the virus & violence that you would be abundantly blessed with prosperity, protection, peace, hope, faith, wisdom, guidance & strength. I pray for double protection for all our medical workers. In the name of Jesus, as a child of God, covered in His blood, protected by Jesus, sealed by the Holy Spirit & as a warrior of Christ I command, rebuke & cast this virus, violence, fear, all agents of evil & the devil away from you this very moment. By the name of Christ they must obey & leave now! They have no other option. Greater is He who is in us than he who is in the world & as it is written if we resist the devil he must flee from us. I thank You Father for our coming victory. I claim all these things in Your Holy, majestic, powerful, everlasting & precious name I pray Lord Jesus, Amen!

Warriors! It's the middle of the week & we can be at peace knowing that Jesus is in complete control & on the Throne. I may say this every day but we're again 24 hours closer to victory then we were yesterday at this same time. I'll say this to all of you, just hang in there, be strong & have faith. We WILL get through these uncertain times & we WILL triumph. Through Christ all things are possible & nothing is too difficult for Jesus. Let not your heart be troubled! We press forward again & will continue to move forward! Victory is coming! We're all in this together! Be safe! Be healthy! Be strong! Have hope! Have faith! Have prosperity! Have joy! May God bless all of you!

DAY 143
August 6th, 2020

Good evening my friends. The weekend is almost here & we're closing out Thursday, August 6th, 2020. Where ever you are in the world reading this, I hope you are safe, healthy & well. Before I begin tonight I want to say this. This virus is terrible & has claimed so many lives around the world. Take a moment & pray that anyone who has contracted this disease will fully recover. In a world where we are so divided on so much, we should come together on this & still value each other as life is precious & we've already lost so much this year.

Dear Heavenly Father, I come to You tonight with Heavenly praise & thanksgiving. Thank You Lord that no matter what we're facing today that You are in complete & total control. Thank You Father that through You we shall see victory & be delivered. I'm praying for all those afflicted by this terrible virus that they're fully restored to complete health. I pray that each of you is surrounded by a hedge of protection that encompasses you & that no evil can penetrate. In the name of Jesus, I claim Psalm 91, Psalm 23, Psalm 116:7, Psalm 62:5-8, Isaiah 26:3, Psalm 25:20-21, Psalm 46:10, Psalm 56:3, Psalm 61:2, 2 Chronicles 7:14, 2 Timothy 1:7, Jeremiah 30:17, Philippians 4:7-9, Romans 12:18, John 14:27, Isaiah 43:2, Isaiah 54:17 & Isaiah 53:5 over all of you & all you love. I pray that all the families, businesses, medical workers, all our leaders & all who have been affected by this virus & violence that you would be abundantly blessed with protection, peace, prosperity, hope, faith, guidance, wisdom & strength through these difficult times. In the name of Jesus, as a child of the Living God, protected by Jesus, sealed by the Holy Spirit & as a warrior of Christ by His name I command, rebuke, come against & cast this virus, the violence, the spirit of fear, all agents of evil & the devil away from you as far as the east is from the west so that it never touches or comes near you. By His name it MUST GO NOW! I thank You Father. I claim all these things in Your Holy majestic, powerful, everlasting, eternal, & precious name I pray Lord Jesus, Amen!

Warriors! Don't let the hourly news that comes in dishearten, distract or worry you. Everything is completely in God's hands & everything that is happening all around us is not a surprise to God. Storms will surround us as this world is fallen but we need not fear. We need only to let go of our own understanding & only trust that God will deliver us. Take your eyes off the storm & fix them only on Christ. I know everything going on is frightening, I know everything seems out of control, I know everything seems uncertain… BUT be certain in Christ. He alone deserves this honor & He will never fail you. He will never forsake you. Let not your heart be troubled. We stand united! We stand firm! We stand on faith! We stand for Christ! Be safe! Be healthy! Be strong! Have hope! Have faith! Have prosperity! Have joy! May God bless all of you!

DAY 144
August 7th, 2020

Good evening my friends. The weekend's here & we're closing out Friday, August 7th, 2020 & wherever you are, as always I hope this message finds you safe, healthy & well.

Dear Heavenly Father, I come to You tonight with Heavenly praise & thanksgiving. Thank You Father for another day to praise You & for the blessings You've given us. In the name of Jesus, I claim Psalm 91, Psalm 23, Psalm 116:7, Psalm 62:5-8, Isaiah 26:3, Psalm 25:20-21, Psalm 46:10, Psalm 56:3, Psalm 61:2, 2 Chronicles 7:14,

2 Timothy 1:7, Jeremiah 30:17, Philippians 4:7-9, Romans 12:18, John 14:27, Isaiah 43:2, Isaiah 54:17 & Isaiah 53:5 over all of you & all you love. I pray you are surrounded by a spiritual hedge of protection & that all that have been afflicted by this virus will be restored to complete & full health. I pray that Your calming hands will cover this nation & that peace is restored throughout the land. I pray for all the families, businesses & medical workers that you're abundantly blessed with protection, peace, prosperity, hope, faith, guidance, wisdom & strength through all these uncertain days. I pray for a safe & powerful vaccine to be developed & the complete eradication of this virus from the Earth. In the name of Jesus, as a child of the Living God, covered in His blood, protected by Jesus, sealed by the Holy Spirit & as a devout warrior of Christ, I command, rebuke & cast this virus, violence, all agents of evil, fear & the devil away from you & all you love, this very moment. They must leave by His now. As it is written, if we resist the devil he must flee through the name & power of Jesus Christ. I thank You Father. I claim all these things in Your Holy, majestic, everlasting & precious name I pray Lord Jesus, Amen!

Warriors! The weekend is here & I pray for continued protection & blessings over you tonight, tomorrow night & the next night. It's been an interesting week to say the least but know this, no matter what comes your way, trust that Christ will deliver you. When adversity comes, and it will, look at it as a chance to truly trust that God is in control. Don't rely on your own understanding but know that God will walk with you each step of the journey, no matter what you are going through. We're all in unprecedented times, but those times are perfect for God to show His miraculous & infinite power! We're going to get through this everyone! All things are possible with Jesus Christ! Just hold on we're gonna make it! Be safe! Be healthy! Be strong! Have hope! Have faith! Have prosperity! Have joy! May God bless all of you!

DAY 145
August 8th, 2020

Good evening my friends. I hope you're all having a wonderful weekend & we're closing out Saturday, August 8th, 2020. I hope that wherever you are in the world reading this, that you & your loved ones are safe, healthy & well.

Dear Heavenly Father, I come before You tonight with Heavenly praise, love & thanksgiving. Thank You Jesus for Your blessings through this difficult time we're all facing. Thank You Father that You've gone before us to clear the path for our deliverance. In the name of Jesus, I claim Psalm 91, Psalm 23, Psalm 116:7, Psalm 62:5-8, Isaiah 26:3, Psalm 25:20-21, Psalm 46:10, Psalm 56:3, Psalm 61:2, 2 Chronicles 7:14, 2 Timothy 1:7, Jeremiah 30:17, Philippians 4:7-9, Romans 12:18, John 14:27, Isaiah 43:2, Isaiah 54:17 & Isaiah 53:5 over all of you & all you love. I pray that you & your loved ones are surrounded by an impenetrable spiritual hedge of protection. I pray for all the afflicted that they're restored to complete & full health & that a powerful & safe vaccine is developed swiftly. I pray for all the families, businesses, medical workers, our leaders & first responders that you're all abundantly blessed with protection, peace, prosperity, health, hope, faith, guidance, wisdom & strength to persevere through these difficult times & triumph against adversity. I pray that Your calming hands will cover every inch of this nation & please restore peace to our lands & people. In the name of Jesus, as a child of the true Living God, covered in His blood, protected by Jesus, sealed by the Holy Spirit & as a warrior of Christ, I command, rebuke & cast this virus, all the violence, the spirit of fear, all agents of evil & the devil away from you & your loved ones this very moment & by His name & power they MUST GO NOW! I thank You Father for our coming victory & deliverance through You. I claim all these things in Your Holy, majestic, powerful, everlasting & precious name I pray Lord Jesus, Amen!

Warriors! Tonight we stand tall & firm against the powers of darkness that come against us. While these storms surround us seemingly on all sides, fear not because God is more powerful than anything in the known & unknown universe. Through Christ we shall prevail & through Christ we WILL make it through this time. We're another 24 hours closer to victory than we were at this same time yesterday. Soon, very soon, all of this will be behind us & we must hold on & be strong. Going through this time we're all a part of history that will be taught to your children & grandchildren. We're united in a way unlike anything in our lifetimes. We must continue to be vigilant but we're pressing forward with each day, week, month all the way to victory! We're going to make it! We're going to get through this! We're going to see victory! Be safe! Be healthy! Be strong! Have hope! Have faith! Have prosperity! Have joy! May God bless all of you!

DAY 146
August 9th, 2020

Good evening my friends. I apologize for the lateness getting this up tonight but I was battling a rather bad migraine but that's not stopping me from praying over you. At any rate, we're nearing the beginning of a new week & we're closing out Sunday, August 9th, 2020. Wherever you are in the world reading this, I pray that you & your loved ones are safe, healthy & well.

Dear Heavenly Father, I come to You tonight with Heavenly praise, & thanksgiving. Thank You Jesus for all the blessings You have given us, for loving us unconditionally & for salvation through You. In the name of Jesus, I claim Psalm 91, Psalm 23, Psalm 116:7, Psalm 62:5-8, Isaiah 26:3, Psalm 25:20-21, Psalm 46:10, Psalm 56:3, Psalm 61:2, 2 Chronicles 7:14, 2 Timothy 1:7, Jeremiah 30:17, Philippians 4:7-9, Romans 12:18, John 14:27, Isaiah 43:2, Isaiah 54:17 & Isaiah 53:5 over all of you & all you love. I pray that each of you & your loved ones is surrounded by a hedge of protection. I pray that all who are afflicted by the virus are restored to full & complete health & for a powerful & safe vaccine to be developed faster than thought possible. I pray for all the families, people, businesses, our leaders & medical workers would be abundantly blessed with protection, prosperity, peace, hope, faith, wisdom, guidance & strength through these difficult times. I pray for our nation & that Your calming hands would completely cover every inch of our lands & people with peace

& restoration. In the name of Jesus, as a child of the Living God, covered in His blood, protected by Jesus, sealed by the Holy Spirit & as a warrior of Christ I command, rebuke & cast this virus, the violence, the spirit of fear, all agents of evil & the devil away from you this very moment & by His name they must obey & leave now. I pray that each of you is covered by peace that surpasses all understanding & that all anxiety dissolves. I thank You Father for our coming victory! I claim all these things in the Holy, majestic, powerful, everlasting & precious name I pray Lord Jesus, Amen!

Warriors! As we begin a new week we must continue to be strong & vigilant through these uncertain times. But let not your heart be troubled as we press forward. Any storms we face this week will pass & we'll continue to move forward to victory. No matter what comes against us, always take your eyes off the storm & place them only on God. He will see us through for all things are possible with Christ. We must only be still & know that He is God. (Psalm 46:10) You never know what amazing advances could be developed this week. With each day we're closer to victory. It could be tonight, tomorrow or the next day but victory is coming. Just hold on & be strong! We're gonna get through this. We're all in this together! Be safe! Be healthy! Be strong! Have hope! Have faith! Have prosperity! Have joy! May God bless all of you!

DAY 147
August 10th, 2020

Good evening my friends. It's a brand new week & we're now closing out Monday, August 10th, 2020. As with each & every night, I pray that wherever you are reading this, that you're safe, healthy & well.

Dear Heavenly Father, I come to You tonight with Heavenly praise, a humble heart & thanksgiving. Thank You Jesus for Your infinite wisdom, power & grace through these difficult times we find ourselves. Father, please cover this divided nation & please restore our lands & cover its people with peace. In the name of Jesus, I claim Psalm 91, Psalm 23, Psalm 116:7, Psalm 62:5-8, Isaiah 26:3, Psalm 25:20-21,

Psalm 46:10, Psalm 56:3, Psalm 61:2, 2 Chronicles 7:14, 2 Timothy 1:7, Jeremiah 30:17, Philippians 4:7-9, Romans 12:18, John 14:27, Isaiah 43:2, Isaiah 54:17 & Isaiah 53:5 over all of you & all you love. I pray for all the sick & afflicted that they'll be fully restored to complete health. I pray this virus is eradicated & that a safe vaccine is developed faster than ever thought possible. I pray that each of you & your loved ones are surrounded by a hedge of protection that no evil can penetrate. I pray for all the families, citizens, businesses & medical workers that all of you will be abundantly blessed with prosperity, peace, protection, hope, faith, wisdom, guidance & strength. In the name of Jesus, as a child of God, covered in His blood, protected by Jesus, sealed by the Holy Spirit & as a warrior of Christ I command, rebuke & cast this virus, the violence, fear, all agents of evil & the devil away from you & your loved ones this very moment. By His name and power they must GO NOW! I thank You Father for our coming victory through You! I claim all these things in Your Holy, majestic, powerful, everlasting, eternal & precious name I pray Lord Jesus, Amen!

Warriors! Stand tall tonight & ready as we're facing a new week. Storms will come but we will weather every single one of them because with Christ all things are possible & we shall prevail. I know how frustrated, depressed & angry many of you are but we will get through this valley. This journey has taken us through unknown territory & continues to do so but in the end we will see victory. It's not been easy but when victory comes, it will the greatest cause for celebration! While weeping endures for the night, joy comes in the morning. Tonight say a prayer for someone you love & as you pray turn over all your burdens to God. He will perfect that which concerns you. We're gonna get through this time everyone! VICTORY IS COMING! VICTORY IS COMING! Be safe! Be healthy! Be strong! Have hope! Have faith! Have prosperity! Have joy! May God bless all of you!

DAY 148
August 11th, 2020

Good evening my friends. It was another hot summer day outside & as we close out Tuesday, August 11th, 2020 I hope that wherever you are reading this, you & your loved ones are safe, healthy & well.

Dear Heavenly Father, I come to You with Heavenly praise & thanksgiving. Thank You Jesus for the blessings You've given us, our protection from You & for loving us unconditionally. I'm praying for our nation tonight. Father please restore our lands & please cover this country with Your calming hands & peace. I pray for all the afflicted that they would be completely restored to full health. I pray for a safe & powerful vaccine & for this virus to be completely eradicated. I pray for all the people, families, businesses & medical workers that You would abundantly bless them with protection, peace, prosperity, hope, faith, wisdom, guidance & strength to get through these uncertain times & to be a blessing to others. In the name of Jesus, I claim Psalm 91, Psalm 23, Psalm 116:7, Psalm 62:5-8, Isaiah 26:3, Psalm 25:20-21, Psalm 46:10, Psalm 56:3, Psalm 61:2, 2 Chronicles 7:14, 2 Timothy 1:7, Jeremiah 30:17, Philippians 4:7-9, Romans 12:18, John 14:27, Isaiah 43:2, Isaiah 54:17 & Isaiah 53:5 over all of you & all you love. I pray that you & your loved ones are surrounded by an impenetrable hedge of protection that no evil can possibly pierce. In the name of Jesus, as a child of the Living God, covered in His blood, protected by Jesus, sealed by the Holy Spirit & as a warrior of Christ I command, rebuke & cast this virus, the violence, all agents of evil & the devil away from you & your loved ones as far as the east is from the west & by His name & power they must go NOW! I thank You Father! I claim all these things in Your Holy, majestic, everlasting, powerful & precious name I pray Lord Jesus, Amen!

Warriors! Shout with me tonight. VICTORY IS COMING! We're not created with a spirit of fear but a spirit of strength. Greater is He who is in us than he who is in the world & we're going to get through this time through the very power of Jesus Christ. He is on the Throne &

in complete control so let not your hearts be troubled. Nothing that is going on is a surprise to God. There is coming a day when every knee shall bow & every tongue confess that Christ is Lord. And as I say again Shout with me! VICTORY IS COMING! Be safe! Be healthy! Be strong! Have hope! Have faith! Have prosperity! Have joy! May God bless all of you!

DAY 149
August 12th, 2020

Good evening my friends. We're through the middle of the week & as we close out Wednesday, August 12, 2020 I hope as always that you're safe, healthy & well.

Dear Heavenly Father, I come to You with Heavenly praise & thanksgiving. Thank You Jesus that You always take care of us & have promised to never leave us or forsake us. In the name of Jesus, I claim Psalm 91, Psalm 23, Psalm 116:7, Psalm 62:5-8, Isaiah 26:3, Psalm 25:20-21, Psalm 46:10, Psalm 56:3, Psalm 61:2, 2 Chronicles 7:14, 2 Timothy 1:7, Jeremiah 30:17, Philippians 4:7-9, Romans 12:18, John 14:27, Isaiah 43:2, Isaiah 54:17 & Isaiah 53:5 over all of you & all you love. I pray that each of you is continually surrounded by an impenetrable hedge of protection. I pray that all the afflicted are supernaturally restored to full health, that a vaccine is swiftly developed & that this virus is completely eradicated. I pray for all the people, families, businesses & medical workers that you would be abundantly blessed with protection, peace, prosperity, faith, hope, guidance, love, wisdom & strength through these uncertain times. I pray for our nation that You'll please restore our lands & bring peace back to our country & people. In the name of Jesus, as a child of the true Living God, covered in His blood, protected by Jesus, sealed by the Holy Spirit & as a warrior of Christ I command, rebuke & cast this horrible virus, all the violence, the spirit of fear, all agents of evil & the devil completely away from you to the farthest ends of the earth. By His name and power they have no claim, authority or power over you and MUST LEAVE NOW. Thank You Father for our coming delivery & victory! I claim all these things in Your Holy, majestic, powerful, everlasting & precious name I pray Lord Jesus, Amen!

Warriors! As we continue to press forward through the valley & storms let not your hearts be troubled. Always know that with Christ all things are possible & He is in complete & total control & on the Throne. This season will come to an end, this valley will come to an end, this pandemic will come to an end and soon, very soon, we'll be on top of the mountain shouting victory as we prevail! We must continue to hold on. We must tell our loved ones how much we care about them. We must forgive others who have wronged us. We're going to get through this everyone! We're all in this together! Once again, say it with me.. VICTORY IS COMING! Be safe! Be healthy! Be strong! Have hope! Have faith! Have prosperity! Have joy! May God bless all of you!

DAY 150
August 13th, 2020

Good evening my friends. As we're on the eve of Friday, we're closing out Thursday, August 13th, 2020 & I pray that you & your family are safe, healthy & well.

Dear Heavenly Father, I come to You tonight with Heavenly praise, love & thanksgiving. We thank You Lord Jesus for being our Lord & savior & for the blessings You've given us. Father, I pray that You'll restore our lands & bring peace back to this nation & its people. In the name of Jesus, I claim Psalm 91, Psalm 23, Psalm 116:7, Psalm 62:5-8, Isaiah 26:3, Psalm 25:20-21, Psalm 46:10, Psalm 56:3, Psalm 61:2, 2 Chronicles 7:14, 2 Timothy 1:7, Jeremiah 30:17, Philippians 4:7-9, Romans 12:18, John 14:27, Isaiah 43:2, Isaiah 54:17 & Isaiah 53:5 over all of you & all you love. I pray that you & your loved ones are completely surrounded by a hedge of protection. I'm praying for all the people, families, businesses & medical workers that you are all abundantly & absolutely blessed through these difficult times so that you may be a blessing to others & your loved ones. I pray that all the afflicted will be completely healed, that this virus is eradicated & for the development for a safe & fully effective vaccine. In the name of Jesus, as a child of God, covered in His blood, protected by Jesus, sealed by the Holy Spirit & as a warrior of Christ I command, rebuke, come against & cast this virus, the violence, all agents of evil, the spirit of fear & the devil away from you & your loved ones this very moment. By His name they must leave NOW. Greater is He who is in us than he who is in the world & as it's written, through the name and power of Christ, if we resist the devil he must flee from us. Thank You Father. I claim all these things in Your Holy, majestic, powerful, everlasting & precious name I pray Lord Jesus, Amen!

Warriors! As we look around, we may see ravaging storms but fear not because we're mere observers. Through the power of Christ, we shall prevail & we WILL see victory. I know everything still seems out of control but we'll make it through this difficult time. We must all stay united & stand tall, stand firm & hold fast. Do not let the fear of the unknown cause anxiety! Do not let the fear for the future depress you! Do NOT let this time destroy you! We ALL will overcome this time. We do NOT have a spirit of fear but of strength because of what Christ has done on the Cross. Through Christ you are strong! Through Christ you are powerful! Through Christ you will overcome! Through Christ we WILL PREVAIL! VICTORY IS COMING! Be safe! Be healthy! Be strong! Have hope! Have faith! Have prosperity! Have joy! May God bless all of you!

DAY 151
August 14th, 2020

Good evening my friends. I hope all of you & your loved ones are safe, healthy & well as we close out Friday, August 14th, 2020.

Dear Heavenly Father, I come to You tonight with Heavenly praise, love & thanksgiving. Thank You Jesus for our blessings, for Your perfect peace that surpasses all understanding, for loving us unconditionally even in our worst moments & for being our Lord & savior. Father, I lift up all the families, businesses & people that have been affected by the violence, the virus, the increase in stress, the state of being overwhelmed at everything going on & I pray that You abundantly bless them with peace, prosperity, hope, love, faith, protection, guidance, wisdom & strength. Please let them feel Your presence so they know everything is going to be okay. I pray for all the afflicted that they're supernaturally restored to full health, for the development of a powerful vaccine & for the eradication of this virus from the surface of the earth. I pray for all our medical workers that they're double protected during dangerous & difficult shifts. I pray that a hedge of protection surrounds you and Your families that no evil can penetrate. I pray that Your calming hands restore peace to our lands. In the name of Jesus, I claim Psalm 91, Psalm 23, Psalm 116:7, Psalm 62:5-8, Isaiah 26:3, Psalm 25:20-21, Psalm 46:10, Psalm 56:3, Psalm 61:2, 2 Chronicles 7:14, 2 Timothy 1:7, Jeremiah 30:17, Philippians 4:7-9, Romans 12:18, John 14:27, Isaiah 43:2, Isaiah 54:17 & Isaiah 53:5 over all of you & all you love. In the name of Jesus, as a child of the true Living God, covered in His blood, protected by Jesus, sealed by the Holy Spirit & as a warrior of Christ I command this virus, the violence, fear, all agents of evil & the devil away from you & your loved ones this very moment. They have NO claim to you & by the name & power of Christ they must obey & GO NOW! Thank You Father! I claim all these things in Your Holy, powerful, majestic, everlasting & precious name I pray Lord Jesus, Amen!

Warriors! The weekend has arrived & we're another week closer to victory than last week! This coming Monday will make 5 months since I started praying over all of you & I'll be continuing to do so. We're getting through this difficult time & through the power of Christ we'll make it through. I know how difficult this has been for all of you, my self included, but we must continue to hold on. This WILL end I promise you. This is only for a season & then this will all be over. The world may have changed but that doesn't mean that we won't see victory through this & prevail. Christ is in control! Christ is on the Throne! Christ will deliver us! Shout it with me again! OUR GOD IS GOD!! Be safe! Be healthy! Be strong! Have hope! Have faith! Have prosperity! Have joy! May God bless all of you!

If you've never invited Jesus Christ into your heart, there's no better time to do it than right now & you can trust Him as your Savior. Just pray this prayer right now with me, just simply say, "God, I'm a sinner. I'm sorry for my sins. I ask that You forgive me, and I believe that Jesus Christ is Your Son, and I want to invite Him to come into my heart and trust Him with my life. I'm willing to trust Him as my Savior and follow Him as my Lord forever, and I pray this in Jesus' Name.'"

DAY 152
August 15th, 2020

Good evening my friends. It's amazing how fast this summer is going by as we close out Saturday, August 15th, 2020. Wherever you are in the world reading this I pray that you're safe, healthy & well.

Dear Heavenly Father, I come to You tonight with Heavenly praise & thanksgiving. Thank You Father for all You have blessed us with & for walking with us each step of this difficult journey. In the name of Jesus, I claim Psalm 91, Psalm 23, Psalm 116:7, Psalm 62:5-8, Isaiah 26:3, Psalm 25:20-21, Psalm 46:10, Psalm 56:3, Psalm 61:2, 2 Chronicles 7:14, 2 Timothy 1:7, Jeremiah 30:17, Philippians 4:7-9, Romans 12:18, John 14:27, Isaiah 43:2, Isaiah 54:17 & Isaiah 53:5 over all of you & all you love. I pray you & your loved ones are surrounded by a spiritual & impenetrable hedge of protection. I pray for all those afflicted that they're restored to full health, for the eradication of this virus & for a powerful vaccine to be developed swiftly. I pray for all the people, families, businesses & medical workers that have been affected by the virus, violence & difficulties that you're abundantly blessed with protection, peace, prosperity, love, guidance, hope, faith, wisdom & strength through these difficult & uncertain times. I pray that Your calming hands cover this nation and it's people & restore peace to every corner. In the name of Jesus, as a child of God, covered in His blood, protected by Jesus, sealed by the Holy Spirit & as a warrior of Christ I command & cast this virus, violence, fear, all agents of evil & the devil away from you & your loved ones right now. I pray that supernatural peace fills all your hearts, knowledge that everything is going to be okay & that we're going to make it through this. I thank You Father! I claim all these things in Your Holy, majestic, powerful, everlasting & precious name I pray Lord Jesus, Amen!

Warriors! Today we continue to press forward through this valley step by step & we will make it to the other side. Through the power of Christ we shall prevail because Christ is on the Throne & in total control. We need not lean on our own understanding but let go &

trust God. He will never let you down & He will guide us to victory & deliverance. As with every day, we must continue to be vigilant & strong but there will be an end to this difficult season & joy will soon return. Let not your hearts be troubled! We're all in this together & we will make it through! Victory is coming! Be safe! Be healthy! Be strong! Have hope! Have faith! Have prosperity! Have joy! May God bless all of you!

DAY 153
August 16th, 2020

Good evening my friends. As we approach a brand new week, we're closing out Sunday, August 16th, 2020 & I hope wherever you are reading this that you & your loved ones are safe, healthy & well.

Dear Heavenly Father, I come to You with Heavenly praise & thanksgiving. Thank You Father for another day to praise You, for Your infinite wisdom, the blessings You've given us & Your infinite love. I lift up all the afflicted with this virus that they may be restored to full health, for our doctors & scientists to develop a powerful & safe vaccine to eradicate the earth from this virus. I pray for all our medical workers to be double protected & given strength to keep fighting. I lift up our nation & pray that Your calming hands restore peace & prosperity to this nation & its people. I pray for all the families, people & businesses affected by the virus, the violence & uncertainty that You would abundantly bless them with everything they need, as well as perfect peace. In the name of Jesus, I claim Psalm 91, Psalm 23, Psalm 116:7, Psalm 62:5-8, Isaiah 26:3, Psalm 25:20-21, Psalm 46:10, Psalm 56:3, Psalm 61:2, 2 Chronicles 7:14, 2 Timothy 1:7, Jeremiah 30:17, Philippians 4:7-9, Romans 12:18, John 14:27, Isaiah 43:2, Isaiah 54:17 & Isaiah 53:5 over all of you & all you love. I pray for a continued hedge of protection to surround you & all you love. In the name of Jesus, as a child of God, covered in His blood, protected by Jesus, sealed by the Holy Spirit & as a warrior of Christ I command, rebuke & cast this virus, the violence, fear, anxiety, all agents of evil, sickness & the devil away from you & your loved ones this very moment & they have no other option but to obey. Greater is He who is in us than he who is in the world & as it's written, if we resist the devil by His name & power he must flee. I thank You Father for our coming victory! I claim all these things in Your Holy, majestic, precious, powerful, everlasting & precious name I pray Lord Jesus, Amen!

Warriors! As we begin a brand new week, we must continue to be vigilant & strong. We've taken another step forward & we're that much closer to victory. We're all facing uncertain times & the future is unknown but I do know this... With Christ all things are possible & we shall triumph! Tonight take a moment to pray for someone who needs it. There's power in prayer & when Christians begin to pray, the devil shudders. Do you realize we have a direct line to the creator of the universe! Whatever you're facing, He's aware & will perfect that which concerns you. We need only let go & let God take care of it. He will never leave or forsake you. We're going to get through this everyone! Let not your hearts be troubled! Victory is coming! Be safe! Be healthy! Be strong! Have hope! Have faith! Have prosperity! Have joy! May God bless all of you!

DAY 154
August 17th, 2020

Good evening my friends. It's a brand new week & we're closing out Monday, August 17th, 2020. As with each night, I hope this message once again finds you, healthy, safe & well.

Dear Heavenly Father, I come to You with Heavenly praise, love & thanksgiving. Thank You Father for Your wisdom, peace, unconditional love & blessings. I'm praying tonight for all the afflicted that they'd be super naturally healed & restored. I'm praying that this virus is eradicated, that a powerful vaccine will be developed & that you & your loved ones will be completely shielded from it. I'm praying for our nation tonight as violence continues to spread across our country & the world that Your calming hands will restore our lands & peace to the people. I pray for all the people, families, businesses & medical workers affected by the pandemic & violence that you'll be abundantly blessed with protection, prosperity, peace, restoration, health, wisdom, guidance, faith, hope & strength through these uncertain times. I pray that you & all of your loved ones will be surrounded by a hedge of protection. In the name of Jesus, I claim Psalm 91, Psalm 23, Psalm 116:7, Psalm 62:5-8, Isaiah 26:3, Psalm 25:20-21, Psalm 46:10, Psalm 56:3, Psalm 61:2, 2 Chronicles 7:14, 2 Timothy 1:7, Jeremiah 30:17, Philippians 4:7-9, Romans 12:18, John 14:27, Isaiah 43:2, Isaiah 54:17 & Isaiah 53:5 over all of you & all you love. In the name of Jesus as a child of the true Living God, covered in His blood, protected by Jesus, sealed by the Holy Spirit & as a warrior of Christ I command, rebuke & cast this virus, violence, fear, anxiety, hatred, all agents of evil & the devil away from you & your loved ones & by His name & power they MUST GO NOW! Greater is He who dwells in us than he who is in the world & as it is written, if we resist the devil he MUST flee from us. I thank You Father for our coming deliverance & victory. I claim all these things in Your Holy, powerful, majestic, everlasting & precious name I pray Lord Jesus, Amen!

Warriors! It's a new week full of possibilities. Despite all the storms that surround us & uncertainty, know that God is on control & fear not but trust God & have peace. I know it can be difficult to let go of control. I've had this same problem myself. But I have learned that when we let go & place everything in our current situations completely in God's hands, He always comes through with the perfect outcome. Sometimes it's not what we expect, but when you look back over the course of your life, you realize how God was directing your steps even if you didn't realize it. So during these difficult times, just know that it's going to be okay. We're going to get through this. Victory IS coming! Let not your hearts be troubled! Shout with me! OUR GOD IS GOD! Be safe! Be healthy! Be strong! Have hope! Have faith! Have prosperity! Have joy! May God bless all of you!

DAY 155
August 18th, 2020

Good evening my friends. We're approaching the middle of the week & we're closing out Tuesday, August 18th, 2020. I hope wherever you are reading this, that you & your loved ones are safe, healthy & well.

Dear Heavenly Father, I come to You tonight with Heavenly praise, love & thanksgiving. Thank You Father for protecting us, blessing us & for guiding us through these uncertain times. In the name of Jesus, I claim Psalm 91, Psalm 23, Psalm 116:7, Psalm 62:5-8, Isaiah 26:3, Psalm 25:20-21, Psalm 46:10, Psalm 56:3, Psalm 61:2, 2 Chronicles 7:14, 2 Timothy 1:7, Jeremiah 30:17, Philippians 4:7-9, Romans 12:18, John 14:27, Isaiah 43:2, Isaiah 54:17 & Isaiah 53:5 over all of you & all you love. I pray that all of you are surrounded by a hedge of protection that no evil, this virus or violence can penetrate. I pray for all the people sick with the virus that they'd be supernaturally restored to full health. I pray for the eradication of this virus & for a vaccine to be swiftly developed. I pray for Your calming hands to restore our lands & bring peace back to its people. I pray for all the families, businesses, people & medical workers that they would be abundantly blessed with protection, prosperity, faith, hope, love, wisdom, guidance & strength. In the name of Jesus, as a child of the true Living God, covered in His blood, protected by Jesus, sealed by the Holy Spirit & as a warrior of Christ, I command, come against, rebuke & cast this virus, the violence, the spirit of fear, all agents of evil & the devil away from you as far as the east is from the west. It has no claim, power or authority over you & by His name & power it must GO NOW! BE GONE & NEVER RETURN! I thank You Father! I claim all these things in Your Holy, powerful, everlasting & precious name I pray Lord Jesus, Amen!

Warriors! Do not look at the storms around us! Only keep your eyes focused on Christ. We need not worry or be concerned because we do not fight for victory but from victory! We've already won & we're going to get through this time. All things are possible with Christ & He is in complete and total control! As of this time tomorrow, we shall be another step closer to victory! It's coming! I know it's been tough! I know it's been hard! I know it's been heartbreaking! But we WILL prevail through this time & season. We need only to stay focused on God. Let not your hearts be troubled! VICTORY IS COMING! Be safe! Be healthy! Be strong! Have hope! Have faith! Have prosperity! Have joy! May God bless all of you!

DAY 156
August 19th, 2020

Good evening my friends. The weekend is quickly approaching & we're closing out Wednesday, August 19th, 2020. Wherever you are reading this, I hope this message finds you & your loved ones healthy, safe & well.

Dear Heavenly Father, I come to You tonight with Heavenly praise, love & thanksgiving. Thank You Father that we're through another day, that victory through You is coming & that You're walking with us each step of this journey. Jesus, I pray to You tonight to please restore our lands, bring back prosperity & peace to all its people. I pray that all the afflicted would be restored to full health. I pray that this virus will be eradicated & that a powerful & safe vaccine will be swiftly developed. I pray for all the people, families, businesses, first responders, our leaders & medical workers that all of you will be abundantly blessed with protection, peace, prosperity, hope, faith, love, guidance, wisdom & strength. In the name of Jesus, I claim Psalm 91, Psalm 23, Psalm 116:7, Psalm 62:5-8, Isaiah 26:3, Psalm 25:20-21, Psalm 46:10, Psalm 56:3, Psalm 61:2, 2 Chronicles 7:14, 2 Timothy 1:7, Jeremiah 30:17, Philippians 4:7-9, Romans 12:18, John 14:27, Isaiah 43:2, Isaiah 54:17 & Isaiah 53:5 over all of you & all you love. I pray that all of you are surrounded by a hedge of protection that this virus & no evil can penetrate. In the name of Jesus, covered in His blood, protected by Jesus, sealed by the Holy Spirit & as a warrior of Christ, I command, rebuke & cast this virus, violence, anxiety, fear, all agents of evil & the devil away from & by His name & power they MUST GO NOW & NEVER COME BACK! I thank You Father for our coming victory & I claim all these things in Your Holy, majestic, powerful, everlasting & precious name I pray Lord Jesus, Amen!

Warriors! As we press forward each day, we're staying strong through the storms. These times may be unprecedented & it seems like everyday there is something even stranger occurring than the day before. This year will always be remembered through the books of history & the people who lived in it. But I believe that history will remember most of all that we persevered no matter what came against us. Our victory will come through & by Christ. So do not worry about what storm may come tomorrow but know that no matter what comes along & things will come along, that we WILL make it through that too. With Christ, not some but ALL things are possible! Say it with me again! VICTORY IS COMING! Be safe! Be healthy! Be strong! Have hope! Have faith! Have prosperity! Have joy! May God bless all of you!

DAY 157
August 20th, 2020

Good evening my friends. We're approaching the weekend & we're closing out Thursday, August 20th, 2020 & wherever you are reading this in the world, I pray you & your loved ones are safe, healthy & well.

Dear Heavenly Father, I come to You with Heavenly praise, love & thanksgiving. Thank You Father that we can pray directly to You, that You love us unconditionally & guide our steps. In the name of Jesus, I claim Psalm 91, Psalm 23, Psalm 116:7, Psalm 62:5-8, Isaiah 26:3, Psalm 25:20-21, Psalm 46:10, Psalm 56:3, Psalm 61:2, 2 Chronicles 7:14, 2 Timothy 1:7, Jeremiah 30:17, Philippians 4:7-9, Romans 12:18, John 14:27, Isaiah 43:2, Isaiah 54:17 & Isaiah 53:5 over all of you & all you love. I pray that you & your loved ones are surrounded by an impenetrable hedge of protection. I pray that all the afflicted with the virus would be supernaturally healed & that a powerful vaccine will be developed faster than thought possible. I pray for all the families, businesses, people & medical workers that you would be protected & abundantly blessed to be a blessing to others. I pray for our nation that You would lay Your calming hands over our country & restore our lands & bring peace back to its people. In the name of Jesus, as a child of the Living God, covered in His blood, protected by Jesus, sealed by the Holy Spirit & as a warrior of Christ, I command, rebuke & cast this virus, violence, anxiety, hatred, destruction, the spirit of fear, all agents of evil & the devil away from all of you & by His name & power it MUST GO NOW! Greater is He who lives in us than he who is in the world & as it is written through the power of Christ, if we resist the devil, he MUST flee. I thank you Father & I claim all these things in Your Holy, majestic, powerful, everlasting & precious name I pray Lord Jesus, Amen!

Warriors! The weekend is almost here & we're another day closer to victory. I truly pray for each of your protection from the storms & evil that surround us. But despite the storms, have hope because we are protected by Christ & through Him we shall be victorious! It's not even a question. We WILL be delivered & victorious! As I say almost every night, take your eyes off the storm & place them firmly & locked on God. He will not let you down. Let not your hearts be troubled because ALL things are possible with Christ. We're going to get through this difficult time. Say it with me again! VICTORY IS COMING! Be safe! Be healthy! Be strong! Have hope! Have faith! Have prosperity! Have joy! May God bless all of you!

DAY 158
August 21st, 2020

Good evening my friends. The weekend is here & we're closing out Friday, August 21st, 2020. As with each night, wherever you are reading this in the world, I pray you are safe, healthy & well.

Dear Heavenly Father, I come to You with Heavenly praise & thanksgiving on this summer night as I pray for protection & blessings on those reading this post. Thank You Father, for Your wisdom, love, guidance & strength. In the name of Jesus, I claim Psalm 91, Psalm 23, Psalm 116:7, Psalm 62:5-8, Isaiah 26:3, Psalm 25:20-21, Psalm 46:10, Psalm 56:3, Psalm 61:2, 2 Chronicles 7:14, 2 Timothy 1:7, Jeremiah 30:17, Philippians 4:7-9, Romans 12:18, John 14:27, Isaiah 43:2, Isaiah 54:17 & Isaiah 53:5 over all of you & all you love. I pray for all the afflicted that they'll be restored to full health with no long term effects. I pray for the swift development of a powerful vaccine & the eradication of this virus. I pray each of you & you're loved ones are surrounded by a hedge of protection. I pray that the people, families, businesses & medical workers will be abundantly blessed with protection, peace, hope, faith, prosperity, guidance, wisdom & strength through these difficult times. I pray that You will lay Your calming hands on this nation & restore our lands & peace. In the name of Jesus, as a child of the Living God, covered in His blood, protected by Jesus, sealed by the Holy Spirit & as a warrior of Christ, I come against, command, rebuke & cast this virus away from you & all your loved ones & by His name, power & authority, it MUST obey! BE GONE! I thank You Father for our coming delivery & I claim all these things in Your Holy, majestic, powerful, everlasting & precious name I pray Lord Jesus, Amen!

Warriors! As we enter the weekend, we're through another week & soon we'll be through another month. The numbers are continuing to come down across the country in terms of the virus, but we need to continue to be vigilant & strong. Christ is clearing the path for our deliverance & He's leading us to victory! Let not your hearts be troubled as we press forward. With each step forward we get closer to our victory & it is coming. Through Christ all things are possible & He didn't bring us this far to leave us now. Through Christ we WILL PREVAIL! Tonight, I'm asking that each of you take a moment & say a prayer of hope for someone hurting tonight. Shout with me tonight GOD IS GOOD! VICTORY IS COMING! Be safe! Be healthy! Be strong! Have hope! Have faith! Have prosperity! Have joy! May God bless all of you!

DAY 159
August 22nd, 2020

Good evening my friends. It's the middle of the weekend & we're closing out Saturday, August 22nd, 2020. Wherever you are in the world reading this, as always, I hope & pray that you & your loved ones are safe, healthy & well.

Dear Heavenly Father, I come to You tonight with Heavenly Praise, love & thanksgiving. Thank You Father that we're another day closer to victory, for the blessings You give us & for being our Lord & Savior. In the name of Jesus, I claim Psalm 91, Psalm 23, Psalm 116:7, Psalm 62:5-8, Isaiah 26:3, Psalm 25:20-21, Psalm 46:10, Psalm 56:3, Psalm 61:2, 2 Chronicles 7:14, 2 Timothy 1:7, Jeremiah 30:17, Philippians 4:7-9, Romans 12:18, John 14:27, Isaiah 43:2, Isaiah

54:17 & Isaiah 53:5 over all of you & all you love. I pray that you & all your loves ones are surrounded by an impenetrable hedge of protection. I pray for all the sick & afflicted with the virus that you'll be supernaturally restored to complete & full health. I pray for all the families, businesses, people & medical workers that you'll be protected & abundantly blessed with prosperity, hope, faith, wisdom, guidance & strength. I pray that Your calming hands will stretch across the country & bring peace & restoration to our lands & people. In the name of Jesus, as a child of the Living God, covered in His blood, protected by Jesus, sealed by the Holy Spirit & as a warrior of Christ, I come against, command, rebuke & cast this virus, violence, destruction, hatred, all agents of evil, & the devil away from you & your loved ones & by His name, power & authority, it MUST OBEY & leave now! I thank You Father & I claim all these things in Your Holy Majestic, powerful, all knowing, everlasting & precious name I pray Lord Jesus, Amen!

Warriors! Tomorrow is a new day & as we approach a new week know that when the storms come, that Christ is in command & you will get through whatever comes against you. We may be living in uncertain times but we can be absolutely certain in the love & power of Jesus Christ. One day VERY soon all of this will be behind us. Until then we must hold on & be vigilant! We WILL get through this time. When you feel discouraged, take your eyes off the storms & lies of the enemy & focus them on Christ. He only wants the best for you & through Christ ALL things are possible! Say it with me again! VICTORY IS COMING! Be safe! Be healthy! Be strong! Have hope! Have faith! Have prosperity! Have joy! May God bless all of you!

DAY 160
August 23rd, 2020

Good evening my friends! We're on the eve of a new work week & we're closing out Sunday, August 23rd, 2020 & I hope where you're reading this that you, your family & loved ones are all safe, healthy & well.

Dear Heavenly Father, I come to You tonight once again with love, Heavenly praise & thanksgiving. Thank You Father for eternal life through You & for always unconditionally loving us, even at our worst moments. In the name of Jesus, I claim Psalm 91, Psalm 23, Psalm 116:7, Psalm 62:5-8, 1 John 4:4, Isaiah 26:3, Psalm 25:20-21, Psalm 46:10, Psalm 56:3, Psalm 61:2, 2 Chronicles 7:14, 2 Timothy 1:7, Jeremiah 30:17, Philippians 4:7-9, Romans 12:18, John 14:27, Isaiah 43:2, Isaiah 54:17 & Isaiah 53:5 over all of you & all you love. I pray for a never ending, spiritual hedge of protection to surround you & your loved ones. I pray for protection & abundant overflowing blessings for the families, businesses, people & medical workers affected by the virus & violence. I pray for all the afflicted that they'll be restored to complete & full health. I pray that this virus is completely & utterly eradicated from the earth. I pray for our nation that You will please restore our lands & bring peace back to its people. In the name of Jesus, as a child of the Living God, covered in His blood, protected by Jesus, sealed by the Holy Spirit & as a warrior of Christ, I once again come against, command, rebuke & cast this virus, this violence, destruction, hatred, anxiety, animosity, all agents of evil, & the devil away from you & your loved ones & by His name, power & authority, it MUST OBEY & leave now! Greater is He who lives in us than he who is in the world. I thank You Father for our coming victory & I claim all these things in Your Holy, powerful, everlasting & precious name I pray Lord Jesus, Amen!

Warriors! We're on the eve of a new week and as we continue to press forward, always know that no matter what comes against you, we have the ultimate and greatest power in the known & unknown universe fighting our battles. We need only let go & let God. It took me a while to understand that but when the pandemic hit and all I had to rely on was Christ for everything and I let go of my control and understanding, did I really realize what that means. Christ wants us to turn our burdens over to Him and He WILL take care of everything. It may be in a different way than we think it should go but when you look back over how everything turns out you suddenly realize why this happened this way, why this piece of the puzzle fit here, why this person came into or out of your life. When you look back you see how God was truly directing your steps. We're gonna get through this everyone! SAY IT WITH ME AGAIN! VICTORY IS COMING! Be

safe! Be healthy! Be strong! Have hope! Have faith! Have prosperity! Have joy! May God bless all of you!

DAY 161
August 24th, 2020

Good evening my friends. It's the beginning of a brand new week & we're closing out Monday, August 24th, 2020. Wherever you & your loved ones are, I pray that you're all safe, healthy & well.

Dear Heavenly Father, I come to You with Heavenly praise, love & thanksgiving. Thank You Father that as we move forward, that you are with us each & every step of this journey. In the name of Jesus, I claim Psalm 91, Psalm 23, Psalm 116:7, Psalm 62:5-8, 1 John 4:4, Isaiah 26:3, Psalm 25:20-21, Psalm 46:10, Psalm 56:3, Psalm 61:2, 2 Chronicles 7:14, 2 Timothy 1:7, Jeremiah 30:17, Philippians 4:7-9, Romans 12:18, John 14:27, Isaiah 43:2, Isaiah 54:17 & Isaiah 53:5 over all of you & all you love. I pray that you & your loved ones are surrounded by a hedge of protection. I pray that Your calming hands restore our lands with peace from this violence. I pray for all the sick & afflicted that all of you are restored to complete and full health. I pray for all the people, families, businesses, medical workers, police, firefighters & our leaders that you'll be abundantly blessed with protection, peace, prosperity, hope, faith, love, wisdom, guidance & strength through these difficult days we face. In the name of Jesus, as a child of the true Living God, covered in His blood, protected by Jesus, sealed by the Holy Spirit & as a warrior of Christ, I come against, command, rebuke & cast this virus, this violence, destruction, hatred, anxiety, animosity, all agents of evil, & the devil away from you & your loved ones & by His name & through the full power & authority of Christ, it MUST OBEY & leave now! I thank You Father for our coming delivery & victory & I claim all these things in Your Holy, powerful, majestic, everlasting & precious name I pray Lord Jesus, Amen!

Warriors! It's a new week & as we continue to battle against unprecedented storms, always know that in the end, through the power of Christ we WIN! Storms will come to try to dishearten you, but God will give you beauty for ashes Isaiah 61:3. So no matter what you or your loved ones are going through, you're going to be okay & you're going to make it through. Each day we take another step & another & another, until we reach our final goal! It's coming everyone! Victory is coming! We must hold on & have faith that through Christ we shall prevail! And say it with me again! OUR GOD IS GOD! VICTORY IS COMING! Be safe! Be healthy! Be strong! Have hope! Have faith! Have prosperity! Have joy! May God bless all of you!

DAY 162
August 25th, 2020

Good evening my friends. As we approach the middle of the week, we're closing out Tuesday, August 25th, 2020 & I pray all of you are healthy, safe & well.

Dear Heavenly Father, I come to You with Heavenly praise, love & thanksgiving. Thank You Father that through the storms of life, You're a bright & shinning beacon, guiding us in the way we should go. In the name of Jesus, I claim Psalm 91, Psalm 23, Psalm 116:7, Psalm 62:5-8, 1 John 4:4, Isaiah 26:3, Psalm 25:20-21, Psalm 46:10, Psalm 56:3, Psalm 61:2, 2 Chronicles 7:14, 2 Timothy 1:7, Jeremiah 30:17, Philippians 4:7-9, Romans 12:18, John 14:27, Isaiah 43:2, Isaiah 54:17 & Isaiah 53:5 over all of you & all you love. I pray that you & your loved ones are continually surrounded by a hedge of protection. I pray for the afflicted by the virus that they're restored to full health & that a powerful vaccine is developed. I pray for all the families, businesses & medical workers that they would be protected & abundantly blessed through these difficult times to be able to be a blessing to others. I pray for our country that peace would return to our lands & people. In the name of Jesus, as a child of the true Living God, covered in His blood, protected by Jesus, sealed by the Holy Spirit & as a warrior of Christ, I command this virus, this violence, destruction, hatred, animosity, all agents of evil, & the devil to leave now & by His name & power it must obey and BE GONE! I thank You Father & I claim all these things in Your Holy, powerful, majestic, everlasting & precious name I pray Lord Jesus, Amen!

Warriors! Tonight, as we press forward through the week, please say a prayer for someone in need. As the storms of life try to ravage us, we can shelter under the wings of Christ. He's promised to never leave us nor forsake us & He always keeps His promises. Soon, all will be made right but until that day, we must remain vigilant, strong & keep the faith. As I say nearly every night, through Christ all things are possible. Do not let the lies of the enemy steal your joy. Take your eyes off the storm & place them on God. Let not your hearts be troubled! It's going to be okay because victory is coming! Be safe! Be healthy! Be strong! Have hope! Have faith! Have prosperity! Have joy! May God bless all of you!

DAY 163
August 26th, 2020

Good evening my friends. Tonight as we close out Wednesday, August 26th, 2020 I pray you & your loved ones are safe, healthy & well.

Dear Heavenly Father, I come to You with Heavenly praise & thanksgiving. Thank You Father for all the blessings You give us & for the gift of eternal life through Christ Jesus. In the name of Jesus, I claim Psalm 91, Psalm 23, Psalm 116:7, Psalm 62:5-8, 1 John 4:4, Isaiah 26:3, Psalm 25:20-21, Psalm 46:10, Psalm 56:3, Psalm 61:2, 2 Chronicles 7:14, 2 Timothy 1:7, Jeremiah 30:17, Philippians 4:7-9, Romans 12:18, John 14:27, Isaiah 43:2, Isaiah 54:17 & Isaiah 53:5 over all of you & all you love. I pray for a hedge of protection to surround you & your loved ones. I pray for the eradication of this virus, that all the afflicted are healed & for the development of a powerful vaccine. I pray for protection & abundant blessings through these difficult times for all the families, businesses, people & medical workers affected by this virus & violence. I pray for & lift up all the people in the way of the hurricane that they will be safe & protected. I pray for peace to be restored to our lands & people. In the name of Jesus, as a child of the true Living God, covered in His blood, protected by Jesus, sealed by the Holy Spirit & as a warrior of Christ, I command this virus, this violence, destruction, hatred, animosity, all agents of evil, & the devil to leave now & by His name & power it must obey and BE GONE! And I thank You Father & I claim all these things in Your Holy, powerful, majestic, eternal, everlasting & precious name I pray Lord Jesus, Amen!

Warriors! Tonight I'm simply asking this. Please pray for all the people in the way of the hurricane in the Gulf States. Pray for their safety, pray for their protection, please pray. This too shall pass. Through the power of Christ all things are possible & I lift up everyone in harms way in the name of Jesus. Be safe! Be healthy! Be strong! Have hope! Have faith! Have prosperity! Have joy! May God bless all of you!

DAY 164
August 27th, 2020

Good evening my friends. We're approaching the weekend & we're closing out Thursday, August 27th, 2020. Wherever you are reading this, I pray you & your loved ones are safe, healthy & well. I apologize for the lateness of the prayer tonight. It's been a busy day & been fighting another migraine but that won't stop me from praying over you tonight.

Dear Heavenly Father, I come to You tonight with Heavenly praise, love & thanksgiving. Thank You Father for the gift of life through Your son Christ Jesus. In the name of Jesus, I claim Psalm 91, Psalm 23, Psalm 116:7, Psalm 62:5-8, 1 John 4:4, Isaiah 26:3, Psalm 25:20-21, Psalm 46:10, Psalm 56:3, Psalm 61:2, 2 Chronicles 7:14, 2 Timothy 1:7, Jeremiah 30:17, Philippians 4:7-9, Romans 12:18, John 14:27, Isaiah 43:2, Isaiah 54:17 & Isaiah 53:5 over all of you & all you love. I pray for a spiritual & impenetrable hedge of protection around you & your loved ones. I pray for the afflicted to be restored & completely healed, the complete eradication of this virus & for the swift development of a powerful vaccine. I pray that all the families, businesses, people & medical workers would have full protection & abundance of blessings through these difficult days. I pray for & lift up all the people that their towns have been ravaged by the hurricanes. I pray for peace to be restored to our lands & people. In the name of Jesus, as a child of the true Living God, covered in His blood, protected by Jesus, sealed by the Holy Spirit & as a warrior of Christ, I command this virus, this violence, destruction, hatred, animosity, all agents of evil, & the devil to leave now & by His name & power it must obey and BE GONE! It has no option but to obey and go! I thank You Father & I claim all these things in Your Holy, powerful, majestic, eternal, everlasting & precious name I pray Lord Jesus, Amen!

Warriors! The weekend approaches & we're almost through another week of this pandemic & the numbers are getting better each day. We have to keep fighting it, remain strong & vigilant but through the power of Christ we shall prevail! Tonight once again, please pray that peace will overtake this nation, for someone in need & for all the people affected by the hurricanes. Each day of 2020 has been a challenge for so many people around the world, but know & have faith that this season will pass & victory is coming soon! Let not your hearts be troubled! We're another day closer! Be safe! Be healthy! Be strong! Have hope! Have faith! Have prosperity! Have joy! May God bless all of you!

DAY 165
August 28th, 2020

Good evening my friends. It's finally the weekend & as we close out Friday, August 28th, 2020, I pray this message & prayer finds you healthy, safe & well.

Dear Heavenly Father, I come to You tonight with Heavenly praise, love & thanksgiving. Thank You Father for all the blessings You've given us & thank You for Your guiding wisdom in these difficult times. Tonight, I pray for all the people in Louisiana, Texas & all the states affected by the hurricanes. We all stand united with you. I pray that Your perfect peace overtakes our lands, people & that our nation is restored. In the name of Jesus, I claim Psalm 91, Psalm 23, Psalm 116:7, Psalm 62:5-8, 1 John 4:4, Isaiah 26:3, Psalm 25:20-21, Psalm 46:10, Psalm 56:3, Psalm 61:2, 2 Chronicles 7:14, 2 Timothy 1:7, Jeremiah 30:17, Philippians 4:7-9, Romans 12:18, John 14:27, Isaiah 43:2, Isaiah 54:17 & Isaiah 53:5 over all of you & all you love. I pray for a continual hedge of protection to surround you & your loved ones. I pray for the eradication of this virus, that all the afflicted will be healed, for the development of a powerful vaccine & for protection and strength for all our brave medical workers. I pray for all the families, businesses & people affected by the virus & violence that you would be protected & abundantly blessed through these uncertain days. In the name of Jesus, as a child of the true Living God, covered in His blood, protected by Jesus, sealed by the Holy Spirit & as a warrior of Christ, I come against, command, rebuke & cast this virus, violence, destruction, hatred, animosity, all agents of evil, & the devil to leave & through His name & ALL His power it must obey and BE GONE NOW! I thank You Father & I claim all these things in Your Holy, powerful, everlasting, eternal & precious name I pray Lord Jesus, Amen!

Warriors! As with the storms of life, this too shall pass. The virus will be eradicated, peace will return, life will return to normal & you & your loved ones are going to make it through this difficult time stronger than before. It's never fun to go through it, but when you come out on the other side of difficult or seemingly impossible situations, you will be far stronger than when you went in. Adversity builds character, tenacity & perseverance. Through Christ ALL things are possible & He will deliver us to victory. Let not your hearts be troubled! Be safe! Be healthy! Be strong! Have hope! Have faith! Have prosperity! Have joy! May God bless all of you!

DAY 166
August 29th, 2020

Good evening my friends. It's the middle of the weekend & once again we're closing out Saturday, August 29th, 2020. Wherever you are reading this, I pray & hope you & your loved ones are safe, healthy & well.

Dear Heavenly Father, I come to You tonight with Heavenly praise, love & thanksgiving. Thank You Father for Your unconditional love, Your infinite wisdom, guidance & perfect peace. In the name of Jesus, I claim Psalm 91, Psalm 23, Psalm 116:7, Psalm 62:5-8, 1

John 4:4, Isaiah 26:3, Psalm 25:20-21, Psalm 46:10, Psalm 56:3, Psalm 61:2, 2 Chronicles 7:14, 2 Timothy 1:7, Jeremiah 30:17, Philippians 4:7-9, Romans 12:18, John 14:27, Isaiah 43:2, Isaiah 54:17 & Isaiah 53:5 over all of you & all you love. I pray for all the afflicted that they're restored to perfect health & for a safe & powerful vaccine to be developed. I pray that you & all your loved ones are surrounded by a spiritual hedge of protection. I pray for all the families, businesses, people & medical workers that they would be fully protected & abundantly blessed to be a blessing to many others. I pray for Your perfect peace to cover this nation & its people. In the name of Jesus, as a child of the true eternal Living God, covered in His blood, protected by Jesus, sealed by the Holy Spirit & as a warrior of Christ, I command, rebuke & cast this virus, destruction, violence, hatred, animosity, all agents of evil, & the devil to leave and BE GONE NOW! I thank You Father & I claim all these things in Your Holy, powerful, everlasting, eternal & precious name I pray Lord Jesus, Amen!

Warriors! As we press forward through each day, know that when the storms come, and they will, that you'll make it to the other side because of the power & authority of Christ Jesus. No matter what you face, Christ is in complete control & on the Throne. With each step of our journey, not only will we make it to the other side, but you're growing stronger with each step. Tomorrow is a brand new day & joy is coming in the morning. Please say a prayer for someone tonight, tell loved ones how much you care about them & forgive those who have wronged you. Place everything in God's hands & He will fight your battles, defend & protect you. Let not your hearts be troubled. Victory is coming! Be safe! Be healthy! Be strong! Have hope! Have faith! Have prosperity! Have joy! May God bless all of you!

DAY 167
August 30th, 2020

Good evening my friends. As we approach a new week we're closing out Sunday, August 30th, 2020 & as with each night, wherever you are reading this, I hope you & your loved ones are safe, healthy & well.

Dear Heavenly Father, I come to You tonight with Heavenly praise, love & thanksgiving. Thank You Father for this new day, this new coming week & this coming month that we may praise Your name through these difficult times. Thank You that You're our Savior & Redeemer & have eternal life through Your Son Christ Jesus. In the name of Jesus, I claim Psalm 91, Psalm 23, Psalm 116:7, Psalm 62:5-8, 1 John 4:4, Isaiah 26:3, Psalm 25:20-21, Psalm 46:10, Psalm 56:3, Psalm 61:2, 2 Chronicles 7:14, 2 Timothy 1:7, Jeremiah 30:17, Philippians 4:7-9, Romans 12:18, John 14:27, Isaiah 43:2, Isaiah 54:17 & Isaiah 53:5 over all of you & all you love. I pray for an impenetrable hedge of protection to surround you & your loved ones. In the name of Jesus, as a child of the true Living God, covered in His blood, protected by Jesus, sealed by the Holy Spirit & as a warrior of Christ, I command & cast this virus, destruction, violence, hatred, animosity, all agents of evil, & the devil to leave & never return. I pray that this virus is eradicated, that all the afflicted are restored to full health & for a powerful & safe vaccine to be created. I pray that peace covers every corner of this land & its people. I pray for all the families, businesses, people & medical workers that you are fully protected & abundantly blessed so you can be a blessing to others. I thank You Father & I claim all these things in Your Holy, majestic, powerful & precious name I pray Lord Jesus, Amen!

Warriors! As we come to the start of a new week, we're another day, another week & shortly, another month closer to victory! It's coming everyone! I know all of you're all frustrated, tired, fed up, restless but just hold on strong. We're going to get through this everyone! Christ is guiding us through each day & each step & we will be victorious! Always remember, that no matter what happens, Christ is in control & on the Throne! One day, you will be able to tell your families, children, friends that you were here during this time & survived through everything that came against us. History books, music & films will be written about this time. What we went through in 2020 is historic & you're part of this history. It's all going to be okay! We're all in this together! Let not your heart be troubled! Victory is coming! Be safe! Be healthy! Be strong! Have hope! Have faith! Have prosperity! Have joy! May God bless all of you!

DAY 168
August 31st, 2020

Good evening my friends. It's a brand new week & as we close out Monday, August 31st, 2020 I hope you & your families are safe, healthy & well.

Dear Heavenly Father, I come to You with Heavenly praise, love & thanksgiving. Thank You Father for Your infinite peace that surpasses all understanding, for Your perfect wisdom & for loving us unconditionally. Father, I pray for our nation tonight as the violence & this terrible virus ravage our lands. Please Father, forgive our sins, restore our lands & bring peace back to the people. I pray for an impenetrable hedge of protection to surround you & your loved ones that no evil can penetrate. I pray for all the afflicted that they will be restored to full health, for the development of a powerful vaccine & that this virus will be eradicated. I lift up & pray for all the families, people, businesses & medical workers affected by the virus & violence that all of you will be protected & abundantly blessed with peace, prosperity, hope, faith, wisdom, love, guidance & strength to be a blessing to many others during these uncertain times. In the name of Jesus, I claim Psalm 91, Psalm 23, Psalm 116:7, Psalm 62:5-8, 1 John 4:4, Isaiah 26:3, Psalm 25:20-21, Psalm 46:10, Psalm 56:3, Psalm 61:2, 2 Chronicles 7:14, 2 Timothy 1:7, Jeremiah 30:17, Philippians 4:7-9, Romans 12:18, John 14:27, Isaiah 43:2, Isaiah 54:17 & Isaiah 53:5 over all of you & all you love. In the name of Jesus, as a child of the true Living God, covered in His blood, protected by Jesus, sealed by the Holy Spirit & as a warrior of Christ, I command, rebuke, come against & cast this virus, destruction, violence, hatred, animosity, all agents of evil, & the devil to leave & never return. Greater is He who is in us than he who is in the world. I thank You Father & I claim all these things in Your Holy, powerful, everlasting & precious name I pray Lord Jesus, Amen!

Warriors! We're approaching a new month and we continue to press forward despite the continual onslaught of storms that come against us. This journey is tough but we WILL make it through and prevail! All of this is going to be history soon. Through the power and authority of Christ, we WILL be victorious! As I've said many nights, we MUST take our eyes off the storm & focus on Christ. Let go and let God. He will never leave you or forsake you. What concerns you, concerns Him & He has a plan for you and your life. Let not your heart be troubled! Victory is coming! Be safe! Be healthy! Be strong! Have hope! Have faith! Have prosperity! Have joy! May God bless all of you!

The Sinner's Prayer

If you are not yet saved I want to personally invite you to read this prayer below. This could be the most profound decision of your entire life. This is a decision only you can make, as I am on a messenger. Please don't put off to tomorrow what can be done right now. Because tomorrow may never come.

If you would like to be saved, please read the prayer below out loud & believing in your heart.

"God, I'm a sinner. I'm sorry for my sins. I ask that You forgive me, and I believe that Jesus Christ is Your Son, and I want to invite Him to come into my heart and trust Him with my life. I'm willing to trust Him as my Savior and follow Him as my Lord forever, and I pray this in Jesus' Name.'"

DAY 169
September 1st, 2020

Good evening my friends. I hope you're having a great week & as we close out Tuesday, September 1st, 2020, I pray this message once again finds you & your loved ones healthy, safe & well.

Dear Heavenly Father, I come to You tonight with a humble heart, Heavenly praise, love & thanksgiving. Thank You Father for our blessings, for walking with us each day of this journey, for never leaving us & for Your unconditional love even at our worst moments. In the name of Jesus, I claim Psalm 91, Psalm 23, Psalm 46:10, Psalm 62:5-8, Psalm 116:7, 1 John 4:4, Isaiah 26:3, Psalm 25:20-21, Psalm 56:3, Psalm 61:2, 2 Chronicles 7:14, 2 Timothy 1:7, Jeremiah 30:17, Philippians 4:7-9, Romans 12:18, John 14:27, Isaiah 43:2, Isaiah 54:17 & Isaiah 53:5 over all of you & all you love. I pray that you're completely surrounded by an impenetrable hedge of protection that no evil can penetrate. I pray for all the afflicted by the virus that they'd be completely restored to full health, that a powerful vaccine will be swiftly developed & for the eradication of this virus from the face of the earth. I pray for all the countless people, families, businesses & medical workers that you'll be given protection, & abundantly blessed with prosperity, peace, hope, faith, love, guidance, wisdom & strength so you can be a blessing to many others who need it during these uncertain times. I pray for Your perfect peace to fill & cover this land & its people. In the name of Jesus, as a child of the true Living God, covered in His blood, protected by Jesus, sealed by the Holy Spirit & as a warrior of Christ, I command, rebuke, come against & cast this virus, destruction, violence, hatred, animosity, all agents of evil, & the devil to leave & never return. By the name of Jesus, it MUST OBEY & leave now! As it is written, by His name & power, if we resist the devil he must flee from us. I thank You Father & I claim all these things in Your Holy, powerful, everlasting & precious name I pray Lord Jesus, Amen!

Warriors! Our number of prayer warriors is increasing & when we pray the devil shudders. Prayer is truly powerful & allows us to directly speak to the Creator of the universe. As we walk through this long valley we've been in for a long time, know that there is end to this season. This journey has been difficult, frustrating & it seems like every day there is a new storm just on the horizon. But despite all of this, Christ is on the Throne & in control! We're going to get through this time & everything will be okay. Life is going to return to normal! Peace will return! This virus will be eradicated! We must stay strong & vigilant. Let not your hearts be troubled! Shout it with me again! VICTORY IS COMING BECAUSE OUR GOD IS GOD! Be safe! Be healthy! Be strong! Have hope! Have faith! Have prosperity! Have joy! May God bless all of you!

DAY 170
September 2nd, 2020

Good evening my friends. It's the middle of the week & as we close out Wednesday, September 2nd, 2020 I hope this message & prayer finds you & your loved ones all safe, healthy & well.

Dear Heavenly Father, I come to You with a humble heart, Heavenly praise, love & thanksgiving. Thank You Father that we have this day to praise You & for our blessings from You. In the name of Jesus, I claim Psalm 91, Psalm 23, Psalm 46:10, Psalm 62:5-8, Psalm 116:7, 1 John 4:4, Isaiah 26:3, Psalm 25:20-21, Psalm 56:3, Psalm 61:2, 2 Chronicles 7:14, 2 Timothy 1:7, Jeremiah 30:17, Philippians 4:7-9, Romans 12:18, John 14:27, Isaiah 43:2, Isaiah 54:17 & Isaiah 53:5 over all of you & all you love. I pray that you & your loved ones are completely surrounded by a spiritual & impenetrable hedge of protection that no evil or virus can penetrate. I pray that all the afflicted with the virus are supernaturally healed & restored to complete health. I pray for all the families, people, businesses & medical workers that all of you will be abundantly blessed with protection, peace, prosperity, hope, faith, love, guidance, wisdom & strength. I pray that You will restore our nation & cover every inch of country with Your calming hands & perfect peace. In the name of Jesus, as a child of the true Living God, covered in His blood, protected by Jesus, sealed by the Holy Spirit & as a warrior of Christ, I command & cast this virus, destruction, violence, hatred, animosity, all agents of evil, & the devil to GO NOW! As it is written, greater is

He who is in us than he who is in the world & if we resist the devil he must flee. I thank You Father & I claim all these things in Your Holy, powerful, majestic, everlasting & precious name I pray Lord Jesus, Amen!

Warriors! It's the middle of the week & we're now into September. It's amazing how fast these past months have gone by. We're continuing to move forward. I want you to think about something, at this time next year, all of this will be a distant memory. 2020 has been difficult in almost every single way & every day we find something new but this season will pass. With each day and every step we take we're that much closer to deliverance & victory. Christ is in control & on the Throne and He has a plan for victory. 24 hours from now, we'll be even closer. As the saying goes, how do you eat an elephant? One bite at a time. We're gonna get through this time. It's a slow journey, but we WILL make it! Say it with me! GOD IS GOOD! Be safe! Be healthy! Be strong! Have hope! Have faith! Have prosperity! Have joy! May God bless all of you!

DAY 171
September 3rd, 2020

Good evening my friends. We're coming up on the weekend & as we close out Thursday, September 3rd, 2020 I hope you & your loved ones are safe, healthy & well.

Dear Heavenly Father, I come to You with Heavenly praise, love & thanksgiving. Thank You Father that You sent Your only Son to die for us that we may have eternal life through Christ. In the name of Jesus, I claim Psalm 91, Psalm 23, Psalm 46:10, Psalm 62:5-8, Psalm 116:7, 1 John 4:4, Isaiah 26:3, Psalm 25:20-21, Psalm 56:3, Psalm 61:2, 2 Chronicles 7:14, 2 Timothy 1:7, Jeremiah 30:17, Philippians 4:7-9, Romans 12:18, John 14:27, Isaiah 43:2, Isaiah 54:17 & Isaiah 53:5 over all of you & all you love. I pray that each of you is surrounded by a spiritual hedge of protection that no evil can penetrate. I lift up and pray for all the people, families businesses & medical workers that they'd be fully protected & abundantly blessed with prosperity, peace, love, faith, wisdom, guidance & strength. I pray that Your perfect calming hands will restore peace to this nation. I pray for all the afflicted with the virus that they'd be restored to complete health. I pray for the development of a safe, powerful & effective vaccine against the virus. In the name of Jesus, I come to You as a child of the true Living God, covered in His blood, protected by Jesus, sealed by the Holy Spirit & as a warrior of Christ, I command, rebuke & cast this virus, this destruction, violence, hatred, animosity, all agents of evil, & the devil to GO NOW! By His name & power it MUST obey and leave. It has no other option but to go. I thank You Father & I claim all these things in Your Holy, majestic, powerful, everlasting & precious name I pray Lord Jesus, Amen!

Warriors! As we approach the weekend, we must continue to remain strong & vigilant. We've been at this for months now & I know that we're all ready to be done with this pandemic, violence & everything else that has been going on in 2020 but know that this too shall pass. We MUST take our eyes OFF the raging storm around us & only focus on God. ONLY He can deliver us to victory. ONLY He can restore our lands. ONLY He can restore peace & the complete eradication of the virus. But no matter what happens in the remaining months of this year, God WILL bring us to victory. I PROMISE you we're going to get through this. Let not your heart be troubled! Be safe! Be healthy! Be strong! Have hope! Have faith! Have prosperity! Have joy! May God bless all of you!

DAY 172
September 4th, 2020

Good evening my friends. The weekend is finally here & as we're closing out Friday, September 4th, 2020. I hope & pray wherever you are reading this, that you & your loved ones are safe, healthy & well.

Dear Heavenly Father, I come to You with a humble heart, Heavenly praise, love & thanksgiving. Thank You Father for loving us unconditionally, guiding our steps & that You have a personal destiny for each of us. In the name of Jesus, I claim Psalm 91, Psalm 23, Psalm 46:10, Psalm 62:5-8, Psalm 116:7, 1 John 4:4, Isaiah 26:3,

Psalm 25:20-21, Psalm 56:3, Psalm 61:2, 2 Chronicles 7:14, 2 Timothy 1:7, Jeremiah 30:17, Philippians 4:7-9, Romans 12:18, John 14:27, Isaiah 43:2, Isaiah 54:17 & Isaiah 53:5 over all of you & all you love. I lift up & pray for all the afflicted that they'll be fully restored, that the virus will be eradicated & that a powerful vaccine will be developed. I pray that you are surrounded by an impenetrable hedge of protection that no evil, virus or violence can penetrate where you're merely an observer. I pray for all the countless people, families, businesses whose lives & livelihoods have been affected by this virus, violence & storms of uncertainty that they'll be abundantly blessed with protection, prosperity, peace, hope, faith, love, guidance, wisdom & strength. I pray that Your perfect calming hands will cover this nation & restore our lands & bring peace back to the people. In the name of Jesus, I come to You as a child of the true Living God, covered in His blood, protected by Jesus, sealed by the Holy Spirit & as a warrior of Christ, I command, come against, rebuke & cast this virus, this destruction, violence, hatred, animosity, all agents of evil, & the devil away from you & your loved ones and that it HAS TO GO NOW! Greater is He who is in us than he who is in the world & as it is written that through the power of Christ if we resist the devil he must flee from us. I thank You Father & I claim all these things in Your Holy, majestic, powerful, everlasting & precious name I pray Lord Jesus, Amen!

Warriors! We're truly living in historic & unprecedented times, but that doesn't mean that we must fear the terrors of the night. When we're weak we are strong with Christ. This time down here is a mere blink in terms of eternity & when we trust in Christ as our Lord & Savior we never need to fear anything. That doesn't mean that bad things won't happen as we're in a fallen world, but it does mean that no matter what the storm that comes, no matter what happens, God will walk with you every single step of the journey & you will come out victorious. It's difficult when walking through the valley, uncertain of what is happening around you & what the future will bring but when you turn everything over to Christ, He'll NEVER let you down. We're going to get through this time everyone! We're all in this together! Let not your heart be troubled! Be safe! Be healthy! Be strong! Have hope! Have faith! Have prosperity! Have joy! May God bless all of you!

DAY 173
September 5th, 2020

Good evening my friends. It's Labor Day weekend & as we're closing out Saturday, September 5th, 2020. I hope & pray that wherever you're reading this message, that you & your loved ones are safe, healthy & well.

Dear Heavenly Father I come to You with Heavenly praise & thanksgiving. Thank You Father for this wonderful day & that You have a special destiny planned for each of us. In the name of Jesus, I claim Psalm 91, Psalm 23, Psalm 46:10, Psalm 62:5-8, Psalm 116:7, 1 John 4:4, Isaiah 26:3, Psalm 25:20-21, Psalm 56:3, Psalm 61:2, 2 Chronicles 7:14, 2 Timothy 1:7, Jeremiah 30:17, Philippians 4:7-9, Romans 12:18, John 14:27, Isaiah 43:2, Isaiah 54:17 & Isaiah 53:5 over all of you & all you love. I pray you & your loved ones are completely surrounded by a hedge of protection against all evil, violence & the virus. I pray for all the afflicted that you'll be completely & fully restored to health, that a vaccine will be swiftly developed & that all our medical workers will be protected & given strength during their difficult & dangerous shifts. I lift up & pray for all the people, families & businesses affected by the virus, violence & uncertainties that you'll be completely protected & abundantly blessed so you can be a blessing to many others. I pray that Your calming hands cover this entire nation & bring peace back to its people. In the name of Jesus, I come to You as a child of the true Living God, covered in His blood, protected by Jesus, sealed by the Holy Spirit & as a warrior of Christ, with the full authority & power of Jesus Christ I command, come against, rebuke & cast this virus, this destruction, violence, hatred, animosity, all agents of evil, & the devil away from you & your loved ones & that it HAS TO LEAVE HERE AND NEVER RETURN! I thank You Father & I claim all these things in Your Holy, powerful, everlasting & precious name I pray Lord Jesus, Amen!

Warriors! It's Labor Day weekend & fall is quickly approaching. It's been a difficult year to say the least, but we're continuing to press forward. We must be vigilant but we'll also prevail through the power of Christ. If you're worried about tomorrow, let go & let God. It took me until this year when all you have left is God to rely on to understand this. Despite everything going on, we continue to press forward to victory & we WILL see deliverance. This season will pass & life will return to normal. I know how many of you are worried, I know how many of you are scared of tomorrow & what it may bring but know this, when we place our trust in God Almighty, there is nothing in this world, the universe known & unknown that is more powerful than God. We're going to get through this. It's a tough journey but through the power of Christ WE ARE STRONG & WE CAN DO THIS!! Let not your heart be troubled! Be safe! Be healthy! Be strong! Have hope! Have faith! Have prosperity! Have joy! May God bless all of you!

DAY 174
September 6th, 2020

Good evening my friends. We're approaching a brand new week & as we close out Sunday September 6th, 2020 I hope this message once again finds you & your loved ones healthy, safe & well.

Dear Heavenly Father, I come to You tonight with a humble heart, Heavenly praise, love & thanksgiving. Thank You Father for the blessings You give us, the wisdom You freely give, Your guidance & infinite love. In the name of Jesus, I claim Psalm 91, Psalm 23, Psalm 46:10, Psalm 62:5-8, Psalm 116:7, 1 John 4:4, Isaiah 26:3, Psalm 25:20-21, Psalm 56:3, Psalm 61:2, 2 Chronicles 7:14, 2 Timothy 1:7, Jeremiah 30:17, Philippians 4:7-9, Romans 12:18, John 14:27, Isaiah 43:2, Isaiah 54:17 & Isaiah 53:5 over all of you & all you love. I lift up & pray for all the afflicted that they'll be restored to full health, that this virus will finally be eradicated & that a powerful & safe vaccine will be swiftly developed. I pray that you & your loved ones are surrounded by a spiritual & impenetrable hedge of protection that this virus can't penetrate. I lift up before You Father all the people, families, businesses & medical workers that You would abundantly bless them with protection, peace, prosperity, hope, faith, love, guidance, wisdom & strength. I pray for our country that You would place Your calming hands on every inch of this nation bringing peace back to our lands & people. In the name of Jesus, I come to You as a child of the true Living God, covered in His blood, protected by Jesus, sealed by the Holy Spirit & as a warrior of Christ, with the full authority & power of Jesus Christ I command, come against, rebuke & cast this virus, this evil destruction, violence, hatred, animosity, all agents of evil, & the devil away from you & your loved ones & by You name & power they must go now! It has no authority, claim or power of you & your loved ones & by His name this evil must leave now. I thank You Father & I claim all these things in Your Holy, powerful, majestic, everlasting & precious name I pray Lord Jesus, Amen!

Warriors! This week when the storms come, do not fear! When worry for the future comes, do not fear! When the waves of uncertainty come, DO NOT FEAR! What concerns you, concerns God & when God is on your side, there isn't anything that can come between you & the destiny that God has for you. He works in your life only for good. Though it can be like wandering in the dark sometimes, God will always guide you to safety. As we enter the fall, we must remain vigilant & strong but know that this season does have an end to it! This dark valley will open up into light & this time of uncertainty will soon be over! We must continue to have faith & we will make it! Always remember, ALL things are possible with Christ! Let not your heart be troubled! Be safe! Be healthy! Be strong! Have hope! Have faith! Have prosperity! Have joy! May God bless all of you!

DAY 175
September 7th, 2020

Good evening my friends. It's Labor Day & the start of a brand new week & as we close out Monday, September 7th, 2020 I hope this finds you & your loved ones healthy, safe & well.

Dear Heavenly Father, I come to You tonight with a humble heart, Heavenly praise, love & thanksgiving. Thank You Father for Your guidance through the darkness we face like a bright beacon of light leading us forward. Father, I pray that You cover this nation with Your perfect calming hands & please restore peace. In the name of Jesus, I claim Psalm 91, Psalm 23, Psalm 46:10, Psalm 62:5-8, Psalm

116:7, 1 John 4:4, Isaiah 26:3, Psalm 25:20-21, Psalm 56:3, Psalm 61:2, 2 Chronicles 7:14, 2 Timothy 1:7, Jeremiah 30:17, Philippians 4:7-9, Romans 12:18, John 14:27, Isaiah 43:2, Isaiah 54:17 & Isaiah 53:5 over all of you & all you love. I pray that you & your loved ones are surrounded by a continual, spiritual & impenetrable hedge of protection that no evil can even approach. I lift up & pray for all the people, all the families, businesses & medical workers that you abundantly bless & protect them through all the storms we're facing so you can be a blessing to many others. In the name of Jesus, I come to You as a child of the true Living God, covered in His blood, protected by Jesus, sealed by the Holy Spirit & as a warrior of Christ, with the full authority & power of Jesus Christ I command, come against, rebuke & cast this virus, this evil destruction, violence, hatred, animosity, all agents of evil, & the devil away from you & your loved ones & by You name & power they must go now! As it's written greater is He who is in us than he who is in the world & if we resist the devil he must flee from us. I thank You Father for our coming deliverance & I claim all these things in Your Holy, majestic, powerful, everlasting & precious name I pray Lord Jesus, Amen!

Warriors! It's a new week & as we end the summer & enter the fall we'll continue to press forward. We WILL not be stopped, we WILL not be deterred, we WILL NOT falter because of the power & guidance of Jesus Christ. When the storms come we can know & have faith that everything will be okay. We're going to get through all of this everyone. Soon, very soon, all of this will pass. We must hold on & keep our eyes focused on God. Don't let the storms distract you! Don't look at the storms, only look to God. Say it with me OUR GOD IS GOD! Let not your heart be troubled! Be safe! Be healthy! Be strong! Have hope! Have faith! Have prosperity! Have joy! May God bless all of you!

DAY 176
September 8th, 2020

Good evening my friends. As we close out Tuesday, September 8th, 2020, as with each night, I hope this message finds you & your loved ones healthy, safe & well.

Dear Heavenly Father, I come to You with Heavenly praise, love & thanksgiving. Thank You Father for all You have blessed us with, thank You for Your infinite wisdom, guidance & unconditional love. In the name of Jesus, I claim Psalm 91, Psalm 23, Psalm 46:10, Psalm 62:5-8, Psalm 116:7, 1 John 4:4, Isaiah 26:3, Psalm 25:20-21, Psalm 56:3, Psalm 61:2, 2 Chronicles 7:14, 2 Timothy 1:7, Jeremiah 30:17, Philippians 4:7-9, Romans 12:18, John 14:27, Isaiah 43:2, Isaiah 54:17 & Isaiah 53:5 over all of you & all you love. I pray that all of you are surrounded by an impenetrable hedge of protection. I pray that You place Your calming hands on this nation & restore peace. I lift up & pray for all the people, families, businesses & medical workers that all of you will be abundantly blessed & protected so you can be a blessing to many others who are in need. I pray for all the afflicted that they would be restored to full health, for a vaccine to be swiftly developed & that this virus will be completely eradicated. In the name of Jesus, I come to You as a child of the true Living God, covered in His blood, protected by Jesus, sealed by the Holy Spirit & as a warrior of Christ, with the full authority & power of Jesus Christ I command, come against, rebuke & cast this virus, violence, this evil destruction, hatred, animosity, all agents of evil, & the devil away from you & your loved ones & by Your name & power they must go now! As it's written, Greater is He who is in us than he who is in the world & if we resist the devil he must flee. I thank You Father for our coming victory & deliverance & I claim all these things in Your Holy, powerful, everlasting & precious name I pray Lord Jesus, Amen!

Warriors! Right now there are countless people across the country who are frustrated & angry & like many of, I am too, but what keeps me going forward is my belief in Christ that He WILL deliver us to victory. I know how hard this season has been but know that this time will end & joy will replace it. Right now, wherever you are reading this message, take a moment & pray for someone in need. When God's people pray mountains are moved, when God's people pray, breakthroughs occur & when God's people pray the devil shudders because he knows his time is short. Despite these uncertain times we face, we can be certain in God. We're gonna get through this everyone! Let not your heart be troubled! Be safe! Be healthy! Be strong! Have hope! Have faith! Have prosperity! Have joy! May God bless all of you!

DAY 177
September 9th, 2020

Good evening my friends. I hope you're having a great day & as we close out Wednesday, September 9th, 2020, I pray this message finds you & your loved ones healthy, safe & well.

Dear Heavenly Father, I come to You with Heavenly praise, love & thanksgiving. Thank You Father that even when we don't understand events in our lives, You have a plan, are in total control & on the Throne. Father, I lift up & pray for this country that You will place Your calming hands on this nation & restore peace. I pray for all the afflicted that they would be restored in full & complete health, that this virus will be eradicated & that a powerful & safe vaccine will be swiftly developed. I lift up & pray for all the people, families, businesses & medical workers that you would be abundantly blessed with protection, peace, prosperity, hope, faith, love, guidance, wisdom & strength. In the name of Jesus, I claim Psalm 91, Psalm 23, Psalm 46:10, Psalm 62:5-8, Psalm 116:7, 1 John 4:4, Isaiah 26:3, Psalm 25:20-21, Psalm 56:3, Psalm 61:2, 2 Chronicles 7:14, 2 Timothy 1:7, Jeremiah 30:17, Philippians 4:7-9, Romans 12:18, John 14:27, Isaiah 43:2, Isaiah 54:17 & Isaiah 53:5 over all of you & all you love. I pray that you & your loved ones are completely surrounded by a spiritual & impenetrable hedge of protection. In the name of Jesus, I come to You as a child of the true Living God, covered in His blood, protected by Jesus, sealed by the Holy Spirit & as a warrior of Christ, with the full authority & power of Jesus Christ I command & cast this virus, violence, destruction, hatred, all agents of evil, & the devil away from you & your loved ones & by Your name & power they must go now! By His name & power it has no other option but to leave! I thank You Father & I claim all these things in Your Holy, powerful, everlasting & precious name I pray Lord Jesus, Amen!

Warriors! It's the middle of the week & as we continue to move forward, don't let the storms distract you. We're going to get through this time. We move as a unified force through each day guided by Christ & through His power we shall prevail. No matter what happens, it's going to be okay. Just think, tomorrow a major breakthrough could happen. It's only a matter of time but this season shall end & this will all be over soon. We must do our part & continue to be vigilant & hold on but we will be victorious! All things are possible through Christ & He is in total control. Let not your heart be troubled! Victory is coming! Be safe! Be healthy! Be strong! Have hope! Have faith! Have prosperity! Have joy! May God bless all of you!

DAY 178
September 10th, 2020

Good evening my friends. I hope you're having a great Thursday and as we close out the day, it's September 10th, 2020. As with each night, I pray this message finds you and your loved ones healthy, safe and well.

Dear Heavenly Father, I come to You tonight with Heavenly praise, love & thanksgiving. Thank You Father that we are another day closer to victory & that no matter what storm comes against us, You're there to protect and guide us. Father, I lift up this nation and pray that Your calming hands will restore peace to our lands and people. I pray for all the sick that they'll be restored to full health, that this virus will finally be eradicated and that a powerful and safe vaccine will be swiftly developed. I pray for all the families, people, businesses and medical workers that you will be protected and abundantly blessed to be a blessing to others. In the name of Jesus, I claim Psalm 91, Psalm 23, Psalm 46:10, Psalm 62:5-8, Psalm 116:7, 1 John 4:4, Isaiah 26:3, Psalm 25:20-21, Psalm 56:3, Psalm 61:2, 2 Chronicles 7:14, 2 Timothy 1:7, Jeremiah 30:17, Philippians 4:7-9, Romans 12:18, John 14:27, Isaiah 43:2, Isaiah 54:17 & Isaiah 53:5 over all of you & all you love. I pray that you and your loved ones are surrounded by a spiritual hedge of protection, shielding you from all evil, violence and this virus. In the name of Jesus, I come to You as a child of the true Living God, covered in His blood, protected by Jesus, sealed by the Holy Spirit and as a warrior of Christ, with the full authority and power of Jesus Christ I command, rebuke and cast this virus, violence, all agents of evil, and the devil away from you and your loved ones and by Your name and power they must go now! I thank You Father and I claim all these things in Your Holy, majestic, powerful, everlasting and precious name I pray Lord Jesus, Amen!

Warriors! Do not fear these uncertain times, for they will pass. Do not look at the storms but focus solely on God. And know that no matter what, Christ is on the Throne & in control. As with each day, we're another day closer & that means one less hurdle to jump. All of us are ready for this to be over soon, but in the mean time, take a moment & thank God for what you have & pray for those who are hurting. Every day seems like there is something new coming against us, but like each of those storms, know that there is no match for God. He is more powerful than anything in the known & unknown universe & through His power we WILL prevail! Also & this might be hard for all of us, but tonight, take a moment & forgive someone who wronged you in the past. Let go of that anger, that animosity & make a conscious effort to forgive them & give it to God. It will be freeing. It's time for all of us to start healing. We're gonna get through this everyone! Let not your heart be troubled! Victory is coming! Be safe! Be healthy! Be strong! Have hope! Have faith! Have prosperity! Have joy! May God bless all of you!

DAY 179
September 11th, 2020

Good evening my friends. As we close out another day of 2020, the date is Friday, September 11th, 2020 & I pray this message finds you & your loved ones healthy, safe & well.

Dear Heavenly Father, I come to You tonight with a humble heart, Heavenly praise, love & thanksgiving. Thank You Father for being our Rock when we haven't anywhere else to turn, that You always are welcoming us back no matter what we have done & that You love us unconditionally. Thank You for being our Father. I pray for all the afflicted that they will be supernaturally healed & restored to complete & full health. I lift up & pray for our nation that Your calming hands will cover every corner & bring peace back to our lands & people. In the name of Jesus, I claim Psalm 91, Psalm 23, Psalm 46:10, Psalm 62:5-8, Psalm 116:7, 1 John 4:4, Isaiah 26:3, Psalm 25:20-21, Psalm 56:3, Psalm 61:2, 2 Chronicles 7:14, 2 Timothy

1:7, Jeremiah 30:17, Philippians 4:7-9, Romans 12:18, John 14:27, Isaiah 43:2, Isaiah 54:17 & Isaiah 53:5 over all of you & all you love. I pray that you & your loved ones are continually surrounded by a hedge of protection. I pray that this virus & violence never comes near you or your loved ones & that you are shielded from it. I pray for all the people, families, businesses & medical workers that you are all blessed with protection & abundantly blessed so you can be a blessing to others around you. In the name of Jesus, I come to You as a child of the true Living God, covered in His blood, protected by Jesus, sealed by the Holy Spirit & as a warrior of Christ, I command, rebuke & cast this virus, violence, all agents of evil, & the devil away from you & your loved ones & by Your name & power they must leave. Greater is He who is in us than he who is in the world & as it's written if we resist the devil he must flee. I thank You Father & I claim all these things in Your Holy, powerful, everlasting & & precious name I pray Lord Jesus, Amen!

Warriors! Today is always a sad day in America but we must always remember & never forget all the people & brave first responders who died on that terrible morning of September 11th, 2001. Even on that morning when all of us were afraid for what tomorrow would bring, God was in control. Even on that day when we though the world might be coming to an end before our eyes, God was in control. And today, when everything seems completely uncertain, out of control & not knowing what tomorrow brings, GOD is still in control! Refuse to entertain the terror of the storms that surround us & focus only on God. All things are possible with Christ & whatever you are going through right now, this very moment, Christ knows & what concerns you concerns Him. It's going to be okay. Let not your heart be troubled! Victory is coming! Be safe! Be healthy! Be strong! Have hope! Have faith! Have prosperity! Have joy! May God bless all of you!

DAY 180
September 12th, 2020

Good evening my friends. It's the weekend & as we close out Saturday, September 12th, 2020, I hope & pray this message finds you & your loved ones healthy, safe & well.

Dear Heavenly Father, I come to You tonight with Heavenly praise, love & thanksgiving. Thank You Father for another day here on earth, thank You for Your wisdom & for being our Lord & Savior. In the name of Jesus, I claim Psalm 91, Psalm 23, Psalm 46:10, Psalm 62:5-8, Psalm 116:7, 1 John 4:4, Isaiah 26:3, Psalm 25:20-21, Psalm 56:3, Psalm 61:2, 2 Chronicles 7:14, 2 Timothy 1:7, Jeremiah 30:17, Philippians 4:7-9, Romans 12:18, John 14:27, Isaiah 43:2, Isaiah 54:17 & Isaiah 53:5 over all of you & all you love. I pray that you are surrounded by a hedge of protection that no evil, virus or violence can pass through. I pray for all the afflicted that they would be completely restored to complete & full health. I lift up & pray for all the people, families, businesses & medical workers that they would be abundantly blessed with protection, peace, prosperity, health, love, hope, faith, wisdom, guidance & strength to get through these difficult days. I pray for our country that Your perfect calming hands would cover this nation & people with Your perfect peace that surpasses all understanding. In the name of Jesus, I come to You as a child of the true Living God, covered in His blood, protected by Jesus, sealed by the Holy Spirit & as a warrior in the Army of Christ, I command, rebuke & cast this virus, violence, all agents of evil, & the devil away from you & your loved ones & by Your name & power they must leave. I thank You Father & I claim all these things in Your Holy, powerful, everlasting & precious name I pray Lord Jesus, Amen!

Warriors! The weekend is here & wherever you are, whatever you are facing today big & small, I pray for a blessing for you that what concerns you will be completely taken care of by the will & power of Christ. As we stand united tonight against the powers of darkness & evil, know that our Lord Jesus is in total control & there isn't anything that is a surprise to God. He will guide us to victory! Tonight, take a moment to say a prayer again for someone in need & shout with me again. OUR GOD IS GOD!! Victory is coming! Be safe! Be healthy! Be strong! Have hope! Have faith! Have prosperity! Have joy! May God bless all of you!

DAY 181
September 13th, 2020

Good evening my friends. It's the end of the weekend & as we close out Sunday, September 13th, 2020, I pray this message finds you & your loved ones healthy, safe & well.

Dear Heavenly Father, I come to You with a humble heart, Heavenly praise, love & thanksgiving. Thank You Father for the blessings You've given us, for Your infinite wisdom & for loving us even at our worst moments. In the name of Jesus, I claim Psalm 91, Psalm 23, Psalm 46:10, Psalm 62:5-8, Psalm 116:7, 1 John 4:4, Isaiah 26:3, Psalm 25:20-21, Psalm 56:3, Psalm 61:2, 2 Chronicles 7:14, 2 Timothy 1:7, Jeremiah 30:17, Philippians 4:7-9, Romans 12:18, John 14:27, Isaiah 43:2, Isaiah 54:17 & Isaiah 53:5 over all of you & all you love. I pray for a continual hedge of protection to be placed around you & your loved ones that no evil, virus or violence can pass through. I lift up & pray for the families, businesses, people & medical workers to be given full protection & abundantly blessed in these uncertain times. I lift up & pray for all the afflicted that all of you will be restored to complete & full health. I pray for our nation that Your calming hands will restore peace to every corner. In the name of Jesus, I come to You as a child of the true Living God, covered in His blood, protected by Christ Jesus, sealed by the Holy Spirit & as a warrior in the Army of Christ, I command, come against, rebuke & cast this virus, violence, all agents of evil, & the devil away from you & your loved ones & by Your name & power they must leave. They have no other option but to obey. I thank You Father for our coming deliverance & I claim all these things in Your Holy, powerful, majestic, everlasting & precious name I pray Lord Jesus, Amen!

Warriors! As we start a new week, walk forward with the confidence that when God is for you, there isn't anything that can be against you. Storms will come in this fallen world, but through the power & might of God, WE SHALL PREVAIL! We stand united & we won't stop! We hold our ground & we will not be deterred or retreat! God has not given us a spirit of fear but of power, love & discipline! (2 Timothy 1:7). No matter what comes against us, won't stop your destiny!

No matter what tells you, you aren't good enough, nothing will ever change or just give up, doesn't know the awesome & amazing power of Christ Jesus. And as we say it in a loud voice, have faith to believe it! OUR GOD IS GOD! Victory is coming! Be safe! Be healthy! Be strong! Have hope! Have faith! Have prosperity! Have joy! May God bless all of you!

DAY 182
September 14th, 2020

Good evening my friends. It's a brand new week & as we're closing out Monday, September 14th, 2020, I pray this message once again finds you & your loved ones healthy, safe & well.

Dear Heavenly Father, I come to You with a humble heart, Heavenly praise, love & thanksgiving. Thank You Father for walking with us along this difficult journey & that You have a plan for our victory & deliverance. Lord Jesus, tonight I lift up all the afflicted with this virus & pray that You'll completely restore all of them to complete & full health. I pray this virus is eradicated, that a powerful & effective vaccine will be swiftly developed. I lift up & pray for all the people, all the families, all the businesses that they would be abundantly blessed with protection, peace, prosperity, hope, health, faith, love, wisdom, guidance & strength to get through these difficult days & to be a blessing to others. In the name of Jesus, I claim Psalm 91, Psalm 23, Psalm 46:10, Psalm 62:5-8, Psalm 116:7, 1 John 4:4, Isaiah 26:3, Psalm 25:20-21, Psalm 56:3, Psalm 61:2, 2 Chronicles 7:14, 2 Timothy 1:7, Jeremiah 30:17, Philippians 4:7-9, Romans 12:18, John 14:27, Isaiah 43:2, Isaiah 54:17 & Isaiah 53:5 over all of you & all you love. I pray that each of you & your loved ones are surrounded by an impenetrable hedge of protection. I pray for this country that You would please place Your perfect calming hands on this nation & return peace to our lands & people. In the name of Jesus, I come to You as a child of the Living God, covered in His blood, protected by Jesus, sealed by the Holy Spirit & as a warrior of Christ, I command & cast this virus, violence, all agents of evil, & the devil away from you & your loved ones & by Your name & power they must leave now. As it is written, greater is He who is in us than he who is in the world & if we resist the devil he MUST flee. I thank You Father & I claim these things in Your Holy, everlasting, powerful, majestic & precious name I pray Lord Jesus, Amen!

Warriors! As we enter into this new week, we'll face certain challenges, but every challenge can be conquered by the power of Christ. What concerns you concerns God. But don't fear about what you are facing, but place it in the hands of God almighty. Let His will be done in your life. Take a moment again tonight & please pray for someone in need. Through these storms we've developed character & good will come of this time. We all want everything to go back to normal, myself included, but know that this season will end & life will return to normal. We're gonna get through this because we're all in this together! Shout it with me again tonight! PRAISE CHRIST! VICTORY IS COMING! Be safe! Be healthy! Be strong! Have hope! Have faith! Have prosperity! Have joy! May God bless all of you!

DAY 183
September 15th, 2020

Good evening my friends. I hope all of you are having a great day & as we close out Tuesday, September 15th, 2020, I pray this message once again finds you & your loved ones healthy, safe & well.

Dear Heavenly Father, I come to You with a humble heart, Heavenly praise & thanksgiving. Thank You Father that You have each of our lives, situations & concerns in Your perfect hands. In the name of Jesus, I claim Psalm 91, Psalm 23, Psalm 46:10, Psalm 62:5-8, Psalm 116:7, 1 John 4:4, Isaiah 26:3, Psalm 25:20-21, Psalm 56:3, Psalm 61:2, 2 Chronicles 7:14, 2 Timothy 1:7, Jeremiah 30:17, Philippians 4:7-9, Romans 12:18, John 14:27, Isaiah 43:2, Isaiah 54:17 & Isaiah 53:5 over all of you & all you love. I pray that each of you & your loved ones are protected by an impenetrable hedge of protection that this virus, violence & evil cannot penetrate. I pray for all the afflicted that they'll be completely restored to full health, that this virus will be eradicated & that an effective vaccine will be swiftly developed. I pray for all the people, families, businesses, medical workers &

our leaders that you will be abundantly blessed & protected through these difficult & uncertain times. I pray for our country that Your calming hands of peace will cover this nation & all it's people. In the name of Jesus, I come to You as a child of the Living God, covered in His blood, protected by Jesus, sealed by the Holy Spirit & as a warrior of Christ, I command, rebuke & cast this virus, violence, all agents of evil, & the devil away from you & your loved ones & by Your name & power they must leave now. BE GONE! I thank You Father & I claim all these things in Your Holy, everlasting, powerful, majestic & precious name I pray Lord Jesus, Amen!

Warriors! We may face great storms & the situations around the country continue to change on an hour by hour basis, but despite all this, Christ is still in control & on the Throne! He's walking us through a long, difficult valley where all we have left is to depend on Him. But when we reach this point where we're completely dependant on Him, we come to realize how much we truly need God. I tell you deliverance & victory is coming. It's not been easy & will continue to not be easy but this season will end & I believe will end soon. A year from this very day this could be all a distant memory. We'll exchange stories of how we survived this time in our history. Books will be written, films made & you are all part of this history. Stay strong & hold on! We're going to get through this everyone! We're one day closer! Be safe! Be healthy! Be strong! Have hope! Have faith! Have prosperity! Have joy! May God bless all of you!

DAY 184
September 16th, 2020

Good evening my friends. I hope all of you are having a great middle of the week & as we close out Wednesday, September 16th, 2020, I pray this message once again finds you & your loved ones healthy, safe & well.

Dear Heavenly Father, I come to You tonight with Heavenly praise, love & thanksgiving. Thank You Father that You love us unconditionally even at our worst moments & that You only want the best for our lives. In the name of Jesus, I claim Psalm 91, Psalm 23, Psalm 46:10, Psalm

62:5-8, Psalm 116:7, 1 John 4:4, Isaiah 26:3, Psalm 25:20-21, Psalm 56:3, Psalm 61:2, 2 Chronicles 7:14, 2 Timothy 1:7, Jeremiah 30:17, Philippians 4:7-9, Romans 12:18, John 14:27, Isaiah 43:2, Isaiah 54:17 & Isaiah 53:5 over all of you & all you love. I pray you & your loved ones are surrounded by a spiritual hedge of protection that no evil can penetrate. I pray for & lift up all the afflicted that they will all be restored to full health & for the development of a safe & effective vaccine. I pray for all the people, families, businesses & medical workers that you'd be abundantly blessed with protection, peace, prosperity, hope, faith, love, health, guidance, wisdom & strength. I pray that You will place Your calming hands on this country & restore our lands & peace. In the name of Jesus, I come to You as a child of the true Living God, covered in His blood, protected by Jesus, sealed by the Holy Spirit & as a warrior of Christ, I command, come against, rebuke & cast this virus, violence, all agents of evil, & the devil away from you & your loved ones & by Your name & power they must leave now. Greater is He who is in us than he who is in the world & by his name if we resist the devil he must flee from us. I thank You Father & I claim all these things in Your Holy, everlasting, powerful, majestic & precious name I pray Lord Jesus, Amen!

Warriors! Tonight we continue to press forward through the storms & through the very name & power of Jesus Christ we shall prevail! God is the creator of the universe & there isn't anything in the known or unknown universe that is more powerful that God! If He can create the universe, surely He can take care of the concerns that you face each day, and when we place our entire trust in His hands, He always does. Fear not! We're going to get through this time in our history! We're all in this together! We're one day closer! VICTORY IS COMING! Be safe! Be healthy! Be strong! Have hope! Have faith! Have prosperity! Have joy! May God bless all of you!

DAY 185
September 17th, 2020

Good evening my friends. We're approaching the weekend & as we close out Thursday, September 17th, 2020, I pray this message once again finds you & your loved ones healthy, safe & well.

Dear Heavenly Father, I come to You tonight with Heavenly praise, love & thanksgiving. Thank You Father for all the blessings You've given us & that even when times seem uncertain, You're still in complete control. In the name of Jesus, I claim Psalm 91, Psalm 23, Psalm 46:10, Psalm 62:5-8, Psalm 116:7, 1 John 4:4, Isaiah 26:3, Psalm 25:20-21, Psalm 56:3, Psalm 61:2, 2 Chronicles 7:14, 2 Timothy 1:7, Jeremiah 30:17, Philippians 4:7-9, Romans 12:18, John 14:27, Isaiah 43:2, Isaiah 54:17 & Isaiah 53:5 over all of you & all you love. I pray that you & your loved ones are surrounded by a continual & spiritual hedge of protection. I lift up & pray for all the afflicted that they will be fully restored & that an effective vaccine will be swiftly developed. I pray for all the people, families, businesses & medical workers that you'll be given complete protection & abundantly blessed so you can be a blessing to many others. I pray for this nation that You will restore our lands & bring back peace. In the name of Jesus, I come to You as a child of the true Living God, covered in His blood, protected by Christ Jesus, sealed by the Holy Spirit & as a warrior of Christ, I command & cast this virus, violence, all agents of evil, & the devil away from you & your loved ones & by Your name & power they must leave now. BE GONE! I thank You Father & I claim all these things in Your Holy, majestic, everlasting, powerful & precious name I pray Lord Jesus, Amen!

Warriors! As we approach the weekend & as we enter into the fall, we must continue to be strong & vigilant. We're all ready for this to be over, myself included. Each day we're another day closer & closer to having this all be behind us. I know how hard it is to go through each day not knowing what tomorrow may bring. But know this, even when times seem uncertain, be certain that God has a plan. When we're in the middle of something that is difficult or terrible it's easy to lose focus that God is truly in control & when we surrender our lives to Him, He only wants what's best for us. Sometimes we go through difficult times to help our faith grow & strength us, sometimes it's the enemy attacking us but if we remain strong in God we always will make it through. VICTORY IS COMING! Be safe! Be healthy! Be strong! Have hope! Have faith! Have prosperity! Have joy! May God bless all of you!

DAY 186
September 18th, 2020

Good evening my friends. Alright the weekend is finally here & as we close out Friday, September 18th, 2020, I pray this message finds you & your loved ones healthy, safe & well.

Dear Heavenly Father, I come to You tonight with a humble heart, Heavenly praise, love & thanksgiving. Thank You Father for continuing to guide us & walk with us along this difficult journey & through each step we are one day closer. I lift up all the afflicted to You Father that You'd restore them to complete & full health, that this virus will be eradicated & that a safe & effective vaccine will be developed. I pray for all the families, people, businesses & medical worker that they'd be abundantly blessed with complete protection, prosperity, peace, hope, faith, purpose, love, guidance, wisdom & strength so they can be a blessing to many others. I pray that you & your loved ones are completely surrounded by a spiritual hedge of protection that never ceases & shields you from all evil. I pray for our nation that Your calming hands will restore peace & our country. In the name of Jesus, I claim Psalm 91, Psalm 23, Psalm 46:10, Psalm 62:5-8, Psalm 116:7, 1 John 4:4, Isaiah 26:3, Psalm 25:20-21, Psalm 56:3, Psalm 61:2, 2 Chronicles 7:14, 2 Timothy 1:7, Jeremiah 30:17, Philippians 4:7-9, Romans 12:18, John 14:27, Isaiah 43:2, Isaiah 54:17 & Isaiah 53:5 over all of you & all you love. In the name of Jesus, I come to You as a child of the true Living God, covered in His blood, protected by Christ Jesus, sealed by the Holy Spirit & as a warrior of Christ, I command & cast this virus, violence, hatred, the spirit of fear, all agents of evil, & the devil away from you & your loved ones & by Your name & power they must leave now. I thank You Father for our coming victory through You & I claim all these things in Your Holy, majestic, everlasting, powerful & precious name I pray Lord Jesus, Amen!

Warriors! It's the weekend & as I said earlier, I pray you & your loved ones are all safe & healthy. Everything is starting to look up & we must continue to be positive through these difficult times. I know that's easier said than done & sometimes we're just so frustrated that we can't take anymore. I've been there. But know that even though this has been difficult, and it has, that this will come to an end. It's a difficult long road & I think about the long 40 year journey Moses led & what they went through but even that long journey came to an end & so will this. Be strong & vigilant & have faith because all things are possible with Christ & this whole thing could be over tomorrow. We're gonna make it because of Christ & because we have each other. This is not like anything we've ever been through & 2020 keeps throwing new surprises at us, but we keep pushing forward & with God WE WILL PREVAIL! Be safe! Be healthy! Be strong! Have hope! Have faith! Have prosperity! Have joy! May God bless all of you!

DAY 187
September 19th, 2020

Good evening my friends. I apologize for being really late tonight I was gone all day but that won't stop me from praying over all of you again tonight as promised. As we close out Saturday, September 19th, 2020, I pray this message once again finds you & your loved ones healthy, safe & well.

Dear Heavenly Father, I come to You tonight with a humble heart, Heavenly praise, love & thanksgiving. Thank You Father that we're another day closer to victory & that You are in control & on the Throne! In the name of Jesus, I claim Psalm 91, Psalm 23, Psalm 46:10, Psalm 62:5-8, Psalm 116:7, 1 John 4:4, Isaiah 26:3, Psalm 25:20-21, Psalm 56:3, Psalm 61:2, 2 Chronicles 7:14, 2 Timothy 1:7, Jeremiah 30:17, Philippians 4:7-9, Romans 12:18, John 14:27, Isaiah 43:2, Isaiah 54:17 & Isaiah 53:5 over all of you & all you love. I pray for a continual hedge of protection to surround you & your loved ones. I lift up & pray for the sick they they'd be fully restored to complete health, that this virus is eradicated & that a safe & effective vaccine is developed. I pray for all the people, families, businesses & medical workers that they would be fully protected & abundantly blessed through these uncertain times. I pray for our country that Your calming hands would restore peace to this nation. In the name of Jesus, I come to You as a child of the true Living God, covered in His blood, protected by Christ Jesus, sealed by the Holy Spirit &

as a warrior of Christ, I command, come against, rebuke & cast this virus, violence, hatred, the spirit of fear, all agents of evil, & the devil away from you & your loved ones & by Your name & power they must leave now. I thank You Father for our coming victory through You & I claim all these things in Your Holy, powerful, majestic, everlasting & precious name I pray Lord Jesus, Amen!

Warriors! It's the middle of the weekend & as we continue to press forward through the storms don't be dismayed by any setbacks that come along. There will always be obstacles we face every day that try to hinder our progress, but how we react to those obstacles is what's important. Don't rely on your own understanding of the events that take place but rather, place them in God's hands & will. This time in our lives is very difficult for everyone, some more than others, but we will prevail through this because of Christ. Let not your hearts be troubled! Say it with me! GOD IS GOOD! Be safe! Be healthy! Be strong! Have hope! Have faith! Have prosperity! Have joy! May God bless all of you!

DAY 188
September 20th, 2020

Good evening my friends. As we close out the weekend, it's Sunday, September 20th, 2020 & as always I pray this message finds you & your loved ones healthy, safe & well.

Dear Heavenly Father, I come to You tonight with Heavenly praise, love & thanksgiving. Thank You Father for getting us through another day, for always supplying our needs & guiding us along the path that is Your will. In the name of Jesus, I claim Psalm 91, Psalm 23, Psalm 46:10, Psalm 62:5-8, Psalm 116:7, 1 John 4:4, Isaiah 26:3, Psalm 25:20-21, Psalm 56:3, Psalm 61:2, 2 Chronicles 7:14, 2 Timothy 1:7, Jeremiah 30:17, Philippians 4:7-9, Romans 12:18, John 14:27, Isaiah 43:2, Isaiah 54:17 & Isaiah 53:5 over all of you & all you love. I pray for a continual hedge of protection tonight, tomorrow night & the next night to surround you & your loved ones. I pray for peace to be restored to this nation from Your perfect calming hands. I lift up all the afflicted that they'll be fully restored to full health. I pray for the families, people, businesses & medical workers that you will be abundantly blessed with protection, peace, prosperity, hope, faith, love, wisdom, guidance & strength. In the name of Jesus, I come to You as a child of the Living God, covered in His blood, protected by Jesus, sealed by the Holy Spirit & as a warrior in the army of Christ, I command & cast this virus, violence, hatred, the spirit of fear, all agents of evil, & the devil away from you & your loved ones & by Your name & power they must leave now. I thank You Father & I claim all these things in Your Holy, powerful, majestic, everlasting & precious name I pray Lord Jesus, Amen!

Warriors! As we're on the eve of a new week, know that at this time next week, next month, next season, next year all of this could be over & be far behind us. As I've said each week, 2020 has been certainly a year for the history books & we're all a part of that history. It's been trying, difficult & heartbreaking but there has also been good that has come out of this time too. Miracles we don't hear about on the news, situations in peoples lives that have completely turned around & healing of loved ones. So no matter how difficult the storm is, always try to know that even in the worst moments we face, there is always some good even if it's just beneath the surface. You showing kindness to someone you've never met can sometimes make the difference in someone's life. They may be having a horrible day or dealing with a lot of stress but you can be a blessing from God to them in the midst of the storm. These storms will pass because God is in control & He WILL deliver us to victory because all things are possible through Christ. Hang in there everyone. Be safe! Be healthy! Be strong! Have hope! Have faith! Have prosperity! Have joy! May God bless all of you!

DAY 189
September 21st, 2020

Good evening my friends. It's a brand new week & as we close out Monday, September 21st, 2020 I pray this message finds you & your loved ones healthy, safe & well.

Dear Heavenly Father, I come to You tonight with Heavenly praise, love & thanksgiving. Thank You Father for the beautiful day out today in North East Ohio & that even in the midst of the storms we face, You are in complete & total control. Tonight, In the name of Jesus, I come to You as a child of the Living God, covered in His blood, protected by Jesus, sealed by the Holy Spirit & as a warrior of Christ, I command, come against & cast this horrible virus, violence, hatred, the spirit of fear, all agents of evil, & the devil away from you & your loved ones & by Your name & power they must leave now. Greater is He who is in us that he who is in the world. When we resist the devil because of Christ, he must flee. I lift up all the afflicted that they will be restored to complete & full health, that this virus is eradicated & that a powerful vaccine is developed & available for everyone who wants it. I pray for our nation that Your calming hands will restore peace to every single corner through the country. I pray for all the people affected by this virus from individuals, families, businesses, medical workers & our leaders that all of you will be protected & abundantly blessed throughout these difficult days we face. In the name of Jesus, I claim Psalm 91, Psalm 23, Psalm 46:10, Psalm 62:5-8, Psalm 116:7, 1 John 4:4, Isaiah 26:3, Psalm 25:20-21, Psalm 56:3, Psalm 61:2, 2 Chronicles 7:14, 2 Timothy 1:7, Jeremiah 30:17, Philippians 4:7-9, Romans 12:18, John 14:27, Isaiah 43:2, Isaiah 54:17 & Isaiah 53:5 over all of you & all you love. I pray for a never ending hedge of protection to surround you & your loved ones. I thank You Father & I claim all these things in Your Holy, powerful, majestic, everlasting, eternal & precious name I pray Lord Jesus, Amen!

Warriors! It's a new week & it's amazing how fast this month is going. As we stay vigilant & strong through the days ahead, know that no matter what storm comes against you, when you place it in God's hands He will always deliver you. It may not be in the way that you envision, but it will be what's best for you. God only wants the best for you. I'll say it again, we must take our eyes off the storm & focus only on God. Do not fear because Christ, your Savior, is in complete & total control. There isn't anything that your facing that God can't handle. It's going to be okay. Say it with me again tonight! OUR GOD IS GOD & VICTORY IS COMING! Let not your hearts be troubled. Be safe! Be healthy! Be strong! Have hope! Have faith!

Have prosperity! Have joy! May God bless all of you!

Tonight, If you've never invited Jesus Christ into your heart, there's no better time to do it than right now, and you can trust Him as your Savior. Just pray this prayer right now with me, just simply say, "God, I'm a sinner. I'm sorry for my sins. I ask that You forgive me, and I believe that Jesus Christ is Your Son, and I want to invite Him to come into my heart and trust Him with my life. I'm willing to trust Him as my Savior and follow Him as my Lord forever, and I pray this in Jesus' Name.'"

DAY 190
September 22nd, 2020

Good evening my friends. As we close out Tuesday, September 22nd, 2020, I pray this message finds you & your loved ones healthy, safe & well.

Dear Heavenly Father, I come to You tonight with Heavenly praise, love & thanksgiving. Thank You Father for the blessings You've given us, Your unconditional love, wisdom & peace that surpasses all understanding. In the name of Jesus, I claim Psalm 91, Psalm 23, Psalm 46:10, Psalm 62:5-8, Psalm 116:7, 1 John 4:4, Isaiah 26:3, Psalm 25:20-21, Psalm 56:3, Psalm 61:2, 2 Chronicles 7:14, 2 Timothy 1:7, Jeremiah 30:17, Philippians 4:7-9, Romans 12:18, John 14:27, Isaiah 43:2, Isaiah 54:17 & Isaiah 53:5 over all of you & all you love. Father I lift up all the afflicted & pray for their full restoration, that this virus will be eliminated, rendered extinct & that a powerful vaccine will be swiftly developed & available for all who need it. I pray for our nation that peace will return & that You'll restore our lands. I pray for all the families, businesses, medical workers & all who have been affected by the past several months that they will be given protection & abundantly blessed through these difficult & uncertain times we live in. I pray that a continual spiritual & impenetrable hedge of protection surrounds you & your loved ones. In the name of Jesus, I come to You as a child of the true Living God, covered in His blood, protected by Jesus, sealed by the Holy Spirit & as a warrior of Christ, I command & cast this horrible virus, violence, hatred, the spirit of fear, all agents of evil, & the devil away from you & your loved ones & by Your name & power they must leave now. THIS EVIL MUST LEAVE in the name of Jesus! I thank You Father & I claim all these things in Your Holy, powerful, majestic, everlasting, eternal & precious name I pray Lord Jesus, Amen!

Warriors! Each day of this year, at one point or another, we've all been frustrated, angry & afraid. But we also have had moments of joy, prayers answered & miraculous prayers answered. I mentioned this before but we must always look at the good in every difficult situation. During these uncertain times, we must keep a good attitude, stay strong & vigilant. Despite the storms we face on a daily basis, we must always have faith that no matter what happens, Christ is in control & on the Throne. No matter what comes against us, we've already won the spiritual war. We don't fight for victory! We fight from victory! Always remember, ALL things are possible with Christ! We're going to get through this everyone! We're all in this together! Be safe! Be healthy! Be strong! Have hope! Have faith! Have prosperity! Have joy! May God bless all of you!

DAY 191
September 23rd, 2020

Good evening my friends. As we close out Wednesday, September 23rd, 2020, I pray this message finds you & your loved ones healthy, safe & well.

Dear Heavenly Father, I come to You tonight with a humble heart, Heavenly praise, love & thanksgiving. Thank You Father for walking with us each step of this long journey & thank You that through You, we'll be victorious! In the name of Jesus, I claim Psalm 91, Psalm 23, Psalm 46:10, Psalm 62:5-8, Psalm 116:7, 1 John 4:4, Isaiah 26:3, Psalm 25:20-21, Psalm 56:3, Psalm 61:2, 2 Chronicles 7:14, 2 Timothy 1:7, Jeremiah 30:17, Philippians 4:7-9, Romans 12:18, John 14:27, Isaiah 43:2, Isaiah 54:17 & Isaiah 53:5 over all of you & all you love. I pray that you & your loved ones are completely surrounded by a hedge of protection that this virus cannot penetrate. I lift up all the afflicted that they would be completely restored to full health with no lasting effects, that this virus is eliminated & that a powerful & safe vaccine is swiftly developed. I pray for all the people, families, businesses & medical workers affected by the virus & violence that all of you will be abundantly blessed with prosperity, peace, protection, health, love, hope, faith, wisdom, guidance & strength through these uncertain times. I pray for our nation that Your perfect calming hands will restore our lands & peace to the people. In the name of Jesus, I come to You as a child of the true Living God, covered in His blood, protected by Jesus, sealed by the Holy Spirit & as a warrior of Christ, I command & cast this virus, violence, the spirit of fear, all agents of evil & the devil away from you & your loved ones & by Your name & power they must leave now. I thank You Father & I claim all these things in Your Holy, powerful, majestic, everlasting & precious name I pray Lord Jesus, Amen!

Warriors! Do not be afraid for the future. When we put our trust in God, no matter what comes against us, we shall prevail because of the work of Christ. Storms will come but they will not overwhelm you because we take refuge in God. Do not focus on the storm but rather on God alone. There is not one problem that is too difficult for God to conquer. He is more powerful that anything in the known & unknown universe. As I've said many nights during this pandemic, ALL things are possible with Christ. Not some things but ALL things. We're going to get through this time & soon, very soon all of this will be behind us as a distant memory. I don't know about you, but I am ready for that! We live in difficult times, but when we place our trust in God, we are strong & WE SHALL SEE VICTORY! I swear to you, it's coming. Be vigilant & strong through the coming days. We're all in this together! Be safe! Be healthy! Be strong! Have hope! Have faith! Have prosperity! Have joy! May God bless all of you!

DAY 192
September 24th, 2020

Good evening my friends. As we close out Thursday, September 24th, 2020, as with each night, I pray this message finds you & your loved ones healthy, safe & well.

Dear Heavenly Father, I come to You tonight with a humble heart, Heavenly praise, love & thanksgiving. Thank You Father that even when we face an uncertain world that we can be certain in You. In the name of Jesus, I claim Psalm 91, Psalm 23, Psalm 46:10, Psalm 62:5-8, Psalm 116:7, 1 John 4:4, Isaiah 26:3, Psalm 25:20-21, Psalm 56:3, Psalm 61:2, 2 Chronicles 7:14, 2 Timothy 1:7, Jeremiah 30:17, Philippians 4:7-9, Romans 12:18, John 14:27, Isaiah 43:2, Isaiah 54:17 & Isaiah 53:5 over all of you & all you love. I pray for all the people, families, businesses & medical workers affected by the virus & violence that all of you will be given complete protection & abundantly blessed so you can be a blessing to many others. I pray you are surrounded by an impenetrable & spiritual hedge of protection that this virus & no evil can penetrate. I lift up & pray for our nation that You will restore peace to the people & our lands. I pray for all the sick & afflicted with this virus that they will be restored to full & complete health with no lasting effects. In the name of Jesus, I come to You as a child of the true everlasting Living God, covered in His Holy blood, protected by Jesus, sealed by the Holy Spirit & as a warrior in the army of Christ, I command, come against, rebuke & cast this virus, violence, the spirit of fear, hatred, all agents of evil & the devil away from you & your loved ones & by Your name & power they must leave now. BE GONE NOW! I thank You Father for our coming victory & deliverance & I claim all these things in Your Holy, powerful, majestic, everlasting & precious name I pray Lord Jesus, Amen!

Warriors! As we approach another weekend, please continue to be strong & vigilant. We live in dangerous & uncertain times & we can't let our guard down for even a moment. This season & difficult journey will end but until then we must do our part. All things are possible with Christ & only by His name & power will we be victorious & we shall prevail. And victorious we WILL BE! We continue to stand united & we will keep pressing forward no matter what comes against us! Storms will come but they will pass. Let not your hearts be troubled! Victory is coming everyone! We're all in this together! Be safe! Be healthy! Be strong! Have hope! Have faith! Have prosperity! Have joy! May God bless all of you!

DAY 193
September 25th, 2020

Good evening my friends. The weekend is here & as we close out Friday, September 25th, 2020, I pray this message finds you & your loved ones healthy, safe & well.

Dear Heavenly Father, I come to You tonight with Heavenly praise, love & thanksgiving. Thank You Father for this day that we may praise You, for the blessings You give us & for Your perfect peace. Father, please cover this nation with Your perfect calming hands & restore our nation & peace to the people. I lift up all the afflicted that they would be restored to full health. I pray for the development of a safe, powerful & effective vaccine. I pray for all the people, families, businesses & medical workers that they would be given full protection & abundantly blessed through these difficult & uncertain times. I pray for a spiritual hedge of protection to surround you & your loved ones that this virus & no evil can penetrate. In the name of Jesus, I claim Psalm 91, Psalm 23, Psalm 46:10, Psalm 62:5-8, Psalm 116:7, 1 John 4:4, Isaiah 26:3, Psalm 25:20-21, Psalm 56:3, Psalm 61:2, 2 Chronicles 7:14, 2 Timothy 1:7, Jeremiah 30:17, Philippians 4:7-9, Romans 12:18, John 14:27, Isaiah 43:2, Isaiah 54:17 & Isaiah 53:5 over all of you & all you love. In the name of Jesus, I come to You as a child of the true Living God, covered in His Holy blood, protected by Jesus, sealed by the Holy Spirit & as a warrior in the army of Christ, I command & cast this virus, violence, the spirit of fear, hatred, all agents of evil & the devil away from you & your loved ones & by Your name & power they must leave now. I thank You Father & I claim all these things in Your Holy, powerful, majestic, everlasting & precious name I pray Lord Jesus, Amen!

Warriors! This is a powerful weekend & tomorrow is a national & global day of prayer. Please take a moment & pray for our nation tomorrow. As we continue to press forward through these uncertain times, please know that there is an end to this & through the very power of Christ WE SHALL PREVAIL! I can't state that enough. Men will fail you but God will NEVER fail you. He hasn't brought you this far in your life to let go of you & your destiny now. Though these storms around us are powerful, they are no match for the power of God! No matter what comes! WE'VE ALREADY WON! No matter what happens! WE'VE ALREADY WON! No matter what we face! WE'VE!! ALREADY!! WON!! Victory is coming! Be safe! Be healthy! Be strong! Have hope! Have faith! Have prosperity! Have joy! May God bless all of you!

DAY 194
September 26th, 2020

Good evening my friends. This is a very important day as we close out Saturday, September 26th, 2020, I pray this message finds you & your loved ones healthy, safe & well on the day of the Return.

Dear Heavenly Father, I come to You tonight with Heavenly praise, love & thanksgiving. Thank You Father for this amazing day & that we can turn to You to always forgive our sins. It doesn't matter what we've done or how far we've fallen, You are always there ready to forgive us & welcome us home. Father, I pray for our nation tonight, that You'll forgive our sins & please restore our lands & bring peace back to its people. I pray that a hedge of protection surrounds all of you that NO evil can penetrate. I pray for all the people, families, businesses, our leaders & medical workers that you'll be abundantly blessed with protection, peace, prosperity, health, hope, faith, love, thanksgiving, wisdom, guidance & strength through these difficult days. I lift up & pray for the afflicted that they'll be restored to complete & full health & that a powerful, safe & effective vaccine will be swiftly developed. In the name of Jesus, I claim Psalm 91, Psalm 23, Psalm 46:10, Psalm 25:20-21, Psalm 56:3, Psalm 62:5-8, Psalm 116:7, 1 John 4:4, Isaiah 26:3, Psalm 61:2, 2 Chronicles 7:14, 2 Timothy 1:7, Jeremiah 30:17, Philippians 4:7-9, Romans 12:18, John 14:27, Isaiah 43:2, Isaiah 54:17 & Isaiah 53:5 over all of you & all you love. I pray for Your perfect will for us. In the name of Jesus, I come to You as a child of the true Living eternal God, covered in His Holy blood, protected by Jesus, sealed by the Holy Spirit & as a warrior in the army of Christ, I command, come against, rebuke & cast this virus, violence, the spirit of fear, hatred, all agents of evil & the devil away from you & your loved ones & by Your name & power they must leave now. I thank You Father for our coming victory & deliverance & I claim all these things in Your Holy, powerful, majestic, everlasting & precious name I pray Lord Jesus, Amen!

Warriors! We continue to press forward with everything we have! Today was truly an amazing day. It's the day that millions of Christians around the entire earth prayed for the restoration of nations, people & for forgiveness. I do believe that this day marks the day where everything will begin to turn around. We've been on this journey for a long time but I believe deep in my heart that things are going to start getting better. Thank You Father, Thank You Jesus, thank You to the creator of the universe. Tonight, after you're done reading this take a moment to just thank Jesus for our coming victory. We're going to get through this everyone! Let not your hearts be troubled! Victory is coming! Be safe! Be healthy! Be strong! Have hope! Have faith! Have prosperity! Have joy! May God bless all of you!

DAY 195
September 27th, 2020

Good evening my friends. It's the end of the weekend & as we close out Sunday, September 27th, 2020, I pray this message & prayer once again finds you & your loved ones healthy, safe & well.

Dear Heavenly Father, I come to You tonight with Heavenly praise, love & thanksgiving. Thank You Father for this day & thank You that in these uncertain times we can always be certain in You. Father, I pray for the afflicted that they'd be restored to complete & full health & that this pandemic will soon be over. I pray for a hedge of protection to surround you & your loved ones that blocks any attack, the virus, or any form of evil. In the name of Jesus, I claim Psalm 91, Psalm 23, Psalm 46:10, Psalm 25:20-21, Psalm 56:3, Psalm 62:5-8, Psalm 116:7, 1 John 4:4, Isaiah 26:3, Psalm 61:2, 2 Chronicles 7:14, 2 Timothy 1:7, Jeremiah 30:17, Philippians 4:7-9, Romans 12:18, John 14:27, Isaiah 43:2, Isaiah 54:17 & Isaiah 53:5 over all of you & all you love. I pray for all the people, families, businesses & medical workers that they would be given complete protection & fully & abundantly blessed through these uncertain & difficult days we face. I lift up this nation before You Father I pray that You will restore our lands & bring peace back to the people. In the name of Jesus, I come to You as a child of the Living God, covered completely in His Holy blood, protected by Jesus, sealed by the Holy Spirit & as a warrior of Christ, I command & cast this virus, violence, the spirit of fear, all agents of evil & the devil away from you & your loved ones & by Your name & power they must leave now. BE GONE! I thank You Father for our coming deliverance & I claim all these things in Your Holy, powerful, majestic, everlasting & precious name I pray Lord Jesus, Amen!

Warriors! As we enter a brand new week, there will be brand new opportunities for us. We continue to press forward through whatever comes our way because of the power of Christ. I want to mention tonight, if you are feeling alone or afraid, please know that it's going to be okay. When everyone else fails you, Jesus will never fail you, never leave you, never forsake you & He's there anytime you need Him. He wants us to rely on Him & cast our burdens on Him. When we do & trust Him, He gives us perfect peace that surpasses all understanding. So today if you're in need of hope for tomorrow. It's available right now. This difficult season will pass & through Christ we shall prevail. Victory is coming! Be safe! Be healthy! Be strong! Have hope! Have faith! Have prosperity! Have joy! May God bless all of you!

DAY 196
September 28th, 2020

Good evening my friends. It's a brand new week & as we close out Monday, September 28th, 2020, I hope & pray this message finds you & your loved ones healthy, safe & well.

Dear Heavenly Father, I come to You tonight with a humble heart, Heavenly praise, love & thanksgiving. Thank You Father that even at our worst moments You still love us unconditionally & for our blessings that You've given us. In the name of Jesus, I claim Psalm 91, Psalm 23, Psalm 46:10, Psalm 25:20-21, Psalm 56:3, Psalm 61:2, Psalm 62:5-8, Psalm 116:7, 1 John 4:4, 2 Chronicles 7:14, 2

Timothy 1:7, Jeremiah 30:17, Philippians 4:7-9, Romans 12:18, John 14:27, Isaiah 26:3, Isaiah 43:2, Isaiah 53:5 & Isaiah 54:17 over all of you & all you love. Father, I lift up to You all the sick & afflicted with the virus & pray that You'll restore all of them to complete & full health. I pray for the development of a powerful, safe, & effective vaccine. I pray that all of you are surrounded by an impenetrable & spiritual hedge of protection that no evil pass through. I pray for all the people, families, businesses & medical workers that they'd be abundantly blessed with protection, peace, prosperity, health, hope, faith, love, thanksgiving, wisdom, guidance & strength through these difficult times. I pray for this nation & I pray that You'll restore our lands & bring peace back to the people. In the name of Jesus, I come to You as a child of the true Living God, covered in His Holy blood, protected by Jesus, sealed by the Holy Spirit & as a warrior of Christ, I command & cast this virus, violence, the spirit of fear, all agents of evil & the devil away from you & your loved ones & by Your name & power they must leave now. I thank You Father for our coming victory & I claim all these things in Your Holy, powerful, majestic, everlasting & precious name I pray Lord Jesus, Amen!

Warriors! Tonight, please take a moment & pray for someone in need & please pray for our nation. Every day of 2020 seems to bring with it something unprecedented but know that this will come to a close soon. We must hold on & continue to be strong & vigilant. We'll make it through this time through the power & might of Christ Jesus. It's been difficult & I'm sure like myself, you're all exhausted & frustrated, but we're going to make it through, we just need to keep pressing forward no matter what happens. Storms will come but they'll not overtake you! Stay focused on God & not the storm! Trust me when I say, Victory is coming! Be safe! Be healthy! Be strong! Have hope! Have faith! Have prosperity! Have joy! May God bless all of you!

DAY 197
September 29th, 2020

Good evening my friends. It's a brand new week & as we close out Tuesday, September 29th, 2020, I hope this message finds you & your loved ones healthy, safe & well.

Dear Heavenly Father, I come to You tonight with Heavenly praise, love & thanksgiving. Thank You Father that no matter what we face, You are still on the Throne & in control. I pray for all the afflicted that they will be completely & fully restored to full health & for the development of a powerful & effective vaccine. I pray for a hedge of protection to surround you & your loved ones. I pray for our nation that You'll lay Your calming hands over every inch of this country & restore our lands & bring peace back to the people. In the name of Jesus, I claim Psalm 91, Psalm 23, Psalm 46:10, Psalm 25:20-21, Psalm 56:3, Psalm 61:2, Psalm 62:5-8, Psalm 116:7, 1 John 4:4, 2 Chronicles 7:14, 2 Timothy 1:7, Jeremiah 30:17, Philippians 4:7-9, Romans 12:18, John 14:27, Isaiah 26:3, Isaiah 43:2, Isaiah 53:5 & Isaiah 54:17 over all of you & all you love. I pray for all the people, families, businesses and medical workers that they will be given full protection and completely & abundantly blessed through this difficult time. In the name of Jesus, I come to You as a child of the true Living God, covered in His blood, protected by Jesus, sealed by the Holy Spirit & as a warrior of Christ, I command & cast this virus, violence, the spirit of fear, all agents of evil & the devil away from you & your loved ones & by Your name & power they must leave now. I thank You Father & I claim all these things in Your Holy, powerful, majestic, everlasting & precious name I pray Lord Jesus, Amen!

Warriors! We're approaching the middle of the week & tonight we draw a line in the sand tonight & we must stand firm & stand fast against the attacks & lies of the enemy. Know this, that no matter how intense the storm that comes, you will weather it because of the work of Christ. All things are possible with Christ. There isn't anything that is more powerful than God. We must hold on and have faith because this season is going to pass us by. We're going to make it through this everyone! Let not your heart be troubled! Victory is coming! Be safe! Be healthy! Be strong! Have hope! Have faith! Have prosperity! Have joy! May God bless all of you!

DAY 198
September 30th, 2020

Good evening my friends. As we close out Wednesday, September 30th, 2020, I hope this message once again finds you & your loved ones healthy, safe & well.

Dear Heavenly Father, I come to You tonight with a humble heart, Heavenly praise, love & thanksgiving. Thank You Father that no matter what we face on a day to day basis that You're always our constant, source of wisdom & guidance & that You will never leave or forsake us ever. In the name of Jesus, I claim Psalm 91, Psalm 23, Psalm 46:10, Psalm 25:20-21, Psalm 56:3, Psalm 61:2, Psalm 62:5-8, Psalm 116:7, 1 John 4:4, 2 Chronicles 7:14, 2 Timothy 1:7, Jeremiah 30:17, Philippians 4:7-9, Romans 12:18, John 14:27, Isaiah 26:3, Isaiah 43:2, Isaiah 53:5 & Isaiah 54:17 over all of you & all you love. I pray that you & your loved ones are completely surrounded by a hedge of protection. I lift up & pray for all the afflicted by the virus & pray for their complete restoration to full health. I pray for the development of a powerful, safe & effective vaccine & that this virus will be completely eradicated. I pray for all the families, people, businesses & medial workers that you'll be abundantly blessed with protection, prosperity, peace, faith, health, hope, love, guidance, wisdom & strength so you can be a blessing to many others. I lift up our nation tonight & pray that You will restore our lands & please return peace to the people. In the name of Jesus, I come to You as a child of the Living God, covered in His blood, protected by Jesus, sealed by the Holy Spirit & as a warrior of Christ, I command & cast this virus, violence, the spirit of fear, all agents of evil & the devil away from you & your loved ones. Greater is He who is in us than he who is in the world & if we resist the devil he must flee from us because of the name & authority of God. I thank You Father & I claim all these things in Your Holy, powerful, majestic, everlasting & precious name I pray Lord Jesus, Amen!

Warriors! I want to start with this tonight. Let not your hearts be troubled! Like many of you out there, myself included, we're all frustrated, angry, depressed & ready for everything to go back to normal. It's like we're running a race & we have to have the endurance & perseverance to cross the finish line. It's not easy, it's tough & like all runners you eventually feel like you've hit a wall. But what runners have to do is press forward through the wall. With our current situation, we all have to press forward through the wall. This time will end & this season will pass but we must hold on & have faith that God will bring us through to deliverance & victory. This journey will come to an end & life will return to normal. Shout this with me. OUR GOD IS GOD! Victory is coming! Be safe! Be healthy! Be strong! Have hope! Have faith! Have prosperity! Have joy! May God bless all of you!

DAY 199
October 1st, 2020

Good evening my friends. It's a new month & as we close out Thursday, October 1st, 2020, I pray this message finds you & your loved ones healthy, safe & well.

Dear Heavenly Father, I come to You tonight with Heavenly praise, love & thanksgiving. Thank You Father that when we're in distress we can always take refuge in You & be blessed with peace that surpasses all understanding. Father, I pray for our nation that You will please restore our lands & restore peace to our people. I pray for all the afflicted that they will be completely restored to full health. I pray that you & your loved ones will be surrounded by a spiritual & impenetrable hedge of protection from all evil. I pray for all the people, families, businesses & medical workers that you will be completely & abundantly blessed with protection, peace, prosperity, faith, hope, health, love, wisdom, guidance & strength. In the name of Jesus, I claim Psalm 91, Psalm 23, Psalm 25:20-21, Psalm 46:10, Psalm 56:3, Psalm 61:2, Psalm 62:5-8, Psalm 116:7, 1 John 4:4, 2 Chronicles 7:14, 2 Timothy 1:7, Jeremiah 30:17, Philippians 4:7-9, Romans 12:18, John 14:27, Isaiah 26:3, Isaiah 43:2, Isaiah 53:5 & Isaiah 54:17 over all of you & all you love. In the name of Jesus, I come to You as a child of the Living God, covered in His blood, protected by Jesus, sealed by the Holy Spirit & as a warrior of Christ, I command, come against & cast this virus, violence, the spirit of fear, hatred, all agents of evil & the devil away from you & your loved ones. By the Holy name of Christ, this evil must flee now! I thank You Father & I claim all these things in Your Holy, powerful, majestic, everlasting & precious name I pray Lord Jesus, Amen!

Warriors! It's a new month & we're starting to approach the end of 2020. This year has flown by & is truly one for the history books. And we still have 3 months to go... But despite everything that has happened in this year, God is still in control & on the throne. He is outside of time, our understanding & everything truly happens for a reason & by His purpose. This time will pass but we must continue to be strong & vigilant. The devil knows his time is short in this world

& has been unleashing destruction & fear everywhere. I do not know one person who hasn't been going through something. But it's going to all be okay because of the victory in Christ! Please tonight say a prayer for someone in need & if they don't know Jesus, there's no better time to discuss it. Let not your hearts be troubled. Victory is coming! Be safe! Be healthy! Be strong! Have hope! Have faith! Have prosperity! Have joy! May God bless all of you!

DAY 200
October 2nd, 2020

Good evening my friends. The weekend is here & as we close out Friday, October 2nd, 2020, I pray this message finds you & your loved ones healthy, safe & well.

Dear Heavenly Father, I come to You tonight with a humble heart, Heavenly praise, love & thanksgiving. Thank You Father that though the storms will come, You are always a shield of protection & refuge against the attacks of the enemy. Father, I pray for all the families, people, businesses, our leaders & medical workers, that You'll abundantly bless them & give them protection to get through these difficult & uncertain times. I pray for an impenetrable hedge of protection that completely surrounds you & your loved ones that no evil can pass through. I lift up the sick & the afflicted that You will restore them to complete & full health, that this virus is eradicated & that a safe, powerful & effective vaccine is swiftly developed. Father, as I pray tonight & as we're a very divided people in a very politically charged environment, as people & Christians, there are times to set all of that aside & pray for each other no matter what side of the aisle we're on. In the name of Jesus, I pray for the healing of President Trump, the First Lady, for the protection of Presidential candidate Joe Biden & the healing & restoration of all our senators, congressmen, governors, mayors, all our first responders & all our leaders across this nation who have been afflicted by this horrible virus. In the name of Jesus, I claim Psalm 91, Psalm 23, Psalm 25:20-21, Psalm 46:10, Psalm 56:3, Psalm 61:2, Psalm 62:5-8, Psalm 116:7, 1 John 4:4, 2 Chronicles 7:14, 2 Timothy 1:7, Jeremiah 30:17, Philippians 4:7-9, Romans 12:18, John 14:27, Isaiah 26:3, Isaiah 43:2, Isaiah 53:5 &

Isaiah 54:17 over all of you & all you love. I pray for Your calming hands to restore our lands & peace to the people. In the name of Jesus, I come to You as a child of the eternal Living God, covered in His blood, protected by Jesus, sealed by the Holy Spirit & as a warrior of Christ, I command, come against & cast this virus, violence, the spirit of fear, hatred, all agents of evil & the devil away from you & your loved ones. By the Holy name of Christ, this evil must flee now! BE GONE! I thank You Father & I claim all these things in Your Holy, powerful, majestic, everlasting & precious name I pray Lord Jesus, Amen!

Warriors! The weekend is here & we once again WILL continue to press forward through these difficult times & adversity. Our Lord & Savior is in command, in complete control & we WILL make it through all of this. Tonight, take a moment to pray for someone who is hurting & in need. I know how frustrated, afraid & angry all of us are in these uncertain times but one thing we all need to do is learn to love each other again. We've lost so much this year, but that doesn't mean that tomorrow will come at more cost to us. As we take a stand tonight, join with me & shout to the true God of the universe, who created everything from the beginning of time & is the ONLY ONE Who has the power to turn everything around. THIS SEASON WILL PASS & GREAT TIMES ARE COMING! DELIVERANCE IS COMING! VICTORY!! IS!! COMING!! Be safe! Be healthy! Be strong! Have hope! Have faith! Have prosperity! Have joy! May God bless all of you!

DAY 201
October 3rd, 2020

Good evening my friends. It's a wonderful evening tonight & as we close out Saturday, October 3rd, 2020, I pray that this message finds you & your loved ones healthy, safe & well.

Dear Heavenly Father, I come to You tonight with a Heavenly praise, love & thanksgiving. Thank You Father for all the blessings You've given us, for Your unconditional love & for guiding us each day. Father, I pray that You'll place Your calming hands on this nation &

please restore our lands & bring peace back to the people. I pray for a spiritual hedge of protection that completely surrounds you & your loved ones that no evil of any kind can pass through. I lift up & pray for all the afflicted that they'll be completely restored to full health, for the development of a vaccine & for the complete eradication of this virus from the Earth. I pray for all the families, people, our leaders, first responders, businesses & medical workers that all of you will be abundantly blessed with protection, peace, prosperity, hope, health, love, faith, wisdom, guidance & strength through these difficult days. I pray for the continued healing, restoration & protection of all of our leaders affected by this virus. In the name of Jesus, I claim Psalm 91, Psalm 23, Psalm 25:20-21, Psalm 46:10, Psalm 56:3, Psalm 61:2, Psalm 62:5-8, Psalm 116:7, 1 John 4:4, 2 Chronicles 7:14, 2 Timothy 1:7, Jeremiah 30:17, Philippians 4:7-9, Romans 12:18, John 14:27, Isaiah 26:3, Isaiah 43:2, Isaiah 53:5 & Isaiah 54:17 over all of you & all you love. In the name of Jesus, I come to You as a child of the true Living God, covered in His Holy blood, protected by Jesus, sealed by the Holy Spirit & as a warrior of Christ, I command, come against, rebuke & cast this virus, violence, the spirit of fear, hatred, all agents of evil & the devil away from you & your loved ones. THEY MUST LEAVE NOW! I thank You Father & I claim all these things in Your Holy, powerful, majestic, everlasting & precious name I pray Lord Jesus, Amen!

Warriors! It's the middle of the weekend & we're continuing forward. We will not be stopped, deterred or falter in our course guided by Christ. Always know, when we're in His will, even when things look at their darkest, Jesus always comes through & on time in the most perfect way that we couldn't have ever thought possible. And this is something to know, when we go through difficult times & adversity, its normal to want to be out of that situation as fast as possible. But sometimes, we need that adversity & situation, bad as it may be, to grow into the person we're meant to be. It's never fun, it's not comfortable, but looking back on my life at things I've had to face along the way, sometimes devastating, have crafted me into who I am & that is what is most important. God is more concerned about crafting you into the being He has destined you for, rather than taking away something that in the end will give you strength in the areas that you need to be strong in. So know that even through the storm,

God is in control, aware of what you are going through & will deliver you on the other side of the problem stronger than when you went in. We're going to get through this time too everyone! Be safe! Be healthy! Be strong! Have hope! Have faith! Have prosperity! Have joy! May God bless all of you!

DAY 202
October 4th, 2020

Good evening my friends. As we're on the eve of a new week & we're closing out Sunday, October 4th, 2020, I pray that this message finds you & your loved ones healthy, safe & well.

Dear Heavenly Father, I come to You tonight with a Heavenly praise, love & thanksgiving. Thank You Father for sending Your only Son that we may have eternal life through Christ when we accept Him as our Lord & Savior. In the name of Jesus, I claim Psalm 91, Psalm 23, Psalm 25:20-21, Psalm 46:10, Psalm 56:3, Psalm 61:2, Psalm 62:5-8, Psalm 116:7, 1 John 4:4, 2 Chronicles 7:14, 2 Timothy 1:7, Jeremiah 30:17, Philippians 4:7-9, Romans 12:18, John 14:27, Isaiah 26:3, Isaiah 43:2, Isaiah 53:5 & Isaiah 54:17 over all of you & all your loved ones. I pray for a continual hedge of protection to surround you and your loved ones. I lift up and pray for all the afflicted with the virus that they'd be completely restored to complete and full health. I pray for a powerful, safe & effective vaccine to be swiftly developed. I pray for all the people, families, businesses and medical workers across this nation that they would all be abundantly blessed with protection, prosperity, peace, faith, health, hope, love, thanksgiving, wisdom, guidance and strength to get through these difficult days and to be a blessing to many others. Father I pray for this nation that You'd please cover every single inch of this country and please restore our lands and restore peace to the people. In the name of Jesus, I come to You tonight as a child of the true Living God, covered in His Holy blood, protected by Jesus, sealed by the Holy Spirit and as a warrior of Christ, I command and cast this virus, violence, the spirit of fear, hatred, anxiety, anger, all agents of evil and the devil away from you and your loved ones. THEY MUST GO NOW! I thank You Father and I claim all these things in Your Holy, powerful, majestic, everlasting and precious name I pray Lord Jesus, Amen!

Warriors! As we approach a new week, stand with strength & confidence that Your Lord has everything in control. I know it's been a long time & we're all ready for the pandemic to be over & life to return to normal. I know there are countless people hurting across this nation & I ask everyone here tonight to pray for them because we've all been there this past year. No matter what comes against you know that no weapon formed against you shall prosper (Isaiah 54:17) & we ARE going to get through this difficult journey. One day soon, when this is completely over, there will be books, films, music, documentaries, etc about this time in history & you'll be able to say you lived through this time & you can shout to the heavens that YOU MADE IT! With Christ, ALL things are possible & we're gonna get through this! Be safe! Be healthy! Be strong! Have hope! Have faith! Have prosperity! Have joy! May God bless all of you!

DAY 203
October 5th, 2020

Good evening my friends. As we start a new week, we're closing out Monday, October 5th, 2020 & as with each night, I pray that this message finds you & your loved ones healthy, safe & well.

Dear Heavenly Father, I come to You with Heavenly praise, love & thanksgiving. Thank You Father for the blessings You've given us, for your unconditional love & peace that surpasses all understanding. Father, I pray for our nation tonight that You'll restore our lands & restore peace to the people. I lift up & pray for all that have been afflicted by the virus that they'd be fully restored to complete health & for the swift development of a powerful & effective vaccine. In the name of Jesus, I claim Psalm 91, Psalm 23, Psalm 25:20-21, Psalm 46:10, Psalm 56:3, Psalm 61:2, Psalm 62:5-8, Psalm 116:7, 1 John 4:4, 2 Chronicles 7:14, 2 Timothy 1:7, Jeremiah 30:17, Philippians 4:7-9, Romans 12:18, John 14:27, Isaiah 26:3, Isaiah 43:2, Isaiah 53:5 & Isaiah 54:17 over all of you & all your loved ones. I pray that you & all you love are completely surrounded by an impenetrable hedge of protection that shields you from all evil. I pray for all the families, people, businesses & medial workers that they'd be given full protection & abundantly blessed through these uncertain times. In the name of Jesus, I come to You tonight as a child of the true Living eternal God, covered in His Holy blood, protected by Jesus, sealed by the Holy Spirit & as a warrior of Christ, I command, come against, rebuke & cast this virus, violence, the spirit of fear, hatred, all agents of evil & the devil away from you & your loved ones. Greater is He who is in us that he who is in the world & as it's written through the name & power of Christ, if we resist the devil he MUST flee. I thank You Father & I claim all these things in Your Holy, powerful, majestic, everlasting & precious name I pray Lord Jesus, Amen!

Warriors! It's a new week & it's full of new possibilities. We again take another step forward & right now, we're 24 hours closer to victory than yesterday & tomorrow we'll be even closer. I know it's a slow climb, but through the power of Jesus Christ, Who has everything in complete & total control, we shall prevail. Trust in the Lord with all your heart & lean not on your own understanding. (Proverbs 3:5) As I say every night & I can't stress this enough. This difficult season will come to an end & life will return to normal. We are so very close to it, I can feel it. But as we wait for everything to go back to normal we must continue to be strong & vigilant. Our deliverance & victory are near! Let not your heart be troubled! Be safe! Be healthy! Be strong! Have hope! Have faith! Have prosperity! Have joy! May God bless all of you!

DAY 204
October 6th, 2020

Good evening my friends. As we're closing out Tuesday, October 6th, 2020 & I hope & pray that this message finds you & your loved ones healthy, safe & well.

Dear Heavenly Father, I come to You with Heavenly praise, love & thanksgiving. Thank You Father that You sent Your only Son to die so that we may have eternal life. I lift up & pray for all the afflicted with this virus that they'd be fully restored to complete health. I pray for our nation that You would place Your calming hands on this country & please restore our lands & peace to the people. Father I pray for all the families, people, businesses, our leaders, first responders & medical workers that You would abundantly bless them with protection, prosperity, peace, faith, health, hope, love, wisdom, guidance & strength through these uncertain times. In the name of Jesus, I claim Psalm 91, Psalm 23, Psalm 25:20-21, Psalm 46:10, Psalm 56:3, Psalm 61:2, Psalm 62:5-8, Psalm 116:7, 1 John 4:4, 2 Chronicles 7:14, 2 Timothy 1:7, Jeremiah 30:17, Philippians 4:7-9, Romans 12:18, John 14:27, Isaiah 26:3, Isaiah 43:2, Isaiah 53:5 & Isaiah 54:17 over all of you & all your loved ones. I pray that you & your loved ones are completely surrounded by a hedge of protection. In the name of Jesus, I come to You tonight as a child of the true Living God, covered in His blood, protected by Jesus, sealed by the Holy Spirit & as a warrior of Christ, I command & cast this virus, violence, the spirit of fear, all agents of evil & the devil away from you & your loved ones to the farthest ends of the earth. By His name & power they MUST leave now & not return. I thank You Father & I claim all these things in Your Holy, powerful, majestic, everlasting & precious name I pray Lord Jesus, Amen!

Warriors! Tonight, as we press onward through the storms we face, please take a moment & pray for someone in need again. When God's people pray the devil shudders & mountains are moved. Each of you is truly a warrior, equipped with real power through the Name & power of Christ. As it is written in (Matthew 17:20) 20 He replied, "Because you have so little faith. Truly I tell you, if you have faith as small as a mustard seed, you can say to this mountain, 'Move from here to there,' and it will move. Nothing will be impossible for you." Remember all things are possible with God. We're going to get through this difficult time & be stronger than ever before. I know it's been tough & will be for a time, but this season of pain will end & be replaced with total joy! Let not your heart be troubled! Be safe! Be healthy! Be strong! Have hope! Have faith! Have prosperity! Have joy! May God bless all of you!

DAY 205
October 7th, 2020

Good evening my friends. It's the middle of the week & we're closing out Wednesday, October 7th, 2020 & I pray that this message finds you & your loved ones healthy, safe & well.

Dear Heavenly Father, I come to You with Heavenly praise, love & thanksgiving. Thank You Father for guiding us along this difficult journey. In the name of Jesus, I claim Psalm 91, Psalm 23, Psalm 25:20-21, Psalm 46:10, Psalm 56:3, Psalm 61:2, Psalm 62:5-8, Psalm 116:7, 1 John 4:4, 2 Chronicles 7:14, 2 Timothy 1:7, Jeremiah 30:17, Philippians 4:7-9, Romans 12:18, John 14:27, Isaiah 26:3, Isaiah 43:2, Isaiah 53:5 & Isaiah 54:17 over all of you & all your loved ones. I lift up & pray for all the afflicted that they would be completely restored to full health, that this virus will be fully eradicated & for the swift development of a safe & powerful vaccine. I pray for all the people, families, businesses & medical workers that they would be given full protection & abundantly blessed through these difficult times. I pray that all of you will be surrounded by an impenetrable hedge of protection. I pray that You Father, would place Your calming hands on this nation and restore our lands & bring peace to the people. In the name of Jesus, I come to You tonight as a child of the true Living God, covered in His blood, protected by Jesus, sealed by the Holy Spirit & as a warrior of Christ, I command & cast this virus, violence, the spirit of fear, all agents of evil & the devil away from you & your loved ones. By His name and power they MUST GO now & not return. I thank You Father and I claim all these things in Your Holy, powerful, majestic, everlasting & precious name I pray Lord Jesus, Amen!

Warriors! Do not focus on the storms that surround us but take refuge under the wings of Christ. The phrase that keeps resonating in my mind is Psalm 46:10 "Be still & know that I am God" I know that we're all dealing with unprecedented & uncertain times but I know one thing that we can be certain in & that is the Name, power & love of Jesus Christ. We've all been afraid, frustrated & worried this year, but this storm will pass & this season will end. All things are possible with Christ & He is in total control & on the Throne! Stand firm, stand tall stand ready! We're all in this together! Let not your heart be troubled! Be safe! Be healthy! Be strong! Have hope! Have faith! Have prosperity! Have joy! May God bless all of you!

DAY 206
October 8th, 2020

Good evening my friends. As its Friday eve, we're closing out Thursday, October 8th, 2020 & I pray that this message finds you & your loved ones healthy, safe & well.

Dear Heavenly Father, I come to You with a humble heart, Heavenly praise, love & thanksgiving. Thank You Lord Father for the peace You give us that surpasses all understanding, for the wisdom You freely give & for Your Son who died so that we may have eternal life. Father, I lift up & pray for all the afflicted that they'd be completely healed from this virus & for the development of powerful & safe vaccine so no one needs to ever suffer from this sickness again. In the name of Jesus, I claim Psalm 91, Psalm 23, Psalm 25:20-21, Psalm 46:10, Psalm 56:3, Psalm 61:2, Psalm 62:5-8, Psalm 116:7, 1 John 4:4, 2 Chronicles 7:14, 2 Timothy 1:7, Jeremiah 30:17, Philippians 4:7-9, Romans 12:18, John 14:27, Isaiah 26:3, Isaiah 43:2, Isaiah 53:5 & Isaiah 54:17 over all of you & all your loved ones. I pray for Your perfect calming hands to be placed on this nation & restore our lands & bring peace to its people. I pray for all the people, the families, the businesses & all the medical workers that they'd be abundantly blessed with protection, peace, prosperity, faith, health, hope, love, wisdom, guidance & supernatural strength to get through each day of these uncertain times. I pray that all of you will be surrounded by an impenetrable hedge of protection that no evil can pass through. In the name of Jesus, as a child of the true Living God, covered in His Holy blood, protected by Jesus, sealed by the Holy Spirit & as a warrior in the army of Christ, I command, come against, rebuke & cast this virus, violence, the spirit of fear, hatred, anger, anxiety, all agents of evil & the devil away from you & your loved ones. I thank You Father & I claim all these things in Your Holy, powerful, majestic, everlasting & precious name I pray Lord Jesus, Amen!

Warriors! We're coming up on the weekend & it's amazing how fast this month is already going by. And in that, it's just a matter of time before this difficult season will pass by. Just think how far we've come since this all started. It seems like forever ago, but as we've stayed vigilant & strong we've continued to press forward to victory no matter what has come against us. It's not been easy at all but as warriors, we haven't backed down for even a moment. Our Lord & Savior Jesus Christ has guided us along this journey & despite the storms we continue forward to deliverance & victory. With Christ all things are possible & through the power of Jesus, WE SHALL PREVAIL! THIS TOO SHALL PASS! Let not your heart be troubled! Be safe! Be healthy! Be strong! Have hope! Have faith! Have prosperity! Have joy! May God bless all of you!

DAY 207
October 9th, 2020

Good evening my friends. The weekend has finally arrived, it was a beautiful fall day out & we're closing out Friday, October 9th, 2020 & as with each night, I pray that this message finds you & your loved ones healthy, safe & well.

Dear Heavenly Father, I come to You with Heavenly praise, love & thanksgiving. Thank You Lord Father that despite the storms we face, You're in complete control & on the Throne. In the name of Jesus, I claim Psalm 91, Psalm 23, Psalm 25:20-21, Psalm 46:10, Psalm 56:3, Psalm 61:2, Psalm 62:5-8, Psalm 116:7, Joel 2:25-26, 1 John 4:4, 2 Chronicles 7:14, 2 Timothy 1:7, Jeremiah 30:17, Philippians 4:7-9, Romans 12:18, John 14:27, Isaiah 26:3, Isaiah 43:2, Isaiah 53:5 & Isaiah 54:17 over all of you & all your loved ones. I pray for all the afflicted with the virus, that they'd be completely restored to full health & for the development of powerful & safe vaccine. I pray for our country that Your calming hands would be placed on this nation & restore our lands & bring peace to the people. I pray for all the people, the families, the businesses, our leaders & all the medical workers that they'd be given complete & full protection from the virus & evil and that they'd be abundantly blessed through these difficult & uncertain times so that they would know that You are the source. I pray that all of you & your families will be surrounded by an impenetrable hedge of protection that no evil can pass through. In the name of Jesus, as a child of the true Living God, covered in His Holy blood, protected by Jesus, sealed by the Holy Spirit & as a warrior of Christ, I command & cast this virus, violence, the spirit of fear, hatred, anger, anxiety, all agents of evil & the devil away from you & all your loved ones. I thank You Father & I claim all these things in Your Holy, powerful, majestic, everlasting, eternal & precious name I pray Lord Jesus, Amen!

Warriors! The weekend is here & as you read this tonight, please say for a prayer for all those on our Gulf coast as hurricane Delta makes landfall. We pressed forward again today & took another step forward. Each & every day is another day closer to victory & the end of this season. But as each day passes, just know how far we've come & how God has provided. He knows what You need before you even ask & though these times are difficult, through the very power of Christ. WE SHALL PREVAIL! We WILL NOT go quietly into the night & this dark valley will soon open into light & victory. Don't be dismayed but hold on with all you've got. We're going to get through this time! Let not your heart be troubled! Be safe! Be healthy! Be strong! Have hope! Have faith! Have prosperity! Have joy! May God bless all of you!

DAY 208
October 10th, 2020

Good evening my friends. It's the middle of the weekend & we're closing out Saturday, October 10th, 2020 & I pray that this message finds you & your loved ones healthy, safe & well. Let's begin tonight.

Dear Heavenly Father, I come to You with Heavenly praise, love & thanksgiving. Thank You Lord Father that You love us so much that even when we stray, even when we have gone to a point where we feel there is no return, that You still are always there ready to welcome us back & forgive us. In the name of Jesus, I claim Psalm 91, Psalm 23, Psalm 25:20-21, Psalm 46:10, Psalm 56:3, Psalm 61:2, Psalm

62:5-8, Psalm 116:7, Joel 2:25-26, 1 John 4:4, 2 Chronicles 7:14, 2 Timothy 1:7, Jeremiah 30:17, Philippians 4:7-9, Romans 12:18, John 14:27, Isaiah 26:3, Isaiah 43:2, Isaiah 53:5 & Isaiah 54:17 over all of you & all your loved ones. I pray that you & your loved ones will be completely surrounded by an impenetrable hedge of protection that no evil can pass through. I pray for all the afflicted, that they'd be completely restored to full & complete health, for the eradication of this virus & for the swift development of powerful & safe vaccine. I pray for our country that You would place Your perfect calming hands on this nation & restore our lands & bring peace to the people. I pray for all the people, the families, the businesses, our leaders & all the medical workers that they'd be abundantly blessed with protection, prosperity, peace, faith, hope, health, love, thanksgiving, wisdom, guidance & strength through these difficult times. In the name of Jesus, as a child of the true Living God, covered in His Holy blood, protected by Jesus, sealed by the Holy Spirit & as a warrior of Christ, I command, come against, rebuke & cast this virus, violence, the spirit of fear, hatred, anxiety, all agents of evil & the devil away from you & all your loved ones. I thank You Father & I claim all these things in Your Holy, powerful, majestic, everlasting, eternal & precious name I pray Lord Jesus, Amen!

Warriors! Wherever you are in the world this very moment, know that your prayers have been heard by God & He will perfect that which concerns you. There is real power in prayer. Think about this for a moment, prayer is truly the ability to talk directly to the Creator of the universe & not only that but that He hears what you are praying for. When God's people pray, the devil shudders & prayer is something that we sometimes go to as a last resort, but the time to pray is the very first thing you should do in any situation. With Christ ALL things are possible & He WILL provide your needs during these difficult times. Through the name & power of Christ VICTORY IS COMING! Let not your heart be troubled! Be safe! Be healthy! Be strong! Have hope! Have faith! Have prosperity! Have joy! May God bless all of you!

DAY 209
October 11th, 2020

Good evening my friends. We're upon a brand new week & as we're closing out Sunday, October 11th, 2020, as with each night, I pray that this message finds you & your loved ones healthy, safe & well.

Dear Heavenly Father, I come to You with a humble heart, Heavenly praise, love & thanksgiving. Thank You Lord Father that through the daily storms that come against us, that You have the final say & that we can take refuge with You. I pray that you & all your loved ones will be surrounded by a spiritual & impenetrable hedge of protection that no evil can pass through. I pray for our nation that You would place Your perfect calming hands on every single inch & restore our lands & bring peace back to the people. I pray for all the sick & afflicted, that they'd be completely restored to full health & for the swift development of a safe, powerful & effective vaccine. In the name of Jesus, I claim Psalm 91, Psalm 23, Psalm 25:20-21, Psalm 46:10, Psalm 56:3, Psalm 61:2, Psalm 62:5-8, Psalm 116:7, Joel 2:25-26, 1 John 4:4, 2 Chronicles 7:14, 2 Timothy 1:7, Jeremiah 30:17, Philippians 4:7-9, Romans 12:18, John 14:27, Isaiah 26:3, Isaiah 43:2, Isaiah 53:5 & Isaiah 54:17 over all of you & all your loved ones. I pray for all the people, the families, the businesses & all the medical workers that they'd be blessed with protection & abundantly blessed through these uncertain & difficult times. In the name of Jesus, as a child of the eternal true Living God, covered in His Holy blood, protected by Jesus, sealed by the Holy Spirit & as a warrior of Christ, I command, come against, rebuke & cast this virus, violence, the spirit of fear, hatred, anxiety, all agents of evil & the devil away from you & all your loved ones. They have no other option but to leave this very moment. I thank You Father & I claim all these things in Your Holy, powerful, majestic, everlasting, eternal & precious name I pray Lord Jesus, Amen!

Warriors! We're upon a new week & despite everything that's going on all around us we're another day closer to victory. I know how tired & frustrated all of you are, myself included, but do not rely on your own understanding but wait patiently on the Lord. I know how hard that is to do but we have to continue to hold on. I can't tell you how excited I am for the day we no longer need the masks, that we no longer need social distancing, that we no longer need to live in fear & paranoia of those around us. I'm a people person & love a good welcome hug & I have really missed that over the past year. But I find joy in that when we can, it will be that much better. Truly all things are possible with Christ & He will deliver us to victory. We just have to stay strong. We can all do this & we have each other to back us all up. Let not your heart be troubled! Be safe! Be healthy! Be strong! Have hope! Have faith! Have prosperity! Have joy! May God bless all of you!

DAY 210
October 12th, 2020

Good evening my friends. The new week is here & we're closing out Monday, October 12th, 2020 & I pray that this message finds you & your loved ones healthy, safe & well.

Dear Heavenly Father, I come to You with Heavenly praise, love & thanksgiving. Thank You Lord Father that You sent Your only Son to die on the cross so that we may be saved & have eternal life through Christ. I pray for all the afflicted around this nation & the world, that they'd be completely restored to full health, for the swift development of a safe, powerful & effective vaccine & for the complete eradication of this virus from the earth. I pray for our country that You would please restore our lands & bring peace back to the people. I pray that you & all your loved ones will be completely surrounded by a spiritual & impenetrable hedge of protection where you are only an observer & that no evil can come near you. In the name of Jesus, I claim Psalm 91, Psalm 23, Psalm 25:20-21, Psalm 46:10, Psalm 56:3, Psalm 61:2, Psalm 62:5-8, Psalm 116:7, Joel 2:25-26, 1 John 4:4, 2 Chronicles 7:14, 2 Timothy 1:7, Jeremiah 30:17, Philippians 4:7-9, Romans 12:18, John 14:27, Isaiah 26:3, Isaiah 43:2, Isaiah 53:5 & Isaiah 54:17 over all of you & all your loved ones. I pray for all the people, the families, the businesses & all the medical workers that they'd be abundantly blessed with protection, peace, prosperity, faith, health, hope, love, thanksgiving, joy, wisdom, guidance & strength so that they can be a blessing to many other people. In the name of Jesus, as a child of the true Living God, covered in His blood, protected by Jesus, sealed by the Holy Spirit & as a warrior of Christ, I command & cast this virus, violence, the spirit of fear, hatred, all agents of evil & the devil away from you & all your loved ones. Greater is He who is in Us than he who is in the world & as it is written, if we resist the devil he must flee from us. I thank You Father & I claim all these things in Your Holy, powerful, majestic, everlasting, eternal & precious name I pray Lord Jesus, Amen!

Warriors! It's a new week & as with each day we continue to press forward through this dark valley & through the storms. Through the name & power of Christ we shall prevail & we'll be triumphant through any storm, any tribulation, any problem that comes our way! As I say each night, VICTORY IS COMING! Take your focus off the storm & focus on God. We can take refuge in Him, He will never forsake or leave you & no matter what you have done in your life Christ is there, right now, waiting for you to come to or come back to Him. All you have to do is open the door to Him. He's knocking right now. That pull on your soul right now is Christ wanting to have a relationship with you. He loves you & He will always love you. Let not your heart be troubled! Be safe! Be healthy! Be strong! Have hope! Have faith! Have prosperity! Have joy! May God bless all of you!

DAY 211
October 13th, 2020

Good evening my friends. It's a beautiful night in NE Ohio & we're closing out Tuesday, October 13th, 2020 & I pray that this message finds you & your loved ones healthy, safe & well.

Dear Heavenly Father, I come to You with Heavenly praise, love & thanksgiving. Thank You Lord Father that no matter what we face in this life, when we put our faith & trust in You & Your will, You always lead us to victory. Father, I pray for our country that You would place Your calming hands on this nation & that You would please restore our lands & bring peace back to the people. I pray for all the afflicted around this country & world, that they'd be completely restored to full health & for the swift development of a safe, powerful & effective vaccine. I pray that you & all your loved ones will be completely surrounded by a spiritual & impenetrable hedge of protection where no evil can come anywhere near you. In the name of Jesus, I claim Psalm 91, Psalm 23, Psalm 25:20-21, Psalm 46:10, Psalm 56:3, Psalm 61:2, Psalm 62:5-8, Psalm 116:7, Joel 2:25-26, 1 John 4:4, 2 Chronicles 7:14, 2 Timothy 1:7, Jeremiah 30:17, Philippians 4:7-9, Romans 12:18, John 14:27, Isaiah 26:3, Isaiah 43:2, Isaiah 53:5 & Isaiah 54:17 over all of you & all your loved ones. Father there are a lot of people hurting & I pray for all the people, the families, the businesses & all the medical workers that they'd be abundantly blessed with protection, peace, prosperity, faith, health, hope, love, thanksgiving, joy, wisdom, guidance & strength through these difficult & uncertain times. In the name of Jesus, as a child of the Living God, covered in His blood, protected by Jesus, sealed by the Holy Spirit & as a warrior of Christ, I command & cast this virus, violence, the spirit of fear, hatred, all agents of evil & the devil away from you & all your loved ones. By the power & name of Jesus Christ, IT MUST LEAVE NOW!! I thank You Father & I claim all these things in Your Holy, powerful, majestic, everlasting, eternal & precious name I pray Lord Jesus, Amen!

Warriors! As we approach the middle of the week we're nearing 7 months that I've been praying over all of you & I WILL continue to do so. As we move constantly forward, we move as a unified force under the will, power & name of Jesus Christ. Through Christ we shall prevail, we will be delivered & we will see victory! And no matter what happens, there is no power in the known or unknown universe that's stronger than God. He's sovereign over all. Not some but ALL. When we are weak He is strong, when we feel like it's over, there's always a new beginning. When we place our faith & trust in God, WE WILL SEE VICTORY! Let not your heart be troubled! Be safe! Be healthy! Be strong! Have hope! Have faith! Have prosperity! Have joy! May God bless all of you!

DAY 212
October 14th, 2020

Good evening my friends. It's the middle of the week & we're closing out Wednesday, October 14th, 2020 & I hope & pray that this message finds you & your loved ones healthy, safe & well.

Dear Heavenly Father, I come to You with Heavenly praise, love & thanksgiving. Thank You Lord Father that through the storms of life, You are always right by our sides, leading us forward to victory. In the name of Jesus, I claim Psalm 91, Psalm 23, Psalm 25:20-21, Psalm 46:10, Psalm 56:3, Psalm 61:2, Psalm 62:5-8, Psalm 116:7, Joel 2:25-26, 1 John 4:4, 2 Chronicles 7:14, 2 Timothy 1:7, Jeremiah 30:17, Philippians 4:7-9, Romans 12:18, John 14:27, Isaiah 26:3, Isaiah 43:2, Isaiah 53:5 & Isaiah 54:17 over all of you & all your loved ones. Father, I pray that all of you & your loved ones will be surrounded by a spiritual & impenetrable hedge of protection that no evil can pass through. I pray for all the afflicted that they'd be completely restored to full health, for the swift development of a safe, powerful & effective vaccine & that this virus will be completely eradicated. Father, I pray that You would place Your calming hands on this nation & that You would please restore our lands & bring peace back to the people. Father, I pray for all the people, the families, the businesses & all the medical workers that they'd be given complete protection & abundantly blessed through these difficult & uncertain times so that they may be a blessing to many others. In the name of Jesus, as a child of the Living God, covered in His blood, protected by Jesus, sealed by the Holy Spirit & as a warrior of Christ, I command & cast this virus, violence, the spirit of fear, hatred, all agents of evil & the devil away from you & all your loved ones. As it is written Greater is He who is in us than he who is in the world & if we resist the devil, through the power of Christ, he must flee from us. I thank You Father & I claim all these things in Your Holy, powerful, majestic, everlasting, & precious name I pray Lord Jesus, Amen!

Warriors! It's the middle of the week & we're another 24 hours closer to victory. It seems like every single day there is a new storm forming but despite all this, God is still in complete control. Through these storms we must do our part & continue to be strong & vigilant, but these difficult days & this season will come to an end & life will go back to normal. I have complete faith that God will deliver us through these uncertain times. I know that even when the storms come, that peace will replace it. I know that the brightest day comes after the darkest night & through the power & majesty of Christ WE SHALL PREVAIL! Let not your heart be troubled! Be safe! Be healthy! Be strong! Have hope! Have faith! Have prosperity! Have joy! May God bless all of you!

DAY 213
October 15th, 2020

Good evening my friends. We're approaching the end of the week & we're closing out Thursday, October 15th, 2020 & I pray that this message once again finds you & your loved ones healthy, safe & well.

Dear Heavenly Father, I come to You with Heavenly praise, love & thanksgiving. Thank You Lord Father that You promised to stay by our side & that You'd never leave us or forsake us. I pray that all of you & your loved ones will be completely surrounded by a spiritual & impenetrable hedge of protection that no evil can pass through or come near you. In the name of Jesus, I claim Psalm 91, Psalm 23, Psalm 25:20-21, Psalm 46:10, Psalm 56:3, Psalm 61:2, Psalm 62:5-8, Psalm 116:7, Joel 2:25-26, 1 John 4:4, 2 Chronicles 7:14, 2 Timothy 1:7, Jeremiah 30:17, Philippians 4:7-9, Romans 12:18, John 14:27, Isaiah 26:3, Isaiah 43:2, Isaiah 53:5 & Isaiah 54:17 over all of you & all your loved ones. I pray for all the afflicted that they'd be fully & completely restored to full health & for the swift development of a safe, powerful & effective vaccine. Father, I pray deeply that You would place Your calming hands on this nation & that You'd please restore our lands & bring peace back to our people. Father, I pray for all the people, the families, the businesses & all the medical workers that they'd be abundantly blessed with protection, peace, prosperity, faith, health, hope, love, wisdom, guidance & strength to get through these difficult & uncertain times. In the name of Jesus, as a child of the eternal & true Living God, covered in His precious blood, protected by Jesus, sealed by the Holy Spirit & as a warrior in the army of Christ, I command, come against, rebuke & cast this virus, violence, the spirit of fear, hatred, anxiety, animosity, all agents of evil & the devil away from you & all your loved ones to the farthest ends of the earth. I thank You Father & I claim all these things in Your Holy, powerful, majestic, everlasting, & precious name I pray Lord Jesus, Amen!

Warriors! Tonight, as we continue to press forward, I want to talk about why I believe what I believe. I'll go into this deeper some night but briefly, I was raised in a Christian home by two amazing parents & I was taught early on about Christ & God. Along with my upbringing, I've seen things first hand which solidify my faith. We all have had moments when we ask, God are You there? Do You know what is happening in my life? God how am I going to get through this? Why am I here? Etc. And looking back through my life, I can truly tell you that I see how God brought me to where I stand today. Though I have dealt with a myriad of serious health problems throughout my life which could have killed me multiple times, despite all that, I'm still here by the very grace of God, praising His name & I thank Jesus. I've personally felt the very power of God flow through me. The path of my life has shown me signs and wonders that God is SO very real. I do not believe in coincidence, everything happens for a reason, both good & bad and ultimately those good & bad times form us into who we are to become. We all would love things to go easy & smoothly but if you are to become who God wants you to be, it's only when we go through times of adversity that develops & builds our faith & character. That adversity, when placed it in God's hands, not ours, shows the true love & amazing power of God to bring us through any situation we face. I DO believe that Jesus is the Son of God, I do believe that He died for my sins, that I may have eternal life through Him & that He has a plan & destiny for my life just as he has a plan & destiny for each of you. He didn't bring you this far in life only to stop now. We're going to get through this time difficult time everyone! Let not your heart be troubled! Be safe! Be healthy! Be strong! Have hope! Have faith! Have prosperity! Have joy! May God bless all of you!

DAY 214
October 16th, 2020

Good evening my friends. The weekend is here & we're closing out, what was a beautiful Friday, October 16th, 2020 & I pray that this message finds you & your loved ones healthy, safe & well.

Dear Heavenly Father, I come to You with a humble heart, Heavenly praise, love & thanksgiving. Thank You Father that even at our lowest & darkest moments You're there to help us & still love us unconditionally. Lord Jesus, I pray that a spiritual & impenetrable hedge of protection would be placed around all reading this & their loved ones. In the name of Jesus, I claim Psalm 91, Psalm 23, Psalm 25:20-21, Psalm 46:10, Psalm 56:3, Psalm 61:2, Psalm 62:5-8, Psalm 116:7, Joel 2:25-26, 1 John 4:4, 2 Chronicles 7:14, 2 Timothy 1:7, Jeremiah 30:17, Philippians 4:7-9, Romans 12:18, John 14:27, Isaiah 26:3, Isaiah 43:2, Isaiah 53:5 & Isaiah 54:17 over all of you & all your loved ones. I pray for all the sick & afflicted that they'd be fully restored to health, for the eradication of this virus & for the swift development of a safe & effective vaccine. I pray that You would place Your calming hands on this entire nation & that You'd please restore our lands & bring peace back to the people. Father, I pray for all the people, the families, the businesses & all the medical workers that they'd be given complete supernatural protection & abundantly blessed through these difficult & uncertain times so they can be a blessing to others. In the name of Jesus, as a child of true Living God, covered in His precious blood, protected by Jesus, sealed by the Holy Spirit & as a warrior of Christ, I command & cast this virus, violence, the spirit of fear, hatred, anxiety, all agents of evil & the devil away from you & all your loved ones. I thank You Father & I claim all these things in Your Holy, powerful, majestic, everlasting, eternal & precious name I pray Lord Jesus, Amen!

Warriors! The weekend is here & we're not backing down for even a moment. As warriors we must pray as warriors, definitively, strategically, powerfully, with authority & with a purpose. As we move forward each day guided by the power of Jesus Christ, victory & deliverance will be ours. As I've said before we do NOT fight for victory but FROM victory! The fight, the battle, the war has already been won because of the work of Christ & we are not victims in this world but champions. There will come a day when every knee shall bow & every tongue confess that Jesus Christ is Lord! I know how hard this past year has been but know that what's on the other side of all of this is absolutely worth the fight. Let not your heart be troubled! Be safe! Be healthy! Be strong! Have hope! Have faith! Have prosperity! Have joy! May God bless all of you!

DAY 215
October 17th, 2020

Good evening my friends. It's the middle of the weekend & we're closing out, what was another beautiful day in NE Ohio & it's Saturday, October 17th, 2020 & I pray that this message finds you & your loved ones healthy, safe & well.

Dear Heavenly Father, I come to You with Heavenly praise, love & thanksgiving. Thank You Father for all the blessings You've given us & for Your perfect peace that surpasses all understanding. I pray that a spiritual & impenetrable hedge of protection will be placed around all of you & your loved ones tonight, tomorrow & the next night. In the name of Jesus, I claim Psalm 91, Psalm 23, Psalm 25:20-21, Psalm 46:10, Psalm 56:3, Psalm 61:2, Psalm 62:5-8, Psalm 116:7, Joel 2:25-26, 1 John 4:4, 2 Chronicles 7:14, 2 Timothy 1:7, Jeremiah 30:17, Philippians 4:7-9, Romans 12:18, John 14:27, Isaiah 26:3, Isaiah 43:2, Isaiah 53:5 & Isaiah 54:17 over all of you & all your loved ones. I pray for all the afflicted that they'd be fully restored to health & for the swift development of a safe & effective vaccine. I pray that You would place Your perfect calming hands on every inch of this nation & that You'd please restore our lands & bring peace back to the people. Father, I pray for all the people, the families, the businesses & all the medical workers that they'd be abundantly blessed with protection, peace, prosperity, faith, health, hope, love, wisdom, guidance & strength through these difficult & uncertain times. In the name of Jesus, as a child of true Living God, covered in His blood, protected by Jesus, sealed by the Holy Spirit & as a warrior of Christ, I command, come against, rebuke & cast this virus, violence, the spirit of fear, hatred, anxiety, animosity, every single agent of evil & the devil away from you & all your loved ones. I thank You Father for our coming deliverance & I claim all these things in Your Holy, powerful, majestic, everlasting, eternal & precious name I pray Lord Jesus, Amen!

Warriors! We're another 24 hours closer to victory as we continue to press forward. There's coming a day when the chaos of this world passes away. It's going to be glorious. For all of you that are afraid of tomorrow, know that God already knows what you need before you even ask or pray about it. He will always provide what you need. The enemy will try to tell you lies that you don't matter to God & that He won't hear your prayers but God knows you better than you know you & even knows the very number of hairs on your head. He is aware of your present situation & no matter what you are facing today, He already has a plan & provision prepared to take care of you. It can be difficult in the moment, but stay strong & have faith that He will provide. These past several months have been extremely difficult but through the power of Christ, victory & deliverance are coming! Let not your heart be troubled! Be safe! Be healthy! Be strong! Have hope! Have faith! Have prosperity! Have joy! May God bless all of you!

DAY 216
October 18th, 2020

Good evening my friends. It's the eve of a brand new week & we're closing out, Sunday, October 18th, 2020 & with each night, I pray that this message finds you & your loved ones healthy, safe & well.

Dear Heavenly Father, I come to You with Heavenly praise, love & thanksgiving. Thank You Father that in this chaotic world we find ourselves in at this time in history that You have never changed & that You are in complete & total control. Father, I pray for all the people, the families, the businesses & all the medical workers that they'd be abundantly blessed with protection, peace, prosperity, faith, health, hope, love, wisdom, guidance & strength through these difficult days.

For those who don't know You, let their eyes be opened & hearts receptive to You Lord Jesus. I pray that a spiritual & impenetrable hedge of protection will be placed around all of you & your loved ones that no evil can pass through. In the name of Jesus, I claim Psalm 91, Psalm 23, Psalm 25:20-21, Psalm 46:10, Psalm 56:3, Psalm 61:2, Psalm 62:5-8, Psalm 116:7, Joel 2:25-26, 1 John 4:4, 2 Chronicles 7:14, 2 Timothy 1:7, Jeremiah 30:17, Philippians 4:7-9, Romans 12:18, John 14:27, Isaiah 26:3, Isaiah 43:2, Isaiah 53:5 & Isaiah 54:17 over all of you & all your loved ones. Father, I pray for this country & that You would place Your calming hands on this nation & that You'd please restore our lands & bring peace back to the people. I pray for all the sick & afflicted that they'd be fully restored to health & for the swift development of a safe & effective vaccine to combat this terrible virus. In the name of Jesus, as a child of the eternal true Living God, covered in His Holy blood, protected by Jesus, sealed by the Holy Spirit & as a warrior of Christ, I command & cast this virus, violence, the spirit of fear, hatred, anxiety, animosity, destruction, all agents of evil & the devil away from you & all your loved ones. Greater is He who dwells in us that he who is in the world & as it is written if we resist the devil he must flee from us. I thank You Father & I claim all these things in Your Holy, powerful, majestic, everlasting, eternal & precious name I pray Lord Jesus, Amen!

Warriors! As we begin a new week, we continue forward & not backward! We will not look at the storms that come but to God & we will not give in to fear but have faith in Christ our Savior! These days are difficult, but they're not a surprise to God & He already has a plan for our deliverance. We must hold fast & have faith that no matter what comes against us, through the name & power of Christ WE SHALL PREVAIL! This time shall end, this season will pass away but we shall be stronger on the other side of this time in history. We are the living, breathing witnesses to the greatness of God as He leads us to total & complete victory! Let not your heart be troubled! Be safe! Be healthy! Be strong! Have hope! Have faith! Have prosperity! Have joy! May God bless all of you!

DAY 217
October 19th, 2020

Good evening my friends. The new week has started & we're closing out, Monday, October 19th, 2020 & I pray that this message finds you & your loved ones healthy, safe & well.

Dear Heavenly Father, I come to You with Heavenly praise, love & thanksgiving. Thank You Father that through the storms we face, You are in complete control & on the Throne. In the name of Jesus, I claim Psalm 91, Psalm 23, Psalm 25:20-21, Psalm 46:10, Psalm 56:3, Psalm 61:2, Psalm 62:5-8, Psalm 116:7, Joel 2:25-26, 1 John 4:4, 2 Chronicles 7:14, 2 Timothy 1:7, Jeremiah 30:17, Philippians 4:7-9, Romans 12:18, John 14:27, Isaiah 26:3, Isaiah 43:2, Isaiah 53:5 & Isaiah 54:17 over all of you & all your loved ones. I pray that a spiritual hedge of protection will be placed around all of you & your loved ones that's impenetrable. For those around the world who don't know You, let their eyes be opened & hearts receptive to You Lord Jesus. Father, I pray for all the people, the families, the businesses & all the medical workers that they'd be given complete protection & abundantly blessed through these difficult days we face. Father, I pray for this country & that You'll place Your perfect calming hands on this nation & that You'd please restore our lands & bring peace back to the people. I pray for all the sick & afflicted that they'd be fully restored to health & for the swift development of a safe & effective vaccine. In the name of Jesus, as a child of the true Living God, covered in His blood, protected by Jesus, sealed by the Holy Spirit & as a warrior of Christ, I command & cast this virus, violence, the spirit of fear, hatred, anxiety, animosity, destruction, all agents of evil & the devil away from you & all your loved ones. Greater is He who dwells in us that he who is in the world & as it is written, if we resist the devil he must flee from us. I thank You Father & I claim all these things in Your Holy, powerful, majestic, everlasting, eternal & precious name I pray Lord Jesus, Amen!

Warriors! We may live in unprecedented times but even in the midst of a global pandemic & the unyielding chaos around the world, there are miracles happening everywhere around us. We must not look at the storms that surround us on all sides but only look to & hold fast to God. He is the ONLY way to salvation. Through the power of Christ we'll traverse this dark valley but we still have a ways to go & we must hold on, stay strong & vigilant. This time will pass but we must keep our focus on God alone. Don't listen to white noise of this world but focus on the true word of God. Through Christ WE SHALL PREVAIL! Let not your heart be troubled! Be safe! Be healthy! Be strong! Have hope! Have faith! Have prosperity! Have joy! May God bless all of you!

DAY 218
October 20th, 2020

Good evening my friends. We're approaching the middle of the week & we're closing out, Tuesday, October 20th, 2020 & I pray that this message once again finds you & your loved ones healthy, safe & well.

Dear Heavenly Father, I come to You with a humble heart, Heavenly praise, love & thanksgiving. Thank You Father that You are the God of power, love, forgiveness miracles & justice. Thank You Lord that You're in complete control of everything & on the Throne. For those around the world who don't know You as their Lord, let their eyes be opened & hearts receptive to You Jesus. I pray that a spiritual & impenetrable hedge of protection will be placed around all of you & your loved ones tonight, tomorrow & the next day. In the name of Jesus, I claim Psalm 91, Psalm 23, Psalm 25:20-21, Psalm 46:10, Psalm 56:3, Psalm 61:2, Psalm 62:5-8, Psalm 116:7, Joel 2:25-26, 1 John 4:4, 2 Chronicles 7:14, 2 Timothy 1:7, Jeremiah 30:17, Philippians 4:7-9, Romans 12:18, John 14:27, Isaiah 26:3, Isaiah 43:2, Isaiah 53:5 & Isaiah 54:17 over all of you & all your loved ones. Father, I pray for all the people, the families, the businesses & all the medical workers around this country & world, that they'd be abundantly blessed with protection, prosperity, peace, faith, health, hope, love, thanksgiving, wisdom, guidance & strength to get through these uncertain times. I pray for this country & that You'll place Your calming hands on this nation & that You'd please restore our lands & bring peace back to the people. I pray for all the sick & afflicted that they'd be fully restored to health, for the eradication of this virus & for the swift development of a safe & effective vaccine. In the name of Jesus, as a child of the eternal true Living God, covered in His Holy blood, protected by Jesus, sealed by the Holy Spirit & as a warrior in the army of Christ, I command, come against, rebuke & cast this virus, violence, the spirit of fear, hatred, anxiety, animosity, destruction, all agents of evil & the devil away from you & all your loved ones. BE GONE & NEVER RETURN! I thank You Father & I claim all these things in Your Holy, powerful, majestic, everlasting, eternal & precious name I pray Lord Jesus, Amen!

Warriors! We're living in very tumultuous times & everyone I know is going through something. But great storms usually come before great blessings. The devil knows he has very very little time left down here & he is running wild around the world trying to disrupt everything. Take joy & peace knowing that "when these things begin to come to pass, then look up, and lift up your heads; for your redemption draweth nigh." (Luke 21:28) As I have said many nights doing this. The storms will come, but as it is written through the power & name of Christ if we resist the devil HE MUST FLEE! In these uncertain times, be certain in the power of Jesus. No matter what happens, Christ is in control & on the throne! He WILL deliver us to victory! Let not your heart be troubled! Be safe! Be healthy! Be strong! Have hope! Have faith! Have prosperity! Have joy! May God bless all of you!

DAY 219
October 21st, 2020

Good evening my friends. It's the middle of the week & we're closing out, Wednesday, October 21st, 2020 & I pray that this message finds you & your loved ones healthy, safe & well.

Dear Heavenly Father, I come to You with Heavenly praise, love & thanksgiving. Thank You Father that even when we don't understand the current circumstances we face that You Father, have a unique destiny for each of us & I praise Your Holy name Lord Jesus. I pray that all of you & your loved ones will be surrounded by a spiritual

& impenetrable hedge of protection. For those around the world who don't know You as their Lord, let their eyes be opened & hearts receptive to You Jesus. Father, I pray for all the people, the families, the businesses & all the medical workers around this country & world, that they'd be given full protection & abundantly blessed to get through these difficult days. In the name of Jesus, I claim Psalm 91, Psalm 23, Psalm 25:20-21, Psalm 46:10, Psalm 56:3, Psalm 61:2, Psalm 62:5-8, Psalm 116:7, Joel 2:25-26, 1 John 4:4, 2 Chronicles 7:14, 2 Timothy 1:7, Jeremiah 30:17, Philippians 4:7-9, Romans 12:18, John 14:27, Isaiah 26:3, Isaiah 43:2, Isaiah 53:5 & Isaiah 54:17 over all of you & all your loved ones. I pray for this country & that You'll place Your perfect calming hands on this nation & that You'd please restore our lands & bring peace back to the people. I pray for all the afflicted that they'd be fully restored to health & for the development of a safe & effective vaccine. In the name of Jesus, as a child of the Living God, covered in His blood, protected by Jesus, sealed by the Holy Spirit & as a warrior of Christ, I command & cast this virus, violence, the spirit of fear, hatred, anxiety, animosity, destruction, all agents of evil & the devil away from you & all your loved ones. I thank You Father & I claim all these things in Your Holy, powerful, majestic, everlasting, eternal & precious name I pray Lord Jesus, Amen!

Warriors! It's the middle of the week & today we're another step closer to victory. Tomorrow we'll be 24 hours even closer! Soon, all of this will be behind us & like all of you, I cannot wait for that day. It's going to be amazing. The thing to remember is that even when things seem at their lowest, darkest or seemingly impossible, God can still bring it to pass. ALL things are possible with God of the universe & He is in total control & on the Throne. We must continue to hold on & be strong. I know how tired & frustrated all of us are but we must continue to hold on, be strong & vigilant. It's all going to be okay. Shout with me! VICTORY IS COMING! Let not your heart be troubled! Be safe! Be healthy! Be strong! Have hope! Have faith! Have prosperity! Have joy! May God bless all of you!

DAY 220
October 22nd, 2020

Good evening my friends. We're nearing the end of the week & we're closing out Thursday, October 22nd, 2020 & I pray that this message finds you & your loved ones healthy, safe & well.

Dear Heavenly Father, I come to You with a humble heart, Heavenly praise, love & thanksgiving. Thank You Father that when we put our entire trust & faith in You, that You take over, take care of us & lead us to victory. I pray for our country & that You'll place Your calming hands on this nation & that You'd please restore our lands & bring peace back to the people. We need You more than ever Father. I pray for all the sick & afflicted that they'd be fully restored to health, for the eradication of this virus & for the development of a safe & effective vaccine. I pray that You will surround all those reading this & their loved ones with a spiritual & impenetrable hedge of protection against all evil. For those around the world who don't know You as their Lord, please let their eyes be opened & hearts receptive to You Jesus. Father, I pray for all the people, the families, the businesses & all the medical workers that they'd be abundantly blessed with protection, prosperity, peace, faith, health, hope, love, wisdom, guidance & strength through these difficult times. In the name of Jesus, I claim Psalm 91, Psalm 23, Psalm 25:20-21, Psalm 46:10, Psalm 56:3, Psalm 61:2, Psalm 62:5-8, Psalm 116:7, Joel 2:25-26, 1 John 4:4, 2 Chronicles 7:14, 2 Timothy 1:7, Jeremiah 30:17, Philippians 4:7-9, Romans 12:18, John 14:27, Isaiah 26:3, Isaiah 43:2, Isaiah 53:5 & Isaiah 54:17 over all of you & all your loved ones. In the name of Jesus, as a child of the true Living God, covered in His blood, protected by Jesus, sealed by the Holy Spirit & as a warrior of Christ, I command, come against, rebuke & cast this virus, violence, the spirit of fear, hatred, anxiety, animosity, destruction, all agents of evil & the devil away from you & all your loved ones. I thank You Father & I claim all these things in Your Holy, powerful, majestic, everlasting, eternal & precious name I pray Lord Jesus, Amen!

Warriors! Even in the midst of the worst storm, God is STILL in control! Even when ALL seems lost, God is still on the Throne! As we walk through this chaotic world, GOD IS IN COMPLETE CONTROL & WILL deliver us to victory! God's will be done, not ours. This time in history has rattled the world to the core & has shown us just how frail we really are but through the name & power of Christ, WE ARE STRONG & WILL PREVAIL! No matter what happens, what comes, what may be, we're going to get through all of this together through the power & name of Jesus Christ. He is the ONLY way, truth & the light. Let not your heart be troubled! Be safe! Be healthy! Be strong! Have hope! Have faith! Have prosperity! Have joy! May God bless all of you!

DAY 221
October 23rd, 2020

Good evening my friends. The weekend is finally here & we're closing out Friday, October 23rd, 2020 & as with each night, I pray that this message finds you & your loved ones healthy, safe & well.

Dear Heavenly Father, I come to You tonight with Heavenly praise, love & thanksgiving praising Your name. Thank You Father that You sent Your only begotten son that only through Christ may we have eternal life. For those around this country & world who don't know You as their Lord & Savior, please let their eyes be opened & hearts receptive to accept You Lord Jesus into their hearts & be saved. I pray for all the afflicted that they'd be fully restored to complete health & for the continued swift development of a safe & effective vaccine. I pray for all those reading this prayer & message tonight that You would surround them & their loved ones with a spiritual & impenetrable hedge of protection. I pray for our nation that You will restore our lands & bring peace back to the people. Let Your will, above all others, be done Lord Jesus. Father, I pray for all the people, the families, the businesses, our leaders & all the medical workers that they'd be abundantly blessed with protection, prosperity, peace, faith, health, hope, love, wisdom, guidance & strength through these difficult times & days ahead. In the name of Jesus, I claim Psalm 91, Psalm 23, Psalm 25:20-21, Psalm 46:10, Psalm 56:3, Psalm 61:2, Psalm 62:5-8, Psalm 116:7, Joel 2:25-26, 1 John 4:4, 2 Chronicles 7:14, 2 Timothy 1:7, Jeremiah 30:17, Philippians 4:7-9,

Romans 12:18, John 14:27, Isaiah 26:3, Isaiah 43:2, Isaiah 53:5 & Isaiah 54:17 over all of you & all your loved ones. In the name of Jesus, as a child of the Living God, completely covered in His blood, protected by Jesus, sealed by the Holy Spirit & as a warrior in the army of Christ, I command & cast this virus, violence, the spirit of fear, hatred, anxiety, animosity, destruction, all agents of evil & the devil away from you & all your loved ones. I thank You Father for our coming victory through You & I claim all these things in Your Holy, powerful, majestic, everlasting, eternal & precious name I pray Lord Jesus, Amen!

Warriors! We are through another week of this pandemic & though we have a ways to go, each step forward is one step closer to the end of this difficult season. With all the numbers fluctuating everywhere up & down, we still must continue to be strong, hold on & be vigilant. Know that this season is only temporary. This too shall pass & life will go back to normal. This year has shown us our true frailty but with Christ ALL things are possible. Please take a moment tonight to pray for someone who is really hurting tonight as there are countless people in need of a lifeline through this storm. You can be that lifeline even if it's a silent prayer, a quick call, a text, something to show someone you care. We as a country, as a state, as a city, as a neighborhood need to learn to love & care for each other again. We're going to get through this time! Let not your heart be troubled! Be safe! Be healthy! Be strong! Have hope! Have faith! Have prosperity! Have joy! May God bless all of you!

DAY 222
October 24th, 2020

Good evening my friends. It's the middle of another weekend & we're closing out Saturday, October 24th, 2020 & I pray that this message finds you & your loved ones healthy, safe & well. I apologize for my lateness tonight.

Dear Heavenly Father, I come to You tonight with Heavenly praise, love & thanksgiving. Thank You Father that through each storm in life, You always have a plan for deliverance & victory. I pray for our nation that You will restore our lands & bring peace back to the people. Let Your will, above all others, be done Lord Jesus. For those who don't know You as their Lord & Savior, please let their eyes be opened & hearts receptive to accept You Lord Jesus into their hearts & be saved. I pray for all the sick & afflicted with the virus that they'd be fully restored to complete health, for the eradication of this virus & for the continued swift development of a safe & effective vaccine. Father, I pray for all the people, the families, the businesses, our leaders & all the medical workers that they'd be abundantly blessed & given full protection through these difficult times. I pray for all those reading this prayer & message tonight that You would surround them & their loved ones with a spiritual & impenetrable hedge of protection that no evil can pass through or come near. In the name of Jesus, I claim Psalm 91, Psalm 23, Psalm 25:20-21, Psalm 46:10, Psalm 56:3, Psalm 61:2, Psalm 62:5-8, Psalm 116:7, Joel 2:25-26, 1 John 4:4, 2 Chronicles 7:14, 2 Timothy 1:7, Jeremiah 30:17, Philippians 4:7-9, Romans 12:18, John 14:27, Isaiah 26:3, Isaiah 43:2, Isaiah 53:5 & Isaiah 54:17 over all of you & all your loved ones. In the name of Jesus, as a child of the true Living God, covered in His blood, protected by Jesus, sealed by the Holy Spirit & as a warrior in the army of Christ, I command & cast this virus, violence, the spirit of fear, hatred, anxiety, animosity, destruction, all agents of evil & the devil away from you & all your loved ones. I thank You Father for our coming victory through You & I claim all these things in Your Holy, powerful, majestic, everlasting, eternal & precious name I pray Lord Jesus, Amen!

Warriors! We do not fight for victory but from victory! From the work done on the Cross, Christ paid the sin debt for all of you past, present & future & to receive this forgiveness & eternal life, all you have to do to is accept that Jesus is the Son of God, that He died for your sins & accept Him into Your heart as Your Lord & Savior. It takes only a moment but could be the most important decision in your entire life. Only through the name & power of Jesus Christ WE SHALL PREVAIL! At the bottom of this message tonight I am going to put a simple prayer that you can pray to have eternal life through Christ Jesus. Let not your heart be troubled! Be safe! Be healthy! Be strong! Have hope! Have faith! Have prosperity! Have joy! May God bless all of you!

If you've never invited Jesus Christ into your heart, there's no better time to do it than right now, and you can trust Him as your Savior. Just pray this prayer right now with me, just simply say, "God, I'm a sinner. I'm sorry for my sins. I ask that You forgive me, and I believe that Jesus Christ is Your Son, and I want to invite Him to come into my heart and trust Him with my life. I'm willing to trust Him as my Savior and follow Him as my Lord forever, and I pray this in Jesus' Name.'"

DAY 223
October 25th, 2020

Good evening my friends. We're on the eve of another new week of possibilities & we're closing out Sunday, October 25th, 2020 & I hope & pray this message finds you & your loved ones healthy, safe & well.

Dear Heavenly Father, I come to You tonight with a humble heart, Heavenly praise, love & thanksgiving. Thank You Father that You are the God who created the universe & that You are in complete control of everything. Father, I pray for all the people, the families, the businesses & all the medical workers that they'd be abundantly blessed with protection, prosperity, peace, faith, health, hope, love, wisdom, guidance & strength. I pray that You will place Your perfect calming hands on this country & that You would please restore our lands & bring peace back to the people. Let Your will be done Lord Jesus. I pray for all the afflicted that they'd be completely & fully restored to health. For those who don't know You as their Lord & Savior, please Father, call to them, let their eyes be opened & hearts receptive to accept You Lord Jesus so they may be saved. I pray that You will surround all reading this & their loved ones with a protective hedge that no evil may come near or pass through. In the name of Jesus, I claim Psalm 91, Psalm 23, Psalm 25:20-21, Psalm 46:10, Psalm 55:22, Psalm 56:3, Psalm 61:2, Psalm 62:5-8, Psalm 116:7, Joel 2:25-26, 1 John 4:4, 2 Chronicles 7:14, 2 Timothy 1:7, Jeremiah 30:17, Philippians 4:7-9, Romans 12:18, John 14:27, Isaiah 26:3, Isaiah 43:2, Isaiah 53:5 & Isaiah 54:17 over all of you & all your loved ones. Father, please guide us through this difficult time. In the name of Jesus, as a child of the Living God, covered in His Holy blood, protected by Jesus, sealed by the Holy Spirit & as a warrior of Christ, I command, come against, rebuke & cast this virus, violence, the spirit of fear, hatred, anxiety, animosity, destruction, all agents of evil & the devil away from you & all your loved ones. Greater is He who is in us than he who is in the world & by Your name & power Lord Jesus they MUST FLEE! I thank You Father for our coming victory & I claim all these things in Your Holy, powerful, majestic, everlasting, eternal & precious name I pray Lord Jesus, Amen!

Warriors! As we begin a new week & as we come near to another month, please take a moment tonight to pray for our country. Pray for God's will to be done & not our own. Though we are all frustrated, stressed, afraid, tired & wondering what tomorrow may bring, know that we WILL make it through this valley, this season will end, life will return to normal, & that above all else God is in control & on the Throne. Through the coming months we need to take a step back & learn to love each other again. We must not let blind hatred cloud our minds & judgments. This message tonight focuses around one word, "forgiveness". The reason forgiveness is so key is because when you allow anger & hatred to consume you. While it may seem empowering at the time, in the end, it will completely & utterly destroy & rot you from the inside out. I'm going to ask something difficult of you tonight & I'm not lying here, it's going to be hard for you. Tonight, please say a prayer for your enemy, whoever that is & here is the hard part… Whatever wrong has been done to you in any capacity, while whatever it was is not right, you don't have to forget it, you don't have to ever talk to that person again, but try to let that pain go & forgive them. Give ALL of it to God & let Him take care of the situation for you. It won't be easy & I'm sure many of you like myself have gone through something at one point or another that you feel you just can't let go. I'm not saying it'll be easy or that you'll be successful on the first try. But try to forgive them. This world is in such chaos, that we need to heal. Just try tonight. Trust me, you'll feel better. Let not your heart be troubled! Be safe! Be healthy! Be strong! Have hope! Have faith! Have prosperity! Have joy! May God bless all of you!

DAY 224
October 26th, 2020

    Good evening my friends. On this evening of this new we're closing out Monday, October 26th, 2020 & I hope & pray this message finds you & your loved ones healthy, safe & well.

Dear Heavenly Father, I come to You tonight with Heavenly praise, love & thanksgiving. Thank You Father that when we're weak You are strong, when we don't see a way You make the impossible, possible & that You love us unconditionally even at our worst moments. I pray that You'll surround everyone reading this & their loved ones with a spiritual & impenetrable hedge of protection. Father, I pray for all the people, the families, the businesses & all the medical workers that they'd be abundantly blessed & given complete & full protection in these uncertain times. I pray for our nation & that You would please restore our lands & bring peace back to the people. Let Your will, not ours, be done Lord Jesus. I pray for all the sick & afflicted that they'd be completely & fully restored to health, that this virus will be completely eradicated & for the swift development of a powerful, safe & effective vaccine. For those who don't know You as their Lord & Savior, please Father, call to them, let their eyes be truly opened & hearts completely receptive to accept You Lord Jesus in their hearts so they may be saved. In the name of Jesus, I claim Psalm 91, Psalm 23, Psalm 25:20-21, Psalm 46:10, Psalm 55:22, Psalm 56:3, Psalm 61:2, Psalm 62:5-8, Psalm 116:7, Joel 2:25-26, 1 John 4:4, 2 Chronicles 7:14, 2 Timothy 1:7, Jeremiah 30:17, Philippians 4:7-9, Romans 12:18, John 14:27, Isaiah 26:3, Isaiah 43:2, Isaiah 53:5 & Isaiah 54:17 over all of you & all your loved ones. In the name of Jesus, as a child of the Living God, covered in His blood, protected by Jesus, sealed by the Holy Spirit & as a warrior of Christ, I command & cast this virus, violence, the spirit of fear, hatred, anxiety, animosity, destruction, all agents of evil & the devil away from you & all your loved ones. This evil MUST LEAVE NOW!! I thank You Father & I claim all these things in Your Holy, powerful, majestic, everlasting, eternal & precious name I pray Lord Jesus, Amen!

Warriors! Tonight we stand again united & strong against the forces of evil that surround us. Through the name & power of Christ WE SHALL PREVAIL! We will NOT bow down to adversity! We will NOT shudder in the face of fear! We will NOT tremble at the unknown! We WILL see VICTORY! We WILL be delivered! We WILL get through this time & because all things are possible with Christ, WE WILL WIN! Hold on everyone! Stay strong & vigilant & have faith! We place all of this in the hands of Christ because HE will NEVER let you down. Let not your heart be troubled! Be safe! Be healthy! Be strong! Have hope! Have faith! Have prosperity! Have joy! May God bless all of you!

DAY 225
October 27th, 2020

Good evening my friends. It's Tuesday & we're closing out October 27th, 2020 & I hope & pray this message finds you & your loved ones healthy, safe & well.

Dear Heavenly Father, I come to You tonight with Heavenly praise, love & thanksgiving. Thank You Father that through these difficult days, that You are walking with us & guiding us to victory. In the name of Jesus, I claim Psalm 91, Psalm 23, Psalm 25:20-21, Psalm 46:10, Psalm 55:22, Psalm 56:3, Psalm 61:2, Psalm 62:5-8, Psalm 116:7, Joel 2:25-26, 1 John 4:4, 2 Chronicles 7:14, 2 Timothy 1:7, Jeremiah 30:17, Philippians 4:7-9, Romans 12:18, John 14:27, Isaiah 26:3, Isaiah 43:2, Isaiah 53:5 & Isaiah 54:17 over all of you & all your loved ones. I pray that you & your loved ones will be completely surrounded by a hedge of protection that no evil can come near or pass through. Father, I pray for all the people, the families, the businesses & all the medical workers that they'd be supernaturally & abundantly blessed & protected through these difficult days. I pray for our nation that You will restore our lands, bring peace back to the people & reunify us. Above all else, let Your will, not ours, be done Lord Jesus. I pray for all the afflicted with the virus that they'd be supernaturally restored to complete & full health. For all those who don't know You as their Lord & Savior, Father, please call to them, let their eyes be opened & hearts receptive to see the truth & accept You as their Lord & Savior so they may be saved. In the name of Jesus, as a child of the Living God, covered in His Holy blood, protected by Jesus, sealed by the Holy Spirit & as a warrior of Christ, I command & cast this virus, violence, the spirit of fear, hatred, anxiety, animosity, destruction, all agents of evil & the devil away from you & all your loved ones. By the name & power of Christ, I command this evil to leave & by His name IT MUST GO! I thank You Father & I claim all these things in Your Holy, powerful, majestic, everlasting, eternal & precious name I pray Lord Jesus, Amen!

Warriors! As we press forward through each day, each storm, each difficulty, know that through the name & power of Christ, We WILL prevail! There isn't any power in the known & unknown universe, greater than God. He is Sovereign over ALL. Whatever you are facing today, place it in God's hands. He will never let you down. The path might not go the way you might think, but when you look back you will see the true perfection in each along the way. He's brought you too far to leave you now. There's soon coming a time when everything will be made right in this fallen world. Until that day, we must continue to hold on, be strong & be vigilant. We're going to make it through this time! Let not your heart be troubled! Be safe! Be healthy! Be strong! Have hope! Have faith! Have prosperity! Have joy! May God bless all of you!

DAY 226
October 28th, 2020

Good evening my friends. It's the middle of the week & we're closing out Wednesday, October 28th, 2020 & I pray this message finds you & your loved ones healthy, safe & well.

Dear Heavenly Father, I come to You again tonight with a humble heart, Heavenly praise, love & thanksgiving. Thank You Father for Your unconditional love, guidance, wisdom & peace that surpasses all understanding. In the name of Jesus, I claim Psalm 91, Psalm 23, Psalm 25:20-21, Psalm 46:10, Psalm 55:22, Psalm 56:3, Psalm 61:2, Psalm 62:5-8, Psalm 116:7, Joel 2:25-26, 1 John 4:4, 2 Chronicles 7:14, 2 Timothy 1:7, Jeremiah 30:17, Philippians 4:7-9,

Romans 12:18, John 14:27, Isaiah 26:3, Isaiah 43:2, Isaiah 53:5 & Isaiah 54:17 over all of you & all your loved ones. Father, I pray for all the people, the families, the businesses, our leaders & all the medical workers that they'd be supernaturally & abundantly blessed with protection, peace, prosperity, faith, health, hope, love, wisdom, guidance & strength so you may be a blessing to others in need. I pray that You will surround all those reading this tonight with a hedge or protection that's impenetrable. I pray for our nation that You will place Your perfect & peaceful hands on this nation, that You will restore our lands, bring peace back to the people & reunify us. Above all else, let Your will, not ours, be done in these uncertain times. I pray for all the sick & afflicted that they'd be supernaturally restored to complete & full health, for the eradication of this virus & for the swift development & distribution of a safe, powerful & effective vaccine. For all those who don't know You as their Lord & Savior, Father, please call to them, let their eyes be opened & hearts receptive to see the truth & accept You as their Lord & Savior so they may be saved & have eternal life. In the name of Jesus, as a child of the Living God, covered in His Holy blood, protected by Jesus, sealed by the Holy Spirit & as a warrior of Christ, I command & cast this virus, violence, the spirit of fear, hatred, anxiety, animosity, destruction, all agents of evil & the devil away from you & all your loved ones. Truly greater is He who dwells in us than he who is in this world & by Your name & power he & all evil must flee now! I thank You Father & I claim all these things in Your Holy, powerful, majestic, everlasting, eternal & precious name I pray Lord Jesus, Amen!

Warriors! It's the middle of the week & we're closing in on another month of this pandemic. I know it goes without saying but we must continue to hold on and be vigilant. But also know that this time is but temporary & these difficult days will end. Throughout history there have been many times when we as a people or even this world have faced impossible situations that we thought were never going to end but they did end. The waters receded from the ark, the end came to two devastating World Wars & this pandemic WILL come to an end as well. We're going to prevail through the power & name of Jesus. So as the warriors we are, do not be afraid! Do not be dismayed! DO NOT GIVE IN TO FEAR! We're going to get through this! We're all in this together! Let not your heart be troubled! Be

safe! Be healthy! Be strong! Have hope! Have faith! Have prosperity! Have joy! May God bless all of you!

DAY 227
October 29th, 2020

Good evening my friends. We're approaching the weekend & we're closing out Thursday, October 29th, 2020 & I pray this message, once again, finds you & your loved ones healthy, safe & well.

Dear Heavenly Father, I come to You tonight with Heavenly praise, love & thanksgiving. Thank You Father that we can prosper through You in these difficult times. Above all else that we pray Father, let Your will be done Father. In the name of Jesus, I claim Psalm 91, Psalm 23, Psalm 25:20-21, Psalm 46:10, Psalm 55:22, Psalm 56:3, Psalm 61:2, Psalm 62:5-8, Psalm 116:7, Joel 2:25-26, 1 John 4:4, 2 Chronicles 7:14, 2 Timothy 1:7, Jeremiah 30:17, Philippians 4:7-9, Romans 12:18, John 14:27, Isaiah 26:3, Isaiah 43:2, Isaiah 53:5 & Isaiah 54:17 over all of you & all your loved ones. I pray for our nation that You will place Your calming hands on this nation, that You will restore our lands, bring peace back to the people. I pray that You will surround everyone reading this & their loved ones with an impenetrable hedge or protection that no evil can come near or pass through. Father, I pray for everyone affected by this terrible pandemic & all the chaos around our country & world that You will give them full protection & abundantly bless them through these uncertain days. I pray for all the afflicted for their complete & full recovery by You the Great Physician. Please heal all those who are sick tonight. For all those who don't know You as their Lord & Savior, Father, please call to them, let their eyes be opened & hearts receptive to see the truth & accept You as their Lord & Savior so they may be saved & have eternal life. In the name of Jesus, as a child of the Living God, covered in His blood, protected by Jesus, sealed by the Holy Spirit & as a warrior of Christ, I command, come against, rebuke & cast this virus, violence, the spirit of fear, hatred, anxiety, animosity, destruction, all agents of evil & the devil away from you & all your loved ones. By His name & power IT MUST GO! LEAVE NOW & NEVER RETURN! I thank You Father & I claim all these things in

Your Holy, powerful, majestic, everlasting, eternal & precious name I pray Lord Jesus, Amen!

Warriors! Each & every day of 2020 continues to be unprecedented but do not let the fear of the unknown make you tremble or be afraid. Though we're surrounded by storms on all sides, truly I tell you, these storms, no matter how great, will soon be no more. God is the ultimate power in the known & unknown universe & there isn't anything that is a match for God. He's in complete & total control! God exists outside of time & already knows what's going to happen. We must hold on with everything we've got with all our strength. We're going to get through this time & we're going to make it. Join with me & shout OUR GOD IS GOD! Let not your heart be troubled! Be safe! Be healthy! Be strong! Have hope! Have faith! Have prosperity! Have joy! May God bless all of you!

DAY 228
October 30th, 2020

Good evening my friends. The weekend is here & we're closing out Friday, October 30th, 2020 & I hope & pray this message, wherever you are in the world, finds you & your loved ones healthy, safe & well. Let's begin.

Dear Heavenly Father, I come to You tonight with Heavenly praise, love & thanksgiving. Thank You Father that in the midst of the storm we face tonight that You're in complete & total control. I thank You Father for Your word & in the name of Jesus, I claim Psalm 91, Psalm 23, Psalm 25:20-21, Psalm 46:10, Psalm 55:22, Psalm 56:3, Psalm 61:2, Psalm 62:5-8, Psalm 116:7, Joel 2:25-26, 1 John 4:4, 2 Chronicles 7:14, 2 Timothy 1:7, Jeremiah 30:17, Philippians 4:7-9, Romans 12:18, John 14:27, Isaiah 26:3, Isaiah 43:2, Isaiah 53:5 & Isaiah 54:17 over all of you & all your loved ones. I thank You Father that even as I pray this tonight You are placing Your calming hands on this nation & that if it be Your will that You are restoring our lands & bringing peace back to the people. I pray that You will surround everyone reading this tonight & their loved ones with a supernatural, spiritual & completely impenetrable hedge or protection that no evil can come near or pass through. Father, I pray for everyone afflicted with the virus & affected from the violence that is spreading throughout our country & around the world & I thank You Lord Jesus that You are restoring the sick to full health, guiding the scientists to develop a vaccine & I thank You that this virus WILL be fully eradicated. For all those who don't know You as their Lord & Savior, Father, please call to them, let their eyes be opened & hearts receptive to see the truth & accept You as their Lord & Savior so they may be saved & have eternal life. In the name of Jesus, as a child of the Living God, covered in His Holy blood, protected by Jesus, sealed by the Holy Spirit & as a warrior of Christ, I command, come against, rebuke & cast this virus, violence, the spirit of fear, hatred, anxiety, animosity, destruction, all agents of evil & the devil away from you & all your loved ones. As it's written, greater is He who is in us than he who is in the world & by His name & power, if we resist the devil he must flee from us! I thank You Father and I claim all these things in Your Holy, powerful, majestic, everlasting, eternal & precious name I pray Lord Jesus, Amen!

Warriors! Tonight, please take a moment to give thanks to Jesus, King of Kings and Lord of Lords. Though this journey continues onward, we're guided by Christ and we will make it across this dark expanse & walk into victory. We've been shown how frail we truly are & how we need Jesus above all else. Do not look at the storm but focus on God. Do not be afraid but have faith in Christ. Do not flee in terror but stand with courage! Through the Name & Power of Christ WE SHALL PREVAIL! The creator of the universe will deliver us to victory. Join with me once again & shout GOD IS GOOD AND VICTORY IS COMING! Let not your heart be troubled! Be safe! Be healthy! Be strong! Have hope! Have faith! Have prosperity! Have joy! May God bless all of you!

DAY 229
October 31st, 2020

Good evening my friends. It's late in the middle of the weekend, on the eve of a new month & we're closing out Saturday, October 31st, 2020 and I pray this message finds you and your loved ones healthy, safe & well.

Dear Heavenly Father, I come to You tonight with a humble heart, Heavenly praise, love & thanksgiving. Thank You Father that even though these days seem so uncertain that we can be certain in You. I pray that You will place a hedge of protection around everyone reading this & there loved ones. In the name of Jesus, I claim Psalm 91, Psalm 23, Psalm 25:20-21, Psalm 46:10, Psalm 55:22, Psalm 56:3, Psalm 61:2, Psalm 62:5-8, Psalm 116:7, Joel 2:25-26, 1 John 4:4, 2 Chronicles 7:14, 2 Timothy 1:7, Jeremiah 30:17, Philippians 4:7-9, Romans 12:18, John 14:27, Isaiah 26:3, Isaiah 43:2, Isaiah 53:5 & Isaiah 54:17 over all of you & all your loved ones. I pray for our nation that You will place Your calming hands on every inch of this country, that You will please restore our lands & bring peace back to the people. Father, I pray for all the afflicted that they would be completely restored to full health & for the swift development of the coming vaccines. For all those who don't know You as their Lord & Savior, Father, please call to them, let their eyes be opened & hearts receptive to see the truth & accept You as their Lord & Savior so they may be saved & have eternal life. In the name of Jesus, as a child of the Living God, covered in His blood, protected by Jesus, sealed by the Holy Spirit & as a warrior in the army of Christ, I command, rebuke & cast this virus, violence, the spirit of fear, hatred, anxiety, animosity, destruction, all agents of evil & the devil away from you & all your loved ones. THIS EVIL MUST LEAVE NOW!! I thank You Father & I claim all these things in Your Holy, powerful, majestic, everlasting, eternal & precious name I pray Lord Jesus, Amen!

Warriors! As we enter into a new month, we must continue to hold on, be strong & vigilant. The coming week will have storms that come, but do not be disheartened, dismayed, deterred or fearful. God goes before us to guide us to victory. Through the name &

power of Christ ALL things are possible & God will perfect that which concerns you. Do not let the fear of what could be, but know that no matter what happens God is in control. We must stand tall & stand firm in the face of adversity. We must shout a collective yell at our coming victory & above all else do not be afraid but keep your eyes on God. Place everything in His hands because "And when these things begin to come to pass, then look up, and lift up your heads; for your redemption draweth nigh.! (Luke 21:28) Warriors! THROUGH CHRIST WE HAVE WON! Let not your heart be troubled! Be safe! Be healthy! Be strong! Have hope! Have faith! Have prosperity! Have joy! May God bless all of you!

The Sinner's Prayer

If you are not yet saved I want to personally invite you to read this prayer below. This could be the most profound decision of your entire life. This is a decision only you can make, as I am on a messenger. Please don't put off to tomorrow what can be done right now. Because tomorrow may never come.

If you would like to be saved, please read the prayer below out loud & believing in your heart.

"God, I'm a sinner. I'm sorry for my sins. I ask that You forgive me, and I believe that Jesus Christ is Your Son, and I want to invite Him to come into my heart and trust Him with my life. I'm willing to trust Him as my Savior and follow Him as my Lord forever, and I pray this in Jesus' Name.'"

DAY 230
November 1st, 2020

Good evening my friends. It's a brand new month & we're closing out Sunday, November 1st, 2020 & I pray this message finds you & your loved ones healthy, safe & well.

Dear Heavenly Father, I come to You tonight with a humble heart, Heavenly praise, love & thanksgiving. Thank You Father that no matter what we're facing today, that when we place our faith in You & place everything in Your hands, You always take care of us. I pray for our nation that Your will be done Father & that You will place Your calming hands on every inch of this country, that You will please restore our lands & bring peace back to the people. I pray that You will place a hedge of protection around everyone reading this & there loved ones tonight tomorrow night & the day after that. In the name of Jesus, I claim Psalm 91, Psalm 23, Psalm 25:20-21, Psalm 46:10, Psalm 55:22, Psalm 56:3, Psalm 61:2, Psalm 62:5-8, Psalm 116:7, Joel 2:25-26, 1 John 4:4, 2 Chronicles 7:14, 2 Timothy 1:7, Jeremiah 30:17, Philippians 4:7-9, Romans 12:18, John 14:27, Isaiah 26:3, Isaiah 43:2, Isaiah 53:5 & Isaiah 54:17 over all of you & all your loved ones. Father, I pray for all the sick & afflicted that they would be completely restored to full health & for the swift development of a safe & effective vaccine. For all those who don't know You as their Lord & Savior, Father, please call to them, let their eyes be opened & hearts receptive to see the truth & accept You as their Lord & Savior so they may be saved & have eternal life. In the name of Jesus, as a child of the eternal true Living God, covered in His Holy blood, protected by Jesus, sealed by the Holy Spirit & as a warrior in the army of Christ, I command, come against, rebuke & cast this virus, violence, the spirit of fear, hatred, anxiety, animosity, destruction, all agents of evil & the devil away from you & all your loved ones. As it it's written & because of the power of Christ if we resist the devil, he must flee from us. I thank You Father & I claim all these things in Your Holy, powerful, majestic, everlasting, eternal & precious name I pray Lord Jesus, Amen!

Warriors! It's a new day, a new week & a brand new month. We continue to press forward through each day & will continue to press through with everything we've got. We're being guided by the hand of Christ & through His power & name WE WILL PREVAIL! I can't say that enough times. I know how everyone is stressed out, frustrated, angry & afraid but know that God is in complete control & no matter what may come, when you accept Christ into your heart as your Lord & Savior, He will take care of you & deliver you to victory! Fear not & take your eyes off the storm. Please take a moment to pray for someone in need tonight. Victory is coming! Let not your heart be troubled! Be safe! Be healthy! Be strong! Have hope! Have faith! Have prosperity! Have joy! May God bless all of you!

DAY 231
November 2nd, 2020

Good evening my friends. As we enter into a new month we're closing out, Monday, November 2nd, 2020 & I hope & pray this message finds you & your loved ones healthy, safe & well as with each night.

Dear Heavenly Father, I come to You tonight with a humble heart, Heavenly praise, love & thanksgiving. Thank You that You are in complete control & on the Throne. Let Your will be done. In the name of Jesus, I claim Psalm 91, Psalm 23, Psalm 25:20-21, Psalm 46:10, Psalm 55:22, Psalm 56:3, Psalm 61:2, Psalm 62:5-8, Psalm 116:7, Psalm 121:2, Joel 2:25-26, 1 John 4:4, 2 Chronicles 7:14, 2 Timothy 1:7, Jeremiah 30:17, Philippians 4:7-9, Romans 12:18, John 14:27, Isaiah 26:3, Isaiah 43:2, Isaiah 53:5 & Isaiah 54:17 over all of you & all your loved ones. I pray for all who are reading this tonight that they & their loved ones would be completely surrounded by a spiritual & impenetrable hedge of protection where you are merely an observer of what happens around you & that you are completely safe from all evil. I pray for our nation Father & we repent of our sins & pray that You would please restore our lands & bring peace back to the people. Father, I pray for all the sick & afflicted with the virus that they'd be completely restored to full health, for the eradication of this virus & for the swift development of a safe & effective vaccine. For all those who don't know You as their Lord & Savior, Father, please call to them, let their eyes be opened & hearts receptive to see the truth & accept You as their Lord & Savior so they may be saved & have eternal life. In the name of Jesus, as a child of the eternal true Living God, covered in His Holy blood, protected by Jesus, sealed by the Holy Spirit & as a warrior in the army of Christ, I command, come against, rebuke & cast this virus, violence, the spirit of fear, hatred, anxiety, animosity, destruction, all agents of evil & the devil away from you & all your loved ones to the farthest corners of the world. Greater is He who is in us than he who is in the world & through the name & power of Christ I command this evil to LEAVE NOW!! BE GONE THIS INSTANT! I thank You Father & I claim all these things in Your Holy, powerful, majestic, everlasting, eternal & precious name I pray Lord Jesus, Amen!

Warriors! Stand with me tonight praying to Lord Jesus that not our will, but His will be done. Stand with me as we pray for forgiveness & ask for His Devine intervention. Stand with me as we shout a mighty shout to the King of Kings & Lord of Lords that He is the way, the Truth & the Light & that NO ONE comes to the Father accept through Him. Stand firm with me on the belief in Christ is the Son of God! Stand with me as we resist the chaos & evil that have surrounded us & that we will NOT fear the storms! That we will not fear the unknown! That we will NOT go quietly into the night but that we STAND STRONG in & for Christ! That we STAND WITH COURAGE in Christ! That we STAND IN FAITH in Christ! That we STAND FOR GOOD & NOT EVIL! And through the name & power of Christ WE SHALL PREVAIL! SHOUT WITH ME, VICTORY IS COMING! Let not your heart be troubled! Be safe! Be healthy! Be strong! Have hope! Have faith! Have prosperity! Have joy! May God bless all of you!

DAY 232
November 3rd, 2020

Good evening my friends. As we enter into a new month we're closing out, Tuesday, November 3rd, 2020 & I pray this message finds you & your loved ones healthy, safe & well as with each night.

Dear Heavenly Father, I come to You tonight with a humble heart, Heavenly praise, love & thanksgiving. Thank You Father that even in the midst of the storm You are God & in complete control of everything. In the name of Jesus, I claim Psalm 91, Psalm 23, Psalm 25:20-21, Psalm 46:10, Psalm 55:22, Psalm 56:3, Psalm 61:2, Psalm 62:5-8, Psalm 116:7, Psalm 121:2, Joel 2:25-26, 1 John 4:4, 2 Chronicles 7:14, 2 Timothy 1:7, Jeremiah 30:17, Philippians 4:7-9, Romans 12:18, John 14:27, Isaiah 26:3, Isaiah 43:2, Isaiah 53:5 & Isaiah 54:17 over all of you & all your loved ones. Father, as I come to You tonight, I pray for our entire nation & we repent of all our sins & we pray that You would please restore our lands & bring peace back to our country. Father, I pray for all the afflicted that they would be completely & fully restored to health & for the development of a safe & powerful vaccine. Lord Jesus, I pray for all who are reading this message tonight You will surround them with a hedge of protection that no evil can pass through. For all those who don't know You as their Lord & Savior, Father, please call to them, let their eyes be opened & hearts receptive to see the truth & accept You as their Lord & Savior so they may be saved & have eternal life. In the name of Jesus, as a child of the Living God, covered in His Holy blood, protected by Jesus, sealed by the Holy Spirit & as a warrior of Christ, I command, come against, rebuke & cast this virus, violence, the spirit of fear, hatred, anxiety, animosity, destruction, all agents of evil & the devil away from you & all your loved ones to the farthest corners of the world. Greater is He who is in us than he who is in the world & through the name & power of Christ I command this evil to LEAVE NOW!! BE GONE THIS INSTANT! As it's written through the power of God if we resist the devil he must flee from us. I thank You Father & I claim all these things in Your Holy, powerful, majestic, everlasting, eternal & precious name I pray Lord Jesus, Amen!

Warriors! We are another day closer to victory! Do not be afraid, do not let the spirit of fear take you over, do not let the storms around you overwhelm you but look to God & focus only on Him. He's guiding us through the valley to deliverance & victory. As I've said many times, through the name and power of Christ ALL things are possible. We're going to get through this everyone. We stand firm against evil and we stand firm with Christ! Shout with me again everyone! GOD IS GOOD & VICTORY IS COMING! Let not your heart be troubled! Be

safe! Be healthy! Be strong! Have hope! Have faith! Have prosperity! Have joy! May God bless all of you!

DAY 233
November 4th, 2020

Good evening my friends. It was a beautiful day here in NE Ohio & we're closing out Wednesday, November 4th, 2020 & I pray this message finds you & your loved ones healthy, safe & well. If you are new to seeing these posts, as promised I'm praying over all of you throughout this pandemic each & every night. Let's begin.

Dear Heavenly Father, I come to You tonight with a humble heart, Heavenly praise, love & thanksgiving. Thank You Father that You are the God of miracles & that you can make the impossible possible, the unlikely certain & that He is always perfectly on time. Father, as I come to You tonight, I pray for our entire nation & we repent of all our sins & we pray that You would please restore our lands & bring peace back to our country once again. In the name of Jesus, I claim Psalm 91, Psalm 23, Psalm 25:20-21, Psalm 46:10, Psalm 55:22, Psalm 56:3, Psalm 61:2, Psalm 62:5-8, Psalm 116:7, Psalm 121:2, Joel 2:25-26, 1 John 4:4, 2 Chronicles 7:14, 2 Timothy 1:7, Jeremiah 30:17, Philippians 4:7-9, Romans 12:18, John 14:27, Isaiah 26:3, Isaiah 43:2, Isaiah 53:5 & Isaiah 54:17 over all of you & all your loved ones. Father, tonight I pray for You to call to all those who do not You as their Lord & Savior, that You would allow their hearts to be receptive & that they would accept that You died on the Cross for their sins, to accept You as their Lord so they may be saved & have eternal life. Father, I pray for all the sick & afflicted that they would be completely & fully restored to health, for the eradication of the virus & for the development of a safe & powerful vaccine. I pray for all the families, people, businesses, our leaders & all medical workers that You would bless them with protection & abundantly bless through these difficult times we face. Lord Jesus, I pray for all who are reading this prayer & message tonight You will completely surround them with an impenetrable hedge of protection that no evil can pass through or even come near. In the name of Jesus, as a child of the true & only Living God, covered in His Holy blood, protected by

Jesus, sealed by the Holy Spirit & as a warrior of Christ, I command, come against, rebuke & cast this virus, violence, the spirit of fear, hatred, anxiety, animosity, destruction, lies, all agents of evil & the devil away from you & all your loved ones to the farthest corners of the world. Greater is He who is in us than he who is in the world & through the name & power of Christ I command this evil to GO!! LEAVE NOW! As it's written through the name & power of Christ, if we resist the devil he must flee from us. I thank You Father & I claim all these things in Your Holy, powerful, majestic, everlasting, eternal & precious name I pray Lord Jesus, Amen!

Warriors! I pray that you will be blessed from God with His peace that surpasses all understanding. I keep hearing one passage from the Bible over & over again in my head & I have it listed below but I keep hearing, "BE STILL & KNOW THAT I AM GOD". Whatever you are facing today this very moment, whatever fears, anxieties, anger, etc give it to God & then watch what happens. We're living in a very uncertain time but I can say this that through the uncertainty, we have grown to understand just how frail we really are, that we have no power & that we truly need Christ. Powerful things are happening this very moment! Tonight, pray with authority! Pray with confidence! Pray for victory! Because VICTORY IS COMING!!! Let not your heart be troubled! Be safe! Be healthy! Be strong! Have hope! Have faith! Have prosperity! Have joy! May God bless all of you!

DAY 234
November 5th, 2020

Good evening my friends. It was another beautiful day here in NE Ohio & we're closing out Thursday, November 5th, 2020 & I pray this message finds you & your loved ones healthy, safe & well.

Dear Heavenly Father, I come to You tonight with a humble heart, Heavenly praise, love & thanksgiving. Thank You Father for Your peace that surpasses all understanding & from the joy it brings even in the midst of apparent turmoil. Father, I once again pray for our entire nation tonight. Lord Jesus, we repent of all our sins & we pray that You would please restore our lands & bring peace & reunification back to our country & people. In the name of Jesus, I claim Psalm 91, Psalm 23, Psalm 25:20-21, Psalm 46:10, Psalm 55:22, Psalm 56:3, Psalm 61:2, Psalm 62:5-8, Psalm 116:7, Psalm 121:2, Joel 2:25-26, 1 John 4:4, 2 Chronicles 7:14, 2 Timothy 1:7, Jeremiah 30:17, Philippians 4:7-9, Romans 12:18, John 14:27, Isaiah 26:3, Isaiah 43:2, Isaiah 53:5 & Isaiah 54:17 over all of you & all your loved ones. I pray that you & your loved ones will completely surrounded by an impenetrable hedge of. I pray for all the families, the people, the businesses, our leaders & all medical workers that You would abundantly bless them with protection, prosperity, peace, faith, health, hope, love, wisdom, guidance, wisdom & strength through this difficult time. Father, I pray for You to call to all those who do not You as their Lord & Savior, that You would allow their hearts to be receptive & that they would accept that You died on the Cross for their sins, to accept You as their Lord so they may be saved & have eternal life. Father, I pray for all the afflicted that they would be completely & fully restored to complete health & for the development of a safe & powerful vaccine. In the name of Jesus, as a child of the true eternal & only Living God, covered in His Holy blood, protected by Jesus, sealed by the Holy Spirit & as a warrior in the army of Christ, I command, come against, rebuke & cast, through the full power of Jesus Christ, this virus, violence, the spirit of fear, hatred, anxiety, animosity, destruction, all agents of evil & the devil away from you & all your loved ones. Truly, greater is He who is in us than he who is in the world & through the name & power of Christ I command this evil to LEAVE NOW! I thank You Father & I claim all these things in Your Holy, powerful, majestic, everlasting, eternal & precious name I pray Lord Jesus, Amen!

Warriors! Do NOT be afraid of this world! Do NOT fear the unknown! Do NOT tremble from the terrors of the night! DO NOT FEAR! As warriors of Christ, you are not a victim, you are not weak & through the power of Christ you're not defeated. Join with me & from the depths of your soul, shout NO!! MORE!! against the evil & storms that have surrounded & invaded us. Tell them they have no right or authority over you. Tell them, by the name & power of Christ, THEY MUST GO NOW! We're in the middle of a immense spiritual battle on all fronts against the forces of evil & darkness. Right now, this moment, pray that God's will be done! Pray with authority! Pray with conviction! Pray! Pray! Pray! We're gonna get through this everyone! VICTORY IS COMING!!! Let not your heart be troubled! Be safe! Be healthy! Be strong! Have hope! Have faith! Have prosperity! Have joy! May God bless all of you!

DAY 235
November 6th, 2020

Good evening my friends. It was yet another beautiful day here in NE Ohio & we're closing out Friday, November 6th, 2020 & I pray this message finds you & your loved ones healthy, safe & well.

Dear Heavenly Father, I come to You tonight with Heavenly praise, love & thanksgiving. Thank You Father that You are truly the God that can make the impossible into the possible. I pray again for all the families, the people, the businesses, our leaders & all medical workers that You would be given full protection & abundantly blessed so they can be a true blessing to many other people in need. Father, I pray that You will surround all reading this message tonight with a spiritual, powerful & impenetrable hedge of protection that no evil can even come near. Father, I pray for You to call to all those who do not You as their Lord & Savior, & that they would accept that You died on the Cross for their sins, to accept You as their Lord so they may be saved & have eternal life. Father, I pray for our entire nation tonight. Lord Jesus, we repent of all our sins & we pray that You would please restore our lands. In the name of Jesus, I claim Psalm 91, Psalm 23, Psalm 25:20-21, Psalm 46:10, Psalm 55:22, Psalm 56:3, Psalm 61:2, Psalm 62:5-8, Psalm 116:7, Psalm 121:2, Joel 2:25-26, 1 John 4:4, 2 Chronicles 7:14, 2 Timothy 1:7, Jeremiah 30:17, Philippians 4:7-9, Romans 12:18, John 14:27, Isaiah 26:3, Isaiah 43:2, Isaiah 53:5 & Isaiah 54:17 over all of you & all your loved ones. Father, I pray for all the sick & afflicted around this nation & around the world that they would be completely & fully restored to complete health & for the development of a safe & powerful vaccine. In the name of Jesus, as a child of the true Living God, covered in His blood, protected by Jesus, sealed by the Holy Spirit & as a warrior of Christ, I command, come against, rebuke & cast, through the full power of Jesus Christ, this virus, violence, the spirit of fear, hatred, anxiety, corruption, animosity, destruction, all agents of evil & the devil away from you & all your loved ones. BE GONE NOW!! I thank You Father & I claim all these things in Your Holy, powerful, majestic, everlasting, eternal & precious name I pray Lord Jesus, Amen!

Warriors! The weekend is finally here & we are another step closer to victory & deliverance. I know so many of you are so ready for the pandemic to be over & soon it will be. We have to keep staying strong & vigilant. This year has been difficult for all of us, but through the power & name of Christ, WE SHALL PREVAIL & BE VICTORIOUS! Always remember, ALL things are possible through Christ even when it seems completely impossible. He is always perfectly on time, never a second early or a second late. Just like the parting of the Red Sea when the Egyptians were chasing the Israelites, God came through at the perfect moment to save Israel. Shout with me again! VICTORY IS COMING!!! Let not your heart be troubled! Be safe! Be healthy! Be strong! Have hope! Have faith! Have prosperity! Have joy! May God bless all of you!

DAY 236
November 7th, 2020

Good evening my friends. It's the middle of the weekend & we're closing out Saturday, November 7th, 2020 & I pray this message finds you & your loved ones healthy, safe & well.

Dear Heavenly Father, I come to You tonight with a humble heart, Heavenly praise, love & thanksgiving. Thank You Father that even in the darkest of storms You are on the Throne & in control. Thank You Father that You are the God of possible impossibilities. Thank You Father that You are Lord & Sovereign over all. One day every knee shall bow & every tongue confess that Jesus Christ is LORD! Father, I pray that You will surround every single person reading this message tonight & their loved ones with a spiritual, powerful & impenetrable hedge of protection. Father, as I pray to You tonight, please call to all those who do not You as their Lord & Savior, & that they would accept that You died on the Cross for their sins, to accept You into their hearts & as their Lord so they may be saved & have eternal life. Father, I lift up & pray for our entire nation tonight. Lord Jesus, we repent of all our sins & we pray that You would please restore our lands. In the name of Jesus, I claim Psalm 91, Psalm 23, Psalm 25:20-21, Psalm 46:10, Psalm 55:22, Psalm 56:3, Psalm 61:2, Psalm 62:5-8, Psalm 116:7, Psalm 121:2, Joel 2:25-26, 1 John 4:4, Luke 12:2-3, 2 Chronicles 7:14, 2 Timothy 1:7, Jeremiah 30:17, Philippians 4:7-9, Romans 12:18, John 14:27, Isaiah 26:3, Isaiah 43:2, Isaiah 53:5 & Isaiah 54:17 over all of you & all your loved ones. I pray again for all the families, the people, the businesses & all medical workers that You would bless & protect all of them so they can be a true blessing to many other people in need during these difficult days. Father, I pray for all the afflicted around this nation & around the world that they would be completely & fully restored to complete health & for the development of a safe & powerful vaccine. In the name of Jesus, as a child of the true Living God, covered in His blood, protected by Jesus, sealed by the Holy Spirit & as a warrior of Christ, I command, come against, rebuke & cast, through the full power of Jesus Christ, this virus, violence, the spirit of fear, hatred, anxiety, corruption, animosity, destruction, all agents of evil & the devil away from you & all your loved ones. BE GONE NOW!! I pray for Your eternal justice Father. I thank You Father & I claim all these things in Your Holy, powerful, majestic, everlasting, eternal & precious name I pray Lord Jesus, Amen!

Warriors! As we continue to press forward through these difficult times we face, know that whatever you facing today, whatever you fear, whatever tribulations come, God is in complete & total control. Fear not the storm but look to God & focus on Him alone. Dread not the unknown because Christ has you in the palm of His hand. Do NOT be afraid but stand with conviction & courage for victory draws near & deliverance is coming swiftly. The years we walk on this planet are a mere twinkle in the eye of time in comparison to eternity. What we see in our physical realm is minuscule compared to what is coming. Through the name & power of Christ, WE SHALL PREVAIL! VICTORY IS COMING!!! Let not your heart be troubled! Be safe! Be healthy! Be strong! Have hope! Have faith! Have prosperity! Have joy! May God bless all of you!

DAY 237
November 8th, 2020

     Good evening my friends. It's the end of the weekend & we're closing out Sunday, November 8th, 2020 & I pray this message, once again, finds you & your loved ones healthy, safe & well.

Dear Heavenly Father, I come to You tonight with a humble heart, Heavenly praise, love & thanksgiving. Thank You Father that Your will be done, that You are Sovereign over all & that man cannot stop, deter or delay what You have ordained. Father, I lift up & pray for our entire nation tonight. Lord Jesus, we repent of all our sins & we pray that You would please restore our lands & bring peace back to our people. One day, not some, not most, not a few, but that once again EVERY knee shall bow & EVERY tongue confess that Jesus Christ IS LORD! Father, I pray that You will surround every single person reading this message tonight & their loved ones with a powerful, spiritual & impenetrable hedge of protection that no evil can pass through or even come near. In the name of Jesus, I claim Psalm 91, Psalm 23, Psalm 25:20-21, Psalm 46:10, Psalm 55:22, Psalm 56:3, Psalm 61:2, Psalm 62:5-8, Psalm 116:7, Psalm 121:2, Joel 2:25-26, 1 John 4:4, Luke 12:2-3, 2 Chronicles 7:14, 2 Timothy 1:7, Jeremiah 30:17, Philippians 4:7-9, Romans 12:18, John 14:27, Isaiah 26:3, Isaiah 43:2, Isaiah 53:5 & Isaiah 54:17 over all of you & all your loved ones. Father, I pray that you would please call to all those who do not You as their Lord & Savior. Call them that they would accept that You died on the Cross for their sins. Call them to accept You into their hearts & as their Lord so they may be saved & have eternal life forever & not cast into the lake of fire. I pray again for all the families, the people, the businesses & all medical workers that You would abundantly bless them & give them complete peace & protection through these difficult days. Father, I pray for all the sick & afflicted around this nation & around the world that they would be completely & fully restored to complete health, for the development of a safe & powerful vaccine & that this virus would be completely eradicated from the earth once & for all. In the name of Jesus, as a child of the everlasting & eternal true Living God, covered in His Holy blood, protected by Jesus, sealed by the Holy Spirit & as a warrior of Christ, I command, come against, rebuke & cast, through the full power of Jesus Christ, this virus, violence, lies, division, the spirit of fear, hatred, anxiety, corruption, animosity, destruction, all agents of evil, evil of truly any kind & the devil away from you & all your loved ones. BE GONE NOW!! Let the pure justice of God rain down on all the evil done & bring to light that which has been in the dark! I thank You Father & I claim all these things in Your Holy, powerful, majestic, everlasting, eternal & precious name I pray Lord Jesus, Amen!

(Tonight read this with authority, strength & conviction!)
Warriors! We stand ready! We stand firm! We stand confidently in You! Our knees are bowed before You! Our courage & strength come from You! We shout a roar as a mighty lion as we tell this evil that has surrounded us TO BE GONE! We tell it, it has no right! No authority! No claim! No control! And by the name of Christ Jesus WE SHALL PREVAIL! WE SHALL OVERCOME! WE SHALL PERSEVERE! We shall NOT back down! We shall NOT be deterred! We shall NOT give in to fear, terror or destruction! We WILL move forward! We WILL conquer through the name & power of Christ! WE!! WILL!! TRIUMPH!! SHOUT WITH ME NOW!! OUR GOD IS GOD!!! Let not your heart be troubled! May God strengthen You! May God give you courage! May God give you peace! May God bless all of you!

DAY 238
November 9th, 2020

Good evening my friends. It's a brand new week & we're closing out Monday, November 9th, 2020 & I pray this message, finds you & your loved ones healthy, safe & well.

Dear Heavenly Father, I come to You tonight with Heavenly praise, love & thanksgiving. Thank You Father that truly no weapon formed against us shall prosper because of You. In the name of Jesus, I claim Psalm 91, Psalm 23, Psalm 25:20-21, Psalm 46:10, Psalm 55:22, Psalm 56:3, Psalm 61:2, Psalm 62:5-8, Psalm 116:7, Psalm 121:2, Joel 2:25-26, 1 John 4:4, Luke 12:2-3, 2 Chronicles 7:14, 2 Timothy 1:7, Jeremiah 30:17, Philippians 4:7-9, Romans 12:18, John 14:27, Isaiah 26:3, Isaiah 43:2, Isaiah 53:5 & Isaiah 54:17

over all of you & all your loved ones. I pray that you & your loved ones will be completely surrounded by a hedge of protection that is impenetrable to the enemy. I pray for all the families, the people, the businesses & all medical workers that You abundantly bless them with protection, peace, prosperity, faith, health, healing, hope, love, wisdom, guidance & strength. Father, I once again lift up & pray for our entire nation tonight. Lord Jesus, we repent of all our sins & we pray that You would please restore our lands & bring peace back to our people. Truly I say, a day is coming very soon when EVERY knee shall bow & EVERY tongue confess that Jesus Christ IS LORD! Something very big is coming soon. Because of this, Father, I pray that you would please call to all those who do not You yet as their Lord & Savior. Call them that they would accept that You died on the Cross for their sins. Call them to accept You into their hearts & as their Lord so they may be saved & have eternal life forever & not cast into the lake of fire. Father, I pray for all the afflicted with the virus that You, the Great Physician, will completely heal & restore them. In the name of Jesus, as a child of the only true Living God, covered in His Holy blood, protected by Jesus, sealed by the Holy Spirit & as a warrior of Christ, I command, come against, rebuke & cast, this virus, violence, lies, division, the spirit of fear, hatred, anxiety, corruption, animosity, destruction, all agents of evil, evil of truly any kind & the devil away from you & all your loved ones. Let the pure justice of God rain down on all the evil done & bring to light that which has been in the dark! I thank You Father for our coming victory, deliverance & I claim all these things in Your Holy, powerful, majestic, everlasting, eternal & precious name I pray Lord Jesus, Amen!

Warriors! As of today, we have moved another day closer to victory & we will continue to press forward no matter what comes against us. Storms will rage but we have shelter under the wings of Christ. In an uncertain future we can be certain in Christ. God's character never changes; He is the same yesterday, today & tomorrow. What you are facing today, let go of your own understanding & give it to God. Stand tall & know that God has the final say & when God has a destiny for you, there isn't anything that can be done to stop it. We must completely let go & trust & have faith in the truly awesome power of God. Something big is about to happen. SHOUT WITH ME AGAIN!! OUR GOD IS GOD!!! Let not your heart be troubled! May

God strengthen You! May God give you courage! May God give you peace! May God bless all of you!

DAY 239
November 10th, 2020

Good evening my friends. It's Tuesday evening, we're closing out November 10th, 2020 & I pray this message, finds you & your loved ones healthy, safe & well.

Dear Heavenly Father, I come to You tonight with a humble heart, Heavenly praise, awe, love & thanksgiving. Thank You Father that in the midst of the storm, You can completely calm the waters of adversity. I pray that all of you & your loved ones will be completely surrounded by a spiritual & impenetrable hedge of protection. I feel in the depths of my soul that something very big is coming soon. Because of this, Father, I pray that you would please call to all those who do not You yet as their Lord & Savior. Call them that they would accept that You died on the Cross for their sins. Call them to accept You into their hearts & as their Lord so they may be saved & have eternal life forever before it's too late where its beyond the time to choose. In the name of Jesus, I claim Psalm 91, Psalm 23, Psalm 25:20-21, Psalm 46:10, Psalm 55:22, Psalm 56:3, Psalm 61:2, Psalm 62:5-8, Psalm 116:7, Psalm 121:2, Joel 2:25-26, 1 John 4:4, Luke 12:2-3, 2 Chronicles 7:14, 2 Timothy 1:7, Jeremiah 30:17, Philippians 4:7-9, Romans 12:18, John 14:27, Isaiah 26:3, Isaiah 43:2, Isaiah 53:5 & Isaiah 54:17 over all of you & all your loved ones. Father, I lift up & pray for the nation tonight. Lord Jesus, we bow before You, we repent of all our sins & we pray that You would please restore our lands & bring peace back. Father, I pray for all the afflicted with this terrible pestilence that You will completely heal, cure & restore everyone. I pray for all the families, the people, the businesses & all medical workers that You abundantly bless them & give them complete protection from the uncertainties we face. I will say it again, a day is coming very soon when EVERY knee shall bow & EVERY tongue confess that Jesus Christ IS LORD! In the name of Jesus, as a child of the Living God, covered in His blood, protected by Jesus, sealed by the Holy Spirit & as a warrior of Christ,

I command & cast, this virus, violence, lies, division, the spirit of fear, hatred, anxiety, corruption, animosity, destruction, all agents of evil & the devil away from you & all your loved ones. Let the pure justice of God completely rain down on all the evil done & bring to light that which has been in the dark! I thank You Father for our coming deliverance & victory & I claim all these things in Your Holy, powerful, majestic, everlasting, eternal & precious name I pray Lord Jesus, Amen!

Warriors! Another day has passed and we continue to march forward to victory. Christ guides us, step by step, day by day until we are at the very door of deliverance. I believe this day is coming very soon. Tonight, I know many of you, if not all, still fear for the future, uncertain about tomorrow and afraid for even today. Place your burdens & concerns before God, give it to Him and let go of control. God will never let you down ever. What concerns you, concerns Him. What matters to you, matters to Him. Have faith that no matter what comes, He is in control. We're all going through uncharted waters but God is still on the Throne guiding us forward. So tonight, pray for someone in need, don't allow yourself to be a victim, but stand firm, stand tall & command this evil to be gone! Truly I tell you that greater is He who is in us than he who is in this world & as we move forward we do not fight for victory but from victory! We're already won the war because of the work on the cross! SHOUT WITH ME AGAIN!! VICTORY IS COMING! VICTORY IS COMING!! VICTORY IS COMING!!! Let not your heart be troubled! May God strengthen You! May God give you courage! May God give you peace! May God bless all of you!

If you would like to be saved simply say this prayer with me right now, out loud with our mouth.

"God, I'm a sinner I'm sorry for my sins. I ask that You forgive me, and I believe that Jesus Christ is Your Son, and I want to invite Him to come into my heart and trust Him with my life. I'm willing to trust Him as my Savior and follow Him as my Lord forever, and I pray this in Jesus' Name.'"

DAY 240
November 11th, 2020

      Good evening my friends. It's the middle of the week & we're closing out Wednesday, November 11th, 2020 & I pray this message, finds you & your loved ones healthy, safe & well. I also want to say Happy Veterans Day to all our brave men & women.

Dear Heavenly Father, I come to You tonight with Heavenly praise, awe, love & thanksgiving. Thank You Father that no matter what we're facing in these uncertain times, we can always be certain & have faith in You. Father, I lift up & pray for the nation again tonight. Lord Jesus, we all bow before You, we all repent of all our sins & we all pray that You would please restore our lands & bring peace back to our country & people. Father, I pray that you would call to all those around the country & world who do not know You as their Lord & Savior. Please call them that they'd accept that You died on the Cross for their sins. Call them to accept You into their hearts & as their Lord so they may be saved & have eternal life. A day is coming very soon when truly EVERY knee shall bow & EVERY tongue confess that Jesus Christ IS LORD! In the name of Jesus, I claim Psalm 91, Psalm 23, Psalm 25:20-21, Psalm 46:10, Psalm 55:22, Psalm 56:3, Psalm 61:2, Psalm 62:5-8, Psalm 116:7, Psalm 121:2, Joel 2:25-26, 1 John 4:4, Luke 12:2-3, 2 Chronicles 7:14, 2 Timothy 1:7, Jeremiah 30:17, Philippians 4:7-9, Romans 12:18, John 14:27, Isaiah 26:3, Isaiah 43:2, Isaiah 53:5 & Isaiah 54:17 over all of you & all your loved ones. Father, I pray that You will place an impenetrable hedge of protection around all those reading this & their loved ones so that no evil or the virus can pass through it or even come near to them. Father, I pray for all the afflicted that You will completely heal, cure & restore them to complete health with no lasting effects. I pray for all the families, the people, the businesses & all medical workers that You abundantly & completely bless them & give them full protection during these difficult days. In the name of Jesus, as a child of the true Living God, covered in His blood, protected by Jesus, sealed by the Holy Spirit & as a warrior of Christ, I command & cast, this virus, violence, lies, division, the spirit of fear, hatred, anxiety, corruption, animosity, destruction, all agents of evil &

the devil away from you & all your loved ones. I pray to You Lord that Your pure justice will completely rain down on all the evil being done & bring to light that which has been in the dark! I thank You Father for our coming deliverance & victory & I claim all these things in Your Holy, powerful, majestic, everlasting, eternal & precious name I pray Lord Jesus, Amen!

Warriors! It's the middle of the week & as we continue to stand firm, we have moved yet another day closer to victory. I know there is so much going on all around us, but even as these storms seem to surge, toss & throw us about, through the power of Jesus Christ, WE SHALL PREVAIL! I know this has been probably the most difficult year for all of you, myself included, but I truly I tell you, THIS TOO SHALL PASS! This season will come to an end & I can't wait for that day. Let me offer this, God knows what you are going through & as a child of God, He has you in the palm of His hand. He's going to help get you through this. Just hold on! VICTORY IS COMING!!! Let not your heart be troubled! May God strengthen You! May God give you courage! May God give you peace! May God bless all of you!

DAY 241
November 12th, 2020

Good evening my friends. We're nearing the weekend & we're closing out Thursday, November 12th, 2020 & I pray this message, finds you & your loved ones healthy, safe & well.

Dear Heavenly Father, I come to You tonight with Heavenly praise, love & thanksgiving. Thank You Father that though we may not see what is going on in the spiritual realm, that You are aligning everything perfectly. In the name of Jesus, I claim Psalm 91, Psalm 23, Psalm 25:20-21, Psalm 46:10, Psalm 55:22, Psalm 56:3, Psalm 61:2, Psalm 62:5-8, Psalm 116:7, Psalm 121:2, Joel 2:25-26, 1 John 4:4, Luke 12:2-3, 2 Chronicles 7:14, 2 Timothy 1:7, Jeremiah 30:17, Philippians 4:7-9, Romans 12:18, John 14:27, Isaiah 26:3, Isaiah 43:2, Isaiah 53:5 & Isaiah 54:17 over all of you & all you love & hold dear. Father, I pray that You will once again place a spiritual & impenetrable hedge of protection around each & everyone reading this tonight that no evil or virus can pass through or come near. Father, I pray for all the sick & afflicted that You will completely restore them to complete health, for the development of a safe & power vaccine & for the complete eradication of this virus. Father, I pray that you would call to all those around the world who do not know You as their Lord & Savior. Please call them that they'd accept that You died on the Cross for their sins. Call them to accept You into their hearts & as their Lord so they may be saved & have eternal life. Father, I lift up & pray for the nation once again tonight. Lord Jesus, we need You more than ever. Please help us Lord Jesus & we thank You for our coming deliverance. I pray for all the families, the people, the businesses & all medical workers that You abundantly & completely bless them with protection, peace, prosperity, faith, health, hope, health, love, thanksgiving, wisdom, guidance & strength so you can be a blessing to many others. In the name of Jesus, as a child of the true Living God, covered in His Holy blood, protected by Jesus, sealed by the Holy Spirit & as a warrior in the army of Christ, I command, come against, rebuke & cast, this virus, violence, lies, division, the spirit of fear, hatred, anxiety, corruption, animosity, destruction, all agents of evil & the devil away from you & all your loved ones. Greater is He who is in us than he who is in the world & through Your name & power I command this evil to go now! I pray to You Lord that Your pure & absolute justice will completely rain down on all the evil being done & bring into the light that which has been done in the dark! I thank You Father for our coming victory & I claim all these things in Your Holy, powerful, majestic, everlasting, eternal & precious name I pray Lord Jesus, Amen!

Warriors! Tonight, wherever you are in the world reading this, take a moment & pray for God's will to be done. Take a moment & pray for someone hurting & in deep need. Take a moment… And… Pray! Prayer is the weapon the devil shudders at because when God's people pray, mountains move! When God's people pray, barriers are broken! When God's people pray, evil strongholds are destroyed! And when God's people pray, miracles truly come to light. As we press forward & we will continue to move forward we must remember that the one who deserves all the glory & praise from us is God. Christ is in complete control & on the throne & we're about to see something monumental occur. Stand strong! Stand firm! Stand ready! VICTORY IS COMING!!! Let not your heart be troubled! May God strengthen You! May God give you courage! May God give you peace! May God bless all of you!

DAY 242
November 13th, 2020

Good evening my friends. The weekend is here & we're closing out Friday, November 13th, 2020 & I pray this message, finds you & your loved ones healthy, safe & well.

Dear Heavenly Father, I come to You tonight with a humble heart, Heavenly praise, love & thanksgiving. Thank You Father that You are in control, You are on the throne & not man's but Your will be done. I pray for all the afflicted with the virus that You will completely & fully restore them to complete health, for the continued development of a safe & power vaccine & for the complete & total eradication of this virus. Father, once again, I lift up & pray for our nation. Lord, we need You more than ever. Father, Please help us Lord & we thank You for our coming deliverance & victory. I pray for everyone reading this tonight that You would give them full protection & that You would completely &abundantly bless them through these difficult times. In the name of Jesus, I claim Psalm 91, Psalm 23, Psalm 25:20-21, Psalm 46:10, Psalm 55:22, Psalm 56:3, Psalm 61:2, Psalm 62:5-8, Psalm 116:7, Psalm 121:2, Joel 2:25-26, 1 John 4:4, Luke 12:2-3, 2 Chronicles 7:14, 2 Timothy 1:7, Jeremiah 30:17, Philippians 4:7-9, Romans 12:18, John 14:27, Isaiah 26:3, Isaiah 43:2, Isaiah 53:5 & Isaiah 54:17 over all of you & all you love & hold dear. Father, I pray that You will once again place a spiritual & impenetrable hedge of protection around all of you & your loved ones. Father, I pray that you would call to all those who do not know You as their Lord & Savior. Please call them that they'd accept that You died on the Cross for their sins. Call them to accept You into their hearts & as their Lord so they may be saved & have eternal life. In the name of Jesus, as a child of the true Living God, covered in His blood, protected by Jesus, sealed by the Holy Spirit & as a warrior of Christ, I command & cast, this virus, violence, lies, division, the spirit of fear, hatred, anxiety, corruption, animosity, destruction, all agents of evil & the devil away from you & all your loved ones. I pray to You Lord that Your pure & absolute justice will completely rain down on all the evil being done & bring into the light that which has been done in the dark! I thank You Father for our coming victory & I claim all these things in Your Holy, powerful, perfect, majestic, everlasting, eternal & precious name I pray Lord Jesus, Amen!

Warriors! Tonight! Right now! We're going to start with shout to almighty God. OUR GOD IS GOD & THY WILL BE DONE!! Know that whatever you are facing right now, God hears your prayers & something amazing is coming. No matter how improbable or seemingly impossible, God is able to do anything. His will, not ours be done. Through the power & name of Christ WE SHALL PREVAIL. Do NOT fear these storms around us, but stay focused on God & keep praying. As I have said before, there is extreme power in prayer & when you have faith the size of even a mustard seed & truly believe, mountains will be moved! I'm telling you right now, mountains are about to move in a mighty way! Shout with me again! VICTORY IS COMING!!! Let not your heart be troubled! May God strengthen You! May God give you courage! May God give you peace! May God bless all of you!

DAY 243
November 14th, 2020

Good evening my friends. It's now the middle of the weekend & we're closing out Saturday, November 14th, 2020 & I pray this message, finds you & your loved ones healthy, safe & well.

Dear Heavenly Father, I come to You tonight with Heavenly praise, love & thanksgiving. Thank You Father for Your unconditional love of us even when we are at our worst moments & that You're always wanting to welcome us back home. In the name of Jesus, I claim Psalm 91, Psalm 23, Psalm 25:20-21, Psalm 46:10, Psalm 55:22, Psalm 56:3, Psalm 61:2, Psalm 62:5-8, Psalm 116:7, Psalm 121:2, Joel 2:25-26, 1 John 4:4, Luke 12:2-3, 2 Chronicles 7:14, 2 Timothy 1:7, Jeremiah 30:17, Philippians 4:7-9, Romans 12:18, John 14:27, Isaiah 26:3, Isaiah 43:2, Isaiah 53:5 & Isaiah 54:17 over all of you &

all you love & hold dear. Father, I pray that You'll surround all those reading this tonight & their loved ones with an impenetrable & spiritual hedge of protection blocking all attacks from the evil one. I pray for all the sick & afflicted that You will fully restore them to health, for the continued development of a safe & power. Father, I pray that you would call to all those who do not know You as their Lord & Savior. Please call them that they'd accept that You died on the Cross for their sins. Call them to accept You into their hearts & as their Lord so they may be saved & have eternal life. Father, I lift up & pray for our nation & people. Lord, we need You Father. Please help us Lord Jesus & we thank You for our coming deliverance & victory from the storms that ravage our people & lands. I pray that You would abundantly bless all reading this with protection, prosperity, peace, faith, health, hope, love, wisdom, guidance & strength. In the name of Jesus, as a child of the Living God, covered in His Holy blood, protected by Jesus, sealed by the Holy Spirit & as a warrior of Christ, I command & cast, this virus, violence, lies, division, the spirit of fear, hatred, anxiety, corruption, animosity, destruction, all agents of evil & the devil away from you & all your loved ones. As it is written through Your name if we resist the devil he must flee from us. I pray to You Lord that Your pure & absolute justice will completely rain down on all the evil being done & bring into the light that which has been done in the dark! I thank You Father for our coming victory & I claim all these things in Your Holy, powerful, perfect, majestic, everlasting, eternal & precious name I pray Lord Jesus, Amen!

Warriors! We're in the middle of the month & though everything seems chaotic, know that God is still in control & still on the Throne. There isn't anything going on anywhere in this universe that He is not aware of. These days may seem difficult but this too shall pass. Keep believing, keep praying, have faith & be expecting things to get better. Thank God for the deliverance that is coming & the pure victory! We are truly an army with God as our Leader & because of His name & power, WE SHALL PREVAIL! We've already won the war & the battle! SHOUT WITH ME AGAIN! VICTORY IS COMING!!! Let not your heart be troubled! May God strengthen You! May God give you courage! May God give you peace! May God bless all of you!

DAY 244
November 15th, 2020

Good evening my friends. We're on the eve of a brand new week of possibilities & we're closing out Sunday, November 15th, 2020 & as always, I pray this message, finds you & your loved ones healthy, safe & well.

Dear Heavenly Father, I come to You again tonight with Heavenly praise, love & thanksgiving. Thank You Father that You calm the storms of life, You heal the afflicted, You triumph in all matters & that You are the King of Kings & lord of Lords. Father, I lift up & pray deeply for our nation. We are so divided & as it's written, "Any kingdom that is divided against itself is being laid waste; and no city or house divided against itself will [continue to] stand" (Mathew 12:25). Lord, we need You Father more than ever. Please help us Lord Jesus. Please restore our lands & people I pray to You Lord that Your pure & absolute justice will completely rain down on all the evil being done & bring into the light that which has been done in the dark! In the name of Jesus, I claim Psalm 91, Psalm 23, Psalm 25:20-21, Psalm 46:10, Psalm 55:22, Psalm 56:3, Psalm 61:2, Psalm 62:5-8, Psalm 116:7, Psalm 121:2, Joel 2:25-26, 1 John 4:4, Luke 12:2-3, 2 Chronicles 7:14, 2 Timothy 1:7, Jeremiah 30:17, Philippians 4:7-9, Romans 12:18, John 14:27, Isaiah 26:3, Isaiah 43:2, Isaiah 53:5 & Isaiah 54:17 over all of you & all you love & hold dear. I pray that you & your loved ones will be completely encapsulated & surrounded by a hedge of protection that is impenetrable. I pray that You would abundantly bless all reading this with protection, prosperity, peace, faith, health, hope, love, wisdom, guidance & strength to get through these difficult days. I pray for all the afflicted that You will fully restore them to health. Father I pray that anyone reading this who doesn't know You, in that they haven't accepted You as their Savior, that You would call to them & allow their hearts to be receptive to You so they may have eternal life. In the name of Jesus, as a child of the Living God, covered in His Holy blood, protected by Jesus, sealed by the Holy Spirit & as a warrior in the army of Christ, I command & cast, this virus, violence, lies, division, the spirit of fear, hatred, anxiety, corruption, animosity, destruction, all agents of evil & the devil away from you & all your loved ones. EVIL BE GONE!! I thank You Father & I claim all these things in Your Holy, powerful, perfect, majestic, everlasting, eternal & precious name I pray Lord Jesus, Amen!

Warriors! As we approach a new week, please take a moment & pray for someone in need, our nation & even our enemies. As we stare into the face of evil we will not fear, be deterred, not be intimidated or destroyed because we're not victims, we're strong in Christ & as it's written through the name & power of Christ, when we resist the devil, he must flee. He has no power over us. Bad things will happen in this fallen world, but one day, quite soon, that will all be made right. Lean not on your own understanding but trust that God will be right on time & have faith & knowledge that He will take care of you. Stay strong & hold on! VICTORY IS COMING!!! Let not your heart be troubled! May God strengthen You! May God give you courage! May God give you peace! May God bless all of you!

DAY 245
November 16th, 2020

Good evening my friends. We've started a new week & we're closing out Monday, November 16th, 2020 & as always, I pray this message, finds you & your loved ones healthy, safe & well.

Dear Heavenly Father, I come to You again tonight with a humble heart, Heavenly praise, love & thanksgiving. Thank You Father that no matter what, You have the final say! We stand with You Lord Jesus! In the name of Jesus, I claim Psalm 91, Psalm 23, Psalm 25:20-21, Psalm 46:10, Psalm 55:22, Psalm 56:3, Psalm 61:2, Psalm 62:5-8, Psalm 116:7, Psalm 121:2, Joel 2:25-26, 1 John 4:4, Luke 12:2-3, 2 Chronicles 7:14, 2 Timothy 1:7, Jeremiah 30:17, Philippians 4:7-9, Romans 12:18, John 14:27, Isaiah 26:3, Isaiah 43:2, Isaiah 53:5 & Isaiah 54:17 over all of you & all you love & hold dear. I pray that all of you reading this tonight & your loved ones will be completely surrounded by an impenetrable hedge of protection. I pray for all the sick & afflicted with this horrible virus that You will fully restore them to complete health with no lasting effects. I pray that You will give all those reading this complete protection & abundantly bless them through these difficult times so they may be a blessing to many others in need. Father, I pray for our nation. Please restore our lands & people I pray to You Lord that Your pure & absolute justice will completely rain down on all the evil being done & bring into the light that which has been done in the dark! Father I pray for everyone reading this, if they do not know You as their Lord & Savior, that You would call to them so they may be saved & have eternal life. In the name of Jesus, as a child of the Living God, covered in His blood, protected by Jesus, sealed by the Holy Spirit & as a warrior of Christ, I command & cast, this virus, violence, lies, division, the spirit of fear, hatred, anxiety, corruption, animosity, destruction, all agents of evil & the devil away from you & all your loved ones. I thank You Father & I claim all these things in Your Holy, powerful, perfect, majestic, everlasting, eternal & precious name I pray Lord Jesus, Amen!

Warriors! Stand courageous! Stand firm! Stand unified! I will say it again! Through the power of Jesus we shall prevail because all things are possible with Christ! We must continue to hold on & be strong & don't give up! We're getting through these difficult days & yes, this season will pass too! I know how frustrated, tired & angry all of you are & I am as well. The world is in complete & total chaos but in this uncertain world that surrounds us, be certain in God & that He is in control. It's hard to know what to believe these days but I know this. God's character is the same yesterday, today & tomorrow. He WILL deliver us to victory! Throughout history there have been unprecedented times & though we're in one now, I believe that this time will come to an end. Tonight, take a moment & thank God for your blessings no matter how big or small. No matter what happens, we must always take a moment to put things in perspective. We're going to get through this everyone! VICTORY IS COMING!!! Let not your heart be troubled! May God strengthen You! May God give you courage! May God give you peace! May God bless all of you!

DAY 246
November 17th, 2020

     Good evening my friends. As of today, this marks 8 months of praying for you & we're closing out Tuesday, November 17th, 2020 & again as always, I pray this message, finds you & your loved ones healthy, safe & well.

Dear Heavenly Father, I come to You tonight with Heavenly praise, love, faith & thanksgiving. Thank You Father for all the blessings, talents & abilities You've given us to further Your Kingdom. In the name of Jesus, I come to You tonight as a child of the true Living God, covered in His blood, protected by Jesus, sealed by the Holy Spirit & as a warrior of Christ, I command, come against, rebuke & cast, this virus, violence, lies, division, the spirit of fear, hatred, anxiety, corruption, animosity, destruction, all agents of evil & the devil away from you & all your loved ones with the full authority of God. This evil MUST leave now! It has no right, no authority, no place, no claim & as it's written, Through the power & name of Jesus Christ, when we resist the devil he must flee from us. In the name of Jesus, I claim Psalm 91, Psalm 23, Psalm 25:20-21, Psalm 46:10, Psalm 55:22, Psalm 56:3, Psalm 61:2, Psalm 62:5-8, Psalm 116:7, Psalm 121:2, Joel 2:25-26, 1 John 4:4, Luke 12:2-3, 2 Chronicles 7:14, 2 Timothy 1:7, Jeremiah 30:17, Philippians 4:7-9, Romans 12:18, John 14:27, Isaiah 26:3, Isaiah 43:2, Isaiah 53:5 & Isaiah 54:17 over all of you & all you love. I pray for the families, people, businesses, our leaders & our medical workers that they would be truly abundantly blessed with protection, peace, prosperity, faith, health, hope, love, wisdom, guidance & strength to keep pressing forward. Father, I once again pray for our nation. Please restore our lands, our people & I pray that Your pure & absolute justice will rain down on all the evil being done bringing into the light that which has been done in the dark! Father I pray for everyone reading this, if they do not know You as their Lord & Savior, that You would call to them so they may be saved & have eternal life. I pray that all of you reading this & your loved ones will be completely surrounded by a spiritual & impenetrable hedge of protection that evil can't pass through or even come close to. I pray for all the afflicted that You will fully restore them to complete health with no lasting effects & for the eradication of this virus. I thank You Father for Your guidance & strength & I claim all these things in Your Holy, powerful, perfect, majestic, everlasting, eternal & precious name I pray Lord Jesus, Amen!

Warriors! Because of what Christ has done on the cross, as children of God, we're an invincible army through the power & name of Jesus. Every day we hear rumors of more destruction around the planet. But fear not, because though these raging storms surround us, Christ is in complete control & on the Throne. As we take shelter under the very wings of Christ, we're mere observers of the chaos that ensues. We're all tired, angry, frustrated, exhausted & many still very afraid for the future. But I know this, if you are still alive down here, God is not finished with you yet. Though the future is uncertain, know that even when we go through moments in life where we don't understand what is happening, God is right there walking each step with you. I view victory as true accomplishment & if everything was merely given to us, we wouldn't appreciate it nearly as much. Christ is leading us to victory! We're in a spiritual battle right now & we have to be strong, be vigilant & keep fighting with everything we've got! LET GO & LET GOD! VICTORY IS COMING!!! Let not your heart be troubled! May God strengthen You! May God give you courage! May God give you peace! May God bless all of you!

DAY 247
November 18th, 2020

Good evening my friends. It's the middle of the week & we're closing out, Wednesday, November 18th, 2020 & I pray this message, finds you & your loved ones healthy, safe & well.

Dear Heavenly Father, I come to You again tonight with Heavenly praise, love, faith & thanksgiving. Thank You Father for Your infinite wisdom, Your guidance, & unconditional love for all of us. In the name of Jesus, I claim Psalm 91, Psalm 23, Psalm 25:20-21, Psalm 46:10, Psalm 55:22, Psalm 56:3, Psalm 61:2, Psalm 62:5-8, Psalm 116:7, Psalm 121:2, Joel 2:25-26, 1 John 4:4, Luke 12:2-3, 2 Chronicles 7:14, 2 Timothy 1:7, Jeremiah 30:17, Philippians 4:7-9, Romans

12:18, John 14:27, Isaiah 26:3, Isaiah 43:2, Isaiah 53:5 & Isaiah 54:17 over all of you & all you love. I pray for all the afflicted with the virus that You will reach down & touch them with Your healing hand completely restoring them. I pray that all of you & your loved ones will be surrounded by a spiritual hedge of protection that this virus & evil can't penetrate. I pray for the families, people, businesses & our medical workers that they would be given complete protection from the virus & abundantly blessed through these difficult days. Father, I pray that You will please restore our nation & bring peace back to the people. I pray that Your pure & absolute justice will rain down on all the evil being done bringing into the light that which has been done in the dark! Father I pray for everyone who do not know You as their Lord & Savior, that You would please call to them so they may be saved & have eternal life through Jesus. In the name of Jesus, I come to You tonight as a child of the Living God, covered in His blood, protected by Jesus, sealed by the Holy Spirit & as a warrior of Christ, I command & cast, this virus, violence, lies, division, the spirit of fear, hatred, anxiety, corruption, animosity, destruction, all agents of evil & the devil away from you & all your loved ones with the full authority of God. I thank You Father & I claim all these things in Your Holy, powerful, perfect, majestic, everlasting & precious name I pray Lord Jesus, Amen!

Warriors! As we press through each day of this difficult journey we've been on now for over 8 months, we're continuing to make headway & despite the chaos on all sides, we're pushing through. Only through the name & power of Christ will we prevail & prevail we will! Know this, this season will end, this pandemic will end, life will return to normal & this will all be because of the power of Christ. This pandemic has shown us how much we need God. With each day that passes we are that much closer to victory. Tomorrow, we'll be even closer! These times are difficult, trying & frustrating for all of us. Even so, we can still prosper in the desert. We can't give up, we can't give in & we can't stop holding on! We're going to get through this everyone! Have faith & trust that God will deliver us! VICTORY IS COMING!!! Let not your heart be troubled! May God strengthen You! May God give you courage! May God give you peace! May God bless all of you!

DAY 248
November 19th, 2020

Good evening my friends. We're once again nearing the weekend & we're closing out, Thursday, November 19th, 2020 & I pray this message, finds you & your loved ones healthy, safe and well.

Dear Heavenly Father, I come to You again tonight with Heavenly praise, love & thanksgiving. Thank You Father for the doors that You open & for the doors that You close knowing what is best for us always. I pray that every one of you & your loved ones will be completely surrounded by a spiritual hedge of protection that no evil or this virus can penetrate. In the name of Jesus, I claim Psalm 91, Psalm 23, Psalm 25:20-21, Psalm 46:10, Psalm 55:22, Psalm 56:3, Psalm 61:2, Psalm 62:5-8, Psalm 116:7, Psalm 121:2, Joel 2:25-26, 1 John 4:4, Luke 12:2-3, 2 Chronicles 7:14, 2 Timothy 1:7, Jeremiah 30:17, Philippians 4:7-9, Romans 12:18, John 14:27, Isaiah 26:3, Isaiah 43:2, Isaiah 53:5 & Isaiah 54:17 over all of you & all whom you love. Father I pray for everyone reading this who do not yet know You as their Lord & Savior, that You would please call to their soul so they may be saved and have eternal life through Christ Jesus. I pray for all the afflicted that You will completely restore them to full health without any lasting effects. Lord Father, I pray that You will please restore our nation and bring peace back to the people once again. I pray that Your pure, complete and absolute justice will rain down on all the evil being done bringing into the light that which has been done in the dark! I pray for the families, people, businesses and all our brave medical workers that they would be given complete protection from the virus and abundantly blessed through these difficult days to be a blessing to many others. In the name of Jesus, I come to You tonight as a child of the Living God, covered in His Holy blood, protected by Jesus, sealed by the Holy Spirit and as a warrior of in the army of Christ, I command, cast and come against this virus, violence, lies, division, the spirit of fear, hatred, anxiety, corruption, animosity, destruction, all agents of evil and the devil away from you and all your loved ones with the full authority of God. This evil MUST leave now! It has no other option but to leave! I thank You Father and I claim all these things in Your Holy, powerful, perfect, majestic, everlasting and precious name I pray Lord Jesus, Amen!

Warriors! The weekend is quickly approaching. Can you believe how far this journey has taken us. No matter what comes against us, we continue to move & press forward. With Christ as our guide we WILL not fail & we shall prevail through this deep valley. We are merely passing through this uncertain season & we will be far stronger on the other side. Although this has been a difficult time, there has been a lot of good that has come of it as well. We must always remember even in the storm there can be joy! Even in the desert there can be prosperity! Even in the valley, there is abundant life! This time shall pass & our coming victory will be only because of Jesus. We are one day closer & even though we may not know exactly when this will end, when we look back there will be a point that we look to that we crossed over the half way mark & didn't even know it. Even in the unknown, we are ever closer to victory & deliverance! Stay strong everyone! VICTORY IS COMING!!! Let not your heart be troubled! May God strengthen You! May God give you courage! May God give you peace! May God bless all of you!

DAY 249
November 20th, 2020

Good evening my friends. The weekend is finally here & we're closing out, Friday, November 20th, 2020 & with each night, I pray this message, finds you & your loved ones healthy, safe & well.

Dear Heavenly Father, I come to You tonight with a humble heart, Heavenly praise, love & thanksgiving. Thank You Father that You are always working behind the scenes aligning everything perfectly through Your infinite wisdom & plan for our lives. Lord Jesus, I pray that Your pure, complete & absolute justice will rain down on all the evil being done bringing into the light that which has been done in the dark! Father, I pray for the countless families, people, businesses & all our brave medical workers that they would be abundantly blessed with prosperity, peace, protection, faith, health, hope, love, wisdom, guidance & strength through these difficult times. Father, I thank

You that this very moment You are reaching down & healing all those whom are afflicted & restoring them to complete health. I thank You Father that You are surrounding all those reading this message right now with an impenetrable hedge of protection that no evil can even come near. Father I lift up & pray for all those who do not yet know You as their Lord & savior that You would call to their souls & that they're hearts would be receptive so they may accept You as their Lord & Savior & have eternal life through You. In the name of Jesus, I claim Psalm 91, Psalm 23, Psalm 25:20-21, Psalm 46:10, Psalm 55:22, Psalm 56:3, Psalm 61:2, Psalm 62:5-8, Psalm 116:7, Psalm 121:2, Joel 2:25-26, 1 John 4:4, Luke 12:2-3, 2 Chronicles 7:14, 2 Timothy 1:7, Jeremiah 30:17, Philippians 4:7-9, Romans 12:18, John 14:27, Isaiah 26:3, Isaiah 43:2, Isaiah 53:5 & Isaiah 54:17 over all of you & all whom you love. I pray, in the name of Jesus, I come to You as a child of the Living God, covered in His blood, protected by Jesus, sealed by the Holy Spirit & as a warrior of Christ, I command & cast this virus, violence, lies, division, the spirit of fear, hatred, anxiety, corruption, animosity, destruction, all agents of evil & the devil away from you & all your loved ones with the full authority of God. Truly greater is He who is in us than he who is in the world & by His name & power this evil MUST GO NOW! I thank You Father & I claim all these things in Your Holy, powerful, majestic, everlasting & precious name I pray Lord Jesus, Amen!

Warriors! As we stand on another mountain, know that all the chaos in the world is not a surprise to God. In fact, all of what we're seeing right now was prophesied nearly 2,000 years ago & must come to pass. (Matthew 24:6-7) "6 You will hear of wars and rumors of wars, but see to it that you are not alarmed. Such things must happen, but the end is still to come. 7 Nation will rise against nation, and kingdom against kingdom. There will be famines and earthquakes in various places." But d NOT be afraid! God is in complete control. We need to have faith that God's promises will come to pass. When you fly on an jet, you trust that the pilot will get you from point A to point B. There might be some turbulence along the way, but when you land, you realize that you have trusted your life to a machine and a human flying over 500MPH at 30,000 feet in the air. God knows everything You need before You even ask & He will supply your necessities. We're all in a difficult season but know that through Christ all things are possible & WE SHALL PREVAIL! We shall continue to press forward no matter the storm, no matter the turbulence. WE WILL CONTINUE ONWARD!! VICTORY IS COMING!!! Let not your heart be troubled! May God strengthen You! May God give you courage! May God give you peace! May God bless all of you!

DAY 250
November 21st, 2020

Good evening my friends. It's a chilly evening out & we're closing out, Saturday, November 21st, 2020 & I hope & pray this message, finds you & your loved ones healthy, safe & well.

Dear Heavenly Father, I come to You tonight with Heavenly praise, love & thanksgiving. Thank You Father that in these uncertain times, that we can always be certain in You. In the name of Jesus, I claim Psalm 91, Psalm 23, Psalm 25:20-21, Psalm 46:10, Psalm 55:22, Psalm 56:3, Psalm 61:2, Psalm 62:5-8, Psalm 116:7, Psalm 121:2, Joel 2:25-26, 1 John 4:4, Luke 12:2-3, 2 Chronicles 7:14, 2 Timothy 1:7, Jeremiah 30:17, Philippians 4:7-9, Romans 12:18, John 14:27, Isaiah 26:3, Isaiah 43:2, Isaiah 53:5 & Isaiah 54:17 over all of you & all whom you love. Father, I pray, in the name of Jesus, I come to You as a child of the true Living God, covered in His Holy blood, protected by Lord Jesus, sealed by the Holy Spirit & as a warrior in the army of Christ, I command, come against, rebuke & cast this virus, violence, countless lies, division, the spirit of fear, hatred, anxiety, corruption, animosity, destruction, all agents of evil & the devil away from you & all your loved ones with the full authority of God. THIS EVIL MUST GO NOW! Father I lift up & pray for all those souls who do not yet know You as their Lord & Savior that You would call to them & that they're hearts would be receptive so they may accept You as their Lord & Savior & have eternal life through You. Father, I pray for the hurting families, people, businesses & all our medical workers that You would comfort them, give them complete protection & abundantly bless them through these difficult times. I thank You Father that You are completely surrounding all those reading this tonight with an impenetrable hedge of protection that no evil can even come near & that you are shielded from the virus. Father, I pray that Your pure, complete & absolute justice will rain down on all the evil being done bringing into the light that which has been done in the dark! Father, I thank You that You're reaching down touching & healing all those whom are afflicted with this virus & restoring them to complete health. I thank You Father & I claim all these things in Your Holy, powerful, majestic, everlasting & precious name I pray Lord Jesus, Amen!

Warriors! It's the middle of the weekend & as we approach the week of Thanksgiving, please take a moment to thank God for your blessings & for the people in your lives, even if they're at a distance. I pray for a blessing over anyone reading this tonight. There has been so much loss this year but we still have each other & I know how exhausted, stressed out & frustrated all of you are, myself included. But know, that soon this will be over. With each day, we're another step closer. Think of it like you have to walk 10 miles to reach a goal. It may seem completely daunting as you approach it as the whole. But once you start walking, while it may be a long journey on foot, step by step, you WILL eventually make it to your destination. This time, while difficult, has shown us just how much we need God in our lives. Through Christ we WILL make it to our destination & along the way we are growing deeper in Him. We're going to make it everyone! We're all in this together! Shout with me again! VICTORY IS COMING!!! Let not your heart be troubled! May God strengthen You! May God give you courage! May God give you peace! May God bless all of you!

DAY 251
November 22nd, 2020

Good evening my friends. We're on the eve of a new week & we're closing out, Sunday, November 22nd, 2020 & I pray this message, finds you & your loved ones healthy, safe & well.

Dear Heavenly Father, I come to You tonight with Heavenly praise, love & thanksgiving. Thank You Father for all the blessings You have given us both seen & unseen. Thank You for always watching over us & that You are in complete control over everything. I pray that all of you & your loved ones will be surrounded by a spiritual hedge of protection. Father I pray for all the afflicted that they would be healed & completely restored to health with no lasting effects. I pray for the development of a safe & powerful vaccine & for the complete eradication of this virus from the planet. Father, I pray for the countless & hurting families, people, businesses & all our medical workers that You would please comfort them, give them complete & full protection & abundantly & overflowing bless them so they may be a blessing to many others. In the name of Jesus, I claim Psalm 91, Psalm 23, Psalm 25:20-21, Psalm 46:10, Psalm 55:22, Psalm 56:3, Psalm 61:2, Psalm 62:5-8, Psalm 116:7, Psalm 121:2, Joel 2:25-26, 1 John 4:4, Luke 12:2-3, 2 Chronicles 7:14, 2 Timothy 1:7, Jeremiah 30:17, Philippians 4:7-9, Romans 12:18, John 14:27, Isaiah 26:3, Isaiah 43:2, Isaiah 53:5 & Isaiah 54:17 over all of you & all whom you love. Father I lift up & pray for all those souls who do not yet know You as their Lord & Savior that You would please call them to You & that they're hearts would be receptive so they may accept You as their Lord & Savior & have eternal life & be forgiven through You. Father I pray for our nation, please restore our lands & bring peace back to the people. Father, I pray that Your pure, complete & absolute justice will rain down on all the evil being done bringing into the light that which has been done in the dark! In the name of Jesus, I come to You as a child of the true Living God, covered in His blood, protected by Jesus, sealed by the Holy Spirit & as a warrior of Christ, I command & cast this virus, violence, division, the spirit of fear, hatred, anxiety, corruption, animosity, destruction, all agents of evil & the devil away from you & all your loved ones with the full authority of God. It has no place here & through the name of Jesus this evil must leave now! I thank You Father for our coming deliverance & I claim all these things in Your Holy, powerful, majestic, everlasting & precious name I pray Lord Jesus, Amen!

Warriors! A new week is upon us & we're continuing to press forward with everything we've got. We must continue to hold on & be vigilant but deliverance is coming! 2020 continues to prove to be a year of unprecedented events & many of us have been through more than most go through in a lifetime. Still, despite the challenges that we face on all sides. We are strong in Christ & though the storms of rage with destructive force surround us, we need not fear because we are protected by Christ. And no matter what happens let God's will, not our own be done. From the time we're born to the time we pass on is a mere blink in the scope of eternity but there is so much more waiting for us & if you do not know Christ there is no better time than to say the prayer below right now. Don't put off the single greatest decision in your life. If you aren't saved & you are reading this, it's not coincidence. This is your chance right now to accept Christ as Your Lord & savior. Below you will see a simple prayer. Say it out loud & believe it in your heart. VICTORY IS COMING!!! Let not your heart be troubled! May God strengthen You! May God give you courage! May God give you peace! May God bless all of you!

Just pray this prayer right now with me, just simply say, "God, I'm a sinner. I'm sorry for my sins. I ask that You forgive me, and I believe that Jesus Christ is Your Son, and I want to invite Him to come into my heart and trust Him with my life. I'm willing to trust Him as my Savior and follow Him as my Lord forever, and I pray this in Jesus' Name.'"

DAY 252
November 23rd, 2020

Good evening my friends. As we begin this new week, we're closing out Monday, November 23rd, 2020 & I pray this message, finds you & your loved ones healthy, safe & well.

Dear Heavenly Father, I come to You tonight with a humble heart, Heavenly praise, love & thanksgiving. Thank You Father that You make the seemingly impossible, completely possible! In the name of Jesus, I claim Psalm 91, Psalm 23, Psalm 25:20-21, Psalm 46:10, Psalm 55:22, Psalm 56:3, Psalm 61:2, Psalm 62:5-8, Psalm 116:7, Psalm 121:2, Joel 2:25-26, 1 John 4:4, Luke 12:2-3, 2 Chronicles 7:14, 2 Timothy 1:7, Jeremiah 30:17, Philippians 4:7-9, Romans 12:18, John 14:27, 2 Samuel 22:40, Isaiah 26:3, Isaiah 43:2, Isaiah 53:5 & Isaiah 54:17 over all of you & all whom you love. I pray for our nation tonight. Father, please restore our lands & people. Father, I pray that Your pure, complete & absolute justice will rain down on all the evil being done bringing into the light that which has been done in the dark! Father, I pray for all the families, people, businesses & medical workers that You would please abundantly bless them with prosperity, peace, protection, courage, faith, hope, love, health, wisdom, guidance & strength. Please give us all perseverance. Father I pray for all those who do not yet know You as their Lord & Savior. I pray that You would call them to You & that they're hearts would be open & receptive so they may accept You as their Lord & Savior & have eternal life. I pray that all of you & your loved ones will be surrounded by a spiritual & impenetrable hedge of protection. Father I pray for all the afflicted with the virus that they would be restored to complete & full health without any lasting effects & for the continued development of a powerful vaccine. Please give our doctors & scientists wisdom beyond themselves. In the name of Jesus, I come to You as a child of the Living God, covered in His blood, protected by Jesus, sealed by the Holy Spirit & as a warrior of Christ, I once again command & cast this virus, violence, division, the spirit of fear, hatred, anxiety, corruption, animosity, destruction, all agents of evil & the devil away from you & all your loved ones with the full authority of God. THIS EVIL MUST LEAVE! I thank You Father & I claim all these things in Your Holy, powerful, majestic, everlasting & precious name I pray Lord Jesus, Amen!

Warriors! Tonight, once again, take a moment to pray for someone in need & prayer for God's will to be done. We're living in a very unique time period unlike any other time in our lifetimes. You're literally seeing history unfold before your eyes every day. Do not be afraid of the uncertain & unknown but trust in God's plan & deliverance. We need to pray like we've never prayed before. The storms that surround us are mighty & great but they are no match for God. ALL things are possible with Christ! Stay focused on God & His promises. We're going to get through this! DELIVERANCE, VICTORY & JUSTICE ARE COMING!!! Let not your heart be troubled! May God strengthen You! May God give you courage! May God give you peace! May God bless all of you!

DAY 253
November 24th, 2020

Good evening my friends. As we near the middle of the week, we're closing out Tuesday, November 24th, 2020 & I pray this message, finds you & your loved ones healthy, safe & well.

Dear Heavenly Father, I come to You tonight with Heavenly praise, love & thanksgiving. Thank You Father that You are Lord over all & man has no power over Your will! Father, I pray that Your will be done & Your pure, complete & absolute justice will rain down on all the evil being done bringing into the light that which has been done in the dark! So let it be! I pray for our nation tonight. Father, please restore our lands & people. In the name of Jesus, I claim Psalm 91, Psalm 23, Psalm 25:20-21, Psalm 46:10, Psalm 55:22, Psalm 56:3, Psalm 61:2, Psalm 62:5-8, Psalm 116:7, Psalm 121:2, Joel 2:25-26, 1 John 4:4, Luke 12:2-3, 2 Chronicles 7:14, 2 Timothy 1:7, Jeremiah 30:17, Philippians 4:7-9, Romans 12:18, John 14:27, 2 Samuel 22:40, Isaiah 26:3, Isaiah 43:2, Isaiah 53:5 & Isaiah 54:17 over all of you & all whom you love. Father please surround everyone reading this with an impenetrable hedge of protection & give all those reading this peace that surpasses all understanding. Please give us all perseverance & tenacity. Father, I pray for all the families, people, businesses & medical workers that You would please overly & abundantly bless them with prosperity, peace, protection, courage, faith, hope, love, health, wisdom, guidance & strength. Father I pray for all the afflicted that they'd be restored to complete & full health. Father I pray for all those who do not yet know You as their Lord & Savior. I pray that You'd please call them to You & that they're hearts would be open & receptive so they may accept You as their Lord & Savior. In the name of Jesus, I come to You as a child of the true Living God, covered in His Holy blood, protected by Jesus, sealed by the Holy Spirit & as a warrior in the army of Christ, with the full & total authority & power of God, I command, rebuke, come against & cast this virus, violence, division, the spirit of fear, hatred, anxiety, corruption, animosity, destruction, all agents of evil & the devil away from you & all your loved ones. I stand on God's word & through His name & power THIS EVIL MUST LEAVE NOW!! You are not welcome, you have no authority, you have no claim & BE GONE NOW!! I thank You Father & I claim all these things in Your Holy, powerful, majestic, everlasting & precious name I pray Lord Jesus, Amen!

Warriors! Tonight as I stand here, I am asking everyone to get on your knees & pray. Pray for your family, friends, even your enemies & our nation. Prayer is the most powerful spiritual defense & offense against the evil one because when God's people begin to pray, the devil & all his agents of evil begin to shudder. As God's children, we're protected but we must put on spiritual armor daily to fight back. While he can't take your soul, he will try to take your joy. Don't let him! If you feel you are under a spiritual attack & I know many people who are, myself included, tell the enemy, "Greater is He who is in me than he who is in the world & by the name & power of Jesus Christ, you & all your agents of evil MUST leave my presence & my family alone, as I command you to be gone & never return. As it's written if we resist the devil he MUST flee! Enemy I say to you, you are defeated & I claim victory over you as I stand my ground in the name of Jesus Christ! Amen!" There's a spiritual war going on all around us & one day soon, this will end! Keep the faith, never give up, stand strong & know that what God has ordained no one can stop! DELIVERANCE, VICTORY & JUSTICE ARE COMING!!! Let not your heart be troubled! May God strengthen You! May God give you courage! May God give you peace! May God bless all of you!

DAY 254
November 25th, 2020

Good evening my friends. It's the eve before Thanksgiving & we're closing out Wednesday, November 25th, 2020 & I hope & pray this message, finds you & your loved ones healthy, safe & well.

Dear Heavenly Father, I come to You tonight on the evening before Thanksgiving 2020 with Heavenly praise, love & thanksgiving. Thank You Father that even though this is a difficult & uncertain time, that You are guiding our steps & walking with us each step of this journey. In the name of Jesus, I claim Psalm 91, Psalm 23, Psalm 25:20-21,

Psalm 46:10, Psalm 55:22, Psalm 56:3, Psalm 61:2, Psalm 62:5-8, Psalm 116:7, Psalm 121:2, Joel 2:25-26, 1 John 4:4, Luke 12:2-3, 2 Chronicles 7:14, 2 Timothy 1:7, Jeremiah 30:17, Philippians 4:7-9, Romans 12:18, John 14:27, 2 Samuel 22:40, Isaiah 26:3, Isaiah 43:2, Isaiah 53:5 & Isaiah 54:17 over all of you & all whom you love. Father I pray for all the sick & afflicted that they'd be restored to complete & full health & for the complete eradication of this virus. Father I pray for all those who do not yet know You as their Savior & I pray that You'd please call to their souls & that they're hearts would be open & receptive so they may accept You as their Lord & Savior & have eternal life. Father there are a lot of hurting people all across our country who are afraid, for the future & for their families. Please give us all perseverance & tenacity to keep pushing forward. Father, I pray for all the families, people, businesses & medical workers that You would please overly & abundantly bless them with prosperity, peace, protection, courage, faith, hope, love, health, wisdom, guidance & strength through these difficult days. I pray for our nation tonight. Father, please restore our lands & bring calming peace back to the people. Father, I pray that Your complete & perfect will be done & Your pure & absolute justice will rain down on all the evil being done bringing into the light that which has been done in the dark! I pray that each of you & your loved ones this Thanksgiving will be completely surrounded by a hedge of protection that this virus or evil can't penetrate or even come near. In the name of Jesus, I come to You as a child of the Living God, covered in His blood, protected by Jesus, sealed by the Holy Spirit & as a warrior of Christ, with the full & total authority & power of God, I command & cast this virus, violence, division, the spirit of fear, hatred, anxiety, corruption, animosity, destruction, all agents of evil & the devil away from you & all your loved ones. Truly as it's written, greater is He who is in us than he who is in the world & through His name & power the devil MUST flee from you now. I thank You Father for this coming Thanksgiving & I claim all these things in Your Holy, powerful, majestic, everlasting & precious name I pray Lord Jesus, Amen!

Warriors! As it's the night before Thanksgiving 2020, please take a moment & thank God for whom you have in your life & the blessings that God has blessed you with. We must always put everything in perspective, be humble & thankful. On Thanksgiving, please take a moment to pray for someone in need & because a lot of us have been so isolated over the past 8 months, maybe tomorrow send a quick text out to your friends letting them know how much they mean to you. As we continue to press forward know that God is still in control & that this season of difficulty will end. We're pushed through yet another day which makes us 24 hours closer to victory than yesterday. Shout with me again, THANKS BE TO GOD & DELIVERANCE, VICTORY & JUSTICE ARE COMING!!! Let not your heart be troubled! May God strengthen You! May God give you courage! May God give you peace! May God bless all of you!

DAY 255
November 26th, 2020

Good evening my friends. It's Thanksgiving 2020 & we're closing out Thursday, November 26th, 2020 & I pray this message, finds you & your loved ones healthy, safe & well.

Dear Heavenly Father, I come to You this Thanksgiving Day 2020 with a humble heart, Heavenly praise, love & thanksgiving. Thank You Father for all of our families, for this Thanksgiving & for Your only Son, Christ Jesus. Father, I pray for all the countless families, businesses & medical workers across our nation that You would overly & abundantly bless them & give them complete protection through these uncertain times. Father I pray for all the sick & afflicted with the virus that they'd be restored to complete & full health, for the development for a safe & powerful vaccine & for the complete eradication of this terrible virus. In the name of Jesus, I claim Psalm 91, Psalm 23, Psalm 25:20-21, Psalm 46:10, Psalm 55:22, Psalm 56:3, Psalm 61:2, Psalm 62:5-8, Psalm 116:7, Psalm 121:2, Joel 2:25-26, 1 John 4:4, Luke 12:2-3, 2 Chronicles 7:14, 2 Timothy 1:7, Jeremiah 30:17, Philippians 4:7-9, Romans 12:18, John 14:27, 2 Samuel 22:40, Isaiah 26:3, Isaiah 43:2, Isaiah 53:5 & Isaiah 54:17 over all of you & all whom you love. I pray that each of you & your loved ones on this Thanksgiving Day will be surrounded by a spiritual & impenetrable hedge of protection. I pray that each of you has God peace that surpasses all understanding. Father I pray for all those who do not yet know You as their Savior. I pray that You will call to their souls & that they're hearts will be receptive so they may accept You as their Lord & Savior & have eternal life. Father there are so many hurting people & families across our nation who are afraid, for the future. Please give us all strength, wisdom, perseverance, hope & tenacity to keep pushing forward. Father, I pray for our country. Please restore our lands & bring calming peace back to the people. Father, I pray that Your complete & perfect will be done & Your pure & absolute justice will rain down on all the evil being done bringing into the light that which has been done in the dark! In the name of Jesus, I come to You as a child of the Living God, covered in His blood, protected by Jesus, sealed by the Holy Spirit & as a warrior in the army of Christ, with the full & total authority & power of God, I command, rebuke & cast this virus, violence, division, the spirit of fear, hatred, anxiety, corruption, animosity, destruction, all agents of evil & the devil away from you & all your loved ones to the farthest corners of the earth. This evil MUST obey & leave now & never return! I thank You Father for this Thanksgiving Day in 2020 & I claim all these things in Your Holy, powerful, majestic, everlasting & precious name I pray Lord Jesus, Amen!

Warriors! Happy Thanksgiving to all of you! For many of us this is a very different kind of Thanksgiving where families are separated across the nation, but through the power of Christ, this too shall pass. I believe that this difficult season will come to an end soon. It's been a hard year for all of us, but we have each other & we have God. Through Him we are strong & through Him we will make it through to the other side of this void. I can't wait for the day that we can all shout a collective voice of victory when this enemy is brought to destruction. We all stand unified & we won't be stopped, anxious or deterred in our resolve. We will ultimately triumph because of the deliverance, victory, guidance & power of Jesus Christ. Through the name of Jesus, we MUST Rebuke the storms that come & stay completely focused on God. We WILL get through this everyone! Stay strong! VICTORY & JUSTICE ARE COMING!!! Let not your heart be troubled! May God strengthen You! May God give you courage! May God give you peace! May God bless all of you!

DAY 256
November 27th, 2020

    Good evening my friends. The weekend is here & we're closing out Friday, November 27th, 2020 & I pray this message, once again, finds you & your loved ones healthy, safe & well.

Dear Heavenly Father, I come to You Heavenly praise, love & thanksgiving. Thank You Father that the no matter how messed up or broken our lives may become, You are always there ready to put them back together perfectly. In the name of Jesus, I claim Psalm 91, Psalm 23, Psalm 25:20-21, Psalm 46:10, Psalm 55:22, Psalm 56:3, Psalm 61:2, Psalm 62:5-8, Psalm 116:7, Psalm 121:2, Joel 2:25-26, 1 John 4:4, Luke 12:2-3, 2 Chronicles 7:14, 2 Timothy 1:7, Jeremiah 30:17, Philippians 4:7-9, Romans 12:18, John 14:27, 2 Samuel 22:40, Isaiah 26:3, Isaiah 43:2, Isaiah 53:5 & Isaiah 54:17 over all of you & all whom you love. I pray that God blesses all of you reading this with peace that surpasses all understanding. Father I pray for all those who do not yet know You as their Savior or those who have maybe drifted away. I pray that You will call to their souls & that they're hearts will be receptive so they may accept You as their Lord & Savior, be restored & have eternal life. Father, I pray for all the families, businesses & medical workers that You would abundantly bless them with protection, prosperity, peace, faith, hope, health, joy, love, wisdom, guidance & strength through these difficult times. Father I pray for all the afflicted that they'd be completely restored to full health & for the complete eradication of this terrible virus. Father, I pray for our country. Please place Your perfect calming hands on this nation & restore our lands & bring calming peace back to the people. Father, I pray that Your complete & perfect will be done & Your pure & absolute justice will rain down on all the evil being done bringing into the light that which has been done in the dark! I pray that each of you & your loved ones will be completely surrounded by a hedge of protection that no evil can pass through or even come close to. In the name of Jesus, I come to You as a child of the Living God, covered in His blood, protected by Jesus, sealed by the Holy Spirit & as a warrior of Christ, I command, rebuke & cast this virus, violence, division, the spirit of fear, hatred, anxiety, corruption, animosity, destruction, all agents of evil & the devil away from you & all your loved ones with the full & total authority & power of God. THIS EVIL MUST GO NOW! I thank You Father & I claim all these things in Your Holy, powerful, majestic, everlasting & precious name I pray Lord Jesus, Amen!

Warriors! We're approaching a new month & as we continue to press forward, always remember that no matter what we face day by day that God is still in control of everything & He will guide you through the storm. It's hard to imagine that we are a little over 1 month away from a new year. So much has occurred in this year & I'm sure many of you are ready for this one to be over with. Remember though, that through the difficulties of this year God has shown us how much we need Him & that He has brought you through all the difficulties and you are now stronger than when this started. So although it's been a hard year for all of us, some more than others, this time has strengthened & hardened you into a warrior. Each day the clock ticks closer to victory. Just think what tomorrow may bring. As I've said many times on here. ALL things are possible with Christ! We're gonna get through this! We're going to win & through the name & power of Jesus, WE SHALL PREVAIL!! VICTORY & JUSTICE ARE COMING!!! Let not your heart be troubled! May God strengthen You! May God give you courage! May God give you peace! May God bless all of you!

DAY 257
November 28th, 2020

Good evening my friends. It was a beautiful day in NE Ohio & we're closing out Saturday, November 28th, 2020 & I pray this message, finds you & your loved ones healthy, safe & well.

Dear Heavenly Father, I come to You again tonight with Heavenly praise, love & thanksgiving. Thank You Father we're seeing Your awesome power at work all around us each and every day & that You are in complete control of everything. In the name of Jesus, I come to You as a child of the true eternal Living God, covered in His Holy blood, protected by Lord Jesus, sealed by the Holy Spirit

& as a warrior in the army of Christ, I command, rebuke & cast this virus, violence, division, the spirit of fear, hatred, anxiety, corruption, animosity, destruction, all agents of evil & the devil away from you & all your loved ones with the full & total authority & power of God. I thank You Father that You are defending Your people & that Your will be done! In the name of Jesus, I claim Psalm 91, Psalm 23, Psalm 25:20-21, Psalm 46:10, Psalm 55:22, Psalm 56:3, Psalm 61:2, Psalm 62:5-8, Psalm 116:7, Psalm 121:2, Joel 2:25-26, 1 John 4:4, Luke 12:2-3, 2 Chronicles 7:14, 2 Timothy 1:7, Jeremiah 30:17, Philippians 4:7-9, Romans 12:18, John 14:27, 2 Samuel 22:40, Isaiah 26:3, Isaiah 43:2, Isaiah 53:5 & Isaiah 54:17 over all of you & all whom you love. I thank You Father that You are healing the sick & afflicted all over this country & world. I thank You that You are eradicating this virus & for guiding our scientists to develop power vaccines. I thank You Father that You are blessing all those reading this tonight abundantly through these uncertain times. I thank You Lord Jesus that You have surrounded Your children with a hedge of protection that's truly impenetrable. I thank You Father that You are calling countless souls who do not know You yet to be saved by You Father. I thank You Father that You are restoring our lands & bringing peace back to this nation & people. Father, I pray & thank You that Your complete & perfect will be done & Your pure & absolute justice will rain down on all the evil being done bringing into the light that which has been done in the dark! I thank You Father & I claim all these things in Your Holy, powerful, majestic, everlasting & precious name I pray Lord Jesus, Amen!

Warriors! We're living in pure historic times & though the days ahead may seem uncertain, feel the peace & joy that God gives that let's you all know that everything is going to be okay. When we are not focused on God or try to lean on our own corporeal understanding we can become anxious & distraught over circumstances that are beyond our control. But God is the God of impossible possibilities. There isn't anyone or anything more powerful in the known or unknown universe than God. One thing to remember is the devil doesn't have equal evil powers opposite of God. He's not omniscient. He's the opposite of the angel Michael as the devil is a fallen angel. Always know that no matter what is happening in your life, that God is MORE powerful than what we're facing & will deliver you to victory. We're going to be okay everyone! VICTORY & JUSTICE ARE COMING!!! Let not your heart be troubled! May God strengthen You! May God give you courage! May God give you peace! May God bless all of you!

DAY 258
November 29th, 2020

Good evening my friends. As it's the eve of another week, we're closing out Sunday, November 29th, 2020 & as with each night, I pray this message, finds you & your loved ones healthy, safe & well.

Dear Heavenly Father, I come to You tonight with a humble heart, Heavenly praise, love & thanksgiving. Thank You Father for guiding us through another week & that You continue to walk with us & guide us through these unknown waters. In the name of Jesus, I claim Psalm 91, Psalm 23, Psalm 25:20-21, Psalm 46:10, Psalm 55:22, Psalm 56:3, Psalm 61:2, Psalm 62:5-8, Psalm 116:7, Psalm 121:2, Joel 2:25-26, 1 John 4:4, Luke 12:2-3, 2 Chronicles 7:14, 2 Timothy 1:7, Jeremiah 30:17, Philippians 4:7-9, Romans 12:18, John 14:27, 2 Samuel 22:40, Isaiah 26:3, Isaiah 43:2, Isaiah 53:5 & Isaiah 54:17 over all of you & all whom you love. I thank You Father that You are going before & defending Your people & that Your will be done! I pray for all the afflicted that Your healing hands will touch them & restore them to complete & full health. I thank You Lord Jesus that You are continuing to surrounded Your children with a spiritual hedge of protection that's completely impenetrable. Father, I pray that Your pure & absolute justice will completely rain down on all this evil being done bringing into the light that which has been done in the dark! I pray for all the countless souls that have not yet accepted You as their Savior & that they will accept You into their hearts. I pray Father that You will abundantly bless all those reading this tonight through these uncertain times & so they can be a massive blessing to many others. In the name of Jesus, I come to You as a child of the Living God, covered in His Holy blood, protected by Lord Jesus, sealed by the Holy Spirit & as a warrior of Christ, I command, rebuke & cast this virus, violence, division, the spirit of fear, hatred, anxiety, corruption, animosity, destruction, all agents of evil & the devil away from you

& all your loved ones with the full & total authority & power of God. THIS EVIL MUST GO!! I thank You Father & I claim all these things in Your Holy, powerful, majestic, everlasting & precious name I pray Lord Jesus, Amen!

Warriors! When others say give up! I say press forward! When others say it's impossible! I say, ALL things are possible with Christ! When the father of lies says it's over! I say, greater is He who is in me than he is in the world & by the Name & power of Christ I command you & all your agents of evil away from me! Christians everywhere are under similar attacks, including myself, but we need not fear the storm but know who we are in Christ. We are God's children & He will always protect & shield you. There will be times we need to go on the spiritual offensive to push back the evil that surrounds us. But fear not because Christ is your strength & protector. Persecution, accusations, lies, corruption will come but soon, very soon, this will all be made right. We're all in the midst of a massive global spiritual battle because the devil knows his time draws short. Though our foe is formidable he is NOT all powerful & as it's written, if we resist the devil through the name & power of Christ, the devil MUST obey & flee! This coming week, storms will come but you have strength through Jesus. Keep your eyes focused on God no matter what happens! And know deep down that soon, VICTORY & JUSTICE ARE COMING!!! Let not your heart be troubled! May God strengthen You! May God give you courage! May God give you peace! May God bless all of you!

DAY 259
November 30th, 2020

Good evening my friends. It's the start of another new week & we're closing out Monday, November 30th, 2020 & I hope & pray this message, finds you & your loved ones healthy, safe & well.

Dear Heavenly Father, I come to You tonight with Heavenly praise, love & thanksgiving. Thank You Father that You are the God of new beginnings, forgiveness & justice. Father, I pray that Your pure & absolute justice will completely rain down on all this evil being done bringing into the light that which has been done in the dark! Father, I pray that Your perfect will, shall be done! I pray Father that You will abundantly bless all those reading this tonight with peace, prosperity, protection, faith, health, hope, love, thanksgiving, wisdom, guidance & strength. I pray for all the afflicted that Your perfect healing hands will touch them & restore all of them to complete & full health. I pray for all the souls that do not know you & have not yet accepted You as their Savior & that they will accept You into their hearts & have eternal life & forgiveness. I thank You Lord Jesus that You are continuing to surround Your children with a spiritual hedge of protection that's completely impenetrable. In the name of Jesus, I claim Psalm 91, Psalm 23, Psalm 25:20-21, Psalm 46:10, Psalm 55:22, Psalm 56:3, Psalm 61:2, Psalm 62:5-8, Psalm 116:7, Psalm 121:2, Joel 2:25-26, 1 John 4:4, Luke 12:2-3, 2 Chronicles 7:14, 2 Timothy 1:7, Jeremiah 30:17, Philippians 4:7-9, Romans 12:18, John 14:27, 2 Samuel 22:40, Isaiah 26:3, Isaiah 43:2, Isaiah 53:5 & Isaiah 54:17 over all of you & all whom you love. In the name of Jesus, as a child of the Living God, protected & covered in His Holy blood, sealed by the Holy Spirit & as a warrior of Christ, I command & cast this virus, violence, division, the spirit of fear, hatred, anxiety, corruption, animosity, destruction, all agents of evil & the devil away from you & all your loved ones with the full & total authority & power of God. Truly greater is He who is in us than he who is in the world. I thank You Father & I claim all these things in Your Holy, powerful, majestic, everlasting & precious name I pray Lord Jesus, Amen!

Warriors! We are in a brand new week & we're another day closer to victory. With each passing day we're getting closer & soon we will reach the end of this difficult season. I know it's been hard to hold on through all these months, but all difficult seasons do come to an end & joy will replace it. We've all been frustrated, tired & more than ready for this to be over. Through this time, we have gained strength & perseverance. We'll continue to push forward with everything we've got! And when that day of deliverance arrives we'll shout a collective roar of a lion that through the power of Christ we made it through to the other side of this valley! I want the entire earth to shake on that day! It's going to be glorious! 2020 is almost over & on the eve of a new month please take a moment to pray for everyone who is in need, who is struggling & who are afraid for the future. We'll lift them up along with us. God is good & He will deliver us through the storm. ALL things are possible through Christ! Stay strong everyone! We're gonna get through this! VICTORY, DELIVERANCE & JUSTICE ARE COMING!!! Let not your heart be troubled! May God strengthen You! May God give you courage! May God give you peace! May God bless all of you!

The Sinner's Prayer

If you are not yet saved I want to personally invite you to read this prayer below. This could be the most profound decision of your entire life. This is a decision only you can make, as I am on a messenger. Please don't put off to tomorrow what can be done right now. Because tomorrow may never come.

If you would like to be saved, please read the prayer below out loud & believing in your heart.

"God, I'm a sinner. I'm sorry for my sins. I ask that You forgive me, and I believe that Jesus Christ is Your Son, and I want to invite Him to come into my heart and trust Him with my life. I'm willing to trust Him as my Savior and follow Him as my Lord forever, and I pray this in Jesus' Name.'"

DAY 260
December 1st, 2020

Good evening my friends. It's that time of year, Christmas time & as we begin a brand new month we're closing out Tuesday, December 1st, 2020 & I pray this message, finds you & your loved ones warm, healthy, safe & well.

Dear Heavenly Father, I come to You tonight with Heavenly praise, love, the joy of the Christmas season & thanksgiving. Thank You Father for Christmas & the birth of Your only begotten Son Jesus Christ that we may be saved through Him & have eternal life. In the name of Jesus, I claim Psalm 91, Psalm 23, Psalm 25:20-21, Psalm 46:10, Psalm 55:22, Psalm 56:3, Psalm 61:2, Psalm 62:5-8, Psalm 116:7, Psalm 121:2, Joel 2:25-26, 1 John 4:4, Luke 12:2-3, 2 Chronicles 7:14, 2 Timothy 1:7, Jeremiah 30:17, Philippians 4:7-9, Romans 12:18, John 14:27, 2 Samuel 22:40, Isaiah 26:3, Isaiah 43:2, Isaiah 53:5 & Isaiah 54:17 over all of you & all whom you love. Father throughout this last month of 2020, please continue to strengthen & surround your children with a spiritual hedge of protection. I pray for all the sick & afflicted with this terrible virus, that You, the Great Physician will reach down with Your perfect healing hands & restore all of them to complete & full health. I pray Father for all the countless families, people, businesses & medical workers, that You will abundantly bless them with peace, prosperity, protection, faith, health, hope, love, thanksgiving, wisdom, guidance & strength. I pray for all the souls that do not know You as their Savior & that they will accept You into their hearts & have eternal life & forgiveness. Father, I pray that Your pure & absolute justice will completely rain down on all this evil being done bringing into the light that which has been done in the dark! Father, I pray that Your perfect will, shall be done in our lands & people! In the name of Jesus, as a child of the Living God, protected & covered in His Holy blood, sealed by the Holy Spirit & as a warrior in the army of Christ, I command, come against, rebuke & cast this virus, violence, division, the spirit of fear, hatred, anxiety, corruption, animosity, destruction, all agents of evil and the devil away from you & all your loved ones with the full & total authority & power of Mighty God. Through His name this evil MUST

LEAVE NOW! I thank You Father & I claim all these things in Your Holy, powerful, majestic, everlasting & precious name I pray Lord Jesus, Amen!

Warriors! As we enter the last month of the year please take a moment to thank God for all that He has blessed you with over the past few months. We're all going through something right now but know this, God will provide. The future may seem uncertain for all of us, but be certain in God. He is always perfectly right on time, never a second too early & never a second too late. As humans, we have a tendency to only see what's right in front of us, rather than thinking of the spiritual realm & how faith is a major part of that. I know faith can be difficult amidst the powerful storms & uncertainty that encircle us, but as it is written (Mathew 17:20) "Truly I tell you, if you have faith as small as a mustard seed, you can say to this mountain, 'Move from here to there,' and it will move. Nothing will be impossible for you." Remember to keep your eyes focused on God, not the storm, not the circumstance & not the seeming impossibility. All things are possible with Christ! Say that with me again "ALL THINGS ARE POSSIBLE WITH CHRIST! For all of you afraid & hurting tonight, God, your Heavenly Father, is telling you, It's going to be alright. Shout with me again, VICTORY, DELIVERANCE & JUSTICE ARE COMING PRAISE BE TO GOD!!! Let not your heart be troubled! May God strengthen You! May God give you courage! May God give you peace! May God bless all of you!

DAY 261
December 2nd, 2020

Good evening my friends. It's the middle of the week & we're closing out Wednesday, December 2nd, 2020 & I pray this message, finds you & your loved ones warm, healthy, safe & well.

Dear Heavenly Father, I come to You again tonight with Heavenly praise, love, & thanksgiving. Thank You Father that You are a God of miracles, love & justice! I pray for all the people, all the souls that do not know You as their Savior & that they will accept You into their hearts & have eternal life & forgiveness. I pray that each of you are completely surrounded by a spiritual hedge of protection that is impenetrable. In the name of Jesus, I claim Psalm 91, Psalm 23, Psalm 25:20-21, Psalm 46:10, Psalm 55:22, Psalm 56:3, Psalm 61:2, Psalm 62:5-8, Psalm 116:7, Psalm 121:2, Joel 2:25-26, 1 John 4:4, Luke 12:2-3, 2 Chronicles 7:14, 2 Timothy 1:7, Jeremiah 30:17, Philippians 4:7-9, Romans 12:18, John 14:27, 2 Samuel 22:40, Isaiah 26:3, Isaiah 43:2, Isaiah 53:5 & Isaiah 54:17 over all of you & all whom you love. I pray for all the families, people, businesses & medical workers, that You'll be abundantly blessed with peace, prosperity, protection, faith, health, hope, love, thanksgiving, wisdom, guidance & strength. I pray for all the afflicted that You will restore all of them to complete and full health. Father, I pray that Your perfect will, shall be done in our lands and people! Father, I pray that Your pure & absolute justice will completely rain down on all this evil being done bringing into the light that which has been done in the dark! In the name of Jesus, as a child of the Living God, protected & covered in His Holy blood, sealed by the Holy Spirit and as a warrior in the army of Christ, I command & cast this virus, violence, division, the spirit of fear, hatred, anxiety, corruption, animosity, destruction, all agents of evil & the devil away from you & all your loved ones with the full & total authority & power of Mighty God to the farthest ends of the earth, never to return again. I thank You Father & I claim all these things in Your Holy, powerful, majestic, everlasting & precious name I pray Lord Jesus, Amen!

Warriors! Tonight! We once again are another day closer to victory! Don't be dismayed and fearful about tomorrow because Christ has you in the palm of His hand. He knows your personal needs before you even pray for them and even knows precisely how many hairs are on your head. No matter what happens God will always provide. We need to always remember that God wants us to place our burdens in His hands and rely on Him. When we try to do things our own way, we eventually will run into a wall or many walls. When we let go and let God, though the journey could be difficult, you will be in a far better place on the other side of the problem and be victorious. Keep your eyes continually focused on God and not the storm. Do not fear because God is your deliverer and through the power of Christ WE SHALL PREVAIL! VICTORY, DELIVERANCE and JUSTICE ARE COMING!!! Let not your heart be troubled! May God strengthen

You! May God give you courage! May God give you peace! May God bless all of you!

DAY 262
December 3rd, 2020

Good evening my friends. We're nearing the weekend & we're closing out Thursday, December 3rd, 2020 & I pray this message, finds you & your loved ones warm, healthy, safe & well.

Dear Heavenly Father, I come to You tonight praising You with Heavenly praise, love, & thanksgiving. Thank You Father that You when everything seemingly collapses around us that not only are You there to pick up the pieces but even then, You can still bring us to victory & our destiny! In the name of Jesus, I claim Psalm 91, Psalm 23, Psalm 25:20-21, Psalm 46:10, Psalm 55:22, Psalm 56:3, Psalm 61:2, Psalm 62:5-8, Psalm 116:7, Psalm 121:2, Joel 2:25-26, 1 John 4:4, Luke 12:2-3, 2 Chronicles 7:14, 2 Timothy 1:7, Jeremiah 30:17, Philippians 4:7-9, Romans 12:18, John 14:27, 2 Samuel 22:40, Isaiah 26:3, Isaiah 43:2, Isaiah 53:5 & Isaiah 54:17 over all of you & all whom you love. I pray that each of you are completely surrounded by a spiritual & impenetrable hedge of protection against all evil. I pray for all the sick & afflicted with this horrible virus that You will restore all of them to complete & full health with no long term problems. Father, I pray that Your perfect will, shall be done in our lands & people! Father, I pray that Your pure & absolute justice will completely rain down on all this evil being done bringing into the light that which has been done in the dark! I pray for all the people all over the world that do not know You as their Savior & that they will accept You into their hearts & have eternal life & forgiveness. I pray for all the families, people, businesses, our leaders & medical workers, that You'll be abundantly & completely protected through these uncertain days. In the name of Jesus, as a child of the Living God, protected & covered in His Holy blood, sealed by the Holy Spirit & as a warrior of Christ, I command & cast this virus, violence, division, the spirit of fear, hatred, anxiety, corruption, animosity, destruction, all agents of evil & the devil away from you & all your loved ones with the full & total authority & power of Mighty GOD! THIS EVIL MUST GO NOW!

I thank You Father & I claim all these things in Your Holy, powerful, majestic, everlasting & precious name I pray Lord Jesus, Amen!

Warriors! The weekend is coming up fast & we need to continue to be strong & vigilant. I know so many people who are struggling & we must remember to pray for all those who are in need tonight, as well as our friends & family. But despite everything going on, know this... God is STILL in control & on the throne. Through the name & power of Christ WE SHALL & WE WILL PREVAIL! Christ didn't bring you this far in life to let you go now. He has a plan for each of you & when we seek God's will for our lives, you WILL reach your appointed destiny set forth from God. There isn't anything in the known or unknown universe that can stop God's plan for your life. We're going to get through this everyone. It's a long journey but we WILL PERSEVERE! Shout with me once again! VICTORY, DELIVERANCE & JUSTICE ARE COMING!!! Let not your heart be troubled! May God strengthen You! May God give you courage! May God give you peace! May God bless all of you!

DAY 263
December 4th, 2020

Good evening my friends. With the weekend finally here, we're closing out Friday, December 4th, 2020 & I pray this message, finds you & your loved ones warm, healthy, safe & well.

Dear Heavenly Father, I come to You tonight with a humble heart, praising You with Heavenly praise, love, & thanksgiving. Thank You Father that in the midst of the storm, You are in complete control & on the Throne! I pray for all the afflicted with the virus that You will miraculously restore all of them to complete & full health. I pray that each of you are completely surrounded by a spiritual & impenetrable hedge of protection against all evil & this virus that it can't even come near you or your loved ones. In the name of Jesus, I claim Psalm 91, Psalm 23, Psalm 25:20-21, Psalm 46:10, Psalm 55:22, Psalm 56:3, Psalm 61:2, Psalm 62:5-8, Psalm 116:7, Psalm 121:2, Joel 2:25-26, 1 John 4:4, Luke 12:2-3, 2 Chronicles 7:14, 2 Timothy 1:7, Jeremiah 30:17, Philippians 4:7-9, Romans 12:18, John 14:27, 2 Samuel

22:40, Isaiah 26:3, Isaiah 43:2, Isaiah 53:5 & Isaiah 54:17 over all of you & all whom you love. In the name of Jesus, I come before You as a child of the Living God, protected & covered in His Holy blood, sealed by the Holy Spirit & as a warrior of Christ, I command, come against, rebuke & cast this virus, violence, division, the spirit of fear, hatred, anxiety, corruption, animosity, destruction, all agents of evil & the devil away from you & all your loved ones with the full & total authority & power of GOD! Greater is He who is in us than he who is in the world & by His name & power this evil must flee now! Father, I pray that Your will shall be done in our lands & people! Father, I pray that Your pure & absolute justice will completely rain down on all this evil being done bringing into the light that which has been done in the dark! I pray for all the people all over this country & world that do not yet know You as their Savior & that they will accept You into their hearts as their Lord. I pray for all the families, people, businesses, our leaders & medical workers, that You'll be abundantly blessed & completely protected so you can be a blessing to many others. I thank You Father & I claim all these things in Your Holy, powerful, majestic, everlasting & precious name I pray Lord Jesus, Amen!

Warriors! As we close out another week, we once again stand on the mountain praising Your name & thanking You that we're another day closer to victory. As we walk through this valley, step by step, we know Your guidance will bring us safely through to the other side. No matter what happens we know that You have the final say, You're in control & You are the God of Justice! My friends, this season will pass. This difficult time will end! Life will return to normal! Through Christ, WE SHALL PREVAIL! Shout with me again tonight OUR GOD IS GOD & VICTORY, DELIVERANCE & JUSTICE ARE COMING!!! Let not your heart be troubled! May God strengthen You! May God give you courage! May God give you peace! May God bless all of you!

DAY 264
December 5th, 2020

Good evening my friends. On this cold winter night in NE Ohio we're closing out Saturday, December 5th, 2020 & I pray this message, finds you & your loved ones warm, healthy, safe & well.

Dear Heavenly Father, I come to You tonight praising You with Heavenly praise, love, & thanksgiving. Thank You Father that You are the Great Healer, the Great Physician, the Lord Almighty & there isn't anything too difficult for you! I pray that You will perfect that which concerns everyone reading this message tonight. Father, I pray that you will surround everyone reading this & their loved ones with an impenetrable hedge of protection. I pray for all the sick & afflicted that You will miraculously restore all of them to complete & full health. I pray that You will heal all those suffering tonight be it human or even pet. In the name of Jesus, I claim Psalm 91, Psalm 23, Psalm 25:20-21, Psalm 46:10, Psalm 55:22, Psalm 56:3, Psalm 61:2, Psalm 62:5-8, Psalm 116:7, Psalm 121:2, Joel 2:25-26, 1 John 4:4, Luke 12:2-3, 2 Chronicles 7:14, 2 Timothy 1:7, Jeremiah 30:17, Philippians 4:7-9, Romans 12:18, John 14:27, 2 Samuel 22:40, Isaiah 26:3, Isaiah 43:2, Isaiah 53:5 & Isaiah 54:17 over all of you & all whom you love. I pray that You will give deep wisdom to those seeking answers. I pray for all the people all over this country & world that do not yet know You as their Savior & that they will accept You into their hearts as their Lord. I pray for all the families, people, businesses, our leaders & medical workers, that You'll be abundantly blessed & completely protected & prosperous so you can be a blessing to many others. Father, I pray that Your perfect will shall be done in our lands & people! Father, I pray that Your pure & absolute justice will completely & totally rain down on all this evil being done bringing into the light that which has been done in the dark! In the name of Jesus, as a child of the Living God, protected, covered & sealed by the Holy Spirit & His blood I command & cast this virus, violence, division, the spirit of fear, hatred, anxiety, corruption, animosity, destruction, sickness, all agents of evil & the devil away from you & all your loved ones with the full & total authority & power of GOD! This evil MUST leave NOW! This destruction MUST leave NOW! I thank You Father & I claim all these things in Your Holy, powerful, majestic, everlasting & precious name I pray Lord Jesus, Amen!

Warriors! Tonight, pray for those in need! Pray for those hurting! Pray for those who are sick! Pray for those who are against us. In a simple word, pray. There is real power in prayer & I believe that this moment God is breaking down barriers, healing the sick, restoring what the locusts have eaten, answering prayers & working everything for your good. It's been a difficult journey, but through the grace of God, we're still fighting! We live in a fallen world, but know that soon, this will all be made right. There are so many people hurting tonight everywhere but as warriors in Christ, a prayer from you, right this moment, can make the total difference in someone's life. We have to stay strong through these difficult times. We're all struggling right now, some more than others, but if God is for us, who can be against us. God promised to NEVER leave or forsake you & His character is the same yesterday, today & tomorrow. As difficult as it can sometimes be, have faith that He will deliver you. I pray for God to bless you tonight. I pray that God will supply all of your needs & give you strength to keep fighting through to victory & deliverance. With Christ, not some things but ALL things are possible. Through Christ, WE SHALL PREVAIL! Stand firm! Stand tall! Stand ready! Stand with Christ! VICTORY, DELIVERANCE & JUSTICE ARE COMING!!! Let not your heart be troubled! May God strengthen You! May God give you courage! May God give you peace! May God bless all of you!

DAY 265
December 6th, 2020

Good evening my friends. It's the eve of a brand new week & we're closing out Sunday, December 6th, 2020 & I pray this message, finds you & your loved ones warm, healthy, safe & well.

Dear Heavenly Father, I come to You tonight with Heavenly praise, love, & thanksgiving. Thank You Father that this very moment You are working miracles for people all over the world & for Your unconditional love. I once again pray that You will perfect that which concerns everyone reading this message tonight & heal all those suffering from even pets to humans. Father I pray for all the afflicted that You will reach down into them & heal every molecule of their bodies & miraculously restore them to complete & full health. In the name of Jesus, I claim Psalm 91, Psalm 23, Psalm 25:20-21, Psalm 46:10, Psalm 55:22, Psalm 56:3, Psalm 61:2, Psalm 62:5-8, Psalm 116:7, Psalm 121:2, Joel 2:25-26, 1 John 4:4, Luke 12:2-3, 2 Chronicles 7:14, 2 Timothy 1:7, Jeremiah 30:17, Philippians 4:7-

9, Romans 12:18, John 14:27, 2 Samuel 22:40, Isaiah 26:3, Isaiah 43:2, Isaiah 53:5 & Isaiah 54:17 over all of you & all whom you love. Father, I pray that you will surround everyone reading this & their loved ones with a spiritual & impenetrable hedge of protection that neither this virus or any form of evil can pass through. I pray that You will give deep spiritual wisdom to those seeking answers. I pray for all the people all over this country & world that do not yet know You as their Savior & that they will accept You into their hearts as their Lord. Father, I pray that Your perfect will shall be done in our lands & people! Father, I pray that Your pure & absolute justice will completely rain down on all this evil being done bringing into the light that which has been done in the dark stopping it in its tracks! I pray for all the families, people, businesses, our leaders & medical workers, that You'll abundantly bless them with complete protection, peace, prosperity, faith, health, hope, love, thanksgiving, wisdom, guidance & strength. In the name & power of Jesus, as a warrior in the army of Christ, covered, sealed & protected by His Blood & the Holy Spirit I command this evil that has spread throughout our lands & people be cast to the farthest ends of the world, never to return or harass you again. THIS EVIL MUST GO NOW! I thank You Father & I claim all these things in Your Holy, powerful, majestic, everlasting & precious name I pray Lord Jesus, Amen!

Warriors! We're approaching a new week & there are so many of us that need prayer tonight. Please take a moment to say a prayer that would cover everyone reading this message. There is pure, spiritual power in prayer & it is the most effective means of victory & deliverance. God hears Your prayers. God knows what you are going through this very moment & He already has a plan for deliverance & victory for you. This time has been one of the most difficult & could be the most difficult we have or ever will face in our lifetimes, but I also believe that this season will come to an end & joy will replace it. We're not only fighting this virus around the planet but we're fighting the very forces of darkness trying to overtake this world. Behind the scenes, there is a spiritual war going on all around us at any one moment. But know this! We do NOT fight for victory but FROM victory! We've already won the war & everything you are seeing right now is leading to EVERYTHING being made right soon. We MUST stay strong! We MUST hold on! We MUST have faith!

Through Christ, WE SHALL PREVAIL! VICTORY, DELIVERANCE & JUSTICE ARE COMING!!! Let not your heart be troubled! May God strengthen You! May God give you courage! May God give you peace! May God bless all of you!

DAY 266
December 7th, 2020

Good evening my friends. As we start this brand new exciting week, we're closing out Monday, December 7th, 2020 & I hope & pray this message, finds you & your loved ones warm, healthy, safe & well.

Dear Heavenly Father, I come to You tonight with a humble heart, Heavenly praise, love, & thanksgiving. Thank You Father that in the midst of the storm, you're in complete & total control of everything going on & thank You that You will deliver us to victory. In the name of Jesus, I claim Psalm 91, Psalm 23, Psalm 25:20-21, Psalm 46:10, Psalm 55:22, Psalm 56:3, Psalm 61:2, Psalm 62:5-8, Psalm 116:7, Psalm 121:2, Joel 2:25-26, 1 John 4:4, Luke 12:2-3, 2 Chronicles 7:14, 2 Timothy 1:7, Jeremiah 30:17, Philippians 4:7-9, Romans 12:18, John 14:27, 2 Samuel 22:40, Isaiah 26:3, Isaiah 43:2, Isaiah 53:5 & Isaiah 54:17 over all of you & all whom you love. Father, I pray that Your perfect will shall be done in our lands & people! Father, I pray that Your pure & absolute justice will completely rain down on all this evil being done bringing into the light that which has been done in the dark! In the name & power of Jesus Christ, as a warrior in the army of Christ, covered, sealed & protected by His Blood & the Holy Spirit I command this pure evil that has been spreading throughout our lands & people & I come against, command, rebuke & cast it to the farthest ends of the world with the full authority & power of God. Greater is He who is in us than he who is in the world & as it's written if we resist the devil he MUST FLEE! I pray that You will give spiritual wisdom to those seeking answers. I pray for all the people all over this country & world that do not yet know You as their Savior & that they will accept You into their hearts as their Lord. Father I pray for all the sick that You will completely restore & heal all who are afflicted with this virus. I pray for all the families, people, businesses, our leaders & medical workers, that You'll abundantly bless them & protect them through these difficult days. Father, I pray that you will surround everyone reading this & their loved ones with a spiritual & impenetrable hedge of protection. I thank You Father & I claim all these things in Your Holy, powerful, majestic, everlasting & precious name I pray Lord Jesus, Amen!

Warriors! Tonight, I'm asking that you once again pray for some one in need, pray for our nation & pray for victory & deliverance. We're another day closer to victory by the grace of Lord Jesus. I will say this every single night. Through the name & power of Christ WE SHALL PREVAIL! These are difficult & dangerous times we live in, but I also believe that deliverance, victory & justice are coming. We're on the edge of times prophesied in the Bible nearly 2,000 years ago. But be not afraid, all this must happen but know that God is still in control & on the Throne! We're going to make it through this time! This season will come to an end! This virus will be eradicated & very soon all wrongs will be made right. Tonight, fear not, have faith & praise the name of our Lord & Savior, Jesus Christ that VICTORY, DELIVERANCE & JUSTICE ARE COMING!!! Let not your heart be troubled! May God strengthen You! May God give you courage! May God give you peace! May God bless all of you!

DAY 267
December 8th, 2020

Good evening my friends. We're another closer to victory & we're closing out Tuesday, December 8th, 2020 & I pray this message, finds you & your loved ones warm, healthy, safe & well.

Dear Heavenly Father, I come to You tonight with Heavenly praise, love, & thanksgiving. Thank You Father You sent Your only begotten Son to die on the cross for our sins, that we may be saved & have eternal Life. Father, I pray that Your will shall be done in our lands & people! Father, I pray that Your pure & absolute justice will completely rain down on all this evil being done bringing into the light that which has been done in the dark exposing everything that is unknown! I pray for all the people all over the world that do not yet know You as their Savior & that they will accept You into their hearts as their Lord. I pray that all the afflicted will be completely restored to full health. In the name of Jesus, as a warrior in the army of Christ, covered, sealed & protected by His Blood & the Holy Spirit I command this unbridled evil that has been spreading throughout our nation & I come against, command, rebuke & cast it to the farthest ends of the world with the full authority & power of God. EVIL GO NOW! In the name of Jesus, I claim Psalm 91, Psalm 23, Psalm 25:20-21, Psalm 46:10, Psalm 55:22, Psalm 56:3, Psalm 61:2, Psalm 62:5-8, Psalm 116:7, Psalm 121:2, Joel 2:25-26, 1 John 4:4, Luke 12:2-3, Ephesians 6:10-18, 2 Chronicles 7:14, 2 Timothy 1:7, Jeremiah 30:17, Philippians 4:7-9, Romans 12:18, John 14:27, 2 Samuel 22:40, Isaiah 26:3, Isaiah 43:2, Isaiah 53:5 & Isaiah 54:17 over all of you & all whom you love. I pray for all the families, people, businesses, our leaders & medical workers, that they'll be abundantly blessed with protection, prosperity, peace, faith, love, health, hope, wisdom, guidance, perseverance & strength!. Father, I pray that you will surround everyone reading this & their loved ones with a spiritual & impenetrable hedge of protection against all evil. I thank You Father & I claim all these things in Your Holy, powerful, majestic, everlasting & precious name I pray Lord Jesus, Amen!

Warriors! In 9 days I will have been praying over you for 9 months solid & by the grace of God we're still here & fighting forward! Christians everywhere are under attack both in the physical & spiritual realm. But through the name & power of Christ, we have strength, strength & we shall prevail. As Paul the Apostle said, we must put on the whole armor of God that we may be able to stand against the devil's schemes. We're in the middle of an all out spiritual war & while we are protected by Christ, there are times we need to go on the offensive to push back against the enemy. As I've said many times. Greater is He who is in us than he who is in the world & if we resist the devil by the name, power & authority of Christ, the devil must flee. While our enemy is formidable he is not all powerful & as children of God we can cast him away from us. But fear not because with each day we're closer to victory & though weeping may endure for a night, joy comes in the morning. We're on a journey through a deep valley & all are affected but we must hold on, stay strong & have unwavering faith even when all seems impossible. But know this truth! VICTORY, DELIVERANCE & JUSTICE ARE COMING!!! Let not your heart be troubled! May God strengthen You! May God give you courage! May God give you peace! May God bless all of you!

DAY 268
December 9th, 2020

Good evening my friends. As we venture through this week during the Christmas season, we're closing out Wednesday, December 9th, 2020 & I pray this message, finds you & your loved ones warm, healthy, safe & well.

Dear Heavenly Father, I come to You tonight with Heavenly praise, love, & thanksgiving. Thank You Father for all the blessings, talents & gifts You have blessed us with. In the name of Jesus, I claim Psalm 91, Psalm 23, Psalm 25:20-21, Psalm 46:10, Psalm 55:22, Psalm 56:3, Psalm 61:2, Psalm 62:5-8, Psalm 116:7, Psalm 121:2, Joel 2:25-26, 1 John 4:4, Luke 12:2-3, Ephesians 6:10-18, 2 Chronicles 7:14, 2 Timothy 1:7, Jeremiah 30:17, Philippians 4:7-9, Romans 12:18, John 14:27, 2 Samuel 22:40, Isaiah 26:3, Isaiah 43:2, Isaiah 53:5 & Isaiah 54:17 over all of you & all whom you love. I pray that you & your loved ones are surrounded by an impenetrable hedge of protection. I pray for all the families, people, businesses, our leaders & medical workers, that they'll be abundantly blessed & completely protected through these uncertain days we face. Lord Jesus, I pray that Your will shall be done in our lands & people! Father, I pray that Your pure & absolute justice will completely rain down on all this evil & bring into the light that which has been done in the dark. I pray for all the people all over the world that do not yet know You as their Savior & that they will accept You into their hearts as their Lord. I pray that all the sick & afflicted will be completely restored to full health with no long term effects & for a power & safe vaccine. In the name of Jesus, as a warrior in the army of Christ, covered, sealed & protected by His Blood & the Holy Spirit I command, come against, rebuke & cast this evil in all forms completely away from you & your loved ones! I thank You Father for our coming deliverance, victory & I claim all these things in Your Holy, powerful, majestic, everlasting & precious name I pray Lord Jesus, Amen!

Warriors! As we approach the end of 2020, I know how many you are happy about this, myself included, take a moment to thank God for the blessings that have come in the midst of the storm. In every difficult or dark situation, we must always try to look for the good in the moment. Life is difficult but our approach to the circumstances can make a huge difference. We're all in a rough season, but take joy in that this season will come to an end & with each day we ARE closer to victory. These uncertain times will end! Through the name & power of Christ we shall prevail & everything going on right now is not a surprise to God. He has a plan for victory, he knows exactly what each of you is going through & he will always supply your needs. We are His children & He only wants what's best for us. Through every difficult situation, there is something to be learned. His ways aren't always easy but they are always BEST. Always remember to keep your eyes focused on God through the storm & I'm calling everyone to pray like you've never prayed before. VICTORY, DELIVERANCE & JUSTICE ARE COMING!!! Let not your heart be troubled! May God strengthen You! May God give you courage! May God give you peace! May God bless all of you!

DAY 269
December 10th, 2020

Good evening my friends. We're approaching the end of the week during this Christmas season & we're closing out Thursday, December 10th, 2020 & I pray this message, finds you & your loved ones warm, healthy, safe & well.

Dear Heavenly Father, I come to You tonight with Heavenly praise, love, & thanksgiving. Thank You Father that when all seems impossible, You're still in complete control & can bring about miracles. I pray for all the families, people, businesses, our leaders & medical workers, that they'll be abundantly blessed with protection, peace, prosperity, faith, hope, health, love, thanksgiving, wisdom, guidance & strength. I pray that you & all your loved ones are completely surrounded by an impenetrable hedge of protection against all forms of evil. I pray that all the afflicted will be completely restored to full health, that this virus will be completely eradicated & for powerful & safe vaccines. Father,

I pray that Your will shall be done in our lands & people! Father, I pray that Your pure & absolute justice will completely rain down on all this evil & bring into the light that which has been done in the dark. In the name of Jesus, as a warrior in the army of Christ, covered, sealed & protected by His Blood & the Holy Spirit I command, come against, rebuke & cast this evil in every & all forms completely away from you & your loved ones! I pray for all the people all over the world that do not yet know You as their Savior & that they will accept You into their hearts as their Lord. In the name of Jesus, I claim Psalm 91, Psalm 23, Psalm 25:20-21, Psalm 46:10, Psalm 55:22, Psalm 56:3, Psalm 61:2, Psalm 62:5-8, Psalm 116:7, Psalm 121:2, Joel 2:25-26, 1 John 4:4, Luke 12:2-3, Ephesians 6:10-18, 2 Chronicles 7:14, 2 Timothy 1:7, Jeremiah 30:17, Philippians 4:7-9, Romans 12:18, John 14:27, 2 Samuel 22:40, Isaiah 26:3, Isaiah 43:2, Isaiah 53:5 & Isaiah 54:17 over all of you & all whom you love. I thank You Father for our coming miraculous deliverance, victory & I claim all these things in Your Holy, powerful, majestic, everlasting & precious name I pray Lord Jesus, Amen!

Warriors! We're continuing to press forward & we're yet another 24 hours closer to victory. We're so close! We need to continue to be strong & vigilant & not let our guard down. We're fighting forward & we will not be stopped, deterred or lose focus. With Christ as our leader, guiding us forward, we shall prevail! (John 8:32) Then you will know the truth, and the truth will set you free. Tonight, please take a moment to pray for someone in need, prayer for our nation, pray for your enemy & pray for your friends & family. The one thing that is certain in this uncertain world is Christ Jesus. Take your eyes off the storm & focus them on Christ! Shout with me again tonight! VICTORY, DELIVERANCE & JUSTICE ARE COMING!!! Let not your heart be troubled! May God strengthen You! May God give you courage! May God give you peace! May God bless all of you!

DAY 270
December 11th, 2020

Good evening my friends. The weekend is finally here on this night in the Christmas season & we're closing out Friday, December

11th, 2020 and I pray this message, finds you & your loved ones warm, healthy, safe & well.

Dear Heavenly Father, I come to You tonight with a humble heart, Heavenly praise, love, & thanksgiving. Thank You Father that You make a way when there appears to not be a way, that You break down the walls of Jericho, that You are the God of the infinite universe & that You & only You have the final say in all things. Father, I pray that Your perfect will shall be done in & throughout our lands & people! Father, I pray that Your pure & absolute perfect justice will rain down on all this evil & bring into the light that which has been done in the dark. In the name of Jesus, as a warrior in the army of Christ, covered, sealed & protected by His Blood & the Holy Spirit I command, come against, rebuke & cast this evil, the spirit of fear, anger, corruption, lies, anxiety, destruction, all agents of evil & the devil away from you & your loves ones this very instant! I pray for all the families, people, businesses, our leaders & medical workers, that they'll be abundantly blessed &given full protection during these chaotic times. I pray that all the afflicted will be completely restored to full health & that this virus will soon be completely eradicated. I pray that you & all your loved ones are surrounded by an impenetrable hedge of protection against all forms of evil & the virus. I pray for all the people who do not yet know You as their Savior & that they will accept You into their hearts as their Lord & have forgiveness & eternal life. In the name of Jesus, I claim Psalm 91, Psalm 23, Psalm 25:20-21, Psalm 46:10, Psalm 55:22, Psalm 56:3, Psalm 61:2, Psalm 62:5-8, Psalm 116:7, Psalm 121:2, Joel 2:25-26, 1 John 4:4, Luke 12:2-3, Ephesians 6:10-18, 2 Chronicles 7:14, 2 Timothy 1:7, Jeremiah 30:17, Philippians 4:7-9, Romans 12:18, John 14:27, 2 Samuel 22:40, Isaiah 26:3, Isaiah 43:2, Isaiah 53:5 & Isaiah 54:17 over all of you & all whom you love. I thank You Father for our still coming miraculous deliverance, victory & I claim all these things in Your Holy, powerful, majestic, everlasting & precious name I pray Lord Jesus, Amen!

Warriors! Tonight shout with me that WE STAND WITH CHRIST! Storms have come! We're still standing! Destruction has come! We're still standing! And no matter what comes tomorrow! Through the name & power of Jesus Christ! WE ARE STILL STANDING! As it is written in Psalm 118:6, The LORD is with me; I will not be afraid.

What can mere mortals do to me? This passage is true to the core! When all seems lost, when all seems impossible, when everything nerve in your body tries to make you stop! Stand firm with faith that God is in control! God has the final word! God's WILL BE DONE! In the world we live in today, faith can be difficult to come by, but when you are before the Red Sea in front of you & the Egyptian army closing in behind you, when all seems lost, when all the safe harbors of this world fail, when all hope in our understanding is gone & all you have left is God & Your faith in God's deliverance. MIRACLES OCCUR!! Have faith! Have trust! Have peace! And know that OUR GOD IS GOD!! VICTORY, DELIVERANCE & JUSTICE ARE COMING!!! Let not your heart be troubled! May God strengthen You! May God give you courage! May God give you peace! May God bless all of you!

DAY 271
December 12th, 2020

Good evening my friends. On this Christmas season evening, we're closing out Saturday, December 12th, 2020 & I pray this message once again, finds you & your loved ones warm, healthy, safe & well.

Dear Heavenly Father, I come to You tonight with, Heavenly praise, love, & thanksgiving. Thank You Father that like the falling of the walls of Jericho, nothing can stand in Your way, nothing can stop Your will & nothing is more powerful than You. Father, I lift up or nation tonight. We are so divided right now & I pray Father that You will please bring peace back, restore our lands & reunite our people. Father, I pray that Your perfect will shall be done in & throughout our lands & people! Father, I pray that Your pure & absolute perfect justice will rain down on all this evil & bring into the light that which has been done in the dark. In the name of Jesus, I claim Psalm 91, Psalm 23, Psalm 25:20-21, Psalm 46:10, Psalm 55:22, Psalm 56:3, Psalm 61:2, Psalm 62:5-8, Psalm 116:7, Psalm 121:2, Joel 2:25-26, 1 John 4:4, Luke 12:2-3, Ephesians 6:10-18, 2 Chronicles 7:14, 2 Timothy 1:7, Jeremiah 30:17, Philippians 4:7-9, Romans 12:18, John 14:27, 2 Samuel 22:40, Isaiah 26:3, Isaiah 43:2, Isaiah 53:5

& Isaiah 54:17 over all of you & all whom you love. I pray for our friends, family, coworkers & people we've never met who are sick & afflicted, with this horrible virus will be fully restored with no long term effects & that this virus will soon be completely eradicated. I pray for all the families, people, businesses, our leaders & medical workers, that they'll be abundantly blessed & given complete protection from the virus & violence during these uncertain days. In the name of Jesus, as a warrior in the army of Christ, completely covered, sealed & protected by His Blood & the Holy Spirit I command, come against, rebuke & cast this horrible evil in all forms away from you & all your loved ones! Greater is He who is in Us than he who is in this world & as it's written through the name & power of Christ, when we resist the devil HE MUST FLEE! I pray that you & all your loved ones are surrounded by a continued & impenetrable hedge of protection. I pray for all the people who do not yet know You as their Savior & that they will accept You into their hearts as their Lord & have forgiveness & eternal life. I thank You Father for our coming miraculous deliverance, victory & I claim all these things in Your Holy, powerful, majestic, everlasting & precious name I pray Lord Jesus, Amen!

Warriors! As 2021 is fast approaching, please take a moment to thank God for your blessings & that He's watched over you & your loved ones this past year. Truly all things are possible with Christ & only through Him will we prevail through these difficult times. This past year a spirit of evil, confusion, anxiety & destruction has tried to knock us down. But by the very Grace of God, we're still here & join with me as we tell this evil spirit by the name and power of Christ! IT MUST GO NOW!! It has no place or claim here or to you! No matter what happens continue to hold strong & stand firm. As we move forward with strength & vigilance we must always remember it is God who guides us through this valley. I tell you this difficult time will come to an end. We have been brought to the point where all we have left is faith that God will deliver us. But that is where miracles begin & ALL the glory goes to almighty God. We're going to get through this time everyone! Just HOLD ON! WITH ALL YOU'VE GOT! VICTORY, DELIVERANCE & JUSTICE ARE COMING!!! Let not your heart be troubled! May God strengthen You! May God give you courage! May God give you peace! May God bless all of you!

DAY 272
December 13th, 2020

      Good evening my friends. On another Christmas season evening, we're closing out Sunday, December 13th, 2020 & I pray this message continues to find you & your loved ones warm, healthy, safe & well.

Dear Heavenly Father, I come to You tonight with, Heavenly praise, love, & thanksgiving. Thank You Father that even when our strength fails, that we can be strong in & through You. Father, I lift up our divided nation tonight. I pray that You'll bring peace back, restore our lands & reunite our people. In the name of Jesus, I claim Psalm 91, Psalm 23, Psalm 25:20-21, Psalm 35, Psalm 46:10, Psalm 55:22, Psalm 56:3, Psalm 61:2, Psalm 62:5-8, Psalm 116:7, Psalm 121:2, Joel 2:25-26, 1 John 4:4, Luke 12:2-3, Ephesians 6:10-18, 2 Chronicles 7:14, 2 Timothy 1:7, Jeremiah 30:17, Philippians 4:7-9, Romans 12:18, John 14:27, 2 Samuel 22:40, Isaiah 26:3, Isaiah 43:2, Isaiah 53:5 & Isaiah 54:17 over all of you & all whom you love. I lift up & pray for all our friends, family, coworkers & people we've never met who are afflicted with this virus, that they'll be fully restored to health with no long term effects & for effectiveness & safety of the vaccines. I pray for all the families, people, businesses, our leaders & medical workers around this country & world, that they'll be abundantly blessed & given complete protection from the virus & violence. Father, I pray that Your perfect will shall be done! Father, I pray that Your absolute perfect justice will rain down on all this evil & bring into the light that which has been done in the dark. I pray that you & all your loved ones are surrounded by an impenetrable hedge of protection. In the name of Jesus, as a warrior in the army of Christ, completely covered, sealed & protected by His Blood & the Holy Spirit I once again command & cast this horrible evil in all forms away from you & all your loved ones! THIS EVIL MUST GO NOW! Father, I pray for all the people who do not yet know You as their Savior & that they will accept You into their hearts as their Lord & have forgiveness & eternal life. I thank You Father for our coming miraculous deliverance, victory & I claim all these things in Your Holy, powerful, majestic, everlasting & precious name I pray Lord Jesus, Amen!

Warriors! On this cold winters night during the Christmas Season, a new year is upon us soon. I want to pray a blessing over all of you that in the coming year & the rest of this year that you & your loved ones will be truly blessed & taken care of in good ways that you could never have thought possible. I pray for all of you hurting tonight & who are afraid for their futures that you will be given supernatural peace. I pray that strength will fill your minds & spirits with wisdom beyond yourself. I pray that all of you will come into a season of abundance & joy. We stand united in Christ & through Jesus & only Jesus will we prevail! God bless all of you tonight & keep you safe in the coming week. And remember no matter what happens, keep your eyes on Christ & not the storm because... VICTORY, DELIVERANCE & JUSTICE ARE COMING!!! Let not your heart be troubled! May God strengthen You! May God give you courage! May God give you peace! May God bless all of you!

DAY 273
December 14th, 2020

Good evening my friends. On this Christmas season at the beginning of the week, we're closing out Monday, December 14th, 2020 & I pray this message finds you & your loved ones warm, healthy, safe & well.

Dear Heavenly Father, I come to You tonight with, Heavenly praise, love, & thanksgiving. Thank You Father for all the blessings You've given us, for Your infinite wisdom & for Your unconditional love. In the name of Jesus, I claim Psalm 91, Psalm 23, Psalm 25:20-21, Psalm 35, Psalm 46:10, Psalm 55:22, Psalm 56:3, Psalm 61:2, Psalm 62:5-8, Psalm 116:7, Psalm 121:2, Joel 2:25-26, 1 John 4:4, Luke 12:2-3, Ephesians 6:10-18, 2 Chronicles 7:14, 2 Timothy 1:7, Jeremiah 30:17, Philippians 4:7-9, Romans 12:18, John 14:27, 2 Samuel 22:40, Isaiah 26:3, Isaiah 43:2, Isaiah 53:5 & Isaiah 54:17 over all of you & all whom you love. I pray that You will surround everyone reading this message with a hedge of protection that's impenetrable. Lord Jesus, I pray for all our friends, family, coworkers & people we've never met who's afflicted with this virus, that they'll be fully restored to health with no long term effects. Thank You Jesus for the coming vaccines. I pray for all the families, people, businesses, our leaders & medical workers around this country & world, that they'll be abundantly blessed & protected from evil in all forms. In the name of Jesus, as a warrior in the army of Christ, completely covered, sealed & protected by His Blood & the Holy Spirit I once again command & cast this horrible evil in all forms away from you & all your loved ones! As it's written if we resist the devil, by the name & power of Christ, he must flee. I pray that You will restore peace & our lands, reunite our people & that Your perfect will shall be done! Father, I pray that Your absolute perfect justice will rain down on all this evil & bring into the light that which has been done in the dark. Father, I pray for all the people who don't yet know You as their Savior & that they'll accept You into their hearts as their Lord, have forgiveness & eternal life. I thank You Father for our coming miraculous deliverance, victory & I claim all these things in Your Holy, powerful, majestic, everlasting & precious name I pray Lord Jesus, Amen!

Warriors! Tonight! Stand with me and make a shout that can be heard from coast to coast. By the power of Christ! The evil in this land MUST GO NOW! The most powerful weapon we have against the powers of darkness is prayer. Please take a moment to pray for all those in need tonight. We're all frustrated & stressed right now. But there is peace available from God. All you have to do is ask for His peace that surpasses all understanding. This has been a year that has taken us to the edge in many aspects but God will deliver us from the precipice to victory, from the valley to mountain & from the pit to the palace. This season will end! God is in control & God is good all the time! Shout with me again! OUR GOD IS GOD & VICTORY, DELIVERANCE & JUSTICE ARE COMING!!! Let not your heart be troubled! May God strengthen You! May God give you courage! May God give you peace! May God bless all of you!

DAY 274
December 15th, 2020

Good evening my friends. With Christmas fast approaching, we're closing out Tuesday, December 15th, 2020 & I pray this message finds you & your loved ones warm, healthy, safe & well.

Dear Heavenly Father, I come to You tonight with a humble heart, Heavenly praise, love, & thanksgiving this Christmas season night. Thank You Father in the midst of the raging storms around us, You are our protector, strength & defender. Father, I pray that You will surround everyone reading this message & their loved ones with a powerful, spiritual & impenetrable hedge of protection. Father I pray for all who are afflicted with this terrible virus that You would completely heal & restore them. Thank You Jesus that vaccines are on the way & being delivered. I pray for all the families, people, businesses & medical workers that through these uncertain days, that they will be completely & abundantly blessed with protection, prosperity, peace, faith, hope, health, love, wisdom, guidance & strength. Lord Jesus, I pray that You will bring peace back, restore our lands, reunite our people & that Your perfect will shall be done! Father, I pray that Your absolute perfect justice will rain down on all this evil & bring into the light that which has been done in the dark. In the name of Jesus, as a warrior in the army of Christ, completely covered, sealed & protected by His Blood, the full armor of God & the Holy Spirit I command & cast this insidious evil that is raging all around us in all forms away from you & all your loved ones! As it is written, greater is He who is in us than he who is in the world & through the name & power of Jesus Christ I say to this evil be gone & never return! In the name of Jesus, I claim Psalm 91, Psalm 23, Psalm 25:20-21, Psalm 35, Psalm 46:10, Psalm 55:22, Psalm 56:3, Psalm 61:2, Psalm 62:5-8, Psalm 116:7, Psalm 121:2, Joel 2:25-26, 1 John 4:4, Luke 12:2-3, Ephesians 6:10-18, 2 Chronicles 7:14, 2 Timothy 1:7, Jeremiah 30:17, Philippians 4:7-9, Romans 12:18, John 14:27, 2 Samuel 22:40, Isaiah 26:3, Isaiah 43:2, Isaiah 53:5 & Isaiah 54:17 over all of you & all whom you love. Father, I pray for all the people who do not yet know You as their Savior & that they will accept You into their hearts as their Lord & have forgiveness & eternal life. I thank You Father & I claim all these things in Your Holy, powerful, majestic, everlasting & precious name I pray Lord Jesus, Amen!

Warriors! As we quickly approach Christmas, take a moment to remember the true meaning of Christmas. And we are in for a true Christmas treat. On December 21st, Saturn & Jupiter are aligning to form what is being called the "Star of Bethlehem" or "Christmas Star."

This is the first time, in 800 years, that this conjunction has occurred & honestly in 2020 we need some Christmas joy. As with each day, we're closer to victory & we continue to press forward through each day. But we are closer to victory now than ever before & tomorrow we'll be even closer. We need to stay strong through this time & not become complacent. We will make it through this. Soon this will all be a distant memory. It's been hard, difficult, heart breaking & brought us to the edge but by the grace & guidance of Christ, we will come out of this season stronger than ever before. Remember, all things are possible with Christ & through Him we will be delivered to victory! Each night say it loud! Say it strong! VICTORY, DELIVERANCE & JUSTICE ARE COMING!!! Let not your heart be troubled! May God strengthen You! May God give you courage! May God give you peace! May God bless all of you!

DAY 275
December 16th, 2020

      Good evening my friends. It's the middle of the week & we're closing out Wednesday, December 16th, 2020 & I pray this message finds you & your loved ones warm, healthy, safe & well.

Dear Heavenly Father, I come to You tonight with Heavenly praise, love, & thanksgiving this Christmas season evening. Thank You Father that You always have the final word, that You are in complete control & on the Throne. In the name of Jesus, I claim Psalm 91, Psalm 23, Psalm 25:20-21, Psalm 35, Psalm 46:10, Psalm 55:22, Psalm 56:3, Psalm 61:2, Psalm 62:5-8, Psalm 116:7, Psalm 121:2, Joel 2:25-26, 1 John 4:4, Luke 12:2-3, Ephesians 6:10-18, 2 Chronicles 7:14, 2 Timothy 1:7, Jeremiah 30:17, Philippians 4:7-9, Romans 12:18, John 14:27, 2 Samuel 22:40, Isaiah 26:3, Isaiah 43:2, Isaiah 53:5 & Isaiah 54:17 over all of you & all whom you love. In the name of Jesus, as a warrior in the army of Christ, covered, sealed & protected by His Blood, the full armor of God & the Holy Spirit, I command & cast this treacherous & insidious evil that is raging around us in all forms, away from you & all your loved ones! This moment, this evil MUST GO NOW! Jesus, I pray that You'll bring peace back, restore our lands, reunite our people & that Your perfect will shall be done! Father, I pray that Your absolute perfect justice will rain down on all this evil & bring into the light that which has been done in the dark. I pray that You'll surround everyone reading this message & their loved ones with a powerful, spiritual & impenetrable hedge of protection that the virus & evil can't even come near. I pray for all who are afflicted with this terrible virus that You will completely heal & restore them. I pray for all the families, people, businesses & medical workers they'll be abundantly blessed with protection, prosperity, peace, faith, hope, health, love, wisdom, guidance & strength. Father, I pray for all the people who do not yet know You as their Savior & that they will accept You into their hearts as their Lord & have forgiveness & eternal life. I thank You Father & I claim all these things in Your Holy, powerful, majestic, everlasting & precious name I pray Lord Jesus, Amen!

Warriors! In the chaotic world we find ourselves, I'm asking that You pray tonight for God's will to be done, not ours. As we move forward through this valley, with each step we come closer to deliverance. Through Christ, ALL things are possible & you never know what tomorrow may bring. Know this, even though everything seems out of control, Christ has everything in the palms of His hands & has a plan for victory & deliverance. We must not lean on our own understanding but have trust & faith in God. Remember in the spiritual battles we all face daily, we've already won the war & that we fight from victory not for victory! They say hindsight is always 2020 & there is truth in that. We will always remember 2020 in full detail. But fear not because our Savior is more powerful than anything in the universe! We're going to make it everyone! VICTORY, DELIVERANCE, VINDICATION & JUSTICE ARE COMING!!! Let not your heart be troubled! May God strengthen You! May God give you courage! May God give you peace! May God bless all of you!

DAY 276
December 17th, 2020

Good evening my friends. We're coming up on the weekend & we're closing out Thursday, December 17th, 2020 & I pray this message finds you & your loved ones warm, healthy, safe & well.

Dear Heavenly Father, I come to You tonight with a humble heart, giving You Heavenly praise, love, & thanksgiving this Christmas season evening. Thank You Father that You are God of the universe, that You have the final word, that You are in complete control & that You are delivering us to victory & justice. Jesus, I come before You tonight, please restore our lands & let Your perfect will be done! Lord Jesus, I pray that Your absolute perfect justice will rain down on all this evil spreading across our nation & bring into the light that which has been done in the dark. In the name of Jesus, as a warrior in the army of Christ, being covered, sealed & protected by His Blood, the full armor of God & the Holy Spirit, I command, come against, rebuke & cast this treacherous & insidious evil that surrounds us away from you & all your loved ones to the farthest corners of the Earth, NEVER to return! I pray that You'll surround everyone reading this message with a continual, powerful, spiritual & impenetrable hedge of protection. I pray for all who are sick & afflicted that You will completely heal & restore them. In the name of Jesus, I claim Psalm 91, Psalm 23, Psalm 25:20-21, Psalm 35, Psalm 46:10, Psalm 55:22, Psalm 56:3, Psalm 61:2, Psalm 62:5-8, Psalm 116:7, Psalm 121:2, Joel 2:25-26, 1 John 4:4, Luke 12:2-3, Ephesians 6:10-18, 2 Chronicles 7:14, 2 Timothy 1:7, Jeremiah 30:17, Philippians 4:7-9, Romans 12:18, John 14:27, 2 Samuel 22:40, Isaiah 26:3, Isaiah 43:2, Isaiah 53:5 & Isaiah 54:17 over all of you & all whom you love. I pray that You will abundantly bless & protect all the families, people, businesses & medical workers & give all strength in the coming days ahead. Father, I pray for all the people who do not yet know You as their Savior & that they will accept You into their hearts as their Lord & have forgiveness & eternal life. In the times we live, this is the most important decision you could ever make. I thank You Father & I claim all these things in Your Holy, powerful, majestic, everlasting & precious name I pray Lord Jesus, Amen!

Warriors! Storms may surround us, THEY WILL PASS! Darkness may come, LIGHT WILL ABOUND! And as evil attempts to destroy us, IT WILL NOT SUCCEED! By the name & power of Christ WE SHALL PREVAIL! Do not listen to the lies of the enemy! Do not fear the night, for it will be replaced with joy of the morning. We have safety & refuge under the wings of Christ. He's our shield, fortress & He will never leave nor forsake you. His character is same past, present &

future! Hold firm & strong in your faith! We're approaching a time prophesied nearly 2,000 years ago, but we need never fear because Christ is in control & on the Throne! No matter what happens, just hold on with everything you've got! Shout with me again! VICTORY, DELIVERANCE, VINDICATION & JUSTICE ARE COMING!!! Let not your heart be troubled! May God strengthen You! May God give you courage! May God give you peace! May God bless all of you!

DAY 277
December 18th, 2020

Good evening my friends. Well the weekend is here on this snowy Christmas season evening & we're closing out Friday, December 18th, 2020 & I pray this message finds you & your loved ones warm, healthy, safe & well.

Dear Heavenly Father, I come to You tonight with Heavenly praise, love, & thanksgiving. Thank You Father that You are our protector, redeemer, Heavenly Father & almighty God. In the name of Jesus, I claim Psalm 91, Psalm 23, Psalm 25:20-21, Psalm 35, Psalm 46:10, Psalm 55:22, Psalm 56:3, Psalm 61:2, Psalm 62:5-8, Psalm 116:7, Psalm 121:2, Joel 2:25-26, 1 John 4:4, Luke 12:2-3, Ephesians 6:10-18, 2 Chronicles 7:14, 2 Timothy 1:7, Jeremiah 30:17, Philippians 4:7-9, Romans 12:18, John 14:27, 2 Samuel 22:40, Isaiah 26:3, Isaiah 43:2, Isaiah 53:5 & Isaiah 54:17 over all of you & all whom you love. I pray for all who are afflicted with this terrible virus, that God will restore you & completely heal you. Father, I pray that You'll surround everyone reading this message with a spiritual & impenetrable hedge of protection against all evil & the virus. Jesus, please restore our lands & let Your perfect will be done! Father, I pray that Your absolute perfect justice will rain down on all this evil & bring into the light that which has been done in the dark. Lord Jesus, I pray that You will truly abundantly bless & protect all who are reading this message tonight & their loved ones. Father, I pray for all the souls who do not know You as their Savior & that they will all accept You into their hearts as their Lord so they would receive eternal life. In the name of Jesus, as a warrior in the army of Christ, being covered, sealed & protected by

His Blood, the full armor of God & the Holy Spirit, I command & cast this insidious evil that surrounds us away from you & all your loved ones. As it's written through the name & power of Christ, if we resist the devil he must flee from us. I thank You Father & I claim all these things in Your Holy, powerful, majestic, everlasting & precious name I pray Lord Jesus, Amen!

Warriors! The weekend is here & as of today, I am 9 months & 1 day in praying over all of you & I will continue to do so through this pandemic. We live in unprecedented & chaotic times. But as I say many times on here, fear not, do not look at the storm but have faith, courage & strength knowing that Your Lord & Savior goes before you to clear the path to victory. This year will never be forgotten but will fade away. We are all indelibly linked together through this time in history & soon when this pandemic is over you'll be part of history & know that it was God that brought you through the mire. We must keep fighting with everything we've got. The enemy will try his best to steal your joy because he cannot have your soul & knows that he has very little time left. There is true evil in this world but evil's grasp has already been defeated at the cross. Soon, very soon, all of the injustices of this world will be made right by God. So shout with me again! OUR GOD IS GOD! VICTORY, DELIVERANCE, VINDICATION & JUSTICE ARE COMING!! Let not your heart be troubled! May God strengthen You! May God give you courage! May God give you peace! May God bless all of you! Merry Christmas everyone.

DAY 278
December 19th, 2020

      Good evening my friends. We're in the middle of another weekend at Christmas & we're closing out Saturday, December 19th, 2020 & I pray this message once again finds you & your loved ones warm, healthy, safe & well.

Dear Heavenly Father, I come to You tonight with Heavenly praise, love, & thanksgiving. Thank You Father for all the blessings You've given us & for walking with us each step of this difficult journey, leading us to victory. Father, tonight I pray for all the souls reading this message & all they love that You will surround each & everyone of them with a power, spiritual & impenetrable hedge of protection against all evil. In the name of Jesus, I claim Psalm 91, Psalm 23, Psalm 25:20-21, Psalm 35, Psalm 46:10, Psalm 55:22, Psalm 56:3, Psalm 61:2, Psalm 62:5-8, Psalm 116:7, Psalm 121:2, Joel 2:25-26, 1 John 4:4, Luke 12:2-3, Ephesians 6:10-18, 2 Chronicles 7:14, 2 Timothy 1:7, Jeremiah 30:17, Philippians 4:7-9, Romans 12:18, John 14:27, 2 Samuel 22:40, Isaiah 26:3, Isaiah 43:2, Isaiah 53:5 & Isaiah 54:17 over all of you & all whom you love. Father, I pray for all the lost souls who do not know You as their Savior & that they're eyes would be opened & that all will accept You into their hearts as their Lord so they would receive forgiveness & eternal life. Father, I pray for all who are sick &afflicted, that You will restore them to complete health & for the eradication of this virus. I pray that You will abundantly bless all who are reading this message tonight & their loved ones with protection, peace, prosperity, faith, love, thanksgiving, health, hope, wisdom, guidance & strength through these difficult & uncertain times. Father, we're in the middle of a massive spiritual battle & in the name of Jesus, as a warrior in the army of Christ, being covered, sealed & protected by His Blood, the full armor of God & the Holy Spirit, I command & cast this insidious evil that seeks to destroy us away from you & all your loved ones. As it's written, greater is He who resides in us than he who is in the world & by His name & authority, this evil must go! Jesus, please restore our lands & let Your perfect will be done! Father, I pray that Your absolute perfect justice will rain down on all this evil & bring into the light that which has been done in the dark. I thank You Father for our coming victory, deliverance & I claim all these things in Your Holy, powerful, majestic, everlasting & precious name I pray Lord Jesus, Amen!

Warriors! We continue to march forward! We continue to hold strong! We continue to have faith & we continue to praise Almighty God in Heaven through these uncertain times. While the events of tomorrow are still unknown, know today, that no matter what comes; God is in complete control of all. And for all those who are asking questions… Know that you are not here by accident, you DO have a great future & we will get through this time. God hears & answers prayers according to His will. We must hold on and have faith because our time table is not always the same as God's but there is nothing that can stop what God has planned for you. You have a unique destiny that ONLY you can accomplish. We all have a tendency to want control over all our circumstances, but we have to release that into God's hands & time frame. That can be difficult, but when we let things happen the way God wants them to, in the end, they are far better. The phrase of today is, "Let Go & Let God". But know this, when your time comes in the will of God, there isn't anything that can stop be it. Keep praying, be prepared & have faith! And know this! VICTORY, DELIVERANCE, VINDICATION & JUSTICE ARE COMING!!! Let not your heart be troubled! May God strengthen You! May God give you courage! May God give you peace! May God bless all of you! Merry Christmas everyone.

DAY 279
December 20th, 2020

Good evening my friends. We're on the eve of a new week during this Christmas season & we're closing out Sunday, December 20th, 2020 & I pray this message finds you & your loved ones warm, healthy, safe & well.

Dear Heavenly Father, I come to You tonight with a humble heart, giving You Heavenly praise, love, & thanksgiving. Thank You Father that even at our worst moments You still love us unconditionally & that You are just waiting for us to return to You. In the name of Jesus, I claim Psalm 91, Psalm 23, Psalm 25:20-21, Psalm 35, Psalm 46:10, Psalm 55:22, Psalm 56:3, Psalm 61:2, Psalm 62:5-8, Psalm 116:7, Psalm 121:2, Joel 2:25-26, 1 John 4:4, Luke 12:2-3, Ephesians 6:10-18, 2 Chronicles 7:14, 2 Timothy 1:7, Jeremiah 30:17, Philippians 4:7-9, Romans 12:18, John 14:27, 2 Samuel 22:40, Isaiah 26:3, Isaiah 43:2, Isaiah 53:5 & Isaiah 54:17 over all of you & all whom you love. Father, we truly find ourselves in the middle of a global spiritual battle. In the name of Jesus, as a warrior in the army of Christ, continually being covered, sealed & protected by His Blood, the full armor of God & the Holy Spirit, I command, come against, rebuke & cast this insidious evil that seeks to destroy us away from you & all your loved ones. Greater is He who is in us than he who is in the world & by Your name Father we tell this evil to GO NOW! Father, I pray for all who are afflicted, that You will restore them to complete health & I thank You for their deliverance & restoration. I pray for all reading this message & all they love that You will surround all of them with a powerful, spiritual & impenetrable hedge of protection. Jesus, as I come to You tonight I pray that You'll abundantly bless all who are reading this with protection & everything they need during this pandemic. Father, I pray for all who don't know You as their Lord & Savior & that they're eyes would be opened & that all will accept You into their hearts as their Lord so they will receive eternal life. Father, I pray for all the lost souls who do not know You as their Savior & that they're eyes would be opened & that all will accept You into their hearts as their Lord so they would receive forgiveness & eternal life. Father, as we pray to You, please restore our lands & let Your perfect will be done! Father, I pray that Your perfect justice will rain down on all this evil & bring into the light that which has been done in the dark. I thank You & I claim all these things in Your Holy, powerful, majestic, everlasting & precious name I pray Lord Jesus, Amen!

Warriors! It's Christmas week & even though the future seems uncertain, be certain in the provision, protection & victory in Christ! The journey we've been on has been long are tiring but no matter what may come, we will continue to press forward & by the very grace of God, WE SHALL PREVAIL! Not by our own hands or understanding but by the will of Christ. Take a moment tonight to pray for the protection of your friends & family. I pray that as you are reading this tonight that God fills you with courage & renewed strength as we press forward. Always know that even when it seems impossible, God can make a way because all things are possible with Christ. Stay strong my friends, stay vigilant & keep holing on. The word of today is Forward! Shout with me again! VICTORY, DELIVERANCE, VINDICATION & JUSTICE ARE COMING!!! Let not your heart be troubled! May God strengthen You! May God give you courage! May God give you peace! May God bless all of you! Merry Christmas everyone.

DAY 280
December 21st, 2020

     Good evening my friends. It's a brand new week during this Christmas season & we're closing out Monday, December 21st, 2020 & I pray this message finds you & your loved ones warm, healthy, safe & well.

Dear Heavenly Father, I come to You tonight with Heavenly praise, love, & thanksgiving. Thank You Father that despite all the chaos & storms that surround us that You've the final say & that You're in full control of everything. Father, I pray that You'll please restore our lands & let Your perfect will be done! Father, I thank You that Your justice will rain down on all this evil & bring into the light that which has been done in the dark. Lord Jesus, I pray for every lost soul who doesn't know You as their Savior & that they're eyes would be truly opened & they'll accept You into their hearts as their Lord & Savior. Father, I pray for all the afflicted with this horrible virus & that You'll touch each of them, healing them completely & restoring them. I pray for the complete eradication of this virus. Father, I pray for a spiritual, powerful & impenetrable hedge of protection that surrounds all of you & all you love against this evil. Father I pray for & thank You that You're abundantly blessing all in need with protection, peace, prosperity, faith, love, health, hope, love, wisdom, guidance & strength during these trying times. I pray for the full protection of all our medical workers. Father, we find ourselves in the middle of a massive spiritual battle against the forces of good & evil. In the name of Jesus, as a warrior of Christ, covered, sealed & protected by His Blood, the full armor of God & the Holy Spirit, I command & cast this insidious evil that seeks to destroy us away from you & all your loved ones. By Your name I cast it to the farthest ends of the earth. In the name of Jesus, I claim Psalm 91, Psalm 23, Psalm 25:20-21, Psalm 35, Psalm 46:10, Psalm 55:22, Psalm 56:3, Psalm 61:2, Psalm 62:5-8, Psalm 116:7, Psalm 121:2, Joel 2:25-26, 1 John 4:4, Luke 12:2-3, Ephesians 6:10-18, 2 Chronicles 7:14, 2 Timothy 1:7, Jeremiah 30:17, Philippians 4:7-9, Romans 12:18, John 14:27, 2 Samuel 22:40, Isaiah 26:3, Isaiah 43:2, Isaiah 53:5 & Isaiah 54:17 over all of you & all whom you love. Father, I thank You & I claim all these things in Your Holy, powerful, majestic, everlasting & precious name I pray Lord Jesus, Amen!

Warriors! It's the week of Christmas & I pray a blessing over all of you tonight that you will have a wonderful Christmas & an abundant 2021. It's been quite a year & we still have a little bit left to go. Let us all pray that 2021 will be a far better year for all of us. But no matter what comes in the days, weeks & months ahead, we will continue to press forward to victory. We all knew this would be a difficult journey, and though it continues, this season too shall pass! We must continue to have faith in Christ as we move forward. We must continue to be strong and vigilant! We must turn from the storms! The enemy will tell you circumstances in your life are impossible but I'm here to tell you that ALL things are possible with Christ! Not some things, but ALL things. Push back against the lies of the enemy & turn your eyes to Christ. He WILL guide us to victory! Shout with me tonight GOD'S WILL BE DONE! And know this! VICTORY, DELIVERANCE, VINDICATION & JUSTICE ARE COMING!!! Let not your heart be troubled! May God strengthen You! May God give you courage! May God give you peace! May God bless all of you! Merry Christmas everyone.

DAY 281
December 22nd, 2020

Good evening my friends. As we approach Christmas 2020 we're closing out Tuesday, December 22nd, 2020 & I pray this message, once again, finds you & your loved ones warm, healthy, safe & well.

Dear Heavenly Father, I come to You with Heavenly praise, love, & thanksgiving on this Christmas season evening. Thank You Father that when the storms of life try to defeat us, You are there to defend & guide us to victory. In the name of Jesus, I claim Psalm 91, Psalm 23, Psalm 25:20-21, Psalm 35, Psalm 46:10, Psalm 55:22, Psalm 56:3, Psalm 61:2, Psalm 62:5-8, Psalm 116:7, Psalm 121:2, Joel 2:25-26, 1 John 4:4, Luke 12:2-3, Ephesians 6:10-18, 2 Chronicles 7:14, 2 Timothy 1:7, Jeremiah 30:17, Philippians 4:7-9, Romans 12:18, John

14:27, 2 Samuel 22:40, Isaiah 26:3, Isaiah 43:2, Isaiah 53:5 & Isaiah 54:17 over all of you & all whom you love. Father, I pray for the full protection of all our medical workers & I pray for all the afflicted that You'll heal & restore all who are sick. Father, I pray that You'll place a spiritual hedge of protection around all reading this message & their loved ones. Father I pray that You'll abundantly bless all in need tonight across our nation. Father, I pray that You'll please restore our lands, that Your perfect will be done & that Your justice will rain down on all this evil & bring into the light that which has been done in the dark! Father, there are so many lost souls around this world & I pray that You'll call to them so they may receive You into their hearts to be saved & have eternal life. Father, we truly find ourselves in the middle of a massive spiritual battle against the forces of good & evil. In the name of Jesus, as a warrior of Christ, covered, sealed & protected by His Blood, the full armor of God & the Holy Spirit, I command & cast this insidious evil that seeks to destroy us away from all of you! Father, I thank You for our coming victory & I claim all these things in Your Holy, powerful, majestic, everlasting & precious name I pray Lord Jesus, Amen!

Warriors! Tonight, stand with courage as we once again draw a line in the sand against the storms that surround us. Tonight, stand with Christ, hand in hand, an impenetrable wall as we continue to move forward & not retreat! Tonight, put your faith in that God will deliver us. Lean not on your own understanding but trust that God is always on time, never a second too early or late! All that we are facing shall pass! All that has brought us to the brink will pass! All that has sought to destroy us will fail! And all goes to the glory & majesty of Christ! The spiritual war may rage all around us but when we shelter under the wings of Christ we're protected as God has already defeated the enemy at the cross! Storms, fire & destruction may come but we tell it to be gone as it has no claim to us as we are children of the Most High God! So as we take another step forward, know that you are not alone as there are hundreds, thousands, millions of us moving together as one & with Christ as our leader, WE SHALL PREVAIL! GOD'S WILL BE DONE! VICTORY, DELIVERANCE, VINDICATION & JUSTICE ARE COMING!!! Let not your heart be troubled! May God strengthen You! May God give you courage! May God give you peace! May God bless all of you! Merry Christmas everyone!!

DAY 282
December 23rd, 2020

Good evening my friends. It's the middle of the week & we're closing out Wednesday, December 23rd, 2020 & I pray this message finds you & your loved ones warm, healthy, safe & well.

Dear Heavenly Father, I come to You with a humble heart, Heavenly praise, love, & thanksgiving on this Christmas season evening. Thank You Father for all the blessings, gifts & talents You've given us & that even we are at our worst, You still love us unconditionally with open arms. Father, I thank You that even though we're in the middle of a massive spiritual battle on all sides, that You're in complete control, protecting us & getting ready to do something miraculous. In the name of Jesus, as a warrior of Christ, covered, sealed & protected by His Blood, the full armor of God & the Holy Spirit, I command & cast this insidious evil that seeks to destroy us away from all of you & your loved ones! Father, I pray that You'll restore our lands, that Your perfect will shall be done & that Your perfect justice will rain down on all this evil & bring into the light that which has been done in the dark! Father, please place an impenetrable hedge of protection around all reading this tonight & their loved ones. Father, I pray for Your complete & full protection of all our medical workers. Father, I pray that You'll abundantly bless all in need tonight across our nation. Father, this Christmas season please call to all the lost souls so that their hearts would be receptive & accept You as their Lord & Savior. In the name of Jesus, I claim Psalm 91, Psalm 23, Psalm 25:20-21, Psalm 35, Psalm 46:10, Psalm 55:22, Psalm 56:3, Psalm 61:2, Psalm 62:5-8, Psalm 116:7, Psalm 121:2, Joel 2:25-26, 1 John 4:4, Luke 12:2-3, Ephesians 6:10-18, 2 Chronicles 7:14, 2 Timothy 1:7, Jeremiah 30:17, Philippians 4:7-9, Romans 12:18, John 14:27, 2 Samuel 22:40, Isaiah 26:3, Isaiah 43:2, Isaiah 53:5 & Isaiah 54:17 over all of you & all whom you love. Father, thank You for our coming victory & deliverance & I claim all these things in Your Holy, powerful, majestic, everlasting & precious name I pray Lord Jesus, Amen!

Warriors! Do not let the fear of what tomorrow may bring paralyze you tonight. For tomorrow has it's own problems, but tonight look to

Christ that you may have peace and joy. Fear not the storms as they come & go for they too shall pass as will this difficult season we're in. Don't be dismayed at the uncertainty of the future but be most certain in the greatness of God. What I'm saying is, no matter what happens. Stay focused on God, know that He is in control & that He alone has the final say in all. I know many of you, myself included, are still frustrated at the chaos going on, but I know deep down that deliverance & victory are truly coming! Just hold on with all you've got. Through Christ WE SHALL PREVAIL & soon, very soon, every knee shall bow & every tongue confess that Jesus Christ is Lord. Events that are swiftly unfolding that were prophesied nearly 2,000 years ago are about to show the entire world that OUR GOD IS GOD! Let not your heart be troubled! May God strengthen You! May God give you courage! May God give you peace! May God bless all of you! Merry Christmas everyone!

DAY 283
December 24th, 2020

Good evening my friends. It's Christmas Eve & we're closing out Thursday, December 24th, 2020 & as with every night I have been praying over you, I pray this message finds you & your loved ones warm, healthy, safe & well. On tonight's prayer we're going to do something a little different. Tonight as I pray over you we're going to thank God for everything.

Dear Heavenly Father, I come to You with a humble heart, Heavenly praise, love, & thanksgiving on this Christmas Eve night. Thank You Father for sending Your Son that He would be born tomorrow & come to seek & save the lost of this world. Father I thank You that You're abundantly blessing, protecting & healing all in need & afflicted. I thank You Father that as You surround all reading this with a hedge of protection, that You're driving the enemy away, shielding us from evil, the virus & restoring our lands. I thank You Father that You are in complete control of all that goes on & that You have the final word in all. I thank You That through You we shall prevail, see justice, victory & deliverance. I thank You Father that at this moment You are calling to all those who don't know You so they may be saved.

In the name of Jesus, I claim Psalm 91, Psalm 23, Psalm 25:20-21, Psalm 35, Psalm 46:10, Psalm 55:22, Psalm 56:3, Psalm 61:2, Psalm 62:5-8, Psalm 116:7, Psalm 121:2, Joel 2:25-26, 1 John 4:4, Luke 12:2-3, Ephesians 6:10-18, 2 Chronicles 7:14, 2 Timothy 1:7, Jeremiah 30:17, Philippians 4:7-9, Romans 12:18, John 14:27, 2 Samuel 22:40, Isaiah 26:3, Isaiah 43:2, Isaiah 53:5 & Isaiah 54:17 over all of you & all whom you love. Most of all, I thank You for this Christmas Eve night & for what tomorrow truly means & what the true meaning of Christmas is. Father, thank You for our coming victory & deliverance & I claim all these things in Your Holy, powerful, majestic, everlasting & precious name I pray Lord Jesus, Amen!

Warriors! On this night before Christmas, please take a moment to pray for your family, friends, all in need & your enemies. Thank God for all He has blessed you with through this pandemic. Thank God for sending His only begotten Son so that we may eternal salvation through Christ. Tonight, just thank God for everything. This year has been a difficult journey for all of us, but always remember that Christmas isn't about the presents, it's not about the lights, dinners or Santa. The true meaning of Christmas is celebrating the birth of our Savior, Jesus Christ, our King. For those of you who feel alone tonight. Know that we are with you, we love you, God is with you, He loves you & we're going to get through this time together. And remember this, God is good all the time & all the time, God is good. Keep praying everyone Let not your heart be troubled! May God strengthen You! May God give you courage! May God give you peace! May God bless all of you! Merry Christmas everyone!!

DAY 284
December 25th, 2020

Good evening my friends. It's Christmas Day & we're closing out Friday, December 25th, 2020. Hallelujah Christ is born & I pray this message finds you & your loved ones warm, healthy, safe & well. Please pray for those in Nashville tonight.

Dear Heavenly Father, I come to You with a humble heart, Heavenly praise, love, & thanksgiving this Christmas Day 2020. Thank You

Father that 2,020 years ago that You sent Your only begotten Son that we may be saved through Him & have eternal life. In the name of Jesus, I claim Psalm 91, Psalm 23, Psalm 25:20-21, Psalm 35, Psalm 46:10, Psalm 55:22, Psalm 56:3, Psalm 61:2, Psalm 62:5-8, Psalm 116:7, Psalm 121:2, Joel 2:25-26, 1 John 4:4, Luke 12:2-3, Ephesians 6:10-18, 2 Chronicles 7:14, 2 Timothy 1:7, Jeremiah 30:17, Philippians 4:7-9, Romans 12:18, John 14:27, 2 Samuel 22:40, Isaiah 26:3, Isaiah 43:2, Isaiah 53:5 & Isaiah 54:17 over all of you & all whom you love. Father this has been a tough year for so many people across this world & I pray that You will abundantly bless, protect & heal all who are reading this, their loved ones & that You'll place a hedge of protection around them. Father I pray that You'll restore our lands, bring peace back to the people & that through You, we'll see true justice, victory & deliverance. Father, I pray that You'll call to all those souls that are lost that they may be saved by accepting You as their Lord & Savior. In the name of Jesus, protected by You & through Your power I command & cast this evil away that surrounds us. Thank You Lord Jesus for this Christmas Day & I claim all these things in Your Holy, powerful, majestic, everlasting & precious name I pray Lord Jesus, Amen!

Warriors! This day we celebrate the birth of our Lord & Savior, Jesus Christ. He has led us through probably the most difficult journey we've ever been on & while it's not over yet, this season too shall pass. Through these storms are fierce, our God is far more powerful. As we stand united together, Christ is leading us to victory. Take a moment tonight & thank Jesus for all He has done for you this year & reflect on the true meaning of this day. For God came to earth to reestablish a relationship with us. He was born so that through Him we could have eternal life if we accept Him as our Lord & Savior. As I said yesterday, many of you feel alone this time of year. But know that when you accept Jesus into your hearts, you will never be alone again. Your creator is their right now calling you to Him. As a child of God, you mean the world to your Heavenly Father. All you have to do is say this prayer & it will truly change your life forever. Don't put off today what God is calling you to do right now. "God, I'm a sinner. I'm sorry for my sins. I ask that You forgive me, and I believe that Jesus Christ is Your Son, and I want to invite Him to come into my heart and trust Him with my life. I'm willing to trust Him as my Savior and follow Him as my Lord forever, and I pray this in Jesus' Name.'" That's all it takes to be truly born again. Shout with me again! OUR GOD IS GOD! Let not your heart be troubled! May God strengthen You! May God give you courage! May God give you peace! May God bless all of you! Merry Christmas everyone!!

DAY 285
December 26th, 2020

Good evening my friends. It's the day after Christmas & we're closing out Saturday, December 26th, 2020. Once again, I pray this message finds you & your loved ones warm, healthy, safe & well. Please continue to pray for those in Nashville tonight.

Dear Heavenly Father, I come to You with Heavenly praise, love, and thanksgiving. Thank You Father for the wisdom You freely give, for guiding us along this difficult journey and for loving us unconditionally. Father, I pray that You'll restore our divided lands, bring peace back to the people & that through You, we will see true justice, victory and deliverance from the evil that's been done. Father, I pray that You will abundantly bless, protect and heal all who are reading this, their loved ones and that You will place a hedge of protection around them that is completely impenetrable. In the name of Jesus, as a child of God, covered, protected & sealed by Your Blood & the Holy Spirit and with the full authority of God, I come against, command, rebuke and cast this evil away from you and your loved ones to the farthest corners of the earth. Greater is He who is in us than he who is in the world. This evil must leave NOW. Father, I pray that You will call to all the lost souls that don't know You yet and that their hearts will be receptive to accept You as their Lord and Savior. In the name of Jesus, I claim Psalm 91, Psalm 23, Psalm 25:20-21, Psalm 35, Psalm 46:10, Psalm 55:22, Psalm 56:3, Psalm 61:2, Psalm 62:5-8, Psalm 116:7, Psalm 121:2, Joel 2:25-26, 1 John 4:4, Luke 12:2-3, Ephesians 6:10-18, 2 Chronicles 7:14, 2 Timothy 1:7, Jeremiah 30:17, Philippians 4:7-9, Romans 12:18, John 14:27, 2 Samuel 22:40, Isaiah 26:3, Isaiah 43:2, Isaiah 53:5 & Isaiah 54:17 over all of you and all whom you love. Thank You Father for our coming deliverance and victory and I claim all these things in Your

Holy, powerful, majestic, everlasting and precious name I pray Lord Jesus, Amen!

Warriors! As we near the end of 2020, our fight will continue into 2021 but I believe that victory & deliverance is swiftly coming. We all must continue to be strong, vigilant & never complacent. Every single day we move another step closer to our inevitable victory through the guidance, power & name of Jesus Christ. This has been a very tough year for so many of us but when this is over, and it will be, there will be untold joy throughout the planet. Please take a moment to pray for all those in need again tonight & to thank God that He is in control & on the Throne. Tomorrow may be uncertain but know that we can be certain in Christ. As I say every day and will continue to say every day, we're going to make it through this. Just hold on strong! We're all in this together! VICTORY, DELIVERANCE & JUSTICE ARE COMING! Let not your heart be troubled! May God strengthen You! May God give you courage! May God give you peace! May God bless all of you!

DAY 286
December 27th, 2020

Good evening my friends. As we approach the final week of 2020 we're closing out Sunday, December 27th, 2020 & I hope & pray this message finds you & your loved ones warm, healthy, safe & well.

Dear Heavenly Father, I come to You with Heavenly praise, love, & thanksgiving. Thank You Father for the peace You give that surpasses all understanding, especially in these stressful times. In the name of Jesus, I claim Psalm 91, Psalm 23, Psalm 25:20-21, Psalm 35, Psalm 46:10, Psalm 55:22, Psalm 56:3, Psalm 61:2, Psalm 62:5-8, Psalm 116:7, Psalm 121:2, Joel 2:25-26, 1 John 4:4, Luke 12:2-3, Ephesians 6:10-18, 2 Chronicles 7:14, 2 Timothy 1:7, Jeremiah 30:17, Philippians 4:7-9, Romans 12:18, John 14:27, 2 Samuel 22:40, Isaiah 26:3, Isaiah 43:2, Isaiah 53:5 & Isaiah 54:17 over all of you & all whom you love. Father, tonight I'm praying that You will call to everyone who doesn't know You. I pray that their hearts will be receptive to accept You as their Lord & Savior. Father, I pray that You will & continue to abundantly bless, protect & heal all who are reading this, their loved ones & that You'll place a spiritual & impenetrable hedge of protection around them. I pray for the complete eradication of this virus. Father I pray for our nation, that You'll restore our divided lands, bring peace back to the people & that through You, we'll see justice, victory & deliverance from the evil that has been done & let it be brought forth into the light. In the name of Jesus, as a child of God, covered, protected & sealed by Your Blood & the Holy Spirit & with the full authority of God, I command & cast this pure evil away from you & all your loved ones. As it's written if we resist the devil, he MUST flee from you through the name & power of Christ. Thank You Father & I claim all these things in Your Holy, powerful, majestic, everlasting & precious name I pray Lord Jesus, Amen!

Warriors! As we're on the eve of a brand new week & the last week of 2021, I'm sure that all of you are ready to see the end of 2020. While our journey will continue into 2021, I believe through the name & power of Christ we will prevail & break through. No matter what comes we must have faith that God will deliver us. I think back to what the Israelites must have felt being up against the Red Sea and Pharos army closing in. I'm sure in the terror of the moment, they felt they were done for, before seeing deliverance as the Red Sea parted. But tonight, I'm asking that you use every once of strength from your souls & reenergize your faith that God will deliver us. Sometimes we hit a wall where we can't keep going but in those moments, we need to draw strength that only God can & will give you to break through. I'm telling you all now, something big is coming swiftly. I don't know what it is yet, but I can feel it in the very marrow of my bones and into the depths of my soul. Through God's grace & might, we're going to make it through this season! Shout with me again! VICTORY, DELIVERANCE & JUSTICE ARE COMING! Let not your heart be troubled! May God strengthen You! May God give you courage! May God give you peace! May God bless all of you!

DAY 287
December 28th, 2020

Good evening my friends. It's the beginning of a brand new exciting week & we're closing out Monday, December 28th, 2020. As with each and every single night I'm praying over all of you, I hope this message finds you & your loved ones warm, healthy, safe & well.

Dear Heavenly Father, I come to You with Heavenly praise, a humble heart, love, & thanksgiving. Thank You Father that You're the King of Kings, the Lord of Lords, that You have final say, that You're in complete control & that You are on the Throne. Father, for all the people, families, businesses & medical workers that are in need, I pray that You will to abundantly bless, protect & heal them & their loved ones. I pray that You'll place a spiritual & impenetrable hedge of protection continually around them, guarding them from all evil. Lord Jesus, I pray for the complete & total eradication of this virus & the end of the chaos in our country. Father, I pray again deeply for our nation, that You'll restore our lands, bring peace to the people & that through You, we'll see pure justice, victory & deliverance from the evil that has been done & let it be brought forth into the light. In the name of Jesus, as a child of the true Living God, covered, protected & sealed by Your Blood & the Holy Spirit & with the full authority of God, I command & cast this evil in all forms away from you & all your loved ones. By His name & power it MUST go now! Father, I'm praying that You will call to everyone who doesn't know You & that their hearts will be receptive to accept You as their Lord & Savior & have eternal life through Your Son Jesus Christ. In the name of Jesus, I claim Psalm 91, Psalm 23, Psalm 25:20-21, Psalm 35, Psalm 46:10, Psalm 55:22, Psalm 56:3, Psalm 61:2, Psalm 62:5-8, Psalm 116:7, Psalm 121:2, Joel 2:25-26, 1 John 4:4, Luke 12:2-3, Ephesians 6:10-18, 2 Chronicles 7:14, 2 Timothy 1:7, Jeremiah 30:17, Philippians 4:7-9, Romans 12:18, John 14:27, 2 Samuel 22:40, Isaiah 26:3, Isaiah 43:2, Isaiah 53:5 & Isaiah 54:17 over all of you & all whom you love. Thank You Father for coming deliverance & I claim all these things in Your Holy, powerful, majestic, everlasting & precious name I pray Lord Jesus, Amen!

Warriors! As we step onto the battlefield this week, put on the full armor of God that You may be protected from the attacks of the enemy. One thing we must always remember that as we go about our daily lives, unfolding all around us at any one moment is a spiritual battle of truly Biblical proportions. We need not fear it but know that there are forces at work trying to deceive, distract & destroy us. But God does give us spiritual offensive weapons & daily we need to tell the enemy that through the power and name of Jesus Christ, he must go now & that he has no claim or authority over you or your loved ones, because you are a child of the Living God. It's written that by the name of Christ if we resist the devil, he MUST flee from you. He has no other option but to obey. While our foe is formidable, God is far more powerful. So tonight before you go to bed, I want you all to tell the enemy to go, that he has no authority over you & by the name & power of Jesus, you command him & all his agents of evil away from you this very moment & to leave you alone. These storms will pass but we need to do our part. We're going to get through this everyone! Shout with me again! OUR GOD IS GOD! VICTORY, DELIVERANCE & JUSTICE ARE COMING! Let not your heart be troubled! May God strengthen You! May God give you courage! May God give you peace! May God bless all of you!

DAY 288
December 29th, 2020

Good evening my friends. We're nearing the end of the year & we're closing out Tuesday, December 29th, 2020 & I pray this message finds you & your loved ones warm, healthy, safe & well.

Dear Heavenly Father, I come to You with Heavenly praise, love, & thanksgiving. Thank You Father that through every season, both joyous & difficult, that You're with us each step of the journey. In the name of Jesus, I claim Psalm 91, Psalm 23, Psalm 25:20-21, Psalm 35, Psalm 46:10, Psalm 55:22, Psalm 56:3, Psalm 61:2, Psalm 62:5-8, Psalm 116:7, Psalm 121:2, Joel 2:25-26, 1 John 4:4, Luke 12:2-3, Ephesians 6:10-18, 2 Chronicles 7:14, 2 Timothy 1:7, Jeremiah 30:17, Philippians 4:7-9, Romans 12:18, John 14:27, 2 Samuel 22:40, Isaiah 26:3, Isaiah 43:2, Isaiah 53:5 & Isaiah 54:17 over all of you

& all whom you love. Father, I pray again for our nation, that You'll restore our lands & that through You, we'll see pure justice, victory & deliverance from all the evil that has been done. Let it be brought forth into the light for all to see. In the name of Jesus, as a child of the true Living God, covered, protected & sealed by Your Blood & the Holy Spirit & with the full authority of God, I come against, command, rebuke & cast this insidious evil in all forms away from you & all your loved ones. This evil must GO NOW & never return! I pray that You'll place a continual spiritual hedge of protection around all reading this message tonight that's impenetrable. Father, I'm praying for all the people, families, businesses & medical workers that are in need, I pray that You will to abundantly bless, protect & heal them & their loved ones during these uncertain times. Father, I'm praying that You'll call to all who do not know You & that their hearts will be open to accept You as their Lord & Savior. I thank You Father & I claim all these things in Your Holy, powerful, majestic, everlasting & precious name I pray Lord Jesus, Amen!

Warriors! Each day we're closing in on the end of this year & as we begin a new year, we need to reflect & always remember what happened in 2020. This was a humbling year to say the least & allows us to realize just how fragile we really are & how we truly need God. But through the difficulties of this year we've also gained an appreciation for what we have & the people in our lives even if it is only seeing them on a screen. When this season has passed we'll appreciate each day forward. Tonight, pray for someone that has been on your mind. This season is going to pass because all things are possible with Christ & He is leading us forward all the way through this deep valley. But soon we will stand on the mountain top, in the light & shout with a collective yell! And remember, DELIVERANCE, VICTORY & JUSTICE ARE COMING! Let not your heart be troubled! May God strengthen You! May God give you courage! May God give you peace! May God bless all of you!

DAY 289
December 30th, 2020

Good evening my friends. 2021 is ever nearer & we're closing out Wednesday, December 30th, 2020 & I pray this message, once again, finds you & your loved ones warm, healthy, safe & well.

Dear Heavenly Father, I come to You with Heavenly praise, a humble heart, love, & thanksgiving. Thank You Father that You have guided us through this year and that we are about to see victory & deliverance in 2021. Father, I'm praying for all the people, families, businesses & medical workers that are in need, I pray that You will to abundantly bless, protect, prosper, guide & heal them & their loved ones. Father, as I pray tonight I thank You that You are placing an impenetrable hedge of protection around all reading this and their loved ones. In the name of Jesus, as a child of the true Living God, covered, protected & sealed by Your Blood & the Holy Spirit & with the full authority of God almighty, I come against, command, rebuke & cast this insidious evil in all forms away from you & all your loved ones to the absolute farthest corners of the earth. Truly greater is He who is in us than he who is in the world & as it's written, through the name & power of Jesus Christ, when we resist the devil he must flee from us. In the name of Jesus, I claim Psalm 91, Psalm 23, Psalm 25:20-21, Psalm 35, Psalm 46:10, Psalm 55:22, Psalm 56:3, Psalm 61:2, Psalm 62:5-8, Psalm 116:7, Psalm 121:2, Joel 2:25-26, 1 John 4:4, Luke 12:2-3, Ephesians 6:10-18, 2 Chronicles 7:14, 2 Timothy 1:7, Jeremiah 30:17, Philippians 4:7-9, Romans 12:18, John 14:27, 2 Samuel 22:40, Isaiah 26:3, Isaiah 43:2, Isaiah 53:5 & Isaiah 54:17 over all of you & all whom you love. Father, I'm praying again that You'll please call to all who do not know You & that their hearts will be truly open to accept You as their Lord & Savior to have eternal life. Father, I pray for our nation, that You'll restore our lands & that through You, we'll see pure justice, victory & deliverance from all the evil that has been done. Let it be brought forth into the light for all to see. I thank You Father & I claim all these things in Your Holy, powerful, majestic, everlasting & precious name I pray Lord Jesus, Amen!

Warriors! It's the middle of week and we're on the cusp of a brand new year. But as we once again draw a line in the sand, we tell these storms, this evil, this chaos around us to leave in one collective voice & through the power of Christ, this too shall pass & this evil will go. This journey is long, difficult, treacherous & uncertain but we can be absolutely certain in the wisdom & guidance of Christ. He will deliver us to victory, He will protect us, He will guide us & through Christ, WE SHALL PREVAIL! The storms we face are great, but our God is greater! This evil is formidable, but our God always triumphs! This difficult time will end & joy will come again. Stay strong! Hold on! We're going to get through this time. When God is for us, there is nothing in the universe that can stop it! PERIOD! Tonight, I pray that a renewed sense of strength fills your mind, spirit & body. Tonight, I pray that as we approach a new year that this coming year will be an absolute blessing to all of you. Tonight, I know that through Christ WE WILL WIN! Shout with me again!! DELIVERANCE, VICTORY & JUSTICE ARE COMING! Let not your heart be troubled! May God strengthen You! May God give you courage! May God give you peace! May God bless all of you!

DAY 290
December 31st, 2020

Good evening my friends. It's New Years Eve & we're closing out Thursday, December 31st, 2020 & I pray this message, finds you & your loved ones warm, healthy, safe & well going into the new year.

Dear Heavenly Father, I come to You with Heavenly praise, a humble heart, love, & thanksgiving this New Years Eve. Thank You Father that throughout this past year that You've sustained, guided & provided for us. Father, I lift up & pray for all reading this tonight that You'll bring prosperity to all reading this and their loved ones. This year I claim victory for all of you & that the Lord will make you the head and not the tail (Deuteronomy 28:13). I'm praying for all the people, families, businesses & medical workers that You'll to abundantly bless, protect, prosper, guide & heal them & their loved ones through the coming year. Please bless them so their cups will overflow with blessings from You Father. In the name of Jesus, I claim Psalm 91, Psalm 23,

Psalm 25:20-21, Psalm 35, Psalm 46:10, Psalm 55:22, Psalm 56:3, Psalm 61:2, Psalm 62:5-8, Psalm 116:7, Psalm 121:2, Deuteronomy 28:13, Joel 2:25-26, 1 John 4:4, Luke 12:2-3, Ephesians 6:10-18, 2 Chronicles 7:14, 2 Timothy 1:7, Jeremiah 30:17, Philippians 4:7-9, Romans 12:18, John 14:27, 2 Samuel 22:40, Isaiah 26:3, Isaiah 43:2, Isaiah 53:5 & Isaiah 54:17 over all of you & all whom you love. Father, I pray that in the coming year You'll surround all reading this & their loved ones with an impenetrable hedge of protection. On this New Years Eve, I pray for our nation, that You'll restore our lands & that through You, we'll see pure justice, victory & deliverance from all the evil that's been done. Let it be brought forth into the light for all to see & let eyes & ears be opened to the truth of God. Father, I'm praying that You'll please call to all who don't know You & that their hearts will be open to accept You as their Lord & Savior. Father finally, In the name of Jesus, as a child of the true Living God, covered, protected & sealed by Your Blood & the Holy Spirit & with the full authority of God almighty, I come against, command, rebuke & cast this insidious evil in all forms away from you & all your loved ones. By Your power & Name, this evil has to leave now & never return! I thank You Father for this coming year & I claim all these things in Your Holy, powerful, majestic, everlasting & precious name I pray Lord Jesus, Amen!

Warriors! As we enter into 2021, know that God has brought you through one of the hardest years, if not the hardest year we've ever faced, but we're still here & we're continuing to press forward through the storm! While the events in 2020 will permeate into 2021, I know that this difficult time will come to an end & life will return to normal. While 2020 was a year we'll never forget for all the bad in it, there was a lot of good as well & we mustn't dwell on the negative but remember the good & the positive. Always remember, it wasn't us who got us through this year, but God almighty. While storms will come, God will deliver us to victory as all things are possible with Christ. It's inevitable. We must not be complacent, but continue to be vigilant, strong & moving forward. Shout this with me again going into 2021. GOD IS GOOD ALL THE TIME & ALL THE TIME GOD IS GOOD! Remember! DELIVERANCE, VICTORY & JUSTICE ARE COMING! Let not your heart be troubled! May God strengthen You! May God give you courage! May God give you peace! May God bless all of you!

DAY 291
January 1st, 2021

Good evening my friends. It's the first day of the new year & we're closing out Friday, January 1st, 2021 & I pray this message, finds you & your loved ones warm, healthy, safe & well. I apologize that I'm a little late getting this out tonight.

Dear Heavenly Father, I come to You with Heavenly praise, a humble heart, love, & thanksgiving. Thank You Father that even though storms have come that You can calm the wind, the rain and the lightning of the chaos we face. Father, I feel that something big is on the horizon & I don't know what that is yet but I ask & pray that Your perfect will be done in all things. I pray that You will surround all reading this with an impenetrable hedge of protection & that You would bless, , prosper, guide & heal them & their loved ones in the coming days ahead. Father, I'm praying that You'll please call to everyone who doesn't know You & that their hearts will be open to accept You as their Lord & Savior. I pray that You will restore our lands & bring justice, victory, deliverance, truth & peace back to the people. Let that which has been done in the dark be brought into the light for all to see. In the name of Jesus, I claim Psalm 91, Psalm 23, Psalm 25:20-21, Psalm 35, Psalm 46:10, Psalm 55:22, Psalm 56:3, Psalm 61:2, Psalm 62:5-8, Psalm 116:7, Psalm 121:2, Deuteronomy 28:13, Joel 2:25-26, 1 John 4:4, Luke 12:2-3, Ephesians 6:10-18, 2 Chronicles 7:14, 2 Timothy 1:7, Jeremiah 30:17, Philippians 4:7-9, Romans 12:18, John 14:27, 2 Samuel 22:40, Isaiah 26:3, Isaiah 43:2, Isaiah 53:5 & Isaiah 54:17 over all of you & all whom you love. In the name of Jesus, as a child of the eternal Living God, covered, protected & sealed by Your Blood & the Holy Spirit & with the full authority of God, I come against, command & cast this insidious evil in all forms away from you & all your loved ones. As it's written if we resist the devil he must flee from us as children of God & through His name & power! I thank You Father for our coming victory and I claim all these things in Your Holy, powerful, majestic, everlasting and precious name I pray Lord Jesus, Amen!

Warriors! Storms are on the horizon, but fear not because God is in control & He alone has the final say. We stand united tonight, hand in hand, arm in arm against the powers of evil & darkness that surround us. We will not go quietly into the night! We will not lay down & give up! We will not surrender to the forces that want our unmitigated destruction. In the coming days, be strong! Be vigilant! Be faithful! The spiritual battle that continues around us will ultimately fail because of the cross. I've said this before but we do not fight for victory but from victory! All glory be to God that He is more powerful & awesome than anything in the known & unknown universe. All of what you are seeing right now was prophesied nearly 2000 years ago but tonight, I want you to raise your hands & thank God that through His might & power that we shall be victorious! Evil strongholds are being destroyed as we speak. Vices & addictions that have been a yoke on the backs of many are being cleansed! Evil is on the run & soon will be no more. And beyond the shadow of a doubt, I know one thing above all else! OUR! GOD! IS! GOD!!! DELIVERANCE, VICTORY & JUSTICE ARE COMING! Let not your heart be troubled! May God strengthen You! May God give you courage! May God give you peace! May God bless all of you!

DAY 292
January 2nd, 2021

Good evening my friends. The weekend is here & we're closing out Saturday, January 2nd, 2021 & as with each and every night, I pray this message, finds you & your loved ones warm, healthy, safe & well.

Dear Heavenly Father, I come to You with Heavenly praise, love, & thanksgiving. Thank You Father for all the blessings You've given us & for the miracles about to unfold. I pray for Your perfect will to be done & that You will restore our lands, bring justice, victory, deliverance, truth & peace back to the people. Let that which has been done in the dark be brought into the light for all to see. Give courage to those whom You've called to do Your will without hesitation on their part. In the name of Jesus, I claim Psalm 91, Psalm 23, Psalm 25:20-21, Psalm 35, Psalm 46:10, Psalm 55:22, Psalm 56:3, Psalm 61:2, Psalm

62:5-8, Psalm 116:7, Psalm 121:2, Deuteronomy 28:13, Joel 2:25-26, 1 John 4:4, Luke 12:2-3, Ephesians 6:10-18, 2 Chronicles 7:14, 2 Timothy 1:7, Jeremiah 30:17, Philippians 4:7-9, Romans 12:18, John 14:27, 2 Samuel 22:40, Isaiah 26:3, Isaiah 43:2, Isaiah 53:5 & Isaiah 54:17 over all of you & all whom you love. I pray that You'll surround all reading this with an impenetrable hedge of protection & that You will abundantly bless, prosper, guide & heal them & their loved ones in the coming days & weeks ahead. Father, I lift up all who don't know You yet & I pray that You'll call to their souls & allow their hearts to be receptive to accept You as their Lord & Savior. In the name of Jesus, as a child of the Living God, covered, protected & sealed by Your Blood & the Holy Spirit & with the full authority of God, I command & cast this horrific & insidious evil in all forms away from you & all your loved ones. Greater is He who is in us than he who is in the world & by Your name & power this evil must go now! I thank You Father for our coming deliverance, victory & I claim all these things in Your Holy, powerful, majestic, everlasting & precious name I pray Lord Jesus, Amen!

Warriors! As we venture into the New Year, know that when God is for us, there isn't anything that can stop us. As it's written ALL things are possible with Christ. As we press forward, we need to have faith that God will deliver us to victory. In the world we live in, faith can be a hard thing to come by these days. But as it's written in the Bible, if you have faith even the size of a mustard seed, you can move mountains according to the will of God. Prayer is one of our most effective weapons against the enemy because when God's people pray, strongholds are shattered, lives are delivered, seemingly impossibility become reality & victory achieved! Don't let current circumstances knock you down in the dust but get up again and again and again if necessary & keep pressing forward thanking God that you will see victory through Him. We're going to get through this season! Shout with me yet again! DELIVERANCE, VICTORY & JUSTICE ARE COMING! Let not your heart be troubled! May God strengthen You! May God give you courage! May God give you peace! May God bless all of you!

DAY 293
January 3rd, 2021

Good evening my friends. We're coming up on a brand new week & we're closing out Sunday, January 3rd, 2021 & I pray this message, finds you & your loved ones warm, healthy, safe & well.

Dear Heavenly Father, I come to You with a humble heart, Heavenly praise, love, & thanksgiving. Thank You Father that in the midst of the storm, You can calm the waters & bring peace where there once was chaos. Father, please give strength & courage to those whom You've called to do Your will. Father, I pray that You'll surround all reading this with a continual, spiritual & impenetrable hedge of protection. Father, I pray that You will supernaturally & abundantly bless, prosper, strengthen, guide & heal all reading this & their loved ones through these uncertain times. I pray for Your perfect will to be done & that You will restore our lands, bring justice, victory, deliverance, truth & peace back to the people. Let this evil that which has been done in the dark be brought into the light for all to see. In the name of Jesus, I claim Psalm 91, Psalm 23, Psalm 25:20-21, Psalm 35, Psalm 46:10, Psalm 55:22, Psalm 56:3, Psalm 61:2, Psalm 62:5-8, Psalm 116:7, Psalm 121:2, Deuteronomy 28:13, Joel 2:25-26, 1 John 4:4, Luke 12:2-3, Ephesians 6:10-18, 2 Chronicles 7:14, 2 Timothy 1:7, Jeremiah 30:17, Philippians 4:7-9, Romans 12:18, John 14:27, 2 Samuel 22:40, Isaiah 26:3, Isaiah 43:2, Isaiah 53:5 & Isaiah 54:17 over all of you & all whom you love. In the name of Jesus, as a child of the eternal Living true God, covered, protected & sealed by Your Blood, the Holy Spirit & with the full authority of God almighty, I command, come against, rebuke & cast this insidious evil in all forms away from you & all your loved ones. By the name & power of Christ this evil MUST GO NOW! Father, I lift up all who don't know You yet & I pray that You'll call to their souls & allow their hearts to be receptive to accept You as their Lord & Savior. I thank You Father & I claim all these things in Your Holy, powerful, majestic, everlasting & precious name I pray Lord Jesus, Amen!

Warriors! As we embark on a new week, remember to guard your thoughts & mind. A lot of the battle against us is directly targeting your thoughts. Don't allow the enemy to get a foothold in your mind. The world will tell you to give up, it's over, it's never going to happen. But remember, we serve a God of real miracles & justice. Man has no say over the will of God. What God ordained WILL come to pass. So no matter what you are facing today, place it entirely in God's perfect hands. Don't listen to what the world tells you but focus solely on God & the word of God. The storms of anxiety, lies & fear may come but stand firm & on the authority of Christ's name tell those lies & evil to go. Truly greater is He who is in us than he who is in the world & when we resist the devil through the name of Jesus Christ, IT MUST GO! This season has been hard for all of us, but soon this will all be a distant memory. We'll never forget this time in our lives but know that you are stronger on the other side because God has brought you through the night & into the light. DELIVERANCE, VICTORY & JUSTICE ARE COMING! Let not your heart be troubled! May God strengthen You! May God give you courage! May God give you peace! May God bless all of you!

DAY 294
January 4th, 2021

Good evening my friends. A new week of pressing forward to victory is here & we're closing out Monday, January 4th, 2021 & I pray this message, finds you & your loved ones warm, healthy, safe & well.

Dear Heavenly Father, I come to You with, Heavenly praise, love, and thanksgiving. Thank You Father for the victory & deliverance that is coming & that You have the ultimate final say in all things. Father, please give supernatural strength and courage to those whom You've called to do Your will. In the name of Jesus, I claim Psalm 91, Psalm 23, Psalm 25:20-21, Psalm 35, Psalm 46:10, Psalm 55:22, Psalm 56:3, Psalm 61:2, Psalm 62:5-8, Psalm 116:7, Psalm 121:2, Deuteronomy 28:13, Joel 2:25-26, 1 John 4:4, Luke 12:2-3, Ephesians 6:10-18, 2 Chronicles 7:14, 2 Timothy 1:7, Jeremiah 30:17, Philippians 4:7-9, Romans 12:18, John 14:27, 2 Samuel 22:40, Isaiah 26:3, Isaiah 43:2, Isaiah 53:5 & Isaiah 54:17 over all of you and all whom you love. Father, I pray for Your will to be done in all that is affecting us now & that You will restore our lands, bring justice, victory, deliverance, truth & peace back to the people. Let this horrific evil that which has been done in the dark be brought into the light for all to see. Father, I pray that You'll completely surround all reading this with a continual, spiritual & impenetrable hedge of protection that no evil can even approach. In the name of Jesus, as a child of the eternal true Living true God, covered, protected and sealed by Your Blood, the Holy Spirit & with the full authority of God, I command and cast this insidious evil in all forms away from you and all your loved ones. As it is written in (Isaiah 59:19) "When the enemy comes in like a flood, The Spirit of the Lord will lift up a standard against him." Father, I pray that You will abundantly bless, prosper, protect, strengthen, guide & heal all reading this and their loved ones through these uncertain times. Father, I pray that You'll call to all the souls who do not yet know you and allow their hearts to be receptive to accept You as their Lord & Savior. I thank You Father for our coming victory and I claim all these things in Your Holy, powerful, majestic, everlasting and precious name I pray Lord Jesus, Amen!

Warriors! I just want to saw thank you for all your wonderful messages I've received. I want you all to know that I do read each & every message. I started this because I felt highly compelled and directed by God to start these prayers & we're continuing onward into 2021! And with that, tonight, say a prayer for your friends, family and all in need. We're another step forward & another day closer to victory. God is continuing to guide us through this difficult terrain and though it may be difficult & frustrating He only has our good in mind. Challenges are where we grow & this past year has been a year to grow our faith. Storms may come but with Christ leading us, we WILL see the promise land of victory on the other side. Tomorrow may be uncertain but take assurance in the certainty of God. He is always right on time, rarely early and never late. He hears your prayers & knows your individual needs. And when all of this chaos began, God already had a plan ready. You're not reading this by coincidence & He wants you all to know that it's going to be alright. Everything is going to be alright. Tonight, raise a hand wherever you are and say thank You to God almighty. And with your hand up! Shout with me! DELIVERANCE, VICTORY AND JUSTICE ARE COMING! Let not your heart be troubled! May God strengthen You! May God give you courage! May God give you peace! May God bless all of you!

DAY 295
January 5th, 2021

Good evening my friends. As we venture into the week we're closing out Tuesday, January 5th, 2021 & I pray this message, finds you & your loved ones warm, healthy, safe & well.

Dear Heavenly Father, I come to You with, a humble heart, Heavenly praise, faith, love, & thanksgiving. Thank You Father that You're shielding & protecting Your children during these difficult times & that we can take refuge in You. Father, I pray for Your absolute perfect will to be done in all that is affecting us now & that You'll restore our lands, bring justice, victory, deliverance, truth & peace back to the people. Let this horrific evil that which has been done in the dark be brought into the light for all to see. Father, I pray that You'll give supernatural strength & courage to those whom You've called to do Your will & that they'll be moved by Your perfect guidance. Father, I pray that all reading this tonight will be completely surrounded by an impenetrable, spiritual & continual hedge of protection by You where we're merely observers. In the name of Jesus, I claim Psalm 91, Psalm 23, Psalm 25:20-21, Psalm 35, Psalm 46:10, Psalm 55:22, Psalm 56:3, Psalm 61:2, Psalm 62:5-8, Psalm 116:7, Psalm 121:2, Deuteronomy 28:13, Joel 2:25-26, 1 John 4:4, Luke 12:2-3, Ephesians 6:10-18, 2 Chronicles 7:14, 2 Timothy 1:7, Jeremiah 30:17, Philippians 4:7-9, Romans 12:18, John 14:27, 2 Samuel 22:40, Isaiah 26:3, Isaiah 43:2, Isaiah 53:5 & Isaiah 54:17 over all of you & all whom you love. In the name of Jesus, as a child of the eternal true Living true God, covered, protected & sealed by Your Blood, the Holy Spirit & with the full authority of God almighty, I command, rebuke, come against & cast this insidious evil in all forms away from you & all your loved ones. Truly greater is He who is in us than he who is in the world & as it's written, if we resist the devil through the power & name of Jesus Christ, the devil must flee! Father, I pray that You'll absolutely & abundantly bless, prosper, protect, strengthen, guide

& heal all reading this & their loved ones through these uncertain times. Father, I pray that You'll call to all the souls who do not yet know you as their Lord & allow their hearts to be receptive to accept You as their Lord & Savior. I thank You Father for our coming victory & I claim all these things in Your Holy, powerful, majestic, everlasting & precious name I pray Lord Jesus, Amen!

Warriors! Tonight we stand at the edge of the storms that surround us on all sides. These are powerful, formidable & seemingly unyielding storms. But despite this, God is more powerful than anything that can come against us. Through the Name & will of God we shall prevail! We draw an indelible line in the sand, cut deep into the bedrock as we stand against the forces of darkness & evil that want nothing more than our unmitigated destruction. Tonight, wherever you are right now, I want you to let out a roar like you've never shouted before praising the name of Christ, letting the forces of darkness know that we have had enough, causing them to tremble to the core! Because we stand with Christ, we do not fear! We are not anxious! We will not be deterred! We will not retreat! We will not falter! We will not bend! We will not break! We will not give in! We will not surrender! We WILL prevail! We WILL see justice! We WILL see deliverance! WE! WILL! SEE! VICTORY!! Let not your heart be troubled! May God strengthen You! May God give you courage! May God give you peace! May God bless all of you!

DAY 296
January 6th, 2021

Good evening my friends. On this winter night we're closing out Wednesday, January 6th, 2021 & I pray this message, finds you & your loved ones warm, healthy, safe & well.

Dear Heavenly Father, I come to You tonight with, a humble heart, Heavenly praise, faith, love, & thanksgiving. Thank You Father that You are the One who can do miracles in the face of the impossible. I thank You Father that You are the One who walked on water, healed the sick, brought Lazarus back from the dead even after 4 days & that You & only You have the final authority in all things. In the name of Jesus, I claim Psalm 91, Psalm 23, Psalm 25:20-21, Psalm 35, Psalm 46:10, Psalm 55:22, Psalm 56:3, Psalm 61:2, Psalm 62:5-8, Psalm 116:7, Psalm 121:2, Deuteronomy 28:13, Joel 2:25-26, 1 John 4:4, Luke 12:2-3, Job 13:15, Ephesians 6:10-18, 2 Chronicles 7:14, 2 Timothy 1:7, Jeremiah 30:17, Philippians 4:7-9, Romans 12:18, John 14:27, 2 Samuel 22:40, Isaiah 26:3, Isaiah 43:2, Isaiah 53:5 & Isaiah 54:17 over all of you & all whom you love. Father, I pray that You will surround all reading this with a hedge of protection that no evil can penetrate. Father, I pray for Your true, absolute & perfect will to be done in all that is affecting us now & that You'll restore our lands, bring justice, victory, deliverance, truth & peace back to the people. Let this horrific evil that which has been done in the dark be brought into the light for all to see. Father, I pray that You'll give them strength & courage to those whom You've called to do Your will & that they'll be moved by Your perfect guidance. In the name of Jesus, as a child of the true Living God, covered, protected & sealed by Your Blood, the Holy Spirit & with the full authority of God almighty, I command & cast this insidious evil in all forms away from you & all your loved ones. Father, I pray that You'll abundantly bless, prosper, protect, strengthen, guide & heal all reading this & their loved ones through these uncertain times. Father, I pray that You'll call to all the souls who do not yet know you as their Lord & allow their hearts to be receptive to accept You as their Lord & Savior. I thank You Father for our coming victory & I claim all these things in Your Holy, powerful, majestic, everlasting & precious name I pray Lord Jesus, Amen!

Warriors! Today as we face the storms that continue to surround us, please take a moment to get on your knees & really pray. Pray for your friends, your family, our nation & your enemies. Pray for the restoration of our lands & for peace. Pray for our deliverance, God's intervention & for victory. Pray for the end of virus. Pray for the end of the violence & chaos. Pray that above all else, that the will of God will be done. These are difficult & dangerous times we live in but I also know that God is still in control & still on the Throne. None of this is a surprise to God. We may not know what tomorrow brings but tonight, wherever you are in the world reading this. Know that God knows your fears, your anxieties, your frustration, your circumstances & He does have a plan of deliverance for you. He knows the very number of hairs on your head & He hears your prayers. Tonight have faith & know that you can trust God. We're going to get through this time everyone. No matter how everything seems, it's going to be okay. Victory is coming. Let not your heart be troubled! May God strengthen You! May God give you courage! May God give you peace! May God bless all of you!

DAY 297
January 7th, 2021

Good evening my friends. We're nearing the end of the week & we're closing out Thursday, January 7th, 2021 & I pray this message truly finds you & your loved ones warm, healthy, safe & well.

Dear Heavenly Father, I come to You tonight with Heavenly praise, faith, love, & thanksgiving. Thank You Father for Your guidance, wisdom, unconditional love & peace that surpasses all understanding. Father, I pray that You'll surround everyone reading this & their loved ones with a hedge of protection that is completely impenetrable. Father, I pray for absolute & perfect will to be done in all that is affecting us now & that You'll restore our lands, bring justice, victory, deliverance, truth & peace back to the people. I pray that this evil that surrounds us like a great storm to be annihilated by Your name & power. Father, I pray that You'll give supernatural courage & strength to those whom You've called to do Your will. In the name of Jesus, as a child of the true Living God, covered, protected & sealed by Your Blood, the Holy Spirit & with the full authority of God, I command & cast this insidious evil in all forms away from you & all your loved ones again. Greater is He who is in us than he who is in the world & as it's written, through the name & power of Jesus Christ, if we resist the devil, he must flee from us. Father, I pray that You'll abundantly bless, prosper, protect, strengthen, guide & heal all reading this & their loved ones through this difficult season. Father, I pray that You'll call to all the souls who do not yet know you as their Lord & allow their hearts to be receptive to accept You as their Lord & Savior so they will have eternal salvation. In the name of Jesus, I claim Psalm 91, Psalm 23, Psalm 25:20-21, Psalm 35, Psalm 46:10, Psalm 55:22, Psalm 56:3, Psalm 61:2, Psalm 62:5-8, Psalm 116:7, Psalm 121:2, Deuteronomy 28:13, Joel 2:25-26, 1 John 4:4, Luke 12:2-3, Job 13:15, Ephesians 6:10-18,

2 Chronicles 7:14, 2 Timothy 1:7, Jeremiah 30:17, Philippians 4:7-9, Romans 12:18, John 14:27, 2 Samuel 22:40, Isaiah 26:3, Isaiah 43:2, Isaiah 53:5 & Isaiah 54:17 over all of you & all whom you love. I thank You Father for our coming victory & I claim all these things in Your Holy, powerful, majestic, everlasting & precious name I pray Lord Jesus, Amen!

Warriors! Do not fear these uncertain times we find ourselves in, because no matter what tomorrow brings, God is in control, asking us to trust Him & will provide for His children. Faith can be a difficult to find in the world we live in, but it's at the core of those particular moments that we must have the strongest faith. As I've said many times on here, prayer is one of our greatest weapons against the enemy. When God's people pray, the devil & his demons shudder. The one thing to always remember is that as we go about our daily lives, we're in the middle of a spiritual battle on a great spiritual battlefield. This is a fallen world but one day soon, very soon, all will be made, right. There will be no more tears, no more sorrow, no more fear. It will be continual and endless joy. While I know it's difficult for our corporeal forms as humans to understand this concept. It truly is coming. Please take a moment to pray for your loved ones tonight. Stay strong everyone! Victory is coming! Let not your heart be troubled! May God strengthen You! May God give you courage! May God give you peace! May God bless all of you!

DAY 298
January 8th, 2021

Good evening my friends. The weekend is here & we're closing out Friday, January 8th, 2021 & I pray this message truly finds you & your loved ones warm, healthy, safe & well. I know this is a little late, I'm battling a massive headache that I've been dealing with for 2 days now. But that's not stopping me from praying over all of you.

Dear Heavenly Father, I come to You tonight with a humble heart, Heavenly praise, faith, love, & thanksgiving. Thank You Father that in the middle of the great storm, you can calm the waters to pure glass. In the name of Jesus, I claim Psalm 91, Psalm 23, Psalm 25:20-21, Psalm 35, Psalm 46:10, Psalm 55:22, Psalm 56:3, Psalm 61:2, Psalm 62:5-8, Psalm 116:7, Psalm 121:2, Deuteronomy 28:13, Joel 2:25-26, 1 John 4:4, Luke 12:2-3, Job 13:15, Ephesians 6:10-18, 2 Chronicles 7:14, 2 Timothy 1:7, Jeremiah 30:17, Philippians 4:7-9, Romans 12:18, John 14:27, 2 Samuel 22:40, Isaiah 26:3, Isaiah 43:2, Isaiah 53:5 & Isaiah 54:17 over all of you & all whom you love. Father, I pray that You'll absolutely & abundantly bless, prosper, protect, strengthen, guide & heal all reading this & their loved ones through this difficult season. Thank You Father that You are restoring the sick to complete health now. Father, I pray that You'll completely surround everyone reading this & their loved ones with a spiritual hedge of protection that is impenetrable & where evil can't even approach. Father, I pray that You'll give supernatural courage, wisdom & strength to those whom You've called to do Your will. Father I pray that You will intercede & drive off the forces of evil that wish our destruction. Father, I pray for Your absolute will to be done in all that is affecting us now & that You'll restore our lands, bring justice, victory, deliverance, truth & peace back to the people. Father, I pray that You'll call to all the souls who do not yet know you as their Lord & allow their hearts to be receptive to accept You as their Lord & Savior. In the name of Jesus, as a child of the Living God, covered, protected & sealed by Your Blood, the Holy Spirit & with the full authority of God, I command & cast this insidious evil in all forms away from you & all your loved ones again. I command the spirit of fear & anxiety away from You in the name of Jesus. I thank You Father for our coming victory & I claim all these things in Your Holy, powerful, majestic, everlasting & precious name I pray Lord Jesus, Amen!

Warriors! Tonight, take a moment to pray for your friends & family. Take a moment & thank God for what He has blessed you with. Take a moment to command the evil that tries to destroy you, through the name & power of Christ, to be gone! Take a moment to breath. We're all under a tremendous about of stress many different forms but they are all valid because they are affecting you tonight. I want you to give that anxiety, that fear, that burden to God right now. Place it at His feet & talk to Him, telling Him that you can't deal with this and to please help & to please take this burden from you. He wants you to place your problems in His hands so He can truly show you His power. Sometimes, difficult situations are in our lives to help us grow, but sometimes, they become overwhelming & we can't do it without Him. We've all had our share of that this past year. But also know, that this difficult season will also pass. We're going to get through this everyone! Victory is coming! Let not your heart be troubled! May God strengthen You! May God give you courage! May God give you peace! May God bless all of you!

DAY 299
January 9th, 2021

      Good evening my friends. It was a beautiful day out in NE Ohio & we're closing out Saturday, January 9th, 2021 & I pray this message truly finds you & your loved ones warm, healthy, safe & well. Thank you for your prayers for my headache. Much better today. It's still hanging on but dissipating.

Dear Heavenly Father, I come to You tonight with a humble heart, Heavenly praise, faith, love, & thanksgiving. Thank You Father that when up against the Red Sea, You always deliver us to victory & safety. Father I pray that You will intercede & drive off the forces of darkness & evil that wish our unmitigated destruction. Father, I pray for Your absolute perfect will to be done in all that is transpiring now & that You'll restore our lands, bring justice, victory, deliverance, truth & peace back to the people. Father, I pray that You'll give supernatural courage, wisdom & strength to those whom You've called to do Your will. Thank You Father that You are restoring the afflicted with the virus to complete health now. Father, I pray that You'll completely & abundantly bless, prosper, protect, strengthen, guide & heal all reading this & their loved ones through this difficult season. In the name of Jesus, I claim Psalm 91, Psalm 23, Psalm 25:20-21, Psalm 35, Psalm 46:10, Psalm 55:22, Psalm 56:3, Psalm 61:2, Psalm 62:5-8, Psalm 116:7, Psalm 121:2, Deuteronomy 28:13, Joel 2:25-26, 1 John 4:4, Luke 12:2-3, Job 13:15, Ephesians 6:10-18, 2 Chronicles 7:14, 2 Timothy 1:7, Jeremiah 30:17, Philippians 4:7-9, Romans 12:18, John 14:27, 2 Samuel 22:40, Isaiah 26:3, Isaiah 43:2, Isaiah 53:5 & Isaiah 54:17 over all of you & all whom you love. Father, I pray that all reading this tonight will be surrounded with an impenetrable spiritual hedge of protection by You Father. In the name of Jesus, as a child of the Living God, covered, protected & sealed by Your Blood, the Holy Spirit & with the full authority of God, I command & cast this insidious evil in all forms away from you & all your loved ones. BE GONE NOW! Father, I pray that You'll call to all the souls who do not yet know you as their Lord & allow their hearts to be receptive to accept You as their Lord & Savior. I thank You Father for our coming deliverance & I claim all these things in Your Holy, powerful, majestic, everlasting & precious name I pray Lord Jesus, Amen!

Warriors! As we take another step forward we must continue to be strong as the storms around us rage. But know this. When God is for you, there isn't anything that can stop you and we will, by the shear grace of God, be victorious and push through. Christ is guiding us safely along the path to deliverance. Along this path there are dangers but we are shielded from those dangers. This being said, we need to continue to be strong, vigilant & not complacent even for a moment. For those of you who are tired, frustrated, afraid, alone & anxious, know that Christ is fully aware of your anxieties, your fears, your circumstances & He will help you. Whatever your burdens are tonight, give it to God. Whatever your fears are tonight, give it to God. Whatever your circumstances are, give it to God. We must learn to let go and let God. There isn't anything in the known or unknown universe that's more powerful than God. Above all else, HIS WILL BE DONE! VICTORY IS COMING! Let not your heart be troubled! May God strengthen You! May God give you courage! May God give you peace! May God bless all of you!

DAY 300
January 10th, 2021

Good evening my friends. It was another beautiful day out in NE Ohio & we're closing out Sunday, January 10th, 2021 & I pray this message truly finds you & your loved ones warm, healthy, safe & well.

Dear Heavenly Father, I come to You tonight with a humble heart, Heavenly praise, faith, love, & thanksgiving. Thank You Father for your guidance, strength, & peace that You give to us whenever we ask. Thank You Father that You're above all things & completely in control. Thank You Father that Your will, will be done. Father I pray that You'll intercede & drive off the forces of darkness & evil that wish our unmitigated destruction. In the name of Jesus, I claim Psalm 91, Psalm 23, Psalm 25:20-21, Psalm 35, Psalm 46:10, Psalm 55:22, Psalm 56:3, Psalm 61:2, Psalm 62:5-8, Psalm 116:7, Psalm 121:2, Deuteronomy 28:13, Joel 2:25-26, 1 John 4:4, Luke 12:2-3, Job 13:15, Ephesians 6:10-18, 2 Chronicles 7:14, 2 Timothy 1:7, Jeremiah 30:17, Philippians 4:7-9, Romans 12:18, John 14:27, 2 Samuel 22:40, Isaiah 26:3, Isaiah 43:2, Isaiah 53:5 & Isaiah 54:17 over all of you & all whom you love. Father, I pray that You'll give absolute supernatural courage, wisdom & strength to those whom You've called to do Your will in all things. Father, I pray that You'll restore our lands, bring justice, victory, deliverance, truth & peace back to the people. Father, bring forth all into the light, that which has been done in the dark! I pray Father that You'll heal all the afflicted & completely restore them. Father, I pray that You'll abundantly bless, prosper, protect, strengthen, guide & heal all Your children, all reading this & their loved ones through this difficult season. Father, I pray that You'll surround all Your children tonight, tomorrow night & the next night with an impenetrable hedge of protection. In the name of Jesus, as a child of the eternal true Living God, covered, protected & sealed by Your Blood, the Holy Spirit & with the full authority of God, I command, rebuke, come against & cast this insidious evil in all forms away from you & all your loved ones. Greater is He who is in us than he who is in the world & as it's written, through the name of Christ, if we resist the devil, he must flee from us. Father, I pray that You'll call to all the souls who do not yet know you as their Lord & allow their hearts to be receptive to accept You as their Lord & Savior before it's too late. I thank You Father for our coming deliverance & I claim all these things in Your Holy, powerful, majestic, everlasting & precious name I pray Lord Jesus, Amen!

Warriors! I have this message for all of you tonight. No matter what storm comes, no matter what evil tries, no matter what happens, be strong, be vigilant, have faith, believe & know above all else that

Jesus Christ is Lord above ALL. God is in complete control. All things are possible with Christ! Man may make plans but God directs his steps. We collectively pray for deliverance, victory & justice. This time here is but a blink in comparison to eternity. We're all tired, frustrated, on edge, anxious & angry. This has been the hardest year for so many, but I also know that while weeping endures for a night, there is joy in the morning. This season will pass. This difficult & uncertain time will end. But we also have to trust & have faith that God's will be done! God is with you & your family. I'm here to continue praying every night. We're gonna get through this. Be safe my friends. HIS WILL BE DONE! VICTORY IS COMING! Let not your heart be troubled! May God strengthen You! May God give you courage! May God give you peace! May God bless all of you!

DAY 301
January 11th, 2021

Good evening my friends. It's the start of a brand new week & we're closing out Monday, January 11th, 2021 & I pray this message truly finds you & your loved ones warm, healthy, safe & well.

Dear Heavenly Father, I come to You tonight with Heavenly praise, faith, love, hope & thanksgiving. Thank You Father that You are in control & working behind the scenes, aligning everything in Your perfect will. In the name of Jesus, I claim Psalm 91, Psalm 23, Psalm 25:20-21, Psalm 35, Psalm 46:10, Psalm 55:22, Psalm 56:3, Psalm 61:2, Psalm 62:5-8, Psalm 116:7, Psalm 121:2, Deuteronomy 28:13, Joel 2:25-26, 1 John 4:4, Luke 12:2-3, Job 13:15, Ephesians 6:10-18, 2 Chronicles 7:14, 2 Timothy 1:7, Jeremiah 30:17, Philippians 4:7-9, Romans 12:18, John 14:27, 2 Samuel 22:40, Isaiah 26:3, Isaiah 43:2, Isaiah 53:5 & Isaiah 54:17 over all of you & all whom you love. In the name of Jesus, as a child of the Living God, covered, protected & sealed by Your Blood, the Holy Spirit & with the full authority of God, I once again command & cast this insidious evil in all forms away from you & all your loved ones. Father, I pray that You'll give absolute supernatural courage, wisdom & strength to those whom You've called to do Your will. Father I pray that You'll go before us, intercede & drive away the forces of darkness & evil that wish our complete destruction. Father, I pray that You'll restore our lands, bring justice, victory, deliverance, truth & peace back to the people. I thank You that Your deliverance & victory are coming. Father, bring forth all that has been done in secret into the light, that which has been done in the dark! Father, I pray that You will reach down to all the afflicted & restore their health with no lasting side effects. Father, in these uncertain times, I pray that You'll abundantly bless, prosper, protect, strengthen, guide & heal all reading this & their loved ones through this difficult season. Father, I pray that You'll completely surround everyone & their loved ones with an impenetrable hedge of protection against all evil. Father, I pray that You'll call to all the souls who do not yet know you as their Lord & allow their hearts to be receptive to accept You as their Lord & Savior. I thank You Father & I claim all these things in Your Holy, powerful, majestic, everlasting & precious name I pray Lord Jesus, Amen!

Warriors! As we have moved through another day together, I know how weary all of you are at the length of this journey. It's been hard, difficult, heartbreaking & continual. I know the stress, the frustration, the anxiety that you all feel. Today while I was praying, that soft voice kept saying to me, "Be still & know that I am God" Tonight when I looked to see what verse I would be posting below, it was Psalm 46:10 saying "Be still & know that I am God". So what I am telling you all tonight is, no matter what you are currently facing, this too shall pass. Whatever the circumstances are you are fighting through, this too shall pass. Whatever your fears are for tomorrow, THIS TOO SHALL PASS! God knows what you are going through & while this is difficult, through the very power of Christ & ONLY through the power of Christ, He will deliver us to victory. Your Father in Heaven already knows what you need before you even ask. This time has allowed us to realize how fragile we really are & how we desperately need God in our lives. All of us. He loves you more than you can possibly imagine & He will lead us to victory. Stay strong, vigilant & stay faithful. Above all else keep praying & trust in God's absolute perfect timing! HIS WILL BE DONE! VICTORY IS COMING! Let not your heart be troubled! May God strengthen You! May God give you courage! May God give you peace! May God bless all of you!

DAY 302
January 12th, 2021

Good evening my friends. It a cold winter day here in NE Ohio & we're closing out Tuesday, January 12th, 2021 & I pray this message truly finds you & your loved ones warm, healthy, safe & well.

Dear Heavenly Father, I come to You tonight with a humble heart, Heavenly praise, faith, love, hope & thanksgiving. Thank You Father that when You are for us, there can be none against us. Thank You Father that while we're in the midst of the storm, You are in full control. Thank You Father that no matter what schemes are perpetrated by the enemy, that You thwart those actions. Thank You that above all else, Your will be done! Father, I pray that You'll go before us, intercede & drive away the forces of darkness & evil that wish our destruction. In the Holy name of Jesus, as a child of the eternal true Living God, covered, protected & sealed by Your Blood, the Holy Spirit & with the full authority of God, I command, come against, rebuke & cast this insidious evil in all forms away from you & all your loved ones. Greater is He who is in Us than he who is in the world & by Your name he must go now. Father, I pray that You'll give absolute supernatural courage, guidance, wisdom, peace & strength to those whom You've called to do Your will. Father, I pray that You'll restore our lands, bring absolute justice, absolute victory, absolute deliverance, absolute truth & absolute peace back to the people. I thank You that Your deliverance & victory are coming. Father, bring forth all the evil that has been done in secret, exposed & into the light! In the name of Jesus, I claim Psalm 91, Psalm 23, Psalm 25:20-21, Psalm 34:19, Psalm 35, Psalm 46:10, Psalm 55:22, Psalm 56:3, Psalm 61:2, Psalm 62:5-8, Psalm 116:7, Psalm 121:2, Deuteronomy 28:13, Joel 2:25-26, 1 John 4:4, Luke 12:2-3, Job 13:15, Ephesians 6:10-18, 2 Chronicles 7:14, 2 Timothy 1:7, Jeremiah 30:17, Philippians 4:7-9, Romans 12:18, John 14:27, 2 Samuel 22:40, Isaiah 26:3, Isaiah 43:2, Isaiah 53:5 & Isaiah 54:17 over all of you & all whom you love. Father, I pray that You'll completely surround all Your children & their loved ones with an impenetrable hedge of protection against all evil. Let them be mere observers to the evil & destruction around them, while being fully protected by You. Father, I pray that You'll completely restore all the afflicted to full health. Father, in these truly unprecedented & uncertain times, I pray that You'll truly & absolutely abundantly bless, prosper, protect, strengthen, guide & heal all Your children & their loved ones through this difficult season. Father, I pray that You'll call to all the souls who do not yet know you as their Lord & allow their hearts to be receptive to accept You as their Lord & Savior. I thank You Father & I claim all these things in Your Holy, powerful, majestic, everlasting & precious name I pray Lord Jesus, Amen!

Warriors! This moment right now, we draw another line in the sand. It's indelible & indestructible. Because of the work of Christ, do not be afraid! Do not fear or have anxiety because in the midst of the storm, God is in control. He calms the waters to a glass mirror & restores peace in the heart. Because all things are possible with Christ, have faith & never let go even when all seems lost, but know that God's timing is absolutely perfect. He is never late, rarely early, but always on time, always. We're all in a very difficult & uncertain season but I also know that a time when all will be made right is coming soon. So right now, say a prayer for your family, your friends, our nation & your enemies. Above all else, pray that God's will, not our will, but God's will be done in all things. Stay strong, have faith, have peace! HIS WILL BE DONE! VICTORY IS COMING! Let not your heart be troubled! May God strengthen You! May God give you courage! May God give you peace! May God bless all of you!

DAY 303
January 13th, 2021

Good evening my friends. It's the middle of the week & we're closing out Wednesday, January 13th, 2021 & I pray this message finds you & your loved ones warm, healthy, safe & well.

Dear Heavenly Father, I come to You tonight with a humble heart, Heavenly praise, faith, love, hope & thanksgiving. Thank You Father that Your will above all else will be done & for Your guidance through these unprecedented times. I claim Psalm 91, Psalm 23, Psalm 25:20-

21, Psalm 34:19, Psalm 35, Psalm 46:10, Psalm 55:22, Psalm 56:3, Psalm 61:2, Psalm 62:5-8, Psalm 116:7, Psalm 121:2, Deuteronomy 28:13, Joel 2:25-26, 1 John 4:4, Luke 12:2-3, Job 13:15, Ephesians 6:10-18, 2 Chronicles 7:14, 2 Timothy 1:7, Jeremiah 30:17, Philippians 4:7-9, Romans 12:18, John 14:27, 2 Samuel 22:40, Isaiah 26:3, Isaiah 43:2, Isaiah 53:5 & Isaiah 54:17 over all of you & all whom you love. Father, I pray that You'll fully restore all the sick & afflicted to full health. Father, I pray that this virus will be completely eradicated from the earth. Father, I pray that You will completely surround & encompass all reading this message with a hedge of protection that is completely impenetrable. Father, I pray that You will abundantly bless, prosper, protect, strengthen, guide, give hope, faith, love & heal everyone reading this & their loved ones. Father, I pray that You'll give supernatural courage, guidance, wisdom, peace & strength to those whom You've called to do Your will. Father, I pray that You'll restore our lands, bring justice, victory, deliverance, vindication, truth & peace back to the people. Father, bring forth into the light all the evil that has been done in secret in the dark. Father, I pray that You'll go before us, interceding & driving away the forces of darkness & evil that want our unmitigated destruction. In the name of Jesus, as a child of the true Living God, covered, protected & sealed by Your Blood, the Holy Spirit & with the full authority of God, I command & cast this insidious evil in all forms away from you & your loved ones. By Your name & power this evil needs to GO NOW & never return! Father, I pray that You'll call to all the souls who do not yet know you as their Lord & allow their hearts to be receptive to accept You as their Lord & Savior. I thank You Father & I claim all these things in Your Holy, powerful, majestic, everlasting & precious name I pray Lord Jesus, Amen!

Warriors! As we press through into another day, take a moment to pray for the safety of your family & loved ones during this difficult time. We all have a tendency to stay focused on ourselves when times are difficult, but everyone we know is going through something right now & could use your intercessory prayer. We're caught in the middle of a spiritual battle going on all around us against the forces of good & evil. It's almost tangible as if you can feel or sense it in the air. But I also believe deep down that something big is coming. I don't know what it is & I can't exactly articulate it, but it's in the depths of my soul & I feel it at every moment of every day. The best I can describe it is something massive. It's almost an excitement. That's the best I can describe it right now. But as we continue to move forward, know that God is leading us through this valley to victory. The past year, as difficult as it's been, will be in history books & you all were part of that. And for all of you who are afraid of tomorrow, know that God is in complete control, He knows what you are facing today & will take care of you. Remember if you have the faith of even of a mustard seed you can move mountains according to God's will. Give God your burdens today & let Him take care of the rest. It's going to be okay! HIS WILL BE DONE! VICTORY IS COMING! Let not your heart be troubled! May God strengthen You! May God give you courage! May God give you peace! May God bless all of you!

DAY 304
January 14th, 2021

      Good evening my friends. We're nearing the weekend & we're closing out Thursday, January 14th, 2021 & with each night, I pray this message finds you & your loved ones warm, healthy, safe & well.

Dear Heavenly Father, I come to You tonight with Heavenly praise, faith, love, hope & thanksgiving. Thank You Father for all the blessings You have given us & that You promised to never leave nor forsake us ever. Father, I pray that You'll go before us, interceding & driving away the forces of darkness & evil that wish our destruction. Father, I pray that You'll please restore our lands, bring justice, victory, deliverance, vindication, truth & peace back to the people. Father, I pray that You will expose & bring into the light this evil that has been done in the cover of darkness & secret. Father, I pray that You'll give courage, guidance, wisdom, peace & strength to those whom You've called to do Your will. Father, I pray that You will abundantly bless, prosper, protect, strengthen, guide, give hope, faith, love & heal everyone reading this & their loved ones. Father, I pray for all the sick & afflicted that they would be completely and fully restored to health. Father, I pray that all reading this will be surrounded by a hedge of protection guarding against evil, the virus & that is impenetrable. In the name of Jesus, as a child of the eternal, everlasting, true Living God, covered, protected & sealed by Your Blood, the Holy Spirit & with the full authority of God, I command & cast this insidious evil in all forms away from you & your loved ones. Above all Father, let Your will be done. Father, I pray that You'll call to everyone who does not yet know you as their Lord & allow their hearts to be open & receptive to accept You as their Lord & Savior. I claim Psalm 91, Psalm 23, Psalm 25:20-21, Psalm 34:19, Psalm 35, Psalm 46:10, Psalm 55:22, Psalm 56:3, Psalm 61:2, Psalm 62:5-8, Psalm 116:7, Psalm 121:2, Deuteronomy 28:13, Joel 2:25-26, 1 John 4:4, Luke 12:2-3, Job 13:15, Ephesians 6:10-18, 2 Chronicles 7:14, 2 Timothy 1:7, Jeremiah 30:17, Philippians 4:7-9, Romans 12:18, John 14:27, 2 Samuel 22:40, Isaiah 26:3, Isaiah 43:2, Isaiah 53:5 & Isaiah 54:17 over all of you & all whom you love. I thank You Father & I claim all these things in Your Holy, powerful, majestic, everlasting & precious name I pray Lord Jesus, Amen!

Warriors! As we march onto the spiritual battlefield once again, stand fast, stand firm & stand ready because the forces of darkness that surround us continue to attack. But do not fear them because we're covered & protected by the blood of Christ. We're entering into a time that was prophesied nearly 2000 years ago & it appears to be coming faster than we ever expected. Christ said these things would happen & have to happen. So take joy in that we're nearing complete & total victory & deliverance. All things are possible with Christ & while everything appears to be in complete chaos, God is still in control, on the Throne & with a perfect plan. I know the feeling many of you, if not all of us, have right now as we're worried for the future & uncertain about the times we live. But what we have to do & I need to remind myself as well, is to take our eyes off the storm & focus them on God. He didn't bring you this far in life only to let you go now. He has a perfect spiritual destiny for each of you that only you can accomplish. We need only be still & know that He is God. It's going to be okay everyone. HIS WILL BE DONE! VICTORY IS COMING! Let not your heart be troubled! May God strengthen You! May God give you courage! May God give you peace! May God bless all of you!

DAY 305
January 15th, 2021

Good evening my friends. The weekend is finally here & we're closing out Friday, January 15th, 2021 & I hope & pray this message finds you & your loved ones warm, healthy, safe & well.

Dear Heavenly Father, I come to You tonight with a humble heart, Heavenly praise, faith, love, hope & thanksgiving praising Your Name Father. Thank You Father that when we pray we're directly speaking with You & that You truly hear our prayers. I claim Psalm 91, Psalm 23, Psalm 25:20-21, Psalm 34:19, Psalm 35, Psalm 46:10, Psalm 55:22, Psalm 56:3, Psalm 61:2, Psalm 62:5-8, Psalm 116:7, Psalm 121:2, Deuteronomy 28:13, Joel 2:25-26, 1 John 4:4, Luke 12:2-3, Job 13:15, Ephesians 6:10-18, 2 Chronicles 7:14, 2 Timothy 1:7, Jeremiah 30:17, Philippians 4:7-9, Romans 12:18, John 14:27, 2 Samuel 22:40, Isaiah 26:3, Isaiah 43:2, Isaiah 53:5 & Isaiah 54:17 over all of you & all whom you love. I pray that each of you are fully surrounded by a spiritual hedge of protection. Father, please give supernatural courage, guidance, wisdom, peace & strength to those whom You've called to do Your will. Father, please restore our lands, bring justice, victory, deliverance, vindication, truth & peace back to the people. Father, please expose & bring into the light this evil & deception that has been done in the cover of darkness & secret. Father, I pray that You'll go before us, interceding & driving away the forces of darkness & evil that wish our destruction. Father, please abundantly bless, give prosperity, protect, strengthen, guide, give hope, faith, love & heal everyone reading this & their loved ones. Father, I thank You that You're healing the afflicted & restoring them to full health. Father, I pray that You'll call to everyone who does not yet know You as their Lord & allow their hearts to be open & receptive to accept You as their Lord & Savior. In the name of Jesus, as a child of the true Living God, covered, protected & sealed by Your Blood, the Holy Spirit & with the full authority of God, I once again command & cast this insidious evil in all forms away from you & your loved ones. Above all Father, let Your will be done. I thank You Father & I claim all these things in Your Holy, powerful, majestic, everlasting & precious name I pray Lord Jesus, Amen!

Warriors! As we walk into the weekend we're another 24 hours closer to victory. We will never forget 2020-2021. But I feel that this year we are going to truly see some amazing things. As I've said a few times on here, I feel that something very big is coming. No matter how each day goes, we must stay strong, keep the faith, not let down, stay vigilant, & keep on praying. Prayer has far more power than you can possibly imagine. It is the ability for the believer to talk directly with the creator of the universe. Think about that, you have a direct line to God & He hears your prayers. Remember all things are possible with Christ & He is leading us through this deep long valley but we are completely safe as He will deliver us to the other side. Always remember, God works all things for our good & God's character never changes. He is the same past, present & future & He loves you far greater than you can ever imagine. We may go through difficult times but God will never allow anything you can't handle & He uses those problems in life to grow you & form you into all you were created to be. It's not always pleasant in the moment, but the end result is amazing. We're going to get through this everyone. HIS WILL BE DONE! VICTORY IS COMING! Let not your heart be troubled! May God strengthen You! May God give you courage! May God give you peace! May God bless all of you!

DAY 306
January 16th, 2021

Good evening my friends. It was a cold blustery day in NE Ohio & we're closing out Saturday, January 16th, 2021 & I pray this message finds you & your loved ones warm, healthy, safe & well.

Dear Heavenly Father, I come to You tonight with Heavenly praise, faith, love, hope & thanksgiving praising Your Name Father. Thank You Father that You're the creator of all things & that through belief in Christ Jesus, that He's the Son of God, accepting Him into our hearts as our Lord & Savior who died on the cross for our sin debt & that we may have eternal life. Father, please go before us & restore our lands, bring justice, victory, deliverance, vindication, truth & peace back to the people. Father, I pray that You'll expose & bring into the light this evil & deception that has been done in the cover of darkness

& secret. Father, we are praying for justice & that You will alone be done. I claim Psalm 91, Psalm 23, Psalm 25:20-21, Psalm 34:19, Psalm 35, Psalm 46:10, Psalm 55:22, Psalm 56:3, Psalm 61:2, Psalm 62:5-8, Psalm 116:7, Psalm 121:2, Deuteronomy 28:13, Joel 2:25-26, 1 John 4:4, Luke 12:2-3, Job 13:15, Ephesians 6:10-18, 2 Chronicles 7:14, 2 Timothy 1:7, Jeremiah 30:17, Philippians 4:7-9, Romans 12:18, John 14:27, 2 Samuel 22:40, Isaiah 26:3, Isaiah 43:2, Isaiah 53:5 & Isaiah 54:17 over all of you & all whom you love. Father, I pray that You'll abundantly bless, give prosperity, protection, strengthen, guidance, give hope, faith, love & heal everyone reading this & their loved ones. Father, I thank You that You're healing the afflicted with the virus & restoring them to full health. Father, I pray that You'll surround everyone reading this & their loved ones with an impenetrable hedge of protection. Father, I pray that You'll call to everyone who does not yet know You as their Lord & allow their hearts to be open & receptive to accept You as their Lord & Savior. In the name of Jesus, as a child of the eternal true Living God, covered, protected & sealed by Your Blood, the Holy Spirit & with the full authority of God, I command & cast this insidious evil in all forms away from you & your loved ones. I thank You Father & I claim all these things in Your Holy, powerful, majestic, everlasting & precious name I pray Lord Jesus, Amen!

Warriors! As we continue to press forward into another day, please take a moment to thank God for all He has done for you through this past difficult year. Please take a moment to pray for the needy, your friends & your family. I know how afraid many of you are tonight. I know how many of you are uncertain about tomorrow or the next day. But know this… God is in control. God loves you. God hasn't brought you to this point only to let go of you now. God chose you to be alive right now, when he could have set you down anytime in history. God knows your fears. God knows your needs. God knows everything that could ever be known about you. God loves you. This has been a difficult season for all of us but through Christ we WILL see the other side of this valley. Hold on & stay strong! We're almost there. It's going to be okay. Tonight, place your fears in God's hands & just rest. HIS WILL BE DONE! VICTORY IS COMING! Let not your heart be troubled! May God strengthen You! May God give you courage! May God give you peace! May God bless all of you!

DAY 307
January 17th, 2021

Good evening my friends. We're on the eve of a brand new week & we're closing out Sunday, January 17th, 2021 & I hope & pray this message finds you & your loved ones warm, healthy, safe & well.

Dear Heavenly Father, I come to You tonight with Heavenly praise, faith, love, hope & thanksgiving praising Your Name Father. Thank You Father that even in the midst of the great storms we find ourselves that You are in control at all times & can calm the storms with a single thought. I claim Psalm 91, Psalm 23, Psalm 25:20-21, Psalm 34:19, Psalm 35, Psalm 46:10, Psalm 55:22, Psalm 56:3, Psalm 61:2, Psalm 62:5-8, Psalm 116:7, Psalm 121:2, Deuteronomy 28:13, Joel 2:25-26, 1 John 4:4, Luke 12:2-3, Job 13:15, Ephesians 6:10-18, 2 Chronicles 7:14, 2 Timothy 1:7, Jeremiah 30:17, Philippians 4:7-9, Romans 12:18, John 14:27, 2 Samuel 22:40, Isaiah 26:3, Isaiah 43:2, Isaiah 53:5 & Isaiah 54:17 over all of you & all whom you love. Father I pray for Your protection over this nation & that above all Your will be done. Father, I pray that all reading this message tonight will be surrounded by a supernatural, spiritual & impenetrable hedge of protection. Father, I pray that You'll go before us, restore our lands, bring justice, victory, deliverance, vindication, truth & peace back to the people. Father, I pray that You'll completely expose & bring into the light this evil & deception that has been done in the dark. In the name of Jesus, as a child of the Living God, covered, protected & sealed by Your Blood, the Holy Spirit & with the full authority of God, I command, come against, rebuke & cast this insidious evil in all forms away from you & your loved ones. Greater is He who is us than he who is in the world & as it's truly written, through Your name & power if we resist the devil he must flee from us. Father, I pray that You will heal the afflicted & restore them completely. Father, I pray that You'll abundantly bless, give prosperity, protection, strengthen, guidance, give hope, faith, love & heal everyone reading this & their loved ones throughout these difficult times. Father, I pray that You'll call to everyone who does not yet know You as their Lord and allow their hearts to be open and receptive to accept You as their Lord and Savior. I thank You Father & I claim all these things in Your Holy, powerful, majestic, everlasting & precious name I pray Lord Jesus, Amen!

Warriors! A new week is upon us & no matter what happens, this too shall pass. With each day the world seems more & more chaotic than the day before but do not be afraid for this was all prophesied nearly 2,000 years ago. We are entering into a unique time period in history. Know that through Christ our Savior, we will prevail. Remember we truly fight from victory, not for victory. The enemy has already been defeated from the cross. We must continue to press forward with everything we've got. We must stay strong, vigilant, faithful & believing. When the storms come, turn away & focus on God alone. He is our refuge, our strength & our fortress. We're all in this together & we're going to get through this together by the very grace of God almighty. Fear not! HIS WILL BE DONE! VICTORY IS COMING! Let not your heart be troubled! May God strengthen You! May God give you courage! May God give you peace! May God bless all of you!

DAY 308
January 18th, 2021

Good evening my friends. We have officially started a brand new week & we're closing out Monday, January 18th, 2021 & I hope & pray this message finds you & your loved ones warm, healthy, safe & well.

Dear Heavenly Father, I come to You tonight with a humble heart, Heavenly praise, faith, love, hope & thanksgiving. Thank You Father that You are in complete control of everything & that even when we don't see what's going on, You are working behind the scenes for Your perfect will. Father, I pray that You will place a spiritual & impenetrable hedge of protection around everyone reading this tonight & all their loved ones. Father, I pray that You will place Your perfect hands on our nation, protecting it, restoring it & that You will bring pure justice, victory, deliverance, vindication, truth & peace. Let all the evil that has been done in secret be brought to light & justice served swiftly. I claim Psalm 91, Psalm 23, Psalm 25:20-21, Psalm 34:19, Psalm 35, Psalm 46:10, Psalm 55:22, Psalm 56:3, Psalm 61:2, Psalm 62:5-8, Psalm 116:7, Psalm 121:2, Deuteronomy 28:13, Joel 2:25-26, 1 John 4:4, Luke 12:2-3, Job 13:15, Ephesians 6:10-18, 2 Chronicles 7:14, 2 Timothy 1:7, Jeremiah 30:17, Philippians 4:7-9, Romans 12:18, John 14:27, 2 Samuel 22:40, Isaiah 26:3, Isaiah 43:2, Isaiah 53:5 & Isaiah 54:17 over all of you & all whom you love. Father, I lift up & pray for all the afflicted & ask that You, the Great Physician will heal & restore all those who are sick. Father, there are so many people hurting tonight, I pray that You'll abundantly bless, give prosperity, protection, strengthen, guidance, give hope, peace, faith, love & heal everyone reading this & their loved ones. Father, there are so many lost souls, I pray that You'll call to everyone who does not yet know You as their Lord & allow their hearts to be open & receptive to accept You as their Lord & Savior. In the name of Jesus, as a child of the Living God, covered, protected & sealed by Your Blood, the Holy Spirit & with the full authority of God almighty, I command & cast this insidious evil in all forms away from you & your loved ones. I thank You Father & I claim all these things in Your Holy, powerful, majestic, everlasting & precious name I pray Lord Jesus, Amen!

Warriors! Tonight, as we live in this chaotic fallen world, know that there is a far greater & superior one coming. All that has been wrong will be made right & God's perfect plan will unfold. There is also coming a day when truly every knee shall bow & every tongue confess that Jesus Christ is Lord. And although we live in uncertain times, be certain in the love, power & justice of Christ. As it is written God will not be mocked. Victory & justice are coming swiftly. I also believe that something very big is about to happen. I don't know what that is yet but I know how great & awesome God is. Tonight, pray for your family, your friends, your enemies & our nation. Christ continues to guide us through these uncharted waters to safety. We must continue to have faith & trust in Him. Lean not on your own understanding but have faith that God will deliver us. No matter what we face down here, it is no match for God. He has everything under complete control & He alone has the final say. HIS WILL BE DONE! VICTORY IS COMING! Let not your heart be troubled! May God strengthen You! May God give you courage! May God give you peace! May God bless all of you!

DAY 309
January 19th, 2021

Good evening my friends. It was an absolutely beautiful day out in NE Ohio today & we're closing out Tuesday, January 19th, 2021 & I hope & pray this message finds you & your loved ones warm, healthy, safe & well.

Dear Heavenly Father, I come to You tonight with Heavenly praise, faith, love, hope & thanksgiving. Thank You Father that You make the possible out the impossible, the way where there was no way & truly the only One with the final say in all things. Father I thank You for what is to come swiftly. I thank You Father that justice, victory, deliverance, vindication & the revelation of truth out the hidden dark places brought to light. I thank You Father that Your will alone will be done. I thank You Father that You are surrounding all Your children with an impenetrable spiritual hedge of protection that no evil will even come near. I thank You Father that by Your hand the afflicted are being healed & restored. Father, I pray for all Your children tonight that they would be refreshed, given peace, strength, wisdom, faith, hope & courage. I thank You Father for Michael & his mission ahead. Father I pray that You will call to all the lost souls that they may find eternal life for believing in You as their Lord & Savior & You alone. In the name of Jesus, as a child of the Living God, covered, protected & sealed by Your Blood, the Holy Spirit & with the full authority of God almighty, I command & cast this insidious evil in all forms away from you & your loved ones. In the name of Jesus, I claim Psalm 91, Psalm 23, Psalm 25:20-21, Psalm 34:19, Psalm 35, Psalm 46:10, Psalm 55:22, Psalm 56:3, Psalm 58:10, Psalm 61:2, Psalm 62:5-8, Psalm 116:7, Psalm 121:2, Proverbs 16:18, Deuteronomy 28:13, Joel 2:25-26, 1 John 4:4, Luke 12:2-3, Job 13:15, Ephesians 6:10-18, 2 Chronicles 7:14, 2 Timothy 1:7, Jeremiah 30:17, Philippians 4:7-9, Romans 12:18, John 14:27, 2 Samuel 22:40, Isaiah 26:3, Isaiah 43:2, Isaiah 53:5 & Isaiah 54:17 over all of you and all whom you love. I thank You Father & I claim all these things in Your Holy, powerful, majestic, everlasting & precious name I pray Lord Jesus, Amen!

Warriors! Tonight, we stand with faith, courage & hope. Tonight, we hold fast to our beliefs & to our God. Tonight, we draw a line in the sand once more & shout at this evil that through the power & name of Jesus Christ we will not bend or break! That we will not deter, falter or fall back! That we will not go quietly into the night but rise up with strength from God almighty! Above all else God's will & only God's will be done! From this mountain & through the power of Christ, we stare down evil till it shrinks to nothing. From this mountain God's power will manifest in ways we've never seen before! From this mountain we shout a collective roar of mighty lions & say NO MORE! With Christ ALL things are possible even when it seems darkest before the dawn. We've fought through a very dark season but WE'RE STILL HERE! God WILL deliver us to victory! God WILL bring justice forth! God WILL bring vindication! God WILL expose the plans of the enemy! GOD'S WILL BE DONE! VICTORY IS COMING! Let not your heart be troubled! May God strengthen You! May God give you courage! May God give you peace! May God bless all of you!

DAY 310
January 20th, 2021

Good evening my friends. It's the middle of the week & we're closing out Wednesday, January 20th, 2021 & I hope & pray this message finds you & your loved ones warm, healthy, safe & well.

Dear Heavenly Father, I come to You tonight with Heavenly praise, faith, love, hope & thanksgiving. Thank You Father that even in the midst of the storm that You calm the waters of chaos. In the name of Jesus, I claim Psalm 91, Psalm 23, Psalm 25:20-21, Psalm 34:19, Psalm 35, Psalm 46:10, Psalm 55:22, Psalm 56:3, Psalm 61:2, Psalm 62:5-8, Psalm 116:7, Psalm 121:2, Proverbs 16:18, Deuteronomy 28:13, Joel 2:25-26, 1 John 4:4, Luke 12:2-3, Job 13:15, Ephesians 6:10-18, 2 Chronicles 7:14, 2 Timothy 1:7, Jeremiah 30:17, Philippians 4:7-9, Romans 12:18, John 14:27, 2 Samuel 22:40, Isaiah 26:3, Isaiah 43:2, Isaiah 53:5 & Isaiah 54:17 over all of you & all whom you love. Father I pray that Your justice, victory, deliverance, vindication & the revelation of truth out the hidden dark places will be brought to light. Father let Your will alone will be done. Father I lift up the afflicted that they would be restored to complete health. Father, I pray that You will surround all reading this & their loved ones with an impenetrable hedge of protection. Father I pray that You will abundantly bless, protect, prosper, give faith, love, peace, wisdom, guidance & strength to all reading this. I pray for the complete eradication of this horrible virus. Father I pray that You will call to all the lost souls that they may find eternal life for believing in You as their Lord & Savior & You alone. In the name of Jesus, as a child of the Living God, covered, protected & sealed by Your Blood, the Holy Spirit & with the full authority of God almighty, I command & cast this insidious evil in all forms away from you & your loved ones. I thank You Father & I claim all these things in Your Holy, powerful, majestic, everlasting & precious name I pray Lord Jesus, Amen!

Warriors! Stay strong in the midst of the storm! Stay courageous in the face of evil. Stand firm! Stand Strong! Stand vigilant! Stand ready! Know this, there is a time coming soon when all will be made right. The storms that surround us have no authority & no control! God alone has the final say & is in total control! Tonight, say a prayer for your family & your friends. We're going to continue to press forward & Christ is leading us to victory! GOD'S WILL BE DONE! VICTORY IS COMING! Let not your heart be troubled! May God strengthen You! May God give you courage! May God give you peace! May God bless all of you!

DAY 311
January 21st, 2021

Good evening my friends. It was a beautiful winter day out in NE Ohio & we're closing out Thursday, January 21st, 2021 & I hope & pray this message finds you & your loved ones warm, healthy, safe & well.

Dear Heavenly Father, I come to You tonight with a humble heart, Heavenly praise, faith, love, hope & thanksgiving. Thank You Father that You are always right on time no matter what the circumstance is, You have the final say as all things are possible with You. Father I pray that You'll absolutely & abundantly bless, protect, prosper, give faith, love, peace, wisdom, guidance & strength to all reading this & their loved ones. Father I pray that You will reach down as the You are the Great Physician & heal all those who are afflicted with this terrible virus. Father, I pray that all reading this message will be completely surrounded by a spiritual hedge of protection that is impenetrable. Father I pray that Your pure justice, victory, deliverance, vindication & the revelation of truth out the hidden dark places will be brought to light. Father let Your will alone will be done. In the name of Jesus, I claim Psalm 91, Psalm 23, Psalm 25:20-21, Psalm 34:19, Psalm 35, Psalm 46:10, Psalm 55:22, Psalm 56:3, Psalm 61:2, Psalm 62:5-8, Psalm 116:7, Psalm 121:2, Proverbs 16:18, Deuteronomy 28:13, Joel 2:25-26, 1 John 4:4, Luke 12:2-3, Job 13:15, Ephesians 6:10-18, 2 Chronicles 7:14, 2 Timothy 1:7, Jeremiah 30:17, Philippians 4:7-9, Romans 12:18, John 14:27, 2 Samuel 22:40, Isaiah 26:3, Isaiah 43:2, Isaiah 53:5 & Isaiah 54:17 over all of you & all whom you love. Father, I pray in the name of Jesus, as a child of the eternal, true Living God, covered, protected & sealed by Your Blood, the Holy Spirit & with the full authority of God, I command, come against, rebuke & cast this insidious evil in all forms away from you & your loved ones. As it is written, Greater is He who is in us than he who is in the world & if we resist the devil through Your name & power, he must flee. Father I pray that all the lost souls in this world will come to know You as their Lord & Savior. I pray that You will call to them & let their hearts be receptive to accept You as their Lord & have eternal life through You. I thank You Father & I claim all these things in Your Holy, powerful, majestic, everlasting & precious name I pray Lord Jesus, Amen!

Warriors! As we approach the weekend we must stand firm, be vigilant & strong through these uncertain times. But do not fear these storms as they're not sent from God but from the enemy because while he knows he can not steal your soul, he will try to steal your joy. As a child of God, know that you are protected by Christ & you can command the enemy away through the name & power of Jesus Christ. The devil knows he has a very short time left & has been running wild trying to destroy God's creation but do not fear. Know this, as children of God, we do not fight for victory but from victory because of the work on the cross. Very soon, all will be made right.

We're in the middle of a massive, global spiritual war that has been going on for thousands of years. We will get through this difficult season as we are now 24 hours even closer to victory! It's coming! GOD'S WILL BE DONE! VICTORY IS COMING! Let not your heart be troubled! May God strengthen You! May God give you courage! May God give you peace! May God bless all of you!

DAY 312
January 22nd, 2021

Good evening my friends. The weekend is upon us & we're closing out Friday, January 22nd, 2021 & I hope & pray this message finds you & your loved ones warm, healthy, safe & well.

Dear Heavenly Father, I come to You tonight with Heavenly praise, faith, love, hope & thanksgiving. Thank You Father for the blessings You've given us, for Your guidance, wisdom & unconditional love. In the name of Jesus, I claim Psalm 91, Psalm 23, Psalm 25:20-21, Psalm 34:19, Psalm 35, Psalm 46:10, Psalm 55:22, Psalm 56:3, Psalm 61:2, Psalm 62:5-8, Psalm 116:7, Psalm 121:2, Proverbs 16:18, Deuteronomy 28:13, Joel 2:25-26, 1 John 4:4, Luke 12:2-3, Job 13:15, Ephesians 6:10-18, 2 Chronicles 7:14, 2 Timothy 1:7, Jeremiah 30:17, Philippians 4:7-9, Romans 12:18, John 14:27, 2 Samuel 22:40, Isaiah 26:3, Isaiah 43:2, Isaiah 53:5 & Isaiah 54:17 over all of you & all whom you love. Father there are so many who do not know You yet. I pray that all the lost souls in this world will come to know You as their Lord & Savior. I pray that You will call to them & let their hearts be receptive to accept You as their Lord. Father I pray that Your pure justice, victory, deliverance, vindication & the revelation of truth out the hidden dark places will be brought to light for all to see. Father let Your will alone will be done. I thank You for our coming deliverance. Father, I pray that all reading this message & their loved ones will be encompassed by an impenetrable spiritual hedge of protection. For all those who are afraid tonight I pray that You'll give them peace that surpasses all understanding. Father, I pray that You will heal all afflicted with the virus & completely restore them. Father I pray that You'll absolutely & abundantly bless, protect, prosper, give faith, love, peace, wisdom, guidance & strength to all reading this & their loved ones. Father, I pray in the name of Jesus, as a child of the Living God, covered, protected & sealed by Your Blood, the Holy Spirit & with the full authority of God, I command & cast this insidious evil in every form away from you & your loved ones. I thank You Father & I claim all these things in Your Holy, powerful, majestic, everlasting & precious name I pray Lord Jesus, Amen!

Warriors! There is much chaos going on all over the world. But this too shall pass. Tonight, as we stand firm, pray for your family! Pray for your friends! Pray for our nation! Pray for the world! Even pray for your enemies! Above all else tonight, pray! Prayer is the number one effective weapon against the enemy. Because truly when God's people pray, the devil & all the demons shudder! They know their time is almost up! They know what's coming! They know what awaits them! But fear not, because when you are a child of the Most High God, you are protected & as it's written when we resist the devil, through the name & power of Christ, he must flee. Stand firm! Stand tall! Stand with conviction! We stand with Christ!! When God is for you, who can be against you? No one! We shall press forward! We shall see deliverance! We shall see victory! GOD'S WILL BE DONE! VICTORY IS COMING! Let not your heart be troubled! May God strengthen You! May God give you courage! May God give you peace! May God bless all of you!

DAY 313
January 23rd, 2021

Good evening my friends. It's the middle of the weekend & we're closing out Saturday, January 23rd, 2021 & I pray this message, once again, finds you & your loved ones warm, healthy, safe & well.

Dear Heavenly Father, I come to You tonight with Heavenly praise, faith, love, hope & thanksgiving. Thank You Father that in the middle of the storm, You are in control, You have the final say & You have the final say in all things. Father I pray that Your justice, victory, deliverance, vindication & the revelation of truth out the secret dark places will be brought to light for all to see. Father let Your will be done. I thank You for our coming victory & deliverance. Father, I pray in the name of Jesus, as a child of the Living God, covered, protected & sealed by Your Blood, the Holy Spirit & with the full authority of God, I command, come against, rebuke & cast this insidious evil in every form away from you & your loved ones. Father, I pray that You will heal all the sick & afflicted, completely restore them & that this virus will be completely eradicated. Father I pray that You'll absolutely & abundantly bless, protect, prosper, give faith, love, peace, wisdom, guidance & strength to all reading this & their loved ones through these difficult times. In the name of Jesus, I claim Psalm 91, Psalm 23, Psalm 25:20-21, Psalm 34:19, Psalm 35, Psalm 46:10, Psalm 55:22, Psalm 56:3, Psalm 61:2, Psalm 62:5-8, Psalm 116:7, Psalm 121:2, Proverbs 16:18, Deuteronomy 28:13, Joel 2:25-26, 1 John 4:4, Luke 12:2-3, Job 13:15, Ephesians 6:10-18, 2 Chronicles 7:14, 2 Timothy 1:7, Jeremiah 30:17, Philippians 4:7-9, Romans 12:18, John 14:27, 2 Samuel 22:40, Isaiah 26:3, Isaiah 43:2, Isaiah 53:5 & Isaiah 54:17 over all of you & all whom you love. I pray that everyone reading this message will be surrounded by an impenetrable hedge of protection & that they will be blessed with peace that surpasses all understanding. Father, I pray that all the lost souls will come to know You as their Lord & Savior. I pray that You will call to them & let their hearts be receptive to accept You as their Lord. I thank You Father & I claim all these things in Your Holy, powerful, majestic, everlasting & precious name I pray Lord Jesus, Amen!

Prayer warriors! As of right now we're 24 hours closer to victory & since we just passed the 17th of January, I have been praying over you for over 10 months now & I will continue to do so. We continue to press forward & as we approach a new month we must continue to be strong. We're almost there. Christ continues to guide us through the valley. This season shall pass. We're all tired, we're all frustrated & exhausted but we shall see victory! So whatever you are facing today, place your burdens in God's hands & let Him take care of whatever concerns you. We're going to get through this everyone, we have each other & most importantly, we have God. That is all we need. GOD'S WILL BE DONE! VICTORY IS COMING! Let not your heart be troubled! May God strengthen You! May God give you courage! May God give you peace! May God bless all of you!

DAY 314
January 24th, 2021

Good evening my friends. The end of the weekend is here as we're coming up on a brand new week & we're closing out Sunday, January 24th, 2021 & I pray this message finds you & your loved ones warm, healthy, safe & well.

Dear Heavenly Father, I come to You tonight with a humble heart, Heavenly praise, faith, love, hope & thanksgiving. Thank You Father for the things that You are doing behind the scenes that we do not know but that You are working them for our good. Father I pray that all reading this will given peace that surpasses all understanding & that a spiritual hedge of protection will surround them. Father, as You are the source of all good things, I pray that You'll abundantly bless, protect, prosper, give faith, love, peace, wisdom, guidance & strength to everyone reading this. Father, I thank You & pray that You'll heal all the afflicted & completely restore them. Father above all else let Your perfect will be done. Father I pray that Your justice, victory, deliverance, vindication & the revelation of truth out the secret dark places will be brought to light for all to see. I thank You for our coming victory & deliverance. Father, I pray in the name of Jesus, as a child of the Living God, covered, protected & sealed by Your Blood, the Holy Spirit & with the full authority of God, I command & cast this insidious evil in every form away from you and your loved ones. Father, I pray for all the lost souls that they will come to ask You into their hearts & that You will be come their Lord. In the name of Jesus, I claim Psalm 91, Psalm 23, Psalm 25:20-21, Psalm 34:19, Psalm 35, Psalm 46:10, Psalm 55:22, Psalm 56:3, Psalm 61:2, Psalm 62:5-8, Psalm 116:7, Psalm 121:2, Proverbs 16:18, Deuteronomy 28:13, Joel 2:25-26, 1 John 4:4, Luke 12:2-3, Job 13:15, Ephesians 6:10-18, 2 Chronicles 7:14, 2 Timothy 1:7, Jeremiah 30:17, Philippians 4:7-9, Romans 12:18, John 14:27, 2 Samuel 22:40, Isaiah 26:3, Isaiah 43:2, Isaiah 53:5 & Isaiah 54:17 over all of you and all whom you love. I thank You Father & I claim all these things in Your Holy, powerful, majestic, everlasting & precious name I pray Lord Jesus, Amen!

Warriors! As we embark on a brand new week, storms may come but know that the dawn always comes right after the darkest point of the night. The sun will rise & every day that you wake up is another gift from God. This has been a tough season & a tough start to the new year but we are not weak or timid but children of the most high God. Always know that truly all things are possible with Christ & though things are difficult right now, He will see us through to victory. He is right beside us every step of the journey. The enemy will try to discourage you but guard your thoughts & mind. We're in the fight of our lives right now & we must hold strong. We have a ways to go but through the very grace, name & power of Christ, we shall see victory! GOD'S WILL BE DONE! VICTORY IS COMING! Let not your heart be troubled! May God strengthen you! May God give you courage! May God give you peace! May God bless all of you!

DAY 315
January 25th, 2021

Good evening my friends. It's the first of the week & we're closing out Monday, January 25th, 2021 & I pray this message finds you & your loved ones warm, healthy, safe & well.

Dear Heavenly Father, I come to You tonight with Heavenly praise, faith, love, hope & thanksgiving. Thank You Father for Your infinite wisdom, love, guidance & grace. In the name of Jesus, I claim Psalm 91, Psalm 23, Psalm 25:20-21, Psalm 34:19, Psalm 35, Psalm 46:10, Psalm 55:22, Psalm 56:3, Psalm 61:2, Psalm 62:5-8, Psalm 116:7, Psalm 121:2, Proverbs 16:18, Deuteronomy 28:13, Joel 2:25-26, 1 John 4:4, Luke 12:2-3, Job 13:15, Ephesians 6:10-18, 2 Chronicles 7:14, 2 Timothy 1:7, Jeremiah 30:17, Philippians 4:7-9, Romans 12:18, John 14:27, 2 Samuel 22:40, Isaiah 26:3, Isaiah 43:2, Isaiah 53:5 & Isaiah 54:17 over all of you & all whom you love. Father, I pray that You will call to all that are lost & that they would be receptive & hearts open to receive You as their Lord & Savior. Father, as You are the source of all truth & good things, I pray that You'll abundantly bless, protect, prosper, give faith, love, peace, hope, wisdom, guidance & strength to everyone reading this & their loved ones. Father I pray that all reading this will be blessed with peace that surpasses all understanding & surrounded by spiritual hedge of protection. Father, I thank You & pray that You'll heal the sick, the afflicted & completely restore them. Father I pray that Your justice, victory, deliverance, vindication & that all the evil that had been done in secret will be brought forth into the light of truth. Father above all else let Your perfect will be done. Father, I pray in the name of Jesus, as a child of the Living God, covered, protected & sealed by Your Blood, the Holy Spirit & with the full authority of God, I command, rebuke & cast this insidious evil in every form away from you & your loved ones. I thank You Father and I claim all these things in Your Holy, powerful, majestic, everlasting and precious name I pray Lord Jesus, Amen!

Warriors! Take my hand, hold strong & raise a shout as we command through the power of Christ this evil away! Stand tall with me with courage & conviction that we will not move, that we will not retreat, that we will not falter as we move forward. Shout with me as we shout praises to God almighty who is victorious in all things. Know deep down that what we face before us is nothing compared to the power of God & He already has a plan of deliverance and victory. Something huge is on the horizon. Something glorious! And something even more amazing than you can imagine is coming & all followers and believers in Christ will see it. Do not fear the evils of this world nor fear the evil plots of man because when Christ is for You, nothing can stand against you. Stay strong everyone! GOD'S WILL BE DONE! VICTORY IS COMING! Let not your heart be troubled! May God strengthen you! May God give you courage! May God give you peace! May God bless all of you!

DAY 316
January 26th, 2021

Good evening my friends. It was a cold blustery day here in NE Ohio & we're closing out Tuesday, January 26th, 2021 & I pray this message finds you & your loved ones warm, healthy, safe & well.

Dear Heavenly Father, I come to You tonight with Heavenly praise, faith, love, hope & thanksgiving. Thank You Father that You already know what we need before we even ask & that You have a special plan & destiny for each of our lives that only we can accomplish. Father, I lift up & pray for a special blessing over all who are reading this message tonight. I pray that You will surround them with Your loving arms, a spiritual hedge of protection & peace that surpasses all understanding. Father, I pray for justice, victory & deliverance tonight for all. In the name of Jesus, I claim Psalm 91, Psalm 23, Psalm 25:20-21, Psalm 34:19, Psalm 35, Psalm 46:10, Psalm 55:22, Psalm 56:3, Psalm 61:2, Psalm 62:5-8, Psalm 116:7, Psalm 121:2, Proverbs 16:18, Deuteronomy 28:13, Joel 2:25-26, 1 John 4:4, Luke 12:2-3, Job 13:15, Ephesians 6:10-18, 2 Chronicles 7:14, 2 Timothy 1:7, Jeremiah 30:17, Philippians 4:7-9, Romans 12:18, John 14:27, 2 Samuel 22:40, Isaiah 26:3, Isaiah 43:2, Isaiah 53:5 & Isaiah 54:17 over all of you & all whom you love. Father, I pray that You'll heal the afflicted all across our nation & protect the vulnerable. Father above all else let Your will be done. Father, I pray in the name of Jesus, as a child of the Living God, covered, protected & sealed by Your Blood, the Holy Spirit & with the full authority of God, I command & cast this insidious evil in every form away from you & your loved ones. Greater is He who is in us than he who is in the world & as it's written, through the power of Christ, if we resist the devil he must flee from us. Father, I pray for all the lost that their eyes would be opened to the truth & accept You as their Lord & Savior. Father, I pray that You'll abundantly bless, protect, prosper, give faith, love, peace, hope, wisdom, guidance & strength to everyone reading this & their loved ones. I thank You Father & I claim all these things in Your Holy, powerful, majestic, everlasting & precious name I pray Lord Jesus, Amen!

Warriors! We're another day closer to victory. I know for so many of you, that you have an overwhelming sense of fear, anxiety & uncertainness. But fear not, because God knows your individual circumstances & I pray tonight that He will perfect that which concerns each of you. I pray that a sense of peace that surpasses all understanding envelops you wherever you are reading this. As I've been praying, I keep hearing that soft voice saying, wait, Be still & know that I'm God. No matter what you are facing right now. I want you to know that it's going to be okay. Stay strong, keep the faith, throw doubt to the wind & place everything in God's hands.

He has never lost a battle ever & He is our source, our victory & our Savior! Please take a moment to thank God tonight & pray for your friends & family. It's going to be okay everyone! GOD'S WILL BE DONE! VICTORY IS COMING! Let not your heart be troubled! May God strengthen you! May God give you courage! May God give you peace! May God bless all of you!

DAY 317
January 27th, 2021

Good evening my friends. It's the middle of the week & we're closing out Wednesday, January 27th, 2021 & I pray this message finds you & your loved ones warm, healthy, safe & well.

Dear Heavenly Father, I come to You tonight with a humble heart, Heavenly praise, faith, hope & thanksgiving. Thank You Father that You're the Lord of all creation & that You love us so much that You even know the exact number of hairs on our heads. In the name of Jesus, I claim Psalm 91, Psalm 23, Psalm 25:20-21, Psalm 34:19, Psalm 35, Psalm 46:10, Psalm 55:22, Psalm 56:3, Psalm 61:2, Psalm 62:5-8, Psalm 116:7, Psalm 121:2, Proverbs 16:18, Deuteronomy 28:13, Joel 2:25-26, 1 John 4:4, Luke 12:2-3, Job 13:15, Ephesians 6:10-18, 2 Chronicles 7:14, 2 Timothy 1:7, 2 Thessalonians 3:16, Jeremiah 30:17, Philippians 4:7-9, Romans 12:18, John 14:27, 2 Samuel 22:40, Isaiah 26:3, Isaiah 43:2, Isaiah 53:5 & Isaiah 54:17 over all of you & all whom you love. I pray that You'll surround all reading this with a powerful & impenetrable hedge of protection & peace that surpasses all understanding. Thank You Father that victory, deliverance, vindication, & justice is coming. I pray for & thank You Father that You will be done in all things. Father, there are so many in need and afraid right now, I pray that You'll abundantly bless, protect, prosper, give faith, love, peace, hope, wisdom, guidance & strength to all reading this message tonight. Father, I pray that You'll call to all the lost souls so they may accept You as their Lord & Savior. In the name of Jesus, as a child of the Living God, covered, protected & sealed by Your Blood, the Holy Spirit & with the full authority of God, I command & cast evil in all forms away from you & your loved ones. I thank You Father & I claim all these things in Your Holy, powerful, majestic, everlasting & precious name I pray Lord Jesus, Amen!

Warriors! As we've been on this long journey together, we've been through a lot together & I'll continue praying for all of you as we walk with Christ through this valley. As difficult & frustrating as this has been, we continue to press forward through the mire on our way to victory. But know this, this too shall pass. For all of us the entire world has been flipped on it's head & while we don't know an exact date when all of this will be over, God continues to bless & guide us. All things are truly possible with Christ & through His name & power we shall prevail. History will record this time & people will study it, films will be made, songs & much more. You are part of that history & at the end of this you will be able to say that you made it through this! We're going to get through this time. Just keep holding on. We have each other & we have God. I pray now that peace covers you, your family, your friends & all you hold dear. GOD'S WILL BE DONE! VICTORY IS COMING! Let not your heart be troubled! May God strengthen you! May God give you courage! May God give you peace! May God bless all of you!

DAY 318
January 28th, 2021

Good evening my friends. We are coming up on another weekend & we're closing out Thursday, January 28th, 2021 & I pray this message finds you & your loved ones warm, healthy, safe & well.

Dear Heavenly Father, I come to You tonight with Heavenly praise, faith, hope & thanksgiving. Thank You Father that even in the midst of the storms of chaos You are still completely in control & on the Throne. Father, I pray for all the families, businesses, people & medical workers that You'll abundantly bless, protect, prosper, give faith, love, peace, hope, wisdom, guidance & strength. I pray that You'll surround all reading this & their loved ones with an impenetrable hedge of protection & given peace that surpasses all understanding. Father, I pray that above all else that Your will be done. Thank You Father that victory, deliverance, vindication, & justice are coming. Father, I pray for all the lost souls that they'll truly see the light &

come to accept You as their Lord & Savior. In the name of Jesus, as a child of the true Living God, covered, protected & sealed by Your Blood, the Holy Spirit & with the full authority of God, I command & cast this evil in all forms away from you & your loved ones. In the name of Jesus, I claim Psalm 91, Psalm 23, Psalm 25:20-21, Psalm 34:19, Psalm 35, Psalm 46:10, Psalm 55:22, Psalm 56:3, Psalm 61:2, Psalm 62:5-8, Psalm 116:7, Psalm 121:2, Proverbs 16:18, Deuteronomy 28:13, Joel 2:25-26, 1 John 4:4, Luke 12:2-3, Job 13:15, Ephesians 6:10-18, 2 Chronicles 7:14, 2 Timothy 1:7, 2 Thessalonians 3:16, Jeremiah 30:17, Philippians 4:7-9, Romans 12:18, John 14:27, 2 Samuel 22:40, Isaiah 26:3, Isaiah 43:2, Isaiah 53:5 & Isaiah 54:17 over all of you & all whom you love. I thank You Father & I claim all these things in Your Holy, powerful, majestic, everlasting & precious name I pray Lord Jesus, Amen!

Warriors! As we approach a new weekend, know that despite the storms that ravage. We are guided & shielded by Christ as we move through another day. I know that all of us are going through something right now & know that whatever you are facing today, you are never alone. God knows what your circumstances are & He will never leave you without provision. This has been truly a difficult & hard year but we are still here and continually moving forward through the very Name, power & grace of God almighty. When you woke up today, it was another gift from God. In an uncertain world, you can be certain in Christ. So tonight, stand strong again! Stand firm! Stand ready as we take another step towards victory & deliverance! GOD'S WILL BE DONE! VICTORY IS COMING! Let not your heart be troubled! May God strengthen you! May God give you courage! May God give you peace! May God bless all of you!

DAY 319
January 29th, 2021

Good evening my friends. The weekend is finally here & we're closing out Friday, January 29th, 2021 & I pray this message finds you & your loved ones warm, healthy, safe & well.

Dear Heavenly Father, I come to You tonight with Heavenly praise, faith, hope & thanksgiving. Thank You Father for Your continued blessings, protection, peace & strength through these difficult times. In the name of Jesus, I claim Psalm 91, Psalm 23, Psalm 25:20-21, Psalm 34:19, Psalm 35, Psalm 46:10, Psalm 55:22, Psalm 56:3, Psalm 61:2, Psalm 62:5-8, Psalm 116:7, Psalm 121:2, Proverbs 16:18, Deuteronomy 28:13, Joel 2:25-26, 1 John 4:4, Luke 12:2-3, Job 13:15, Ephesians 6:10-18, 2 Chronicles 7:14, 2 Timothy 1:7, 2 Thessalonians 3:16, Jeremiah 30:17, Philippians 4:7-9, Romans 12:18, John 14:27, 2 Samuel 22:40, Isaiah 26:3, Isaiah 43:2, Isaiah 53:5 & Isaiah 54:17 over all of you & all whom you love. Father, I pray that Your perfect absolute will be done. Father, for all those reading this tonight please surround them with a hedge of protection & peace that surpasses all understanding. Father, I thank You that through the storms You are abundantly blessing all those reading this tonight. Thank You Father that victory, deliverance, vindication, truth & justice are coming. In the name of Jesus, as a child of the eternal Living God, covered, protected & sealed by Your Blood, the Holy Spirit & with the full authority of God, I command & cast this insidious evil away from you & your loved ones. Father, I pray for all the lost souls that they'll truly see the light & come to accept You as their Lord & Savior. I thank You Father for our coming victory & I claim all these things in Your Holy, powerful, majestic, everlasting & precious name I pray Lord Jesus, Amen!

Warriors! In these uncertain times, we can be certain in God. In moments of fear we can take courage that Christ is our protector, Lord & Savior. Though darkness is trying to cover the earth, God's light shines forth illuminating the path to victory & ultimately the destruction of the enemy. I know many of you are afraid tonight, but know that truly victory, deliverance, vindication & revival are coming. In the face of evil we must stand strong, never fall back & command it away through the name & power of Christ. Tonight, pray for your friends, your family, for our nation like you've never prayed before. As God's children, we must do our part & pray. As I've said many times on here, prayer is the most powerful weapon we have against the enemy. God hears our prayers & in God's perfect timing, He will answer them. God will not be mocked & very soon, we will see deliverance through Christ. Hold fast & be strong! GOD'S WILL BE DONE! VICTORY IS COMING! Let not your heart be troubled! May

God strengthen you! May God give you courage! May God give you peace! May God bless all of you!

DAY 320
January 30th, 2021

Good evening my friends. It was a cold blustery day here in NE Ohio & we're closing out Saturday, January 30th, 2021 & I pray this message finds you & your loved ones warm, healthy, safe & well.

Dear Heavenly Father, I come to You tonight with Heavenly praise, faith, hope & thanksgiving. Thank You Father for your wisdom, guidance, unconditional love & salvation through Christ Jesus. Thank You Father that victory, deliverance, vindication, truth & justice are coming. Father, I pray for the people, families, businesses, medical workers & all reading this that You would abundantly bless them with protection, peace, hope, faith, love, prosperity, wisdom, guidance & strength. Father, for everyone reading this prayer tonight please surround them with a hedge of protection & peace that surpasses all understanding. I lift up & pray for all the afflicted that they would be completely restored to full health. Father, I pray that Your perfect absolute will be done. Father, I pray for all the lost souls that You'll call to them so they can accept You as their Lord & Savior. In the name of Jesus, as a child of the Living God, covered, protected & sealed by Your Blood, the Holy Spirit & with the full authority of God, I command & cast this insidious evil away from you & your loved ones. In the name of Jesus, I claim Psalm 91, Psalm 23, Psalm 25:20-21, Psalm 34:19, Psalm 35, Psalm 46:10, Psalm 55:22, Psalm 56:3, Psalm 61:2, Psalm 62:5-8, Psalm 116:7, Psalm 121:2, Proverbs 16:18, Deuteronomy 28:13, Joel 2:25-26, 1 John 4:4, Luke 12:2-3, Job 13:15, Ephesians 6:10-18, 2 Chronicles 7:14, 2 Timothy 1:7, 2 Thessalonians 3:16, Jeremiah 30:17, Philippians 4:7-9, Romans 12:18, John 14:27, 2 Samuel 22:40, Isaiah 26:3, Isaiah 43:2, Isaiah 53:5 & Isaiah 54:17 over all of you & all whom you love. In Your Holy name Father, I declare victory! I thank You Father & I claim all these things in Your Holy, powerful, majestic, everlasting & precious name I pray Lord Jesus, Amen!

Warriors! Tonight as we're approaching a brand new month & week, pray with conviction, pray with authority, pray with purpose as we move forward & combat the storms that continue to surround us on all sides. Thank God for our coming deliverance & victory! Thank God for the miracles coming! Thank God for the strength, courage & peace as we take another step! This difficult time shall pass! Remember, no matter what we face, God is command & on the throne. None of this is a surprise or a coincidence. He is the Alpha & the Omega, the beginning & the end & there is none like Him. He has a perfect plan for all things according to His will & we shall prevail through the name of Christ! GOD'S WILL BE DONE! VICTORY IS COMING! Let not your heart be troubled! May God strengthen you! May God give you courage! May God give you peace! May God bless all of you!

DAY 321
January 31st, 2021

Good evening my friends. As we conclude another weekend & on the eve of a brand new month, we're closing out Sunday, January 31st, 2021 & I pray this message finds you & your loved ones warm, healthy, safe & well.

Dear Heavenly Father, I come to You tonight with a humble heart, Heavenly praise, faith, hope & thanksgiving. Thank You Father that in the midst of the great storm, You are completely in control of everything & on the Throne. In the name of Jesus, I claim Psalm 91, Psalm 23, Psalm 25:20-21, Psalm 34:19, Psalm 35, Psalm 46:10, Psalm 55:22, Psalm 56:3, Psalm 61:2, Psalm 62:5-8, Psalm 116:7, Psalm 121:2, Proverbs 16:18, Deuteronomy 28:13, Joel 2:25-26, 1 John 4:4, Luke 12:2-3, Job 13:15, Ephesians 6:10-18, 2 Chronicles 7:14, 2 Timothy 1:7, 2 Thessalonians 3:16, Jeremiah 30:17, Philippians 4:7-9, Romans 12:18, John 14:27, 2 Samuel 22:40, Isaiah 26:3, Isaiah 43:2, Isaiah 53:5 & Isaiah 54:17 over all of you & all whom you love. Father, I pray for all the lost souls around this country & world, that You'll call to them so they can accept You as their Lord & Savior. Father, I pray that all the afflicted with the virus will be completely restored to full health with no lasting effects. Father, I pray for everyone reading this that You'd surround them with a hedge of protection & give them peace that surpasses all understanding through these difficult days. Thank You Father that victory, deliverance, vindication, truth & justice are coming. Father, I pray for the people, families, businesses, medical workers & all reading this that You would abundantly bless them with protection, peace, hope, faith, love, prosperity, wisdom, guidance & strength. Above all, let Your perfect will be done. In the name of Jesus, as a child of the eternal true Living God, covered, protected & sealed by Your Blood, the Holy Spirit & with the full authority of God, I command, rebuke, come against & cast this insidious evil away from you & your loved ones. Greater is He who is in us than he who is in the world & by the name & power of Christ & as it's written when we resist the devil he must flee from us. In Your Holy name Father, I declare victory! I thank You Father & I claim all these things in Your Holy, powerful, majestic, everlasting & precious name I pray Lord Jesus, Amen!

Warriors! On this cold, stormy winter night, know that God is aligning everything for our victory. We must continue to do our part by holding on, staying strong, being vigilant & continue to pray but know that God has heard our prayers. While the winds of spiritual storms have ravaged us over the past year, through the very grace of God we are still here! We're still fighting forward & pressing on with everything we've got. Always know, while this season has been difficult, it too shall pass. With each day we're another step closer to deliverance. For 321 nights I have been praying over us all & I will continue as we move forward. Tonight, take a moment and give a shout to God as we move into another month & know that ALL things are possible through Christ! We're going get through this everyone! Keep the faith & stay strong! GOD'S WILL BE DONE! VICTORY IS COMING! Let not your heart be troubled! May God strengthen you! May God give you courage! May God give you peace! May God bless all of you!

DAY 322
February 1st, 2021

Good evening my friends. It's a brand new week and month & we're closing out Monday, February 1st, 2021 & I pray this message finds you & your loved ones warm, healthy, safe & well.

Dear Heavenly Father, I come to You tonight with Heavenly praise, faith, hope & thanksgiving. Thank You Father that we're through another month as You guide us to victory in 2021. Above all else Father, let Your perfect will be done. Thank You Father that victory, deliverance, vindication, truth & justice are coming swiftly. I pray that all reading this prayer tonight will be surrounded by a hedge of protection & I pray that all of you will be given peace that surpasses all understanding. Thank You Father that right now You are continuing to heal the afflicted & restoring them. Father, I pray for the vast numbers of lost souls around this country & world, that You'll call to them so they can accept You as their Lord & Savior. Father, I pray for the people, families, businesses, medical workers & all reading this that You would abundantly bless & protect them through these uncertain times. In the name of Jesus, as a child of Living God, covered, protected & sealed by Your Blood, the Holy Spirit & with the full authority of God, I command & cast this insidious evil away from you & your loved ones. In the name of Jesus, I claim Psalm 91, Psalm 23, Psalm 25:20-21, Psalm 34:19, Psalm 35, Psalm 46:10, Psalm 55:22, Psalm 56:3, Psalm 61:2, Psalm 62:5-8, Psalm 116:7, Psalm 121:2, Proverbs 16:18, Deuteronomy 28:13, Joel 2:25-26, 1 John 4:4, Luke 12:2-3, Job 13:15, Ephesians 6:10-18, 2 Chronicles 7:14, 2 Timothy 1:7, 2 Thessalonians 3:16, Jeremiah 30:17, Philippians 4:7-9, Romans 12:18, John 14:27, 2 Samuel 22:40, Isaiah 26:3, Isaiah 43:2, Isaiah 53:5 & Isaiah 54:17 over all of you & all whom you love. In Your Holy name Father, I declare victory! I thank You Father & I claim all these things in Your Holy, powerful, majestic, everlasting & precious name I pray Lord Jesus, Amen!

Warriors! As we venture into a new month & week we continue to move forward towards victory. Each day is full of potential. Each day is a gift from God. Each day we're closer than ever before. Christ continues to guide us through the unknown terrain of 2021 & though storms will come, He will always guide us to safety & protect us. One thing we're learned over the past year, beyond anything else, is how much we need God. Alone we are frail but through the name & power of Christ we are strong! Keep the faith everyone! Onward to victory! GOD'S WILL BE DONE! VICTORY & DELIVERANCE ARE COMING! Let not your heart be troubled! May God strengthen you! May God give you courage! May God give you peace! May God bless all of you!

DAY 323
February 2nd, 2021

Good evening my friends. As we conclude this cold & windy winter day, we're closing out Tuesday, February 2nd, 2021 & I pray this message finds you & your loved ones warm, healthy, safe & well.

Dear Heavenly Father, I come to You tonight with Heavenly praise, faith, hope & thanksgiving. Thank You Father for Your blessings that You give us & for guiding our steps every day. In the name of Jesus, I claim Psalm 91, Psalm 23, Psalm 25:20-21, Psalm 34:19, Psalm 35, Psalm 46:10, Psalm 55:22, Psalm 56:3, Psalm 61:2, Psalm 62:5-8, Psalm 116:7, Psalm 121:2, Proverbs 16:18, Deuteronomy 28:13, Joel 2:25-26, 1 John 4:4, Luke 12:2-3, Job 13:15, Ephesians 6:10-18, 2 Chronicles 7:14, 2 Timothy 1:7, 2 Thessalonians 3:16, Jeremiah 30:17, Philippians 4:7-9, Romans 12:18, John 14:27, 2 Samuel 22:40, Isaiah 26:3, Isaiah 43:2, Isaiah 53:5 & Isaiah 54:17 over all of you & all whom you love. Father, I pray for all the sick & afflicted that they would be supernaturally healed & fully restored to full health. Father, I pray for the people, families, businesses, medical workers & all reading this that You would abundantly bless, heal & protect them. Father, I pray that everyone reading this & their loved ones will be surrounded by a hedge of protection & given peace that truly surpasses all understanding. Father, I'm praying for victory, deliverance, vindication, truth & justice to come swiftly. In the name of Jesus, as a child of Living God, covered, protected & sealed by Your Blood, the Holy Spirit & with the full authority of God, I command & cast this insidious evil away from you & your loved ones.

Let Your will alone be done Father. Father, I pray for all the lost souls around this world, that You'll call to them so they can accept You as their Lord & Savior. In the name of Jesus, I declare victory! I thank You Father & I claim all these things in Your Holy, powerful, majestic, everlasting & precious name I pray Lord Jesus, Amen!

Warriors! Tonight, take a moment to pray for all your family members, your friends & our nation. Tonight, thank God that no matter what comes against us, we continue to press forward guided by Him. Tonight, give a shout to God that He alone is the King of Kings & Lord of Lords & that He has a plan for victory & deliverance through these uncertain times. Everything we're seeing is not a surprise to God & through the power & name of Christ WE SHALL PREVAIL! When God is for us, there is nothing that can stop us. Storms may come but they will dissipate! We must continue to be strong & pray for victory because it's coming soon! Stay strong everyone! Stay vigilant! And Shout with me tonight OUR GOD IS GOD! VICTORY & DELIVERANCE ARE COMING! Let not your heart be troubled! May God strengthen you! May God give you courage! May God give you peace! May God bless all of you!

DAY 324
February 3rd, 2021

Good evening my friends. It's the middle of the week & we're closing out Wednesday, February 3rd, 2021 & I pray this message, once again, finds you & your loved ones warm, healthy, safe & well.

Dear Heavenly Father, I come to You tonight with Heavenly praise, faith, hope & thanksgiving. Thank You Father that we had another day on earth, for Your infinite wisdom & unconditional love. Father, I pray for all the afflicted with the virus that they would be supernaturally healed & restored. Father, I pray that You'll surround all reading this with a hedge of protection & peace that surpasses all understanding. Father, I pray all reading this that You would abundantly bless them with protection, prosperity, faith, hope, love, wisdom, guidance & strength. Father, I'm praying for victory, deliverance, vindication, truth & justice to come swiftly across our nation. In the name of

Jesus, as a child of eternal Living true God, covered, protected & sealed by Your Blood, the Holy Spirit & with the full authority of God, I command & cast this insidious evil away from you & your loved ones. This evil must leave now! Let Your will be done Father. Father, I pray for all the lost souls who don't know You yet, that You'll call to them so they can accept You as their Lord & Savior. In the name of Jesus, I claim Psalm 91, Psalm 23, Psalm 25:20-21, Psalm 34:19, Psalm 35, Psalm 46:10, Psalm 55:22, Psalm 56:3, Psalm 61:2, Psalm 62:5-8, Psalm 116:7, Psalm 121:2, Proverbs 16:18, Deuteronomy 28:13, Joel 2:25-26, 1 John 4:4, Luke 12:2-3, Job 13:15, Ephesians 6:10-18, 2 Chronicles 7:14, 2 Timothy 1:7, 2 Thessalonians 3:16, Jeremiah 30:17, Philippians 4:7-9, Romans 12:18, John 14:27, 2 Samuel 22:40, Isaiah 26:3, Isaiah 43:2, Isaiah 53:5 & Isaiah 54:17 over all of you & all whom you love. In the name of Jesus, I declare victory! I thank You Father & I claim all these things in Your Holy, powerful, majestic, everlasting & precious name I pray Lord Jesus, Amen!

Warriors! In the chaotic world we live in, uncertainness abounds, but know that you can be certain in Christ. His character never changes. It is the same yesterday, today and tomorrow. He knows what your individual circumstances are right now & is already setting everything in motion for your good. Always know that even when circumstances seen tough, God is using those moments to build your character into the person you were made to be. So as we move forward into another day, know that we're that much closer to victory and know that we are that much closer to deliverance! Truly all things are possible with Christ! Hold on strong! Stay vigilant and know that VICTORY & DELIVERANCE ARE COMING! Let not your heart be troubled! May God strengthen you! May God give you courage! May God give you peace! May God bless all of you!

DAY 325
February 4th, 2021

Good evening my friends. This week is going so fast, we're coming up on another weekend & we're closing out February 4th, 2021 & I pray this message finds you & your loved ones warm, healthy, safe & well.

Dear Heavenly Father, I come to You tonight with a humble heart, Heavenly praise, faith, hope & thanksgiving. Thank You Father that as we walk through life, when we have You by our side, You always guide us through the tough times & celebrate the joyful ones. Father, I pray for everyone reading this that You'll abundantly bless & protect them through these difficult days. Father, I pray that each of you are surrounded by an impenetrable hedge of protection & given God's perfect peace that surpasses all understanding. Father, I pray for all the sick & afflicted that they'll be completely healed & restored by Your hand. Father, I'm praying for victory, deliverance, vindication, truth & justice to come swiftly across our nation. Father, I pray for all the lost souls around this world who don't know You yet, that You'll call to them so they can accept You as their Lord & Savior. In the name of Jesus, as a child of Living God, covered, protected & sealed by Your Blood, the Holy Spirit & with the full authority of God almighty, I command, rebuke, come against & cast this insidious evil away from you & your loved ones. In the name of Jesus, I claim Psalm 91, Psalm 23, Psalm 25:20-21, Psalm 34:19, Psalm 35, Psalm 46:10, Psalm 55:22, Psalm 56:3, Psalm 61:2, Psalm 62:5-8, Psalm 116:7, Psalm 121:2, Proverbs 16:18, Deuteronomy 28:13, Joel 2:25-26, 1 John 4:4, Luke 12:2-3, Job 13:15, Ephesians 6:10-18, 2 Chronicles 7:14, 2 Timothy 1:7, 2 Thessalonians 3:16, Jeremiah 30:17, Philippians 4:7-9, Romans 12:18, John 14:27, 2 Samuel 22:40, Isaiah 26:3, Isaiah 43:2, Isaiah 53:5 & Isaiah 54:17 over all of you & all whom you love. In the name of Jesus, Let Your will be done Father & I declare victory! I thank You Father & I claim all these things in Your Holy, powerful, majestic, everlasting & precious name I pray Lord Jesus, Amen!

Warriors! As we approach another weekend let's raise a shout to God as we're another day closer to victory! Things are definitely looking up & we must continue to stay strong, stay vigilant & not become complacent. Tonight, be sure to continue to pray for your family, friends & our nation but also be sure to thank God that through all the storms we've faced together that you woke up this morning & have another day on earth. This walk through life is difficult but together with Christ as our guide, we shall prevail, have deliverance & be victorious! This has truly been a difficult year in all aspects & will continue to be so for a while, but soon, we'll come out of this deep valley to the open fields of victory! Stay strong everyone! We can do this! VICTORY & DELIVERANCE ARE COMING! Let not your heart be troubled! May God strengthen you! May God give you courage! May God give you peace! May God bless all of you!

DAY 326
February 5th, 2021

Good evening my friends. The weekend is finally here & we're closing out Friday, February 5th, 2021 & I pray this message finds you & your loved ones warm, healthy, safe & well.

Dear Heavenly Father, I come to You tonight with Heavenly praise, faith, hope & thanksgiving. Thank You Father that victory, deliverance, vindication, truth & justice are coming swiftly. I pray that each of you reading this tonight & all your loved ones are protected by an impenetrable hedge of protection & given God's absolute perfect peace that surpasses all understanding. Father, I pray for all the afflicted with the virus that they will be completely healed & restored. Father, I pray for all the lost souls around the world that You'll call to them so they can accept You as their Lord & Savior. Father, I pray for everyone reading this that You'll truly abundantly bless, heal, prosper & protect them in these uncertain times. In the name of Jesus, let Your perfect will be done Father & I declare victory & deliverance! In the name of Jesus, as a child of Living God, covered, protected & sealed by Your Blood, the Holy Spirit & with the full authority of God, I command & cast this insidious evil away from you & your loved ones this very moment. In the name of Jesus, I claim Psalm 91, Psalm 23, Psalm 25:20-21, Psalm 34:19, Psalm 35, Psalm 46:10, Psalm 55:22, Psalm 56:3, Psalm 61:2, Psalm 62:5-8, Psalm 116:7, Psalm 121:2, Proverbs 16:18, Deuteronomy 28:13, Joel 2:25-26, 1 John 4:4, Luke 12:2-3, Job 13:15, Ephesians 6:10-18, 2 Chronicles 7:14, 2 Timothy 1:7, 2 Thessalonians 3:16, Jeremiah 30:17, Philippians 4:7-9, Romans 12:18, John 14:27, 2 Samuel 22:40, Isaiah 26:3, Isaiah 43:2, Isaiah 53:5 & Isaiah 54:17 over all of you & all whom you love. I thank You Father & I claim all these things in Your Holy, powerful, majestic, everlasting & precious name I pray Lord Jesus, Amen!

Warriors! As we walk each day through the valleys of uncertainness, know that God has a plan for not only our victory & deliverance, but also has a singular perfect plan for your life as well. Never feel like you don't matter down here, because you are placed here & now at this specific point in history on purpose & not by mistake. God doesn't make mistakes & He has a destiny selected for you that only you can accomplish. When we place our lives in God's hands, amazing things occur. This doesn't mean that life will be perfect as storms & trials will come but realize that is not to destroy you, but to build you up & mold you into all that God has created you to be. While going through difficult times is never fun, that refining makes you into a stronger person. If steel wasn't tempered correctly, it would become brittle & shatter but the refining process makes it strong, unyielding & immensely powerful Always know that God only wants the best for you. As our journey continues through the valley, there is light ahead everyone! Onward to victory through Christ! VICTORY & DELIVERANCE ARE COMING! Let not your heart be troubled! May God strengthen you! May God give you courage! May God give you peace! May God bless all of you!

DAY 327
February 6th, 2021

Good evening my friends. We're in the middle of the weekend & we're closing out this cold Saturday evening, February 6th, 2021 & I pray this message finds you & your loved ones warm, healthy, safe & well.

Dear Heavenly Father, I come to You once again tonight with Heavenly praise, faith, hope & thanksgiving. I will declare it again, thank You Father that victory, deliverance, vindication, truth & justice are coming swiftly. In the name of Jesus, I claim Psalm 91, Psalm 23, Psalm 25:20-21, Psalm 34:19, Psalm 35, Psalm 46:10, Psalm 55:22, Psalm 56:3, Psalm 61:2, Psalm 62:5-8, Psalm 116:7, Psalm 121:2, Proverbs 16:18, Deuteronomy 28:13, Joel 2:25-26, 1 John 4:4, Luke 12:2-3, Job 13:15, Ephesians 6:10-18, 2 Chronicles 7:14, 2 Timothy 1:7, 2 Thessalonians 3:16, Jeremiah 30:17, Philippians 4:7-9, Romans 12:18, John 14:27, 2 Samuel 22:40, Isaiah 26:3,

Isaiah 43:2, Isaiah 53:5 & Isaiah 54:17 over all of you & all whom you love. Father, I pray that You'll abundantly bless all those reading this with protection, prosperity, hope, faith, health, wisdom, guidance & strength. Father, I pray for all the afflicted that they'll be completely restored to full health. I pray that everyone reading this tonight will be fully protected by a hedge of protection & given God's perfect peace that surpasses all understanding. In the name of Jesus, let Your perfect will be done Father. In the name of Jesus, as a child of living true eternal God, covered, protected & sealed by Your blood, the Holy Spirit, shielded with the armor of Christ & with the full authority of God, I command & cast this insidious evil away from you & your loved ones. As it's written when we resist the devil through the power of Christ he must flee! Father, I pray for all the lost souls everywhere that You'll call to them so they can accept You as their Lord & Savior. I thank You Father & I claim all these things in Your Holy, powerful, majestic, everlasting & precious name I pray Lord Jesus, Amen!

Warriors! On this cold winter night, know that the warmth & light of God surrounds you wherever you are anywhere in the world. He knows your individual circumstances & what you are facing today. He even knows the very number of hairs on your head. As we walk through this long valley, He is protecting us & guiding us each step until we reach victory & deliverance. But do not fear the uncertainness or unknown of what lies ahead. Storms will come but through Christ we will prevail. Tonight, give a shout to God & thank Him again for another day as we walk forward into another day on our path to victory. Stand with courage, stand with determination, stand with authority knowing that God is in control of everything & on the throne. VICTORY IS COMING!! Let not your heart be troubled! May God strengthen you! May God give you courage! May God give you peace! May God bless all of you!

DAY 328
February 7th, 2021

Good evening my friends. We're coming up on a new week & we're closing out Sunday, February 7th, 2021 & I pray this message finds you & your loved ones warm, healthy, safe & well.

Dear Heavenly Father, I come to You with Heavenly praise, faith, hope & thanksgiving. Thank You Father that You have something on the horizon coming soon that is astronomical. In the name of Jesus, let Your perfect will be done! Father, as the vaccines are being distributed, I pray for all the afflicted that they'll be completely restored to full health with no lasting effects & for the complete eradication of this virus. I pray that all reading this will be surrounded & protected by a spiritual hedge of protection & given God's absolute perfect peace that surpasses all understanding. Father, I pray that You'll abundantly bless, prosper & protect all reading this & their loved ones. Father, I pray every lost soul will be called by You so they can accept You as their Lord & Savior. In the name of Jesus, as a child of Living God, covered, protected & sealed by Your Blood, the Holy Spirit, shielded with the Armor of Christ & with the full authority of God, I command & cast this insidious evil away from you & your loved ones. In the name of Jesus, I claim Psalm 91, Psalm 23, Psalm 25:20-21, Psalm 34:19, Psalm 35, Psalm 46:10, Psalm 55:22, Psalm 56:3, Psalm 61:2, Psalm 62:5-8, Psalm 116:7, Psalm 121:2, Proverbs 16:18, Deuteronomy 28:13, Joel 2:25-26, 1 John 4:4, Luke 12:2-3, Job 13:15, Ephesians 6:10-18, 2 Chronicles 7:14, 2 Timothy 1:7, 2 Thessalonians 3:16, Jeremiah 30:17, Philippians 4:7-9, Romans 12:18, John 14:27, 2 Samuel 22:40, Isaiah 26:3, Isaiah 43:2, Isaiah 53:5 & Isaiah 54:17 over all of you & all whom you love. I thank You Father for our coming victory & I claim all these things in Your Holy, powerful, everlasting & precious name I pray Lord Jesus, Amen!

Warriors! As we venture into a new week, we've pressed through another day & onwards to another! Each day, each step, we're closer to victory & though the future is unknown, I believe we are on the path to deliverance. Do not fear because Christ goes before us to clear the path forwards. In just over 5 weeks we will be at one year since I started praying over all of you & I will continue to do so beyond that. Remember all things are possible with Christ, even the most impossible ones. Just because we can't necessarily see it with our eyes doesn't mean that it can't happen. I believe big things are about to happen. Stay strong! Stay vigilant! Keep the faith & onward because VICTORY IS COMING!! Let not your heart be troubled! May God strengthen you! May God give you courage! May God give you peace! May God bless all of you!

DAY 329
February 8th, 2021

Good evening my friends. As we begin a brand new week we're closing out Monday, February 8th, 2021 & I pray this message finds you & your loved ones warm, healthy, safe & well.

Dear Heavenly Father, I come to You tonight with Heavenly praise, faith, hope & thanksgiving. Thank You Father for all the blessings You've given us & for the most wonderful gift of salvation through Your Son, Christ Jesus. In the name of Jesus, I claim Psalm 91, Psalm 23, Psalm 25:20-21, Psalm 34:19, Psalm 35, Psalm 46:10, Psalm 55:22, Psalm 56:3, Psalm 61:2, Psalm 62:5-8, Psalm 116:7, Psalm 121:2, Proverbs 16:18, Deuteronomy 28:13, Joel 2:25-26, 1 John 4:4, Luke 12:2-3, Job 13:15, Ephesians 6:10-18, 2 Chronicles 7:14, 2 Timothy 1:7, 2 Thessalonians 3:16, Jeremiah 30:17, Philippians 4:7-9, Romans 12:18, John 14:27, 2 Samuel 22:40, Isaiah 26:3, Isaiah 43:2, Isaiah 53:5 & Isaiah 54:17 over all of you & all whom you love. Father, I pray that You'll abundantly bless, prosper, heal & protect all who are reading this & their loved ones. Father, I pray for all reading this that they'll be surrounded & protected by an impenetrable spiritual hedge of protection & given God's absolute perfect peace that surpasses all understanding. Father, I pray for every lost soul on this planet that You'll call to them so they can accept You as their Lord & Savior. In the name of Jesus, Let Your will be done. Father, I pray for all the afflicted with the virus that they'll be restored to full health, with no lasting effects & even better than before. In the name of Jesus, as a child of Living God, covered, protected & sealed by Your Blood, the Holy Spirit, shielded with the Armor of Christ & with the full authority of God, I command & cast this insidious evil away from you & your loved ones. This evil must leave now & through the name of Christ it must obey! I thank You Father & I claim all these things in Your Holy, powerful, majestic, everlasting & precious name I pray Lord Jesus, Amen!

Warriors! Tonight is a very important night. Every week, like every day has a new beginning & I want you to know that if you don't know Christ as Your Lord & Savior, it doesn't matter what you've done in your life, it doesn't matter how far you feel you've strayed or gone, it just doesn't matter. God is waiting there right now for you to come to Him, ask for His forgiveness, ask Him into Your heart as Your Lord & Savior and then you are saved for all eternity. It's that simple. Like the father of the prodigal son, God is waiting for you with open arms, He loves you more than you can ever know. He's not mad at you, He wants you to come to Him. Accepting Christ is truly the most important decision you can ever make. It only takes a moment & if you're feeling something in the back of your mind pulling at you, that is Christ calling you now. Don't put it off to tomorrow because tomorrow may never come. The storms that come in life are nothing compared to the power of God & while followers of Christ will still face, storms, trials & tribulations, having God with you to walk through those difficulties is the knowledge that no matter what comes against you, through the power of Christ, you will prevail! VICTORY IS COMING!! Let not your heart be troubled! May God strengthen you! May God give you courage! May God give you peace! May God bless all of you!

DAY 330
February 9th, 2021

Good evening my friends. It was a cold blustery day in NE Ohio today & we're closing out Tuesday, February 9th, 2021 & I pray this message finds you & your loved ones warm, healthy, safe & well.

Dear Heavenly Father, I come to You tonight with Heavenly praise, faith, hope, love & thanksgiving. Thank You Father that through the storms of life that come, that You are there right beside us to walk with us & guide us all the way to victory. Father, I pray that You'll abundantly bless, protect, prosper, give health, faith, love, wisdom, guidance & strength through these uncertain times & their loved ones. Father, I pray that Your will be done above all else. Father, I pray for all the sick & afflicted that they'll be restored to complete & full health. I pray that this virus is eradicated. Father, I pray that each of you will be surrounded & protected by a spiritual hedge of protection & given God's absolute perfect peace that surpasses all understanding. In the name of Jesus, as a child of Living God, covered, protected, shielded & sealed by Your Blood, the Holy Spirit, the full Armor of Christ & with the full authority of God, I command & cast this insidious evil away from you & your loved ones. In the name of Jesus, I claim Psalm 91, Psalm 23, Psalm 25:20-21, Psalm 34:19, Psalm 35, Psalm 46:10, Psalm 55:22, Psalm 56:3, Psalm 61:2, Psalm 62:5-8, Psalm 116:7, Psalm 121:2, Proverbs 16:18, Deuteronomy 28:13, Joel 2:25-26, 1 John 4:4, Luke 12:2-3, Job 13:15, Ephesians 6:10-18, 2 Chronicles 7:14, 2 Timothy 1:7, 2 Thessalonians 3:16, Jeremiah 30:17, Philippians 4:7-9, Romans 12:18, John 14:27, 2 Samuel 22:40, Isaiah 26:3, Isaiah 43:2, Isaiah 53:5 & Isaiah 54:17 over all of you & all whom you love. Father, I pray for every lost soul on this planet that You'll call to them so they can accept You as their Lord & Savior. I thank You Father for our coming victory & deliverance & I claim all these things in Your Holy, powerful, majestic, everlasting & precious name I pray Lord Jesus, Amen!

Warriors! Tonight as we continue to press forward, take a moment to say a prayer for your friends, family, our nation & for yourself. Prayer is one of the most powerful weapons we have against the agents of darkness. God truly hears your prayers & is always working towards your good. Prayer is your direct connection to the Creator of the universe. Every night, when I pray for all of you, I truly hope these prayers are helping lift your souls & spirits through this difficult season. Know this, though things feel uncertain right now, God is clearing the path for deliverance & victory through this time. Always know that your have refuge under the wings of Christ & as a promise of God, He will never leave you nor forsake you. He will provide. I know all of you, myself included, are frustrated & exhausted. But know this that this too shall pass. As I've said many times, All things are possible with Christ & He will deliver us. So right now, hold your head up, put a hand in the air & give God a great shout of praise! VICTORY IS COMING!! Let not your heart be troubled! May God strengthen you! May God give you courage! May God give you peace! May God bless all of you!

DAY 331
February 10th, 2021

Good evening my friends. It's the middle of the week & we're closing out Wednesday, February 10th, 2021 & I pray this message finds you & your loved ones warm, healthy, safe & well on this cold winter evening.

Dear Heavenly Father, I come to You tonight with a humble heart, Heavenly praise, faith, hope, love & thanksgiving. Thank You Father that each day is a gift from You, that You're in complete control & that You are on the Throne. In the name of Jesus, I claim Psalm 91, Psalm 23, Psalm 25:20-21, Psalm 34:19, Psalm 35, Psalm 46:10, Psalm 55:22, Psalm 56:3, Psalm 61:2, Psalm 62:5-8, Psalm 116:7, Psalm 121:2, Proverbs 16:18, Deuteronomy 28:13, Joel 2:25-26, 1 John 4:4, Luke 12:2-3, Job 13:15, Ephesians 6:10-18, 2 Chronicles 7:14, 2 Timothy 1:7, 2 Thessalonians 3:16, Jeremiah 30:17, Philippians 4:7-9, Romans 12:18, John 14:27, 2 Samuel 22:40, Isaiah 26:3, Isaiah 43:2, Isaiah 53:5 & Isaiah 54:17 over all of you & all whom you love. Father we're facing many storms on all sides & In the name of Jesus, as a child of Living God, covered, protected, shielded & sealed by Your Blood, the Holy Spirit, the full Armor of Christ & with the full authority of God, I command & cast this insidious evil away from you & your loved ones. I pray that Your will be done in all things. Father, I pray for all the afflicted that You'll heal & restore all of them, that You'll shield Your children with an impenetrable hedge of protection & give peace that surpasses all understanding. Father, there are so many lost souls & I pray that You'll call to them, that their eyes will be opened to the truth & accept You as their Lord & Savior. Father, I pray that You'll abundantly bless, protect, prosper all who read this. I thank You Father & I claim all these things in Your Holy, powerful, majestic, everlasting & precious name I pray Lord Jesus, Amen!

Warriors! Do not fear tomorrow but have faith to move forth into another day as we press onward to victory through the guidance & power of Christ Jesus! Take courage when the storms come because this too shall pass! Do not tremble at the frail words of man but know that God is in control & on the throne! He has the final say!

He decides! He knows the path forward! He knows the outcome! And know that God is more powerful than anything in the universe! Whatever you are facing today, lay your burdens at the feet of God. In times of difficulty & uncertainness, faith builds & the renewal of spring is coming swiftly! Big things are about to happen. So have joy & do not worry about tomorrow. We're all getting through this! VICTORY IS COMING!! Let not your heart be troubled! May God strengthen you! May God give you courage! May God give you peace! May God bless all of you!

DAY 332
February 11th, 2021

Good evening my friends. I'm fighting a massive migraine tonight, but that won't stop me from praying over you. We are coming up on a great weekend & we're closing out Thursday, February 11th, 2021 & I pray this message finds you & your loved ones warm, healthy, safe & well.

Dear Heavenly Father, I come to You tonight with, Heavenly praise, faith, hope, love & thanksgiving. Thank You Father that You are making the crooked paths straight & leading the way to victory. Father, I pray for all the sick & afflicted with the virus that You will heal & restore them, that You will surround everyone reading this with an impenetrable hedge of protection & give them peace that truly surpasses all understanding. Father, I pray that You'll abundantly bless, protect, prosper all who read this tonight & their loved ones. Father, I pray that Your will be done in all things & for the restoration of our lands & people. Father, I pray for all the lost souls & I pray that You will call to them, that their eyes will be opened to the truth & accept You as their Lord & Savior. In the name of Jesus, as a child of true Living God, covered, protected, shielded & sealed by Your Blood, the Holy Spirit, the full Armor of Christ & with the full authority of God, I command & cast this insidious evil away from you & your loved ones. This evil must leave now. In the name of Jesus, I claim Psalm 91, Psalm 23, Psalm 25:20-21, Psalm 34:19, Psalm 35, Psalm 46:10, Psalm 55:22, Psalm 56:3, Psalm 61:2, Psalm 62:5-8, Psalm 116:7, Psalm 121:2, Proverbs 16:18, Deuteronomy

28:13, Joel 2:25-26, 1 John 4:4, Luke 12:2-3, Job 13:15, Ephesians 6:10-18, 2 Chronicles 7:14, 2 Timothy 1:7, 2 Thessalonians 3:16, Jeremiah 30:17, Philippians 4:7-9, Romans 12:18, John 14:27, 2 Samuel 22:40, Isaiah 26:3, Isaiah 43:2, Isaiah 53:5 & Isaiah 54:17 over all of you & all whom you love. I thank You Father & I claim all these things in Your Holy, powerful, majestic, everlasting & precious name I pray Lord Jesus, Amen!

Warriors! As we fight through another day, we are that much closer to the promised land. The journey has been long & full of difficulties but we'll continue to press forward, guided by Christ & we shall prevail. Tonight, pray for your friends, family & our nation. We move as one & through the name & power of Christ we shall arrive as one. Have faith that this difficult time will be over soon. Have courage walking into the unknown of tomorrow. And have peace knowing that no matter what comes against us, that will inevitably fail because God is in complete control & on the throne. Raise up a shout of praise to God because OUR GOD IS GOD! VICTORY IS COMING!! Let not your heart be troubled! May God strengthen you! May God give you courage! May God give you peace! May God bless all of you!

DAY 333
February 12th, 2021

Good evening my friends. Thank you for all the thoughts & prayers about my migraine. I'm feeling much better today. It's Valentine's Day Weekend & we're closing out Friday, February 12th, 2021 & I pray this message finds you & your loved ones warm, healthy, safe & well.

Dear Heavenly Father, I come to You tonight with Heavenly praise, faith, hope, love & thanksgiving. Thank You Father that when the enemy comes in like a flood, You lift a standard against him. In the name of Jesus, I claim Psalm 91, Psalm 23, Psalm 25:20-21, Psalm 34:19, Psalm 35, Psalm 46:10, Psalm 55:22, Psalm 56:3, Psalm 61:2, Psalm 62:5-8, Psalm 116:7, Psalm 121:2, Proverbs 16:18, Deuteronomy 28:13, Joel 2:25-26, 1 John 4:4, Luke 12:2-3, Job 13:15, Ephesians 6:10-18, 2 Chronicles 7:14, 2 Timothy 1:7,

2 Thessalonians 3:16, Jeremiah 30:17, Philippians 4:7-9, Romans 12:18, John 14:27, 2 Samuel 22:40, Isaiah 26:3, Isaiah 43:2, Isaiah 53:5 & Isaiah 54:17 over all of you & all whom you love. Father, I pray that Your will be done & for the complete restoration of our lands. Father, I pray that You'll abundantly bless, protect, prosper, heal, give faith, wisdom, guidance & strength to all reading this tonight. Father, I pray for all the afflicted that You'll heal them, that You will completely surround all reading this with a spiritual hedge of protection & give them peace that surpasses all understanding. In the name of Jesus, as a child of Living God, covered, protected, shielded & sealed by Your Blood, the Holy Spirit, the full Armor of Christ & with the full authority of God, I command & cast this evil away from you & your loved ones. Greater is He who is in us than he who is in the world & by Your name & power the enemy must flee now! Father, I pray for all the lost souls & I pray that You'll call to them, that their eyes will be opened to the truth & accept You as their Lord & Savior. I thank You Father & I claim all these things in Your Holy, powerful, majestic, everlasting & precious name I pray Lord Jesus, Amen!

Warriors! Stand tall! Stand firm! Stand ready! Tonight, shout a praise to God almighty because He is our God! The spirit of fear may come to try to terrorize us but through the name & power of Christ Jesus, we command this evil spirit away. It has no power against you & no claim what so ever. I command through the name of Christ that this cloud of anxiety that has enveloped us be gone! That this evil storm that surrounds us must leave! I declare victory in the name of Christ over all of you & your circumstances & I give all the glory to Christ Jesus. Spring is coming & joy soon! Hold on everyone! Stand strong! VICTORY IS COMING!! Let not your heart be troubled! May God strengthen you! May God give you courage! May God give you peace! May God bless all of you!

DAY 334
February 13th, 2021

Good evening my friends. It's Valentine's Day Eve & we're closing out Saturday, February 13th, 2021 & I pray this message finds you & your loved ones warm, healthy, safe & well.

Dear Heavenly Father, I come to You tonight with a humble heart, Heavenly praise, faith, hope, love & thanksgiving. Thank You Father for Your infinite wisdom, guidance, justice, strength & unconditional love. Father, I pray that Your perfect will be done & for the complete restoration of our lands & people. Father, I pray that You'll abundantly bless, protect, prosper all reading this tonight & all their loved ones. Father, I lift up & pray for all the sick & afflicted that You will completely restore them, that You will surround all reading this with a spiritual hedge of protection & give them pure peace that surpasses all understanding. Father, I pray for all the lost souls around the Earth & I pray that You'll call to them, that their eyes will be truly opened to the truth & accept You as their Lord & Savior. In the name of Jesus, as a child of eternal Living God, covered, protected, shielded & sealed by Your Blood, the Holy Spirit, the full Armor of Christ & with the full authority of God, I command, come against, rebuke & cast this evil away from you & your loved ones. The enemy has no authority over you & by the name of Jesus Christ I command him away from you & your loved ones. As it's written through the name & power of Christ, when we resist the devil he must flee from us. He has no other option but to obey. In the name of Jesus, I claim Psalm 91, Psalm 23, Psalm 25:20-21, Psalm 34:19, Psalm 35, Psalm 46:10, Psalm 55:22, Psalm 56:3, Psalm 61:2, Psalm 62:5-8, Psalm 116:7, Psalm 121:2, Proverbs 16:18, Deuteronomy 28:13, Joel 2:25-26, 1 John 4:4, Luke 12:2-3, Job 13:15, Ephesians 6:10-18, 2 Chronicles 7:14, 2 Timothy 1:7, 2 Thessalonians 3:16, Jeremiah 30:17, Philippians 4:7-9, Romans 12:18, John 14:27, 2 Samuel 22:40, Isaiah 26:3, Isaiah 43:2, Isaiah 53:5 & Isaiah 54:17 over all of you & all whom you love. I thank You Father & I claim all these things in Your Holy, powerful, majestic, everlasting & precious name I pray Lord Jesus, Amen!

Warriors! As we continue to move through this valley, know that joy is on the other side of this season. We started down this tumultuous path nearly 11 months ago & although we've all faced frustrations, anger, anxiety & fear... Because of the grace of God, WE ARE STILL HERE & still moving forward. Even though going through the storm is unpleasant, our faith has grown, our reliance on God has grown & when this time of uncertainty is over we will all be far stronger than when we went in! Don't let this time destroy you, but let it grow you! We all fear the unknown, but when you let go of your own understanding & place it in God's hands, He always works it out for your good. God didn't bring you this far in life only to let you go now. One of His promises to us as His children, and we are His children, is that He will never leave you nor forsake you, ever! So let's move forward with intense courage, strength, tenacity, perseverance, faith & determination! Because, not some things, but ALL things are possible with Christ! Onward!! VICTORY IS COMING!! Let not your heart be troubled! May God strengthen you! May God give you courage! May God give you peace! May God bless all of you!

DAY 335
February 14th, 2021

Good evening my friends. It's Valentine's Day & the eve of a brand new week & we're closing out Sunday, February 14th, 2021 & I pray this message finds you & your loved ones warm, healthy, safe & well.

Dear Heavenly Father, I come to You tonight with Heavenly praise, faith, hope, love & thanksgiving. Thank You Father for this day & thank You for guiding our steps as they come. In the name of Jesus, I claim Psalm 91, Psalm 23, Psalm 25:20-21, Psalm 34:19, Psalm 35, Psalm 46:10, Psalm 55:22, Psalm 56:3, Psalm 61:2, Psalm 62:5-8, Psalm 116:7, Psalm 121:2, Proverbs 16:18, Deuteronomy 28:13, Joel 2:25-26, 1 John 4:4, Luke 12:2-3, Job 13:15, Ephesians 6:10-18, 2 Chronicles 7:14, 2 Timothy 1:7, 2 Thessalonians 3:16, Jeremiah 30:17, Philippians 4:7-9, Romans 12:18, John 14:27, 2 Samuel 22:40, Isaiah 26:3, Isaiah 43:2, Isaiah 53:5 & Isaiah 54:17 over all of you & all whom you love. In the name of Jesus, as a child of the Living God, covered, protected, shielded & sealed by Your Blood, the Holy Spirit, the full Armor of Christ & with the full authority of God, I command & cast this evil away from you & your loved ones. Father, I pray for all the afflicted with the virus that You will completely restore them to full health, that You will surround all reading this with an impenetrable spiritual hedge of protection & give them peace that surpasses all understanding. Father, I pray that You'll abundantly bless, protect, prosper, give health, wisdom & guidance to all reading this tonight & all their loved ones. Father, I pray that Your perfect will be done. Father, I pray for all the lost souls & I pray that You'll call to them, that their eyes will be truly opened & accept You as their Lord & Savior. I thank You Father & I claim all these things in Your Holy, powerful, majestic, everlasting & precious name I pray Lord Jesus, Amen!

Warriors! As we venture into a brand new week we need to continue to be strong & vigilant. Christ already knows what challenges there will be for each of us & know that no matter what comes against you that God already has a plan. And also know that even in storms of uncertainty there are also great blessings that come. This time has been difficult but will end & be replaced with joy. Even in the darkest of moments our attitudes can make the difference. So with each day, take a moment to thank God for every good thing no matter how small because they will add up very quickly. Stay strong everyone! We're gonna get through this and remember above all else. God is in control & God's will be done! VICTORY IS COMING!! Let not your heart be troubled! May God strengthen you! May God give you courage! May God give you peace! May God bless all of you!

DAY 336
February 15th, 2021

Good evening my friends. It's the start of a new week & we're closing out Monday, February 15th, 2021 & I pray this message finds you & your loved ones warm, healthy, safe & well on this snowy winter night.

Dear Heavenly Father, I come to You tonight with a humble heart, Heavenly praise, faith, hope, love & thanksgiving. Thank You Father that when You are for us, no one can be against us. In the name of Jesus, I claim Psalm 91, Psalm 23, Psalm 25:20-21, Psalm 34:19, Psalm 35, Psalm 46:10, Psalm 55:22, Psalm 56:3, Psalm 61:2, Psalm 62:5-8, Psalm 116:7, Psalm 121:2, Proverbs 16:18, Deuteronomy 28:13, Joel 2:25-26, 1 John 4:4, Luke 12:2-3, Job 13:15, Ephesians 6:10-18, 2 Chronicles 7:14, 2 Timothy 1:7, 2 Thessalonians 3:16, Jeremiah 30:17, Philippians 4:7-9, Romans 12:18, John 14:27, 2 Samuel 22:40, Isaiah 26:3, Isaiah 43:2, Isaiah 53:5 & Isaiah 54:17

over all of you & all whom you love. Father, as I pray to You tonight, in Your name Jesus I pray & declare victory over the circumstances that we find ourselves presently in. In the name of Jesus I pray for deliverance from the evil storms that surround us! In the name of & through the power of Christ Jesus, I pray for & declare healing over all the afflicted, that through this difficult time you shall be abundantly blessed, you shall be the head & not the tail & that you shall prosper so that you will lend & not borrow. In the name of Jesus, I pray for & declare protection & peace over all of you with a hedge of protection from God that is impenetrable. In the name of Jesus, as a child of the Living God, covered, protected, shielded & sealed by Your Blood, the Holy Spirit, the full Armor of Christ & with the full authority of God, I command, declare, rebuke, come against & cast this evil away from you & your loved ones. It has no other option but to obey through the name of Christ & be gone now! Father I pray for & declare Your will, not ours, over these lands & people. I pray for, lift up & declare victory over the countless souls that are held in bondage, blind & I pray that their eyes will be opened, that they see the truth & accept You as their Lord & Savior. I thank You Father & I claim all these things in Your Holy, powerful, majestic, everlasting & precious name I pray Lord Jesus, Amen!

Warriors! After everything that has happened over the past year, through the very grace of God, we are still here! Still fighting & through Christ we shall prevail! We do not fight for victory but from victory! The war has already been won from the work on the cross & though storms surround us they will be to no avail as we're fully protected by Christ. He goes before us to make the crooked paths straight, clear the obstacles & guide us. It's not an easy path but each and every day we take another step forward to victory. All things are truly possible with Christ & we must not become complacent but stand firm, stay vigilant & strong. Know this, God always wins! His character is the same yesterday, today & tomorrow. He's guiding us to victory! Keep holding on! VICTORY IS COMING!! Let not your heart be troubled! May God strengthen you! May God give you courage! May God give you peace! May God bless all of you!

DAY 337
February 16th, 2021

Good evening my friends. I hope everyone made it safely through the storm & we're closing out Tuesday, February 16th, 2021 & I pray this message finds you & your loved ones warm, healthy, safe & well on this snowy winter night.

Dear Heavenly Father, I come to You tonight with Heavenly praise, love & thanksgiving. Thank You Father for Your Son Christ Jesus that we may have eternal life through Him. Father, I pray for Your will to be done above all. I pray for the restoration of our lands & people. Father, I pray that all reading this will be surrounded by a hedge of protection, given peace that surpasses all understanding & rest through these difficult days. In the name of Jesus I pray for deliverance from the evil storms that surround us! In the name of & through the power of Christ Jesus, I pray for & declare healing over all the afflicted, that all reading this shall be abundantly blessed, prosperous, protected & given wisdom. In the name of Jesus, as a child of the Living God, covered, protected, shielded & sealed by Your Blood, the Holy Spirit, the full Armor of Christ & with the full authority of God, I command & cast this evil away from you & your loved ones. I pray for the countless souls that are lost, held in bondage, blind & I pray that their eyes will be truly opened, that they see the truth & accept You as their Lord & Savior. In the name of Jesus, I claim Psalm 91, Psalm 23, Psalm 25:20-21, Psalm 34:19, Psalm 35, Psalm 46:10, Psalm 55:22, Psalm 56:3, Psalm 61:2, Psalm 62:5-8, Psalm 116:7, Psalm 121:2, Proverbs 16:18, Deuteronomy 28:13, Joel 2:25-26, 1 John 4:4, Luke 12:2-3, Job 13:15, Ephesians 6:10-18, 2 Chronicles 7:14, 2 Timothy 1:7, 2 Thessalonians 3:16, Jeremiah 30:17, Philippians 4:7-9, Romans 12:18, John 14:27, 2 Samuel 22:40, Isaiah 26:3, Isaiah 43:2, Isaiah 53:5 & Isaiah 54:17 over all of you & all whom you love. I thank You Father & I claim all these things in Your Holy, powerful, majestic, everlasting & precious name I pray Lord Jesus, Amen!

Warriors! On this cold winter night I pray each of you are warm & safe. Tomorrow will make 11 months since I started praying over you

& the journey we continue to be on takes us another day closer to victory. This has been a difficult season but one where faith in God has immensely grown. I know how many of you are ready for this difficult time to be over & soon it will be. Until then we must continue to do our part & hold on strong & be vigilant. Tonight, take a moment to pray for your loved ones & thank God for all He's blessed you with over this past year. We have a ways to go yet but through the very name, power & grace of God will shall prevail. Our season of joy is coming swiftly. His will be done above all & all the glory goes to God. In those anxious moments put all your faith & trust in Christ. I pray that He will cover you with peace that surpasses all understanding. We're gonna get through this everyone! Shout with me! VICTORY IS COMING!! Let not your heart be troubled! May God strengthen you! May God give you courage! May God give you peace! May God bless all of you!

DAY 338
February 17th, 2021

Good evening my friends. It's the middle of the week & we're closing out Wednesday, February 17th, 2021 & I pray this message finds you & your loved ones warm, healthy, safe & well.

Dear Heavenly Father, I come to You tonight with Heavenly praise, love & thanksgiving. Thank You Father that even when we are surrounded by storms on all sides, You can calm the wind, the water & bring total peace. In the name of Jesus, I claim Psalm 91, Psalm 23, Psalm 25:20-21, Psalm 34:19, Psalm 35, Psalm 46:10, Psalm 55:22, Psalm 56:3, Psalm 61:2, Psalm 62:5-8, Psalm 116:7, Psalm 121:2, Proverbs 16:18, Deuteronomy 28:13, Joel 2:25-26, 1 John 4:4, Luke 12:2-3, Job 13:15, Ephesians 6:10-18, 2 Chronicles 7:14, 2 Timothy 1:7, 2 Thessalonians 3:16, Jeremiah 30:17, Philippians 4:7-9, Romans 12:18, John 14:27, 2 Samuel 22:40, Isaiah 26:3, Isaiah 43:2, Isaiah 53:5 & Isaiah 54:17 over all of you & all whom you love. Father, I pray that all reading this & their loved ones will be surrounded by an impenetrable & continual hedge of protection & given Your perfect peace that surpasses all understanding. Father, I pray for our nation & that Your will to be done above all. Father, I pray for victory & deliverance from the evil storms that surround us! In the name of Jesus, as a child of the eternal true Living God, covered, protected, shielded & sealed by Your Blood, the Holy Spirit, the full Armor of Christ & with the full authority of God, I command & cast this evil away from you & your loved ones. As it's written greater is He who is in us than he who is in the world & through the name & power of Christ, when we resist the devil, he must flee from us. Father, I pray for healing over all the sick & afflicted with the virus, that all reading this shall be abundantly blessed, prosperous, protected & given health, guidance, strength & wisdom. Father, I pray for the lost souls around the world & I pray that their eyes will be opened, that they see the truth & accept You as their Lord & Savior. I thank You Father & I claim all these things in Your Holy, powerful, majestic, everlasting & precious name I pray Lord Jesus, Amen!

Warriors! Tonight, join me as we take another step forward & not a step back! Tonight, join me as we collectively shout GLORY BE TO GOD as we stand in the face of evil! Tonight, take courage, without fear knowing that our Savior goes before us to lead us to victory! No one ever said life would be easy, but when God is on our side, there isn't anything that can stand against us. Even when all seems lost & over, God brings victory! Even when the situation is in the realm of the impossible, God brings miracles! And even when evil seems like it's winning, it's already been defeated! Tonight, do not fear what tomorrow may bring but rest because Christ is in control & on the throne. Tomorrow, we take another step forward! Remember this, only God has the final say in all things, not man! God's will be done! Shout with me again! OUR GOD IS GOD! Let not your heart be troubled! May God strengthen you! May God give you courage! May God give you peace! May God bless all of you!

DAY 339
February 18th, 2021

Good evening my friends. We're coming up on another weekend in 2021 & we're closing out Thursday, February 18th, 2021 & I pray this message finds you & your loved ones warm, healthy, safe & well.

Dear Heavenly Father, I come to You tonight with Heavenly praise, love & thanksgiving. Thank You Father for your blessings You give us, Your guidance, wisdom, forgiveness & unconditional love. Father, I pray that You perfect will be done, for our nation & for our people. Father, I pray that You'll surround all reading this with a spiritual & continual hedge of protection & given peace that surpasses all understanding. Father, I pray for all the sick that they will be restored to health, for the eradication of this horrible virus & that You'll abundantly bless, protect, prosper, strengthen & guide all Your children. Father, I pray for the lost souls all over the world that You'll call to them & that they'll accept You as their Lord & Savior. Father, I pray for victory & deliverance from the evil storms that surround us! In the name of Jesus, as a child of Living God, covered, protected, shielded & sealed by Your Blood, the Holy Spirit, the full Armor of Christ & with the full authority of God, I command & cast this evil away from you & your loved ones. In the name of Jesus, I claim Psalm 91, Psalm 23, Psalm 25:20-21, Psalm 34:19, Psalm 35, Psalm 46:10, Psalm 55:22, Psalm 56:3, Psalm 61:2, Psalm 62:5-8, Psalm 116:7, Psalm 121:2, Proverbs 16:18, Deuteronomy 28:13, Joel 2:25-26, 1 John 4:4, Luke 12:2-3, Job 13:15, Ephesians 6:10-18, 2 Chronicles 7:14, 2 Timothy 1:7, 2 Thessalonians 3:16, Jeremiah 30:17, Philippians 4:7-9, Romans 12:18, John 14:27, 2 Samuel 22:40, Isaiah 26:3, Isaiah 43:2, Isaiah 53:5 & Isaiah 54:17 over all of you and all whom you love. I thank You Father and I claim all these things in Your Holy, powerful, majestic, everlasting & precious name I pray Lord Jesus, Amen!

Warriors! As we approach a new weekend, continue to be strong and vigilant. We're so close to this all being over. I truly can't wait. In the interim we mustn't be complacent but do not fear tomorrow because Christ guides us forward. We're yet another day closer. We stand with Christ as a unified force against the powers of evil & darkness and we will not grow weak in the face of adversity because we're strong through Christ. The spirit of fear will try to scare you but through the name of Jesus, you have power to cast it away. Under the wings of Christ we have refuge and through Him we shall prevail! Stand strong, stand firm with your hands raised to God commanding this evil to be gone in the name of Jesus. We're pressing forward again! Shout with me! VICTORY IS COMING! Let not your heart be troubled! May God strengthen you! May God give you courage! May God give you peace! May God bless all of you! ONWARD!!

DAY 340
February 19th, 2021

Good evening my friends. The weekend is finally here & we're closing out Friday, February 19th, 2021 & I pray this message finds you & your loved ones warm, healthy, safe & well.

Dear Heavenly Father, I come to You tonight with a humble heart, Heavenly praise, love and thanksgiving. Thank You Father that even in the midst the great storm, You are still in complete control, on the Throne & can calm the raging waters to mirror like peace. In the name of Jesus, I claim Psalm 91, Psalm 23, Psalm 25:20-21, Psalm 34:19, Psalm 35, Psalm 46:10, Psalm 55:22, Psalm 56:3, Psalm 61:2, Psalm 62:5-8, Psalm 116:7, Psalm 121:2, Proverbs 16:18, Deuteronomy 28:13, Joel 2:25-26, 1 John 4:4, Luke 12:2-3, Job 13:15, Ephesians 6:10-18, 2 Chronicles 7:14, 2 Timothy 1:7, 2 Thessalonians 3:16, Jeremiah 30:17, Philippians 4:7-9, Romans 12:18, John 14:27, 2 Samuel 22:40, Isaiah 26:3, Isaiah 43:2, Isaiah 53:5 & Isaiah 54:17 over all of you & all whom you love. In the name of Jesus, as a child of Living God, covered, protected, shielded and sealed by Your Blood, the Holy Spirit, the full Armor of Christ and with the full authority of God, I command, come against, rebuke & cast this evil away from you & your loved ones. This evil has no claim or authority over you or your loved ones and through the name & power of Christ Jesus, it must go now! Father, I pray for complete and total victory and deliverance from the evil storms that continue to surround us! Father, I pray that Your will be done, for our nation, our future & for our people. Father, I pray that You'll surround all reading this and their loved ones with a spiritual and impenetrable hedge of protection and given peace that surpasses all understanding through these difficult times. Father, I pray for the lost souls that You'll call to them & that they'll accept You as their Lord & Savior. Father, I pray for all the afflicted with the virus that they will be restored to full health and that You'll abundantly bless, protect, prosper, strengthen and guide all reading this. I thank You Father and I claim all these things in Your Holy, powerful, majestic, everlasting and precious name I pray Lord Jesus, Amen!

Warriors! Like on a battlefield we're in a spiritual battle that is all around us that has been going on for thousands of years & continues now. But despite this, do not fear because as children of God, we're protected from the forces of darkness. This doesn't mean that they can't try to attack you, but through the name & power of Christ, you can command this evil force away from you & it must obey. This is spiritual warfare & while the devil can't take your soul, he will try to steal your joy. Don't let him do it. Know who you are as a child of the most High God. Know that as a child of God you have the power to command it away. You need not fear it. As I've said many times on here before, we do not fight for victory but from victory. Soon all will be made right, but until then we must continue to press forward. We will not be deterred, we will not falter we will not retreat. But through the power of Christ, we will continue onward! We WILL persevere & we WILL prevail! Give a good shout of praise to God with me! OUR GOD IS GOD! VICTORY IS COMING! Let not your heart be troubled! May God strengthen you! May God give you courage! May God give you peace! May God bless all of you! WE CONTINUE ONWARD!!

DAY 341
February 20th, 2021

Good evening my friends. It was a beautiful winter day out in NE Ohio & we're closing out Saturday, February 20th, 2021 & I pray this message finds you & your loved ones warm, healthy, safe & well.

Dear Heavenly Father, I come to You tonight with Heavenly praise, love & thanksgiving. Thank You Father for all You bless us with, our talents & gifts. Please let those blessings glorify You in all ways. Father, I'm praying for the lost souls around the world that their eyes will be opened & accept You as their Lord & Savior. Father, I pray that Your will be done in all things. Please restore our lands. Father, I pray that each of you will be surrounded with a spiritual hedge of protection. In the name of Jesus, I claim Psalm 91, Psalm 23, Psalm 25:20-21, Psalm 34:19, Psalm 35, Psalm 46:10, Psalm

55:22, Psalm 56:3, Psalm 61:2, Psalm 62:5-8, Psalm 116:7, Psalm 121:2, Proverbs 16:18, Deuteronomy 28:13, Joel 2:25-26, 1 John 4:4, Luke 12:2-3, Job 13:15, Ephesians 6:10-18, 2 Chronicles 7:14, 2 Timothy 1:7, 2 Thessalonians 3:16, Jeremiah 30:17, Philippians 4:7-9, Romans 12:18, John 14:27, 2 Samuel 22:40, Isaiah 26:3, Isaiah 43:2, Isaiah 53:5 & Isaiah 54:17 over all of you & all whom you love. Father, I pray for total victory & deliverance from the insidious storms that continue to surround us. In the name of Jesus, as a child of Living God, covered, protected, shielded & sealed by Your Blood, the Holy Spirit, the full Armor of Christ & with the full authority of God, I command & cast this evil away from you and your loved ones. BE GONE NOW! Father, I pray for all the that they'll be restored to full health & that You'll abundantly bless, protect, prosper, strengthen & guide them. I thank You Father and I claim all these things in Your Holy, powerful, majestic, everlasting & precious name I pray Lord Jesus, Amen!

Warriors! On this bitterly cold winter night, please pray for all those less fortunate around our nation and pray for all those who still don't have power. We live in truly unprecedented times & every day it seems like something new is occurring that has never happened before. Events like these have been prophesied nearly 2,000 years ago & none of this is a surprise to God. He knows every single circumstance you are all facing and He knows & cares deeply what affects you. What I'm saying is, when there are things that are beyond our control, trust in and turn everything over to God. He will provide for you in ways you never thought possible. Life is not easy, but when you place everything in God's hands it always works out for your good. We serve a good God, a loving God and a just God. Trust His timing. Stay strong everyone! You have a God given purpose and future. VICTORY IS COMING! Let not your heart be troubled! May God strengthen you! May God give you courage! May God give you peace! May God bless all of you! WE CONTINUE ONWARD!!

DAY 342
February 21st, 2021

Good evening my friends. We're coming up on a brand new week & we're closing out Sunday, February 21st, 2021 & I pray this message, once again, finds you & your loved ones warm, healthy, safe & well.

Dear Heavenly Father, I come to You tonight with Heavenly praise, love & thanksgiving. Thank You Father for the gift of eternal life to all those who believe in Your son Jesus Christ, who died on the cross for our sins & was resurrected & whoever accepts Him as their Lord & Savior will have eternal life. Father, I'm praying for the lost souls that their eyes will be opened & accept You as their Lord & Savior. In the name of Jesus, as a child of eternal true Living God, covered, protected, shielded & sealed by Your Blood, the Holy Spirit, the full Armor of Christ & with the full authority of God, I command & cast this evil away from you & your loved ones. It has no other option but to flee. Father, I pray that You will surround all reading this with an impenetrable hedge of protection. In the name of Jesus, I claim Psalm 91, Psalm 23, Psalm 25:20-21, Psalm 34:19, Psalm 35, Psalm 46:10, Psalm 55:22, Psalm 56:3, Psalm 61:2, Psalm 62:5-8, Psalm 116:7, Psalm 121:2, Proverbs 16:18, Deuteronomy 28:13, Joel 2:25-26, 1 John 4:4, Luke 12:2-3, Job 13:15, Ephesians 6:10-18, 2 Chronicles 7:14, 2 Timothy 1:7, 2 Thessalonians 3:16, Jeremiah 30:17, Philippians 4:7-9, Romans 12:18, John 14:27, 2 Samuel 22:40, Isaiah 26:3, Isaiah 43:2, Isaiah 53:5 & Isaiah 54:17 over all of you & all whom you love. Father, I pray that Your perfect will be. Father, I pray for all the afflicted & sick with the virus that they'll be restored to full health & that You'll abundantly bless & protect them. I thank You Father & I claim all these things in Your Holy, powerful, majestic, everlasting & precious name I pray Lord Jesus, Amen!

Warriors! In these unprecedented times, we must all look to God & stay focused on Him. Though tribulation will come, we must take our attention off the storm. There is nothing more powerful than God & all things are truly possible with Christ. Whatever you are facing today, know that when you give it to God, He always takes scare of it. Another important thing to do is to pray. As I've said many times, prayer is one of the most effective & powerful weapons we have against the enemy. We truly need more prayer to God in this world. Tonight, please say a prayer for your friends, family, our nation & even your enemies. In an uncertain world, you can be certain in God. It's going to be okay everyone! Just hold on strong! VICTORY IS COMING! Let not your heart be troubled! May God strengthen you! May God give you courage! May God give you peace! May God bless all of you! ONWARD!!

DAY 343
February 22nd, 2021

Good evening my friends. As we venture into a new week, we're closing out Monday, February 22nd, 2021 & I pray this message finds you & your loved ones warm, healthy, safe & well.

Dear Heavenly Father, I come to You tonight with Heavenly praise, love & thanksgiving. Thank You Father that even when we don't know which way to go, You always guide us in the right direction. Father, I come before You tonight praying for all the people reading this tonight that You will watch over & keep them protected. I pray that You will give their souls rest & peace through these chaotic times. I pray that You will surround them with an impenetrable hedge of protection & place guardian angles around them to keep them safe. Father, I pray above all that Your will be done in all things. Father, I pray for the restoration of our lands & people. Father, I'm praying for all the souls who do not yet know You as their Lord & that they would accept You as their Lord & Savior. Father, I pray that the storms of evil be held back & that Your perfect justice will be carried out. In the name of Jesus, as a child of Living God, covered, protected, shielded & sealed by Your Blood, the Holy Spirit, the full Armor of Christ & with the full authority of God, I command & cast this evil away from you & your loved ones. In the name of Jesus, I claim Psalm 91, Psalm 23, Psalm 25:20-21, Psalm 34:19, Psalm 35, Psalm 46:10, Psalm 55:22, Psalm 56:3, Psalm 61:2, Psalm 62:5-8, Psalm 116:7, Psalm 121:2, Proverbs 16:18, Deuteronomy 28:13, Joel 2:25-26, 1 John 4:4, Luke 12:2-3, Job 13:15, Ephesians 6:10-18, 2 Chronicles 7:14, 2

Timothy 1:7, 2 Thessalonians 3:16, Jeremiah 30:17, Philippians 4:7-9, Romans 12:18, John 14:27, 2 Samuel 22:40, Isaiah 26:3, Isaiah 43:2, Isaiah 53:5 & Isaiah 54:17 over all of you & all whom you love. Father, there are so many that are still sick with the virus & I pray that Your healing hands will reach down & restore them. I thank You Father & I claim all these things in Your Holy, powerful, majestic, everlasting & precious name I pray Lord Jesus, Amen!

Warriors! In the chaotic world we find ourselves in, know that their truly is only one answer & that is Christ Jesus. Know that even though these times are uncertain we can be certain in God. Know that despite the storms that rage around us we do not need to fear them. Know that Your Father in Heaven loves you more than you can possible imagine & that He will always provide. Know that one day soon, all will be made right. Know that the evil in this world will one day be eliminated for all eternity. Know that this virus will be defeated. Know that God knows your circumstances & knows your frustration, fear, anxiety & wants to help you. Know that our God is God! Know that there isn't anything more powerful than God. And know this… VICTORY IS COMING! Let not your heart be troubled! May God strengthen you! May God give you courage! May God give you peace! May God bless all of you! ONWARD!!

DAY 344
February 23rd, 2021

Good evening my friends. It was a beautiful day here in NE Ohio & we're closing out Tuesday, February 23rd, 2021 & I pray this message finds you & your loved ones warm, healthy, safe & well.

Dear Heavenly Father, I come to You once again tonight with Heavenly praise, love & thanksgiving. Thank You Father that You make the possible out of the impossible, the way where there was no way & a miraculous victory when all seems lost. In the name of Jesus, I claim Psalm 91, Psalm 23, Psalm 25:20-21, Psalm 34:19, Psalm 35, Psalm 46:10, Psalm 55:22, Psalm 56:3, Psalm 61:2, Psalm 62:5-8, Psalm 116:7, Psalm 121:2, Proverbs 16:18, Deuteronomy 28:13, Joel 2:25-26, 1 John 4:4, Luke 12:2-3, Job 13:15, Ephesians

6:10-18, 2 Chronicles 7:14, 2 Timothy 1:7, 2 Thessalonians 3:16, Jeremiah 30:17, Philippians 4:7-9, Romans 12:18, John 14:27, 2 Samuel 22:40, Isaiah 26:3, Isaiah 43:2, Isaiah 53:5 & Isaiah 54:17 over all of you & all whom you love. Father, I pray for all reading this who are anxious & afraid tonight that You will calm their souls & give them Your perfect peace that surpasses all understanding. I pray that you & your loved ones are shielded with an impenetrable hedge of protection that no evil can even come near. Father, I pray that Your will be done & for the restoration of our lands & people. Father, I pray for complete & healing for all those with the virus around our country & world. Father, through these uncertain times, I pray that You will abundantly bless & protect all reading this tonight. I pray for all the families, people, businesses & medical workers around our country. In the name of Jesus, as a child of the eternal Living God, covered, protected, shielded & sealed by Your Blood, the Holy Spirit, the full Armor of Christ & with the full authority of God, I command, come against, rebuke & cast this evil away from you this very moment. Father, I'm praying for all the lost souls, that their eyes would be opened to the truth & accept You as their Lord & Savior. I thank You Father & I claim all these things in Your Holy, powerful, majestic, everlasting & precious name I pray Lord Jesus, Amen!

Warriors! Each and every day, we're nearer to victory. And soon, we will take the last step into victory & deliverance. Until then, we need to continue to be strong, vigilant & never become complacent. Next month will make 1 full year since we started this journey together & while we have a ways to go yet, by the very grace of God almighty, we shall prevail. I know many of you & absolutely exhausted, but just hold on because deliverance is growing closer. We're going to make it. Always know that God is leading us forward, has a perfect plan & already knows the outcome. Nothing happening here is a surprise to God. He lives outside of time & can see all at once. He hasn't brought you this far to leave you now. Do not fear this world, but have faith in Your Savior. All things are possible with Christ! Tonight, say a prayer & thank God for all He has done for you this past year & let's all give a mighty shout to God! OUR GOD IS GOD! VICTORY IS COMING! Let not your heart be troubled! May God strengthen you! May God give you courage! May God give you peace! May God bless all of you! ONWARD!!

DAY 345
February 24th, 2021

Good evening my friends. It was another beautiful day here in NE Ohio & we're closing out Wednesday, February 24th, 2021 & I pray this message finds you & your loved ones warm, healthy, safe & well.

Dear Heavenly Father, I come to You tonight with a humble heart, Heavenly praise, love & thanksgiving. Thank You Father for guiding us through this difficult & unfamiliar terrain as we move forward to victory & deliverance. Father, above all else, I pray that Your will be done. Let Your justice rain down on the evil storms that want our utter destruction. Father, I pray for complete restoration for all those who are afflicted with the virus. Father, I pray that You will abundantly bless, protect & guide all reading this tonight & their loved ones. Father, let Your perfect peace envelope & surround all who are anxious & afraid. I pray that you & your loved ones are shielded with an impenetrable spiritual hedge of protection. Father, I pray that all the lost souls will come to know You as their Lord & Savior. In the name of Jesus, as a child of the true Living God, covered, protected, shielded & sealed by Your Blood, the Holy Spirit, the full Armor of Christ & with the full authority of God, I command & cast this evil away from you this very moment. Greater is He who is in us than he who is in the world & as it's written, through the name & power of Christ, when we resist the devil he must flee from us. In the name of Jesus, I claim Psalm 91, Psalm 23, Psalm 25:20-21, Psalm 34:19, Psalm 35, Psalm 46:10, Psalm 55:22, Psalm 56:3, Psalm 61:2, Psalm 62:5-8, Psalm 116:7, Psalm 121:2, Proverbs 16:18, Deuteronomy 28:13, Joel 2:25-26, 1 John 4:4, Luke 12:2-3, Job 13:15, Ephesians 6:10-18, 2 Chronicles 7:14, 2 Timothy 1:7, 2 Thessalonians 3:16, Jeremiah 30:17, Philippians 4:7-9, Romans 12:18, John 14:27, 2 Samuel 22:40, Isaiah 26:3, Isaiah 43:2, Isaiah 53:5 & Isaiah 54:17 over all of you & all whom you love. I thank You Father & I claim all these things in Your Holy, powerful, majestic, everlasting & precious name I pray Lord Jesus, Amen!

Warriors! Tonight, I pray for your protection! Tonight, we stand unified! Tonight, we thank God for our coming victory! Tonight, we take another step forward towards deliverance! Know this, that when the storms come, take your eyes off the storm & focus on God. Only through Christ will we see victory! He guides our steps & directs us toward deliverance. When Christ is for us, nothing can be against us. I know it's been a long journey, but as we move into another day, know that we're that much closer. Please say a prayer for your loved ones this evening. If you are anxious & afraid, I stand & pray with you tonight that God will give you and your family complete peace that surpasses all understanding & I'm here to tell you now that no matter how the circumstances appear to be, it's going to be okay. And know this, VICTORY IS COMING! Let not your heart be troubled! May God strengthen you! May God give you courage! May God give you peace! May God bless all of you! ONWARD!!

DAY 346
February 25th, 2021

Good evening my friends. As we're quickly coming up on another weekend, we're closing out Thursday, February 25th, 2021 & I pray this message finds you & your loved ones warm, healthy, safe & well.

Dear Heavenly Father, I come to You tonight with, Heavenly praise, love & thanksgiving. Thank You Father for another day here on earth to praise Your name. In the name of Jesus, I claim Psalm 91, Psalm 23, Psalm 25:20-21, Psalm 34:19, Psalm 35, Psalm 46:10, Psalm 55:22, Psalm 56:3, Psalm 61:2, Psalm 62:5-8, Psalm 116:7, Psalm 121:2, Psalm 135:14, Proverbs 16:18, Deuteronomy 28:13, Joel 2:25-26, 1 John 4:4, Luke 12:2-3, Job 13:15, Ephesians 6:10-18, 2 Chronicles 7:14, 2 Timothy 1:7, 2 Thessalonians 3:16, Jeremiah 30:17, Philippians 4:7-9, Romans 12:18, John 14:27, 2 Samuel 22:40, Isaiah 26:3, Isaiah 43:2, Isaiah 53:5 & Isaiah 54:17 over all of you & all whom you love. I pray that all of you & your loved ones are surrounded by a spiritual hedge of protection & given God's perfect peace that surpasses all understanding. Father, I pray that You will abundantly bless, prosper, protect, guide, give health, wisdom, guidance & strength to all reading this. Father, I pray for complete healing & full restoration for all those who are afflicted with no long term effects. Father, I pray that all the lost souls will come to know You as their Lord & Savior. In the name of Jesus, as a child of the Living God, covered, protected, shielded & sealed by Your Blood, the Holy Spirit, the full Armor of Christ & with the full authority of God, I command & cast this evil away from you & all your loved ones. This evil must go now! Father, above all else, I pray that Your will be done. Let Your justice rain down. I thank You Father & I claim all these things in Your Holy, powerful, majestic, everlasting & precious name I pray Lord Jesus, Amen!

Warriors! As we conclude another day, know that no matter what you're personally facing today, that when you place everything in God's hands, He always works it out for your good. We live in a fallen world in very chaotic & uncertain times, but know that God is in complete control of everything & is on the throne. He has a perfect plan for each & every one of you. Do not fear this world for this is only but a drop in the ocean of eternity. When God is for you, there isn't anything that can be against you. This long season will come to an end soon & joy will return. Just keep holding on! We're going to make it through this together. With Christ as our guardian we shall only prevail! PRAISE BE TO GOD! VICTORY IS COMING! Let not your heart be troubled! May God strengthen you! May God give you courage! May God give you peace! May God bless all of you! ONWARD!!

DAY 347
February 26th, 2021

Good evening my friends. The weekend is finally here, it was a beautiful day out in NE Ohio & we're closing out Friday, February 26th, 2021 & I pray this message finds you & your loved ones warm, healthy, safe & well.

Dear Heavenly Father, I come to You tonight with, Heavenly praise, love & thanksgiving. Thank You Father for Your infinite wisdom, guidance & unconditional love. Father, I pray that Your will be done in all things. Father, I pray for all those afflicted with the virus that they'll be fully restored to health. In the name of Jesus, I claim Psalm 91, Psalm 23, Psalm 25:20-21, Psalm 34:19, Psalm 35, Psalm 46:10, Psalm 55:22, Psalm 56:3, Psalm 61:2, Psalm 62:5-8, Psalm 116:7, Psalm 121:2, Psalm 135:14, Proverbs 16:18, Deuteronomy 28:13, Joel 2:25-26, 1 John 4:4, Luke 12:2-3, Job 13:15, Ephesians 6:10-18, 2 Chronicles 7:14, 2 Timothy 1:7, 2 Thessalonians 3:16, Jeremiah 30:17, Philippians 4:7-9, Romans 12:18, John 14:27, 2 Samuel 22:40, Isaiah 26:3, Isaiah 43:2, Isaiah 53:5 & Isaiah 54:17 over all of you & all whom you love. Father, I pray that You will abundantly bless, prosper, protect, guide, give health, wisdom, guidance & strength, I pray that you will surround all reading this & their loved ones with a hedge of protection & peace that surpasses all understanding. Father, I pray that all the lost souls will come to know You & accept You as their Lord & Savior. In the name of Jesus, as a child of the Living God, covered, protected, shielded & sealed by Your Blood, the Holy Spirit, the full Armor of Christ & with the full authority of God, I command & cast this evil away from you & all your loved ones. I thank You Father & I claim all these things in Your Holy, powerful, majestic, everlasting & precious name I pray Lord Jesus, Amen!

Warriors! As we approach a new month, please take a moment & thank God for all He's blessed you with over the past month. Know that when this is all over that it was God who guided us through this long valley all the way to victory. This past year has been trying in all ways but soon it will come to an end. All of us have been tired, stressed & frustrated but think how amazing everything will be when this virus is fully eradicated. Joy is coming. Always know that all things are possible with Christ. There is nothing more powerful than God in the known & unknown universe. His character has never & will never change. He is the same yesterday, today & tomorrow. He loves you more than you can possibly know. So tonight as we stand on yet another step forward, shout with me! VICTORY IS COMING! Let not your heart be troubled! May God strengthen you! May God give you courage! May God give you peace! May God bless all of you! ONWARD!!

DAY 348
February 27th, 2021

Good evening my friends. It's the middle of the weekend & we're closing out Saturday, February 27th, 2021 & I pray this message finds you & your loved ones warm, healthy, safe & well.

Dear Heavenly Father, I come to You tonight with a humble heart, Heavenly praise, love & thanksgiving. Thank You Father that even we don't see an answer, You already have a plan for victory. In the name of Jesus, I claim Psalm 91, Psalm 23, Psalm 25:20-21, Psalm 34:19, Psalm 35, Psalm 46:10, Psalm 55:22, Psalm 56:3, Psalm 61:2, Psalm 62:5-8, Psalm 116:7, Psalm 121:2, Psalm 135:14, Proverbs 16:18, Deuteronomy 28:13, Joel 2:25-26, 1 John 4:4, Luke 12:2-3, Job 13:15, Ephesians 6:10-18, 2 Chronicles 7:14, 2 Timothy 1:7, 2 Thessalonians 3:16, Jeremiah 30:17, Philippians 4:7-9, Romans 12:18, John 14:27, 2 Samuel 22:40, Isaiah 26:3, Isaiah 43:2, Isaiah 53:5 & Isaiah 54:17 over all of you & all whom you love. Father, I pray that You will abundantly bless, protect, that you will surround all reading this & their loved ones with an impenetrable hedge of protection & given peace that surpasses all understanding in these uncertain times. In the name of Jesus, as a child of the Living God, covered, protected, shielded & sealed by Your Blood, the Holy Spirit, the full Armor of Christ & with the full authority of God, I command, come against & cast this evil away from you & all your loved ones. As it's written through the power of Christ, this evil must leave now! Father, I pray that all the lost souls around the world will see the truth & accept You as their Lord & Savior. Father, I pray for all those sick & afflicted that they'll be fully restored to health with no long term effects. I thank You Father & I claim all these things in Your Holy, powerful, majestic, everlasting & precious name I pray Lord Jesus, Amen!

Warriors! On this late Saturday night we once again have made it through another day! So tonight, say a prayer for your friends, family, our nation & even your enemies. Forgiveness is so key, because when we hold on to anger & unforgiveness, it can destroy you from the inside out. It doesn't mean that you have to forget, but forgiving someone & moving on is so important. As we move into the last day of this month, know that when the storms come, to take your focus off the storms & place it only on God. As Christ leads us forwards, we shall prevail! We must continue to be strong & hold on. We're gonna make it through this everyone! VICTORY & DELIVERANCE IS COMING! Let not your heart be troubled! May God strengthen you! May God give you courage! May God give you peace! May God bless all of you! ONWARD!!

DAY 349
February 28th, 2021

Good evening my friends. It's the eve of a new week & month & we're closing out Sunday, February 28th, 2021 & I pray this message finds you & your loved ones warm, healthy, safe & well.

Dear Heavenly Father, I come to You tonight with Heavenly praise, love & thanksgiving. Thank You Father that You are in complete control & on the Throne. Let Your will be done! Thank You Father that You are going before us to lead us to victory. Thank You Father that You are healing the afflicted, blessing Your children, protecting us, giving us peace that surpasses understanding & walking with us each step of this journey. Thank You Lord Jesus that You are surrounding Your children with a hedge of protection that no evil can pass through. Thank You Lord that You are calling to all the souls on the planet & let those who don't know You accept You as their Lord & Savior. In the name of Jesus, as a child of the Living God, covered, protected, shielded & sealed by Your Blood, the Holy Spirit, the full Armor of Christ & with the full authority of God, I command & cast this evil away from you & all your loved ones. In the name of Jesus, I claim Psalm 91, Psalm 23, Psalm 25:20-21, Psalm 34:19, Psalm 35, Psalm 46:10, Psalm 55:22, Psalm 56:3, Psalm 61:2, Psalm 62:5-8, Psalm 116:7, Psalm 121:2, Psalm 135:14, Proverbs 16:18, Deuteronomy 28:13, Joel 2:25-26, 1 John 4:4, Luke 12:2-3, Job 13:15, Ephesians 6:10-18, 2 Chronicles 7:14, 2 Timothy 1:7, 2 Thessalonians 3:16, Jeremiah 30:17, Philippians 4:7-9, Romans 12:18, John 14:27, 2 Samuel 22:40, Isaiah 26:3, Isaiah 43:2, Isaiah 53:5 & Isaiah 54:17 over all of you & all whom you love. I thank You

Father, I declare victory in &all the glory to Your name & I claim all these things in Your Holy, powerful, majestic, everlasting & precious name I pray Lord Jesus, Amen!

Warriors! As we embark on a new week & month, we're approaching a full year since I started praying over all of you & I will continue to do so. Know that through each day, we're truly living in a historic time & more is yet to come. Everything you're seeing developing around us was truly prophesied nearly 2,000 years ago. But do not fear because God is in control & on the throne. In a chaotic world, you can be certain in Christ. He's never lost a battle & has already defeated the enemy. One day soon, all will be made right, but as we venture into this fallen world, know that there is still joy to be had, peace to prosper & love to abound. It can be hard to see the good when there's such evil storms on the horizon but even in the darkest moments, good always comes to surface. Good will always triumph! God will always triumph! GOD ALWAYS PREVAILS! So tonight! Shout with me a heavenly shout from this mountain once again! VICTORY & DELIVERANCE IS COMING! Let not your heart be troubled! May God strengthen you! May God give you courage! May God give you peace! May God bless all of you! ONWARD!!

DAY 350
March 1st, 2021

Good evening my friends. It's the eve of a new week & month & we're closing out Monday, March 1st, 2021 & I pray this message finds you & your loved ones warm, healthy, safe & well.

Dear Heavenly Father, I come to You tonight with Heavenly praise, hope, love & thanksgiving. Thank You Father that You are the God of miracles, new beginnings, victory, love & justice! Father, I pray for all the countless afflicted with the virus that You will completely restore them & eradicate this virus. In the name of Jesus, I claim Psalm 91, Psalm 23, Psalm 25:20-21, Psalm 34:19, Psalm 35, Psalm 46:10, Psalm 55:22, Psalm 56:3, Psalm 61:2, Psalm 62:5-8, Psalm 116:7, Psalm 121:2, Psalm 135:14, Proverbs 16:18, Deuteronomy 28:13, Joel 2:25-26, 1 John 4:4, Luke 12:2-3, Job 13:15, Ephesians 6:10-18, 2 Chronicles 7:14, 2 Timothy 1:7, 2 Thessalonians 3:16, Jeremiah 30:17, Philippians 4:7-9, Romans 12:18, John 14:27, 2 Samuel 22:40, Isaiah 26:3, Isaiah 43:2, Isaiah 53:5 & Isaiah 54:17 over all of you & all whom you love. Father I pray that You'll surround all reading this with a spiritual hedge of protection against all evil, please give them peace that surpasses all understanding & abundantly bless them through these difficult days. In the name of Jesus, as a child of the Living God, covered, protected, shielded & sealed by Your Blood, the Holy Spirit, the full Armor of Christ & with the full authority of God, I command & cast this evil away from you & all your loved ones. I thank You Father, I declare victory in & all the glory to Your name & I claim all these things in Your Holy, powerful, majestic, everlasting & precious name I pray Lord Jesus, Amen!

Warriors! We're through another day & we've begun a brand new month. One year ago, we didn't know what the remainder of 2020 would be like, but now in 2021, despite everything we've faced, we can thank God that we're still here! We can thank God because He's holding back the powers of darkness! We can thank God for guiding us through the valley! We can thank God for providing through uncertain times! We can thank God for the blessings in the storm, the kindness we didn't expect & the strength to carry on! We can thank God for everything because we woke up this morning to a new day! While our journey is not over yet, because of & only because of Christ, we continue forward! Give God a shout of praise tonight! GLORY BE TO GOD!!! Let not your heart be troubled! May God strengthen you! May God give you courage! May God give you peace! May God bless all of you!

DAY 351
March 2nd, 2021

Good evening my friends. It was a beautiful day out again today & we're closing out Tuesday, March 2nd, 2021 & I pray this message finds you & your loved ones warm, healthy, safe & well.

Dear Heavenly Father, I come to You tonight with a humble heart, Heavenly praise, love & thanksgiving. Thank You Father for all the blessings You've given us, for protecting us, Your unconditional love & guiding us. Father I pray that You'll surround all reading this & their loved ones with a spiritual hedge of protection against all evil, please give them complete peace that surpasses all understanding & abundantly bless, protect, guide & strengthen them. Father I lift up & pray for all the afflicted with the virus that You would fully & completely restore them. In the name of Jesus, I claim Psalm 91, Psalm 23, Psalm 25:20-21, Psalm 34:19, Psalm 35, Psalm 46:10, Psalm 55:22, Psalm 56:3, Psalm 61:2, Psalm 62:5-8, Psalm 116:7, Psalm 121:2, Psalm 135:14, Proverbs 16:18, Deuteronomy 28:13, Joel 2:25-26, 1 John 4:4, Luke 12:2-3, Job 13:15, Ephesians 6:10-18, 2 Chronicles 7:14, 2 Timothy 1:7, 2 Thessalonians 3:16, Jeremiah 30:17, Philippians 4:7-9, Romans 12:18, John 14:27, 2 Samuel 22:40, Isaiah 26:3, Isaiah 43:2, Isaiah 53:5 & Isaiah 54:17 over all of you & all whom you love. In the name of Jesus, as a child of the eternal Living God, covered, protected, shielded & sealed by Your Blood, the Holy Spirit, the full Armor of Christ & with the full authority of God, I command & cast this evil away from you & all your loved ones. Greater is He who is in us than he who is in the world & as it's written if we resist the devil he must flee from us. I thank You Father & I claim all these things in Your Holy, powerful, majestic, everlasting & precious name I pray Lord Jesus, Amen!

Warriors! As we begin the month of March, I find it fitting that it comes in like a Lion. Through the power of Christ we are a unified force moving forward, pressing on through the storms. We do not focus on the problems but God alone. We are strong through Christ because all things are possible with Christ. While these times may seem uncertain, we can be certain in Christ & know that, no matter what happens, He is completely in control. Do not fear! We will not back down! We will not falter! We will not be deterred! Whatever we face tomorrow, know that God will walk with us every step of the journey. Please take a moment to pray for your loved ones this evening. And know this! VICTORY IS COMING! Let not your heart be troubled! May God strengthen you! May God give you courage! May God give you peace! May God bless all of you!

DAY 352
March 3rd, 2021

Good evening my friends. It was another beautiful day out in the middle of the week & we're closing out Wednesday, March 3rd, 2021 & I pray this message finds you & your loved ones warm, healthy, safe & well.

Dear Heavenly Father, I come to You tonight with a humble heart, Heavenly praise, love, faith & thanksgiving. Thank You that even when we all sin & fall short of the glory of Christ, You are always there to forgive us & welcome us back. In the name of Jesus, I claim Psalm 91, Psalm 23, Psalm 25:20-21, Psalm 34:19, Psalm 35, Psalm 46:10, Psalm 55:22, Psalm 56:3, Psalm 61:2, Psalm 62:5-8, Psalm 116:7, Psalm 121:2, Psalm 135:14, Proverbs 16:18, Deuteronomy 28:13, Joel 2:25-26, 1 John 4:4, Luke 12:2-3, Job 13:15, Ephesians 6:10-18, 2 Chronicles 7:14, 2 Timothy 1:7, 2 Thessalonians 3:16, Jeremiah 30:17, Philippians 4:7-9, Romans 12:18, John 14:27, 2 Samuel 22:40, Isaiah 26:3, Isaiah 43:2, Isaiah 53:5 & Isaiah 54:17 over all of you & all whom you love. In the name of Jesus, as a child of the Living God, covered, protected, shielded & sealed by Your Blood, the Holy Spirit, the full Armor of Christ & with the full authority of God, I command & cast this evil away from you & all your loved ones again tonight & every night. Father I pray that You'll surround all reading this message with an impenetrable hedge of protection, peace that surpasses all understanding & abundantly bless them. Father I lift up & pray for all the sick & afflicted that You, the Great Physician will completely restore them to health. I thank You Father & I claim all these things in Your Holy, powerful, majestic, everlasting & precious name I pray Lord Jesus, Amen!

Warriors! It's a good night! A very good night, because as we stand here this evening, we're not only another day closer to victory, but we're also nearing the warm weather of Spring. As we continue to press forward, Christ is continually leading us forward to deliverance. I know the future seems uncertain but I believe that big things are coming & you can be certain in God. This year has been trying for all of us but think of the joy when this pandemic is over. I don't know who needs to hear this tonight but I just want to say, through the power of Christ, it's going to be okay. Whatever the circumstances you find yourself in, it's going to be okay. We're going to get through this thing & we're all going to be stronger on the other side. God is more powerful than anything in the known & unknown universe & what concerns you, concerns Him. He loves you far more than you can possibly imagine. We need to continue to be strong, hold on & be vigilant. Tonight, as we move forward into another day, shout with me once again! OUR GOD IS GOD & VICTORY IS COMING! Let not your heart be troubled! May God strengthen you! May God give you courage! May God give you peace! May God bless all of you!

DAY 353
March 4th, 2021

Good evening my friends. We're coming up on another weekend & we're closing out Thursday, March 4th, 2021 & I pray this message finds you & your loved ones warm, healthy, safe & well.

Dear Heavenly Father, I come to You tonight with Heavenly praise, love & thanksgiving. Thank You Father that You have a planned destiny & purpose for each & every one of us. Father I pray for everyone reading this that they'll be surrounded by an impenetrable hedge of protection, given Your peace that surpasses all understanding & abundantly blessed during these uncertain times. Father, I lift up & pray for all the afflicted that they will be restored to complete & full health & for the eradication of this virus. In the name of Jesus, as a child of the Living God, covered, protected, shielded & sealed by Your Blood, the Holy Spirit, the full Armor of Christ & with the full authority of God, I command & cast this evil away from you & all your loved ones to the farthest ends of the earth. In the name of Jesus, I claim Psalm 91, Psalm 23, Psalm 25:20-21, Psalm 34:19, Psalm 35, Psalm 46:10, Psalm 55:22, Psalm 56:3, Psalm 61:2, Psalm 62:5-8, Psalm 116:7, Psalm 121:2, Psalm 135:14, Proverbs 16:18, Deuteronomy 28:13, Joel 2:25-26, 1 John 4:4, Luke 12:2-3, Job 13:15, Ephesians 6:10-18, 2 Chronicles 7:14, 2 Timothy 1:7, 2 Thessalonians 3:16, Jeremiah 30:17, Philippians 4:7-9, Romans 12:18, John 14:27, 2 Samuel 22:40, Isaiah 26:3, Isaiah 43:2, Isaiah 53:5 & Isaiah 54:17 over all of you & all whom you love. I thank You Father & I claim all these things in Your Holy, powerful, majestic, everlasting & precious name I pray Lord Jesus, Amen!

Warriors! I pray that each of you is at peace in your hearts tonight. I know these times have been trying for all of us & I pray that each of you is well. As we've taken another step forward, we continue on to another day. This whole journey Christ has been at the helm, guiding us forward & protecting us along the way. With every second that passes by we're that much closer to victory. As we move forward in faith, know that God is with us every step of the way & He will guide us to complete deliverance. Know that each of you has a special purpose & destiny that only you can accomplish. You were chosen for this time in history. God could have placed you at any point along the timeline of life, but He chose this time for you & you are a masterpiece in His eyes. God knows the circumstances we face & has a plan for triumph in your life. Tonight, pray for your family & friends & be sure to give God thanks for guiding us through another day. Be strong everyone! VICTORY IS COMING! Let not your heart be troubled! May God strengthen you! May God give you courage! May God give you peace! May God bless all of you!

DAY 354
March 5th, 2021

Good evening my friends. The weekend is here & we're closing out Friday, March 5th, 2021 & I pray this message finds you & your loved ones warm, healthy, safe & well.

Dear Heavenly Father, I come to You tonight with Heavenly praise, love & thanksgiving. Thank You Father for all the blessings, gifts & talents You've given us & for loving us unconditionally. In the name of Jesus, I claim Psalm 91, Psalm 23, Psalm 25:20-21, Psalm 34:19, Psalm 35, Psalm 46:10, Psalm 55:22, Psalm 56:3, Psalm 61:2, Psalm 62:5-8, Psalm 116:7, Psalm 121:2, Psalm 135:14, Proverbs 16:18, Deuteronomy 28:13, Joel 2:25-26, 1 John 4:4, Luke 12:2-3, Job 13:15, Ephesians 6:10-18, 2 Chronicles 7:14, 2 Timothy 1:7, 2 Thessalonians 3:16, Jeremiah 30:17, Philippians 4:7-9, Romans 12:18, John 14:27, 2 Samuel 22:40, Isaiah 26:3, Isaiah 43:2, Isaiah 53:5 & Isaiah 54:17 over all of you & all whom you love. Father, I pray that You will restore our lands & bring peace back to our people. Father, I pray for all the afflicted that they'll be fully restored to health, the distribution of the vaccine & for the eradication of this virus. Father I pray for everyone reading this that they'll be surrounded by a spiritual & impenetrable hedge of protection, given Your full peace that surpasses all understanding & abundantly blessed & given wisdom during these uncertain days. In the name of Jesus, as a child of the true Living God, covered, protected, shielded & sealed by Your Blood, the Holy Spirit, the full Armor of Christ & with the full authority of God, I command & cast the spirit of fear, the devil & all agents of evil away from you & all your loved ones. This evil MUST go now & never return! Greater is He who is in us than he who is in the world & by the power of Christ, as it's written if we resist the devil he must flee from us. I thank You Father & I claim all these things in Your Holy, powerful, majestic, everlasting & precious name I pray Lord Jesus, Amen!

Warriors! The weekend is here & as we venture into another day we need to continue to be strong, hold on & be vigilant. We've been through so much over the past year & each day we're closer to victory! As we stand tonight on another mountain, despite the uncertainty of the times we live in, God is in complete control & on the throne. Do not fear the unknown but trust in the power of Christ. He didn't bring us this far only to leave us & I believe that something amazing is coming on the horizon. We need to keep praying with everything we've got. Prayer is truly the greatest weapon against the enemy. Because when God's people pray, the devil & his demons shudder! So tonight, as we face down this evil give a shout of glory to God almighty! GOD IS GOOD & VICTORY IS COMING! Let not your heart be troubled! May God strengthen you! May God give you courage! May God give you peace! May God bless all of you!

DAY 355
March 6th, 2021

Good evening my friends. It was a beautiful day & we're closing out Saturday, March 6th, 2021 & I pray this message finds you & your loved ones warm, healthy, safe & well.

Dear Heavenly Father, I come to You again tonight with Heavenly praise, love & thanksgiving. Thank You Father for always watching over us, guiding us & strengthening us. Father, I pray for all the sick & afflicted & I pray that You will supernaturally heal all those in need tonight. Father, You are the Great Physician & all things are possible with You. Father I pray that You'll surround all reading this with a hedge of protection, give them peace that surpasses all understanding & abundantly bless them. Father, I pray that You will restore our lands & bring peace back to our people & nation. In the name of Jesus, as a child of the Living God, covered, protected, shielded & sealed by Your Blood, the Holy Spirit, the full Armor of Christ & with the full authority of God, I command & cast this evil away from you and your loved ones. This evil must GO NOW! In the name of Jesus, I claim Psalm 91, Psalm 23, Psalm 25:20-21, Psalm 34:19, Psalm 35, Psalm 46:10, Psalm 55:22, Psalm 56:3, Psalm 61:2, Psalm 62:5-8, Psalm 116:7, Psalm 121:2, Psalm 135:14, Proverbs 16:18, Deuteronomy 28:13, Joel 2:25-26, 1 John 4:4, Luke 12:2-3, Job 13:15, Ephesians 6:10-18, 2 Chronicles 7:14, 2 Timothy 1:7, 2 Thessalonians 3:16, Jeremiah 30:17, Philippians 4:7-9, Romans 12:18, John 14:27, 2

Samuel 22:40, Isaiah 26:3, Isaiah 43:2, Isaiah 53:5 & Isaiah 54:17 over all of you & all whom you love. I thank You Father & I claim all these things in Your Holy, powerful, majestic, everlasting & precious name I pray Lord Jesus, Amen!

Warriors! On this night, I pray that God watches over all of you, keeps you & perfects that which concerns you. I pray that you will have supernatural increase this year! I pray that God will heal you & your loved ones. As we move into another day, no matter what circumstances occur, I pray that you & all you love will victorious because of the power of Christ! While life can be uncertain & every day has it's own set of problems, when we place those burdens in God's hands, He works them for your good. Do not fear tomorrow but have faith that whatever may come that God will walk with you all the way through. Stand firm! Stand tall! And know that Christ goes before you to make the crooked paths straight. He loves you more than you will ever know. Please say a prayer for your family & friends tonight. We're gonna get through this everyone! VICTORY IS COMING! Let not your heart be troubled! May God strengthen you! May God give you courage! May God give you peace! May God bless all of you!

DAY 356
March 7th, 2021

Good evening my friends. As we conclude another weekend & we're closing out Sunday, March 7th, 2021 & I pray this message finds you & your loved ones warm, healthy, safe & well.

Dear Heavenly Father, I come to You again tonight with a humble heart, Heavenly praise, love & thanksgiving. Thank You Father for giving us wisdom, guidance & strength. In the name of Jesus, I claim Psalm 91, Psalm 23, Psalm 25:20-21, Psalm 34:19, Psalm 35, Psalm 46:10, Psalm 55:22, Psalm 56:3, Psalm 61:2, Psalm 62:5-8, Psalm 116:7, Psalm 121:2, Psalm 135:14, Proverbs 16:18, Deuteronomy 28:13, Joel 2:25-26, 1 John 4:4, Luke 12:2-3, Job 13:15, Ephesians 6:10-18, 2 Chronicles 7:14, 2 Timothy 1:7, 2 Thessalonians 3:16, Jeremiah 30:17, Philippians 4:7-9, Romans 12:18, John 14:27, 2

Samuel 22:40, Isaiah 26:3, Isaiah 43:2, Isaiah 53:5 & Isaiah 54:17 over all of you & all whom you love. Father, I pray for all the afflicted & I pray that You will supernaturally heal all those in need tonight & eradicate this virus. Thank You Father that You are the Great Physician & all things are possible with You. In the name of Jesus, as a child of the eternal true Living God, covered, protected, shielded & sealed by Your Blood, the Holy Spirit, the full Armor of Christ & with the full authority of God, I command, come against & cast this insidious evil, in all forms, away from you and your loved ones. Father I pray that You'll surround all reading this & their loved ones with an impenetrable hedge of protection, give them Your perfect peace that surpasses all understanding & abundantly bless them. I thank You Father & I claim all these things in Your Holy, powerful, majestic, everlasting & precious name I pray Lord Jesus, Amen!

Warriors! Tonight, do not fear the unknown! Tonight, do not fear the future! Tonight, do not lean on your own understanding! But have faith that the circumstances that you face, when placed in the hands of God, will always work for your good. When we face adversity, in any form, our natural course is to ask God to remove the problem. However, sometimes God is using those situations to grow you or mold you into all that God wants you to be. It's never pleasant & I won't sugar coat it, it can be heart wrenching while going through. But know this, God may not take away the situation, but He WILL walk with you the entire journey from beginning to the end. You will never be alone, without provision or forsaken. In these situations, difficult as they may be, God is not punishing you. Only when we look back on our lives do we see the scope of God's work in us. We wouldn't be the person we are meant to be if not for these trials. If you are going through something like this right now, I want to pray for you & for the victory that comes at the end of that time. I pray for your strength & endurance! I pray for your mind to look at this as a time to trust in God even when everything seems to be going sideways. You will make it through this situation. And know this, VICTORY IS COMING! Let not your heart be troubled! May God strengthen you! May God give you courage! May God give you peace! May God bless all of you!

DAY 357
March 8th, 2021

Good evening my friends. As we start a new week, it was a beautiful day out today & we're closing out Monday, March 8th, 2021 & I pray this message finds you & your loved ones warm, healthy, safe & well.

Dear Heavenly Father, I come to You again tonight with Heavenly praise, love & thanksgiving. Thank You Father that You hear our prayers, understand our circumstances & have a plan of purpose & destiny for each of us. Father, I pray for all the afflicted & I pray that You will fully restore all suffering tonight. Father, I pray that everyone reading this tonight will be surrounded by a hedge of protection, given peace & abundantly blessed in all areas of their lives during these difficult days. Father, I pray that You'll restore our lands & bring peace back to the people. In the name of Jesus, as a child of the Living God, covered, protected, shielded & sealed by Your Blood, the Holy Spirit, the full Armor of Christ & with the full authority of God, I command & cast this insidious evil, in all forms, away from you and your loved ones. Greater is He who is in us than he who is in the world & as it's written, through the name & power of Christ when we resist the devil he must flee from us. In the name of Jesus, I claim Psalm 91, Psalm 23, Psalm 25:20-21, Psalm 34:19, Psalm 35, Psalm 46:10, Psalm 55:22, Psalm 56:3, Psalm 61:2, Psalm 62:5-8, Psalm 116:7, Psalm 121:2, Psalm 135:14, Proverbs 16:18, Deuteronomy 28:13, Joel 2:25-26, 1 John 4:4, Luke 12:2-3, Job 13:15, Ephesians 6:10-18, 2 Chronicles 7:14, 2 Timothy 1:7, 2 Thessalonians 3:16, Jeremiah 30:17, Philippians 4:7-9, Romans 12:18, John 14:27, 2 Samuel 22:40, Isaiah 26:3, Isaiah 43:2, Isaiah 53:5 & Isaiah 54:17 over all of you & all whom you love. I thank You Father & I claim all these things in Your Holy, powerful, majestic, everlasting & precious name I pray Lord Jesus, Amen!

Warriors! On the start of this new week, if & when the storms of adversity come, do not be afraid but focus your eyes on Christ alone. Only through the name & power of Christ Jesus will we prevail & prevail we shall. With the start of this new day, we're that much closer to victory & with spring & Easter right around the corner, things are beginning to look up. We're not out of the woods yet, but as this long journey through the valley continues, have faith & declare that we will see victory & deliverance on the other side. There is true power in words so rather than focus on the negative of the situation, start declaring victory over the giant before you. I won't lie this can be difficult because at times we feel defeated & do not have the strength to fight back. But at those times, that is time to gain strength from God & shout with all you've got that this too shall pass & that through the name of Christ Jesus, whom all things are possible, I declare victory over this situation! Tonight! Pray for your family & loved ones & know this!! VICTORY IS COMING! Let not your heart be troubled! May God strengthen you! May God give you courage! May God give you peace! May God bless all of you!

DAY 358
March 9th, 2021

Good evening my friends. It was another beautiful day out today & we're closing out Tuesday, March 9th, 2021 & I pray this message finds you & your loved ones warm, healthy, safe & well.

Dear Heavenly Father, I come to You tonight with Heavenly praise, love & thanksgiving. Thank You Father that even when in the midst of the great storm & chaos, You are still in complete control. In the name of Jesus, I claim Psalm 91, Psalm 23, Psalm 25:20-21, Psalm 34:19, Psalm 35, Psalm 46:10, Psalm 55:22, Psalm 56:3, Psalm 61:2, Psalm 62:5-8, Psalm 116:7, Psalm 121:2, Psalm 135:14, Proverbs 16:18, Deuteronomy 28:13, Joel 2:25-26, 1 John 4:4, Luke 12:2-3, Job 13:15, Ephesians 6:10-18, 2 Chronicles 7:14, 2 Timothy 1:7, 2 Thessalonians 3:16, Jeremiah 30:17, Philippians 4:7-9, Romans 12:18, John 14:27, 2 Samuel 22:40, Isaiah 26:3, Isaiah 43:2, Isaiah 53:5 & Isaiah 54:17 over all of you & all whom you love. Father, I lift great Heavenly praise to You tonight that in all our distresses You walk with us each step of the journey. Through all our pain, You tend to us & heal us. And though the enemy tries to destroy us, You protect & shield us. In the name of Jesus, as a child of the Living God, covered, protected, shielded & sealed by Your Blood, the Holy Spirit, the full Armor of Christ & with the full authority of God, I command & cast this insidious evil, in all forms, away from you and your loved ones. And I say it again even louder! Greater is He who is in us than he who is in the world & as it's written, through the name & power of Christ when we resist the devil he must flee from us. Through the name of Christ I command you to leave now! BE GONE EVIL ONE! Father, I pray for all the sick, hurt & afflicted & I pray that You will fully restore all suffering tonight. Father, I pray that You'll restore our lands & bring peace back to the people. Father, I pray that everyone reading this tonight & their loved ones will be surrounded by an impenetrable hedge of protection, given peace that surpasses all understanding & abundantly blessed in all areas of their lives during these difficult days. I thank You Father & I claim all these things in Your Holy, powerful, majestic, everlasting & precious name I pray Lord Jesus, Amen!

Warriors! Look not at the storms of chaos that surround us, but turn away & only focus on God. Have faith that God hears your prayers & has a plan for deliverance in all circumstances. Do not fear the uncertainness of tomorrow but have faith that the future is sound in the hands of Christ. When the spirit of fear tries to terrorize you, through the name & power of Christ, command that spirit away to the farthest corners of the earth. I pray for each of you that you are surrounded by a hedge of protection that no evil of any kind can penetrate. We take another step forward today & as we move forward through the power of Christ. We stare down & command the enemy to flee! The devil is attacking everyone in high magnitude because he knows his times draws very short. Very soon everything will be made right. All that you see now, the pure chaos in the world was prophesied nearly 2,000 years ago but do not fear because these things must happen. God will not leave you without provision. He will walk with us every step of the journey & through Christ WE SHALL PREVAIL! Tonight! Stand firm! Stand tall! Stand ready with the full armor of Christ & command this evil to leave! SHOUT WITH ME! VICTORY IS COMING! Let not your heart be troubled! May God strengthen you! May God give you courage! May God give you peace! May God bless all of you! ONWARD!!!

DAY 359
March 10th, 2021

Good evening my friends. It's the middle of the week & we're closing out Wednesday, March 10th, 2021 & I pray this message finds you & your loved ones warm, healthy, safe & well.

Dear Heavenly Father, I come to You tonight with Heavenly praise, love & thanksgiving. Thank You Father for Your infinite wisdom, guidance & strength through these difficult times. Father, I pray that You'll surround all reading this will be surrounded by a spiritual & impenetrable hedge of protection, given Your perfect peace that surpasses all understanding & abundantly blessed in all areas of their lives. Father, I pray for all the afflicted that You'll fully restore all suffering tonight. Father, I pray that You'll restore our lands. In the name of Jesus, I claim Psalm 91, Psalm 23, Psalm 25:20-21, Psalm 34:19, Psalm 35, Psalm 46:10, Psalm 55:22, Psalm 56:3, Psalm 61:2, Psalm 62:5-8, Psalm 116:7, Psalm 121:2, Psalm 135:14, Proverbs 16:18, Deuteronomy 28:13, Joel 2:25-26, 1 John 4:4, Luke 12:2-3, Job 13:15, Ephesians 6:10-18, 2 Chronicles 7:14, 2 Timothy 1:7, 2 Thessalonians 3:16, Jeremiah 30:17, Philippians 4:7-9, Romans 12:18, John 14:27, 2 Samuel 22:40, Isaiah 26:3, Isaiah 43:2, Isaiah 53:5 & Isaiah 54:17 over all of you & all whom you love. In the name of Jesus, as a child of the Living God, covered, protected, shielded & sealed by Your Blood, the Holy Spirit, the full Armor of Christ & with the full authority of God, I command & cast this insidious evil, in all forms, away from you and your loved ones. I thank You Father & I claim all these things in Your Holy, powerful, majestic, everlasting & precious name I pray Lord Jesus, Amen!

Warriors! We're a 1/3 of the way through the month of March & as we approach Easter it's a good time to reflect on everything we've been through over the past year. The warmth of spring is coming & with each day we keep pressing forward through the chaos & mire. As I've said many times on here, all things are possible with Christ & through His name & power we shall prevail. The attacks of the enemy will come but always remember, we do not fight for victory but from victory. Because of Christ's sacrifice on the cross, we've already won the war. Soon, all will be made right. In the mean time we must continue to press forward, stay strong, hold on & be vigilant. We can't allow ourselves to become complacent. Do not be afraid because though weeping may endure for a night, there comes joy in the morning. Tonight, say a prayer for your loved ones & shout with me once again! VICTORY IS COMING! Let not your heart be troubled! May God strengthen you! May God give you courage! May God give you peace! May God bless all of you! ONWARD!!!

DAY 360
March 11th, 2021

Good evening my friends. We're coming up on a new weekend & we're closing out Thursday, March 11th, 2021 & I pray this message finds you & your loved ones warm, healthy, safe & well.

Dear Heavenly Father, I come to You tonight with a humble heart, Heavenly praise, love & thanksgiving. Thank You Father that even when it seems the darkest, You're always in complete control & on the throne! In the name of Jesus, I claim Psalm 91, Psalm 23, Psalm 25:20-21, Psalm 34:19, Psalm 35, Psalm 46:10, Psalm 55:22, Psalm 56:3, Psalm 61:2, Psalm 62:5-8, Psalm 116:7, Psalm 121:2, Psalm 135:14, Proverbs 16:18, Deuteronomy 28:13, Joel 2:25-26, 1 John 4:4, Luke 12:2-3, Job 13:15, Ephesians 6:10-18, 2 Chronicles 7:14, 2 Timothy 1:7, 2 Thessalonians 3:16, Jeremiah 30:17, Philippians 4:7-9, Romans 12:18, John 14:27, 2 Samuel 22:40, Isaiah 26:3, Isaiah 43:2, Isaiah 53:5 & Isaiah 54:17 over all of you & all whom you love. Father, I pray that You'll restore all our lands & bring peace back to the people. Father, I pray for all the afflicted with the virus that You'll fully restore all suffering & for the eradication of this virus. In the name of Jesus, as a child of the Living God, covered, protected, shielded & sealed by Your Blood, the Holy Spirit, the full Armor of Christ & with the full authority of God, I command & cast this insidious evil, in all forms, away from you and your loved ones. The evil storms that have surrounded us are no match for God almighty! He's more powerful than anything in the universe. Father, I pray that You'll completely surround all reading this with a spiritual & impenetrable hedge of protection & abundantly bless, protect, guide, strength heal & give peace, faith, love & wisdom. I thank You Father & I claim all these things in Your Holy, powerful, majestic, everlasting & precious name I pray Lord Jesus, Amen!

Warriors! On this night, do not be afraid! On this night, stand with praise for God! Tonight, pray from the deepest depths of your heart that the evil that is attacking us will be stopped! No matter what happens, have faith that God is still in control, on the throne & has a perfect plan. We may not understand all that is going on right now, but God can see the whole picture while we only see a small fraction of the whole. But as I've said many times before, do not look at the storm. Turn away and focus only on God & take refuge in Him. God has never lost a battle & never will. It may seem like evil is winning at times, but in the end, evil has already been defeated through the name & power of Christ because we fight from victory, not for victory. Tonight, say a prayer for your loved ones, your friends, our nation & your enemies. We're going to get through this everyone! VICTORY IS COMING! Let not your heart be troubled! May God strengthen you! May God give you courage! May God give you peace! May God bless all of you! ONWARD!!!

DAY 361
March 12th, 2021

Good evening my friends. The weekend is finally here, it was another beautiful day out in NE Ohio & we're closing out Friday, March 12th, 2021 & I pray this message finds you & your loved ones warm, healthy, safe & well.

Dear Heavenly Father, I come to You tonight with Heavenly praise, love & thanksgiving. Thank You Father for guiding us to deliverance & victory, guiding us & walking with us each step of the journey. Father, I pray that You'll surround everyone reading this prayer & their loved ones with a powerful, spiritual & impenetrable hedge of protection & abundantly bless them through these difficult times. Father, I pray that all the sick & afflicted with the virus will be restored to full health. Father, I pray that You'll restore our lands, bring peace back to the people & calm the stormy waters. In the name of Jesus, as a child of the eternal true Living God, covered, protected, shielded & sealed by Your Blood, the Holy Spirit, the full Armor of Christ & with the full authority of God, I command, come against, rebuke & cast this insidious evil away from you and your loved ones. As it's written, through the power & name of Christ when we resist the devil, he MUST flee from us! In the name of Jesus, I claim Psalm 91, Psalm 23, Psalm 25:20-21, Psalm 34:19, Psalm 35, Psalm 46:10, Psalm 55:22, Psalm 56:3, Psalm 61:2, Psalm 62:5-8, Psalm 116:7, Psalm 121:2, Psalm 135:14, Proverbs 16:18, Deuteronomy 28:13, Joel 2:25-26, 1 John 4:4, Luke 12:2-3, Job 13:15, Ephesians 6:10-18, 2 Chronicles 7:14, 2 Timothy 1:7, 2 Thessalonians 3:16, Jeremiah 30:17, Philippians 4:7-9, Romans 12:18, John 14:27, 2 Samuel 22:40, Isaiah 26:3, Isaiah 43:2, Isaiah 53:5 & Isaiah 54:17 over all of you & all whom you love. I thank You Father for our coming victory & I claim all these things in Your Holy, powerful, majestic, everlasting & precious name I pray Lord Jesus, Amen!

Warriors! On this Friday night we're a mere couple of days from one year of these prayers. Though we are all exhausted, frustrated & ready for this season to be done with, we continue to press forward with everything we've got. As we continue to be strong & vigilant, know that this time shall pass & through the power of Christ we shall be victorious! We must continue to pray for God's will to be done & when God's people pray, the devil & all his agents of evil begin to shudder! As I've said before, prayer is one of the most powerful weapons we have against the enemy. When we cry out to God, He hears our prayers. God's will be done in all things! Everyone, though this journey has been long, don't give up! Stand strong & by God's grace, we will make it to the other side of this time! Shout with me again tonight! VICTORY IS COMING! Let not your heart be troubled! May God strengthen you! May God give you courage! May God give you peace! May God bless all of you! ONWARD!!!

DAY 362
March 13th, 2021

      Good evening my friends. It is the middle of an absolutely beautiful weekend & we're closing out Saturday, March 13th, 2021 and I pray this message finds you and your loved ones warm, healthy, safe & well.

Dear Heavenly Father, I come to You tonight with Heavenly praise, love & thanksgiving. Thank You Father that Your will is being done in all things. In the name of Jesus, I claim Psalm 91, Psalm 23, Psalm 25:20-21, Psalm 34:19, Psalm 35, Psalm 46:10, Psalm 55:22, Psalm 56:3, Psalm 61:2, Psalm 62:5-8, Psalm 116:7, Psalm 121:2, Psalm 135:14, Proverbs 16:18, Deuteronomy 28:13, Joel 2:25-26, 1 John 4:4, Luke 12:2-3, Job 13:15, Ephesians 6:10-18, 2 Chronicles 7:14, 2 Timothy 1:7, 2 Thessalonians 3:16, Jeremiah 30:17, Philippians 4:7-9, Romans 12:18, John 14:27, 2 Samuel 22:40, Isaiah 26:3, Isaiah 43:2, Isaiah 53:5 & Isaiah 54:17 over all of you & all whom you love. In the name of Jesus, as a child of the Living God, covered, protected, shielded & sealed by Your Blood, the Holy Spirit, the full Armor of Christ & with the full authority of God, I command & cast this insidious evil away from you and your loved ones. Father, I lift up & pray for the afflicted with the virus that they'll be restored to full health. Father, I pray that You'll restore our lands & bring peace back to the people. Father, I pray that You'll surround & envelope everyone reading this prayer with a powerful & impenetrable hedge of protection & abundantly bless them in all ways. I thank You Father for our coming victory & I claim all these things in Your Holy, powerful, majestic, everlasting & precious name I pray Lord Jesus, Amen!

Warriors! On this day we are another day closer to victory. As the storms continue to rage, fear not, but look to the refuge of God. He has promised to never leave nor forsake you & will always provide. Always remember that all things are possible with Christ and through His name & power, we shall prevail. One day after this all passes, there will be history books written and because we are all indelibly unified through these times, you are now part of that history and you will be able to say you made it through that! We must never become complacent, but continue to be strong and vigilant. This difficult season truly will pass & life will return to normal. Do not let the spirit of fear and anxiety infiltrate your mind and lean not on your own understanding but have faith and trust in God. He's leading us to victory! Shout with me! GOD IS GOOD ALL THE TIME!! Let not your heart be troubled! May God strengthen you! May God give you courage! May God give you peace! May God bless all of you! ONWARD!!!

DAY 363
March 14th, 2021

Good evening my friends. We're coming to the end of another weekend & we're closing out Sunday, March 14th, 2021 & I pray this message, once again, finds you & your loved ones warm, healthy, safe & well.

Dear Heavenly Father, I come to You tonight with Heavenly praise, love & thanksgiving. Thank You Father for all You've blessed us with, our talents & our gifts. I thank You Father that as I pray tonight You're surrounding Your children with a powerful and impenetrable hedge of protection and abundantly blessing them and giving them peace which surpasses all understanding. I thank You Father that You're healing the afflicted and sick with the virus. I thank You Father that You hear our prayers and our restoring our lands. In the name of Jesus, as a child of the Living God, covered, protected, shielded & sealed by Your Blood, the Holy Spirit, the full Armor of Christ & with the full authority of God, I command & cast this insidious evil, fear, anxiety and hatred in all forms away from you and your loved ones. In the name of Jesus, I claim Psalm 91, Psalm 23, Psalm 25:20-21, Psalm 34:19, Psalm 35, Psalm 46:10, Psalm 55:22, Psalm 56:3, Psalm 61:2, Psalm 62:5-8, Psalm 116:7, Psalm 121:2, Psalm 135:14, Proverbs 16:18, Deuteronomy 28:13, Joel 2:25-26, 1 John 4:4, Luke 12:2-3, Job 13:15, Ephesians 6:10-18, 2 Chronicles 7:14, 2 Timothy 1:7, 2 Thessalonians 3:16, Jeremiah 30:17, Philippians 4:7-9, Romans 12:18, John 14:27, 2 Samuel 22:40, Isaiah 26:3, Isaiah 43:2, Isaiah 53:5 & Isaiah 54:17 over all of you and all whom you love. I thank You Father for our coming victory and I claim all these things in Your Holy, powerful, majestic, everlasting and precious name I pray Lord Jesus, Amen!

Warriors! On this night in March, I thank You Father that You're continuing to lead us forward to victory! When the storms come, turn to God! When fear enters your mind, turn to God! When anxiety permeates your soul, turn to God! God wants us to cast our burdens on Him so whatever you are facing today, whatever circumstances have surrounded you, give all your fear, worry, anger to God & let His will be done in Your life. God loves you, no matter how badly you've messed up. Tonight! We stand unified again against the evil forces of darkness & through the power of Christ, we command them to leave this very moment! They have no option but to obey! We're going to get through this season everyone! Stay strong! Have courage! GOD IS IN CONTROL!! Let not your heart be troubled! May God strengthen you! May God give you courage! May God give you peace! May God bless all of you! ONWARD!!!

DAY 364
March 15th, 2021

Good evening my friends. It's the start of a new week & we're closing out Monday, March 15th, 2021 & I pray this message, finds you & your loved ones warm, healthy, safe & well.

Dear Heavenly Father, I come to You tonight with Heavenly praise, love & thanksgiving. Thank You Father that You are the God of new beginnings, justice, love & forgiveness. In the name of Jesus, I claim Psalm 91, Psalm 23, Psalm 25:20-21, Psalm 34:19, Psalm 35, Psalm 46:10, Psalm 55:22, Psalm 56:3, Psalm 61:2, Psalm 62:5-8, Psalm 116:7, Psalm 121:2, Psalm 135:14, Proverbs 16:18, Deuteronomy 28:13, Joel 2:25-26, 1 John 4:4, Luke 12:2-3, Job 13:15, Ephesians 6:10-18, 2 Chronicles 7:14, 2 Timothy 1:7, 2 Thessalonians 3:16, Jeremiah 30:17, Philippians 4:7-9, Romans 12:18, John 14:27, 2 Samuel 22:40, Isaiah 26:3, Isaiah 43:2, Isaiah 53:5 & Isaiah 54:17 over all of you & all whom you love. Father, I pray that You'll surround everyone reading this with a spiritual hedge of protection that no evil can pass through, please give them peace & I pray that You'll abundantly bless all their needs. Father, I lift up & pray for all the sick & afflicted with the virus that they'll be fully restored to complete health. Father I lift up our nation, please restore our lands & bring peace back to the people. In the name of Jesus, as a child of the Living God, covered, protected, shielded & sealed by Your Blood, the Holy Spirit, the full Armor of Christ & with the full authority of God, I command & cast this insidious evil, fear, anxiety & hatred in all forms away from you and your loved ones to the farthest ends of the earth. I thank You Father & I claim all these things in Your Holy, powerful, majestic, everlasting & precious name I pray Lord Jesus, Amen!

Warriors! As we begin a new week, I pray you & your loved ones are safe & at peace. But no matter what the circumstances are that you personally face, know that God has a plan for victory & deliverance from whatever you are facing. We look at life moment by moment & to the past, but God sees the beginning, the middle & the end all at the same time & while we make plans in our lives, He is directing your steps to fulfill your God given destiny in this life. He knows what you need before you even ask for it. In the world we live in, faith can be difficult to come by, but God loves faith & when you put your trust in Him, you will be on an amazing adventure. Life is not easy, but knowing that God only wants the best for you should be comforting when adversity comes that you can be courageous with faith in Him. All things are truly possible with Christ & He is leading us to deliverance. Do not fear but have faith. We're going to get through this everyone! We're all in this together! And shout with me tonight VICTORY IS COMING & GOD IS GOOD ALL THE TIME!! Let not your heart be troubled! May God strengthen you! May God give you courage! May God give you peace! May God bless all of you! AGAIN ONWARD!!!

DAY 365
March 16th, 2021

     Good evening my friends. It was a beautiful day out today & we're closing out Tuesday, March 16th, 2021 & I pray this message, finds you & your loved ones warm, healthy, safe & well.

Dear Heavenly Father, I come to You tonight with Heavenly praise, love & thanksgiving. Thank You Father that You shield us from the storms that surround us. Father, I'm praying tonight for all the afflicted that they may be completely healed & fully restored with no long term lasting effects. Father, I pray that everyone reading this tonight will be shielded by a hedge of protection, given peace that surpasses all understanding, given wisdom, strength & abundantly blessed. In the name of Jesus, I claim Psalm 91, Psalm 23, Psalm 25:20-21, Psalm 34:19, Psalm 35, Psalm 46:10, Psalm 55:22, Psalm 56:3, Psalm 61:2, Psalm 62:5-8, Psalm 116:7, Psalm 121:2, Psalm 135:14, Proverbs 16:18, Deuteronomy 28:13, Joel 2:25-26, 1 John 4:4, Luke 12:2-3, Job 13:15, Ephesians 6:10-18, 2 Chronicles 7:14, 2 Timothy 1:7, 2 Thessalonians 3:16, Jeremiah 30:17, Philippians 4:7-9, Romans 12:18, John 14:27, 2 Samuel 22:40, Isaiah 26:3, Isaiah 43:2, Isaiah 53:5 & Isaiah 54:17 over all of you & all whom you love. Father I pray for our nation that You'll please restore our lands. In the name of Jesus, as a child of the Living God, covered, protected, shielded & sealed by Your Blood, the Holy Spirit, the full Armor of Christ & with the full authority of God, I command & cast this insidious evil, fear, anxiety & hatred in all forms away from you and your loved ones. I thank You Father & I claim all these things in Your Holy, powerful, majestic, everlasting & precious name I pray Lord Jesus, Amen!

Warriors! We are one day away from the year anniversary to when I first started praying over all of you. We've been through so much this past year, but by the very grace of God, we are still here & pressing forward. Very soon this will all be over & life is already starting to return to normal. One thing this past year has truly taught us is just how fragile we are & how we truly need Christ. We will continue to press forward because victory & deliverance are coming! Tonight, please say a prayer for your family, friends & loved ones. Tonight, thank God that you are still here through the tribulations of this past year. Tonight, give a shout of praise to the name of Christ because through Him, VICTORY IS COMING!! Let not your heart be troubled! May God strengthen you! May God give you courage! May God give you peace! May God bless all of you! ONWARD!!!

This completes the first full year (all 365 days) of the pandemic of 2020-2021. As of the writing of this book, we are just shy of year two which I will have a continuation of this book in "Prayers Through the Pandemic : Year Two"

The Sinner's Prayer

If you are not yet saved I want to personally invite you to read this prayer below. This could be the most profound decision of your entire life. This is a decision only you can make, as I am on a messenger. Please don't put off to tomorrow what can be done right now. Because tomorrow may never come.

If you would like to be saved, please read the prayer below out loud & believing in your heart.

"God, I'm a sinner. I'm sorry for my sins. I ask that You forgive me, and I believe that Jesus Christ is Your Son, and I want to invite Him to come into my heart and trust Him with my life. I'm willing to trust Him as my Savior and follow Him as my Lord forever, and I pray this in Jesus' Name.'"

JOHN 14:6

I am the way and the truth and the life. No one comes to the Father except through Me.

BIBLE VERSES USED IN PRAYERS

Psalm 91

Amplified Bible (AMP)
Security of the One Who Trusts in the Lord.

He who dwells in the shelter of the Most High will remain secure and rest in the shadow of the Almighty [whose power no enemy can withstand]. 2 I will say of the Lord, "He is my refuge and my fortress, my God, in whom I trust [with great confidence, and on whom I rely]!" 3 For He will save you from the trap of the fowler, and from the deadly pestilence. 4 He will cover you and completely protect you with His pinions, and under His wings you will find refuge; His faithfulness is a shield and a wall. 5 You will not be afraid of the terror of night, nor of the arrow that flies by day, 6 Nor of the pestilence that stalks in darkness, nor of the destruction (sudden death) that lays waste at noon. 7 A thousand may fall at your side and ten thousand at your right hand, But danger will not come near you. 8 You will only [be a spectator as you] look on with your eyes and witness the [divine] repayment of the wicked [as you watch safely from the shelter of the Most High]. 9 Because you have made the Lord, [who is] my refuge, even the Most High, your dwelling place, 10 No evil will befall you, nor will any plague come near your tent. 11 For He will command His angels in regard to you, to protect and defend and guard you in all your ways [of obedience and service]. 12 They will lift you up in their hands, so that you do not [even] strike your foot against a stone. 13 You will tread upon the lion and cobra; the young lion and the serpent you will trample underfoot. 14 "Because he set his love on Me, therefore I will save him; I will set him [securely] on high, because he knows My name [he confidently trusts and relies on Me, knowing I will never abandon him, no, never]. 15 "He will call upon Me, and I will answer him; I will be with him in trouble; I will rescue him and honor him. 16 "With a long life I will satisfy him and I will let him see My salvation."

Psalm 23
Amplified Bible (AMP)
The Lord, the Psalmist's Shepherd.
A Psalm of David.

The Lord is my Shepherd [to feed, to guide and to shield me], I shall not want. 2 He lets me lie down in green pastures; He leads me beside the still and quiet waters. 3 He refreshes and restores my soul (life); He leads me in the paths of righteousness for His name's sake. 4 Even though I walk through the [sunless] valley of the shadow of death, I fear no evil, for You are with me; Your rod [to protect] and Your staff [to guide], they comfort and console me. 5 You prepare a table before me in the presence of my enemies. You have anointed and refreshed my head with oil; my cup overflows. 6 Surely goodness and mercy and unfailing love shall follow me all the days of my life, and I shall dwell forever [throughout all my days] in the house and in the presence of the Lord.

Psalm 25:20-21
Amplified Bible (AMP)

20 Guard my soul and rescue me; do not let me be ashamed or disappointed, for I have taken refuge in You. 21 Let integrity and uprightness protect me, for I wait [expectantly] for You.

Psalm 34:19
Amplified Bible (AMP)

19 Many hardships and perplexing circumstances confront the righteous, but the Lord rescues him from them all.

Psalm 35
Amplified Bible (AMP)
Prayer for Rescue from Enemies.
A Psalm of David.

Contend, O Lord, with those who contend with me; fight against those who fight against me. 2 Take hold of shield and buckler (small shield), and stand up for my help. 3 Draw also the spear and javelin to meet those who pursue me. Say to my soul, "I am your salvation." 4 Let those be ashamed and dishonored who seek my life; let those be turned back [in defeat] and humiliated who plot evil against me. 5 Let them be [blown away] like chaff before the wind [worthless, without substance], with the angel of the Lord driving them on. 6 Let their way be dark and slippery, with the angel of the Lord pursuing and harassing them. 7 For without cause they hid their net for me; without cause they dug a pit [of destruction] for my life. 8 Let destruction come upon my enemy by surprise; let the net he hid for me catch him; into that very destruction let him fall. 9 Then my soul shall rejoice in the Lord; it shall rejoice in His salvation. 10 All my bones will say, "Lord, who is like You, who rescues the afflicted from him who is too strong for him [to resist alone], and the afflicted and the needy from him who robs him?" 11 Malicious witnesses rise up; they ask me of things that I do not know. 12 They repay me evil for good, to the sorrow of my soul. 13 But as for me, when they were sick, my clothing was sackcloth (mourning garment); I humbled my soul with fasting, and I prayed with my head bowed on my chest. 14 I behaved as if grieving for my friend or my brother; I bowed down in mourning, as one who sorrows for his mother. 15 But in my stumbling they rejoiced and gathered together [against me]; the slanderers whom I did not know gathered against me; they slandered and reviled me without ceasing. 16 Like godless jesters at a feast, they gnashed at me with their teeth [in malice]. 17 Lord, how long will You look on [without action]? Rescue my life from their destructions, my only life from the young lions. 18 I will give You thanks in the great congregation; I will praise You among a mighty people. 19 Do not let those who are wrongfully my enemies rejoice over me; nor let those who hate me without cause wink their eye [maliciously]. 20 For they do not speak peace, but they devise deceitful words [half-truths and lies] against those who are quiet in the land. 21 They open their mouths wide against me; they say, "Aha, aha, our eyes have seen it!" 22 You have seen this, O Lord; do not keep silent. O Lord, do not be far from me. 23 Wake Yourself up, and arise to my right And to my cause, my God and my Lord. 24 Judge me, O Lord my God, according to Your righteousness and justice; and do not let them rejoice over me. 25 Do not let them say in their heart, "Aha, that is what we wanted!" Do not let them say, "We have swallowed him up and destroyed him." 26 Let those be ashamed and humiliated together who rejoice at my distress; let those be clothed with shame and dishonor who magnify themselves over me. 27 Let them shout for joy and rejoice, who favor my vindication and want what is right for me; let them say continually, "Let the Lord be magnified, who delights and takes pleasure in the prosperity of His servant." 28 And my tongue shall declare Your righteousness (justice), And Your praise all the day long.

Psalm 46:10
Amplified Bible (AMP)

10 "Be still and know (recognize, understand) that I am God. I will be exalted among the nations! I will be exalted in the earth."

Psalm 55:22
Amplified Bible (AMP)
22 Cast your burden on the Lord [release it] & He will sustain &uphold you; He will never allow the righteous to be shaken (slip, fall, fail).

Psalm 56:3
Amplified Bible (AMP)

3 When I am afraid, I will put my trust and faith in You.

Psalm 61:2
Amplified Bible (AMP)

2 From the end of the earth I call to You, when my heart is overwhelmed and weak; lead me to the rock that is higher than I [a rock that is too high to reach without Your help].

Psalm 61:2
Amplified Bible (AMP)
Psalm 62:5-8
Amplified Bible (AMP)
5 For God alone my soul waits in silence & quietly submits to Him, for my hope is from Him. 6 He only is my rock and my salvation; my fortress and my defense, I will not be shaken or discouraged. 7 On God my salvation and my glory rest; He is my rock of [unyielding] strength, my refuge is in God. 8 Trust [confidently] in Him at all times, O people; pour out your heart before Him. God is a refuge for us. Selah.

Psalm 116:7
Amplified Bible (AMP)
7 Return to your rest, O my soul, for the Lord has dealt bountifully with you.

Psalm 121:2
Amplified Bible (AMP)
2 My help comes from the Lord, who made heaven and earth.

Psalm 135:14
Amplified Bible (AMP)
14 For the Lord will judge His people and He will have compassion on His servants [revealing His mercy].

Proverbs 16:18
Amplified Bible (AMP)
18 Pride goes before destruction, and a haughty spirit before a fall.

Deuteronomy 28:13
Amplified Bible (AMP)
13 The Lord will make you the head (leader) and not the tail (follower); and you will be above only, and you will not be beneath, if you listen and pay attention to the commandments of the Lord your God, which I am commanding you today, to observe them carefully.

Joel 2:25-26
Amplified Bible (AMP)
25 "And I will compensate you for the years that the swarming locust has eaten, the creeping locust, the stripping locust, and the gnawing locust—My great army which I sent among you. 26 "You will have plenty to eat and be satisfied and praise the name of the Lord your God who has dealt wondrously with you; and My people shall never be put to shame.

1 John 4:4
Amplified Bible (AMP)
4 Little children (believers, dear ones), you are of God and you belong to Him and have [already] overcome them [the agents of the antichrist]; because He who is in you is greater than he (Satan) who is in the world [of sinful mankind].

Luke 12:2-3
Amplified Bible (AMP)
2 But there is nothing [so carefully] concealed that it will not be revealed, nor so hidden that it will not be made known. 3 For that reason, whatever you have said in the dark will be heard in the light, and what you have whispered behind closed doors will be proclaimed on the housetops.

Job 13:15
Amplified Bible (AMP)
15 "Even though He kills me; I will hope in Him. nevertheless, I will argue my ways to His face.

Ephesians 6:10-18
Amplified Bible (AMP)
The Armor of God
10 In conclusion, be strong in the Lord [draw your strength from Him and be empowered through your union with Him] and in the power of His [boundless] might. 11 Put on the full armor of God [for His precepts are like the splendid armor of a heavily-armed soldier], so that you may be able to [successfully] stand up against all the schemes and the strategies and the deceits of the devil. 12 For our struggle is not against flesh and blood [contending only with physical opponents], but against the rulers, against the powers, against the world forces of this [present] darkness, against the spiritual forces of wickedness in the heavenly (supernatural) places. 13 Therefore, put on the complete armor of God, so that you will be able to [successfully] resist and stand your ground in the evil day [of danger], and having done everything [that the crisis demands], to stand firm [in your place, fully prepared, immovable, victorious]. 14 So stand firm and hold your ground, having tightened the wide band of truth (personal integrity, moral courage) around your waist and having put on the breastplate of righteousness (an upright heart), 15 and having strapped on your feet the gospel of peace in preparation [to face the enemy with firm-footed stability and the readiness produced by the good news]. 16 Above all, lift up the [protective] shield of faith with which you can extinguish all the flaming arrows of the evil one. 17 And take the helmet of salvation, and the sword of the Spirit, which is the Word of God. 18 With all prayer and petition pray [with specific requests] at all times [on every occasion and in every season] in the Spirit, and with this in view, stay alert with all perseverance and petition [interceding in prayer] for all God's people.

2 Chronicles 7:14
Amplified Bible (AMP)
14 and My people, who are called by My Name, humble themselves, and pray and seek (crave, require as a necessity) My face and turn from their wicked ways, then I will hear [them] from heaven, and forgive their sin and heal their land.

2 Timothy 1:7
Amplified Bible (AMP)
7 For God did not give us a spirit of timidity or cowardice or fear, but [He has given us a spirit] of power and of love and of sound judgment and personal discipline [abilities that result in a calm, well-balanced mind and self-control].

2 Thessalonians 3:16
Amplified Bible (AMP)
16 Now may the Lord of peace Himself grant you His peace at all times and in every way [that peace and spiritual well-being that comes to those who walk with Him, regardless of life's circumstances]. The Lord be with you all.

Jeremiah 30:17
Amplified Bible (AMP)
17 'For I will restore health to you and I will heal your wounds,' says the Lord, 'because they have called you an outcast, saying: "This is Zion; no one seeks her and no one cares for her."'

Philippians 4:7-9
Amplified Bible (AMP)
7 And the peace of God [that peace which reassures the heart, that peace] which transcends all understanding, [that peace which] stands guard over your hearts and your minds in Christ Jesus [is yours]. 8 Finally, believers, whatever is true, whatever is honorable and worthy of respect, whatever is right and confirmed by God's word, whatever is pure and wholesome, whatever is lovely and brings peace, whatever is admirable and of good repute; if there is any excellence, if there is anything worthy of praise, think continually on these things [center your mind on them, and implant them in your heart]. 9 The things which you have learned and received and heard and seen in me, practice these things [in daily life], and the God [who is the source] of peace and well-being will be with you.

Romans 12:18
Amplified Bible (AMP)
18 If possible, as far as it depends on you, live at peace with everyone.

John 14:27
Amplified Bible (AMP)
27 Peace I leave with you; My [perfect] peace I give to you; not as the world gives do I give to you. Do not let your heart be troubled, nor let it be afraid. [Let My perfect peace calm you in every circumstance and give you courage and strength for every challenge.]

2 Samuel 22:40
Amplified Bible (AMP)
40 "For You have surrounded me with strength for the battle; You have subdued under me those who stood against me.

Isaiah 26:3
Amplified Bible (AMP)
3 "You will keep in perfect and constant peace the one whose mind is steadfast [that is, committed and focused on You—in both inclination and character], because he trusts and takes refuge in You [with hope and confident expectation].

Isaiah 43:2
Amplified Bible (AMP)
2 "When you pass through the waters, I will be with you; snd through the rivers, they will not overwhelm you. When you walk through fire, you will not be scorched, nor will the flame burn you.

Isaiah 53:5
Amplified Bible (AMP)
5 But He was wounded for our transgressions, He was crushed for our wickedness [our sin, our injustice, our wrongdoing]; The punishment [required] for our well-being fell on Him, and by His stripes (wounds) we are healed.

Isaiah 54:17
Amplified Bible (AMP)

17 "No weapon that is formed against you will succeed; And every tongue that rises against you in judgment you will condemn. This [peace, righteousness, security, and triumph over opposition] is the heritage of the servants of the Lord, and this is their vindication from Me," says the Lord.

The Lord's Prayer

"Our Father, who art in heaven, hallowed be thy name; thy kingdom come; thy will be done on earth as it is in heaven. Give us this day our daily bread; and forgive us our trespasses as we forgive those who trespass against us; and lead us not into temptation, but deliver us from evil. For Yours is the kingdom and the power and the glory forever. Amen.'

THE SINNER'S PRAYER

The Sinners Prayer

If you are not yet saved, I want to personally invite you to read this prayer below. This could be the most profound decision of your entire life. This is a decision only you can make, as I am on a messenger. Please don't put off to tomorrow what can be done right now. Because tomorrow may never come.

If you would like to be saved, please read the prayer below out loud & believing in your heart.

"God, I'm a sinner. I'm sorry for my sins. I ask that You forgive me, and I believe that Jesus Christ is Your Son, and I want to invite Him to come into my heart and trust Him with my life. I'm willing to trust Him as my Savior and follow Him as my Lord forever, and I pray this in Jesus' Name.'"

ABOUT THE AUTHOR
JOE VITALE JR

Joe Vitale Jr is a professional musician, producer, artist, audio engineer, photographer, cinematographer, film director, film editor, speaker, laserist & author. But above all these professions & passions, Joe Vitale Jr is a Christian & believer in Jesus Christ.

Joe Vitale Jr was born in 1977 & grew up in a Christian home in Canton, Ohio. His mother would read the Bible to him every night before he went to sleep and even at the young age of seven, Joe gave his life to Christ.

His father is veteran rock drummer Joe Vitale from Joe Walsh, The Eagles, Buffalo Springfield, Crosby Stills & Nash, Peter Frampton, Dan Fogelberg, just to name a few was out on tour with Crosby Stills & Nash and they asked Joe Jr if he wanted to play tambourine on stage on CSN's hit song "Teach Your Children" at Blossom Music Center in Cuyahoga Falls, Ohio. Joe was only 10 years old but he was so excited. He dove at the chance & when he walked on stage and heard the roar of 19,000 people, it changed his life & right then and there he knew what his calling was.

Since that time Joe has fought through a lot of adversity in many areas of his life, but he keeps pressing forward knowing & trusting that God will guide him on the path chosen by God. His message has always been triumph over adversity.

Through his music, artwork, writing & films, he always prays that everything he does brings glory to God in some capacity.

TRIUMPH. OVER. ADVERSITY.

TESTIMONY

I want to start off by saying, my name is Joe Vitale Jr, I'm a Christian, believer in Christ & like all of us, I am a sinner.

From an early age & through my life, I always had a close relationship with God. For the most part, the first 19 years of my life were fairly smooth sailing. My mother used to joke that it was like I had God on speed dial as whatever I prayed for, seemed to come to pass. Then one day in the summer of 1997, I was sitting at a local swimming pool contemplating how God always existed, this is beyond our corporeal intellectual power to fathom & in that moment it felt like my connection with God was pulled out from underneath me. I couldn't feel that connection like I had all those earlier years. I felt a sudden & deep sense of anxiety over the matter. Though I was having a crisis in my faith, as we all do at some point, I never once left God or stopped believing in Him. In the proceeding years after this event, I went through several decades, not days, months or even years, but decades of trials & tribulations in my life. I went through being let go from a major tour, being robbed, my church that I loved, went through a devastating split, events in college that led to me leaving school altogether, career opportunities that fell through, manager & music industry problems, health issues, rocky relationships, major spiritual warfare attacks and dealing with deep depression & anxiety. It was a very dark time in my life.

Around this same time, I was trying to be perfect in life as a Christian, which I soon learned is impossible as we are all sinners & all fall short of the glory of Christ. It took a while, but eventually I came to realize that it is impossible to live perfectly no matter how hard we try & that's the whole reason for why we need Jesus Christ as our Savior. We truly cannot get to Heaven on our own merits or works but only through admitting that we are sinners, believing in our hearts that Jesus Christ is the Son of God, that He died on the cross for our sin debt past, present & future, that he rose from the dead 3 days later & that when we receive Jesus Christ & the Holy Spirit into our hearts & accepting & receiving this free Gift that we may be saved and have eternal life through Him.

Over the years I have seen so many wonders of God's presence in my life from simple to profound events. I've seen how God has protected me from bad decisions. As a modern society we try to rationalize everything but I've also seen things in the supernatural that can't be explained by anything other than God.

Looking back on my life, I can see where God was guiding my steps through the mire of that difficult time. I know deep in my heart that God never left my side through those dark years even when I wasn't the greatest Christian at all. He loved me, despite myself. But through that time I felt that God pulled back from me not to punish me or leave me as it's written that God will never leave nor forsake us, but to test and grow my faith & to strengthen me for my life & career. The path to our God given destiny is different for everyone. Would I have rather not gone through all the difficulty in my life, absolutely, but it's through adversity that grows our character and faith. See, God is more concerned about transforming us into the likeness of Christ & what He envisions for us, rather than our own comfort. He truly sees your full & complete potential even when you don't. Am I there yet, far from it, but with each passing day, God is molding me & transforming me.

God doesn't expect us to be perfect but to at least try. He wants us to put our complete faith & trust in Him, casting our burdens on Him & truly surrendering our life to Him. Of course it's not easy because, like all of us, myself included, we like to have control over what happens to us, but when we surrender our lives to God, He works all things for our good. His ways aren't easiest but they are truly best. None of us are perfect. We all mess up & we all sin. We're human. God knows this & He loves us unconditionally.

Like all of us, I'm a constant work in progress & I still deal with anxiety, stress, spiritual attacks & tribulation but I know that my God is more powerful than anything that comes my way. The devil knows he can't steal your soul so he'll attack you in a multitude of ways with lies & deception to try to steal your joy. Don't allow him to as you do have offensive power to fight back through the Word of God.

The life we live down here is a mere blink of the eye in comparison to eternity & everything comes down to a simple choice. Do we want to spend eternity with the Creator of the universe, a loving God who loves us more than we can ever imagine or do we reject Jesus and spend forever permanently separated from Him. He gives you free will to choose & honors your decision. God doesn't send us to hell, we do by our own choice.

Each day we're alive is a gift but one day when the door closes on your life are you prepared for what comes after. The choice is yours.

The Sinners Prayer

I wanted the last page of this book to be about the salvation of Jesus Christ. God does truly loves you more than you can ever imagine. He uses all circumstances in your life, both the good & the bad, for your good.

If you are not yet saved, I'm not only inviting you, but I truly am pleading with you to read this prayer below. This could truly be the most profound decision of your entire life. This is a decision that only you can make, as I am on a messenger. Please don't put off to tomorrow what can be done right now. Because tomorrow may never come and the hour is late & the clock is ticking.

If you would like to be saved, please read the prayer below out loud & believing in your heart.

"God, I'm a sinner. I'm sorry for my sins. I ask that You forgive me, and I believe that Jesus Christ is Your Son, and I want to invite Him to come into my heart and trust Him with my life. I'm willing to trust Him as my Savior and follow Him as my Lord forever, and I pray this in Jesus' Name.'"